International Conferences e-Society 2024 and Mobile Learning 2024

Held at MCCSIS 2024

Porto, Portugal
9-11 March 2024

Editors:

Piet Kommers
Inmaculada A. Sánchez
Pedro Isaías
Luís Rodrigues

ISBN: 979-8-3313-0141-5

Printed from e-media with permission by:

Curran Associates, Inc.
57 Morehouse Lane
Red Hook, NY 12571

Some format issues inherent in the e-media version may also appear in this print version.

International Association for Development of the Information Society (IADIS)
Rua Sao Sebastiao Da Pedreira
No. 100, 30, 1050-209
Lisbon, Portugal

Phone: 351 21 3151373
Fax: 351 21 3151244

secretariat@iadis.org

Additional copies of this publication are available from:

Curran Associates, Inc.
57 Morehouse Lane
Red Hook, NY 12571 USA
Phone: 845-758-0400
Fax: 845-758-2633
Email: curran@proceedings.com
Web: www.proceedings.com

INTERNATIONAL CONFERENCES
ON
E-SOCIETY 2024
AND
MOBILE LEARNING 2024

PROCEEDINGS OF THE INTERNATIONAL CONFERENCES

on

E-SOCIETY 2024

AND

MOBILE LEARNING 2024

9- 11 MARCH, 2024

Organised by

iadis

international association for development of the information society

As a member of Crossref (a non-profit membership organization for scholarly publishing working with the purpose to make content easy to find, link, cite and assess) each published paper in this book of proceedings will be allocated a DOI (Digital Object Identifier) number for its fast and easy citation and indexation.

Edited by Piet Kommers, Inmaculada Arnedillo Sánchez and Pedro Isaías

Associate Editor: Luís Rodrigues

TABLE OF CONTENTS

FULL PAPERS

e-Society

REFLECTION PAPERS

e-Society

Mobile Learning

POSTERS

e-Society

Mobile Learning

DOCTORAL CONSORTIUM

Mobile Learning

FOREWORD

These proceedings contain the papers and posters of the 22nd International Conference on e-Society (ES 2024) and 20th International Conference on Mobile Learning (ML 2024), organised by the International Association for Development of the Information Society in Porto, Portugal, during 9-11 March 2024.

The e-Society 2024 conference aims to address the main issues of concern within the Information Society. This conference covers both the technical as well as the non-technical aspects of the Information Society. Broad areas of interest are:

- e-Government / e-Governance
- e-Business / e-Commerce
- Technology and Society
- e-Learning
- New Media and E-Society
- e-Health
- Information Systems
- Information Management
- COVID-19 & Digital Transformation

The Mobile Learning 2024 Conference seeks to provide a forum for the presentation and discussion of mobile learning research which illustrate developments in the field. In particular, but not exclusively, we aim to explore the theme of mobile learning under the following topics:

- Learning analytics and mobile learning
- Cloud computing and mobile learning
- Pedagogical approaches, models and theories for mLearning
- mLearning in and across formal and informal settings
- Strategies and challenges for integrating mLearning in broader educational scenarios
- User Studies in mLearning
- Learner mobility and transitions afforded by mlearning
- Socio-cultural context and implications of mLearning
- Mobile social media and user generated content
- Enabling mLearning technologies, applications and uses
- Evaluation and assessment of mLearning
- Research methods, ethics and implementation of mLearning
- Innovative mLearning approaches
- Tools, technologies and platforms for mLearning
- mlearning: where to next and how?

These events received 185 submissions from more than 25 countries. Each submission has been anonymously reviewed by an average of 4 independent reviewers, to ensure the final high standard of the accepted submissions. Out of the papers submitted, 32 received blind referee ratings that signified acceptability for publication as full papers (acceptance rate of 17%), while some other papers were published under the following categories: short, reflection, poster and doctoral. The best papers will be selected for publishing as extended versions in the Interactive Technology and Smart Education (ITSE) journal (ISSN: 1741-5659) and also in the IADIS International Journal on WWW/Internet (ISSN: 1645-7641).

In addition to the papers' presentations, the conferences also feature two keynote presentations. We wish to thank Professor Ashok Jashapara (Royal Holloway – University of London, School of Business & Management, Egham, United Kingdom) and Dr. Inmaculada Arnedillo-Sánchez (Associate Professor in Learning Technologies, Director of Industry Engagement, Trinity College Dublin, The University of Dublin, Ireland) for accepting our invitation as keynote speakers. Furthermore, it is included a Tutorial entitled "Empower Student Tutors in Hybrid teaching Environments" by Melanie Ludwig and Michelle Pippig (ZiLL – Dresden University of Technology, Germany).

As we all know, a conference requires the effort of many individuals. We would like to thank all members of the Program Committee for their hard work in reviewing and selecting the papers that appear in this book. We would also like to thank all the authors who have submitted their papers to this conference. We wish to thank all members of our organizing committee.

Last but not least, we hope that everybody enjoyed the presentations, and we invite all participants for next year's edition of the International Conferences on e-Society and Mobile Learning.

Piet Kommers, University of Twente, The Netherlands
ES 2024 Program Chair

Inmaculada Arnedillo Sánchez, Trinity College Dublin, Ireland
ML 2024 Program Chair

Pedro Isaías, Information Systems & Technology Management School, The University of New South Wales, Australia
ES 2024 and ML 2024 Conference Chair

March 2024

PROGRAM COMMITTEE

E-SOCIETY

PROGRAM CHAIR

Piet Kommers, University of Twente, The Netherlands

CONFERENCE CHAIR

Pedro Isaias, Information Systems & Technology Management School,
The University of New South Wales, Australia

COMMITTEE MEMBERS

Adam Wojciechowski, Poznan University of Technology, Poland
Agapito Ledezma, Universidad Carlos III de Madrid, Spain
Albena Antonova, University of Sofia, Bulgaria
Aleksandar Dimov, University of Sofia St. Kliment Ohridski, Bulgaria
Alexandre Veronese, University of Brasilia, Brazil
Alfredo Pina, Public University of Navarra, Spain
Ali Saberi, Iranian Researchers Network, Iran
Anastasija Nikiforova, University of Tartu, Estonia
Anna Lewandowska, University of Information Technology and Management, Poland
Boong Ryoo, Texas A&M University, USA
Boyan Bontchev, Sofia University St. Kl. Ohridski, Bulgaria
Bruce Chien-ta Ho, National Chung Hsing University, Taiwan
Carina dc Villiers, University of Pretoria, South Africa
Cesar Alberto Collazos, University of Cauca, Colombia
CHRISTOS GEORGIADIS, University of Macedonia, Greece
Christos Kalloniatis, University of the Aegean, Greece
Christos Papatheodorou, National and Kapodistrian University of Athens, Greece
Chun Kit Lok, The University of Hong Kong, Hong Kong
Damiano Distante, University of Rome Unitelma Sapienza, Italy
David Cabrero Souto, University of a Coruña, Spain
Demetrios Sampson, University of Piraeus, Greece
Dessislava Vassileva, Sofia University "St. Kliment Ohridski", Bulgaria
Dorina Kabakchieva, University of National and World Economy, Bulgaria
Egbert Sánchez Vanderkast , National Autonomous University of Mexico, Mexico
Eliza Stefanova, Sofia University, Bulgaria
Eltahir Kabbar, Unitec Institute of Technology, New Zealand
Elvis Mazzoni, University of Bologna, Italy
Eugenia Kovatcheva, University of Library Studies and Information Technologies, Bulgaria
Faton Shabani, University of Tetova, Albania
Fausto Fasano, Università Degli Studi del Molise, Italy
Fernanda Faini, University of Bologna, Italy
Fisnik Dalipi, Linnaeus University, Sweden

Vasiliki Spiliotopoulou, ASPAITE Patras, Greece
Vincent Ng, The Hong Kong Polytechnic University, Hong Kong
Vincenzo Deufemia, Universita' Degli Studi di Salerno, Italy
Vladimir Dimitrov, University of Sofia, Bulgaria
Yi Lu, Queensland University of Technology, Australia
Yongjian Fu, Cleveland State University, USA
Zeki Bayram, Eastern Mediterranean University, Cyprus

MOBILE LEARNING

PROGRAM CHAIR

Inmaculada Arnedillo Sánchez, Trinity College Dublin, Ireland

CONFERENCE CHAIR

Pedro Isaías, Information Systems & Technology Management School, The University of New South Wales, Australia

COMMITTEE MEMBERS

Abdullah Al-Zaghameem, Tafila Technical University, Jordan
Abeer Salim Jamil, Al-mansour University College, Iraq
Adamantios Koumpis, University Hospital Cologne, Germany
Ademiotan Laleye, Adekunle Ajasin University, Akungba-akoko, Nigeria
Agostino Marengo, University of Foggia, Italy
Aiman Ayyal Awwad, Faculty of Information and Communications Technology, Jordan
Alessandro Pagano, University of Bari, Italy
Amedeo Roberto Esposito, Institute of Science and Technology Austria, Austria
Angelos Michalas, University of Western Macedonia, Greece
Antoanela Naaji, Vasile Goldis Western University, Romania
Antonella Carbonaro, Universiy of Bologna, Italy
Ashraf Mousa Saleh, Amman Arab University, Jordan
Aslı Gonenç, Istanbul University, Turkey
Bertil P. Marques, ISEP/IPP, Portugal
Boriss Misnevs, Transport and Telecommunication Institute, Latvia
Celine Llewellyn-Jones, London Metropolitan University and University of East London, United Kingdom
Charalampos Karagiannidis, University of Thessaly, Greece
Christos Bouras, University of Patras, Greece
Claudia Steinberger, University of Klagenfurt, Austria
Demetrios Sampson, University of Piraeus, Greece
Diana Bratić, University of Zagreb, Croatia
Emad Bataineh, Zayed University, United Arab Emirates
Fadi Abuamara, Shenandoah University, USA
Gabor Kiss, J. Selye University, Slovakia
Gazi Zahirul Islam, Southeast University, Bangladesh
George Magoulas, Birbeck College, United Kingdom

KEYNOTE LECTURE

DECODING DECISION MAKING: AI SENSEMAKING AND THE AUTHENTICITY DILEMMA IN IS STRATEGY

Professor Ashok Jashapara
Royal Holloway – University of London
School of Business & Management, United Kingdom

Abstract

The paper explores the strategic implications of generative AI in organizations. It starts with an overview of AI's evolution, highlighting the rise of machine learning, deep learning, and General Adversarial Networks. The paper emphasizes generative AI's transformative role across various sectors while noting the challenges of biases and fake content generation.

The paper introduces the 'Authenticity Dilemma' framework, advocating a knowledge-based approach for strategic AI integration. This framework focuses on AI capabilities in decision-making and sensemaking, distinguishing between authentic and fake processes. The paper presents four levels of strategic positioning – Smoke Screen, Echo Chamber, Chameleon, and Greenhouse – illustrating different organizational approaches to AI application.

In summary, the paper provides a framework for understanding and navigating the complexities of AI in organizational strategy. While offering valuable insights, the paper also acknowledges potential limitations in oversimplifying decision-making complexities and defining 'authentic' versus 'fake' AI applications.

KEYNOTE LECTURE

TWENTY-FIVE YEARS OF MOBILE LEARNING: THE GOOD THE BAD AND THE UGLY

Dr. Inmaculada Arnedillo-Sánchez
Associate Professor in Learning Technologies, Director of Industry Engagement
Trinity College Dublin, The University of Dublin, Ireland

Abstract

Since its first appearance in the educational scene, mobile learning has disrupted education and turned the adoption of technology in educational settings in its head. The educational establishments' 'love hate' relationship with mobile learning has been through phases of scepticism, adjustment, commitment, and acceptance. In recent years arguments against the 'excessive' use of mobile technologies by children and youth are starting to erode the relationship. In fact, governments are beginning to regulate against the use of mobile phones in classrooms. Thus, we are moving backwards rather than moving forward. In this presentation, I will examine the Good, the Bad and the Ugly of mobile learning from a learning and teaching perspective and attempt to outline pitfalls and how to overcome these going forward.

TUTORIAL

EMPOWER STUDENT TUTORS IN HYBRID TEACHING ENVIRONMENTS

Melanie Ludwig and Michelle Pippig
ZiLL – Dresden University of Technology, Mommsenstr. 6, 01069 Dresden, Germany

ABSTRACT

How tutors learn in a practical way how to prepare themselves and their (online) course room in a meaningful way and how to eliminate analogue and digital stumbling blocks. A tutorial including how to set up such a "hybrid room of horrors" as a real life simulation will be shown. Conference participants will be able to try the setting themselves, be it in the real room or on their mobile device. Meaningful learning effects will be transported by showing templates, 360-degree panoramas - and the scientific idea behind and additionally its implementation as Open Educational Practice.

KEYWORDS

Didactics, Student Tutors, Hybrid, Paedagogics, Continuing Education

1. INTRODUCTION

We have often found that tutors step into a seminar room and just start their lesson. Then they trip over cables, the door remains open, or remote participants are frustrated being just in the listener position: the quality for the audience suffers. How can we support student tutors to become aware of these obstacles that have been proven to reduce motivation and learning outcomes in order to promote a good teaching atmosphere, especially in the context of mobile learning environments?

2. A TEMPLATE FOR THE HYBRID ROOM OF HORRORS

Our new learning concept aims to increase awareness of common mistakes. Mobile learning is crucial in today's educational landscape, as it enhances access to education and integrates learners into various contexts. Our "Real life Simulation Approach" (Lateef, 2010) is a playful way to discover where traps for student tutors can lurk everywhere, both analogue and mobile learning (Nome et. Al., 2022). The increasing use of mobile devices and applications in educational institutions presents teachers with unique challenges. Our "hybrid fright room" simulation is designed to teach participants how to integrate mobile technologies into their teaching methods without disruption. This includes aspects such as connecting mobile devices to presentation technology, ensuring that all participants can be actively engaged regardless of their location, and encouraging interaction and collaboration in mobile learning environments. The approach is based on a training concept transferred from the field of medicine, where patient rooms (Pat. Schweiz, 2022) are checked and trip hazards removed in a "Room of Horrors". This is followed by extensive feedback and the participants receive a detailed checklist (Zimmermann et. al., 2020). The tutorial involves participants trying the simulation, experiencing challenging scenarios and moments of success, identifying hidden obstacles in both physical and digital spaces. Subsequently, they learn to implement the "hybrid room of horrors" - an innovative and engaging method for preparing seminar rooms. We provide practical examples during the tutorial and offer the concept as Open Educational Resources (OER) for attendees to access later. Participants can adapt the approach to their teaching contexts and assess their own methods using a provided framework.

3. CONCLUSION

The tutorial is aimed at all those who deal with university didactics, teach themselves or are otherwise active in the field of continuing education. By addressing specific challenges of hybrid learning environments, this tutorial provides valuable insights into creating effective and engaging learning spaces. We look forward to a stimulating discussion.

REFERENCES

Lateef, F.B., 2010. Simulation-based learning: Journal of Emergencies, Trauma and Shock, 3, 348 - 352.

Nome, K., Olsen, M.V., Soleim, H., Geitung, A.B., Johnsgaard, T., & Karlgren, K., 2022. Usability of a VR Simulation Training Concept with Intentional Simulation Errors. 2022 1st IEEE International Conference on Cognitive Aspects of Virtual Reality (CVR), 000037-000042.

Patientensicherheit Schweiz, 2022. *Interaktives Lernen im Room of Horros*, In: https://patientensicherheit.ch/room-of-horrors/ (27.04.2023)

Zimmermann, C., Fridrich, A., & Schwappach, D.L., 2020. Training Situational Awareness for Patient Safety in a Room of Horrors: An Evaluation of a Low-Fidelity Simulation Method. Journal of Patient Safety, 17, e1026 - e1033.

INTERNATIONAL CONFERENCES PROCEEDINGS

2024

9 - 11 March
Porto, Portugal

e-SOCIETY

Edited by

Piet Kommers
Inmaculada Arnedillo Sánchez
Pedro Isaías

MOBILE LEARNING

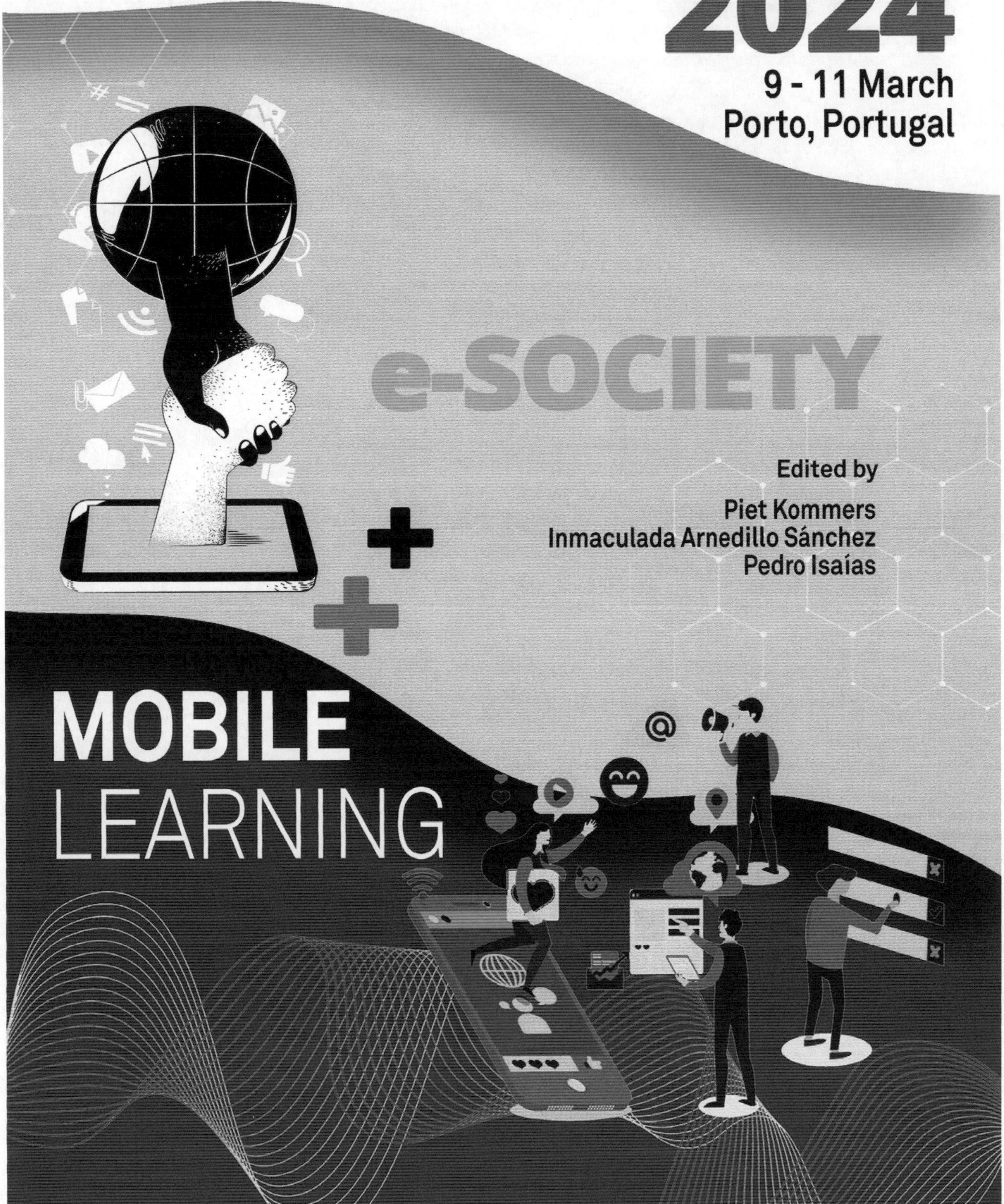

Full Papers

MEDIA DESIGN FOR ADOLESCENTS IN SEPARATION AND DIVORCE SITUATIONS

Mirella Moser, Severine Gomringer and Thomas Keller
ZHAW School of Management and Law, Winterthur, Switzerland

ABSTRACT

This study examines the design of digital media to support adolescents dealing with parental separation and divorce. With increasing mental health issues among youth, there is a need for innovative, accessible mental health services. The study, utilizing Design Science Research methodology, developed a concept for a mobile app tailored to the unique needs and preferences of adolescents aged 15-21. The app integrates features like immediate access to support, personalized coping strategies, interactive elements for peer engagement, and the creation of trust figures in the form of avatars. Validation through focus groups highlighted the app's success in meeting adolescents' requirements for accessibility, personalization, and privacy, while also revealing the need for further adaptation and exploration in future iterations. This research contributes to the field by offering a nuanced understanding of digital mental health services and their potential in addressing specific youth mental health challenges.

KEYWORDS

Divorce and Separation, Adolescent Mental Health, Digital Mental Health Services, Digital Counseling

1. INTRODUCTION

The contemporary landscape in Switzerland presents a concerning trajectory, underscored by a sharp increase in the number of young people struggling with mental health problems (Public Health Schweiz et al., 2023). This trend is further exacerbated by the Covid-19 pandemic (Schuler et al., 2022). Regrettably, these struggling adolescents often find themselves isolated, dealing with their challenges in solitude. Only a fraction actively seeks external help and takes advantage of mental health care services (Barense-Dias et al., 2021). At the same time, there exists an evident undersupply of essential services for these adolescents in Switzerland (von Wyl et al., 2020). This also applies to adolescents suffering from separation and divorce situations. For these young people, access to appropriate therapeutic interventions remains a challenge. Such complications not only exacerbate the individuals' distress, but also impact their immediate environment. Considering a rising divorce prevalence in the country (Bundesamt für Statistik, 2022) and the attendant conflicts, increasing costs for the health sector are expected (Public Health Schweiz et al., 2023).

Addressing such issues is imperative. Current interventions in Switzerland range from helplines, chat-based counseling, to physical counseling centers (Musliu & Edthofer, 2021). Additionally, there have been endeavors to communicate assistance through text-centric media such as brochures or flyers (ZHAW Zürcher Hochschule für Angewandte Wissenschaften, 2021). However, media consumption trends amongst this age bracket in Switzerland suggest a diminishing affinity for text-centered journalistic media (Waller et al., 2021). In contrast, adolescents prefer smartphones and online formats for obtaining information (Külling et al., 2022). This scenario presents a compelling challenge: to design and develop a media offering that the affected young people would genuinely be engaged with and that positively impacts their mental health in a sustainable manner.

2. RESEARCH OBJECTIVES

The research presented in this paper aims to tackle the following question: *What emergent characteristics should a medium exhibit so that adolescents perceive it as a useful and supportive resource in situations of parental separation and divorce?* The media design is aimed at young people aged 15-21.

This age group is in the middle to late adolescence, which is characterized by a striving for greater independence from parents and an increasing emphasis on relationships with peers (Kessels, 2013). At this stage of development, the need for independent support services is particularly high.

The goal of this research extends to testing the following assumptions (hypotheses), which are crucial for the development of a medium that aligns with the needs and preferences of adolescents:

Immediate Availability of Support and Coping Strategies: It is assumed that assistance and coping mechanisms must be readily and directly accessible to adolescents. This immediacy is essential given the urgent nature of support needed in situations of parental separation.

Relevance and Customization of Support: The presumption posits that support offerings become relevant and engaging for adolescents when they are individually tailored to their unique situations. Personalization is key in ensuring that the support is perceived as meaningful and effective.

Peer Interaction in Difficult Situations: The assumption is that adolescents seek to engage with their peers when faced with challenging circumstances. Peer support is thus a critical component of the medium's design.

Trust Figures Within the Medium: The hypothesis is that adolescents require a trust figure within the medium, one that is emotionally resonant and capable of fostering engagement. This figure should provide a sense of reliability and emotional connection.

3. RELATED WORK

In recent years, alongside traditional sources like close acquaintances and professional services, there has been an increase in adolescents seeking support from online platforms (Kupfer & Mayer, 2019). This is since there are more barriers to overcome when seeking help offline than when seeking help online (Pretorius et al., 2019). The widespread ownership and use of cell phones for various communication among adolescents (Külling et al., 2022) further underscores this trend. Contemporary studies indicate that adolescents are effectively engaged through a blend of social media and physical interactions supplemented by digital tools (Amstad et al., 2022). Consequently, digital health and counseling services emerge as promising possibilities to reach more young people and tailor the services to the target group (Jesser et al., 2021).

For online counseling, various channels are used, such as chats, apps, emails, or forums. Platforms like OPEN enable young people between the ages of 14 and 21 to contact so-called peer mentors. It is intended to enable adolescents to talk openly about their problems (Jesser et al., 2021). In Switzerland, platforms like “häschziit” (Verein #häschziit, 2023) or “ciao.ch” (Association romande CIAO, 2023) facilitate anonymous yet trustworthy exchanges for young people and adults. These platforms differ in their approach; some provide peer-to-peer support while others connect users with specialists. Another example for a created artifact in online services is the iFightDepression tool (Arensman et al., 2015). iFightDepression is an internet-based self-management tool for mild to moderate depression cases for young adults. Additionally, mobile applications such as “Wie geht’s dir?” (Trägerschaft Wie geht’s dir-Kampagne, 2023), “Heavy Mental” (Zürcher Hochschule der Künste & Stiftung Sanitas Krankenversicherung, 2023), and “Eda” (Moltrecht et al., 2022) focus on emotional regulation and self-awareness.

However, the long-term use of these mobile applications often falls short of expectations and despite the advancement in digital mental health services, several requirements from adolescents remain unfulfilled. Research highlights, that adolescents seek services that are interactive and engaging, empathetic to their unique experiences and life stages, as well as easily accessible and flexible (Gibson, 2021). Many existing services offer a one-size-fits-all approach, lacking the personalized care and attention that adolescents require. Additionally, some digital services may not fully leverage interactive elements. Moreover, services often miss out on fully understanding the unique contexts and experiences of adolescents, leading to a gap in empathy and connection.

Research has been carried out to understand, how user empowerment is facilitated and constrained by the design of online counseling services (Lundmark & Evaldsson, 2017). The results show that factors such as user interface design, modes of interaction, and overall user experience play a crucial role in promoting young users' engagement and empowerment. Furthermore, the analysis underlines the importance of integrating digital tools with human elements for more effective digital advice. This is in line with other research findings that suggest that guided online services are generally more effective than their non-guided counterparts (Arensman et al., 2015).

This research aims to build on previous research projects by moving beyond current digital mental health services and focusing on long-term effectiveness and usefulness for adolescents, particularly in the context of parental separation and divorce. It emphasizes the need for services that combine digital accessibility with deep empathy, interactivity, and a high degree of personalization, tailored to the unique circumstances of each adolescent. With this, and the goal of combining digital tools with human elements, the study aims to create a more effective digital support system for adolescents facing the complex issues of their parents' separation and divorce, thereby making a significant contribution to the field of adolescent mental health.

4. METHODOLOGY AND APPROACH

This research is anchored in the Design Science Research (DSR) framework. DSR emphasizes both rigor and relevance, operating in a cyclic process of three research cycles to ensure both the scientific validity and practical applicability of its results (Hevner, 2007). The development and validation of the research artifact were guided by the Design Science Research Methodology according to Peffers et al. (2007), involving the following steps:

Problem Identification and Requirement Elicitation was instrumental in formulating the assumptions (hypotheses). To understand the unique challenges and needs of adolescents impacted by parental separation or divorce, qualitative data collection was essential. Semi-structured interviews were conducted with adults (n=7) who had experienced parental separation or divorce in their youth, seeking to gain insights into their behavior and what forms of support could have potentially benefitted them. Additionally, interviews with professionals (n=6) who regularly interact with affected adolescents offered perspectives on the challenges this group faces.

Systematic content analysis (Mayring, 2016) was conducted on these dialogues, leading to the documentation of requirements for the intended media. A literature review complemented this stage to cross-verify the requirements for the media design.

The Design of the Artifact led to the development of concrete solutions in form of mockups addressing the hypotheses. Using the gathered requirements, a media solution in the form of an app was conceptualized. An iterative design process was employed to ensure usability and effectiveness. Mockups of the app were reviewed by both affected adolescents (n=5) and professionals (n=6), whose feedback informed continuous refinements in the app's design.

The Artifact Validation was carried out through focus groups comprising 9 participants (5 females, 4 males; ages 13-20, average age 16.5; German-speaking Switzerland). Due to the sensitive nature of the topic and partially limited availability of affected individuals, the focus groups were not exclusively composed of affected adolescents. Though the intention was to immerse participants in relevant scenarios.

A first focus group intervention (n=6) was conducted, where discussions were structured into two parts: the first part sought to understand general behaviors and needs of adolescents during challenging situations with parents; the second part involved discussing the proposed solutions using the app artifact. Special attention was given to assessing the established hypotheses. In cases where responses and opinions were not uniform, a second, smaller focus group session with other participants (n=3) provided additional insights, aiming to minimize the influence of specific group dynamics on the outcomes.

Data from the focus groups such as audio recordings, transcripts and flipchart documentations were analyzed using Descriptive Coding (Saldaña, 2013).

5. DESIGN OF THE MEDIA

The aim of the design is to genuinely engage adolescents and to positively impact their mental health in a sustainable manner. As outlined in the methodology section, the foundation of the design is formed by feedback from professionals and adolescents impacted by parental separation or divorce, supplemented by extensive literature research. Adapted on the media conception of Döring & Ingerl (2008), this research focuses on the aspects *Why*, *What* and *How*. The artifact is the synthesis of these aspects and visualizes the design in form of mockups.

5.1 Why

This section explores the rationale behind the design of the medium: the intended effects and the impact it should have on the target audience.

In the context of parental separation and divorce, adolescents face numerous challenges and questions. They often withdraw and seek distraction or interaction with people who are not involved in the events. They are also confronted with many uncertainties, such as specific questions about personal rights or the general challenge of future steps. Feelings of guilt, conflicts of loyalty, new responsibilities, and harmful role changes are common.

This research highlights the critical need for a dedicated space focused on the adolescents themselves – a place of trust, personal comfort, and security. This space should enable them to address insecurities and discomforts, ensuring a supportive environment where they can communicate freely, whether with peers or specialists. The intended outcome of the developed artifact is to provide support at crucial moments.

5.2 What

This aspect delves into the content and functionality of the medium.

The design aims to provide relevant, engaging, and practical resources tailored to the unique needs of adolescents during parental separation or divorce. The content and functionality are designed to be adaptable, evolving with the changing needs and feedback of the adolescent users, ensuring ongoing relevance and effectiveness:

Educational Support and Guidance

The medium offers clear, concise information on rights, procedures, and coping strategies to help demystify the complexities associated with parental separation. It incorporates educational material addressing common misconceptions, provides insights into emotional responses, and offers advice on handling new responsibilities and possible role changes. This approach aims to empower adolescents with knowledge and understanding, enabling them to navigate their situations more effectively.

Personalized Support

The support offered within the medium is customized to the individual user. To achieve this, the app gathers information about the situation and needs of the adolescent. Users can select from a range of support options to tailor the app to their specific needs, creating a space that is solely focused on them and aligns with their personal circumstances. An innovative feature is the ability for users to create their own personal avatar, which accompanies and motivates them throughout their journey in the medium. This personalized avatar adds a unique, engaging touch to the experience.

Interactive Features

The medium incorporates interactive elements to foster active participation and engagement. Conversations with the avatar encourage users to reflect on their situation and needs. The inclusion of community elements, including chat capabilities and options to establish or participate in groups, facilitates interaction and external assistance, fostering a community spirit. The medium integrates coping mechanisms with tangible exercises, like relaxation techniques and reflective writing, offering pragmatic approaches for emotional regulation and stress management. These features collectively aim to provide a dynamic and supportive experience for the users.

5.3 How

This section of the conceptual framework outlines the implementation and operational features of the medium, explaining the specific choices made in its design.

Opting for a mobile application is a strategic decision, recognizing that smartphones are central to adolescents' lives (Külling et al., 2022). This choice ensures the help offered is always within reach, providing round-the-clock accessibility. The decision is further supported by the Media Richness Theory, which posits that richer media formats are superior in complex communication scenarios (Daft & Lengel, 1986). An app, with its multimedia capabilities and interactive features, provides the necessary richness and immediacy for effective communication and engagement. A distinctive aspect of the app is its integration of a multimedia mix, encompassing not only digital content but also real-life references, including peers and professionals.

This blend offers a more relatable and engaging user experience, connecting digital interactions with real-world contexts (Amstad et al., 2022). A crucial aspect is that the app is conceptualized as an all-in-one platform, eliminating the need for users to navigate away from the system to access different types of support. This unified approach ensures a seamless user experience and simplifies access to various resources. The app also emphasizes the importance of professionalism in its content and interactions while maintaining user anonymity, ensuring that adolescents can seek help and engage with the app without concerns about privacy or judgment. Professionalism in content and guidance provides reliability and trustworthiness, essential factors for effective support.

5.4 Artifact

The artifact in form of mockups of a mobile application (Gomringer & Moser, 2023) represents the synthesis of the *Why*, *What* and *How* aspects. During the design development phase, the four hypotheses served as the primary guide. Specific solutions were developed and visualized in mockups to address them. The mockups then served as a basis for discussion for input and feedback from adolescents and professionals.

1. Immediate Availability of Support and Coping Strategies

The hypothesis suggests that for adolescents facing the stress of parental separation, support and coping strategies should be readily accessible without delay. The app responds to this need by offering a selection of tools, assistance, and information, along with coping strategies that are immediately accessible, for instance through the home screen (see **Error! Reference source not found.**). It functions as an all-in-one platform, offering resources directly within the app, allowing for private, anytime access without the need for external input or adherence to service hours.

2. Relevance and Customization of Support

The app employs a tailored approach to support, aligning with the hypothesis that relevance and personalization are key for engaging adolescents. Through an initial assessment, the app discerns each user's specific situation and needs. Based on their responses, the app suggests customized support and coping strategies. This process is powered by a learning algorithm working in the background, while the user interacts with a friendly avatar for a personalized experience, as shown in **Error! Reference source not found.**. Additionally, users have the flexibility to update their profiles to reflect any changes in their personal circumstances, ensuring the assistance they receive remains pertinent and effective.

3. Peer Interaction in Difficult Situations

The app supports the hypothesis that adolescents seek peer connections during tough times by incorporating community features. Users can join existing groups or create new communities, fostering valuable exchanges. There is also a functionality to add peers as friends for more direct interaction, as seen in **Error! Reference source not found.**, underlining the app's role in facilitating and encouraging peer support.

4. Trust Figures Within the Medium

The app integrates the concept of a trusted figure by allowing users to create a personalized avatar (see **Error! Reference source not found.**). The avatar, which users can customize down to name, outfit, hairstyle, and facial features, acts as a constant, comforting presence within the app. It accompanies the user through various functionalities, offering advice and support, thereby triggering engagement through its emotive and relatable design. This personalized avatar becomes a digital confidant, fostering a unique relationship that combines reliability with emotional resonance.

Figure 1. Accessible tools and information

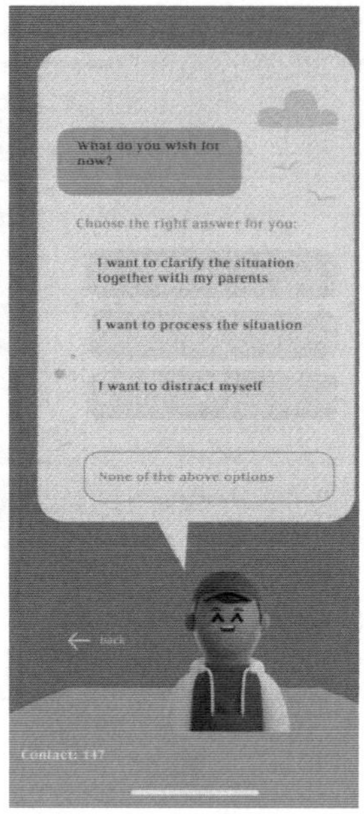

Figure 2. Assessment of personal situation

Figure 3. Exchange through communities and friends

Figure 4. Creating a personal avatar

6. RESULTS

The research went through a first iteration of a design science cycle by using focus groups for validation. This phase was crucial for assessing the feasibility of the developed design and the circumstances under which young people would use the media. The findings allowed for an evaluation of the hypotheses.

6.1 Immediate Availability of Support and Coping Strategies

Results from the focus groups indicate that the young participants greatly valued the direct access to support provided by the mobile application. All participants appreciated the inclusion of specific self-help exercises, such as meditation and diary writing, which they could undertake independently. Equally important to them was the ability to reach out for external support, such as contacting specialists or utilizing emergency numbers, directly through the app. The emergency number 147 was specifically mentioned as an important resource by three participants. They emphasized its importance as an easily accessible option for those who do not know where to turn for a listening ear or immediate assistance. The app's feature of helping users locate nearby specialists was also well received, highlighting the adolescents' desire for accessible professional help within their local context. This local assistance aspect was seen as an extension of the app's comprehensive support network.

Four participants expressed their appreciation for the app's all-in-one platform design, which allowed them to access various services without the need to switch between different apps or websites, enhancing the sense of a secure and integrated support environment. Moreover, the platform was praised by all participants for providing a safe space, which is paramount for young people dealing with sensitive issues.

However, the feedback on the selection of options within the app varied. Just as adolescents have diverse interests and personalities, their preferences for the exercises and content offered by the app differed. Some found certain activities more helpful or appealing than others, reflecting the individualized approach the app strives to offer. This diversity in preferences underscores the need for a wide range of options to accommodate the varied coping mechanisms of different individuals.

6.2 Relevance and Customization of Support

The results underscore the importance of the app being personalized to the unique circumstances of the adolescents. The participants were not explicitly aware of the learning algorithm's role in tailoring their experience, but all of them valued the guided assessment provided as a form of support, aiding in their engagement with the app. Moreover, the feedback of two adolescents highlighted the preference for a concise questionnaire, noting that extensive queries could deter continued engagement.

The option to choose from a curated set of activities was welcomed by seven participants, preventing the feeling of being overwhelmed. However, there was also a desire for the ability to view all available options, rather than being limited to a few suggestions, to allow for informed decision-making. In addition, one participant expressed the need for a personal dashboard to track the progress and to reflect on the personal journey.

However, the aspect of customization extended beyond the functional; it was equally important for all adolescents to personalize the app's look and feel, such as changing the background color, selecting a profile image, or designing their avatar, making the app not just a tool, but a reflection of their identity.

6.3 Peer Interaction in Difficult Situations

The results reveal nuanced insights into the adolescents' communication preferences during difficult situations. While typically reserved about discussing personal struggles openly and personally with friends, the largest part of the group responded positively to the concept of online possibilities such as communities for sharing experiences with others in similar situations. They emphasized the value of authentic peer exchanges in these online spaces, finding comfort in the realization that they are not alone and that their feelings are shared by others. The importance of interacting with real individuals, as opposed to digital entities like bots, was highlighted by two participants, with a preference for peers of similar age to foster a sense of belonging. Furthermore, safety within these communities emerged as a non-negotiable condition for all the adolescents. Privacy and respectful interaction were paramount for them to create an environment where they felt secure to share and interact.

However, opinions diverged on the scope of discussions within these communities. Four participants believed that conversations should focus solely on navigating the challenges directly related to their situation, such as adapting to new family dynamics. In contrast, the five others advocated for the inclusion of diverse topics, like hobbies, to provide a welcome distraction and broader support. Despite varied opinions on content focus within the communities, all the participants concurred that while these online spaces provide a fitting platform for dialogue, engaging actively often involves overcoming personal reservations and the challenge of revealing one's vulnerabilities.

6.4 Trust Figures Within the Medium

The focus group results shed light on the participants' attitudes toward the use of avatars within the app, underscoring their preference for personalization in the digital experience. The ability to customize their avatars was particularly well-received by all the participants, allowing them to infuse their personal identity into the app. Most participants were in favor of the avatar being a human figure. In addition, the idea of an animal, e.g. a pet dog, as a neutral figure detached from family conflicts was also appealing for two adolescents. However, the consensus tended towards a human figure as the avatar.

While the avatar added a personal touch to the app, two of the participants did not see it as necessary for it to be present in all functionalities. They see its most effective use in areas involving personal interactions. For six adolescents, the avatar functioned as a virtual confidant, creating a sense of talking to someone and thereby enhancing the engagement with the app. For them, it provided a feeling of constant companionship, mitigating feelings of isolation. However, there was recognition of three of the participants that the avatar, despite its personal touch, remained a digital figure. This led to expressing the need for human elements within the app, highlighting a desire for a balance between digital interaction and human connection.

6.5 Essential Criteria for Comfort and Usability

The focus group participants articulated several key factors necessary for the app to be considered helpful and comfortable.

A significant emphasis was placed on security, with all the adolescents expressing a strong desire for anonymity and data privacy. The platform being a safe space where they can freely express feelings and be taken seriously was highlighted as crucial. They underscored the importance of creating an environment where they feel protected from any potential harm.

Personalization emerged as another key requirement. Six adolescents showed a keen interest in customizing the platform to reflect their personal tastes and preferences, aspiring to transform the app into a space that feels uniquely theirs. This desire for personalization extended to the functionality and aesthetics of the app, underscoring their need for a deeply individualized experience.

Another feature that five participants found appealing was the idea of a reminder function or regular personalized messages. They liked the notion of the avatar interacting within the app, providing encouragement or suggestions. Outside the app, push notifications could prompt them to re-engage with the app or to complete certain exercises. However, they stressed that the frequency and nature of these reminders should be adjustable to avoid becoming intrusive or overwhelming.

7. CONCLUSIONS

The research conducted within the DSR framework has yielded valuable insights into the media design aimed at supporting adolescents, particularly in situations of parental separation and divorce. However, these results should be viewed in light of certain limitations. Not all participants of the focus groups were directly affected by parental separation, potentially influencing the findings. Additionally, the mixed age composition of the groups makes it difficult to draw definitive conclusions about the app's effectiveness across different adolescent age groups. Moreover, the small number of participants emphasizes the qualitative focus of the study, limiting the scope for broad quantitative conclusions.

Despite these limitations, the results from the focus groups indicate that the hypotheses played a crucial and constructive role in the design process. This has led to the successful functioning of the media design concept, aligning closely with the initial intentions. Particularly, the implementation and operational features outlined in the *How* section emerged as critical components for any future application. This includes the creation of an all-in-one platform, ensuring anonymity, and integrating a media mix that combines digital spaces with human interactions. However, the findings under the *What* section call for a more nuanced approach. The diverse reactions to specific exercises highlight the importance of personalization, allowing adolescents to choose what resonates with them. Similarly, offering flexible use of communities is essential to cater to varied preferences and needs.

A general cognition from the validation process was the difference in perceptions and priorities between adolescents and professionals. The adolescents seemed to underemphasize aspects like educational material and the need for professionalism, possibly perceiving these as basic expectations rather than notable features. This suggests that while these elements are essential, they might not be the primary factors that draw adolescents to the app.

In summary, the implementation of this media design holds the potential to fill a significant gap in current adolescent mental health support. It offers a novel, user-centric approach that blends technological innovation with empathetic human interaction, aiming to engage and support adolescents in a way that traditional methods may not. Future steps, including experimental testing and addressing outstanding questions about app discoverability and data protection, are crucial in refining the concept for optimal impact.

REFERENCES

Amstad, F., Suris, J.-C., Barense-Dias, Y., Dratva, J., Meyer, M., Nordström, K., Weber, D., Bernath, J., Süss, D., Suggs, S., Bucher Della Torre, S., Wieber, F., von Wyl, A., Zysset, A., Schiftan, R., & Wittgenstein Mani, A.-F. (2022). Gesundheitsförderung für und mit Jugendlichen und jungen Erwachsenen—Wissenschaftliche Erkenntnisse und Empfehlungen für die Praxis (9; Gesundheitsförderung Schweiz, p. 118). Gesundheitsförderung Schweiz. https://promozionesalute.ch/sites/default/files/2022-11/Bericht_009_GFCH_2022-11_-_Gesundheitsf%C3%B6rderung%20f%C3%BCr%20und%20mit%20Jugendlichen%20und%20jungen%20Erwachsenen.pdf

Arensman, E., Koburger, N., Larkin, C., Karwig, G., Coffey, C., Maxwell, M., Harris, F., Rummel-Kluge, C., Audenhove, C. van, Sisask, M., Alexandrova-Karamanova, A., Perez, V., Purebl, G., Cebria, A., Palao, D., Costa, S., Mark, L., Tóth, M. D., Gecheva, M., … Hegerl, U. (2015). Depression Awareness and Self-Management Through the Internet: Protocol for an Internationally Standardized Approach. JMIR Research Protocols, 4(3), e4358. https://doi.org/10.2196/resprot.4358

Association romande CIAO. (2023). Ciao.ch. https://www.ciao.ch/

Barense-Dias, Y., Chok, L., & Suris, J.-C. (2021). A picture of the mental health of adolescents in Switzerland and Liechtenstein. https://www.unicef.ch/de/unsere-arbeit/schweiz-liechtenstein/psychische-gesundheit

Bundesamt für Statistik. (2022). Internetnutzung. https://www.bfs.admin.ch/asset/de/23588807

Döring, N., & Ingerl, A. (2008). Medienkonzeption. In B. Batinic & M. Appel (Eds.), Medienpsychologie (pp. 403–424). Springer Berlin Heidelberg. https://doi.org/10.1007/978-3-540-46899-8_17

Gibson, K. (2021). What Young People Want from Mental Health Services: A Youth Informed Approach for the Digital Age. https://doi.org/10.4324/9780429322457

Gomringer, S., & Moser, M. (2023). Media design for adolescents in separation and divorce situations. https://osf.io/anj97/

Hevner, A. R. (2007). A Three Cycle View of Design Science Research. Scandinavian Journal of Information Systems, 19(2).

Jesser, A., Schmalwieser, S., Mädge, A.-L., Culen, C., Schrank, B., & Böckle, M. (2021). Chancen niederschwelliger online Peer-to-Peer Begleitung für Jugendliche am Beispiel der Online-Plattform OPEN. Psychotherapie Forum, 25(3), 154–160. https://doi.org/10.1007/s00729-021-00188-z

Kessels, U. (2013). Jugend. In S. Andresen, C. Hunner-Kreisel, & S. Fries (Eds.), Erziehung: Ein interdisziplinäres Handbuch (pp. 39–44). J.B. Metzler. https://doi.org/10.1007/978-3-476-05023-6_6

Külling, C., Waller, G., Suter, L., Willemse, I., Bernath, J., Skirgaila, P., Streule, P., & Süss, D. (2022). JAMES Jugend | Aktivitäten | Medien – Erhebung Schweiz (Studie 7). ZHAW Zürcher Hochschule für Angewandte Wissenschaften. https://www.zhaw.ch/de/psychologie/forschung/medienpsychologie/mediennutzung/james/

Kupfer, A., & Mayer, M. (2019). Digitalisierung der Beratung. Onlineberatung für Kinder und Jugendliche und die Frage nach Möglichkeiten des Blended Counseling in der Kinder- und Jugendhilfe. Soziale Passagen, 11(2), 243–265. https://doi.org/10.1007/s12592-019-00333-1

Lundmark, S., & Evaldsson, A.-C. (2017). Click-guides and panic buttons: Designed possibilities for youth agency and user empowerment in online youth counselling services. Childhood, 24(2), 260–278. https://doi.org/10.1177/0907568216656761

Mayring, P. (2016). Einführung in die qualitative Sozialforschung: Eine Anleitung zu qualitativem Denken (6., überarbeitete Auflage). Beltz.

Moltrecht, B., Patalay, P., Bear, H. A., Deighton, J., & Edbrooke-Childs, J. (2022). A Transdiagnostic, Emotion Regulation App (Eda) for Children: Design, Development, and Lessons Learned. JMIR Formative Research, 6(1), e28300. https://doi.org/10.2196/28300

Musliu, L., & Edthofer, S. (2021). Jahresbericht 2021 (p. 28). Stiftung Pro Juventute. https://www.projuventute.ch/sites/default/files/2022-05/DT_Jahresbericht_2021_0.pdf

Peffers, K., Tuunanen, T., Rothenberger, M. A., & Chatterjee, S. (2007). A Design Science Research Methodology for Information Systems Research. Journal of Management Information Systems, 24(3), 45–77. https://doi.org/10.2753/MIS0742-1222240302

Pretorius, C., Chambers, D., & Coyle, D. (2019). Young People's Online Help-Seeking and Mental Health Difficulties: Systematic Narrative Review. Journal of Medical Internet Research, 21(11), e13873. https://doi.org/10.2196/13873

Public Health Schweiz, Pro Juventute, SAJV, Ciao.ch, & Unicef. (2023). Tagungswebseite – 24. Mai 2023 – Psychische Gesundheit junger Menschen. https://tagu.ng/

Saldaña, J. (2013). The coding manual for qualitative researchers (2nd ed). SAGE.

Schuler, D., Tuch, A., Sturny, I., Peter, C., & Obsan. (2022). Psychische Gesundheit—Kennzahlen mit Fokus Covid-19. Schweizerisches Gesundheitsobservatorium.

Trägerschaft Wie geht's dir-Kampagne. (2023). Wie geht's dir? https://www.wie-gehts-dir.ch/

Verein #häschziit. (2023, October 31). Häsch Ziit? https://haeschziit.ch/

von Wyl, A., Howard, E. C., Wade-Bohleber, L., Passalacqua, S., Schneebeli, L., Haemmerle, P., & Andreae, A. (2020). Stationäre und tagesklinische Angebote der psychiatrischen Gesundheitsversorgung an der Schnittstelle des Jugend- und Erwachsenenalters in der Schweiz. Eine Bestandesaufnahme bestehender Angebote im Auftrag des BAG. Zürcher Hochschule für Angewandte Wissenschaften.

Waller, G., Süss, D., Suter, L., Willemse, I., Külling, C., Bernath, J., Skirgaila, P., & Löpfe, S. (2021). JAMESfocus—Rückblick auf ein Jahrzehnt Jugendmedienforschung. Zürcher Hochschule für Angewandte Wissenschaften. https://www.zhaw.ch/storage/psychologie/upload/forschung/medienpsychologie/james/jamesfocus/2022/JAMESfocus_Jugendmedienforschung_DE.pdf

ZHAW Zürcher Hochschule für Angewandte Wissenschaften. (2021). Heb der Sorg! Ein Werkzeugkasten für Jugendliche, die aktiv mit Herausforderungen umgehen wollen.

Zürcher Hochschule der Künste & Stiftung Sanitas Krankenversicherung. (2023). Heavy Mental. https://www.heavy-mental.ch/

DIGITAL TRANSFORMATION IN THE HEALTHCARE SECTOR IN BRAZIL AND THE EFFECTS OF THE PANDEMIC ON PUBLIC HEALTH

Luciana Portilho and Manuella Maia Ribeiro
Regional Center for Studies on the Development of the Information Society (Cetic.br), Brazil

ABSTRACT

The Covid-19 pandemic highlighted the need for and the benefits of digital transformation in the healthcare sector. Digital technologies facilitated various actions such as data collection processes, public health monitoring, dissemination of protocols to healthcare professionals, and recommendations to the population. In light of this, this paper analyzes the process of digital transformation in healthcare in Brazil driven by the demands imposed by the Covid-19 pandemic, as well as the sustainability of these advancements in the post-pandemic period, providing benefits to the served population. To achieve this, data regarding the adoption of ICT in public healthcare facilities were analyzed, focusing on ICT infrastructure, the adoption of electronic patient information systems, and telehealth. The results demonstrate that there has indeed been progress in various areas of the Brazilian healthcare system with the increased adoption of digital health, particularly concerning connectivity, electronic availability of patient information, and telehealth. However, challenges remain for achieving complete connectivity in public healthcare facilities, expanding telehealth, and implementing actions aimed at protecting the privacy and personal data of users of the Brazilian healthcare system.

KEYWORDS

Digital Transformation, Digital Health, Healthcare Facilities, Covid-19

1. INTRODUCTION

The digital transformation of the health sector has been advancing in recent years in various countries. With the advent of the Covid-19 pandemic, the urgency of its implementation has become even more evident. During the global health crisis, the use of Information and Communication Technologies (ICT) was essential for the implementation of actions aimed at prevention, detection, and assistance to the population. The digital technologies applied to the processes of information collection, dissemination of protocols to healthcare professionals, and recommendations to the population provided greater efficiency in public health policy actions (World Health Organization [WHO] & International Telecommunication Union [ITU], 2020).

Health information systems were essential for managing data and information quickly, facilitating evidence-based decision-making, and developing and implementing health policies and actions that were better suited to the current needs. Emerging technologies such as artificial intelligence (AI), robotics, and the Internet of Things (IoT) contributed to improving remote patient monitoring and more efficient and faster diagnoses, resulting in significant benefits for public health (Pan American Health Organization [PAHO], 2021). Digital technologies also favored the expansion of telehealth services during this period, especially for non-emergency consultations that did not require direct interaction between the patient and healthcare professionals, reducing resource utilization in healthcare facilities, improving healthcare delivery, and reducing the risk of contagion to the population (Zhai et al., 2020; Chaunan et al., 2020).

In Brazil, progress has been made in the availability of ICT infrastructure, such as computers and the Internet, as well as the adoption of electronic health records. However, significant disparities still existed between private and public healthcare facilities, with public primary healthcare units (PHUs) having less access to digital technologies.

With the emergence of the pandemic, the need for the accelerated adoption of digital technologies in public health became paramount. In addition to addressing the lack of devices and internet access, public policies focused on the development of applications. One of the main programs implemented during this period was

Conecte SUS, launched in 2019 and boosted during the pandemic. This program primarily focuses on expanding the digitization of primary care, improving Internet connectivity for Family Health teams (eSF), and digitizing other levels of care (Brazilian Ministry of Health, 2021). Regarding telehealth, new regulations allowed for teleconsultations (Ministry of Health Ordinance No. 467/2020), which were previously prohibited in the country, and online screening tools proved valuable, contributing to the maintenance of social distancing measures.

It is worth highlighting that Brazil has a public healthcare system that provides universal health coverage for the population. Nevertheless, a portion of the population also has access to the private healthcare sector, approximately 47 million people (24.1%) in 2022, according to the National Supplementary Health Agency (Agência Nacional de Saúde Suplementar, ANS). This means that the majority of the population, nearly 163 million people, depends solely on the public system known as Sistema Único de Saúde (SUS). In this context, the digitization of public healthcare facilities in Brazil has the potential to improve healthcare and the lives of the majority of the Brazilian population and facilitate the monitoring of public health in the country.

In light of the above, this paper aims to analyze the digital transformation of healthcare in Brazil driven by the demands imposed by the COVID-19 pandemic and the sustainability of these advances in the post-pandemic period, providing benefits to the served population. Data on the adoption of ICT in public healthcare facilities were analyzed, including ICT infrastructure, the adoption of electronic patient information systems, and telehealth.

It is expected that this paper will contribute to a better understanding of the advances in the digitization of public health during the pandemic and its effects on the digital transformation process in the health sector in Brazil, with a focus on citizen well-being.

2. METHODOLOGY

The analysis used data from the ICT in Health survey conducted by the Brazilian Internet Steering Committee (CGI.br) for the years 2019, 2021 and 2022. This survey has been conducted since 2013, except for 2020, and investigates the use of ICT in Brazilian healthcare facilities (CGI.br, 2023). The overall goal of the survey has been to understand the stage of ICT adoption in Brazilian healthcare facilities and their appropriation by healthcare professionals. The initiative follows the model survey developed by the Organisation for Economic Co-Operation and Development (OECD) for statistics in the sector (OECD, 2015).

The ICT in Health survey had the Brazilian healthcare facilities as the target population. The survey frame used for selecting the facilities was the National Registry of Health Care Facilities (CNES) maintained by the Health Informatics Department of the Brazilian Unified Health System (DATASUS). The scope of the survey includes public and private legal entities that are registered with the CNES, which is designated exclusively for healthcare-related activities, with at least one physician or nurse (CGI.br, 2023).

The questionnaire prepared to collect the research data was directed to the administrative professionals from the facilities to obtain information on the infrastructure and availability of ICT services in healthcare facilities. All respondents were contacted through the Computer-Assisted Telephone Interviewing (CATI) technique.

The healthcare facilities included in the sample were selected by probability proportional to size sampling. Four categories were considered: type of facility; region; location; and administrative jurisdiction, which made up 80 strata for the survey. These strata allow for representation of all types of facilities, regions, locations, and administrative jurisdictions in the sample, while also enabling analyses of the domains defined by each variable individually. In the 2019 ICT in Health survey, interviews were conducted in 2,427 healthcare facilities. For the 2021 survey, interviews were conducted in 1,524 healthcare facilities and for the ICT in Health 2022 survey, interviews were conducted in 2,103 healthcare facilities.

3. DIGITAL TRANSFORMATION IN THE HEALTH SECTOR

Adequate ICT infrastructure is necessary for new digital solutions to be developed and applied in new contexts, especially in health emergencies. In recent years, some progress has been identified in improving access to devices and internet connectivity in public healthcare facilities in Brazil. However, during the pandemic period, a more accelerated advancement was observed compared to previous years. Between 2019 and 2022, the availability of computers in public facilities increased from 92% to 97%, and internet access increased from 85% to 97%. This means that about 2,000 public healthcare facilities do not have access to computers and the Internet. Primary Healthcare Units (PHUs) deserve special mention, as they showed a more pronounced evolution in the adoption and use of computers and the Internet. In 2019, 91% of them used computers, and 82% had internet access, which increased to 97% in both cases in 2022, leaving an estimated 1300 PHUs without access to computers and the Internet.

Another aspect to consider is the type of device used, especially in primary care, where tablets allow Family Health Teams (eSF) to visit the communities they serve regularly. An increase of 24 percentage points in the use of tablets in public healthcare facilities was observed, rising from 21% to 45% between 2019 and 2022. This increase was particularly notable in PHUs, as more than half gained access to this device (56% in 2022). This rise can be attributed to the greater digitization of PHUs with Family Health Units (USF), and its uses expanded since the beginning of the COVID-19 pandemic. The use of laptops also increased by 18 percentage points, going from 30% in 2019 to 48% in 2022.

In addition to greater availability, there was also an improvement in the type of internet connection. In 2019, 86% of healthcare facilities had cable or fiber optic connections, which increased to 95% in 2022. More stable connections like these contribute to better data storage in electronic health records, faster access, and the possibility of adopting telehealth services.

Another advancement noted was the adoption of electronic health records in healthcare facilities. The use of computerized systems allows for more agile access and exchange of information, improving prioritization of care, analysis of tests, quality of care, patients' and healthcare professionals' experiences, and continuity and monitoring of patient care. Therefore, the adoption of electronic health records in public facilities also increased from 74% to 88% between 2019 and 2022 during the pandemic. PHUs also significantly improved, as 78% of them had electronic health records before the pandemic, rising to 87% in 2022.

This increase in the adoption of electronic information systems positively impacted the availability of patient information in electronic format, decision support functionalities, and the exchange of health information. Among the types of patient information that became more available electronically were nursing notes, detailed clinical notes from encounters with clinicians or medical histories, and allergies, which increased by approximately 20 percentage points between 2019 and 2022. This type of information can assist in making decisions about patient diagnosis and treatment. Patient demographics were the most widely available information electronically (Figure 1).

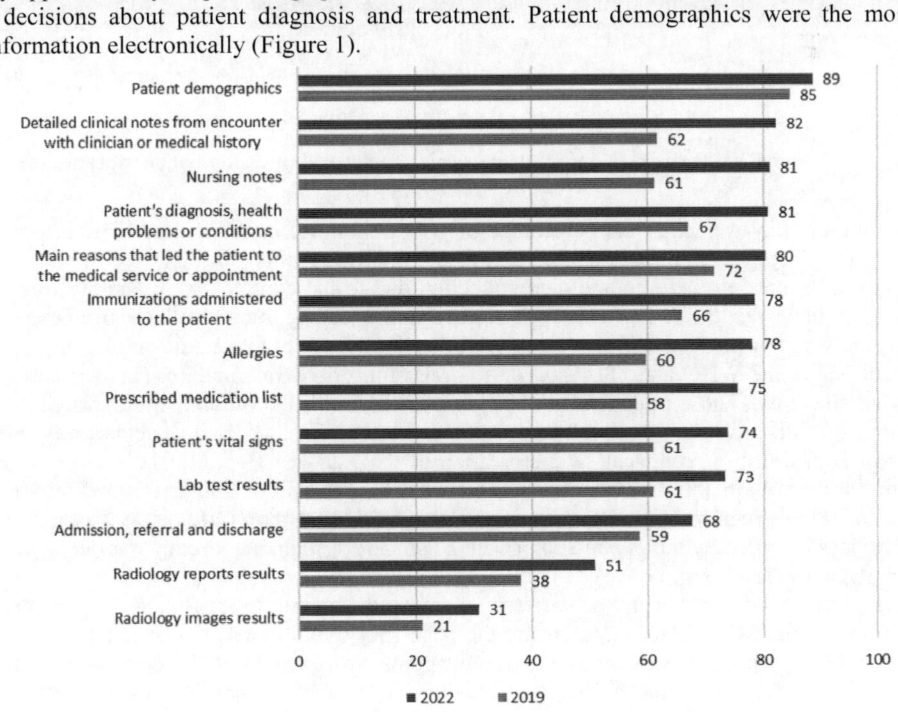

Figure 1. Public healthcare facilities by type of patient data available electronically, 2019-2022 (%)

This increased availability may be associated with the greater digitization of healthcare facilities and the urgency of transmitting patient information during the pandemic. Furthermore, similar proportions of growth were observed in PHUs. Increased digitization of primary care allowed public health authorities to identify the main reasons for patients' spontaneous demand for care and, consequently, develop actions for care-avoiding patients visiting healthcare facilities during a pandemic, contributing to the social distancing measures.

Regarding access to patient information, another point highlighted by the COVID-19 pandemic was the need for reliable and rapid information exchange both between healthcare facilities and from these facilities to the entities responsible for managing the system, such as health departments and the Ministry of Health. In this regard, there is also an increase in information exchange functionalities present in the electronic information systems of public healthcare facilities. The functionalities that recorded the most significant increases were sending or receiving reports on the care provided to patients at the time of discharge or referral to another facility (18 percentage points) and sending or receiving clinical information (13 percentage points), as shown in Figure 2.

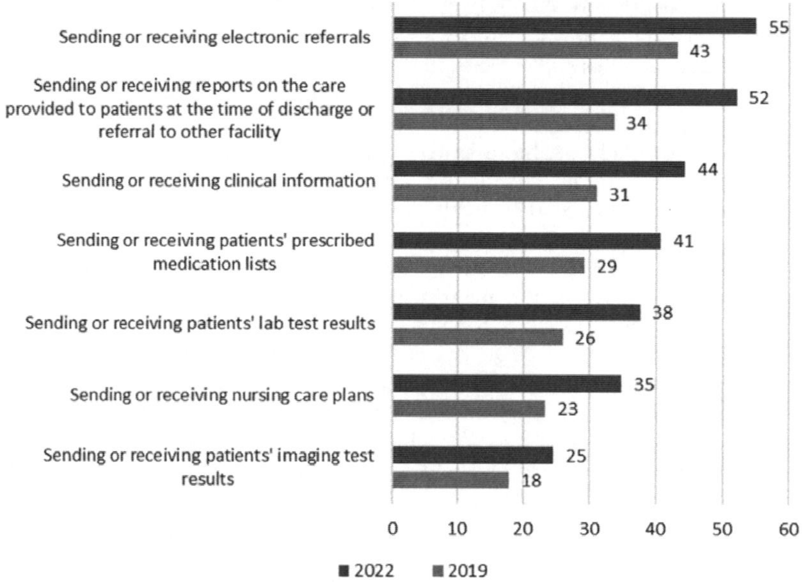

Figure 2. Public healthcare facilities by available electronic healthcare information exchange functionalities, 2019-2022 (%)

Despite the improvements, the percentage of public facilities enabling electronic information exchange remains low. There are significant challenges to the interoperability of electronic information systems, the exchange of patient information, and data collection due to the complexity of healthcare processes and the organization of the healthcare network. Furthermore, a high degree of commitment from managers, healthcare professionals, and system users is also essential for accurate and complete data entry.

According to the WHO and ITU (2020), it is relevant to integrate and ensure interoperability among all digital health systems and applications used by healthcare facilities, professionals, and patients so that they can communicate with each other and exchange data accurately, efficiently, and systematically. Efforts have been made to advance in this area, such as the creation of the National Health Data Network (RNDS), a digital platform for innovation, information, and healthcare services across the country (Brazilian Ministry of Health, 2020). Under this program, the unification of the National Vaccination Card, as well as tests, procedures, and other services provided by the public and private healthcare system, are already in effect and can be accessed through the Conecte SUS app.

During the pandemic, many countries implemented various telehealth service models to meet the population's demands while trying to ensure the necessary social distancing as much as possible. In Brazil, telehealth also contributes to clinical care for remote populations with limited access to healthcare professionals or more complex healthcare centers. Thus, telehealth has become an increasingly effective and accessible tool for reducing the burden on hospitals and expanding access to specialized healthcare.

The availability of these telehealth services varied during and after the pandemic, as shown in Figure 3. Remote patient monitoring services advanced during the most critical period of the health crisis. However, they declined by seven percentage points in 2022, suggesting a return to in-person treatments and monitoring after the pandemic. Teleconsultation services, currently available in about a quarter of healthcare facilities, and telediagnosis, in about a fifth of them, also increased during the pandemic and remained stable.

During the pandemic, many countries implemented various telehealth service models to meet the population's demands while trying to ensure the necessary social distancing as much as possible. In Brazil, telehealth also contributes to clinical care for remote populations with limited access to healthcare professionals or more complex healthcare centers. Thus, telehealth has become an increasingly effective and accessible tool for reducing the burden on hospitals and expanding access to specialized healthcare.

The availability of these telehealth services varied during and after the pandemic, as shown in Figure 3. Remote patient monitoring services advanced during the most critical period of the health crisis. However, they declined by seven percentage points in 2022, suggesting a return to in-person treatments and monitoring after the pandemic. Teleconsultation services, currently available in about a quarter of healthcare facilities, and telediagnosis, in about a fifth of them, also increased during the pandemic and remained stable.

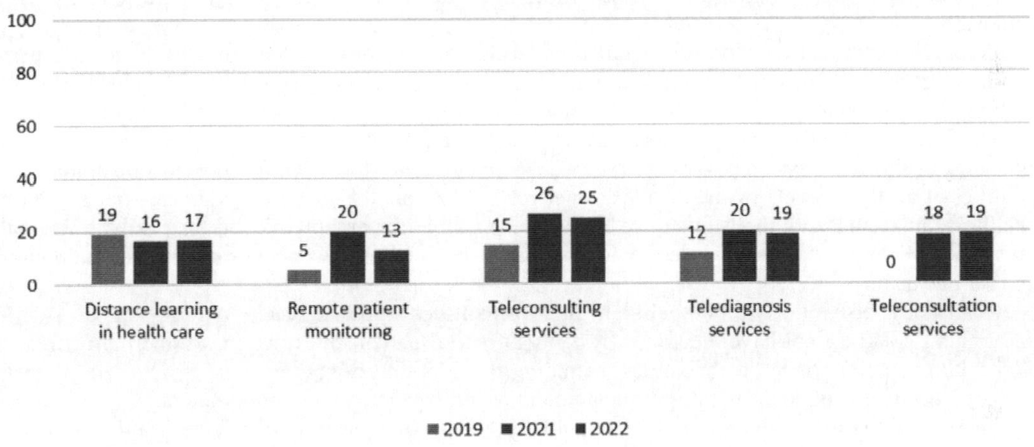

Figure 3. Public healthcare facilities by telehealth services available, 2019-2022 (%)

Regarding teleconsultations, prior to the pandemic, remote consultations without the physical presence of a healthcare professional were prohibited in Brazil. In other words, for an online consultation with a specialist to occur, a nurse or a general practitioner had to be present with the patient. During the pandemic, there was an emergency authorization for entirely online consultation. This remote consultation was well-received by patients and healthcare professionals and was permanently authorized in 2022. It is worth noting that about a fifth of healthcare facilities provided online consultations in 2021 and 2022.

Digital technologies enable the broader dissemination of prevention campaigns, assist in treatment monitoring, and support programs for mental health and awareness of well-being. When combined with electronic information systems that provide secure and reliable data, they can support clinical decisions and expand the coverage of healthcare services.

However, despite the advancements in the adoption and use of digital technologies, attention must also be given to the protection and privacy of patients' personal data. This was an area with little progress during the pandemic. The development of digital health applications must ensure the privacy of shared information, transparency in data usage and security policies, and awareness among professionals working with these technologies. Digital health initiatives should align with existing regulations and a set of best practices that ensure information security for healthcare system users.

The Brazilian General Data Protection Law (LGPD), which came into effect during the pandemic, aims to guarantee the right to privacy and the protection of personal data in both physical and digital environments. However, significant changes in this area were not observed during the pandemic and post-pandemic periods. In 2022, only a quarter of healthcare facilities had an information security policy, with no significant variation compared to 2019. Regarding actions related to LGPD compliance, approximately 3 out of 10 facilities adopted some measures established by the law, such as appointing a Data Protection Officer (DPO), establishing information security policies, developing incident response plans, and conducting awareness campaigns with their employees. Therefore, there is still a long way to go to achieve compliance with the provisions defined by the new regulatory framework.

4. CONCLUSION

With the emergence of the COVID-19 pandemic, countries had to take rapid actions to adapt their healthcare systems to the new health needs. This included attending to a large number of patients, disseminating new clinical protocols to healthcare professionals, developing new tools that allowed patient care while facilitating social distancing, and monitoring the health information of the population to formulate collective healthcare actions.

In Brazil's case, an increase in digital transformation was observed during the pandemic period that persisted in the post-pandemic period. This included increased adoption and use of ICT in healthcare facilities, with more units connected and greater use of electronic systems to record patient information.

The increased availability of patient data in electronic format and functionalities related to information exchange in electronic systems were and continue to be necessary for effective coordination among healthcare facilities at all three levels of the healthcare network. Additionally, it promotes greater integration between healthcare units and with the Ministry of Health, responsible for organizing and formulating national public plans and policies. Consequently, electronic information can potentially enhance population health monitoring and service quality.

However, approximately 2,000 public healthcare facilities still lack access to computers and the Internet, and around 7,000 do not have electronic systems to record patient information. Furthermore, areas such as telehealth or more complex technologies, including the adoption of resources to ensure data protection and privacy, still pose challenges with significant potential for expansion and improvement.

Therefore, it is imperative to implement public policies aimed at fully digitizing healthcare facilities and adopting digital technologies to harness the potential of telehealth in the country's healthcare system. To achieve this, barriers to the adoption of these systems need to be considered, such as financial (high implementation and maintenance costs), technical (the need for computer literacy among professionals), behavioral (related to distrust and fear of loss of autonomy), social (lack of support from healthcare unit management), legal (data security and privacy), and professional practices (resistance to change) (Chiavegatto & Ferrari, 2022).

Finally, another challenge in the adoption of digital healthcare is its regulation. Although regulatory advances have been identified recently, existing international and national legislation still does not cover the full complexity of developing digital healthcare products and services. This can create uncertainties and insecurity regarding the methods and ethics applied and the effective protection of patients' rights, healthcare professionals, companies, and governments.

REFERENCES

Brazilian Internet Steering Committee - CGI.br. (2023). *Survey on the Use of Information and Communication Technologies in Brazilian Healthcare Facilities:* ICT in Health 2022. São Paulo: CGI.br.

Brazilian Ministry of Health. (2020). *Digital health strategy for Brazil 2020-2028.* https:// bvsms.saude.gov.br/bvs/publicacoes/ estrategia_saude_digital_Brasil.pdf

Brazilian Ministry of Health. (2021). *1st Monitoring and Evaluation Report of the Digital Health Strategy for Brazil 2020-2028.* https:// bvsms.saude.gov.br/bvs/publicacoes/relatorio_ monitoramento_estrategia_saude_digital.pdf

Chiavegatto, A., & Ferrari, I. (2022). Uso de Big Data em saúde no Brasil: Perspectivas e desafios de conformidade com a LGPD. In F. Aith, & A. Dallari (Coords.), *LGPD na saúde Digital* (pp. 213-228). Revista dos Tribunais.

Ordinance MS No. 467, of March 20, 2020. (2020). Exceptionally and temporarily provides for Telemedicine actions with the goal of regulating and operationalizing measures to face the public health emergency of international importance foreseen in Article 3 of Law No. 13.979, of February 6, 2020, arising from the COVID-19 epidemic. Brasília, DF. https:// www.in.gov.br/en/web/dou/-/portaria-n- 467-de-20-de-marco-de-2020-249312996.

Organisation for Economic Coorperation and Development – OECD. (2015). *Draft OECD guide to measuring ICTs in the health sector*. http://www.oecd.org/health/health-systems/Draft-oecd-guide-to-measuring-icts-in-the-health-sector.pdf

Pan American Health Organization – PAHO. (2021). *COVID-19 and the importance of strengthening information systems – Department of evidence and intelligence for action in health*. https:// iris.paho.org/handle/10665.2/52127

World Health Organization – WHO, & International Telecommunication Union – ITU. (2020). *Digital health platform handbook: Building a digital information infrastructure (infostructure) for health*. https://apps.who.int/iris/ handle/10665/337449

Zhai, Y., et al. (2020). From isolation to coordination: How can telemedicine help combat the COVID-19 outbreak? *medRxiv*, 2020.

EU RIGHT TO JUSTIFICATIONS FOR POST-SCORING CLASSIFIERS

Diogo Morgado Rebelo[1], Francisco Pacheco de Andrade[1] and Paulo Novais[2]
[1]*JusGov Research Centre, University of Minho, Braga - Portugal*
[2]*Algoritmi Research Centre/ LASI University of Minho, Braga - Portugal*

ABSTRACT

This paper delves into the changing regulatory landscape of consumer credit scoring within Artificial Intelligence (AI) and FinTech. Focusing on crucial European Union (EU) regulations such as the General Data Protection Regulation (GDPR) and the Digital Services Act (DSA), our objective is to unveil ambiguities and emphasize the necessity for adopting practical and uniformised approaches to *eXplainable Artificial Intelligence* (XAI). The goal is to enhance clarity and contestability in Automated Decision-Making (ADM). As such, this study granularly explores both global and local functioning of explainability vis-à-vis interpretability, addressing challenges arising from the opacity of AI-based credit scoring. It sheds light on governing contradictions, including those within GDPR's Automated Decision-Making framework, Arts. 12 and 18(8)(a) of the Directive (EU) 2023/2225 on credit agreements for consumers and repealing Directive 2008/48/EC, dated October 18, 2023, on one hand, and Art. 13 of the Proposal for an Artificial Intelligence Act (AIA) dated April 21, 2021, on the other. Leveraging a comprehensive interpretation of Art. 27(2)(a)(b) in the DSA Regulation, the paper advocates for a more pragmatic approach to AI-based consumer credit scoring. The fulfilment of *justifiability* would entail a focus on the automated disclosure of the critical criteria for the classification process. In conclusion, we suggest an EU-level *right to ex-post justification* through counterfactuals to balance technological innovation and individual rights in the dynamic consumer credit landscape.

KEYWORDS

EU Policymaking, Consumer Creditworthiness Assessment, *eXplainable Artificial Intelligence*

1. INTRODUCTION

Between the 1990s and 1995, credit scoring underwent a transformative shift, extending its reach into realms previously reserved for judgemental systems (Lyn et al., 2002). This period witnessed the emergence of AI software in the assessment of creditworthiness. From the mid-2015s to the present day, the credit industry has evolved with society's adoption of new consumer habits, prompting a demand for innovative digital solutions catering to genuine needs. Currently, consumer credit financing operations are migrating from physical counters to online platforms (i.e., applications or websites), accessible 24 hours to customers. A new cohort of economic players, FinTech, has entered the market (The World Bank Group, 2019). Notably, in the consumer credit sector, besides banking institutions and bureaus like TransUnion or Equifax, start-ups such as FriendlyScore, Lenddo, Tiaxa, Trusting Social, among others, have taken the forefront in delivering data-driven services to end-consumers (Ferretti & Vandone, 2019).

Moreover, despite all the dangers creditors may encounter, service providers increasingly persist in selecting predictive technologies as their preferred tool for consumer credit access (The World Bank Group, 2019). However, AI-based credit scoring systems, while offering benefits such as increased profitability and improved risk management, also present enormous challenges (Morgado Rebelo & Campos Ferreira, 2022). Specifically, the opaque nature of the predictive creditworthiness assessment often results in black-box analyses (Burrel, 2016; Carabantes, 2019). This lack of transparency has already raised concerns to the European Data Protection Supervisor recently (EDPS, 2021).

Through the lens of XAI, we aim to unravel the contradictions in the policy-making both already enshrined and proposed at the EU level. Section 2 covers an approach to the anatomy of data-driven decision-making in the milieu of Credit Scoring and Machine Learning (ML). In Section 3 we explore the differences in the XAI policies of the GDPR, specified in the ADM regime of the Regulation (EU) 2016/679 and in Art. 27(2)(a)(b) of Regulation (EU) 2022/2065, on DSA, dated 19 October 2022. It additionally investigates the interpretations allowed by the AIA proposal dated 21 April 2021- last amended by the European Parliament on June 14, 2023, and by the Council on December 6, 2022, both of which dele Art, 19(2), thus substantiating the application of the conformity assessment set out in Arts 8 to 15 thereof - and, otherwise enshrined in Arts. 12 and 18(8)(a) of the Directive (EU) 2023/2225, of 18 October 2023, following its Recital 45.

2. AI-BASED CONSUMER SCORING

In today's consumer credit market, the core belief is that the near future mirrors the recent past. Oddly enough, the logic of these procedures can be, incredible as it may be, straightforward and intuitive for an average citizen. It involves identifying the link between a group of clients' current compliance or non-compliance and their past information. Once identified, this connection can be applied to infer, predict, and monitor the behaviour of them over time (Morgado Rebelo & Campos Ferreira, 2022). Yet, especially in the era of ML, *predictors* categories such as age, finance, employment, or behaviour (below, section 2.3) might affect their loan eligibility (Vojtek & Koândra, 2006). Many individuals should, once and for all, express apprehension about how their personal information can impact loan approvals. In the contemporary landscape, credit data is critical in lending, mainly when automated *outputs* materially sustain approvals or rejections – i.e., the *outcomes*. Programmers no longer hold the primary roles; instead, personal (often sensitive) data, in collaboration with self-learning models, assumes responsibility for determining 'whom to accept next' (Alpaydin, 2016; Kissinger et al., 2021).

2.1 Understanding AI-Powered Scoring

AI-powered scoring assesses an individual's ability, resulting in a final *score* derived from the *fuzzy correlation* of partial weights assigned to various attributes. This evaluation applies to both those seeking credit for the first time (*application scoring*) and clients with revolving credit (*behavioural scoring*), the latter requesting a loan increase. However, occurrences arise where credit information availability is insufficient. In such cases, a supplementary check of external databases, known as bureau scoring, may suit the greater accuracy of the analysis as a whole well. Bureaus compile payment histories, prioritize them, highlight financial commitments, and assess consumer's expenses by retaining information on credit types, default history, and debt levels. They also validate specific data sets, including the number of data queries, positive registers, georeferentiation, among other factors (Raymond, 2007; Silva, 2011).

2.2 Decoding Decision-Making: Unveiling its 'Anatomy'

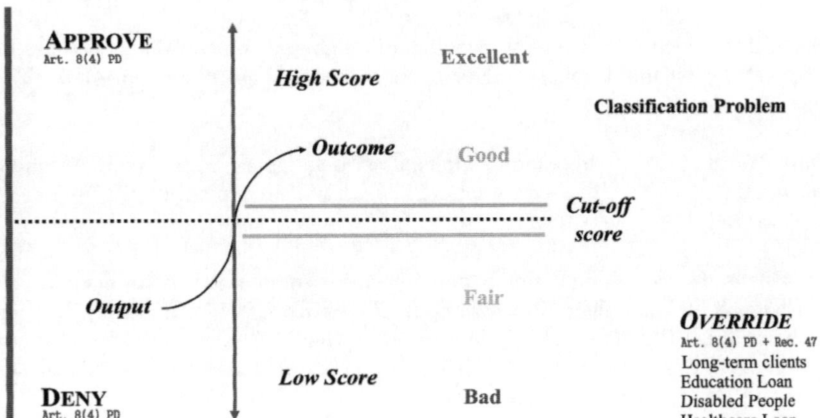

Figure 1. Anatomy of decision-making in consumer credit scoring

In broad terms, the classification procedure, illustrated above, can be summarised as follows:

- Each applicant receives a numeric or categoric *score*, which is then compared to a predefined *cut-off* set by the lenders, usually not revealed to customers. The *cut-off* distinguishes the compliant clientele from the defaulting one. This threshold determination varies from one institution to another, even depending on the macroeconomic context. In terms of administrative policies, establishing this guideline, grounded in technical and financial factors, is essential for both maximizing profitability and enhancing model's generalisation. Overall, the unknown *cut-off* reference dictates if a candidate is accepted or rejected. From this on, we can deduce that the likelihood of success is higher when the *cut-off* stipulated is lower, indicating a predisposition of lenders to take on more significant risks (Abdou & Pointon, 2011).
- Subsequently, an '*excellent*' customer is the one whose predictive performance indicates a low risk (*high score*), whereas a '*bad*' customer is labelled by an *output* indicating a risk of default below the institution's predefined threshold (*low score*).
- Also, suppose the *score* falls within an intermediate range (i.e., '*fair*' or '*good*'), suggesting uncertain future solvency. In that case, the analyst may conduct a *referral*, re-evaluating the client based on his or her genuine needs. There are numerous factors that, given values close to (*high-score override*) or below (*low-score override*) the *cut-off*, could previously validate an arbitrary decision not always justifiable by credit analysts (Raymond, 2007). However, from a legal perspective, the nature of this procedure undergoes a substantial transformation with Art. 18(6) of Directive (EU) 2023/2225, dated October 18, 2023. Compared with Art. 8(1)(2) of the Directive 2008/48/EC, of 23 April, what was formerly an obligation to solely apply the appropriate means in its Art. 8 may now be contingent on the assessment output. Hence, the creditor will only be able to provide loan to consumer "where the result of the creditworthiness assessment indicates that the obligations resulting from the credit agreement (...) are likely to be met in the manner required under that agreement". Still, when interpreted based on its Recital 55, there will be circumstances where the nuances of financial inclusion may let credit to be granted through exceptional *referrals* (Morgado Rebelo & Campos Ferreira, 2022). This *output-outcome differentiation* applies to credit agreements for longstanding customers, to cover student fees, and especially in cases where loans are acquired to cover healthcare expenses or for disabled consumers. Of course, there will always be outstanding situations in which the analyst opts to decline the application despite a satisfactory score from the model, for example, when suspicious or fraudulent activities are perceived. However, most *overrides* commonly serve to approve applications that were initially rejected (Raymond, 2007).

2.3 The Power of Data-Driven Scoring

It is audacious to assert, even theoretically, an optimal ML-based technique for tasks like consumer creditworthiness assessments. What is certain is that those choices hinge on measuring a range of metrics that undergoes enough maturation for, including the accuracy, processing easiness and speed, along with the interpretation of certain explanatory or independent variables (Raymond, 2007).

Regardless of this evidence, it would be beneficial to highlight some advantages these methods - such as Decision Trees (DTs), Neural Networks (NNs), and Genetic Algorithms (GAs) -, offer for tasks like creditworthiness assessment using ML:

- DTs stand out for their ability to combine alphanumeric variables, both continuous and categorical. This strength makes them more well-suited for tasks like *feature selection* (Abdou & Pointon, 2011; Louzada et al., 2016; Silva, 2011).
- NNs demonstrate enhanced classification accuracy, particularly compared to some parametric ones. This method is valuable for modelling complex and non-linear combinations with many predictors (Abdou et al., 2008; Abdou & Pointon, 2011; Louzada et al., 2016; Silva, 2011). However, it struggles to fulfil the transparency criteria (Raymond, 2007; Silva, 2011; Vojtek & Koândra, 2006) on EU policymaking (Morgado Rebelo & Campos Ferreira, 2022). This is the reason why we choose NN as a hypothesis for our problem-solving, i.e., *justificative semi-automata*.
- GAs, geared towards stochastic optimization, contribute to identifying simultaneous alternative solutions and *counterfactual interpretations* in risk prediction (Abdou & Pointon, 2011; Louzada et al., 2016)

However, despite all these technicalities, what ultimately categorises customers as '*good*' or '*bad*' payers?

In fact, beyond the computational techniques employed, the crucial step is identifying which variables are most effective for such problem-solving, which, by the way, has a computational nature. Accordingly, we should bear in mind that predictors selection varies based on cultural and socio-economic traits and, more importantly, on each institution's management and scoring policies (Abdou & Pointon, 2011; Alpaydin, 2016). In 2006, Martin Vojtek and Evïen Koândra summarised the types of predictors applicable in creditworthiness assessment (p. 164), as we outline in Table 1 below, with several adjustments.

Table 1. Predictors or explainable variables

SOCIODEMOGRAPHIC	FINANCIAL	EMPLOYMENT		BEHAVIOURAL
Name	Total assets	Type of employment	TRADITIONAL	Current accounts
Sex	Gross income (household)	Field		Average bank balance
Date of birth	Active assets	Position		Other loan
Civil identification	Passive assets	Length		Delay in payments
Marital status	Monthly household costs	Experience		Number of payments
Naturalness	------------------------------	(Un)employment		Warranties
Nationality	------------------------------	------------------------------	ALTERNATIVE	Income
National register	------------------------------	------------------------------		Online payments
Address	------------------------------	------------------------------		Geolocalisation
Mobile phone	------------------------------	------------------------------		E-mail tracking
Home description	------------------------------	------------------------------		Call registers
Age of housing	------------------------------	------------------------------		Search engine results
Educational degrees	------------------------------	------------------------------		------------------------------
Number of dependants	------------------------------	------------------------------		------------------------------

Ultimately, the answer to what labels a candidate as a '*good*' or '*bad*' payer is case-specific. Collaborative teamwork is essential for identifying prevailing predictors, considering associated costs and time (Morgado Rebelo, 2023).

3. EXPLAINABLE AI IN CONSUMER CREDIT

A key component of socio-ethical and legal considerations is the examination of XAI. Such micro-science exists in an AI-based system whose inductive model provide tailored-made explanations to a specific target audience, also rendering the system's operations transparent and enlightening to the broadest possible range of people (Arrieta et al., 2020). Practically, there are several approaches (McDermid et al., 2021) for explaining a concept to a consumer with a moderate level of digital literacy.

1. First of all, subjectively, these explanations can be tailored to applicants affected by the decision, as well as extended to end users, including credit analysts, teams involved in system design and development, auditors, and, from a governance perspective, regulatory bodies, such as the European Union institutions, the national legislators, and even the Data Protection Authorities.
2. Regarding the timing, these explanations can be given either before or after the solvency profile of a specific applicant is determined.
3. In terms of configuration, it is fundamental to differentiate between agnostic explanations, which are used regardless of the modelling technique, and explanations that rely on specific models, such as Linear and Logistic Regressions or Decision Trees.
4. Regarding how they are provided, *post-hoc* explanations can be presented to the end-user (or even directly to the applicant) mainly in text or visual formats. They may also be examples or simplifications.
5. Finally, and most significantly, through a granular scrutiny, the explanation can be categorized as either focusing on the entire decision-making process (*global explainability*) or on interpreting a particular prediction or the independent variables (*local interpretability*) – see, considerations, below.

In our hypothesis, the NNs depicted in Figures 2 and 3 below do not constitute by themselves explanations. Instead, XAI inductive methods could theoretically demonstrate how a model-agnostic approach could influence the independent variables within the model.

3.1 Global Explainability

The first category, encompassing all stages of the software life cycle, pertains to the overarching technical rationale governing the model's generation and functioning (Bücker et al., 2022). Providing data subjects with such information would yield little practical benefits. Details provided usually relate to the technical logic of the model, rendering them more relevancy to both regulatory institutions and the lender's management bodies (Demajo et al., 2020). The taxonomy to which these explanations allude leads to a higher level of detail within the model. Their validity is primarily confirmed through identifying the architecture's component that significantly impact the output (Arrieta et al., 2020).

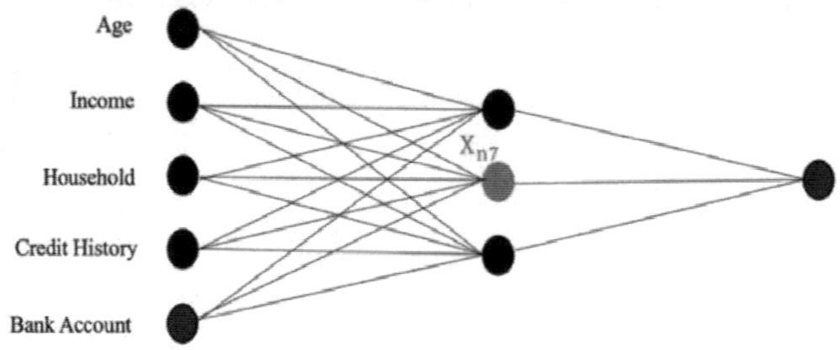

Figure 2. Global Explanation

For instance, according to Figure 2, above, in the model's training phase, it was discovered that the node (X_{n7}) held the most substantial influence in driving the endogenous or dependent variable. Therefore, one can deduce this explanation is advantageous in enhancing a model's performance, especially during the modelling's initial stages. It can effectively address issues like multicollinearity and overfitting. Consequently, this type of explanation primarily caters to data scientists during modelling, not to consumers (Demajo et al., 2020).

3.2 Local Interpretable Model-Agnostic Explanation

The XAI community has already proposed some compliance alternatives to address the requirements of an *ex-post* 'explanation'. In 2018, Sandra Wachter, Brent Mittelstadt, and Chris Russell introduced a model of *counterfactual explanations* (Hulstjn, 2023; Wachter et al., 2018). This second methodology, the so-called Local Interpretable Model-Agnostic Explanation (LIME) constructs linear and localized interpretations of the model by examining sub-hypotheses when specific input elements are adjusted (Ribeiro et al., 2016). The idea is to highlight that LIME works by *perturbing the input data* and observing the local changes in the model's predictions, offering interpretable insights into the decision-making process. In other words, it endeavours to detect *delta values* (i.e., variations or changes in key features or parameters). Updated *delta values* can be particularly useful when examining scenarios close to a score cut-off where small changes in input variables may have a notable impact on the decision outcome (Hamon et al., 2020). According to this approach, it becomes the legal responsibility of the data controller to elucidate to applicants the predictive attributes that could be modified, in case of a rejection, to reverse the decision. This reasoning could also improve understanding the primary factors influencing loan approvals (Hacker & Jan-Hendrik, 2022). Ultimately, the objective is to replicate the results through an experimental process (Carneiro et al., 2020).

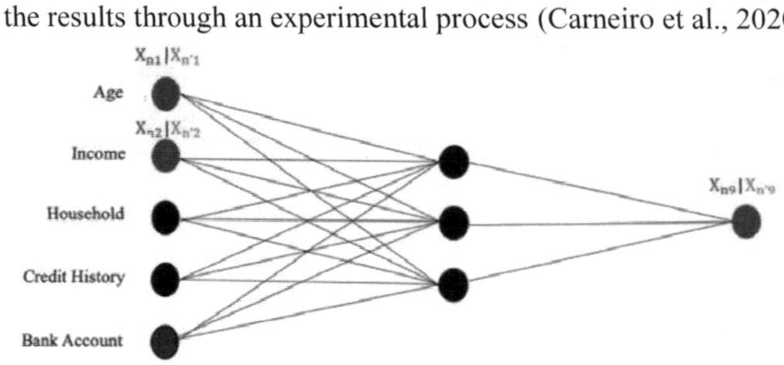

Figure 3. LIME

In the scenario of a consumer credit application, a counterfactual interpretation involves the following logic: the score Y was derived, resulting in either acceptance or rejection (X_{n9}) because the predictor or explanatory variables had specific values ($X_{n1}, X_{n2}, \ldots, . X_n$). However, if the applicant possessed different characteristics ($X_{n\prime 1}, X_{n\prime 2}, \ldots, . X_n$) while keeping all other explanatory attributes constant, the scoring would have led to a different application decision ($X_{n\prime 9}$). In the illustrated scenario, as depicted in Figure 3, above, let us consider customer α, who is single and was rejected because he was 63 years old and earn a salary of only €1,000.00. However, he would have been accepted if he were 60 years old with an income of €1,300.00. With this insight, evidently, he could only contest and induce the alternative outcome by modifying the second parameter.

4. EU RIGHT TO JUSTIFICATIONS FOR POST-SCORING CLASSIFIERS

The existence of a right to an *ex-post* 'explanation' in the GDPR remains unclear, still raising debate since the wording "explanation" in its Recital 71 is not explicitly stated as a "suitable safeguard" in Art. 22(3) thereof, not to mention transparency, information and access duties enshrined in Arts. 12, 13(2)(f), 14(2)(g) and 15(1)(h), all of the GDPR (D. Selbst & Powles, 2017; Goodman & Flaxman, 2016; Kaminski, 2019; Malgieri & Comandé, 2017; Morgado Rebelo & Campos Ferreira, 2022; Sérgio Cabral, 2021; Wachter et al., 2017). Regarding this long-standing quarrel, key conclusive observations (Morgado Rebelo, 2023) include:

a. Practitioners and scholars still struggle to define the extent of information lenders (i.e., the controllers) must provide to consumers (i.e., the data subjects) before and after output extraction. Specifically in AI-based credit scoring, there is ambiguity regarding the lawfulness of creditors delivering personalized recommendations to applicants based on interpretability foundations. These 'suggestions', however, only are possible if there is a later amendment to the initial draft, as per the for a Directive (EU) 2023/2225 on credit agreements for consumers and repealing Directive 2008/48/EC, dated October 18, 2023, Referring to the adequate explanation outlined in Art. 12 – which does not specify whether they should be provided prior to, during or following the creditworthiness assessment – its Recital 45 emphasizes that a proper one "should not [in itself] constitute a personal recommendation". Upon closer examination, the emphasis on consumers' preferences appears to be disregarded even in the European context. Such *contrastive interpretations* are what consumers desire rather than the other way around (Hulstjn, 2023). It would be in the best interests of applicants to have insights into both the reasons for their rejection and, perhaps, the general functioning of these self-learning models. On this subject, Ana Alves Leal recently concluded that "it is not the inherent nature of algorithmic decisions that should be vilified, but rather the manner in which they are integrated into the decision-making process and their alignment with established legal principles and rules" (2024, p. 350).
b. Moreover, given that, according to Art. 6(2), Annex III(5)(b) of the AIA, systems employed for predicting consumer creditworthiness are categorized as high-risk, the approach outlined in Arts. 12 and 18(8)(a) of Directive (EU) 2023/2225 on credit agreements for consumers, of 18 October 2023, directly contradicts Art. 13 of the AIA since the latter explicitly acknowledges interpretability as the suitable method for transparency (Ebers et al., 2021).
c. Also, the right to access in Art. 15(1)(h) of the GDPR still presents uncertainty in not adversely affecting controllers' trade secrets or intellectual property, including software copyright, as highlighted in Recital 63 of the GDPR. The question arises: in a conflict between trade secrets and data subjects' rights, which rules take precedence (Brkan & Bonnet, 2020)?
d. The assumed right to explanation in the GDPR could clash with the *ne bis in idem* principle, a fundamental right protected by European laws. In simple terms, if an AI system's functioning lacks legal explainability, it may violate transparency in Art. 5(1)(a) of the GDPR, breaching simultaneously rights in Arts 12, 13(2)(f), 14(2)(g), 15(1)(h), all of the GDPR, and the (un)suitable safeguard in Art. 22(3), considering its Recital 71. Even from a substantive standpoint, the *ne bis in idem* principle prevents controllers from being penalized twice for the same offence, as per Art. 83(5)(a)(b) of the GDPR. Surprisingly, GDPR fines seemingly allow sanctions on controllers violating their own rights.

Regarding the issue of explainability *versus* interpretability, on March 16, 2023, in Case C-634/21, *OQ v Land Hesse and SCHUFA Holding AG* [ECLI:EU:C:2023:220], the European Court of Justice (ECJ) received an application to decide whether bureau scoring in credit falls under the scope of Art. 22 and other transparency provisions. In paragraph 58 of the opinion, following the WP29 Guideline, adopted on October 2, 2017, as last revised and adopted on February 6, 2018 (p. 27), the Advocate-General Priit Pikamäe "considered that the obligation to provide 'meaningful information about the logic involved' must be understood to include sufficiently detailed explanations of the method used to calculate the score and the reasons for a certain result. In general, the controller should provide the data subject with general information, notably on factors taken into account for the decision-making process and on their respective weight on an aggregate level (…)" (Case C-634/21, 2023).

In any case, the primary question remains to be answered: what constitutes justification, and how are legal challenges addressed by establishing such an EU Right for post-scoring classifiers?

As Hulstijn pinpointed during the 2023 ICAIL Conference, which took place in Braga, it is essential to mark that a *justification* goes beyond a mere explanation. It should contextually elucidate the foundation for the algorithmic decision, a particularly crucial factor when it negatively impacts the individual involved (Hulstjn, 2023). According to social sciences, a suitable explanation must be grounded on reasons or goals comprehensible for human understanding (Miller, 2019). So, with all these in mind, it is our contention that the justification's quality should be contingent upon social and legal factors. This entails not only the antecedent disclosure of the decision-maker's legitimacy but, more crucially, the *post hoc* specifics of case data or decision rules, potentially manifesting a causal chain within the AI-driven evaluation of creditworthiness.

By engineering law in action with a hypothetical scenario, we thus propose the establishing a *right to ex-post justification* at the EU level. Until now, a more effective approach to this AI-based consumer credit scoring jigsaw would be to employ a wide-ranging interpretation of Art. 27(2)(a)(b) of the DSA Regulation to this intended purpose, according to which: "information (…) suggested to the recipient of the service (…) shall include, at least: (a) the criteria which are most significant (…); (b) [and] the reasons for the relative importance of those parameters".

5. CONCLUSION

In conclusion, the evolution of consumer credit scoring, influenced by AI and FinTech, signifies a transformative shift. While online accessibility has increased, AI-based credit scoring poses challenges due to opacity. Our paper explores regulatory contradictions, advocating for XAI to reconcile GDPR and DSA discrepancies. The call for an extended interpretation of Art. 27(2)(a)(b) in the DSA Regulation to this intended purpose suggests a path for a more effective regulatory approach. So, to clarify and contest the *outcome* of a decision (refer to Figure 1), it is essential to articulate the decision-rule mechanism and illustrate how the actual case data shaped the *output* (refer to Figure 3). We believe that solely such level of transparency will promote accountability and trust in algorithmic decisions. However, our hypothetical exploration lacks empirical validation. Future research should delve deeply into real-world implementations to refine regulatory frameworks.

REFERENCES

Abdou, H., & Pointon, J. (2011). Credit scoring, statistical techniques and evaluation criteria: A review of the litera-ture. Intelligent Systems in Accounting and Management, 18, 59–88. https://doi.org/10.1002/isaf.325

Abdou, H., Pointon, J., & El-Masry, A. (2008). Neural nets versus conventional techniques in credit scoring in Egyptian banking. Expert Systems with Applications, 35(3), 1275–1292.

Alpaydin, E. (2016). Machine Learning: The new AI. The MIT Press Essential Knowledge Series.

Arrieta, A., Días-Rodríguez, N., Del Ser, J., Barbado, A., Garcia, S., Gil-Lopez, S., Molina, D., Benjamins, R., Chatila, R., & Herrera, Francisco. (2020). Explainable Artificial Intelligence (XAI): Concepts, taxonomies, opportunities and challenges toward responsible. Fusion, 58, 82–115. https://doi.org/10.1016/j.inffus.2019.12.012

Article 29 Data Protection Working Party. (2017). Guidelines on Automated individual decision-making and Profiling for the purposes of Regulation 2016/679 (wp251rev.01). https://ec.europa.eu/newsroom/article29/items/612053

Brkan, M., & Bonnet, G. (2020). Legal and Technical Feasibility of the GDPR's Quest for Explanation of Algorithmic Decisions: Of Black Boxes, White Boxes and Fata Morganas. 11(1), 18–50. https://doi.org/10.1017/err.2020.10

Bücker, M., Szepannek, G., Gosiewska, A., & Bieck, P. (2022). Transparency, auditability, and explainability of machine learning models in credit scoring. Journal of the Operational Research Society, 73(1), 70–90. https://doi.org/10.1080/01605682.2021.1922098

Burrel, J. (2016). How the machine 'thinks': Understanding opacity in machine learning algorithms. Big Data & Society, 3(1), 1–12. https://doi.org/10.1177/2053951715622512

Carabantes, M. (2019). Black-box artificial intelligence: An epistemological and critical analysis. AI & Society, 35(2), 309–317. https://doi.org/10.1007/s00146-019-00888-w

Carneiro, D., Silva, F., Guimarães, M., Sousa, D., & Novais, P. (2020). Explainable Intelligent Environments. Ambient Intelligence – Software and Applications, 11th, 34–43. https://hdl.handle.net/1822/69252

Case C-634/21, Pikamäe ___ (ECJ 2023). https://curia.europa.eu/juris/document/document.jsf?text=&docid=271343&pageIndex=0&doclang=EN&mode=lst&dir=&occ=first&part=1&cid=650929

Demajo, L., Vella, V., & Dingli, A. (2020). Explainable AI for Interpreting Credit Scoring. ACITY, DPPR, VLSI, WeST, DSA, CNDC, IoTE, AIAA, NLPTA, 185–203. https://doi.org/10.5121/csit.2020.101516

Ebers, M., Hoch, V., Rosenkranz, F., Ruschemeier, H., & Steinrötter, B. (2021). The European Commission's Proposal for an Artificial Intelligence Act—A Critical Assessment by Members of the Robotics and AI Law Society (RAILS). J Multidisciplinary Scientific Journal, 4(4), 509–603. https://doi.org/10.3390/j4040043

EDPS. (2021). Opinion 11/2021 on the Proposal for a Directive on consumer credits. https://edps.europa.eu/data-protection/our-work/publications/opinions/edps-opinion-proposal-directive-consumer-credits_en

Ferretti, F., & Vandone, D. (2019). Personal Debt in Europe: The EU financial market and consumer insolvency,. Cambridge University Press.

Goodman, B., & Flaxman, S. (2016). EU regulations on algorithmic decision-making and a "right to explanation. ICML workshop on human interpretability in machine learning (WHI). https://arxiv.org/abs/1606.08813

Hacker, P., & Jan-Hendrik, P. (2022). Varieties of AI Explanations Under the Law. From the GDPR to the AIA and Beyond. In International Workshop on Extending Explainable AI Beyond Deep Models and Classifiers (pp. 343–373). Springer. https://doi.org/10.1007/978-3-031-04083-2_17

Hamon, R., Jumklewitz, H., & Sanchez, I. (2020). Robustness and Explainability of Artificial Intelligence (Publications Office of the European Union EUR 30040 EN). European Parliament. https://publications.jrc.ec.europa.eu/repository/handle/JRC119336

Hulstjn, J. (2023). Computational Accountability. 19th Procedings of the Conference, 121–130.

Kaminski, M. E. (2019). The Right to Explanation, Explained. Berkeley Technology Law Journal, 34(1), 189–218.

Kissinger, H., Schmidt, E., & Huttenlocher, D. (2021). The Age of AI And Our Human Future (1st ed.). Little, Brown and Company.

Leal, A. A. (2024). Algorithms, Creditworthiness, and Lending Decisions. ICASL 2022: Legal Aspects of Autonomous Systems, 4, 321–353. https://doi.org/10.1007/978-3-031-47946-5_17

Louzada, F., Ara, A., & Fernandes, G. (2016). Classification methods applied to credit scoring: Systematic review and overall comparison. Surveys in Operations Research and Management Science, 21(2), 117–134. https://doi.org/10.1016/j.sorms.2016.10.001

Lyn, T., Edelman, D., & Crock, J. (2002). Credit Scoring and Its Applications: Monographs on Mathematical Modeling and Computation (2nd ed.). Philadelphia PA, Society for Industrial and Applied Mathematics.

Malgieri, G., & Comandé, G. (2017). Why a Right to Legibility of Automated Decision-Making Exists in the General Data Protection Regulation. International Data Privacy Law, 7(4), 243–265. https://doi.org/10.1093/idpl/ipx019

McDermid, J., Jia, Y., Porter, Z., & Habbl, I. (2021). Artificial intelligence explainability: The technical and ethical dimensions. Philosophical Transactions Royal Society A., 379:20200363, 1–18. https://doi.org/10.1098/rsta.2020.0363

Miller, T. (2019). Explanation in Artificial Intelligence: Insights from the social sciences. Artificial Intelligence, 267, 1–38. https://doi.org/10.1016/j.artint.2018.07.007

Morgado Rebelo, D. (2023). Inteligência Artificial e Scoring no Crédito ao Consumo. Almedina.

Morgado Rebelo, D. (2023, April 23). The AI Act Shall say 'Goodbye' to 'GDPR' Jigsaw on Automated Decision-Making. RAILS-Blog. https://blog.ai-laws.org/the-ai-act-shall-say-goodbye-to-gdpr-jigsaw-on-automated-decision-making/

Morgado Rebelo, D., & Campos Ferreira, F. (2022). AI-based consumer's creditworthiness assessment: Era of automation, future of scoring and the EU policymaking on automated decision-making. In Tec. Yearbook—Industry 4.0: Legal Challenges (Eva Sónia Moreira, pp. 77–105). Universidade do Minho. Centro de Investigação em Justiça e Governação (JusGov). https://hdl.handle.net/1822/83161

Raymond, A. (2007). The Credit Scoring Toolkit: Theory and Practice for Retail Credit Risk Manage-ment and Decision Automation. Oxford University Press.

Ribeiro, M., Singh, S., & Guestrin, C. (2016). 'Why should i trust you?' Explaining the predictions of any classifier. Proceedings of the 22nd ACM SIGKDD, 1135–1144. https://doi.org/10.18653/v1/N16-3020

Selbst, A. D., & Powles, J. (2017). Meaningful information and the right to explanation. International Data Privacy Law, 7(4), 233–242. https://doi.org/10.1093/idpl/ipx022

Sérgio Cabral, T. (2021). AI and the Right to Explanation: Three Legal Bases under the GDPR. In Data Protection Artificial Intelligence (Dara Hallinan, Ronald Leenes and Paul De Hert, Vol. 13, pp. 29–56). Hart Publishing.

Silva, F. (2011). Credit Scoring as an Asset for Decision Making in Intelligent Decision Support Systems [Master's Thesis, University of Minho, School of Engineering]. http://hdl.handle.net /1822/27891

The World Bank Group. (2019). Disruptive Technologies in the Credit Information Sharing Industry: Developments and Implications,. Finance Competitiveness & Innovation Global Practice. https://documents1.worldbank.org/curated/en/587611557814694439/pdf/Disruptive-Technologies-in-the-Credit-Information-Sharing-Industry-Developments-and-Implications.pdf

Vojtek, M., & Koândra, E. (2006). Credit Scoring Methods. Czech Journal of Economics and Finance (Finance a Úvěr), 56(3–4), 152–167.

Wachter, S., Mittelstadt, B., & Floridi, L. (2017). Why a Right to Explanation of Automated Decision-Making Does Not Exist in the General Data Protection Regulation. International Data Privacy Law, 7(2), 76–99. https://doi.org/10.1093/idpl/ipx005

Wachter, S., Mittelstadt, B., & Russel, C. (2018). Counterfactual Explanations without Opening the Black Box. Harvard Journal of Law & Technology, 31(2), 841–877.

ELECTRONIC GOVERNMENT AND THE LIMITATIONS OF CITIZEN INTERACTIVITY: A BRAZIL AND PORTUGAL ANALYSIS

Dario de Azevedo Nogueira Júnior[1]
Universidade Federal do Espírito Santo UFES, Brazil

ABSTRACT

This article aims to contribute to the academic debate, seeking to trace a correlation in the pattern adopted in electronic public policies applied to the Brazilian and Portuguese reality. Starting from the aspect of how these governments are thinking about the use of the internet and its relationship with the restrictions of citizen digital interactivity in relation to the use of the internet by these governments.

KEYWORDS

Electronic Government, Digital Public Services, Brazil, Portugal

1. INTRODUCTION

Both in Brazil and in Portugal, digital platforms are increasingly present in the field of public services. It is possible to point out that Brazil has been highlighted in the provision of public services on the Internet, as shown by the study carried out by the World Bank, GovTech Maturity Index 2022. Brazil was referenced as "the second country in the world with the highest maturity in digital government." The assessment is the result of digital public service indices in 198 global economies based on parameters created by the World Bank itself. The ranking of the ten leaders in digital government, according to this study, brings South Korea in first place, followed by Brazil, Saudi Arabia, United Arab Emirates, Estonia, France, India, Lithuania, Mongolia and Russia. That is, Brazil is a leader in this study among Western countries. And, according to the parameters of the World Bank, Brazil stood out among Western countries due to the amount of digital public services offered through the centralized platform called gov.br, which already has 140 million users - which is equivalent to 80% of the Brazilian population over 18 years old. There is a caveat here regarding the high number of users of the gov.br digital platform, given that, among other aspects, access to public services is increasingly migrating from the physical to the digital medium and the State requirement that users make a password, has been in many cases the only way for citizens to access public services. In this way, in order to obtain information, the citizen is almost obliged to have to maintain a relationship with the government through gov.br, which does not mean greater interactivity nor does it provide full transparency of information

Portugal, in turn, has also stood out, as indicated by the eGovernment Factsheets document, which is a comparative study on the development of digital public administration in Europe published by the European Commission's observatory in 2018 (EU, 2018). The study indicates that Portugal, in what confers the usability and availability of online services called user centricity, is scored at 96, on a scale of 100, while the average of European countries measures 70 points in this argument.

Still on the result of the analysis, GovTech Maturity Index 2022 (WB, 2022), promoted by the World Bank, Portugal is in group A, in this particular study, the highlight of Portugal is in the area of "Public Service Delivery Index", that is, Portugal provides a considerable amount in the number of services offered to users on digital platforms in relation to other countries without, however, meaning that these services are fully transparent or interactive as we will see later. However, the simple offer of more digital public services does

[1] Author contact: dazevedojr@yahoo.com.br

not necessarily guarantee an equivalent proportion of benefits to the user in relation to interactivity and transparency with public management is what concludes, paradoxically, the World Bank data.

"Across all 190 countries surveyed, the Digital Citizen Engagement Index scored the lowest (DCEI, 0.449) among the items surveyed. This indicates that economies have focused relatively more on improving the offerings of key government systems and shared platforms for delivering public services than on participation and feedback from digital citizens globally" (World Bank, 2022).

In this sense, Franco (2014) assesses that e-government should not be seen only by offering services over the Internet, but also by the wide range of possibilities for interaction and participation between government and society and by the government's commitment to transparency. Even though Portugal and Brazil already offer various government data publicly, it is necessary to consider that the manager does not always provide all possibilities of information and communication to the user. Castells (2003), when speaking of the Internet as a possibility for digital democracy, indicates that:

"Interactivity makes it possible for citizens to request information, express opinions and request personal responses from their representatives. [...] However, Governments at all levels use the Internet mainly as an electronic bulletin board to disseminate their information without engaging much in real interaction" (2003, p. 17).

Another aspect worth mentioning is how public administrations, in the two countries in question, appropriate, even at the present time, the centralized communication model and offering few channels of possibilities for real interactivity of participatory management to the citizen. Even with many services available on digital platforms, the population does not have truly interactive communication channels that make a real dialogue possible and not a simple dissemination of information in which the State is the only one to determine the form of communicative action or dissemination. In this sense, it is always up to the user to adapt to the State's determinations. Let us take the example of the gov.br platform in Brazil, which even with a significant number of users does not provide even a link in which the citizen can be a participatory agent in the direction of public management, the same effect is also observed in Portugal with the platform simplex.pt.

The following work question is posed: the digital policies adopted only with the expansion in the offer of public services, both in Portugal and in Brazil, provide users with a satisfactory environment so that there is a real participatory citizen interaction of these societies with the State?

2. METHODOLOGY

The study of consolidated data such as: Digitality Index of Economy and Society of the European Commission, National Institute of Statistics, Internet Steering Committee in Brazil, Digital In, Brazilian Institute of Geography and Statistics, Fundação Getúlio Vargas among other sources. Observing a correlation in the standard adopted in electronic public policies applied to the Brazilian and Portuguese reality.

3. DISCUSSION BRAZIL AND PORTUGAL

According to Lopes (2007), the implementation of information access mechanisms in Brazil is very recent., government models that had pre-bureaucratic characteristics still prevailed, preventing any movement in favor of transparency in access to information.

In countries where democratization was delayed, as occurred in Brazil, loyal mechanisms of access to information emerged only after the establishment of minimum democratic conditions. And, following the trend of other governments, Law No. 12,527, popularly known as the Access to Information Law (LAI), was enacted on November 18, 2011, with the purpose of regulating the constitutional right of access to public information in the country. And in its text, the LAI, in force since May 16, 2012, defined the Internet as a mandatory channel for the dissemination of Active Transparency initiatives, (Brasil, 2011).

The Brazilian government has been adopting for some time, mainly in theory, the following concept of electronic government in accordance with the public management model of the Ministry of Planning, Budget and Management (MPOG): "[...] the Electronic Government policy of the Brazilian government follows a set of guidelines based on three fundamental ideas: citizen participation; improvement of the State's internal management; and integration with partners and suppliers" (Brasil, 2017).

However, even in the face of this discourse adopted by the Brazilian government, in the sense of promoting more appropriate means of communicability to the particularities of the different target audiences, that is, in favor of more segmented forms of communication, what is observed in practice is a very opposite, because even with the multiple possibilities generated by digital technologies, the formula of centralizing communication still predominates in the public sector, based on the conception of a mass society, where in many cases what happens is just the simple dissemination of information and not a communication with the citizen.

Due to its continental and population size and its socioeconomic contradictions, among many other particularities, electronic government has become necessary for the functioning and improvement of Brazilian public administration. This is explained by the fact that: "Communication in this new configuration allows all actors to be senders and receivers, in a high level of interactivity between the parties, and, in theory, with the same levels of visibility and opportunity. The Internet, in particular, provoked expansion in the way in which people and organizations relate, given its speed and accessibility. It altered the notion of time and space, the type of access to goods and services, the relationship between the notion of citizenship and the universe of politics" (Brito, 2006, p. 113).

It is worth remembering that among the arguments of NGP theorists is the observation that the Brazilian State would have grown far beyond its desirable size, compromising the development of the economy and public spending. In this sense, the reduction of the State and the implementation of electronic government actions becomes a necessity in the neoliberal conception for the introduction of these administrative reforms:

"By strengthening a rhetorical base that exalted the importance of efficiency in public administration (albeit excessively), the managerial reform project ended up, indirectly, enabling a rapid penetration of electronic government tools within that administration. In other words, the reform was a fundamental element for the functioning (in socio-technical terms) of electronic government in Brazil" (Dias, 2012, p.38).

Following this order, investments in information technologies (IT) constantly increase, being urgent in the expansion of public services. In 2017 alone, the Brazilian government spent BRL 4.8 billion on IT, as stated by the Open Accounts organization (O Globo, 2018). The forecast in 2020, before Covid-19, in specific e-gov programs reached an increase in public resources in the order of 6.2% of the federal government (Terra online, 2020). It is worth noting that these investments follow a logic of profit and cost reduction. As an example of this theoretical management proposal, Florencia Ferrer, from the consultancy e-Strategia Pública, responsible for developing e-gov strategies in the state of São Paulo, states: "Electronic systems are capable of structurally reducing costs for the public machine." Following this logic, Ferrer uses as an example the reformulation of the collection of the tax for the circulation of automobiles (IPVA) in the state of São Paulo. By creating the electronic IPVA, which allows the payment of taxes over the Internet, the initiative showed significant results in improving service delivery and reducing bureaucracy. The measure eliminates paperwork and employees, lowering the cost of IPVA collection for the government from R$16.70 reais to R$1.90 per unit, reducing expenses for the state. That is, the amount to be paid by the taxpayer remained the same and the total savings for the government of São Paulo in 2010 was over 13 million reais (Exame online, 2011).

In this same sense, the central government, with the program "New Digital Government Strategy" published on April 30, 2020, defined the target of 100% of federal government services digitalized by the end of 2022. With the application of the strategy, the estimate is a saving of BRL 38 billion in five years, from 2020 to 2025, including eliminations of hiring personnel for face-to-face assistance, leasing structures, maintaining logistics, among other aspects (Brasil, 2020).

So that we have more elements about the object under study, I also make use of some research with consolidated data. Starting with the 2019 edition "ICT Electronic Government", carried out by the Internet Management Committee in Brazil, (Brasil, 2019), in the cut called "contact through the Internet", the objective is to evaluate the effectiveness of the form of contact made available to users by the websites of the public agencies. The data demonstrate, even with all the communicational potential of digital platforms, clearly the inertia and the absence of a forceful action in the Brazilian electronic management that provides the desired interactivity between citizen and State, let us see some aspects: online service in real time as chats only 8% of federal agencies and 5% of state agencies provide this service. We could question, on the State's side, the expenditure on personnel to implement a more humane and interactive channel. However, even in automated service, with a virtual assistant or chatbots, the project conceived represents an insignificant 9% of services offered by federal agencies and 6% by state agencies. The lack of real communication that is two-way and not just a one-way dissemination of information by the federal and state governments becomes noticeable to the detriment of the restriction of interactivity, largely designed by public managers, distancing from the legitimate fluid possibilities of connectivity, digital platforms, Brazilian taxpayers.

The Digital in 2019 report exposes the contradictions of the numbers and the potential of the actions, which is already public knowledge, 66% of the Brazilian population is a user of social networks. However, paradoxically, ICT (BRASIL, 2019) reinforces the obviousness of the Brazilian State in not being effective in e-gov regarding services on social networks: the real-time chat service in federal agencies represents only 14% of the possibility of communicability and 19% in state agencies. Still in relation to social networks, automated service with a virtual assistant or chatbots represent 10% of the form of contact in federal agencies and 9% in state ones.

The 2020 survey by the Getúlio Vargas Foundation of São Paulo (FGV-SP) defines 234 million smartphones, in use, making it the most consumed multimedia device in the country. Regarding the number of smartphones, the research points out that there is still more than one smartphone per inhabitant. When adding notebooks and tablets, there are 342 million portable devices in June 2020, i.e., 1.6 portable devices per inhabitant. Through the published results, the number of smartphones in use also brings us a dimension of the importance of this technology.

The 2017 IBGE survey reinforces the social importance that cell phones have in Brazilian society as an information and communication tool today. Denoting the most used equipment for Internet access in the country. In 98.7% of households with Internet access, cell phones were used for this purpose. Then there were microcomputers 52.3%.

However, Urupá (2019), among many scholars, when analyzing public policies in the field of communication and technology in an article, recalls that one of the characteristics of the Brazilian State is that it does not provide quality accessibility for a large part of the population.

The analysis of some data on electronic government in the municipalities reinforces a kind of concession on the form of policies adopted based on the guidelines of the "New Public Management". According to the 2019 ICT edition, even with the territorial extension and geographic distances, the survey indicates that all municipalities, 100%, have Internet access, with none being pointed out, in any city, that is off the web. It is worth mentioning that 73% of these have a fiber optic connection and only 3% have a dial-up connection. Among the types of services available on the website by Brazilian municipalities, I highlight the most offered, which is the download of documents or forms, especially for payment of fees and taxes, with more than 80% of access among users. Among the tools that are less available on the websites of city halls are: making appointments for medical-hospital consultations, consultations, services, among others that would be of greater need for citizens with a percentage around 20%.

In order to contextualize the relevance of the current electronic government project, it is necessary to immediately mention the Portuguese Constitution of 1976, in its article 268, which contemplates access to the right to information as the reserve of intimacy and private life, secrecy of justice and issues of national and State security when it states: "Citizens also have the right of access to administrative files and records, without prejudice to the provisions of the law on matters relating to internal and external security, criminal investigation and the privacy of people" among other norms. In this sense, Portugal has rules on access to information, even before using the Internet.

In order to understand the legal system on the subject, the Law of Access to Administrative Documents (LADA), which was first introduced on August 26, 1993, over the decades, has undergone updates and versions. At the moment, Law No. 26/2016, of August 22, is in force, approving the regime for access to administrative and environmental information and the reuse of administrative documents, transposing Directive 2003/4/EC, of the European Parliament and of the Council, of 28 January, and Directive 2003/98/CE, of 17 November.

It is worth mentioning that LADA brings an important aspect when considering that the Public Administration has the duty to publicize information: "The right of access to administrative documents includes not only the right to obtain their reproduction, as well as the right to be informed about its existence and content" (Portugal, 1993).

Another important aspect of LADA was the creation of the Commission for Access to Administrative Documents (CADA), which judges, gives guidance to government bodies and ensures compliance with laws that guarantee access to public information. It is also worth noting that CADA was maintained even with the recurring updates of LADA.

Law n° 46/2007 emphasizes that the documents must be available: "(...) in electronic databases easily accessible to the public through public telecommunications networks" (Portugal, 2007), emphasizing the adoption of digital platforms by the Portuguese State. However, it is worth highlighting Sousa (2016) indicates that Portugal brings the legislation that least discusses the issue of the Internet, even though its text was approved in 2007.

The Portuguese NGO Transparency and Integration indicates that Law No. 26/2016, the most current, is not applied in its entirety.

"Portugal joined the Open Government Partnership in December 2017 and, within the scope of the 1st National Open Administration Plan, we proposed a commitment to reinforce the implementation and monitoring of LADA. Unsurprisingly, this is one of the commitments that made the least progress during the implementation of the plan, which started in 2019" (Transparency and Integration, 2020).

In the study entitled the 2021 Index of Digitality of Economy and Society (DESI) of the European Commission brings the information that "only 48% of digital public services in Portugal are open data, being below compared to the EU average which is of 78%". Which leads us to question whether the public has access to information with full knowledge of where and how to find them and, above all, whether there is an incentive to consult them. After all, nowadays the Internet fully provides this possibility of interactivity between the State and the citizen and vice versa. In this regard, Ramos (2016) criticizes the Portuguese model for making public data available on digital platforms.

"The right to administrative information (procedural and non-procedural) is considered a fundamental right, similar in nature to the rights, freedoms and guarantees provided for in the Constitution, and should not be restricted, except in cases provided for by law. Administration must be open, clear, transparent and accessible, in accordance with national and European legislation" (2016, p.88).

In the field of Finance, Portugal stood out in electronic public management, as the first country in the world to receive the declaration of Income Tax over the Internet, in 1996. Known as the IRS Individual Income Tax. The practice of digital platforms is now adopted as an efficient way to fight fraud and tax evasion, leading, among other events, to the development of the "e-fatura" Program by Decree-Law 198/2012, of 24 August. In this direction, Melo (2018), when analyzing the numbers involved until 2017, indicates that from the implementation of the "e-fatura" program, which began on January 1, 2013, as well as all the measures that were part of it, concludes that even in times of crisis the application of the electronic form leads to a greater collection of tax revenue, by the Portuguese State, if compared to previous numbers, indicating above all, how public management also needs and depends on the tools fingerprints.

"In 2013, we saw an increase of 13.21% compared to the previous period of 2012. In 2014, an increase of 2.34%, in 2015 an increase of 4.66%, in 2016 an increase of 3.59% % and, in 2017, an increase of 4.81%. A final note regarding tax collection, referring to this period of 2017 where tax revenue collects, compared to 2012, where the "e-invoice" measures were not in force, there is a difference in the increase in tax revenue in the order of ten billion euros" (2018, p.74).

The 2021 IDES report adds up to a figure of 3.67 billion Euros invested in digital skills actions in the "digitization of the State as a lever for the sustainability of public finances" (2021, p.04).

It is also worth noting the "Global Strategic Plan for Rationalization and Cost Reduction through ICT in Public Administration" approved by Council of Ministers Resolution No. 12/2012 (Portuguese Republic, 2012). This plan, according to Monteiro (2020), had the ultimate objective of "achieving savings gains in all ministries, which entails lower costs for citizens and companies, and simultaneously reduces public expenditure, especially in the field of ICT". (2020, p.91). In other words, the Portuguese State has a great interest in the implementation of e-government policies as a form of financial control efficiency, but not necessarily creating more interactive communication channels with the population.

The National Institute of Statistics (INE), in the context of the covid-19 pandemic, presents the stage reached by the Portuguese in the most varied activities related to the Web, such as the search for e-government services, in 2020. More than half of the population used from Internet:

"56.9% declared having used the services of Public Administration bodies through a website or Internet application for at least one of the following purposes: downloading or printing official forms or filling out and submitting official forms online" (INE, 2020). The offer of these services is not necessarily the most essential to be offered to the population, since the download of documents or forms are mainly used for payment of fees and taxes or administrative requirements that serve more to control and power of the State than exactly in direct benefit to citizens. As for investments in telecommunications infrastructure, they constitute one of the strong points in the evaluations of Portugal, because if the citizen in general does not have access to the web network, the electronic government project will not be able to prosper. Thus, it is worth mentioning that in November 1999, with the aim of organizing public administration guidelines, the European Union Commission launched eEurope. At this time, Portugal as a Member State, adopted the determinations of the European Union to effectively apply and implement the defined action plans. In addition, the country undertook its own initiatives, mobilizing itself in the establishment of actions. Then, in March 2000, the European Council in Lisbon approved the 2010 Lisbon Strategy, in which it defined that the main public services should be offered on a virtual platform. The use of the Internet began to be reinforced in 2000 with the eEurope 2002 Action Plan and with the use of ICTs by the Stockholm European Council, which was then framed as electronic government. Thus, the European Union's initiatives for electronic public information were guided through a sequence of actions and plans: the eEurope 2005 action plan, the Lisbon Strategy 2010 and i2010, among others. (Bilhime end al., 2007, p.05).

In terms of the use of these infrastructures, in 2020, the data gathered on the National Institute of Statistics (INE) portal shows a society connected to the Internet with a rate of "84.5% of households in Portugal with an Internet connection at home and 81.7% use a broadband connection, which represents a significant increase of over 3.6% compared to the previous year". This increase is mainly explained by the need for communication that was imposed during the pandemic due to the restriction of population movement. However, social inequalities are also expressed in Internet access by income class. In the INE survey, it is observed that: 20% of households with higher incomes are those with higher levels of Internet access (96.8%) and to broadband (94.5%). At the other extreme, in households with the lowest income 20%, the proportions drop to 66.9% with Internet access at home and 62.4% via broadband. Internet connection at home and broadband connection are, in 2020, more frequent in the metropolitan area of Lisbon, in the regions of the Algarve and the autonomous region of Madeira. (INE, 2020). In the IDES report, "in 2019, the percentage of the Portuguese population that does not have at least basic digital skills decreased from 50% to 48%. However, around 26% had no digital competence at all. This remains essentially due to the fact that many people have never used the Internet". (2020, p.06) and the same study shows 22% of people who never used the Internet in 2020.

INE (2020), with regard to the proportion in the use of digital public services, despite being higher than that obtained in 2019, more than 3.1%, remained below the European Union average, which is 62% in 2020. Other A relevant aspect is that before covid-19, the data show a downward trend in the number of people who used public services over the Internet to contact public administration bodies in Portugal: 61.3% in 2017, 55.2% in 2018 and 53.8% in 2019. This demonstrates that users of these services, for some reason, face some difficulty in interactive communicability, and may consider these services non-essential or may even consider their demands unresolved. In this sense, the Deputy Secretary of State and Administrative Modernization, Luís Goes Pinheiro, reveals that "despite the immense availability of online services over the years by the Public Administration, the levels of use are quite low", and expresses how the services offered fail to be effective or interactive for citizens. And he gives examples: "in 2018, 750,000 driving license revalidations were requested, but less than 10% were electronically. The same happened with criminal record requests: there were almost a million requests in 2018, but just over 6% were made online" (TSF, 2019).

The Citizen Portal, which was launched in 2004, was replaced by the ePortugal website in 2019 (www.eportugal.gov.pt), to aggregate and make online public services more visible. One of the objectives of this transformation, determined by the government, is to reach the mark of one million users, surpassing the low use that is registered of the online services and in the expectation of tripling the current 320 thousand users of the portal. The evolution of the Citizen's Portal to ePortugal is a Simples+ 2017 measure, which emerged in the sense of organizing information and electronic services around events in the life of citizens and companies. It is worth mentioning that the Government, when presenting the Simplex 20-21, estimated that it would be able to save 190 million euros with 58 of the 158 measures presented (SAPO, 2020).

As for the main use of the Internet and the set of all activities analyzed during the pandemic in 2020, INE revealed a greater growth in video or voice calls over the Internet from 18% in 2019, rising to 70.5% in 2020. The mobile phone or smartphone was the equipment most mentioned by Internet users (82.5%) to access the Internet while on the move. Therefore, the research does not point to any data, or specific service of digital government, in which the citizen could make a video call with the public administration directly.

4. CONCLUSION

The two countries, on the screen, have many similarities in the way public information is made available on digital platforms, as well as in the way they do not fully provide the possibility of interactive communication between the citizen and the State through the communication potential of the web network. According to

Ruediger (2002), one cannot deny the positive consequences that the availability of digital services represents from the point of view of an improvement in government performance with some positive repercussions for the population. It is observed here, however, that even with the regular use of technology for the publication of online information and the provision of public services, contributing to impact the improvement in Digital Government rankings, this does not necessarily reflect in greater social participation by through government digital platforms.

In this sense, based on the data presented in this analytical section, electronic government is a need for public management and not necessarily a desire of governments to provide interactive citizen communication, both in Brazil and in Portugal. In this context and as a result of the discussion, it is believed that there is an interactivity deficit and that there is still a way to go in the creation of services associated with e-government that are truly interactive.

REFERENCES

Bilhim, J. A. F. e Neves, B. B. (2007). "O Governo electrónico em Portugal: O caso das cidades e regiões digitais" Instituto Superior de Ciências Sociais e Políticas (ISCSP), Universidade Técnica de Lisboa. Retrieved June 2022 https://apdsi.pt/uploads/news/id546/3.8_joao%20bilhim%20+%20barbara .

Brasil. Ministério da Economia. Transformação Digital. (2020). Retrieved June 2022: https://www.gov.br/economia/pt-br/assuntos/noticias/2020/maio/governo-atinge-marca-de-700-servicos-digitalizados-em-17-meses-e-dobra-numero-de-acessos

Brasil. Ministério do Planejamento, Orçamento e Gestão. Centro de Estudos sobre as Tecnologias da Informação e da Comunicação. Panorama Setorial da Interne. Acesso à Internet no Brasil: desafios para conectar toda a população. Universalização do acesso, v. 8. n. 1. Brasil, 2017. Retrieved June 2022:<http://cetic.br/media/docs/publicacoes/6/Panorama_Setorial_11.pdf http://cetic.br/pesquisa/domicilios/>.

Brasil. Ministério do Planejamento, Orçamento e Gestão. Centro de TIC Estudos sobre as Tecnologias da Informação e da Comunicação. Panorama setorial da Internet – Acesso à Internet no Brasil: desafios para conectar toda a população. 2019. Retrieved June 2022: de https://cetic.br/pesquisa/governo-eletronico/http://cetic.br/pesquisa/domicilios/>.

Brasil. Presidência da Republica. Lei n. 12.527, de 18 de novembro de 2011. Regula o acesso à informação. Retrieved June 2022: <http://www.planalto.gov.br/ccivil_03/_ato2011-2014/2011/lei/l12527.htm>.

Brito, I. Política da Qualidade: Gestão de Pequenas e Médias Empresas. Apostila Universidade Salgado de Oliveira. Rio de Janeiro, Brasil: UNSO, 2006.

Castells, M. A Galáxia da Internet: reflexões sobre a Internet, os negócios e a sociedade. Rio de Janeiro, Brasil: Zahar, 2003.

Comissão Européia. Índice de Digitalidade da Economia e da Sociedade (IDES). (2021). Retrieved June 2022: https://ec.europa.eu/commission/presscorner/detail/pt/IP_21_5481. Acesso em: fevereiro 2022.

Comissão Européia. Índice de Digitalidade da Economia e da Sociedade (IDES). (2020). Retrieved June 2022 em:https://ec.europa.eu/commission/presscorner/detail/pt/qanda_20_1022.

Dias, R. Governo eletrônico: ferramenta democrática ou instrumento do neoliberalismo? En. Revista Tecnologia e Sociedade – 2ª Edição, 2012. ISSN: 1984-3526 Retrieved June 2022: https://periodicos.utfpr.edu.br/rts/article/view/2593.

Digital in. We are social 2019. Retrieved June 2022: https://wearesocial.com/global-digital-report-2019 .

Exame. O jeito certo de cortar gastos públicos exagerados. 2011. Retrieved June 2022: https://exame.abril.com.br/revista-exame/o-jeito-certo-de-cortar/ .

FGV. 31ª Pesquisa Anual de Administração e Uso de Tecnologia da Informação nas Empresas, realizada pela Fundação Getúlio Vargas de São Paulo (FGV-SP) 2020. Retrieved June 2022 https://www.gov.br/economia/pt-br/assuntos/noticias/2020/maio/governo-atinge-marca-de-700-servicos-digitalizados-em-17-meses-e-dobra-numero-de-acessos .

Franco, L. Participação digital e governo eletrônico abertura para qual cidadania? Revista Brasileira de Administração Científica, *5*(2), out. 2014. p. 214-225.

Instituto Brasileiro e Geográfico (IBGE). Uso da Internet, televisão e celular no Brasil. 2017. Retrieved June 2022: https://educa.ibge.gov.br/jovens/materias-especiais/20787-uso-de-Internet-televisao-e-celular-no-brasil.html#subtitulo-1 .

Instituto Nacional de Estatística (INE). Sociedade da Informação e do Conhecimento - Inquérito à Utilização de Tecnologias da Informação e da Comunicação nas Famílias 2020. Portugal. Retrieved June 2022: https://www.ine.pt/xportal/xmain?xpid=INE&xpgid=ine_destaques&DESTAQUESdest_boui=415621509&DESTAQUESmodo=2&xlang=pt#:~:text=Portal%20do%20INE&text=Em%202020%2C%2084%2C5%25,em%20rela%C3%A7%C3%A3o%20ao%20ano%20anterior.

Lopes, Cristiano Aguiar. Acesso à informação pública para a melhoria da qualidade dos gastos públicos: literatura, evidências empíricas e o caso brasileiro. Caderno de Finanças Públicas, Brasília, n. 8, p. 5-40, dez. 2007. Retrieved June 2022 <Erro! A referência de hiperlink não é válida.assuntos/ biblioteca/cadernos-de-financas-publicas-1/arquivo.2013-04-18.4951615613>.

Melo, Carlos Miguel Amorim. e-fatura – A reforma digital da AT. Implicações no crescimento da receita fiscal. Dissertação apresentada no âmbito do mestrado para obtenção do Grau de Mestre em Gestão Fiscal no ISG – Instituto Superior de Gestão, Lisboa, 2018. Retrieved June 2022 from: *https://comum.rcaap.pt/bitstream/10400.26/24270/1/Efatura%20%e2%80%93%20A%20reforma%20digital%20da%20AT%20%20Implica%c3%a7%c3%b5es%20no%20crescimento%20da%20receita%20fiscal.pdf*. Acesso em: março 2021.

Monteiro, Ana Rita Batista. Governo Digital – Desafios e Impactos para os Recursos Humanos do Setor Público. Dissertação apresentada à Universidade de Aveiro para cumprimento dos requisitos necessários à obtenção do grau de Mestre em Administração e Gestão Pública, Aveiro, 2020. Retrieved June 2022 from https://ria.ua.pt/bitstream/10773/30327/1/Documento_Ana_Rita_Monteiro.pdf

O Globo. Brasília abriga empresas tecnológicas de fachada que desviam milhões do governo. 2018. Retrieved June 2022: https://oglobo.globo.com/brasil/brasilia-abriga-empresas-tecnologicas-de-fachada-que-desviam-milhoes-do-governo-22956710

Portugal (1976). Constituição da República Portuguesa.

Portugal (1993). Lei nº 65/93, de 26 de agosto de 1993. Lei do Acesso aos Documentos Administrativos, (LADA) 1993. Diário da Repúblical –Série –A, p. 4524.

Portugal (2007). Lei nº 46/2007, de 24 de agosto de 2007. Regula o acesso a documentos administrativos e sua reutilização, 2007. Diário da República –Série, p. 5680. Comissão de Acesso aos Documentos Administrativos (CADA) Retrieved June 2022 from http://www.cada.pt

Portugal (2016). Lei n.º 26/2016, de 22 de agosto. Aprova o regime de acesso à informação administrativa e ambiental e de reutilização dos documentos administrativos, transpondo a Diretiva 2003/4/CE, do Parlamento Europeu e do Conselho, de 28 de janeiro, e a Diretiva 2003/98/CE, do Parlamento Europeu e do Conselho, de 17 de novembro.

Ramos, Alexandra Lemos. O princípio da administração aberta versus o princípio da proteção dos dados pessoais. Dissertação de Mestrado em Direito Administrativo na Faculdade de Direito da Universidade de Lisboa, Lisboa, 2016. Retrieved June 2022 from: https://repositorio.ul.pt/bitstream/10451/37453/1/ulfd136607_tese.pdf

República Portuguesa (2012). Resolução de Conselho de Ministros nº12/2012, Retrieved June 2022 from https://dre.pt/pesquisa/-/search/543701/details/maximized

Ruediger, Marco Aurélio. Governo Eletrônico e Democracia – Uma Análise Preliminar dos Impactos e Potencialidades na Gestão Pública. Encontro da Associação Nacional de Programas de Pós-graduação em Administração (ENANPAD), 26, Salvador-BA, 2002.

Sapo. Estado poupa 190 milhões com o Simplex. 2020. Retrieved June 2022 from: https://sol.sapo.pt/artigo/703093/estado-poupa-190-milhoes-com-o-simplex.

Sousa, Janara et al. A Lei de Acesso à Informação no Brasil, Portugal e Espanha: uso da Internet, transparência e cidadania. Revista Electrónica Razón y Palabra, Cuba, Número 92 Diciembre 2015 – marzo 2016. Retrieved March 2022 from: http://www.razonypalabra.org.mx/N/N92/Varia/20_SousaGeraldes_V92.pdf

Terra Online. Orçamento do emetic tem alta de 6,2%. 2020. Retrieved March 2020 from: http://www.telesintese.com.br/proposta-de-orcamento-do-mctic-para-2020-tem-alta-de-62/

Transparência e Integração. Perguntar não ofende. 2020. Retrieved March, 2022 from: https://transparencia.pt/perguntar-nao-ofende/

TSF. Revalidar a carta de condução ou alterar a morada? O Sigma promete ajudar. 2019. Retrieved: https://www.tsf.pt/economia/novo-portal-do-cidadao-quer-um-milhao-de-utilizadores-e-tem-assistente-virtual-10574076.html.

Urupá, Marcos Francisco. A EPC como referencial teórico-metodológico na análise de políticas públicas de banda larga Revista Eptic vol.21, n.2, mai-ago. 2019. Retrieved: https://seer.ufs.br/index.php/eptic/article/view/11498 .

World Bank *GovTech Maturity Index 20:* Retrieved March 2022 https://www.worldbank.org/en/programs/govtech/2022-gtmi

AN EQUATION OF NO RETURN: CYBERSECURITY + HUMAN FACTORS

Dulce Mourato[1] and Paula Amaro[2]
[1]*Higher Advanced Technological Institute (ISTEC), Lisbon, Portugal*
[2]*Polytechnic of Guarda (IPG), Portugal*

ABSTRACT

It is concerning to observe that individuals, corporations, public services, and healthcare professionals often overlook the importance of Cybersecurity. Cyberattacks, Ransomware, Data Breaches, and Phishing, among others, seem unreal dimension concerns. People often fail to exercise caution when it comes to keeping their computers secure while working. This non-existence of concern raises a critical question, especially among healthcare professionals: How can we make them realize that their actions, or lack thereof, could potentially endanger numerous lives? - Maybe healthcare professionals may not fully comprehend the gravity of the situation, and may not fully grasp the potential risks and consequences that can arise from failing to prioritize Cybersecurity or they are simply unaware of the specific actions they should be taking to ensure the security of their systems.

Faced with these hypotheses, two professors from the Higher Advanced Technological Institute from Lisbon (ISTEC) and Polytechnic of Guarda Institute (IPG), within the scope of promoting Cybersecurity culture among the degrees in Science Computer Engineering, and Multimedia Engineering students, discussed how human factors influence the daily practice of computer security in a health unit.

The first aim of this experience was to assess the level of Cybersecurity awareness among healthcare professionals and determine the feasibility of using a scientific approach. The second aim was to apply an open-ended interview to determine the student's relationship with the subject, examine the daily practice of health professionals to protect confidential computer data and understand how to introduce the human factors in Cybersecurity as technological courses mandatory curriculum taught at the two institutes.

The result of that first phase was a complete failure, from the motivation of the students, the design of the study, and some indifference of health professionals, regarding the subject, however, it focused on the research question: How to minimize the impact of the human factors in terms of computer security, in a health unit, regardless of size through Project Based Learning (PBL)?

Preparatory work and rethinking of the entire study were necessary, together with the students, to identify the themes and daily binding practices of safety procedures, to be tested by health professionals in their daily work and measured by academic quality services. The previous conclusions serve to project a Project Based Learning Workshop tailored-made to be applied.

KEYWORDS

Cybersecurity, Human Factors, Prevention, Privacy, Data

1. INTRODUCTION

Minimize the impact of human factors in terms of computer security, in a health unit, regardless of size through Project Based Learning (PBL), was the main goal of two professors from the Higher Advanced Technological Institute from Lisbon (ISTEC) and Polytechnic of Guarda (IPG), within the scope of promoting Cybersecurity culture among the degrees in Science Computer Engineering and Multimedia Engineering students, discussed how the human factor influences the daily practice of computer security in a local health unit.

Students visit the health care unit to understand what are the real Cybersecurity threats. After carrying out direct observation in the field and surveying requirements, it was possible to verify 'the innocent relaxation' of the various health professionals who, because they were few for so many requests, left their profiles active, on their work computers, without any security safeguards or vigilance.

That information observed by students became crucial to refining the research questions and became a piece of evidence: how to use PBL to prepare students with the knowledge and skills needed to develop secure, private, and ethical software, that could be resilient to human factors?

How to explain potential Cybersecurity threats and privacy data violations, what is confidentiality, and what kind of health information needs to be secure?

What kind of regular and up-to-date education could be provided to health employees to improve Cybersecurity with human factor prevention, and how they can avoid all the risks involved?

Another objective was to integrate Science Computer students and Higher Education Institutions to make available regular Cybersecurity and data privacy awareness training, in the first phase, for healthcare employees and after for continuous Cybersecurity literacy long-life training.

How the students solved the problems of privacy and approach to the institution is what will be described in the following chapters.

2. LITERATURE REVIEW

The article leitmotiv was inquiry-based, which brings all those starting points already highlighted: perceive user behaviour, verify insider threats, and understand technologies systems applications choices that influence decision, manipulation, and defense. The urgent mainstream of making and explaining to health organizations' employees, crucial Cybersecurity policies and procedures and how to transmit every person quality practice, makes possible the implementation of effective technical safety measures such as firewalls, antivirus software, and intrusion detection systems that can really help or prevent cyber-attacks if not exist yet, must be daily based goal as it was expressed in several articles.

The recent COVID-19 Pandemic brings to daylight some concerns in healthcare services:

> One of the main trends established through comparison of all available, recent, and relevant literature is that serious gaps are present in hospitals' approaches to technical, educational, policy, and resource-allocation elements of Cybersecurity. Cybercriminals can access, steal, block, or manipulate screening tools, medication treatments, vital sign alarms, patient records, telecommunication, or clinical supplies, just to name a few. Yet, hospitals lack adequate protection for each of these vulnerabilities. From ineffective measures to advanced innovations that focus on patient care and that neglect the risks such technologies create, to a lack of employee awareness of security protocols, to simply deficient Cybersecurity IT teams, hospitals are no match for savvy, and sometimes even amateur, hackers. The research question, of whether US hospitals are prepared for cyber risks that accompany clinical medicine, can thus be answered with a succinct 'not yet' (Wasserman & Wasserman, 2022, p.14).

Cybersecurity is critical for preserving productivity in all kinds of organizations and needs to adopt a holistic approach, that includes technology, people, and processes to stay ahead of evolving cyber threats: by protecting sensitive data, networks, and systems from cyber-attacks.

Recently, Van Kessel, Haig and Mossialos (2023, p.1) enhanced the importance of this issue worldwide and in particular in Europe: "The European Commission proposed the European Health Data Space (EHDS) in 2022 to enhance care delivery and improve patients' lives by offering all EU citizens control over their personal health data in a private and secure environment". Van Kessel, Haig and Mossialos (2023, p.1) observes that "the EHDS proposal only briefly mentions Cybersecurity as a field that should be coordinated and collaborated with throughout the proposal" and suggesting "One possible solution is to explore the feasibility of incorporating Cybersecurity modules into medical, public health, and digital health curricula and providing retraining and upskilling opportunities for practicing professionals" (Van Kessel, Haig and Mossialos, 2023, p.2).

King et al. (2018, p.2) describe that: "The explicit integration of human factors into Cybersecurity risk assessment is necessary to fully understand and characterize the impact of malicious behavior as it is reflected throughout all levels of society. The way people think and behave is just as important to study as the malicious code used to exploit vulnerabilities in technology".

In order to clarify human factors, king et al. (2018, p.4) inspired and modified from Henshel et al. (2015, p.1120) the above-constructed diagram, which gives some clew to overview and describes the steps to Cybersecurity awareness.

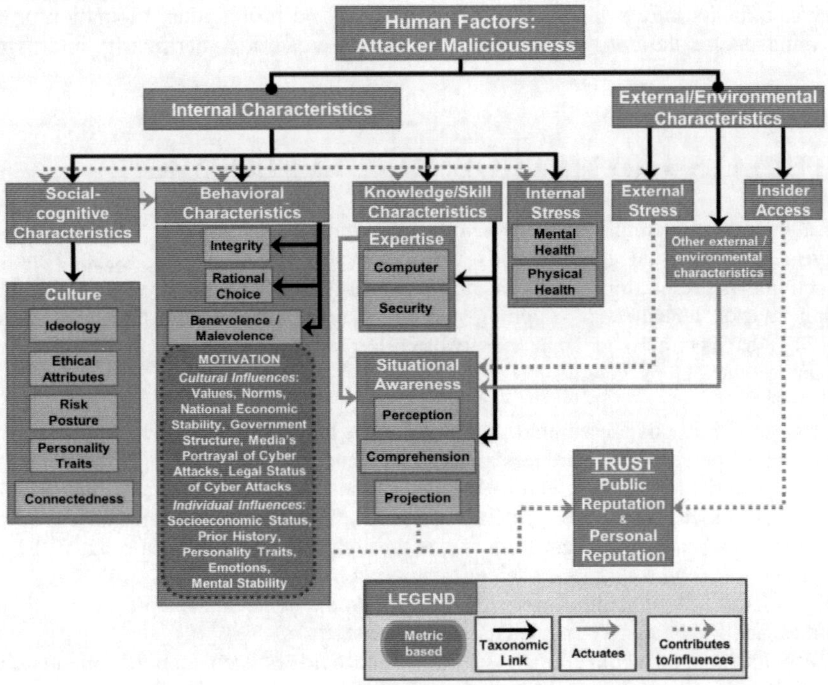

Figure 1. Human factors framework - King et al. (2018, p.4) inspired and modified from Henschel et al. (2015, p.1120) Defender/analyst trust framework.

At the same time that researchers try to find a coherent path between Cybersecurity awareness and standards milestones to get it, King et al. (2018, p.16) explain that:

> Despite progress toward detecting characteristics contributing to maliciousness, little has been done to develop and test a reasonably sized survey or another instrument that can be used to test multiple malicious-related metrics in the same population. Rather, assumptions inferring motivation and intent are drawn indirectly from behavior, making these endpoints more difficult to quantify and validate. It is also difficult to assess the error and uncertainty in the metrics (King et al., 2018, p.16).

Actually, enterprises can minimize interruption of services, avoid damage to reputation and customer trust, and reduce financial losses. The recent implementation of Cloud Computing to promote Cybersecurity services standardization does not avoid global dangers. As Mourato (2021, p.3) explains:

> There are lots of vulnerabilities and threats amplified by cloud infrastructure, more digital assets, and the proliferation of mobile access devices. Security is now connected to the crucial need for confidentiality, integrity, and availability present in data, software, and hardware. As resource sharing, computation outsourcing, and external data warehousing increase, more accuracy turns the security and privacy concerns in order to create new security challenges (Mourato, 2021, p.3).

In the development of this process, which pointed to several clues, the distinction between Cybersecurity and 'cyber safety' also emerged. Is it possible to have the similarity of concepts in networks and in real life? - Security means protecting organizations/people against possible threats/dangers. Safety, in turn, means providing effective protection of someone or a thing from natural or external causes that may cause damage.

Cai (2018, p.5) enlightens that "there is a growing pool of efforts on Cybersecurity education including teaching pedagogies, curriculum materials, lab platforms, and faculty training".

In this case and for health organizations, the awareness of Cybersecurity could be cyber safety goals: identity, privacy, data secure availability, patient privacy, and professional reputation protection. With this thought in mind maybe the only way to progress was to create a Cybersecurity and cyber safety training workshop.

3. MATERIALS AND METHODS OF DEVELOPMENT

As the literature review demonstrated, in healthcare organizations, several vulnerabilities could be put in risk-sensitive equipment, that controls body treatments and measurements, assisted medicines, or human interface tractions, like respiratory management systems, among others. At the same time, it adds other dangers like phishing attacks, human error, opening malicious attachments inside multiple services, and plug-ins brought by USB drives or network apps or software referred by some authors like Cybersecurity balks.
Several methodological steps were taken:

- first, a comprehensive research design needs to be developed for conducting an open-ended interview study on Cybersecurity awareness among healthcare professionals;
- second, clearly define the research objective of the study, which is to assess the level of Cybersecurity awareness among healthcare professionals, the importance of human factors, in terms of computer security, in a health unit, regardless of size through Project Based Learning (PBL), and determine the potential for using a case study scientific approach;
- third, identify participant selection, the ideal sample of healthcare professionals, including doctors, nurses, administrators, IT specialists, and other staff;
- fourth, invest in data collection, observation, and field research. Conduct open-ended interviews with the participants to gather qualitative data;
- fifth, evaluate the feasibility of using this kind of scientific approach to address the identified gaps in knowledge, areas of improvement, the potential for developing evidence-based interventions, training programs, and possible solutions to enhance Cybersecurity practices awareness and practices.

By conducting this open-ended interview study, students can gain valuable insights into the current state of Cybersecurity awareness among healthcare professionals. These findings can inform the development of targeted interventions and strategies to improve Cybersecurity practices for all. Moreover, it can provide a groundwork for future scientific research in this area, contributing to the advancement of knowledge and the protection of patient data.

The main step was to compile the answers to inspire some questions that could be used, as a starting point to research and applied to PBL in order to structure a basic checklist, that reflects requirements gathering, data collection instruments creation, and a sample survey, to determine the degree of professionals' attention, about Cybersecurity regarding the use of technologies in the workplace.

In Table 1 (Interview – Anti-hacking Challenge) it is possible to verify a possible draft of the requirement, gathering, and data sample questions, to establish case study underpinning.

Table 1. First data instrument (Interview – Anti-hacking Challenge) to verify human factor Cybersecurity awareness

Research Categories	Questions
Personal and Professional Profile	1 - How old are you? 2 - What is your background? 3- In which sector of the hospital do you work? 4- How many times do you use your email in a day/night at work? 5- Do you have a personal email or do you usually use just one for everything? 6 - What equipment do you usually work with/use (computer, mobile phone, tablet)
Prevention and Knowledge of Technologies and Cybersecurity	7 - Do you use your personal equipment for work? 8 - Do you usually use the computer to charge you cell phone? 9 - Does the service computer allow the use of a pen to exchange documents between colleagues? 10 - Where did you acquire your training in Cybersecurity?
Procedures for Cybersecurity Events	11 - Have you ever suffered a cyberattack? If yes, what did you do? 12 - What to do when you suffer a cyberattack in any sector of the hospital? And in your sector? 13 - What computer attacks have you received? And what are the most common ones to receive? 14 - How many attacks do you receive per day? 15 - What was the worst attack you have ever received? 16 – If there was training on Cybersecurity, would you like to help?
Knowledge about Privacy and Data Protection and Actions to be taken in case of Cybersecurity Attacks	17 - How do you avoid information leakage? 18 - What usually happens when a worker suffers computer attack? 19 - How is the communication with the other sectors of the hospital, in terms of Cybersecurity? 20 - What are the most frequent individual Cybersecurity problems that characterize those who work in the hospital? And yours? 21 - How careful are you about the information yo receive?

The use of an open-ended semi-structured interview guide ensures consistency while allowing flexibility for in-depth exploration of participants' perspectives, about the knowledge of Cybersecurity, their perception of its importance, their current practices, and any challenges they face in implementing Cybersecurity measures.

Found the proper methodology as qualitative research, supported by PBL, student-centered teaching, and learning approach, to develop skills and work collaboratively on authentic problems and challenges. With qualitative research, it is possible to understand the lived and subjective experiences, perceptions, and participants' perspectives, such as user behaviour and attitudes toward security portraits with a case study.

Cai (2018, p.1) in the article 'Using Case Studies To Teach Cybersecurity Courses' defines the PBL stepstones that could provide interest stimulation:

> Students will look into the details of these attacks, learn how these attacks took place from the beginning to the end, understand what security topics are relevant, and study how these attacks could be prevented or stopped. Students will also be able to replicate some of the breaches in a simulated virtual lab environment using similar tools and methods described in the case studies. Through guided in-class discussion, selected readings, and hands-on lab assignments centered around the case studies, students will explore various Cybersecurity offensive and defensive techniques, and understand best practices and lessons learned in the real world. During the process of case analysis, students will learn how different subsystems interact with each other and obtain a whole picture of integrated Cybersecurity systems. In addition, socio-technical topics including human and business factors are introduced during case analysis (Cai, 2018, p.1).

Every step taken in this research follows privacy and ethical principles and everyone, who answered the interviews, knows that the only purpose was to educate the real importance of paying attention to the details as they do in professional day life. Until this does not happen, the efficacy of the palliative measures must be verified, day by day, but certainly, people could be more conscious about the subject.

4. RESULTS AND DISCUSSIONS

The results were few and beyond expectations (only sixteen - 16 - participants) answered the interviews, and took some time to talk about Cybersecurity and the protection of confidential information. When faced with an insufficiency of data, it can indeed present a challenge to give value to scientific results, however, it was made content analysis coding, categorizing, and confirming text or visual material from observation or research field verification. It was not possible to explore alternative research designs so it is important to consider innovative approaches to gather meaningful insights as transcribing and analyzing the interview and other data using a thematic analysis approach. Identify recurring themes, patterns, and trends related to Cybersecurity awareness among healthcare professionals.

Some of the answers that are transcribed here (Table 2) revealed, limited knowledge of the subject:

Table 2. Participants' Opinions about Cybersecurity in local health unit

	Random Answers to Analyse
Participants	P1 "When you receive emails with suspicious links" P2: "Avoid opening attachments". P3: "I don't know enough". P4: "There are new viruses and new risks". P5: "Beware of suspicious emails and therefore only open work emails and never personal ones". P6: "Be attentive and do not ignore the risks, do not open dubiou emails, and clean files history. Do not write or store passwords in places frequented by more people. Create secure passwords and be careful with personal data, patients' clinical history, and bank data details, as well as be attentive to the security rules of the hospital". P7: "If we have information from all sectors of the hospital, we must be very careful and therefore make weekly backups of all activity". P8 "If there is an attack or something strange, turn off the system/PC, call the Information Technologies department, notify the authorities, report, and alert the Judiciary Police".

The evidence of the participant's answers demonstrates the urgent need for training, specifically in Cybersecurity subjects as a prior issue in human factors prevention. What kind of alert should a health professional have, regarding computer security or the procedure to be adopted in the event of a Cybersecurity threat?

Undoubtedly, the preoccupation with physical security at the local health unit was notorious, in terms of controlling entrances and exits, cleaning spaces, and publicizing basic health rules, such as successive posters reminding that hand washing prevents more than 60 percent of typical infections. However, there is no simple reminder, at the beginning of each professional's session on work computers, to enlighten the measures to be taken to protect the confidentiality and privacy of patients' clinical data protection, to be aware of suspicious personal mail, and must pay attention in the use of networks and interaction with all technologies.

With all these results, using PBL it was possible to trace a methodology working plan and a training workshop, about Cybersecurity mindset and cyber resilience, specifically for healthcare workers.

After planning the Health Cybersecurity PBL Workshop methodology for that specific case study, there are main issues to achieve:

- ✓ Use storytelling, which can be a powerful tool to help someone understand the danger of human factors in Cybersecurity;
- ✓ Identify and share real-life examples, games, and anecdotes of how human error has led to Cybersecurity breaches;
- ✓ Exemplify the potential consequences of not taking Cybersecurity seriously in health data-sensitive areas;
- ✓ Develop a security mindset that provides health professionals intuition plus complex reasoning to perceive that there is something wrong;
- ✓ Demonstrate how phishing attacks have led to data breaches or how weak passwords have allowed hackers to gain access to sensitive information.
- ✓ Present the importance of implementing strong password policies and multi-factor authentication to prevent unauthorized access to sensitive information.
- ✓ Alert that health professionals be aware that all software and systems are kept up-to-date with the latest security patches, which can help prevent vulnerabilities from being exploited.

5. CONCLUSION

The problem identified has little existing related research, so drawing upon and synthesizing relevant findings from other studies, was not possible, in this particular case. Therefore, being transparent about limitations and constraints, was the main challenge as well as validating or testing the results and providing a broader context for interpretation.

It was possible to derive value from the pursued qualitative approaches that provide meaningful insights and contribute to generating other questions for future studies about human factors that influence health professionals' performance and Cybersecurity knowledge prevention. Though, one question remained unanswered: what kind of content, could be useful and determinant to inform practices and guide behaviours about the theme? – Maybe these proposals, could be the first step to changing organizations and universities and creating a pool of resources in order to introduce Cybersecurity soft skills.

REFERENCES

Bhuyan, S. S., Kabir, U. Y., Escareno, J. M., Ector, K., Palakodeti, S., Wyant, D., Kumar, S., Levy, M., Kedia, S., Dasgupta, D., & Dobalian, A. (2020). *Transforming Healthcare Cybersecurity from Reactive to Proactive: Current Status and Future Recommendations*. Journal of medical systems, 44(5), 98. https://doi.org/10.1007/s10916-019-1507-y.

Burrell, D. N. & Nobles, C. (2022). *Discovering the Emergence of Technical Sociology in Human Capital Systems and Technology-Driven Organizations*. International Journal of Human Capital and Information Technology Professionals (IJHCITP), 13(1), 1-15. http://doi.org/10.4018/IJHCITP.300324.

Cai, Yu (2018). *Using Case Studies To Teach Cybersecurity Courses. Journal of Cybersecurity Education, Research and Practice*. Vol. 2018, No. 2, Article 3. Available at: https://digitalcommons.kennesaw.edu/jcerp/vol2018/iss2/3.

Green, Marcus L. (2021). "*Employees Breaking Bad With Technology: An Exploratory Analysis of Human Factors That Drive Cyberspace Insider Threats*". USF Tampa Graduate Theses and Dissertations. https://digitalcommons.usf.edu/etd/9118.

Henshel, D., Cains, M. G., Hoffman, B., and Kelley, T. (2015). *Trust as a human factor in holistic cyber security risk assessment*. Procedia Manuf. 3, 1117–1124. Doi: 10.1016/j.promfg.2015.07.186.

King ZM, Henshel DS, Flora L, Cains MG, Hoffman B and Sample C. (2018). *Characterizing and Measuring Maliciousness for Cybersecurity Risk Assessment*. Front. Psychol. 9:39. doi: 10.3389/fpsyg.2018.00039.

Mourato, D. (2021). *Security and Privacy in Cloud Computing: Simple Checklist to Virtualization*. Edition No. 9, November 22– Kriativ.tech. ISTEC- Portugal. http://www.kriativ-tech.com/?p=66404. DOI: 10.31112/kriativ-tech-2021-10-63.

Nifakos, S., Chandramouli, K., Nikolaou, C. K., Papachristou, P., Koch, S., Panaousis, E., & Bonacina, S. (2021). *Influence of Human Factors on Cyber Security within Healthcare Organisations: A Systematic Review*. Sensors (Basel, Switzerland), 21(15), 5119. https://doi.org/10.3390/s21155119.

Noran Shafik Fouad (2021). *Securing higher education against cyber threats: from an institutional risk to a national policy challenge*. Journal of Cyber Policy, 6:2, 137-154, DOI: 10.1080/23738871.2021.1973526.

Van Kessel, R., Haig, M. & Mossialos, E., (2023). *Strengthening Cybersecurity for Patient Data Protection in Europe*. J Med Internet Res 2023;25:e48824. URL: https://www.jmir.org/2023/1/e48824 DOI: 10.2196/48824

Wasserman, L., & Wasserman, Y. (2022). *Hospital Cybersecurity risks and gaps: Review (for the non-cyber professional)*. Frontiers in digital health, 4, 862221. https://doi.org/10.3389/fdgth.2022.862221.

Yeo, L. H., & Banfield, J. (2022). *Human Factors in Electronic Health Records Cybersecurity Breach: An Exploratory Analysis. Perspectives in health information management*, 19(Spring), 1i. Url: https://pubmed.ncbi.nlm.nih.gov/35692854/.

EXPLORING INFLUENTIAL FACTORS IN KNOWLEDGE SHARING WITHIN INDONESIAN PRISONS

Ejo Imandeka[1], Achmad Nizar Hidayanto[1], Heru Suhartanto[1] and Jan Pidanic[2]
[1]*Department of Computer Science, Faculty of Computer Science, University of Indonesia*
Depok, Indonesia
[2]*Department of Electrical Engineering, Faculty of Electrical Engineering, and Informatics, Pardubice University*
Pardubice, Czechia

ABSTRACT

The exchange of knowledge is widely recognized as a crucial aspect of effective knowledge management. When it comes to sharing knowledge within Prison settings, things get complicated due to various challenges such as limited resources, social stigma, isolation, communication barriers, and security concerns. Additionally, there's a scarcity of resources dedicated to promoting knowledge sharing in secure environments. This study aims to dig deep into the key factors that influence how knowledge is shared in Indonesian prisons. To navigate this intricate terrain, the study uses questionnaires distributed among Prison officers to understand the complex relationship between the identified critical factors and knowledge sharing in Prison. Leadership support, organizational culture, organizational structure, incentives, and individual beliefs emerge as pivotal elements in knowledge sharing. It's also noted that the connection between these critical factors and the intention to share knowledge is significantly influenced by organizational structure. Recognizing and addressing critical factors in knowledge sharing within prisons not only improves rehabilitation within prison walls but also transforms the broader criminal justice system. This approach fosters evidence-based practices, better communication, and a comprehensive understanding of factors leading to successful rehabilitation and reduced recidivism, ultimately creating a more just and effective system.

KEYWORDS

Critical Factors, Knowledge, Knowledge Sharing, Prison, Indonesia

1. INTRODUCTION

Knowledge sharing has been recognized as the most important factor in the success of knowledge management in organizations. Knowledge sharing is a mutual exchange of ideas and information that could influence the way teams learn in organizations (Muniz et al., 2019). Knowledge sharing has been shown to have numerous benefits for organizations and individuals alike. Bock et al., (2005) discovered that knowledge sharing can lead to better decision-making, higher innovation, and improved job performance. Furthermore, knowledge sharing can help reduce redundancies and duplication of effort, resulting in more efficient resource utilization (Kankanhalli et al., 2005). Knowledge sharing is especially crucial in the public sector for increasing the quality of public services and policy. Additionally, knowledge sharing can help build trust and collaboration between different levels of government, leading to more effective and coordinated policy responses (Lin & Lee, 2004; Willem & Buelens, 2007). The effective knowledge sharing requires more than just the availability of information or technology. It also needs a collaborative and open communication environment where staff members are at ease sharing their knowledge and experiences. Social capital and trust were crucial factors in promoting information sharing among employees in a public sector organization. Similarly, a study by Lee found that organizational culture, leadership, and incentives were key factors in promoting knowledge sharing among local government employees (J. C. Lee et al., 2016). Effective knowledge sharing can improve organizational performance, enhance decision-making, and increase innovation (Zhao et al., 2020). In government organizations, knowledge sharing is particularly important as it can lead to better public services and policies, as well as more efficient use of resources. There are several approaches to knowledge sharing in government organizations, including formal training programs, informal mentoring and coaching, and knowledge management systems (Karkoulian et al., 2008). While informal mentoring and coaching can help transfer tacit knowledge and expertise from experienced employees to newer staff members, a formal training program can give employees the knowledge and skills they need to perform their jobs effectively (Swap et al., 2001).

In Indonesia, with a prison population of 228,204 surpassing the designed capacity of 128,656, there is an alarming overcapacity of 77%, as reported by the General Directorate of Corrections (Imandeka & Zulfikri, 2021). The primary focus of criminal justice systems is now on commitments to reduce imprisonment and implement rehabilitative programs. Prisons, as state-run institutions, they are entrusted with the responsibility of incarcerating and rehabilitating individuals convicted of criminal offenses. The treatment and conditions of inmates significantly impact public perception of government legitimacy and effectiveness. Consequently, governments must allocate appropriate resources and conduct monitoring to guarantee just, compassionate, and effective prison operations (Perrin et al., 2008). Knowledge sharing in prisons presents a complex issue involving various stakeholders and considerations (Dell'Anna & Dell'Ovo, 2022). Prisons often grapple with constraints, including limited access to educational materials, books, computers, and training programs. Prison officers, primarily focused on security (Agus & Susanto, 2021), may have limited time and resources for facilitating knowledge-sharing activities. Inadequate staff support further hinders the establishment of educational initiatives promoting knowledge sharing among staff and inmates. Despite these obstacles, there is a growing recognition of the value of knowledge sharing in achieving positive outcomes for incarcerated individuals, ultimately contributing to a reduction in recidivism rates. Recidivism rates can be decreased by up to 43% through the implementation of correctional education programs (Davis et al., 2017). However, effective program necessitates access to high-quality instructional materials, trained instructors, and robust evaluation and feedback mechanisms (Hawley et al., 2013). Sharing best practices and lessons learned enables prison systems to enhance the effectiveness and efficiency of their education and training programs (Al-Alawi et al., 2007). The knowledge sharing involves the distillation of best practices, ensuring the dissemination of effective strategies honed through experience. This multifaceted knowledge exchange not only nurtures the professional growth of individual officers but also significantly contributes to the overall efficiency and safety of the prison environment. Identifying critical factors for effective knowledge sharing is paramount in directing the creation and execution of regulations and plans fostering efficient knowledge sharing (Yew Wong, 2005). This study aims to delve into the critical factors influencing knowledge sharing among prison officers in Indonesian.

2. LITERATURE REVIEWS

Prisons grapple with significant challenges, including overcrowding and insufficient resources resulting from budget constraints (Imandeka & Zulfikri, 2021). These issues have far-reaching effects on inmates, impacting their living conditions, access to education, and opportunities for rehabilitation. Collaborative efforts involving governments, institutions, and communities are essential to enhance prison conditions and safeguard the rights of prisoners (Barreiro-Gen & Novo-Corti, 2015; Belkin, 2020). Despite resource limitations, knowledge sharing plays a pivotal role in the development of inmates. Sharing skills, experiences, and practical knowledge becomes a valuable asset in the rehabilitation process (Chan et al., 2019; Reisdorf & Rikard, 2018). Both expert officers and inmates can contribute by providing training, fostering skill development, and creating potential employment opportunities. Knowledge exchange also facilitates education within prisons, where educated individuals can mentor their peers, improving prospects for inmates upon their release (Behan & UNESCO, 2021; Pulido, 2021). Exploring knowledge management practices in prisons underscores pivotal factors such as leadership support, organizational culture, structure, technology access, individual beliefs, education, and training. Leadership support stands out as crucial, fostering an environment that actively encourages information sharing (Sayogo et al., 2021; Zia et al., 2022). A positive organizational culture, emphasizing knowledge sharing, collaboration, and communication, amplifies this process (Al-Alawi et al., 2007; Wahyudi et al., 2020). The organizational structure in prisons plays a critical role in delineating hierarchical relationships, roles, and responsibilities within the correctional system (Bock et al., 2005). Individual beliefs about knowledge sharing in prison exhibit considerable variability, influenced by personal values, experiences, and the specific context of incarceration (Al-Alawi et al., 2007). Essential for skill development, education, and training programs play a key role, while collaboration between staff and prisoners facilitates seamless information transfer and effective problem-solving (Hawley et al., 2013; Smith et al., 2022). Implementing rewards for information sharing serves as a motivational tool, encouraging both personnel and prisoners to actively contribute to a culture of sharing

(Nguyen & Malik, 2020). Incentives, including recognition programs, rewards, and career advancement opportunities, further stimulate participation (Muniz et al., 2019). Additionally, ensuring access to information and technology is indispensable for facilitating effective knowledge exchange (Mufarreh et al., 2022; Xu, 2021; Zheng, 2021). Addressing these multifaceted factors is crucial for policymakers and practitioners aiming to enhance knowledge sharing in prisons, ultimately contributing to the well-being and successful reintegration of incarcerated individuals into society.

3. METHODOLOGY

This study employed a multi-step process aimed at comprehensively investigating knowledge sharing among prison officers. It employs the Analytic Hierarchy Process (AHP) within the triple-helix approach to identify critical factors influencing knowledge sharing. A validation process was conducted through the Triple Helix approach involving three lecturers, two community representatives, and one prison official. The identified critical factors are leadership support, organizational culture, organizational, structure, individual beliefs, incentives, collaboration and communication, education and training, access to IT, evaluation and feedback, and facilities. A model is meticulously developed based on insights derived from our preliminary study. This model serves as a conceptual framework that articulate the anticipated influence of critical factors on knowledge sharing in prisons. Online questionnaires are distributed to gather insights from a diverse sample of 60 prison officers across various prisons in Indonesia, incorporating Likert scales. Hypotheses are formulated based on existing literature and our initial research. Subsequently, the gathered data undergoes a sophisticated analysis using SmartPLS 4.0 technologies. The primary objective of this analysis is to systematically examine and establish the intricate relationship between critical factors and the phenomenon of knowledge sharing within prison environments. These hypotheses are systematically presented in Table 1.

Table 1. The hypotheses of the critical factors for knowledge sharing in prison

Factor	Item	Description
Leadership support (H. Lee & Choi, 2003)	LS1	The leadership style
	LS2	The leader initiate or become a role model for sharing knowledge
	LS3	The leader support knowledge sharing
Organizational Culture (Argote, 2013; Bock et al., 2005)	OC1	Knowledge sharing initiatives with colleagues
	OC2	Knowledge sharing with colleagues
	OC3	The feeling about sharing your knowledge with others
	OC4	The feel of asking for knowledge from others
Organizational Structure (Huysman & Wulf, 2006)	OS1	The prison engages in knowledge sharing practices that are aligned with organizational goals
	OS2	The organizational structure suitable for implementing knowledge sharing
	OS3	The necessary to add a new organizational structure that is specifically tasked with sharing knowledge
	OS4	The necessary to appoint an employee to be assigned the for managing the knowledge sharing process
Incentives (Alavi & Leidner, 2001; Cabrera & Cabrera, 2002)	IN1	Incentives are available for knowledge sharing
	IN2	Incentive supports knowledge sharing
	IN3	The necessary to have a reward and appreciation system to encourage knowledge sharing among employees
Individual beliefs (Cummings, 2004; Gupta & Govindarajan, 2000; Huysman & Wulf, 2006)	IB1	Trusted information from organization
	IB2	Trusted information from knowledge sharing colleagues
	IB3	The value of sharing knowledge by your colleagues
Education and training (H. Lee & Choi, 2003; Siddiqui et al., 2019)	ET1	Attendance in knowledge sharing
	ET2	Active role in knowledge sharing

	ET3	Open to learning from colleagues
Access to Information technology (Alavi & Leidner, 2001; Chiu et al., 2006; Riege, 2005)	IT1	Easy access to IT for knowledge sharing
	IT2	The use of IT Systems been carried out in the process of sharing knowledge
Collaboration and Communication (Lin, 2007; Willem & Buelens, 2007)	CC1	There is a value of communication for knowledge sharing
	CC2	Leadership's level of communication regarding knowledge sharing initiatives or activities
	CC3	Colleagues' level of communication regarding knowledge sharing initiatives or activities
	CC4	Often to collaborate or cooperate with colleagues in knowledge sharing programs or activities
Evaluation and Feedback (Bock et al., 2005)	EF1	Often receive feedback or recognition for sharing knowledge
	EF2	The effectiveness of knowledge sharing
Facility (Hsu et al., 2007)	FA1	The quality of infrastructure and knowledge-sharing resources
	FA2	Knowledge management systems or tools to share knowledge
	FA3	Easy to use knowledge management system or tool to share knowledge
Knowledge Sharing Intention (Al-Alawi et al., 2007; Cabrera & Cabrera, 2002; Lin & Lee, 2004; Obrenovic et al., 2020)	KS1	The rate of knowledge-sharing culture
	KS2	The level of cultural diversity and its relation to knowledge sharing
	KS3	Actively seek new knowledge

3.1 Result

Upon completion of the model, the calculation of the outer model and significance level commences. All indicators exhibit a convergence ratio of at least 0.7, signifying strong values. The subsequent step involves detailing the path coefficients, as illustrated in Figure 1. Knowledge sharing intention in prisons is positively influenced by collaboration, communication, evaluation, feedback, facility, individual belief, leadership support, organizational culture, and organizational structure. Conversely, education, training, incentive, and information technology indicators negatively impact knowledge sharing intention. The reliability and validity of indicators are assessed using Cronbach alpha and Composite Reliability values, with indicators having values above 0.7 considered highly dependable. Despite some indicators falling below 0.7, the AVE value verifies convergent validity when exceeding 0.5 for each indicator. Discriminant validity is determined, and values exceeding correlation between latent variables indicate good discriminant validity. Model quality is assessed through R square values, with values above 0.26 indicating a fit or excellent model. Additional indicators like f square, model fit, and NFI values also contribute to evaluating model quality, detailed in Figure 2. Following the determination of outer model values for both indicators and latent variables, the significance level is assessed through a process known as bootstrapping. A significant influence of the exogenous variable link is indicated by a t-statistic value exceeding 1.96. The result shows that if MEAN, STDEV, P-Values (<0.05), and path coefficient are positive, the relationship between the indicator and the latent variable is positive. It implies that a higher indicator value corresponds to a greater effect on the latent variable.

	Path coefficients
Collaboration and Communication -> Knowledge Sharing Intention	0.070
Education and Training -> Knowledge Sharing Intention	-0.112
Evaluation and Feedback -> Knowledge Sharing Intention	0.485
Facility -> Knowledge Sharing Intention	0.090
Incentive -> Knowledge Sharing Intention	-0.073
Individual Belief -> Knowledge Sharing Intention	0.139
Information Technology -> Knowledge Sharing Intention	-0.120
Leadership Support -> Knowledge Sharing Intention	0.086
Organizational Culture -> Knowledge Sharing Intention	0.120
Organizational Structure -> Knowledge Sharing Intention	0.394

Figure 1. Path coefficients values

(a)

	R-square	R-square adjusted
Knowledge Sharing Intention	0.903	0.882

(b)

	f-square
Collaboration and Communication -> Knowledge Sharing Intention	0.009
Education and Training -> Knowledge Sharing Intention	0.030
Evaluation and Feedback -> Knowledge Sharing Intention	0.620
Facility -> Knowledge Sharing Intention	0.033
Incentive -> Knowledge Sharing Intention	0.022
Individual Belief -> Knowledge Sharing Intention	0.070
Information Technology -> Knowledge Sharing Intention	0.062
Leadership Support -> Knowledge Sharing Intention	0.022
Organizational Culture -> Knowledge Sharing Intention	0.044
Organizational Structure -> Knowledge Sharing Intention	0.294

(c)

	Saturated model	Estimated model
SRMR	0.100	0.100
d_ULS	4.073	4.073
d_G	3.919	3.919
Chi-square	924.558	924.558
NFI	0.535	0.535

Figure 2. R square (a), f-Square (b), SRMR and NFI values (c)

3.2 Discussion

Knowledge sharing is especially crucial in government organizations since it can lead to better public services and policy, as well as more effective resource utilization. In government organizations, there are numerous techniques to knowledge sharing, including official training program, informal mentorship and coaching, and knowledge management systems. While informal mentoring and coaching can assist in the transfer of tacit knowledge and expertise from experienced employees to newer staff members, formal training program can give employees the skills and knowledge they need to perform their jobs effectively. Government organizations need a culture that promotes teamwork, open communication, and ongoing learning to successfully share knowledge (Karlsson et al., 2021; Lin & Lee, 2004; Siddiqui et al., 2019). Knowledge sharing in prisons is a complex issue that involves multiple stakeholders and considerations (Travis et al., 2013). There is growing recognition of the importance of knowledge sharing in promoting positive outcomes for incarcerated people and lowering recidivism rates. Knowledge sharing among prison officers' spans procedural intricacies, safety protocols, legal procedures, and best practices. This exchange extends to insights and experiences, fostering a comprehensive understanding of effective communication, conflict resolution, and strategies for the well-being of staff and inmates. This collaborative knowledge exchange enhances both individual professional growth and the overall efficiency and safety of the prison environment. According to result, there are prioritized critical factors that lead to effective knowledge sharing in prisons: leadership support, organizational culture, organizational structure, individuals' beliefs, incentives. Organizational structure is found to be more important factor than other critical factors influencing knowledge sharing in Prison. There is a need specifies how roles, rules, authority, and responsibilities are allocated, managed, and coordinated to encourage efficient knowledge exchange in prisons (Willem & Buelens, 2007). It also specifies how information is moved between layers of management (Kuzhabekova & Lee, 2020; Muniz et al., 2019; Nugraha et al., 2021). The organizational structure is a critical element that defines the hierarchical relationships, roles, and responsibilities within the correctional system. This structure serves as the framework for managing operations, maintaining security, and ensuring the effective functioning of the facility. A well-designed organizational structure in prisons provides clarity, accountability, and coordination among staff members, ultimately contributing to the safety, order, and rehabilitation of inmates (Willem & Buelens, 2007). At the top of the organizational structure, there is typically a warden or superintendent who oversees the entire prison facility. The warden is responsible for setting the overall vision, strategic direction, and policies of the prison. Beneath the warden, various departments and units are typically organized. These can include security, operations, programs, healthcare, administration, and support services. Each department has its specific functions and responsibilities. Within each department, there may be supervisors, managers, and line staff who are assigned specific duties and tasks. Supervisors are responsible for overseeing the day-to-day operations, ensuring compliance with policies and procedures, and providing guidance to staff. Managers play a more strategic role, overseeing multiple areas or units within a department and collaborating with other departments to achieve common goals. The organizational structure in prisons also includes specialized units or teams, such as emergency response teams, classification units, or disciplinary boards. These units address specific needs or situations within the prison and play a crucial role in maintaining security, managing inmate behaviour, and enforcing rules and regulations. A well-designed organizational structure in prisons is characterized by clear lines of authority, effective communication channels, and a balance between centralized decision-making and decentralized operations. Finally, an organizational structure supports the mission of the correctional system, which includes maintaining security, promoting inmate rehabilitation, and safeguarding public safety. In this study, numerous factors influenced the online questionnaire participation rate, with a particular emphasis on accessibility and inclusivity to ensure a diverse and representative sample. Implementation of strategies aimed at minimizing bias and accommodating individuals with varying technological proficiency levels underscores the commitment to broadening the applicability of findings and deepening the understanding of the subject matter. Recognizing constraints related to timing and duration for data collection, ethical considerations remained paramount, with measures taken to safeguard respondent confidentiality and privacy. This concerted effort was dedicated to constructing a robust and representative dataset, and interpretation of research findings.

4. CONCLUSION

The critical factors of knowledge sharing in prison are essential components of effective rehabilitation programs for prisoners. The critical factors are leadership support, organizational culture, organizational structure, incentives, and Individuals' beliefs based on the confirmation from academics, policy makers, and communities. The success of knowledge sharing in prison ultimately depends on its ability to manage these factors in a way that supports the safety and well-being of both staff and prisoners. Also, it depends on the support of policymakers to allocate the necessary resources and funding to the programs. Organizational structure is found to be the most important factor than the other factors in prison. The study on knowledge sharing in prisons has broad implications for stakeholders. Prison administrators and policymakers can use insights to enhance rehabilitation programs and inform policy decisions. Academics find value in advancing theoretical models, while communities, advocacy groups, and the public gain insights into positive impacts on public safety and recidivism. Some of the study's considerations led to number of respondents on online questionnaires. Furthermore, several research discussions that were not accommodated in this study will become future observations related to knowledge sharing strategy in prison.

ACKNOWLEDGEMENT

This research is supported by University of Indonesia and LPDP Scholarship, Ministry of Finance, Indonesia.

REFERENCES

Agus, M. A., & Susanto, A. (2021). The Optimization of the Role of Correctional Centers in the Indonesian Criminal Justice System. Jurnal Penelitian Hukum De Jure, 21(3). https://doi.org/10.30641/dejure.2021.v21.369-384

Al-Alawi, A. I., Al-Marzooqi, N. Y., & Mohammed, Y. F. (2007). Organizational culture and knowledge sharing: Critical success factors. Journal of Knowledge Management, 11(2). https://doi.org/10.1108/13673270710738898

Alavi, M., & Leidner, D. E. (2001). Review: Knowledge management and knowledge management systems: Conceptual foundations and research issues. MIS Quarterly: Management Information Systems, 25(1). https://doi.org/10.2307/3250961

Argote, L. (2013). Organizational learning: Creating, retaining and transferring knowledge. In Organizational Learning: Creating, Retaining and Transferring Knowledge. https://doi.org/10.1007/978-1-4614-5251-5

Barreiro-Gen, M., & Novo-Corti, I. (2015). Collaborative learning in environments with restricted access to the internet: Policies to bridge the digital divide and exclusion in prisons through the development of the skills of inmates. Computers in Human Behavior, 51. https://doi.org/10.1016/j.chb.2015.01.076

Behan, C., & UNESCO. (2021). Education in Prison: A Literature Review. UNESCO Institute for Lifelong Learning.

Belkin, L. D. (2020). Challenges with school re-entry for incarcerated youth and inadequacies of collaborative service provision by schools and agencies. In Handbook on Promoting Social Justice in Education. https://doi.org/10.1007/978-3-030-14625-2_115

Bock, G. W., Zmud, R. W., Kim, Y. G., & Lee, J. N. (2005). Behavioral intention formation in knowledge sharing: Examining the roles of extrinsic motivators, social-psychological forces, and organizational climate. MIS Quarterly: Management Information Systems, 29(1). https://doi.org/10.2307/25148669

Cabrera, Á., & Cabrera, E. F. (2002). Knowledge-sharing Dilemmas. In Organization Studies (Vol. 23, Issue 5). https://doi.org/10.1177/0170840602235001

Chan, J. P. S., Yeung, J. H. Y., Wong, N. C. Q., Tan, R. C. H., & Musa, N. (2019). Utilising digital media as enabling technologies for effective correctional rehabilitation. Safer Communities, 18(1). https://doi.org/10.1108/SC-05-2018-0016

Chiu, C. M., Hsu, M. H., & Wang, E. T. G. (2006). Understanding knowledge sharing in virtual communities: An integration of social capital and social cognitive theories. Decision Support Systems, 42(3). https://doi.org/10.1016/j.dss.2006.04.001

Cummings, J. N. (2004). Work Groups, Structural Diversity, and Knowledge Sharing in a Global Organization. In Management Science (Vol. 50, Issue 3). https://doi.org/10.1287/mnsc.1030.0134

Davis, L., Bozick, R., Steele, J., Saunders, J., & Miles, J. (2017). Evaluating the Effectiveness of Correctional Education: A Meta-Analysis of Programs That Provide Education to Incarcerated Adults. In Evaluating the Effectiveness of Correctional Education: A Meta-Analysis of Programs That Provide Education to Incarcerated Adults. https://doi.org/10.7249/rr266

Dell'Anna, F., & Dell'Ovo, M. (2022). A stakeholder-based approach managing conflictual values in urban design processes. The case of an open prison in Barcelona. Land Use Policy, 114. https://doi.org/10.1016/j.landusepol.2021.105934

Gupta, A. K., & Govindarajan, V. (2000). Knowledge flows within multinational corporations. Strategic Management Journal, 21(4). https://doi.org/10.1002/(SICI)1097-0266(200004)21:4<473::AID-SMJ84>3.0.CO;2-I

Hawley, J., Murphey, I., & Souto-Otero, M. (2013). Prison Education and Training in Europe. European Commission, May 2013.

Hsu, M. H., Ju, T. L., Yen, C. H., & Chang, C. M. (2007). Knowledge sharing behavior in virtual communities: The relationship between trust, self-efficacy, and outcome expectations. International Journal of Human Computer Studies, 65(2). https://doi.org/10.1016/j.ijhcs.2006.09.003

Huysman, M., & Wulf, V. (2006). IT to support knowledge sharing in communities, towards a social capital analysis. Journal of Information Technology, 21(1). https://doi.org/10.1057/palgrave.jit.2000053

Imandeka, E., & Zulfikri. (2021). Preventing Coronavirus in Overcrowded Prisons in Indonesia. Proceedings of the 1st International Conference on Law and Human Rights 2020 (ICLHR 2020), 549. https://doi.org/10.2991/assehr.k.210506.022

Kankanhalli, A., Tan, B. C. Y., & Wei, K. K. (2005). Contributing knowledge to electronic knowledge repositories: An empirical investigation. MIS Quarterly: Management Information Systems, 29(1). https://doi.org/10.2307/25148670

Karkoulian, S., Halawi, L. A., & McCarthy, R. V. (2008). Knowledge management formal and informal mentoring An empirical investigation in Lebanese banks. Learning Organization, 15(5). https://doi.org/10.1108/09696470810898384

Karlsson, F., Hedström, K., Frostenson, M., Prenkert, F., Kolkowska, E., & Helin, S. (2021). Attempts to share information between public sector organisations over time: A case-based exploration of value conflicts. Information Polity, 26(3). https://doi.org/10.3233/IP-200234

Kuzhabekova, A., & Lee, J. T. (2020). Internationalization and Local Research Capacity Strengthening: Factors Affecting Knowledge Sharing Between International and Local Faculty in Kazakhstan. European Education, 52(4). https://doi.org/10.1080/10564934.2020.1723422

Lee, H., & Choi, B. (2003). Knowledge management enablers, processes, and organizational performance: An integrative view and empirical examination. In Journal of Management Information Systems (Vol. 20, Issue 1). https://doi.org/10.1080/07421222.2003.11045756

Lee, J. C., Shiue, Y. C., & Chen, C. Y. (2016). Examining the impacts of organizational culture and top management support of knowledge sharing on the success of software process improvement. Computers in Human Behavior, 54. https://doi.org/10.1016/j.chb.2015.08.030

Lin, H. F. (2007). Knowledge sharing and firm innovation capability: An empirical study. International Journal of Manpower, 28(3–4). https://doi.org/10.1108/01437720710755272

Lin, H. F., & Lee, G. G. (2004). Perceptions of senior managers toward knowledge-sharing behaviour. Management Decision, 42(1). https://doi.org/10.1108/00251740410510181

Mufarreh, A., Waitkus, J., & Booker, T. A. (2022). Prison official perceptions of technology in prison. Punishment and Society, 24(3), 410–432. https://doi.org/10.1177/1462474521990777

Muniz, J., Hong, J., Oliveira, S., Wintersberger, D., & Popadiuk, S. (2019). Knowledge sharing in the automotive sector: A comparative study of chinese and brazilian firms. Production, 29. https://doi.org/10.1590/0103-6513.20180084

Nguyen, T. M., & Malik, A. (2020). Cognitive processes, rewards and online knowledge sharing behaviour: the moderating effect of organisational innovation. Journal of Knowledge Management, 24(6). https://doi.org/10.1108/JKM-12-2019-0742

Nugraha, A., Irwansyah, & Purwadi. (2021). How digital knowledge sharing affects innovation work behavior and organizational innovation capability in term of sustainability development goals. IOP Conference Series: Earth and Environmental Science, 716(1). https://doi.org/10.1088/1755-1315/716/1/012058

Obrenovic, B., Jianguo, D., Tsoy, D., Obrenovic, S., Khan, M. A. S., & Anwar, F. (2020). The Enjoyment of Knowledge Sharing: Impact of Altruism on Tacit Knowledge-Sharing Behavior. Frontiers in Psychology, 11. https://doi.org/10.3389/fpsyg.2020.01496

Perrin, C., National Anti-Drugs Agency, UNODC, United Nations Office on Drugs and Crime, Committee, T., Ray, R., Ray, R., Kosals, L., Pavlenko, S., Cheyette, C. M., Condon, L., Hek, G., Harris, F., Fish, D. G., Walker, S. J., Singaravelu, K., Fiore, R., Klopf, L., Hubbard, M. J., … Aye, K. W. (2008). Handbook on strategies to ¬ reduce overcrowding in prisons. Journal of Law, Medicine and Ethics, 14(4).

Pulido, M. L. (2021). Challenges to the Educational "Digital Divide" in Spanish Prisons. European Journal on Criminal Policy and Research. https://doi.org/10.1007/s10610-021-09493-4

Reisdorf, B. C., & Rikard, R. V. (2018). Digital Rehabilitation: A Model of Reentry Into the Digital Age. American Behavioral Scientist, 62(9). https://doi.org/10.1177/0002764218773817

Riege, A. (2005). Three-dozen knowledge-sharing barriers managers must consider. In Journal of Knowledge Management (Vol. 9, Issue 3). https://doi.org/10.1108/13673270510602746

Sayogo, D. S., Gil-Garcia, J. R., & Yuli, S. B. C. (2021). Assessing the role of leadership mechanisms for inter-agency collaboration and information sharing success in Indonesia. EJournal of EDemocracy and Open Government, 13(1). https://doi.org/10.29379/jedem.v13i1.629

Siddiqui, S. H., Rasheed, R., Nawaz, M. S., & Abbas, M. (2019). Knowledge sharing and innovation capabilities: The moderating role of organizational learning. Pakistan Journal of Commerce and Social Science, 13(2), 455–486.

Smith, M. J., Parham, B., Mitchell, J., Blajeski, S., Harrington, M., Ross, B., Johnson, J., Brydon, D. M., Johnson, J. E., Cuddeback, G. S., Smith, J. D., Bell, M. D., Mcgeorge, R., Kaminski, K., Suganuma, A., & Kubiak, S. (2022). Virtual Reality Job Interview Training for Adults Receiving Prison-Based Employment Services: A Randomized Controlled Feasibility and Initial Effectiveness Trial. Criminal Justice and Behavior. https://doi.org/10.1177/00938548221081447

Swap, W., Leonard, D., Shields, M., & Abrams, L. (2001). Using mentoring and storytelling to transfer knowledge in the workplace. Journal of Management Information Systems, 18(1). https://doi.org/10.1080/07421222.2001.11045668

Travis, J., Davis, R., & Lawrence, S. (2013). Exploring the role of the police in prisoner reentry. In Modern Policing: New Paradigms and Perspectives.

Wahyudi, D., Salim, U., Djazuli, A., & Rofiaty, R. (2020). Influence of Organizational Culture, Organizational Trust and Self-Efficacy on Knowledge Sharing Behavior by Mediating Organizational Commitments Study on Auditors of District/City Inspectorates in East Java Province. ARPN Journal of Engineering and Applied Sciences, 15(2). https://doi.org/10.36478/JEASCI.2020.398.409

Willem, A., & Buelens, M. (2007). Knowledge sharing in public sector organizations: The effect of organizational characteristics on interdepartmental knowledge sharing. Journal of Public Administration Research and Theory, 17(4). https://doi.org/10.1093/jopart/mul021

Xu, L. (2021). Application Research of Information Technology in Modern Prison Management. Proceedings - 2021 International Conference on Education, Information Management and Service Science, EIMSS 2021, 333–336. https://doi.org/10.1109/EIMSS53851.2021.00078

Yew Wong, K. (2005). Critical success factors for implementing knowledge management in small and medium enterprises. In Industrial Management & Data Systems (Vol. 105, Issue 3). https://doi.org/10.1108/02635570510590101

Zhao, S., Jiang, Y., Peng, X., & Hong, J. (2020). Knowledge sharing direction and innovation performance in organizations: Do absorptive capacity and individual creativity matter? European Journal of Innovation Management, 24(2). https://doi.org/10.1108/EJIM-09-2019-0244

Zheng, L. (2021). Application of virtual and reality (VR) technology in prison correction. Proceedings - 2021 International Conference on Computer Technology and Media Convergence Design, CTMCD 2021. https://doi.org/10.1109/CTMCD53128.2021.00038

Zia, M. Q., Decius, J., Naveed, M., & Anwar, A. (2022). Transformational leadership promoting employees' informal learning and job involvement: the moderating role of self-efficacy. Leadership and Organization Development Journal, 43(3), 333–349. https://doi.org/10.1108/LODJ-06-2021-0286

SECURITY SYSTEMS IN GREEK HEALTH CARE INSTITUTIONS: A SCOPING REVIEW TOWARDS AN EFFECTIVE BENCHMARKING APPROACH

Savina Mariettou[1], Constantinos Koutsojannis[2] and Vassilis Triantafyllou[3]
[1]University of Peloponnese, Electrical and Computer Engineering Department, Patras, Greece
[2]Professor of Medical Physics & Electrophysiology, Director of Health Physics & Computational Intelligence Laboratory, Physiotherapy Department, School of Health Rehabilitation Sciences, University of Patras, Patras, Greece
[3]Professor of Network Technologies and Digital Transformation lab, Electrical and Computer Engineering Dpt., University of Peloponnese. Patras, Greece

ABSTRACT

Healthcare has undoubtedly brought many advancements through information technology. Specifically, healthcare informatics involves the use of various technologies, data management and communication systems to collect, store, analyze and effectively disseminate information. Therefore, the above serves to improve care as well as patient outcomes, improve efficiency, promote innovation and data analysis, as digitization has become an integral part of our daily lives in today's world. However, with the increased use of interconnected systems and electronic health records, hospitals have become prime targets for cyber-attacks. In this article we will delve into the critical topic of cybersecurity in hospitals as well as nursing facilities. The deepening of this issue was carried out with extensive analysis of the security systems of Greek hospitals. We investigated all their web sites and the security systems already in place on those sites. By checking we found a number vulnerabilities and potential risks. The most important weakness is the lack of legal as well as technical information for all interested citizens and patients. More organizational as well as technical work concerning internal architecture of information systems is needed, towards the improvement of security. In conclusion, we present our proposals on strategies to strengthen healthcare facilities against cyber threats.

KEYWORDS

Healthcare, Information, Systems, Patients, Digitization, Cybersecurity

1. INTRODUCTION

In this article we present an extensive analysis of the security systems of the hospitals of Greece. The main objective of first section is to explain how security became increasingly important, providing a chronological review of the evolution of health information technology including the developing stages of health systems.

1.1 Historical Review of Computer System in Healthcare

Starting in 1960, experts on information systems realized that protecting the organization was not limited to fire hazards and criminal activities (York and MacAlister, 2015). In the 1960s, computers evolved in two stages. At the beginning of mini-computers and along the way they evolved into microcomputers (Berner, Detmer and Simborg, 2005). The late 1960s saw an important period in the development of information systems in hospitals. Some systems integrate patient diagnoses, patient information, and care plans based on physician and nurse orders. This development represents a remarkable step forward in the digitization of healthcare information and the potential for more comprehensive patient care management (Saba, Johnson and Simpson, 1994). In general in the 1960s and 1970s, it was perceived in all departments and functions of the health organization as a time of rebirth (York and MacAlister, 2015). The use of informatics in health care began with the first applications mainly for administrative and fiscal functions in hospital settings. However, there were still hesitations about the use of these systems by experts, as evidenced by the increasing number of pharmaceuticals and the increase in laboratory tests and diagnostic equipment (Berner, Detmer and Simborg,

2005). In the 1970s, object- oriented databases started being used (Gharote et al., 2022). The 1980s was an important era in health informatics (Ambinder, 2005). The volume and complexity of patient data as well as health records increased significantly (Gharote et al., 2022). The methodologies and systems of this period were intended to support clinical decision making in healthcare and focused on clinical diagnosis providing optimal patient care. At the same time, health level 7 (HL7) highlighted the importance of electronic data exchange in healthcare. This has an impact on improved interoperability and information sharing between different healthcare systems. Clearly, the method improved the quality of patient care. However, despite the increased potential, the development of health information systems has faced challenges. Hospitalization-related diagnostic groups and the need for managed care have increased pressure on health care to control costs. This means that, despite the need to integrate information systems in hospitals, the budget was quite limited for the development and maintenance of these systems. As a result, the implementation of health information systems in the 1980s faced funding challenges, despite predictions of improving patient care and reducing costs (Ambinder, 2005). In the 1990s, the rise of healthcare systems was significant (Ambinder, 2005). Health Management Information System has begun to be adopted by more and more countries in the hospital environment (Gharote et al., 2022). The sheer volume of this data allowed users to access this information without controls, and the main issue was how it allowed them to use it. Patient privacy soon emerged as an obstacle. This concern culminated with the passage of (HIPAA) (Ambinder, 2005). HIPAA appeared in 1996, known as the federal law enacted to protect sensitive health information. HIPAA mandatory physical safeguards include the use and security of workstations, device and media controls, and facility access controls (Cs et al., 2017). In the early 2000s, the synergies between Information and Communication Technologies and medical and healthcare practices rapidly converged and enabled a key cornerstone in this field: electronic healthcare (e-health). This development was significant and enabled, among other things, the provision of medical services via the Internet, the management of electronic records by standards and the communication between patients and health professionals. At the same time, it is worth noting that mobile healthcare (m-health) also appeared for patient care. Taken together, they marked a significant shift towards *digitization in healthcare*, which brought greater security challenges and increased awareness of the need to protect patient information. Healthcare organizations have invested in security measures, policies and technologies to protect sensitive personal health data (Batista et al., 2021).

In the 2010s, a defining moment was on 2015. The World Health Organization report on countries and health care organizations around the world noted the priority of information systems in health care (Fernandes et al., 2022). Also, in the first decade of the 21st century, COVID-19 posed a challenge to the global healthcare system (He et al., 2020). From the beginning of the second decade of the 21st century until today, Hospital Management Information Systems have evolved a lot. The main role is to improve healthcare service delivery, patient care and administrative efficiency. Information systems have become a key tool for modern healthcare institutions, supporting them in delivering high-quality care, optimizing operations and adapting to the evolving healthcare landscape. In addition to the above, information systems offer a wide range of software and services integrated into the facilities that a hospital has in order to serve them as best as possible. These information systems range from large hospitals to smaller clinics and nursing homes. Over the years, healthcare delivery, data management (Gharote et al., 2022) and obviously the security of these systems is expected to improve further. Therefore, in general, we can analyze the stages of development of the health system. The time distribution could be recorded as follows.

- ***Healthcare 1.0 (18th - 1920)***: At this stage, the technology was limited but used for basic medical applications such as anesthesia and precision in blood measurements.
- ***Healthcare 2.0 (1920 - 1990)***: This stage was accompanied by the development of the Internet, as well as the industrialization of health care. Internet health applications and online appointments are important.
- ***Healthcare 3.0 (1990 - 2015)***: The third stage focused on the development of the World Wide Web and the interconnection of electronic health data. An increase was also observed in the use of electronic health services.
- ***Healthcare 4.0 (2015 - present)***: During the present phase, artificial intelligence and intelligence have been introduced into medical services. This has led to advanced applications such as autonomous diagnosis and personalized therapy. The goal of improving the quality of care, expanding access to healthcare and enhancing health intelligence are part of this development. Healthcare 4.0 continues to evolve, supporting high-quality care and a customized approach for each patient (Ahmad et al., 2022).

1.1.1 Challenges and Solutions

Reviewing the bibliography and the effort to improve the quality of care, some challenges have been created. The challenges of data security, privacy and trust building are indeed significant in today's cyber-threat-dominated world (Gharote et al., 2022). We identified research which focused clearly on the challenges and solutions in the health sector. At the figure 1 there will be a brief review so that we understand the importance of security in healthcare (He et al., 2020).

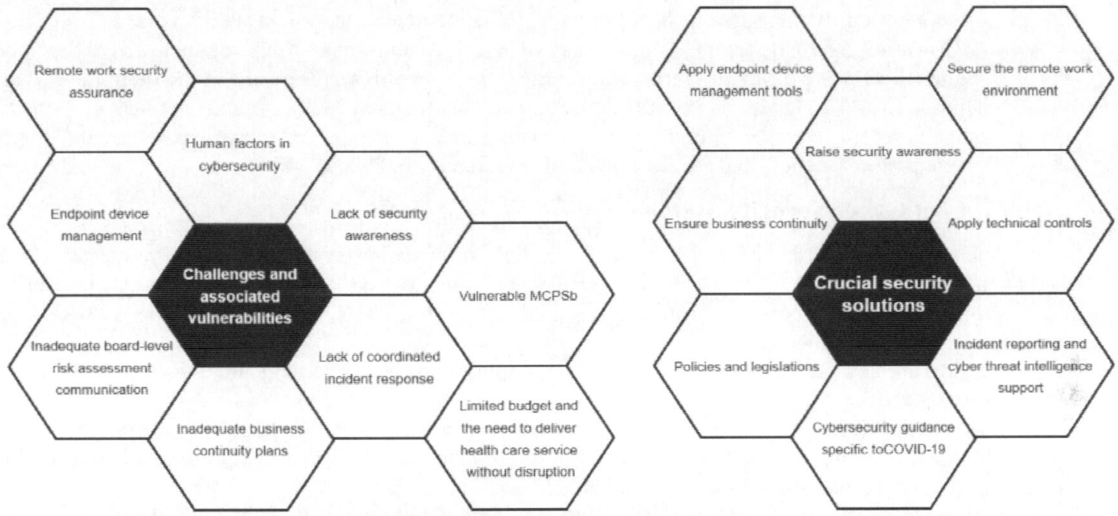

Figure 1. Challenges and solutions in the health sector

2. SECURITY

Based on what we have analyzed above, "*Healthcare 4.0*" specifically addresses the ways in which the 4th Industrial Revolution is reshaping the healthcare industry. But attention should be directed to the security of the systems. Specifically, the qualities CIA trinity (Confidentiality, Integrity and Availability) serve as the basis for designing comprehensive security policies, practices and controls in an organization. The main threats are cyber-attacks, data breach and unauthorized access. For example, there are data protection laws such as GDPR or HIPAA specifically in the health sector. These laws take basic considerations for compliance dealing with (Sarker, 2021):

- ***Confidentiality***: The aspect is concerned with keeping sensitive information confidential and protecting it from unauthorized access. It ensures that only people or systems with appropriate rights can access certain data. Examples include the protection of patient health records in healthcare institutions and intellectual property in research organizations (Al-Issa, Ottom and Tamrawi, 2019).
- ***Integrity***: Maintaining data integrity means ensuring that information remains accurate and reliable. In health care, this violation could lead to incorrect treatment (Gritzalis and Lambrinoudakis, 2004).
- ***Availability***: Availability focuses on ensuring that systems and data are accessible when needed by authorized users. In healthcare, availability is critical because patient data and systems must be accessible 24 hours a day (Computer security for data collection technologies, 2018).

2.1 Cybersecurity and Related Terms

"*Cybersecurity*" and related terms that have separate meanings in practice are very interconnected. Let's clarify these terms:

- ***Information Security***: focuses specifically on the protection of privacy, integrity and availability of information. This security can be divided into digital or physical forms. This term has under its umbrella data security, information systems and risk management related to information management (Sarker, 2021).

- ***Data Security***: is related to information security as we said in the above term. Its main objectives are the protection of data from unauthorized access or illegal use. It includes encryption, access controls, and other measures to protect data at rest, in transit, and during processing (Al-Issa, Ottom and Tamrawi, 2019).
- ***Network Security***: focuses on the security of communication channels. In network protection, we will often see security measures such as firewalls, intrusion detection systems and VPNs.
- ***Internet/IoT Security***: refers to the security of activities and transactions conducted over the Internet (Sarker, 2021). Adapting this term to the context of the health sector results in the Internet of Medical Things (IoMT). IoMT refers to the network of medical devices and applications that are interconnected over the Internet and collect and exchange data to improve patient care, improve operational efficiency, and advance medical research (Lee, 2023).

2.1.1 Types of Cyber Security Systems

According to publications in the HIPAA magazine, how information systems should provide the required security and taking the necessary awareness from what is mentioned, we deepen the types of security of information systems in cyberspace from any kind of cyber-attack (HIPAA Journal, 2018). Therefore, by studying identify the following.

1. Firewalls are key network security devices that monitor and filter incoming and outgoing network traffic (Gharote et al., 2022).

2. The Intrusion Detection System (IDS), defined as a device or software application. Monitors network traffic and systems for any suspicious activity or fraud. It collects data from various sources and thus is able to detect breaches as well as internal and external attacks (Sarker, 2021).

3. Intrusion Prevention Systems (IPS) that receives a threat and the intrusion prevention system (IPS) can be used to avoid and block it. This is achieved in a number of ways, including manual sending, notification sending or automation (Sarker, 2021).

4. Antivirus. A subset of anti-malware tools. Anti-malware software is defined as antivirus software. Its use is to detect and remove computer viruses or malware or even prevention (Sarker, 2021).

5. Email Security Systems as is a primary means of communication in healthcare organizations. Because large amounts of information are stored, email security solutions protect against phishing attacks, spam and email-borne malware, which are common attack vectors.

6. Security Checks, specifically divided into two categories *basic* and *advanced* security controls. Key controls include virus protection, file/data backup and restore, data loss prevention, email gateway, encryption, incident response plan, detection and system intrusion prevention, mobile device management, secure deployment, security awareness training, vulnerability management and web portal. Advanced security controls include anti-theft devices, digital forensics, multi-factor authentication, network segmentation, penetration testing, threat intelligence sharing, vulnerability scans (HIMSS, 2020).

3. METHODOLOGY

In order to gather the relevant information for my review article, I conducted a comprehensive search from 1 May 2023 to 15 November 2023. This search involved investigating a wide range of reliable sources, databases and academic journals to ensure that the information included is timely, reliable and comprehensive. Therefore, the databases used include Google Scholar, Science Direct, IEEE and Hospital Websites.

Finally in this paper we have investigated 126 hospitals, 100% of publicly owned hospitals in Greece according to (Statista, 2023) and representing all Greek Health Regions according to ministry of health division.

4. SECURITY MEASURES IN GREEK HOSPITALS

The components of risk management are variable. It can be safety, environmental safety, worker health, worker safety, patient safety, medical audits, disaster program, infection control, insurance/claims management, product evaluation, evaluation of contracts, incident reporting/review/action, Biomedical Instrument Testing (York and MacAlister, 2015). Before starting our analysis of all hospitals by region, we identified a survey published in 2009. It is based on the integration of IT and communication technologies in all public hospitals in Greece. Specifically, in 132 hospitals, 77% of hospitals have an IT department, while only 52.7% have an Integrated Information System. Finally, the 5th and 6th Health Regional show the greatest shortage in IT departments, since 5 of the 12 hospitals of the 5th (41.7%) and half (11 out of 22) of the 6th (50%), do not have an IT department. On the other hand, the best pictures are presented in the 3rd (93.8%), the 4th (92.9%) and the 1st Health Regional (91.7%) (Stamouli et al., 2009). Based on these, we did research by checking all the websites of the hospitals in Greece, as well as the Goverment Gazettes, observing what information is written about the security of the information systems in each hospital.

Table 1. Analysis of Greek Hospital websites: posted information for patients/ citizens

Hospital Name	Policy Name	Description	Reference
«Evangelismos», «Panagiotis & Aglaia Kyriakou», «Sismanoglio», «Amalia Fleming»	firewalls	security measure that restricts access to the network and protects against unwanted access attempts	(1st YPE, 2023)
«Evangelismos», «Panagiotis & Aglaia Kyriakou», «Children's Penteli Hospital»	intrusion detection and prevention (IDS/IPS)	systems that detect and prevent network intrusions	(1st YPE, 2023)
«Evangelismos», «Panagiotis & Aglaia Kyriakou», «Sismanoglio», «Amalia Fleming», «Sotiria»	cryptography	protect data confidentiality	(1st YPE, 2023)
«Evangelismos», «Agia Eleni - Spiliopouleio», «Agia Sophia Children's Hospital», «Agios Savvas», «Konstantopouleio», »Alexandra», «Hippokrateio», «Pammakaristos», «Gennimatas», «Laiko», «Elena Venizelou», «KAT», «EKA», «Sotiria», «Thessaloniki - Agios Pavlos», «Halkidiki», «Kilkis», «Serres», «Kavala», «Didymoteicho», «Alexandroupolis», «Komotini», «EKA», «Veria», «Edessa», «Kastoria», «Florina», «Bodosakeio», «Giannitsa», «Naousa», «Thebes», «Chalkida», «Kimi», «Karystos», «Karpenissi», «Amfissa», «Lamia», "Kalymnos - Vouvaleio», «Karpathos», «Thira», «Nikaia Piraeus - Agios Panteleimon» , «Syros - Vardakeio and Proio», «Leros - State Sanatorium », «Kos - Hippokrateion», «Chios - Skylitseio», «Samos - Agios Panteleimon», «Mytilene - Vostaneio», «Lemnos», «Ikaria», «Metaxa», «Psychiatric» , «Elefsina - Thriasio», «Dromokaitio», «Argos», «Tripoli», «Ioannina - Chatzikosta», «Preveza», «University Hospital - Ioannina», «Molos», «Amaliada», «University Hospital - Patras», «Rethymno», «University Hospital of Heraklion», «Health Center of Sitia»	personal data, privacy policy	passwords, personal data (GDPR), cookies	(1st YPE, 2023), (2nd YPE, 2023), (3rd YPE.gr, 2023), (4YPE, 2021), (Dypethessaly.gr, 2020), (6th YPE, 2021), (7th YPE Crete, 2012)
«Korgialeneio-Benakeio», «Sismanoglio», «Amalia Fleming», «Sotiria»	infrastructure and communications management	protection of information systems, communications and infrastructure management	(1st YPE, 2023)

«Papanikolaou», «Gennimatas–Agios Dimitrios», «KAT», «Veria», «Edessa», «Mamatsio», «Florina», «Grevena», «Giannitsa», «Papageorgiou», «Thessaloniki - Agios Pavlos», «Serres», «Kavala», «Xanthi», ««University Hospital - Larissa», «Volos», «Trikala», «Karpenissi», «Amfissa», «Lamia», «Argos»,«Nafplio», «Kalamata», «Kyparissia», «Corinth», «Tripoli», «Zakynthos», «Corfu», «Kefalonia», «Lefkada», «Arta», «Ioannina - Chatzikosta», «Preveza», «University Hospital - Ioannina», «Molcs», «Agrinio», «Mesolongi - Chatzi-Kosta», «Aigio», «Kalavryta», «Pyrgos», «Amaliada», «Krestena», «Patras - Agios Andreas», «University Hospital - Patras», «Karamandan», «Heraklion - Venizeleio-Pananeio», «Agios Nikolaos»	integrated information system (organization responsibilities)	(3rd YPE, 2023), (4YPE, 2021), (Dypethessaly.gr, 2020), (6th YPE, 2021), (7th YPE Crete, 2012)
«Evangelismos», «Laiko», «KAT», «Gennimatas», «Sismanoglio», «Amalia Fleming», «Agios Savvas», «Panagiotis & Aglaia Kyriakou», «Children's Penteli Hospital», «Agioi Anargyroi», «Agia Sophia Children's Hospital», «Bodosakeio», «Karpathos», «Naxos», «Samos - Agios Panteleimon», Attikon, «Patras - Agios Andreas», «University Hospital - Patras», «University Hospital - Ioannina», «Health Center of Sitia»	integrated information system	(1st YPE, 2023), (2nd YPE, 2023), (3rd YPE, 2023), (6th YPE, 2021), (7th YPE Crete, 2012), (Uhi.gr, 2023)

Security systems data were collected in details (Table 1). We recorded the main website which shows all hospital websites by Health Regional separately. In particular, in the first Health Regional there are a total of 24 hospitals. In the time frame we worked the «Polyclinic» and «Agioi Anargyri» General Oncology Hospital of Kifissia city, did not have a website available. Even in the «Ophthalmology Hospital» there was no mention of anything related to security and privacy. The rest of the hospitals are ranked as follows four hospitals that report that there are "firewalls", hospitals with (IDS/IPS), 5 hospitals with cryptographic tools, and fourteen that refer to privacy policy. Five that note the protection of information, communications and infrastructure management systems. Another 11 hospitals report that they have a complete information system but in a different source, an article as it was not found to highlight anything on the websites. In the second Health Regional we have a total of 24 general hospitals. The General Hospital of Rhodes Island «Andreas Papandreou» website was not available. At the General Hospital - Health Center of Kythira Island «Trifillio» and General Hospital «Asklepieio Voulas», no relevant information was found on their websites regarding the legal framework or security systems. Also, we have 6 hospitals that refer to patient protection and 4 hospitals that state that they have an integrated information system. In the third and fourth Health Regions we have a total of 16 hospitals and 14 hospitals, respectively. In these two Health Regional there does not seem to be any website running through any issues. Specifically, we have eight in each Health Regions that seem to touch on the issue of privacy policy, respectively. 10 hospitals in the third and four hospitals in the fourth reporting information system responsibilities. In the third in 1 hospital, it states that they have a complete information system. It should be noted that the specific hospital also mentions data protection. Finally in the fourth a single hospital integrated information system. In the fifth Health Regional we have a total of 13 hospitals. At the General Hospital of Livadia town website was not available. We found data protection issues recorded in seven hospitals, only one hospital integrated information system and six hospitals with information system responsibilities. In the sixth Health Regional we have a total of 27 hospitals. At the General Hospital of Krestena town and the General Hospital of Lefkada Island, websites were not available. In this region, in addition to the websites, a check was also made on the corresponding legislations since you indicate these on the Health Regional home page. Specifically, we have eight hospitals that refer to privacy policy, 26 hospitals that state the responsibilities of the information system and three hospitals that state that they have an integrated information system. In the seventh Health Regional, we have a total of 8 hospitals. At the General Hospital - Health Center of Neapolis town, no relevant information was found on their websites regarding the legal framework or security systems. At the General Hospital - Health Center of Ierapetra town, website was not available. All the hospitals that were General Hospitals of Greece were not written the term "General Hospital", just the name was used. On these websites, we found that 3 hospitals recorded issues of privacy policy. A single hospital integrated information system and two hospitals with information system responsibilities. According to our results, the security systems, in the posted information that exists, differ from one facility to another. In addition, you do not record to a degree visible to citizens and patients the protection of personal data and the privacy policy. Furthermore, we should note that they themselves do not know to what extent these information systems are secure, to what extent data and information could be exposed and for what reason.

5. CONCLUSION

Hospital and healthcare facility security systems play a critical role in protecting patients. So, we could focus this article purely on patients, however when we are talking about personal and sensitive medical data both the patients and their environment are exposed. It is worth noting that after our research we found that cyber-attacks, also known as threats or attacks, appeared in the late 1970s, including health care domain. What initially manifested as spam eventually evolved into more malicious forms such as viruses and malware (Cs et al., 2017). However, in this decade, we refer to Healthcare 2.0, as a result of which we realize that security systems have always taken measures, but the issue that arises is whether these measures were enough, whether they kept pace with developments in information systems, and whether all of this ultimately did not lead to risk to patients. Focusing on the public hospitals of Greece, we identified several vulnerabilities in these security systems as several hospitals in Greece there is no complete picture of whether there is an information system or the responsibilities of this department that proves its existence. The most important, the citizen has no knowledge about protection and rights. In particular, he does not know how protected he is and how much he could be exposed if sensitive information is leaked. Even with regard to the General Data Protection Regulation, it is not clear who the Data Protection Officer is and how his data is used. The information posted to the citizen or patient is minimal and not clear. Therefore, between security and accessibility, it is necessary to find the right balance without forgetting cost management.

In the future, for proper communication and data exchange between these systems, the creation of an effective interface should be tested. Secondly we could focus on an architecture that would rely on blockchain technology as a security measure. Finally, benchmarking should be applied, aiming to identify best practices and improve performance (Sponsored by ID Experts, 2016). Certainly, the benefits to such a proposal are many as this strategy will be able to improve workflow efficiency, hospital financial benefits, employee performance, quality of care, patient experience and safety. Focusing more on information system security, according to the bibliography with an integrated software it will be possible to improve the privacy of protected health information and data security by complying with HIPAA regulations (Wagner et al., 2002).

REFERENCES

Ahmad, K.A.B., Khujamatov, H., Akhmedov, N., Bajuri, M.Y., Ahmad, M.N. and Ahmadian, A. (2022). *Emerging trends and evolutions for smart city healthcare systems*. Sustainable Cities and Society, 80, p.103695. doi:https://doi.org/10.1016/j.scs.2022.103695

Al-Issa, Y., Ottom, M.A. and Tamrawi, A. (2019). *eHealth Cloud Security Challenges: A Survey*. Journal of Healthcare Engineering, [online] 2019, pp.1–15. doi:https://doi.org/10.1155/2019/7516035.

Ambinder, E.P. (2005). *A History of the Shift Toward Full Computerization of Medicine*. Journal of Oncology Practice, [online] 1(2), pp.54–56. doi:https://doi.org/10.1200/jop.2005.1.2.54.

Batista, E., Moncusi, M.A., López-Aguilar, P., Martínez-Ballesté, A. and Solanas, A. (2021). *Sensors for Context-Aware Smart Healthcare: A Security Perspective*. Sensors (Basel, Switzerland), [online] 21(20), p.6886. doi:https://doi.org/10.3390/s21206886.

Berner, E.S., Detmer, D.E. and Simborg, D. (2005). *Will the Wave Finally Break? A Brief View of the Adoption of Electronic Medical Records in the United States*. Journal of the American Medical Informatics Association : JAMIA, [online] 12(1), pp.3–7. doi:https://doi.org/10.1197/jamia.M1664.

Computer security for data collection technologies. (2018). *Development Engineering*, [online] 3, pp.1–11. doi:https://doi.org/10.1016/j.deveng.2017.12.002.

Cs, K., B, F., T, J. and Dk, M. (2017). *Cybersecurity in Healthcare: A Systematic Review of Modern Threats and Trends*. [online] Technology and health care : official journal of the European Society for Engineering and Medicine. Available at: https://pubmed.ncbi.nlm.nih.gov/27689562/.

Dypethessaly.gr. (2020). *5th YPE.* [online] Available at: https://www.dypethessaly.gr/#contactnav.

Fernandes, C., Claro, N., Monteiro, S., Pires, I.M. and Gouveia, A.J. (2022). *The evolution of IS/IT in health care in last decades*. Procedia Computer Science, [online] 203, pp.707–713. doi:https://doi.org/10.1016/j.procs.2022.07.105.

Gharote, Y., Jatakia, R. and Nagare, D.G. (2022). *Evolution, Prospects, and Challenges in Hospital Management Information System: Case Studies*. International Journal of Engineering Research & Technology, [online] 11(11). doi:https://doi.org/10.17577/IJERTV11IS110082.

Gritzalis, D. and Lambrinoudakis, C. (2004). *A security architecture for interconnecting health information systems*. International Journal of Medical Informatics, [online] 73(3), p.305. Available at: https://www.academia.edu/19626212/A_security_architecture_for_interconnecting_health_information_systems [Accessed 14 Nov. 2023].

HIMSS (2020). *Cybersecurity in Healthcare.* [online] www.himss.org. Available at: https://www.himss.org/resources/cybersecurity-healthcare.

HIPAA Journal (2018). *HIPAA Compliance Checklist*. [online] HIPAA Journal. Available at: https://www.hipaajournal.com/hipaa-compliance-checklist/.

He, Y., Aliyu, A., Evans, M. and Luo, C. (2020). *Healthcare Cyber Security Challenges and Solutions Under the Climate of COVID19: A Scoping Review (Preprint)*. Journal of Medical Internet Research, [online] 23(4). doi:https://doi.org/10.2196/21747.

Lee, I. (2023). *Analyzing Web Descriptions of Cybersecurity Breaches in the Healthcare Provider Sector: A Content Analytics Research Method.* Computers & Security, p.103185. doi:https://doi.org/10.1016/j.cose.2023.103185.

Saba, V.K., Johnson, J.E. and Simpson, R.L. (1994*). Computers in nursing management*. American Nurses Association Publications, [online] (NP-87 10M), pp.i–x, 1–42. Available at: https://pubmed.ncbi.nlm.nih.gov/8042715/ [Accessed 14 Nov. 2023].

Sarker, I.H. (2021). *AI-Driven Cybersecurity: An Overview, Security Intelligence Modeling and Research Directions*. www.preprints.org. [online] doi:https://doi.org/10.20944/preprints202101.0457.v1.

Sponsored by ID Experts (2016). Sixth Annual Benchmark Study on Privacy & Security of Healthcare Data. Ponemon Institute LLC.

Stamouli, T., Tsikrika, I., Tsikrikas, N., Tsaklakidou, E., Apostolakis, A., & Kyriopoulos, A. (2009). *Informatics in Greek public hospitals: Its use by hospital executives*. Hellenic Statistical Institute, Proceedings of the 22nd Panhellenic Statistical Conference, pp. 191–200.

Statista. (2023). Publicly owned hospitals in Greece 2002-2021. [online] Available at: https://www.statista.com/statistics/557195/publicly-owned-hospitals-in-greece/ [Accessed 17 Nov. 2023].

Uhi.gr. (2023). *Yphresia Informatics– University General Hospital Ioannina*. [online] Available at: https://uhi.gr/ypiresia-pliroforikis/.

Wagner, J.R., Thoman, D.J., Anumalasetty, K., Hardre, P. and Ross-Lazarov, T. (2002). Benchmarking HIPAA compliance. Journal of healthcare information management: JHIM, [online] 16(2), pp.46–50. Available at: https://pubmed.ncbi.nlm.nih.gov/11941920/ [Accessed 17 Nov. 2023].

York, T. W., & MacAlister, D. (2015). *Hospital and Healthcare Security*. In Google Books. Butterworth-Heinemann. https://books.google.gr/books?hl=en&lr=&id=odacBAAAQBAJ&oi=fnd&pg=PP1&#v=onepage&q&f=false

1st YPE, (2023). *Hospital – 1st Regional Health Authority*. [online] Available at: https://www.1dype.gov.gr/?page_id=70.

2nd YPE, (2023). *Public Hospital* – 2nd D.Regional Health Authority Piraeus & Aegean. [online] Available at: https://www.2dype.gov.gr/dimosia-nosokomeia/.

3rd YPE, (2023). *Hospital*. [online] Available at: https://www.3ype.gr/menutop-foreisygeias/menutop-nosokomeia.

4th YPE, (2021). *Hospital Contact Details | 4th YPE Macedonia & Thrace*. [online] Available at: https://www.4ype.gr/e-s-y/stoicheia-epikoinonias-nosokomeion/.

6th YPE (2021). *Legislation – Organizations Hospitals – 6th Regional Health Authority*. [online] Available at: https://www.dypede.gr/%ce%bd%ce%bf%ce%bc%ce%bf%ce%b8%ce%b5%cf%83%ce%b9%ce%b1-%ce%bf%cf%81%ce%b3%ce%b1%ce%bd%ce%b9%cf%83%ce%bc%ce%bf%ce%b9-%ce%bd%ce%bf%cf%83%ce%bf%ce%ba%ce%bf%ce%bc%ce%b5%ce%b9%cf%89%ce%bd/.

7th YPE Crete. (2012). Www.hc-Crete.gr. Retrieved November 15, 2023, from https://www.hc-crete.gr/MonadesYgeias/home/nosokomeia.

TRAINING AN ARTIFICIAL INTELLIGENCE MODEL FOR THE DETECTION OF GESTURES RELATED TO TRICHOTILLOMANIA

Daniel Victor Costa de Gois Paulino and Robinson Luis De Sousa Alves
Instituto Federal de Educação, Ciência e Tecnologia do Rio Grande do Norte, Brazil

ABSTRACT

This article presents an artificial intelligence model capable of identifying actions strongly related to trichotillomania, a psychiatric disorder that causes people to have a desire to pull their hair. The model was trained with images and videos collected and variations generated through artificial intelligence to improve the image database. The work focused on the user's frontal perspective to optimize the construction of the dataset and neural network training. As a result, we obtained 89% precision in the model, which requires further testing and optimization to be used in real applications – still limited – that can provide users with statistics and results related to the disorder for possible treatments or alert the user to decrease their involuntary actions.

KEYWORDS

Artificial Intelligence, Trichotillomania, Behavioral Pattern Recognition, Machine Learning, Image Processing, Computational Psychiatry, Neural Networks

1. INTRODUCTION

Trichotillomania, also known as TTM, is a psychiatric disorder characterized by a persistent and uncontrollable urge to pull one's hair, as identified by J.E. Grant in 2016. Subsequent studies, including those by Jon E. Grant and Jennifer R. Alexander, have linked TTM with heightened anxiety levels, exacerbating its symptoms (Jennifer R. Alexander, 2017). Grant further elaborates on a range of triggers for this disorder, encompassing sensory (such as the texture or length of hair), emotional (including feelings of anxiety, boredom, or anger), and cognitive factors (like concerns over hair appearance or inflexible thinking patterns). These triggers can escalate to more acute issues, including substantial hair loss, skin damage, and in extreme cases, serious infections and gastrointestinal blockages when the condition progresses to trichophagia—the consumption of the pulled hair (J.E. Grant, 2017).

Despite the availability of various treatments, cognitive-behavioral therapy remains the most effective and widely utilized approach, emphasizing habit reversal through self-monitoring, heightened action awareness, and the adoption of healthier stress-relief practices (Sah D.E., 2008).

This article represents a pioneering endeavor as it introduces an innovative approach to the monitoring of trichotillomania using image-based movement detection—a method not previously explored. Drawing parallels with notable works such as "Detection of Involuntary Movement with Wearable Technology" (Yuksel Koseoglu, 2022) and "A Novel System to Monitor Tic Attacks for Tourette Syndrome Using Machine Learning and Wearable Technology: Preliminary Survey Study and Proposal for a New Sensing Device" (Agni Rajinikanth, 2023), which suggest the use of sensor-embedded and AI-integrated solutions for medical monitoring, this study extends the application of such technologies for the specific case of TTM. It endeavors to facilitate self-monitoring and patient awareness through the computerized detection of trichotillomania-related movements.

When training an AI, there are several variables that mainly affect the accuracy of the model, such as dataset size, neural network layers, and the number of neurons. Many of these parameters are adjusted through network pruning and trial and error (CONG, S., 2023), the main methods addressed in this work, along with functions that measure the model's efficiency, to train, evaluate, and test new variables.

2. DEVELOPMENT

The creation of an artificial intelligence model capable of identifying gestures related to trichotillomania in images requires various stages, and in the case of this work, a solid phase in the collection and construction of the data to be trained.

From this section, the various aspects and stages directly related to the development of the work will be addressed, from data collection, information enhancement, optimizations, architectures, training, and everything that was done in the work to create a model that can be used in various environments and applications.

2.1 Data Collection and Dataset Creation

The dataset, essential for training an AI model, was specifically created for this study as no suitable existing dataset was found. It involved video recordings of 12 volunteers performing various gestures, both related and unrelated to trichotillomania. These recordings, transformed into 15,000 images after processing (see Figure 1), were divided into two categories: 'pulling' for hair-pulling gestures and 'not_pulling' for other gestures. This categorization, along with the removal of non-conforming images, was designed to enhance the model's gesture detection capabilities. The dataset evolved from its initial version to a more comprehensive version 2.0, aimed at improving gesture recognition accuracy.

Figure 1. Examples of collected images

2.2 Architectures

Architecture is a fundamental element in training an artificial intelligence model; it is what will calculate and store the machine learning information, and they are very adaptable, each problem requires a specific architecture that will help capture the characteristics of the object to be identified. However, there are various architectures targeted at some problems but work more generally, like VGG16, which was designed for the classification of over 1000 classes, and SqueezeNet, designed to have high accuracy like AlexNet, but with a much lighter output model.

All the pre-existing architectures mentioned are very robust, containing an abundance of neurons and more complex convolutional layers. Consequently, they require more processing power, so this work necessitated testing and developing a proprietary architecture that met the proposed problem and stayed within the available computational power limits.

With the complete dataset, it was possible to test some initial architectures to gather the first results and based on that, continue with tests and modifications of the architecture. Two convolutional layers and two Max Pooling layers alternately were the entry layers of the architecture followed by a Flatten layer that transforms the image matrix into a linear structure, thereby facilitating the next steps, and then a dense layer of 64 neurons followed by the final layer, a dense layer of 1 neuron with the sigmoid activation function (Figure 2), where any input will result in a value between 0 and 1, which suits our problem with values closer to 0 indicating images without trichotillomania-related gestures and closer to 1 when detected.

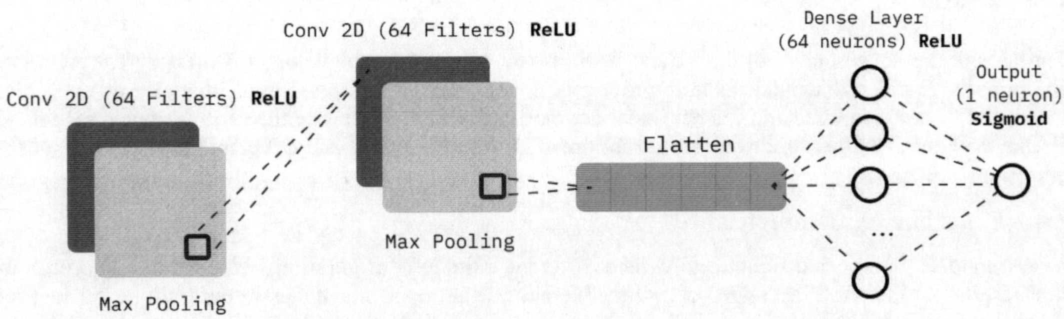

Figure 2. Representation of the initial architecture

The initial tests were encouraging. Good results appeared in the first tests, but soon a problem was detected. The high accuracy percentages of the models were related only to images the artificial intelligence was already familiar with, images used in training or in the validation stage. The model struggled with new images in recognizing the gestures.

To solve this issue, it was necessary to refine the architecture with layers that mitigate specific learning, thereby improving its ability to generalize. Two additional dense layers of 128 neurons each were added, with a Dropout layer between them. This layer is crucial for reducing overfitting; it randomly deactivates some neurons in the dense layers, so the neural network is unable to converge on the same values in the various iterations of training, thus learning in different ways over time.

2.3 Evaluation Parameters

The AI models were automatically tested and produced a report detailing the architecture and four key performance parameters, as depicted in Figure 3. Metrics derived from the confusion matrix include accuracy, which measures the percentage of correct predictions in the test data; recall, indicating the percentage of positive cases correctly predicted; precision, calculating the percentage of positive predictions that were correct; and the F1 Score, a harmonic mean balancing precision and recall.

These metrics are crucial for assessing the model's quality and for advancing to more practical tests. For example, a model with 93% recall and 62% precision effectively identifies most positive gesture cases but also incorrectly flags negative cases as positive, indicating a specialization in positive cases and a failure in generalizing to non-related gestures. The selection of models for further testing is based on achieving a balance and sufficiently high empirical values of these parameters, rather than fixed values.

```
Layer (type)                    Output Shape              Param #
=================================================================
conv2d (Conv2D)                 (None, 254, 254, 64)      640
max_pooling2d (MaxPooling2D)    (None, 127, 127, 64)      0

conv2d_1 (Conv2D)               (None, 125, 125, 64)      36928
max_pooling2d_1 (MaxPooling2D)  (None, 62, 62, 64)        0

flatten (Flatten)               (None, 246016)            0
dense (Dense)                   (None, 128)               31490176
dropout (Dropout)               (None, 128)               0
dense_1 (Dense)                 (None, 128)               16512
dropout_1 (Dropout)             (None, 128)               0
dense_2 (Dense)                 (None, 1)                 129

Total params: 31,544,385
Trainable params: 31,544,385
Non-trainable params: 0
_________________________________________________

Model v58

Accuracy: 83.20%
Recall: 91.18%
F1 Score: 87.01%
Precision: 74.22%
```

Figure 3. Report generated for each model

2.4 Results

Throughout the development of this article, various test models were developed, with different architectures and minor alterations to the dataset to improve the model's metrics and present one that already embodies the essence of what is proposed and can be used for some tests and cases. Among the various trained models, some already had good numbers and were stored for potential future use and study of elements that were successful in refining new models.

2.4.1 Experiments Conducted

87 test models with various architectures and different training configurations were created in search of the best results. As depicted in Figure 4, the timeline shows the main milestones in the training of the models. From the 1st to the 22nd, version 1 of the dataset was used, and the images entered the neural network with a size of 256x256 in RGB colors. Starting with the 23rd model, version 2.0 of the image set was used, which was employed in most of the models.

In the 37th model, the strategy of training the neural network by converting the images to black and white was adopted. This approach, having fewer parameters to calculate, allowed the models to be trained more quickly, and a reduction in the average training time of about 15 to 25% was observed. The use of black and white images also favors performance improvement of the models considering that colors are not relevant for classifying an image as containing or not containing gestures related to trichotillomania. However, this improvement in performance was not confirmed, as the data generated were not sufficient to affirm this hypothesis.

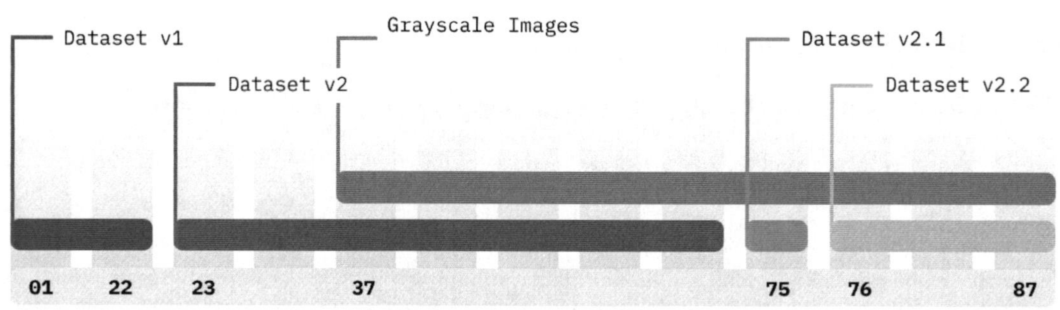

Figure 4. Timeline of major changes throughout the models

Having generated some models with good results using the second version of the dataset, the search for overall improvement of the model began, utilizing versions 2.1 and 2.2 of the image bank, which are much more stringent in terms of image classification. Thus, it also became a challenge for the neural network's learning to capture the minor differences between the two classes of images. Therefore, from model 75 onwards, the new versions of the dataset were used.

The graph above (Figure 5) provides an overview of the metrics of the last 40 trained models, from which we can analyze several factors.

Models with a higher recall rate had lower metrics in other areas, indicating that the model experienced overfitting. This happened due to a higher number of epochs or a lack of parameters that mitigate this occurrence. Therefore, the best models have slightly lower percentages in metrics, but are more balanced, as we can observe towards the end of the graph. The focus of this final period was on obtaining higher-performing models through strategies tested earlier, such as the use of Dropout layers.

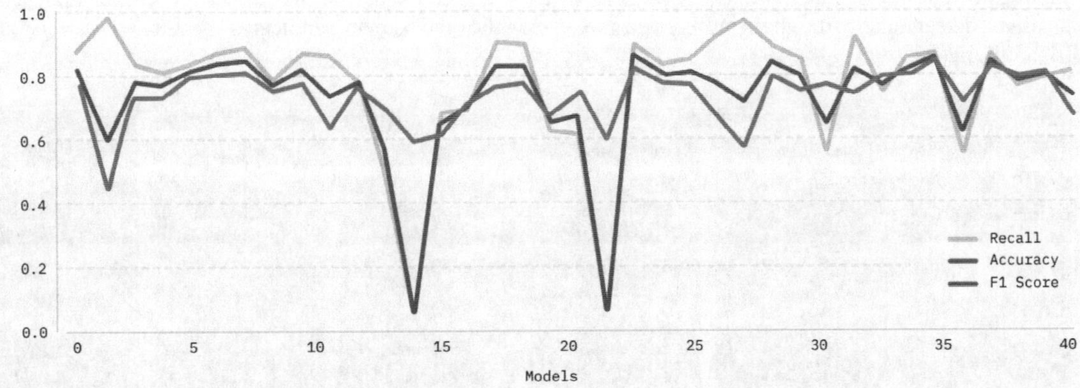

Figure 5. Graph of metrics for the last 40 trained models

Version	Architecture	Accuracy	Recall	Precision	F1 Score	Epochs
v69	c2d64, MP, c2d128, MP, c2d256 F, D128, Dp0.5, D1	85,37%	88,15%	79,01%	83,33%	20
v58	c2d64, MP, c2d64, MP, F, D128, Dp0.5, D128, Dp0.3, D1	83,20%	91,18%	74,22%	81,83%	25
v44	c2d64, MP, c2d64, MP, F, D128, D128	81,37%	90,08%	72,03%	80,05%	15
...	...	...	...	...		...
v50	c2d64, MP, BN, c2d64, MP, BN, F, D128, D128, D1	A 58.51	0,00%	0,00%	00,00%	25

Figure 6. Listing of architectures and their respective metrics

The table above Figure 6 shows some of the best architectures trained and tested, as well as one of the architectures that had the worst performance in metrics. The architecture is represented in a summarized form for a clearer visualization of the image.

- **c2d:** Conv2D layer followed by the number of filters applied in the layer. E.g., c2d64, a convolutional layer with 64 filters.
- **MP:** Max Pooling layer.
- **F:** Flatten layer.
- **D:** Dense layer followed by the number of neurons. E.g., D128.
- **Dp:** Dropout layer followed by the multiplier of neurons that will be deactivated. E.g., Dp0.3.
- **BN:** Batch Normalization layer.

The models with the best results advanced to a new stage of manual testing for a detailed evaluation of the artificial intelligence. The model was imported and connected to webcam frames, allowing for real-time predictions to analyze positions and gestures that are correctly or incorrectly identified. This approach provides insights for improving the training dataset to expand the range of possibilities. Figure 7 consists of some captures of the model functioning in real time, where the green square in the upper left corner represents a positive detection of the hair-pulling gesture, and the red square indicates gestures not related to trichotillomania.

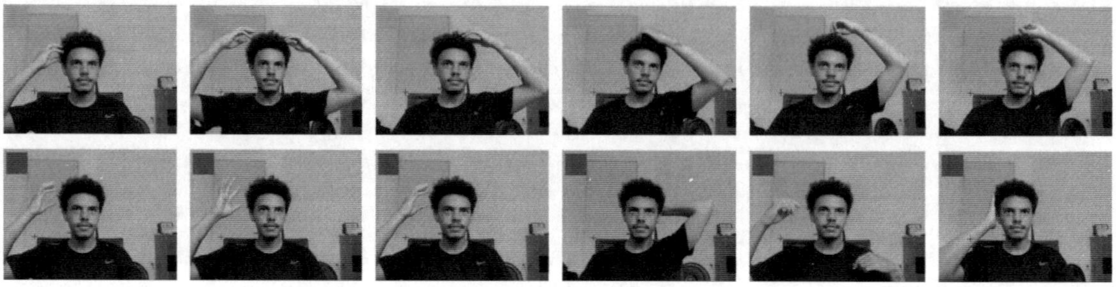

Figure 7. Real time webcam testing

This test was crucial for detecting irregularities in the models, which need to be refined with improvements in the dataset and architecture. However, the results were still above expectations. The main trained model was able to distinguish micro-gestures that varied between pulling hair or not, as shown in Figure 8, where it was evident that the model did not merely detect that the hand was near the hair, but rather the specific gesture of the hand, which had a significant influence on the result.

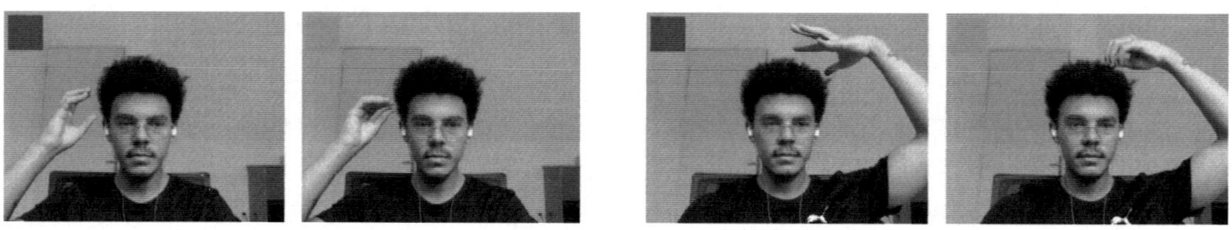

Figure 8. Micro gesture testing

Some tests showed that the dataset needs a greater variety of images in different environments, as the background influenced gesture detection. Additionally, other factors such as distance from the camera, position, and coloration were still crucial for successful predictions.

In this experiment, we achieved a model with 89% accuracy, the highest precision model. However, other metrics must be considered for the model's success, with a recall rate of 77%, meaning that out of 100 images where the user is pulling their hair, it can detect 77 of those cases. This indicates that this model's precision is more related to cases where the user is not performing hair-pulling gestures, highlighting the importance of a balance between accuracy and recall metrics.

The model with the best performance was the 69th test, which had an accuracy rate of 85.37%, recall of 88.15%, and F1 Score of 86.74%, making it the most balanced model. Trained over 20 epochs, it also achieved the best results in practical tests, capable of detecting micro-gestures varying between pulling hair or not. It is important to note that this model does not work in 100% of cases, having its limitations already mentioned, factors that make it less effective.

Accuracy and loss are metrics generated during the training of the model at each epoch. As we can analyze in Figure 9, the best model obtained had its training accuracy approaching 95% and the loss value close to 0.1, which were the best metrics acquired during training.

Its architecture consists of 3 convolutional layers with 64, 128, and 256 filters respectively, and between each of them, a Max Pooling layer, a Flatten layer, a Dropout layer with a rate of 0.5, meaning it will randomly deactivate 50% of the neurons from the fully connected layer, and finally a dense layer of 128 neurons with the ReLU activation function and the output dense layer with one neuron and sigmoid activation function.

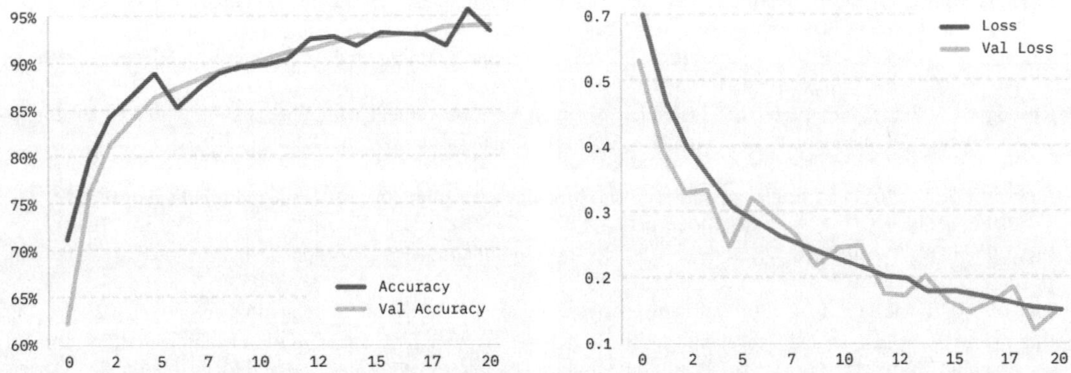

Figure 9. Training graphs of the 69th model

3. CONCLUSION

The aim of this experiment was to create an artificial intelligence model capable of detecting trichotillomania-related gestures through images, by training the machine with images collected in the study.

The main result was a model with 85% accuracy that could predict even minor differences in gestures. However, we must consider the model's inefficiencies. The hardware used was a limitation in refining the architecture and expanding the dataset for more comprehensive training that could potentially yield more effective and comprehensive models. Other training techniques, such as transfer learning, could also be utilized to achieve significant and complete results more quickly.

As per the tests conducted, different backgrounds, lighting, and camera positions still negatively affect the model, making it less effective. Therefore, significant improvements are needed for use in real applications, which will be extremely important for cases where the model is applied in generating reports, interventions, and data that can be provided to individuals with psychiatric disorders and professionals conducting treatments.

One of the key aspects to be addressed in continuing this work is to expand the dataset to increase data variability, differentiating the gestures present in the current dataset. Data collection in different environments, lighting, and even angles will be necessary to enhance the dataset's complexity.

Additionally, more powerful hardware will be needed to accommodate the data increase, the scaling of the architecture, and data augmentation with a greater variety of filters in the model training. The use of a more robust architecture will enable the artificial intelligence to detect the smallest details that differentiate trichotillomania gestures.

REFERENCES

Alexander, J.R., Houghton, D.C., Twohig, M.P., Franklin, M.E., Saunders, S.M., Neal-Barnett, A.M., Compton, S.N. and Woods, D.W. (2017). Clarifying the relationship between Trichotillomania and anxiety. Journal of Obsessive-Compulsive and Related Disorders, 13, pp.30-34. https://doi.org/10.1016/j.jocrd.2017.02.004

Cong, S. and Zhou, Y. (2023). A review of convolutional neural network architectures and their optimizations. Artificial Intelligence Review, 56, pp.1905-1969. https://doi.org/10.1007/s10462-022-10213-5

Deng, L. J., Guo, W. and Huang, T. Z. (2016). Single image super-resolution by approximated Heaviside functions. Information Sciences, 348, pp.107-123. https://doi.org/10.1016/j.ins.2016.02.015

Esteves, T. (2022). The disadvantage of using ReLU. Medium. https://estevestoni.medium.com/the-disadvantage-of-using-relu-4478589ef834

Grant, J. E. and Chamberlain, S. R. (2016). Trichotillomania. American Journal of Psychiatry, 173(9), pp.868-874. DOI: 10.1176/appi.ajp.2016.15111432. https://doi.org/10.1176/appi.ajp.2016.15111432

Grant, J. E., Redden, S. A., Leppink, E. W. and Chamberlain, S. R. (2017). Trichotillomania and co-occurring anxiety. Comprehensive Psychiatry, 72, pp.1-5. https://doi.org/10.1016/j.comppsych.2016.09.005%20

Iberdrola (2023). 'Deep learning': a key concept for taking artificial intelligence to a higher level. https://www.iberdrola.com/innovation/deep-learning

Janiesch, C., Zschech, P. and Heinrich, K. (2021). Machine learning and deep learning. Electronic Markets, 31, pp. 685–695. https://doi.org/10.1007/s12525-021-00475-2

Köseoğlu, Y. and Boyacı, A. (2022). Detection of Involuntary Movement with Wearable Technology. In: International Congress on Human-Computer Interaction, Optimization and Robotic Applications (HORA). Ankara, Turkey: IEEE, pp. 1-5. DOI: 10.1109/HORA55278.2022.9800040

Ludermir, T. B. (2021). Artificial Intelligence and Machine Learning: current status and trends. Advanced Studies, São Paulo, 35(101), pp. 85–94. https://doi.org/10.1590/s0103-4014.2021.35101.007

McCulloch, W. S. and Pitts, W. (1943). A logical calculus of the ideas immanent in nervous activity. The bulletin of mathematical biophysics, 5, pp. 115-133.

Medsker, L. R. and Jain, L. C. (2001). Recurrent neural networks. Design and Applications, 5(64-67), p.2.

Rajinikanth, A., Clark, D. and Kapsetaki, M. (2023). A Novel System to Monitor Tic Attacks for Tourette Syndrome Using Machine Learning and Wearable Technology: Preliminary Survey Study and Proposal for a New Sensing Device. JMIR Neurotech. https://neuro.jmir.org/2023/1/e43351

Rauber, T. W. (2005). Artificial neural networks. Federal University of Espírito Santo, 29.

Sah, D. E., Koo, J. and Price, V. H. (2008). Trichotillomania. Dermatologic Therapy, 21, pp. 13-21. https://doi.org/10.1111/j.1529-8019.2008.00165.x

Thai, L. H., Hai, T. S. and Thuy, N. T. (2012). Image classification using support vector machine and artificial neural network. International Journal of Information Technology and Computer Science, 4(5), pp. 32-38. http://www.mecs-press.org/ijitcs/ijitcs-v4-n5/IJITCS-V4-N5-5.pdf

Vaz, F. (2012). Heaviside, 1850-1925. Electronics and Telecommunications, 5(4), pp. 371-381.

ARTIFICIAL INTELLIGENCE BASED MODULE FOR MELANOMA DETECTION USING DERMOSCOPY IMAGES

Sávio Araújo Carvalho Alves[1], João Augusto Diniz Moura[2] and Robinson Luis de Souza Alves[1]
[1]*Federal Institute of Education, Science and Technology of Rio Grande do Norte*
Senador Salgado Filho avenue, 1559, Tirol - Natal-RN, Brazil
[2]*University Federal do Espírito Santo*
CCS Management - Health Sciences Center Building, Av. Mal. Campos, 1468 - Maruípe, Vitória - ES, Brazil

ABSTRACT

Skin cancer is one of the most common diseases in the world, requiring greater attention especially in relation to melanoma, which is responsible for a large proportion of the deaths caused by this disease. It is widely known in the medical community that early diagnosis is a key factor in increasing patient survival rates. The aim of this work is to progressively develop an artificial intelligence model specialized in predicting melanoma-type skin cancer based on images from dermoscopy exams, which was based on the accuracy metric for its development, achieving a result of 90.31% in order to open up space for other work to be developed based on the improvement options it provides.

KEYWORDS

Convolutional Neural Networks, Skin Cancer, Melanoma

1. INTRODUCTION

Skin cancer is one of the most common types of cancer in the world, accounting for a significant proportion of all cancer cases (Oncoguia, 2022). Currently, the World Health Organization (WHO) states that the highest incidence is the non-melanoma type, which accounts for more than 2 million cases, followed by melanoma with 132.000 cases per year worldwide, in which it is highlighted that for every three types of cancer diagnosed, one is skin cancer (WHO, 2017). This disease occurs when genetic mutations in skin cells, which can be caused by stimulation from endogenous or exogenous factors, such as excessive exposure to sunlight, causing uncontrolled cell reproduction. Skin cancer can be divided into 2 categories: melanoma and non-melanoma (Popim, 2008) which, in turn, can be represented by a series of skin lesions.

It is widely known that early diagnosis is the most effective method available to improve the prognosis of cancer and, consequently, increase the individual's survival rate (De Souza Torres Torres, 2016, p. 60). According to the (Ministério da Saúde, 2022), skin cancer is diagnosed by clinical examination, which one of it's stages is the dermoscopy, which, in turn, consists of using a device to visualize and photograph layers of the skin that may not be visible to the naked eye in order to identify signs that indicate whether or not the lesion in question is skin cancer. The Ministério da Saúde also reinforces the recommendation that, in cases that the patient already has a personal or family history of the disease, follow-up examinations should be carried out periodically, as a way of ensuring an early diagnosis.

Another way of making a pre-diagnosis that is currently being experimented with is through the use of artificial intelligence with the aim of analyzing, through computer vision, the images generated by the dermoscopy exam to identify the signs that indicate the presence of the disease. Due to the fact that this type of examination generates a series of images as a result (Ministério da Saúde, 2022), one of the techniques that is widely used to automate this pre-diagnosis is through the use of convolutional neural networks. This is because this type of artificial intelligence has the ability to extract information from images very efficiently (Gao, 2020).

Even limiting itself to the use of convolutional neural networks for the classification of skin lesions, it is possible to break down this type of artificial intelligence into a wide variety of architectures, as can be seen when analyzing the work of Delazeri (2021), where the results of 4 different types of convolutional neural network architectures are analyzed, including VGG-16, ResNet-101, ResNet-50 and Inception-ResNet, where the importance of using Data Augmentation was highlighted, which according to Shorten (2021, p. 2) "Data augmentation describes a set of algorithms that build synthetic data from an available data set", that is, they are algorithms for manipulating real data in order to increase the number of samples for training, as well as analyzing how they behave with the use of transfer learning generated by the original training of such architectures.

Another implementation of convolutional neural networks can also be analyzed by the work of Utsch (2018) where he uses an Inception-v3 architecture which is made up of 4 main blocks which are: the base, convolutional, Filter Concat and Pool blocks, in addition to using transfer learning and bottlenecks, which, according to Dankers (2023, p.1) "limits the transfer of information between nodes". Adding up all the blocks, it is possible to reach a total of 48 layers fed by images of dimension 299 x 299, and it is also possible to load a module pre-trained by images from the ImageNet dataset (Mathworks, 2023). To calculate the accuracy of his neural network, Utsch (2028) used the TensorFlow and scikit-learn libraries, which returned 86% and 81% respectively.

At the same time, as seen in Vieira's (2022) work, another approach would be to implement the EfficientNet-B7 architecture, in which he carried out several tests with and without Data Augmentation, where in his case its use proved to be more efficient, increasing the confidence in his predictions, as well as using Coarse as a Dropout resource, which, according to Chen (2021) is a technique that increases the probability of a neuron being ignored, which on the one hand increases the network's uncertainty, but helps to deal with Overfitting problems. Overfitting is the process that occurs when artificial intelligence becomes so expert in the training data that it loses its ability to generalize and is unable to improve its results with the validation data (Didática, 2022). Thus, by using all these strategies to build the architecture of his network, Vieira (2022) managed to achieve an accuracy of 86.4%, which is very promising considering the state of the art.

It is therefore possible to see the importance of early diagnosis of skin cancer and how the application of convolutional neural networks can be crucial in reducing the risks and sequelae that the disease can cause. The aim of this work is therefore to develop an artificial intelligence module specialized in detecting skin cancer in dermoscopy images in order to speed up and facilitate the process of pre-diagnosis of the disease and thus save lives.

2. BODY OF PAPER

In order to gain a clearer understanding of the process of developing the neural network proposed in this work, it is necessary to explore the key concepts involved in greater depth, focusing on the theory on which skin cancer studies are based, as well as those of artificial neural networks, so that the decisions made in the development of this work can be better understood.

2.1 Skin Cancer

Skin cancer is "a tumor that affects the skin being the most frequent cancer in Brazil and worldwide" (Ministério da Saúde do Brasil, 2023). In general, cancer is a disease with a multifactorial cause characterized by the uncontrolled reproduction of genetically defective cells, with the ptch1 and p53 genes standing out most (Craythorne, 2017). ptch1 is a gene responsible for controlling cell multiplication (Craythorne, 2017), while p53 is responsible for the process of apoptosis (Fett-Conte, 2002), which is also known as cell death. Thus, defects in these genes generate cells that continue to reproduce even after the end of their lifespan, thus transmitting their genetic flaw to these new cells in an uncontrolled way.

Skin cancers are commonly divided into two groups: melanoma and non-melanoma. The non-melanoma group includes some types of tumors such as basal cell carcinoma, which is the most common type of skin cancer, especially among people over 40 (Craythorne, 2017). Another type of non-melanoma tumor is squamous cell carcinoma, which is often found in squamous regions of the skin or those with mucus, such as the lips, nose and ears (Craythorne, 2017). Melanoma-type tumours can often be characterized by lesions that appear or change rapidly (Craythorne, 2017).

Skin tumors are often lesions in easily visible areas, so the diagnosis of the disease can be made through clinical examination, which can be aided by dermoscopy, which in turn consists of the use of a machine capable of visualizing regions of the skin invisible to the naked eye (Ministério da Saúde, 2022). In general, this examination aims to analyze the morphological characteristics of the skin in order to identify characteristics common to certain types of skin lesions.

The melanoma type, for example, is known for presenting the characteristics present in the ABCDE rule, which are: asymmetry, irregular borders, change in color and if the same is evolving over time (Craythorne, 2017). In the past, the rule also referred to the diameter, when it was equal to or greater than 6 millimeters, but it is no longer used as a reference because several melanoma-type tumors have already been diagnosed that had a diameter smaller than that specified by the rule (Zink, 2014), thus making this characteristic irrelevant to the analysis.

The Ministério da Saúde (2022) points to this rule as a form of self-analysis, making it a very useful tool for the early diagnosis of the disease. If after the clinical examination there is still doubt as to whether or not it is skin cancer, a histological examination should be carried out, which consists of taking a sample of the material to be sent to the pathology laboratory so that a more accurate report can be issued (Ministério da Saúde, 2022).

2.2 Artificial Neural Networks

Although it is not a recent invention, having been created after the Second World War in the 1950s (X2 Inteligência Digital, 2020), artificial intelligence is a technology that has become more popular in recent years, which can be seen with the emergence of technologies such as GPT Chat, which is capable, among other features, of interacting and answering users' questions.

This technology can be defined as any machine or computer system capable of simulating the way the human brain works (MIJWIL, 2021). Artificial intelligence (AI) includes many types of algorithms with this role, such as machine learning algorithms.

These algorithms are known for their ability to learn to make decisions without needing to be explicitly programmed to do so (Bi, 2019). This is due to the fact that, after receiving a set of data for training and what the expected results, they are able to automatically find which algorithm can best reproduce these results (Bi, 2019), thus being able, when receiving a new input, to predict what its output would be.

As part of the set of machine learning algorithms, the group of neural networks stands out. This technology aims to reproduce the way biological neurons work and how their relationships can be created to generate intelligence (Rauber, 2005).

In order to reproduce these biological neurons, the concept of mathematical neurons was created. This mathematical model is made up of a set of input values which are multiplied by their respective synaptic weights and added to the sum of the inputs. The result of this sum is in turn sent to an activation function which has the responsibility of defining whether the signal from this neuron will move on in the network or not (McCulloch W S and Pitts W 1943 apud Mangini, 2020).

In the universe of artificial neural networks, it is possible to find a wide variety of well-known architectures and also to create new models. The simplest existing architecture is the Perceptron, which consists only of its inputs, 1 neuron and its output, and is useful for solving simpler problems such as linear regression.

Another architecture that has come to the fore recently due to its great applicability in computer vision is convolutional neural networks. According to Ferreira (2017, p. 27) "convolution is a mathematical operation between two functions, f and g, producing a third function". Its application in the context of neural networks is to "apply masks to input images, based on the neighborhood pixels." (Santos, 2017, p. 2012). This process is applied at the beginning of the image and passes through it with regular jumps until it passes through the entire image, thus being able to extract characteristics from them (Santos, 2018).

2.3 Method

To make this work possible, it was necessary to go through a series of stages in order to understand the scientific landscape of similar works. This process involved tasks such as identifying possible tools, technologies and strategies for developing an artificial intelligence capable of comparing with the performance of similar networks using the minimum hardware resources as possible, as well as gaining a deeper understanding of this disease.

2.3.1 Dataset

Among the many specific datasets for skin lesion studies that are available for free and with easy access, one that stands out is the HAM 10000. Developed by Philipp Tschandl , Cliff Rosendahl & Harald Kittler, and available from the ISIC archive (https://isic-archive.com/) for the classification challenge at the 2018 MICCAI annual conference in Spain (Tschandl et al, 2018), it consists of more than 10000 dermoscopy images collected over 20 years by the dermatology department of the Medical University of Vienna and Cliff Rosendahl's practical collection (Tschandl et al, 2018).

This dataset was divided into 7 groups: "akiec" which according to Tschandl et al (p. 6, 2018) "is composed of actinic keratosis, intraepithelial carcinoma and Bowen's disease which are variations of squamous cell carcinoma", "bcc" representing basal cell carcinoma, "bkl" being composed of benign keratosis such as seborrheic keratosis, actinic lentigo and lichen planus (Tschandl et al, 2018), "df" representing dermatofibromas, "nv" referring to melanocytic nevus, "mel" which is an abbreviation for melanoma and finally "vasc" referring to vascular skin lesions (Tschandl et al, 2018).

To ensure a reliable classification, four strategies were used to validate the diagnosis of the lesions. The first strategy used was histopathological examination, which was carried out by specialized dermatologists and a survey of how plausible the results obtained for the sample in question are (Tschandl et al, 2018). Another strategy used was confocal microscopy, which consisted of using a confocal microscope to analyze the lesion at an almost cellular level and analyze its characteristics (Tschandl et al, 2018). The remaining strategies were through monitoring the lesions, which, if there was no progression of the disease every 3 visits or after a year and a half, confirmed that it was a benign lesion and finally, if the lesions had characteristics that were benign, a consensus was reached between the authors to guarantee the diagnosis (Tschandl et al, 2018).

Due to the fact that it is a dataset composed exclusively of images from the dermoscopy exam, which, according to Botton (p. 159, 2020) "has a higher diagnostic sensitivity compared to clinical methods, in addition to greater effectiveness and reliability", with a large number of records, in addition to its diagnoses being analyzed by 4 different validation strategies (Tschandl et al, 2018), the HAM 10000 becomes one of the best choices when working on research involving classification of skin lesions assisted by artificial intelligence.

2.3.2 Workflow

The model creation process began with an extensive literature review on the subject. By analyzing it, it was possible to find points of improvement in relation to the state of the art, understand what the performances were found and what level of architectural complexity has been used and why, as well as understanding what technologies and strategies have been used to build these artificial intelligences based on computer vision.

Once the literature review was completed, it was possible to highlight the use of the HAM 10000 dataset due to its distribution and data characteristics, as well as the use of tools such as Keras and Tensorflow, with libraries available for the Python language, to build artificial intelligence models. Another relevant piece of information obtained from this study was the performance possibilities with the use of convolutional layers in the neural network, allowing smaller networks to achieve satisfactory results due to their ability to extract characteristics from images.

To validate the effectiveness of the possible tools, as well as to make the first prototypes of what became the project's base network, the Google Colab platform was used to carry out the tests. At first, using it allowed the simplest tests to be carried out, as well as data organization tasks. However, due to the limitations of the free plan, especially in relation to the session's uptime, which deleted all the files generated after it ended, it was necessary to transfer the project to a personal computer so that it would be possible to carry out training sessions with a greater number of epochs. The computer used was a personal desktop with a 3.00GHz Intel(R) Core(TM) i5-7400 processor, 8GB of 2400MHz RAM and an NVIDIA GeForce GTX 1050 TI graphics card.

After defining the dataset, the best tools and possible structures for the architecture, an initial model was developed to test how it would behave with the chosen data. This initial model was built with 4 convolutional layers followed by another 4 hidden layers using a low number of epochs dividing the data between the possible classifications, but not focusing on melanoma detection.

From this initial network, tests were carried out in order to understand how the network behaved in relation to learning the data and, based on these results, adjustments were made as necessary in order to improve the accuracy of this model. Once a minimally satisfactory result had been achieved, the dataset was reorganized in order to allow the classification of images between melanoma and non-melanoma, and new tests were carried out to verify its accuracy.

From this point, the test execution process was repeated so that new points for improvement could be identified in the network architecture in order to achieve an accuracy in the validation tests as close to 100% as possible.

2.4 Results

The comparisons and improvements made in this work were based on the behavior of the results obtained from the records generated when running the Keras library's training function. During network training, this library provides 4 pieces of information by default regarding the performance achieved at the time, which are the loss values, which represent how far the synaptic weights are from the ideal values, and the accuracy, which refers to the proportion of correct predictions, those relating to the training and validation tests.

For the training to be possible, the data set is divided into 80% of the images for training the network, and the remaining 20% is used to validate whether the network is capable of making coherent predictions with unknown data at the time of training. The accuracy calculation is based on the following formula:

$$(tp + tn) / (tp + tn + fp + fn) = \textit{accuracy}$$

The architecture used for the first melanoma prediction test consisted of a data augmentation layer in which the images were randomly inverted in a horizontal direction, then rotated by 10% in random directions and their data rescaled in a ratio of 1/255. Next, 4 convolutional layers were used followed by batch normalization functions and another 4 dense layers so that both the convolutional and dense layers used 256 neurons and "ReLU" activation functions.

Table 1. Results of test 1

Epoch	Loss	Accuracy	Validation loss	Validation accuracy
102	0,1963	0,9205	0,2546	0,8962
139	0,1583	0,9342	0,2745	0,9031
200	0,1101	0,9566	0,3513	0,8957

According to the results obtained from the first test (table 1), it can be seen that in relation to the loss and accuracy tests with the training data, the epoch that obtained the best result was number 200, achieving 11.01% of loss and 95.66% of accuracy. An important point to note is that the value of its results has been growing evenly, which may be an indication that its training is not yet complete and that it may need a greater number of epochs for the training to find its best result.

Taking the validation data in consideration, there was a divergence as to which epoch obtained the best result. According to the loss values, the 102 epoch was the best, achieving 25.42%, but in terms of accuracy, the 139 epoch was better, achieving 90.31%, which is the best result obtained so far. An important analysis of this training is the distribution of accuracy results over the epochs. It is possible to analyze that, in contradiction to the training results, accuracy began to perform less well after epoch 139. Considering the uncertainty as to whether the training achieved the best possible result with 200 epochs and the distribution of accuracy in validation, tests with a greater number of epochs are necessary to resolve these questions.

Table 2. Results of test 2

Epoch	Loss	Accuracy	Perda da validação	Acurácia validação
12	0,2590	0,8940	0,2772	0,8892
16	0,2505	0,8988	0,2689	0,8842

A new test was then carried out using only 20 epochs (table 2) to confirm that the results were similar. In this scenario, epoch 16 obtained the best training results in both categories (loss and accuracy) where the loss reached 25.05% and the accuracy 89.88%, differing from the previous test since the last epoch was not the best. In the context of validation, there was once again a divergence in terms of the best epoch in relation to the category where the loss in epoch 16 once again obtained the best result with 26.89%, but with regard to accuracy, 88.92% was recorded in epoch 12, which was 0.5% better than epoch 16.

Table 3. Results of test 3

Epoch	Loss	Accuracy	Validation loss	Validation accuracy
68	0,2240	0,9080	0,2482	0,9021
90	0,2128	0,9108	0,2409	0,8987
92	0,2069	0,9172	0,2659	0,8952
96	0,2026	0,9165	0,2458	0,8997

The third test (table 3) was the most heterogeneous of those obtained so far. It used 100 training epochs so that, for each of its results, its best performance is found in different epochs. In relation to the training tests, the loss function performed best in epoch 96, reaching 20.26%, which is already 4.79% lower than the last test. Moving on to training accuracy, 91.72% was achieved in epoch 92, 1.84% better than the previous epoch.

With regard to the validation results, the best result for loss was achieved in epoch 90 with 24.09%, an improvement of 2.8%. The accuracy achieved its best performance at epoch 68 with 90.21%, an improvement of 3.09%. Comparing the results with the previous test, it can be seen that, with the exception of validation accuracy, the results are reaching their peak at times relatively close together, which may indicate that the neural network is learning relatively easily. Furthermore, although the validation accuracy is not keeping up with this result, all the results are improving their performance uniformly as the number of epochs increases, indicating the need for new tests with more epochs.

3. CONCLUSION

Analyzing the progress made in the process of development of the convolutional neural network for the detection of melanoma-type skin cancer proposed in this work, it is possible to conclude that it is feasible to apply this type of tool in the early diagnosis of the disease, due to the fact that it achieved an accuracy of 90.31% while still in the training stage. In addition to being very promising in itself, it is important to note that this network has a tendency to achieve even better results as tests are carried out with more epochs.

Based on these results, as well as the fact that this is a topic that has become more popular in recent years among scientific papers, it is notable that the efforts made in research aimed at developing and improving technologies driven by the benefits of artificial intelligence for the early diagnosis of diseases such as skin cancer can have a major positive impact in the area of health.

However, it is very important to recognize that this area is in development and that there is room for a wide range of improvements, both in terms of the reliability of the predictions generated in such a sensitive area as health, and the feasibility of using such tools can serve as an incentive for computer vision to be present in other studies aimed at helping diagnose other types of disease.

It is important to note that other types of tools can be used for such studies, such as neural networks that use the Vision Transformer, a technology that has achieved interesting results in studies based on computer vision.

REFERENCES

BI et al, 2019. A Primer for the Epidemiologist. *American Journal of Epidemiology*, Vol. 188, No. 12, pp 2222-2239.

Bottom et al, 2020. Relevância da Dermatoscopia para o Diagnóstico Precoce de Melanomas: Uma Revisão de Literatura. *Revista Interdisciplinar de Saúde e Educação*, Vol. 1, No. 2, pp 159-174.

BVSMS (2007) Câncer de pele. Available: https://bvsms.saude.gov.br/cancer-de-pele/ (Accessed 3 December 2023).

Chen, Yuanyuan and Yi, Zhang, 2021. Adaptative Sparce Dropout: Learning the Certainty and Uncertainty in Deep Neural Networks. *Neurocomputing.* Vol. 450, pp 354-361.

Craythorne, Emma and Al-Niami, Firas, 2017. Skin Cancer. *Medicine.* Vol. 45, No. 7, pp 431-434.

Dankers, Verna and Titov, Ivan, 2023. Recursive Neural Networks with Bottlenecks Diagnose (Non-) Compositionality. No publisher. No page.

De Souza Torres et, 2016. A Importância do Diagnóstico Precoce de Câncer Bucal em Idosos. *Ver Soc Bras Clin Med,* Vol. 14, No. 1, pp. 57-62.

Delazeri, Alexandre Valadão and Stevani, Egon Sulivan, 2021. Classificação de Câncer de Pele Usando Redes Neurais Convolucionais: Uma Análise do Desempenho de Classificação em um Conjunto de Dados Desbalanceado. *Universidade Tecnológica Federal do Paraná.* No Publisher.

Didática (2022) Underfitting e Overfitting. Available at: https://didatica.tech/underfitting-e-overfitting/ (Accessed 12 October 2023).

Ferreira, Alessandro dos Santos, 2017. Redes Neurais Convolucionais Profundas na Detecção de Plantas Daninhas em Lavoura de Soja. No Publisher, no pagination.

Fett-Conte, A. C. and Salles, A. B. C. F, 2002. A Importância do Gene P53 na Carcinogênese Humana. *Revista Brasileira de Hematologia e Hemoterapia.* Vol. 24, No. 2, pp. 85-89.

Gao et al, 2020. Extracting Features from Infrared Images Using Convolutional Neural Networks and Transfer Learning. Infrared Physics & Technology, Vol. 105, pp 103-237.

Inca (2022) INCA estima 704 mil casos de câncer por ano no Brasil até 2025. Available at: http://www.gov.br/inca/pt-br/assuntos/noticias/2022/inca-estima-704-mil-casos-de-cancer-por-ano-no-brasil-ate-2025/ (Accessed 3 December 2023).

Mangini et al, 2020. Quantum Computing Model of an Artificial Neuron with Continuously Valued Input Data. *Machine Learning: Science and Technology,* Vol. 1, No. 4, pp. 045008.

Mathworks (2023) Inceptionresnetv2. Available at: https://www.mathworks.com/help/deeplearning/ref/inceptionresnetv2.html/ (Accessed 12 October 2023).

Mathworks (2023) Inceptionv3. Available at: https://www.mathworks.com/help/deeplearning/ref/inceptionv3.html/ (Accessed 12 October 2023).

Mathworks (2023) Resnet101. Available at: https://www.mathworks.com/help/deeplearning/ref/resnet101.html/ (Accessed 12 October 2023).

Mathworks (2023) Resnet50. Available at: https://www.mathworks.com/help/deeplearning/ref/resnet50.html/ (Accessed 12 October 2023).

Mathworks (2023) Vgg16. Available at: HTTPS://WWW.MATHWORKS.COM/HELP/DEEPLEARNING/REF/VGG16.HTML (Accessed 12 October 2023).

Mijwil et al, 2021. Artificial Intelligence: A Survey on Evolution and Feture Trends. *Asian Journal of Applied Sciences*, Vol. 8, No. 2, no pagination.

Ministério da saúde (2022) Diagnóstico. Available at: https://www.gov.br/saude/pt-br/assuntos/saude-de-a-a-z/c/cancer-de-pele/diagnostico/ (Accessed 13 October 2023).

Ministério da saúde (no date) Câncer de pele. Available at: https://www.gov.br/saude/pt-br/assuntos/saude-de-a-a-z/c/cancer-de-pele/ (Accessed 3 December 2023).

Oncoguia (2022) Estimativas de câncer no Brasil. Available at: https://www.oncoguia.org.br/conteudo/estimativas-no-brasil/1705/1/#:~:text=O%20c%C3%A2ncer%20de%20pele%20n%C3%A3o,e%20est%C3%B4mago%20(21.480%20casos)/ (Accessed 12 October 2023).

Popim et al, 2008. Câncer de Pele: Uso de Medidas Preventivas e Perfil Demográfico de um Grupo de Risco na Cidade de Botucatu. *Ciência e Saúde Coletiva,* Vol. 13, pp.1331-1336.

Rauber, 2005. Redes Neurais Artificiais. *Universidade Federal do Espirito Santo*, Vol. 29, no pagination.

Santos et al, 2017. Uma Abordagem de Classificação de Imagens Dermatoscópicas Utilizando Aprendizado Profundo com Redes Neurais Convolucionais. *Anais do XVII Workshop de Informática Médica, n*o pagination.

Shorten et al, 2021. Text Data Augmentation for Deep Learning. *Journal of Big Data*. Vol. 8, pp. 1-34.

Tschandl et al, 2018. The HAM10000 Dataset, A Large Collection of Multi-Source Dermatoscopic Images of Common Pigmented Skin Lesions. *Scientific Data.* Vol. 5, No. 1, pp 1-9.

Utsch, Kaio Giurizatto, 2018. Uso de Redes Neurais Convolucionais para Classificação de Imagens Digitais de Lesões de Pele. *Universidade Federal do Espirito Santo.* No Publisher, Espirito Santo.

Vieira, Elias Queiroga, 2022. Comparação Entre Diferentes Modelos de Redes Neurais Convolucionais para Classificação de Melanoma. No publisher. No pagination.

X2 Inteligência Digital (2020) História da Inteligência Artificial. Available at: https://x2inteligencia.digital/2020/02/20/historia-da-inteligencia-artificial-2/ (Accessed 14 November 2023).

Zink, Beatrix Sabóia, 2014. Câncer de Pele: A Importância do seu Diagnóstico, Tratamento e Prevenção. *Revista Hospital Universitário Pedro Ernesto*. Vol. 13, no pagination.

PREDICTING THE IMPACT OF TIKTOK LIVE STREAMING QUALITY ON PURCHASE INTENTION THROUGH SELF-DETERMINATION THEORY

Arina Aunaka, Fauziah Putri Fajrianti, Mazaya Nur Labiba, Syifa Mumtaz Wazdy, Vania Azria Wardani and Widia Resti Fitriani
Faculty of Computer Science, Universitas Indonesia
Kampus UI Depok, Depok, 16424, Indonesia

ABSTRACT

TikTok has emerged as a dynamic social commerce platform that provides live-streaming features to facilitate engaging and interactive shopping experiences. This study analyzes the factors influencing users' intentions to purchase products on TikTok live-streaming. This study integrates the variable of live streaming quality with the Self-Determination Theory, emphasizing users' intrinsic and extrinsic motivations in performing a specific behavior. Utilizing a quantitative approach, data from 217 respondents were processed using the PLS-SEM method. The findings show that TikTok live streaming quality significantly influences users' perceived competence, relatedness, autonomy, and social influence. The study also proves that users' perceived enjoyment and perceived usefulness directly impact their purchase intentions. However, this study finds insignificant relationships between live streaming quality on network externalities and social influence on perceived usefulness. These findings have theoretical and practical implications for researchers, content creators, marketers, and platform developers to provide engaging and valuable content and technical enhancements in a social commerce platform to encourage users' purchase intention.

KEYWORDS

Live Streaming, Social Commerce, Quality, Self-Determination Theory, Purchase Intention

1. INTRODUCTION

Live streaming has become a dominant phenomenon in social media (Mao *et al.*, 2022). According to the Live Streaming Global Market Report 2022, the global live-streaming market grew from $1.03 billion in 2021 to $1.23 billion in 2022 (The Business Reserach Company, 2022). Projections are even more remarkable, with an expected growth of $2.61 billion by 2026 (Mao *et al.*, 2022). Among many live-streaming platforms available, TikTok has emerged as one of the most popular in Indonesia (We Are Social, 2023). In January 2023, TikTok recorded over 109.9 million users aged 18 and above. Moreover, 69 percent of Indonesian respondents use TikTok to watch live shopping (We Are Social, 2023). These numbers underscore TikTok's dominant position within the social media landscape in this country.

Previous research has provided valuable insights into how live streaming can influence user purchase intention. Zheng *et al.*, 2023 stated the importance of social presence and interactivity in live streaming, affecting purchase intention. Live streaming also impacts user purchase intention by reducing product uncertainty and fostering trust (Lu and Chen, 2021). Research by (Mao *et al.*, 2022) found that entertaining live-streaming content can enhance user purchase intention, mainly when products or services are presented appealingly. In another study, self-determination positively influenced consumers' intention to purchase fashion products from online retailers (Widyarini and Gunawan, 2018). These previous studies emphasize the importance of content quality, interactivity, and trust in live streaming influencing purchase intention.

While previous studies have given significant results, there is a noticeable research gap regarding the specific impact of live streaming quality on TikTok within the framework of Self-Determination Theory (SDT). With the significant growth of TikTok users transitioning from social interaction to live streaming commerce, this research aims to understand how the quality of TikTok live streaming affects user purchase intention through the SDT. By applying the SDT, this research provides a deeper understanding of the intrinsic and extrinsic motivations driving users in their online purchase decisions through live streaming. Additionally, this study recommends companies to design more appealing and interactive content and strengthen consumer trust on the TikTok platform.

2. LITERATURE REVIEW

This section discusses the theoretical concepts used in this paper, including TikTok as a live streaming platform and self-determination theory.

2.1 Tiktok as a Live Streaming Platform

With its real-time recording and interactive engagement between broadcasters and viewers, live streaming has revolutionized information delivery, transforming passive information consumers into active participants (Zhang *et al.*, 2022). It enables viewers to provide immediate feedback and even financial support as a reward for quality content, reshaping the traditional one-way flow of information (Kang *et al.*, 2021). TikTok, a popular social media platform known for its short-form video content, also offers live streaming feature that allows creators to monetize their content through virtual gifts and donations (Xu, Yan and Z. Zhang, 2019). Shoppable ads, in-feed shopping, and seamless product promotion by content creators also make it conducive for businesses to reach a broad and engaged audience.

Previous research highlights the significant impact of live streaming on product sales, reporting a 27.9% increase compared to pre-recorded broadcasts (Chen *et al.*, 2019). Broadcasters enhance their credibility by addressing consumer queries and conveying their brand philosophy in real time (Wongkitrungrueng and Assarut, 2020). Financial incentives such as gifts and commissions on product purchases from viewers motivate broadcasters to improve their communication skills, enhancing the audience's desire to purchase or offer rewards during live streams (Wohn, Freeman and McLaughlin, 2018).

2.2 Self-Determination Theory

The Self-Determination Theory (SDT) sheds light on intrinsic and extrinsic motivations. There are three fundamental psychological needs in SDT: autonomy, competence, and relatedness (Rezvani, Khosravi and Dong, 2017). Autonomy involves the need for self-direction and choice in one's actions, competence pertains to mastery and effectiveness in tasks, and relatedness concerns the need for meaningful interpersonal connections. When these needs are satisfied, individuals experience intrinsic motivation, greater well-being, and enhanced activity engagement (Rezvani, Khosravi and Dong, 2017). Competence is promoted through environments that offer opportunities for skill development and feedback, while relatedness thrives in settings emphasizing positive social connections and a sense of belonging (Rezvani, Khosravi and Dong, 2017).

This study uses SDT to understand how intrinsic and extrinsic motivations can influence TikTok users' purchase intentions within the live streaming feature. Users' fundamental psychological needs can be met by enhancing the quality of live streaming on TikTok, allowing users to feel that they can access content freely and competently (autonomy and competence) (Rezvani, Khosravi and Dong, 2017). Additionally, provided content should be meaningful and relevant to users to satisfy their need for meaningful relationships (relatedness) (Rezvani, Khosravi and Dong, 2017). The use of SDT in this study can help develop a more comprehensive understanding of TikTok users' motivation and behavior related to their purchase intentions following live streaming on the platform.

3. RESEARCH MODEL AND HYPOTHESES

This study presents a research model grounded in the SDT as the theoretical underpinning. The interrelationships among variables are elucidated within the proposed research model in Figure 1.

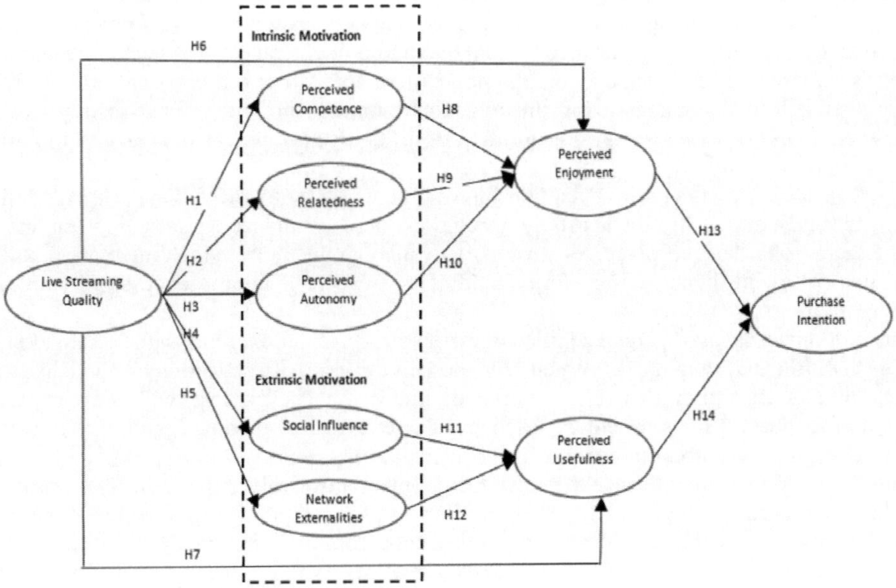

Figure 1. Proposed research model

Intrinsic motivation comprises perceived competence, relatedness, and autonomy. As for extrinsic motivation, this study encompasses social influence and network externalities. Social influence refers to the ability of individuals or groups to influence users' behavior, views, or decisions while participating in live streaming for shopping (Doan, 2020). Meanwhile, network externalities refer to the value of live streaming for users influenced by the number of other individuals also using the platform for shopping (Luo *et al.*, 2021). Users' intrinsic and extrinsic motivations will influence their perceived enjoyment and usefulness in using the live streaming on TikTok, and ultimately driving their intention to make purchases.

A high-quality live streaming enhances the visual and auditory aspects of the content and contributes to the overall satisfaction and engagement of the users (Zhang *et al.*, 2022). When live streaming content is optimally reasonable, appropriate, and easily understood, users have a sense of competence (Nikou and Economides, 2017). In this case, the quality of TikTok live streaming can provide a better user experience that will increase users' feelings of competence in using the platform. Therefore, we propose the following hypothesis: **H1. Live streaming quality significantly influences perceived competence.**

High-quality live streaming on TikTok is also expected to impact the perceived relatedness among users. When users feel that the content is explicit, well-produced, and enjoyable, they will likely feel a stronger relatedness to the creator and the content. Moreover, interactivity within the live streams fosters a sense of community and connectedness among users (Nikou and Economides, 2017). Therefore, we propose the following hypothesis: **H2. Live streaming quality significantly influences perceived relatedness.**

High-quality live streaming in TikTok also provides users a smoother, more immersive experience, allowing them to navigate and engage with content more freely. This enhanced experience may make users feel they have greater control over their interactions with the platform and its content, ultimately contributing to a sense of autonomy (Nikou and Economides, 2017). Therefore, we propose the following hypothesis: **H3. Live streaming quality significantly influences perceived autonomy.**

The quality of live-streaming content on TikTok substantially impacts how users perceive social influence within the platform. When the content is well-produced, enjoyable, and immersive, it may enhance the credibility and persuasiveness of the content creator, potentially increasing their ability to influence users' opinions, preferences, and actions. Therefore, we propose the following hypothesis: **H4. Live streaming quality significantly influences social influence.**

Network externalities is where the value of a product increases as more people adopt or use it, creating a positive feedback loop that attracts even more users (Luo *et al.*, 2021). High-quality live-streaming content is expected to attract a larger audience and retain existing users more effectively. Consequently, the quality of live streaming contributes to more significant network effects. Therefore, we propose the following hypothesis: **H5. Live streaming quality significantly influences network externalities.**

When TikTok live streaming content is of high quality, it creates a more immersive, engaging, and enjoyable viewing experience. The enhanced visual and audio quality and the absence of technical issues can provide users with a more satisfying and entertaining experience. Moreover, users are more likely to perceive such content as helpful in obtaining information, entertainment, or both. Consequently, we propose the following hypotheses: **H6. Live streaming quality significantly influences perceived enjoyment** and **H7. Live streaming quality significantly influences perceived usefulness.**

Perceived competence has a positive relationship with perceived enjoyment in the context of online learning study (Luo, Lin and Yang, 2021). In this study, when users perceive themselves as competent in using the live streaming feature on TikTok, they are likely to derive greater enjoyment from their interactions and experience. Therefore, the following hypothesis is formulated: **H8. Perceived competence significantly influences perceived enjoyment.**

Moreover, a higher level of perceived relatedness may contribute to a more satisfying and enjoyable user experience (Luo, Lin and Yang, 2021). When users perceive a sense of connection or relatedness with content creators and other users within the live-streaming community on TikTok, they will likely experience greater enjoyment during their interactions and experiences. Therefore, the following hypothesis is formulated: **H9. Perceived relatedness significantly influences perceived enjoyment.**

Perceived autonomy can influence perceived enjoyment positively (Luo, Lin and Yang, 2021). This suggests that when users feel a greater sense of autonomy and control in their interactions with live-streaming content on TikTok, they will likely derive more enjoyment from their experiences. Therefore, the following hypothesis is formulated: **H10. Perceived autonomy significantly influences perceived enjoyment.**

Social influence refers to individuals or groups' ability to influence others' behavior, attitudes, and views (Doan, 2020). Social influence is expected to have a significant positive impact on perceived usefulness. This implies that when users are influenced by social factors such as recommendations, opinions, or interactions with others on TikTok's live streaming platform, they are more likely to perceive the platform as beneficial for their needs. Therefore, the following hypothesis is formulated: **H11. Social influence significantly influences Perceived usefulness.**

Network externalities, which refer to the idea that the value of a platform or service increases as more users join or engage with it, play a substantial role in shaping how users perceive the usefulness of that platform or service (Luo *et al.*, 2021). In TikTok live streaming, a larger and more engaged user base enhances users' opportunities for interaction and content discovery, ultimately contributing to their perception of the platform's usefulness because users can derive more value from it. Therefore, the following hypothesis is formulated: **H12. Network externalities significantly influence perceived usefulness.**

Perceived enjoyment can be defined as the level of satisfaction a consumer feels during an online purchase on a particular website in terms of its ability to bring them happiness while excluding the performance they will experience (Luo, Lin and Yang, 2021). The more enjoyable the online shopping process is on a particular platform, the more likely consumers will buy on that platform (Childers *et al.*, 2001). Therefore, the following hypothesis is formulated: **H13. Perceived enjoyment significantly influences purchase intention.**

Finally, individuals who perceive a product, service, or platform as useful and valuable are likelier to do certain behaviors, such as intention to purchase (Yin and Qiu, 2021). In TikTok live streaming, users who perceive the platform as valuable are more likely to express an intention to make purchases. Therefore, the following hypothesis is formulated: **H14. Perceived usefulness significantly influences purchase intention.**

4. METHODOLOGY

This study utilizes a quantitative approach, employing a questionnaire as the primary data collection tool. The questionnaire had 26 items defining nine constructs. Respondents provided their feedback for each item using a five-point Likert scale, ranging from "strongly disagree" (1) to "strongly agree" (5). Respondents are individuals with a TikTok social media account who have participated in live-streaming activities on TikTok. The questionnaire was developed using Google Forms and distributed across various social media platforms to reach a broad and diverse group of participants. Data was collected from March 27, 2023, to June 2, 2023. A total of 217 respondents completed the questionnaire as presented in Table 1. The Partial Least Square - Structural Equation Model (PLS-SEM) with SmartPLS software is used for data analysis to determine the interrelationship between variables in the proposed research model.

Table 1. Demography of respondents

Measure	Items	Frequency	Percentage
Gender	Female	130	59.9%
	Male	87	40.1%
Age (years old)	< 17	3	1.4%
	17 - 25	165	76.0%
	26 - 35	39	18.0%
	36 - 45	10	4.6%
Occupation	Student	134	61.8%
	Self-employed	29	13.4%
	Private emp.	25	11.5%
	Government emp.	29	13.4%

5. RESULTS

The result section is divided into measurement model evaluation and structural model evaluation.

5.1 Measurement Model Evaluation

The initial step in data analysis involves examining the measurement model. Convergent validity is measured from loading factors that should be higher than 0.5 and ideally higher than 0.7 (Hair *et al.*, 2010). The average variance extracted (AVE) value for each latent variable should be greater than 0.5 (Hair *et al.*, 2010) while composite reliability (CR) should have a value greater than 0.7 (Hair *et al.*, 2010). Table 2 presents the respective values for each indicator.

Table 2. Construct validity and reliability

Construct	Parameter	Loading Factor	CR	AVE
Live Streaming Quality (LSQ)	LSQ1	0.756	0.822	0.536
	LSQ2	0.726		
	LSQ3	0.735		
	LSQ4	0.710		
Network Externalities (NE)	NE1	0.730	0.840	0.636
	NE2	0.824		
	NE3	0.835		
Perceived Autonomy (PA)	PA1	0.684	0.700	0.511
	PA2	0.744		
Perceived Competence (PC)	PC1	0.815	0.791	0.560
	PC2	0.716		
	PC3	0.708		
Perceived Enjoyment (PE)	PE1	0.745	0.772	0.629
	PE2	0.839		
Purchase Intention (PI)	PI1	0.713	0.763	0.519
	PI2	0.661		
	PI3	0.783		
Perceived Relatedness (PR)	PR1	0.726	0.708	0.500
	PR2	0.656		
	PR3	0.623		
Perceived Usefulness (PU)	PU1	0.719	0.774	0.533
	PU2	0.746		
	PU3	0.725		
Social Influence (SI)	SI1	0.833	0.809	0.586
	SI2	0.740		
	SI3	0.718		

The AVE square root value of a latent variable must be greater than the correlation value with other latent variables (Hair *et al.*, 2010). In addition, the cross-loading value of each indicator must be greater than the latent variable it describes (Hair *et al.*, 2010). Discriminant validity is also measured by the Fornell Lacker criterion and HTMT (Heterotrait-Monotrait Ratio).

5.2 Structural Model Evaluation

The structural model evaluation comprises hypothesis testing and coefficient determination. Hypothesis testing in this study was carried out in two directions (two-tailed) using a significance level of 5%. Table 3 shows the results of the hypothesis testing of the proposed model. Among 14 initial hypotheses, two of them are rejected, while the rest are accepted.

Table 3. Hypothesis Testing Results

Hypothesis	Path	Original Sample	T-statistics	P-values	Result
H1	LSQ -> PC	0.142	2.033	0.042	Accepted
H2	LSQ -> PR	0.336	5.691	0.000	Accepted
H3	LSQ -> PA	0.174	2.627	0.009	Accepted
H4	LSQ -> SI	0.238	3.603	0.000	Accepted
H5	LSQ -> NE	0.074	1.080	0.280	Rejected
H6	LSQ -> PE	0.197	3.014	0.003	Accepted
H7	LSQ -> PU	0.242	2.905	0.004	Accepted
H8	PC -> PE	0.206	2.716	0.007	Accepted
H9	PR -> PE	0.219	3.202	0.001	Accepted
H10	PA -> PE	0.170	2.105	0.035	Accepted
H11	SI -> PU	0.107	1.309	0.191	Rejected
H12	NE -> PU	0.216	2.457	0.014	Accepted
H13	PE -> PI	0.311	4.712	0.000	Accepted
H14	PU -> PI	0.282	3.265	0.001	Accepted

The coefficient of determination (R^2) for perceived competence, perceived relatedness, perceived autonomy, social influence, network externalities, perceived enjoyment, perceived usefulness, and purchase intention sequentially are 0.02, 0.113, 0.03, 0.057, 0.006, 0.28, 0.158, and 0.241. While the overall research model still exhibits low R^2 values, the R^2 value for the purchase intention can be categorized as reasonably practical for predictive purposes.

6. DISCUSSION

This study found that high-quality live streaming in TikTok substantially influences intrinsic motivation factors such as perceived competence, relatedness, and autonomy. When content is presented in a high-quality manner, users are more likely to be intrinsically motivated to engage with it because they feel capable, connected to others, and in control of their viewing experience, all of which contribute to a more satisfying and fulfilling engagement with the content in TikTok. The findings align with the research conducted by (Nikou and Economides, 2017). This study also found that the quality of live-streaming content notably impacts extrinsic motivation factors, specifically social influence. When the live-streaming content is well-produced, enjoyable, and immersive, it can boost the credibility and persuasiveness of the content creator to influence users' opinions, preferences, and actions. However, this study did not find a similar effect on network externalities, suggesting that live streaming quality alone may not substantially attract a larger audience and retain existing users more effectively in TikTok.

This study found that live streaming quality influences perceived enjoyment and usefulness. High-quality live streams offer an appealing visual, with clear audio and uninterrupted engaging content, which can build users' perception that the content is enjoyable. Live streaming also provides a useful solution to address product uncertainty by allowing sellers to demonstrate products in real time (Lu and Chen, 2021).

This study also proved that intrinsic motivational factors within the SDT framework (i.e., perceived competence, autonomy, and relatedness) collectively contribute to users' perceived enjoyment during TikTok live streaming. The result is aligned with (Luo, Lin and Yang, 2021), suggesting that users' enjoyment increases when they feel competent in navigating and understanding the content, feel connected with the content and other users, and can control their engagement with live streams.

While social influence and network externalities represent extrinsic motivational factors within the SDT framework, this study found that only network externalities influence perceived usefulness. This implies that a larger audience and increased user engagement appear to enhance the perceived usefulness of the platform (Luo *et al.*, 2021). On the other hand, perceived usefulness is not significantly influenced by social influence. This result is supported by (Zheng *et al.*, 2023), which indicates that social influence does not enhance users' perceived usefulness in the Instagram live streaming platform. Social influence is more focused on how individuals are influenced by or influence others in terms of actions or views, and this doesn't necessarily mean that they will perceive a live streaming experience on TikTok as more useful.

Finally, this study proved that perceived enjoyment and usefulness significantly influence purchase intention in TikTok live streaming. This result is aligned with research by (Childers *et al.*, 2001; Yin and Qiu, 2021). It suggests that a satisfying and enjoyable live streaming experience in TikTok can directly contribute to users' intentions to buy products during the live streams. Moreover, users are more likely to consider purchasing products when they see TikTok live streaming as a useful tool for their shopping needs.

The findings of this study have both theoretical and practical implications. This study enriches the understanding of SDT by applying it to the context of TikTok live streaming and social commerce, highlighting the significance of live streaming quality, perceived competence, autonomy, and relatedness in shaping users' purchase intentions. This study also contributes to cross-cultural research by examining Indonesian users. From a practical standpoint, this research offers practical guidance for content creators, marketers, and platform developers to provide live-streaming content that aligns with user interests. Content creators can build community and actively engage with their audience. Platform developers should prioritize technical improvements to enhance streaming quality and user interfaces. Additionally, marketers can design campaigns based on TikTok's principles of enjoyment and usefulness to positively influence users' purchasing decisions.

7. CONCLUSION

This study analyzes the relationships between TikTok live streaming quality, self-determination theory, and user purchase intentions. This study affirmed that TikTok live streaming quality significantly influences users' perceived competence, relatedness, autonomy, and social influence. These intrinsic and extrinsic motivational factors in SDT are pivotal in shaping users' purchase intentions on TikTok. However, the study revealed that live streaming quality did not significantly affect network externalities, and social influence was found to have no significant impact on perceived usefulness. Additionally, the study emphasized that the perceived enjoyment and usefulness of TikTok live streaming directly impacts users' purchase intentions.

This study has several limitations that could be addressed in future research. Firstly, the demographics of the respondents posed a limitation, as most participants were students (59.91%). This limitation can be mitigated in future research by increasing the number and diversity of respondents. Secondly, the scope of the study was confined to the TikTok application alone. Consequently, the findings of this research may not necessarily be representative or applicable to other applications that offer similar live-streaming features. Hence, future studies are encouraged to explore and compare various live-streaming platforms.

ACKNOWLEDGMENT

This work is funded by PUTI Q1 grant No. NKB-293/UN2.RST/HKP.05.00/2023.

REFERENCES

Chen, C. *et al.* (2019). 'Everyone can Be a star: quantifying grassroots online sellers' live streaming effects on product sales', in *Proceedings of the 52nd Hawaii International Conference on System Sciences*. Available at: https://hdl.handle.net/10125/59887.

Childers, T. L. *et al.* (2001). 'Hedonic and utilitarian motivations for online retail shopping behavior', *Journal of Retailing*, 77(4), pp. 511–535. doi: https://doi.org/10.1016/S0022-4359(01)00056-2.

Doan, T. T. (2020). 'Factors affecting online purchase intention: A study of Vietnam online customers. , 10, .', *Management Science Letters*, 10, pp. 2337–2342. doi: https://doi.org/10.5267/j.msl.2020.3.001.

Hair, J. F. *et al.* (2010). *Multivariate Data Analysis*. 7th Editio. Pearson Education Limited.

Kang, K. *et al.* (2021). 'The dynamic effect of interactivity on customer engagement behavior through tie strength: Evidence from live streaming commerce platforms', *International Journal of Information Management*, 56. doi: https://doi.org/10.1016/j.ijinfomgt.2020.102251.

Lu, B. and Chen, Z. (2021). 'Live streaming commerce and consumers' purchase intention: An uncertainty reduction perspective', *Information & Management*, 58(7). doi: https://doi.org/10.1016/j.im.2021.103509.

Luo, Y. *et al.* (2021). 'Examining protection motivation and network externality perspective regarding the continued intention to use m-health apps', *International Journal of Environmental Research and Public Health*, 18(11). doi: 10.3390/ijerph18115684.

Luo, Y., Lin, J. and Yang, Y. (2021). 'Students' Motivation and Continued Intention with Online Self-Regulated Learning: A Self-Determination Theory Perspective.', *Z Erziehungswiss*, 24, pp. 1380–1399. doi: https://doi.org/10.1007/s11618-021-01042-3.

Mao, Z. *et al.* (2022). 'Short-term or long-term cooperation between retailer and MCN? New launched products sales strategies in live streaming ecommerce.', *Journal of Retailing and Consumer Services*, 67(102996). doi: https://doi.org/10.1016/j.jretconser.2022.102996.

Nikou, S. A. and Economides, A. A. (2017). 'Mobile-Based Assessment: Integrating acceptance and motivational factors into a combined model of Self-Determination Theory and Technology Acceptance', *Computers in Human Behavior*, 68, pp. 83–95. doi: https://doi.org/10.1016/j.chb.2016.11.020.

Rezvani, A., Khosravi, P. and Dong, L. (2017). 'Motivating users toward continued usage of information systems: Self-determination theory perspective', *Computers in Human Behavior*, 76, pp. 263–275. doi: https://doi.org/10.1016/j.chb.2017.07.032.

The Business Reserach Company (2022). *Live Streaming Global Market Report 2022*. Available at: https://www.researchandmarkets.com/reports/5646890/live-streaming-global-market-report-2022 (Accessed: 1 September 2023).

We Are Social (2023). *The Changing World of Digital in 2023*. Available at: https://wearesocial.com/uk/blog/2023/01/the-changing-world-of-digital-in-2023/ (Accessed: 5 September 2023).

Widyarini, L. A. and Gunawan, S. (2018). 'Predicting Consumer Purchase Intention on Fashion Products in Online Retailer: Integration of Self Determination Theory and Theory of Planned Behavior', *International Journal of Emerging Research in Management &Technology*, 6(9). doi: doi:10.23956/ijermt.v6i9.78.

Wohn, D. Y., Freeman, G. and McLaughlin, C. (2018).'Explaining viewers' emotional, instrumental, and financial support provision for live streamers', in *Proceedings of the 2018 CHI Conference on Human Factors in Computing Systems*, pp. 1–13. doi: https://doi.org/10.1145/3173574.3174048.

Wongkitrungrueng, A. and Assarut, N. (2020). 'The role of live streaming in building consumer trust and engagement with social commerce sellers', *Journal of Business Research*, 117, pp. 543–556. doi: https://doi.org/10.1016/j.jbusres.2018.08.032.

Xu, L., Yan, X. and Z. Zhang (2019). 'Research on the Causes of the "Tik Tok" App Becoming Popular and the Existing Problems', *J. Adv. Manag. Sci.* doi: doi: 10.18178/joams.7.2.59-63.

Yin, J. and Qiu, X. (2021). 'AI Technology and Online Purchase Intention: Structural Equation Model Based on Perceived Value', *Sustainability*, 13. doi: https://doi.org/10.3390/su13105671.

Zhang, M. *et al.* (2022). 'How to retain customers: Understanding the role of trust in live streaming commerce with a socio-technical perspective', *Computers in Human Behavior*, 127. doi: https://doi.org/10.1016/j.chb.2021.107052.

Zheng, S. *et al.* (2023). 'What motivates users' viewing and purchasing behavior motivations in live streaming: A stream-streamer-viewer perspective', *Journal of Retailing and Consumer Services*, 72(103240). doi: https://doi.org/10.1016/j.jretconser.2022.103240.

EXAMINING THE IMPORTANCE OF LIVE-STREAMING EXPERIENCE ON SOCIAL COMMERCE: IMPACTS ON COMMITMENT AND PURCHASE INTENTION

Alya Annissa Diyantari, Nathasya Shalsabilla Putri, Naura Saffa, Shafira Alya Chairunnisa, Fatimah Azzahro and Achmad Nizar Hidayanto
Faculty of Computer Science, Universitas Indonesia
Kampus UI Depok, Depok, 16418, Indonesia

ABSTRACT

This study aims to explore the multifaceted dimensions of the TikTok live streaming experience and how it influences viewers' emotions, their commitment towards TikTok as a social commerce platform, and their purchase intention. Through empirical research, this study uncovers that information experience influences the feeling of dominance. Additionally, homophily experience influences arousal and dominance, while relationship experience influences pleasure and arousal. All emotional constructs observed in this study affect users' commitment towards the platform, which signifies the willingness to make a purchase. This research contributes valuable insights into the ever-evolving landscape of social commerce, shedding light on how live-streaming experiences on TikTok can profoundly influence user attitudes and behaviors, ultimately affecting their commitment to the platform and their intention to make purchases.

KEYWORDS

Live Streaming Experience, Commitment, Social Commerce, Purchase Intention

1. INTRODUCTION

In today's digital age, social media platforms have evolved into critical channels that extend far beyond mere social interaction (Zhang, Wenyao et al., 2023). Due to its ability to influence consumer purchasing behavior, social media has recently shown massive growth in communicating and promoting products and services (Huang and Benyoucef, 2015). One social media platform that has garnered immense popularity and attention is TikTok. TikTok has transformed into a thriving hub of content creators, influencers, and brands, presenting a unique blend of entertainment and commerce.

TikTok provides users with content in the form of live streams and short video streams, with live streaming has become a more popular choice in online sales. One of the reasons behind this phenomenon is that live streaming allows users to see and obtain comprehensive and transparent product information. This addresses the issue of users relying solely on static images on regular e-commerce websites (Xu et al., 2019). Users are not only captivated by entertaining content but also exposed to product promotions and endorsements during live streams. As users spend more significant time on TikTok's live streaming to make online purchases, it has become increasingly crucial to understand how these live streaming experiences impact users' emotions and, subsequently, their commitment and purchase intentions. Therefore, this research seeks to answer how the emotional responses triggered by TikTok live streaming experiences impact users' commitment to the platform and their intention to make purchases.

Moreover, this study responds to the growing need for research in the context of social commerce. With TikTok emerging as a prominent player in the field, it becomes imperative to investigate the factors that drive user commitment and purchase intentions in this unique social commerce landscape. By examining the emotional dimensions of the TikTok live streaming experience, we aim to provide valuable insights for businesses, marketers, and platform operators seeking to harness the power of TikTok as a social commerce platform.

This research aims to rethink important concepts about users' behavioral intention, especially in the context of live streaming in a social commerce platform. Next, this study develops a conceptual model to study factors that impact users' emotion and how it impacts users' commitment to the platform and intention to purchase. We propose an integrated model that consists of four constructs of live streaming experience (entertainment, relationship, information, and homophily experience), three constructs of users' emotion (pleasure, arousal, and dominance), and two dependent variables, namely commitment and intention to purchase. Using questionnaire data, we employ structural equation modeling to test the research hypotheses.

The paper is organized as follow. In the following section, we review the relevant literature to support our hypotheses development. We then describe our methodology and present our results, ending with a discussion and conclusion of our findings, including our theoretical implication, practical implications, and research limitations.

2. LITERATURE STUDY AND HYPOTHESES DEVELOPMENT

This study proposes an investigation on how the live-streaming experience perceived by viewers may influence their emotions, such as pleasure, arousal, and dominance. To get a more detailed assessment, we observed the live streaming experience using four constructs, namely information experience, entertainment experience, homophily experience, and relationship experience, that are adopted from (Purwandari et al., 2022). Then, we seek to investigate the influence of the emotional dimension on commitment and how commitment affects users' purchase intention. The proposed research model is presented in Figure 1.

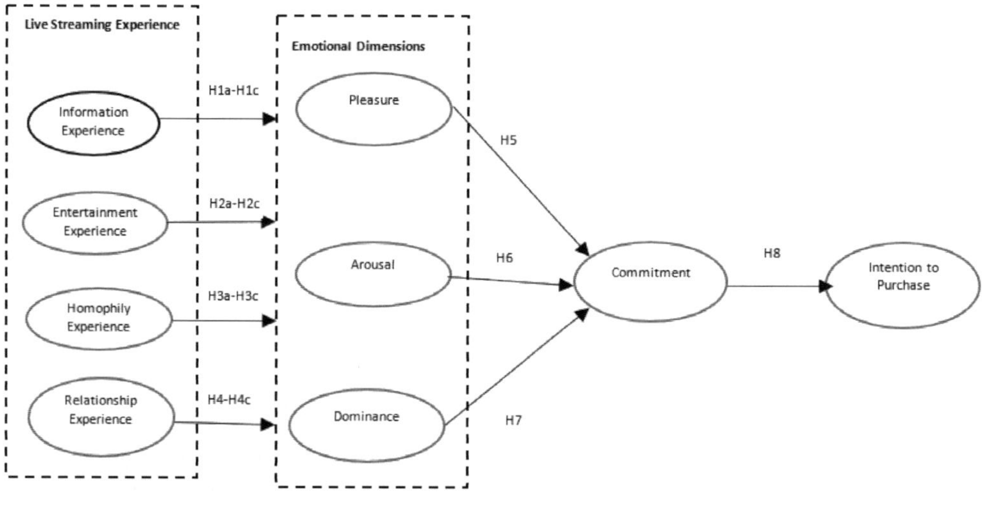

Figure 1. Research Model

Information experience involves users processing and utilizing information presented during live streams (Archer-Brown et al., 2013). Streamers often share valuable insights about products, services, or topics, which create an educational and informative atmosphere during live streams. Viewers have the opportunity to ask questions in real time, facilitating an exchange of knowledge. This information experience empowers users to make informed decisions, explore new ideas, and gain deeper insights into the presented content. Thus, as users perceive the provided information as valuable, they are more likely to derive pleasure from live streams.

Additionally, when consumers feel well-informed during their shopping journey, they are more likely to experience heightened arousal (Purwandari et al., 2022). An engaging information experience is expected to stimulate interest, curiosity, and a sense of excitement, thereby contributing to a more emotionally charged purchase intention. A joyous information experience can also lead to an increased sense of dominance in users (Inan et al., 2022). When consumers feel well-informed and capable of making informed choices based on the information provided, they tend to exhibit a stronger sense of control and influence over their purchase decisions. Therefore, we propose the following hypotheses:

H1a. Information experience affects pleasure significantly.
H1b. Information experience affects arousal significantly.
H1c. Information experience affects dominance significantly.

The entertainment experience is a hallmark of TikTok live streaming. It revolves around enjoyable content that keeps viewers engaged and entertained. Viewers are drawn to live streams that offer not only valuable information but also an element of entertainment, and this, in turn, can positively increase pleasure. Additionally, when TikTok users are exposed to stimulating and exciting content, it triggers a sense of arousal and excitement, which can positively influence their intention to engage with the products or services showcased in the content. Moreover, live streams with great entertainment experiences often offer interaction between streamers and viewers. As TikTok users perceive themselves as active participants in the content and decision-making process, they may also feel dominant and influential, positively affecting their intention to make a purchase on the platform. Based on this, we propose these following hypotheses:
H2a. Entertainment experience affects pleasure significantly.
H2b. Entertainment experience affects arousal significantly.
H2c. Entertainment experience affects dominance significantly.

Homophily refers to the similarity among a group of individuals where they tend to connect or associate themselves with others who are similar to them rather than dissimilar (Lakhan et al., 2021). In our study, homophily experience becomes one of the aspects of the live streaming experience. As a social commerce, TikTok's live streaming platform also fosters a homophily experience, where users connect with like-minded individuals and form communities based on shared interests and values. This experience is driven by the platform's ability to match users with content that aligns with their preferences. As users engage in live streams related to their interests, they feel a sense of belonging with both the streamer and fellow viewers who share similar passions.

When users engage in live streaming experiences with individuals who share similar interests and values, they are more likely to derive pleasure from the content and interactions (Lu, Zhicong et al., 2018). The excitement and engagement derived from interactions with like-minded individuals can also trigger emotional responses and increase arousal during the live-streaming experience. Additionally, when users feel a sense of connection and similarity with others, they may perceive a higher degree of control and influence over their interactions and decisions, leading to a greater sense of dominance during the live stream (Purwandari et al., 2022). Therefore, the following hypotheses are proposed:
H3a. Homophily experience affects pleasure significantly.
H3b. Homophily experience affects arousal significantly.
H3c. Homophily experience affects dominance significantly.

Relationship experience during live streaming on TikTok refers to the quality of interpersonal connections and interactions that viewers and participants establish with content creators (streamers) and other viewers within the TikTok live streaming environment. This experience encompasses the development of social bonds, rapport, and emotional connections during the live stream. Building relationships with content creators and fellow viewers often involves emotional connections. When viewers feel a sense of camaraderie, friendship, or belonging, it generates positive emotions, contributing to pleasure. Additionally, the emotional bonds formed during live streaming can make viewers feel more engaged and excited, leading to heightened arousal and pleasure. Thus, these following hypotheses are proposed:
H4a. Relationship experience affects pleasure significantly.
H5b. Relationship experience affects arousal significantly.
H6c. Relationship experience affects dominance significantly.

According to (Ryu, Sann and Park, Jung Kun, 2020), users who derive pleasure from their interactions and experiences on a social commerce platform are more likely to develop a strong commitment to that platform. Pleasure is associated with positive emotions and satisfaction, which can foster a sense of attachment and loyalty to the platform. Additionally, users who feel a sense of control and influence (dominance) over their interactions in social commerce and experience heightened levels of arousal, such as excitement and engagement, are more likely to develop a strong commitment to the social commerce platform. Arousal signifies active and dynamic interactions and highly aroused users are expected to feel more committed (Purwandari et al., 2022). Accordingly, we proposed the following hypotheses:

H5. Pleasure has a significant effect on commitment.
H6. Arousal has a significant effect on commitment.
H7. Dominance has a significant effect on commitment.

According to Khodabandeh and Lindh, users who demonstrate a higher level of commitment to a live-streaming platform are more likely to exhibit a stronger intention to make purchases (Khodabandeh and Lindh, 2021). Commitment may manifest as a sense of loyalty, engagement, and attachment to the platform, streamers, or the community. Users who are committed may perceive the platform as a valuable source of content and information, which can positively influence their purchase intention. They are more likely to trust recommendations from streamers and the community, leading to a greater likelihood of making purchases during or after a live stream (Wongkitrungrueng and Assarut, 2020). Thus, the following hypotheses can be formulated:

H8. Commitment affects the intention to purchase.

3. RESEARCH AND METHODOLOGY

The research employed a web-based online survey method for data collection. The primary target group for this research consisted of individuals who owned a TikTok social media account and had engaged in live streaming on TikTok. The survey distribution spanned various social media platforms, including LINE, WhatsApp, Instagram, Twitter, and TikTok, with the objective of reaching a diverse pool of respondents. A total of 227 respondents successfully completed the questionnaire, providing valuable primary data for analysis. The profiles of respondents are listed in Table 1.

Table 1. Demography of Respondents

Variable	Items	Frequency	Percentage
Sex	Male	100	44.1%
	Female	127	55.9%
Age (years old)	< 17	15	6.4%
	17 - 25	144	63.4%
	26 - 35	55	24.2%
	>35	13	5.7%
How many times have you made purchases while following live streaming on the TikTok application?	Never	27	11.9%
	1-3 times	109	48%
	4-5 times	54	23.8%
	6-10 times	29	12.8%
	>10 times	8	3.5%

In this empirical study, we analyzed how live streaming experience may affect user's emotions such as pleasure, arousal, and dominance. Live streaming experiences are represented by information experience, entertainment experience, homophily experience, and relationship experience. The items of each construct were adopted from prior studies such as information experience from (Archer-Brown et al., 2013) and (Xu et al., 2020), entertainment experiencefrom (Dholakia et al., 2004) and (Liu et al., 2022), homophily experience from (McPherson et al., 2001), and relationship experience from (Wang et al., 2019). Meanwhile, emotional dimensions are represented by three constructs: pleasure that were adopted from (Huang et al., 2017), arousal, and dominance which was adopted from (Kourouthanassis et al., 2015). Lastly, we used measurement of commitment from (Goutam and Gopalakrishna, 2018) and intention to purchase from (Zheng et al., 2022) and (Huang et al., 2020).

We designed a two-part questionnaire survey to assess our theoretical model. To ensure the meaning remained consistent, we followed Brislin's (Brislin, 2014) procedure by translating and back-translating all measures from English to Bahasa Indonesia. The questionnaire comprised 28 measurements that defined nine constructs. Each item corresponding to a construct was evaluated using a five-point Likert scale, with response options ranging from "strongly disagree" (1) to "strongly agree" (5).

4. RESEARCH RESULTS

The research employed a web-based online survey method for data collection. A total of 227 respondents successfully completed the questionnaire, providing valuable primary data for analysis. After ensuring the reliability and validity of the measurement model (see Table 2), we then evaluated the significance of paths ($p \leq 0.05$) and conducted a hypothesis test. The hypothesis testing was carried out using the two-tailed method and a significance level of 0.05. For each hypothesis, if the T statistics value obtained is greater than 1.96, then the hypothesis will be accepted, and vice versa (Hair et al., 2011). Table 3 exhibits the results of the structural testing of the proposed model. Among 16 initial hypotheses, 4 of them are rejected, while the rest are accepted.

Table 2. The Results of Reliability and Validity Testing for the Constructs

Factors	Items	Loading Factor	AVE	CR	Factors	Items	Loading Factor	AVE	CR
Relationship	RE1	0.904	0.774	0.932	Pleasure	P1	0.893	0.801	0.924
Experience	RE2	0.874				P2	0.898		
	RE3	0.865				P3	0.894		
	RE4	0.874			Arousal	A1	0.898	0.805	0.925
Information	IE1	0.846	0.739	0.895		A2	0.904		
Experience	IE2	0.868				A3	0.890		
	IE3	0.866			Dominance	D1	0.767	0.662	0.854
Homophily	HE1	0.817	0.688	0.869		D2	0.829		
Experience	HE2	0.847				D3	0.843		
	HE3	0.824			Commitment	C1	0.890	0.789	0.918
Entertainment	EE1	0.848	0.791	0.919		C2	0.885		
Experience	EE2	0.913				C3	0.891		
	EE3	0.906			Intention to	ITP1	0.890	0.770	0.909
					Purchase	ITP2	0.904		
						ITP3	0.838		

Furthermore, to evaluate the portion of variability in the dependent variable that can be explained by the independent variable, we followed the recommendations from (Hair et al., 2011) by observing the R-squared for each dependent variable. The R^2 values for arousal, commitment, dominance, pleasure, and intention to purchase are 0.782, 0.797, 0.712, 0.768, and 0.348, respectively. According to Moore, dependent variables achieving an R^2 value exceeding 0.50 are considered favorable, indicating a robust coefficient of determination (Hair et al., 2011). This implies that the existing models possess the capability to forecast the dependent variable, although it is possible to improve the prediction by adding other variables.

5. DISCUSSION AND IMPLICATIONS

Our results show that information experience only influences dominance but not pleasure and arousal. Although this finding is not aligned with prior studies (Purwandari et al., 2022), one may argue that TikTok users often engage with the platform for entertainment and social interaction. When users join a live stream, they may have specific expectations of being entertained or emotionally engaged rather than seeking purely informational content. If the live stream is perceived as more informational, viewers may not experience the expected pleasure or arousal. Meanwhile, informative content in live streams may improve users' knowledge, which may make them feel more capable of making informed choices, which can lead to a heightened sense of dominance.

Additionally, our finding shows that homophily experience affects dominance and arousal but not pleasure. Homophily experience is defined as the similarity among a group of individuals where they tend to connect or associate themselves with others who are similar to them (Lawrence and Shah, 2020). In our study, it refers to the phenomenon where viewers who join a live stream on TikTok share common interests, values, or demography with the content creator (streamer) and other viewers. Homophily experience can provide viewers with validation and positive feedback from their peers who share their interests. This validation can enhance feelings of dominance as viewers receive recognition and affirmation for their contributions and opinions. This is aligned with prior study of (Purwandari et al., 2022). Moreover, sharing interests with others and participating in discussions about those interests can be emotionally engaging, which may heighten arousal as viewers become more emotionally invested in the content and conversations. On the other hand, while homophily experience may contribute to a sense of community and belonging, it might not be the dominant factor in determining overall pleasure. Viewers may derive pleasure from various aspects of the live stream, such as content quality, streamer charisma, and entertainment value.

Table 3. Hypothesis Testing Result

Hypothesis	Path	T-Statistics	*p*	Results
H1a	Information Experience → Pleasure	1.254	0.210	Rejected
H1b	Information Experience → Arousal	0.745	0.456	Rejected
H1c	Information Experience → Dominance	4.339	0.000	Accepted
H2a	Entertainment Experience → Pleasure	7.244	0.000	Accepted
H2b	Entertainment Experience → Arousal	7.059	0.000	Accepted
H2c	Entertainment Experience → Dominance	2.743	0.006	Accepted
H3a	Homophily Experience → Pleasure	1.563	0.118	Rejected
H3b	Homophily Experience → Arousal	3.123	0.002	Accepted
H3c	Homophily Experience → Dominance	4.991	0.000	Accepted
H4a	Relationship Experience → Pleasure	4.603	0.000	Accepted
H4b	Relationship Experience → Arousal	3.965	0.000	Accepted
H4c	Relationship Experience → Dominance	0.442	0.659	Rejected
H5	Pleasure → Commitment	5.982	0.000	Accepted
H6	Arousal → Commitment	5.210	0.000	Accepted
H7	Dominance → Commitment	3.957	0.000	Accepted
H8	Commitment → Intention to Purchase	12.721	0.000	Accepted

Our study also indicates that relationship experience on TikTok is affecting pleasure and arousal, but not dominance. Relationship experience refers to the quality of interpersonal connections and interactions that viewers and participants establish with streamers and other viewers within the TikTok live-streaming environment. This experience encompasses the development of social bonds and emotional connections during the livestream that tend to foster a sense of community and belonging. Still, they may not inherently convey a sense of dominance. Moreover, building relationships with streamer creators and fellow viewers often involves emotional connections. When viewers feel a sense of friendship or belonging, it generates positive emotions, contributing to pleasure. This is aligned with (Purwandari et al., 2022). Also, the emotional bonds formed during live streaming can make viewers feel more engaged and excited, leading to increased arousal.

In terms of entertainment experience during live streaming on TikTok, our study shows that it affects pleasure, arousal, and dominance. When viewers find the content entertaining, they experience a sense of enjoyment and pleasure (Purwandari et al., 2022), (Song et al., 2019). Entertaining content can be dynamic, stimulating, and emotionally engaging. Viewers become emotionally invested in the content, leading to heightened arousal levels. Entertainment experiences often require active participation, such as reacting to funny moments, guessing outcomes, or responding to challenges. This active engagement can create a sense of control and influence (dominance) over the experience, as viewers actively contribute to the entertainment.

Furthermore, pleasure, arousal, and dominance can affect commitment in live streaming on TikTok due to their roles in shaping the overall user experience and influencing user attitudes and behaviors. Users who associate positive emotions (pleasure) with TikTok's live streaming content, feel engaged and excited (arousal) and perceive themselves as active participants with influence (dominance) are more likely to develop a strong commitment to the platform. This is aligned with findings from prior study (Wang et al., 2019). These emotional dimensions create a sense of attachment, satisfaction, and loyalty, ultimately influencing users' willingness to continue using TikTok for live streaming and related activities. Lastly, this study found that commitment to use TikTok will result in higher purchase intention. This result is in accordance with the results of research conducted by (Khodabandeh and Lindh, 2021).

This research contributes both in terms of practical and theoretical aspects. From a practical perspective, this research provides insight for TikTok as a social commerce platform to develop live-streaming features that may enhance user emotions such as pleasure, arousal, and dominance, which may improve users' commitment to the platform and their intention to purchase products using TikTok. Then, from a theoretical point of view, this research provides knowledge about factors influencing users' emotions, commitment, and intention to purchase by using the theory of experience in the context of live streaming on TikTok. We have not found this specific aspect in previous studies.

6. CONCLUSION

This study aimed to investigate the factors influencing users' emotions based on the live streaming experience on TikTok and their subsequent impact on purchase intention. Data collection was executed through an online survey involving a total of 227 participants. Our study found that pleasure was influenced by entertainment experience and relationship experience but not influenced by information experience and homophily experience. Meanwhile, arousal is influenced by entertainment experience, homophily experience, and relationship experience, but is not influenced by information experience. Furthermore, dominance is influenced by information experience, entertainment experience, and homophily experience, but is not influenced by relationship experience. Lastly, we found that users' emotions, such as pleasure, arousal, and dominance, influence users' commitment along with their purchase intention.

Our study has several limitations that provide suggestions for future studies. First, we did not integrate actual usage behavior into the proposed model. Nevertheless, there is substantial empirical research available that addresses the cause-and-effect relationship between behavioral intention and usage behavior (Venkatesh et al., 2012). Second, the demography of respondents was unbalanced as more than 60% of the respondents were students in the 17-25 age range category. Thus, the results of this study may not have represented TikTok users in general. Therefore, in the future, it is recommended to conduct research with a more diverse demographic of respondents so that the research results are more representative. Additionally, future study may investigate if there are differences in the emotional perception and use of live streaming on TikTok social media between different groups.

ACKNOWLEDGEMENT

We would like to thank Universitas Indonesia for the support through PUTI Q1 grant No. NKB-293/UN2.RST/HKP.05.00/2023.

REFERENCES

Archer-Brown, C., Piercy, N., Joinson, A. (2013). Examining the information value of virtual communities: Factual versus opinion-based message content. Journal of Marketing Management. https://doi.org/10.1080/0267257X.2012.732599

Brislin, R. (2014). Applied Cross-Cultural Psychology: An Introduction, in: Applied Cross-Cultural Psychology. https://doi.org/10.4135/9781483325392.n1

Ceci L. (2023). Countries with the most TikTok users 2022. Statisca.com.

Dholakia, U.M., Bagozzi, R.P., Pearo, L.K., 2004. A social influence model of consumer participation in network- and small-group-based virtual communities. International Journal of Research in Marketing. https://doi.org/10.1016/j.ijresmar.2003.12.004

Goutam, D., Gopalakrishna, B.V. (2018). Customer loyalty development in online shopping: An integration of e-service quality model and commitment-trust theory. Management Science Letters. https://doi.org/10.5267/j.msl.2018.8.009

Hair, J.F., Ringle, C.M., Sarstedt, M., 2011. PLS-SEM: Indeed a Silver Bullet. Journal of Marketing Theory and Practice 19, 139–152. https://doi.org/10.2753/MTP1069-6679190202

Huang, L., Bai, L., Gong, S. (2020). The effects of carrier, benefit, and perceived trust in information channel on functional food purchase intention among Chinese consumers. Food Quality and Preference. https://doi.org/10.1016/j.foodqual.2019.103854

Huang, M., Ali, R., Liao, J. (2017). The effect of user experience in online games on word of mouth: A pleasure-arousal-dominance (PAD) model perspective. Computers in Human Behavior. https://doi.org/10.1016/j.chb.2017.05.015

Huang, Z., Benyoucef, M. (2015). User preferences of social features on social commerce websites: An empirical study. Technological Forecasting and Social Change. https://doi.org/10.1016/j.techfore.2014.03.005

Inan, D.I., Hidayanto, A.N., Juita, R., Maulana, A., Putri, D.M.Q., Farhan, M.F., Hasnaa, S.K., Sanglise, M. (2022). The Follower-Influencer Experience Affecting the Intention to Follow Recommendation: PAD Perspective, in: 2022 7th International Conference on Informatics and Computing, ICIC 2022. https://doi.org/10.1109/ICIC56845.2022.10007014

Khodabandeh, A., Lindh, C. (2021). The importance of brands, commitment, and influencers on purchase intent in the context of online relationships. Australasian Marketing Journal 29, 177–186. https://doi.org/10.1016/j.ausmj.2020.03.003

Kourouthanassis, P., Boletsis, C., Bardaki, C., Chasanidou, D. (2015). Tourists responses to mobile augmented reality travel guides: The role of emotions on adoption behavior. Pervasive and Mobile Computing. https://doi.org/10.1016/j.pmcj.2014.08.009

Lakhan, G.R., Ullah, M., Channa, A., Abbas, M., Khan, M.A. (2021). Factors Effecting Consumer Purchase Intention : Live Streaming Commerce. Psychology and Education.

Lawrence, B.S., Shah, N.P. (2020). Homophily: Measures and meaning. Academy of Management Annals. https://doi.org/10.5465/annals.2018.0147

Liu, X., Zhang, L., Chen, Q. (2022). The effects of tourism e-commerce live streaming features on consumer purchase intention: The mediating roles of flow experience and trust. Frontiers in Psychology. https://doi.org/10.3389/fpsyg.2022.995129

Lu, Zhicong, Xia, Haijun, Heo, Seongkook, Wigdor, Daniel. (2018). You watch, you give, and you engage: A study of live streaming practices in China, in: Conference on Human Factors in Computing Systems - Proceedings. Presented at the CHI '18: Proceedings of the 2018 CHI Conference on Human Factors in Computing Systems, Montreal, pp. 1–13. https://doi.org/10.1145/3173574.3174040

McPherson, M., Smith-Lovin, L., Cook, J.M. (2001). Birds of a feather: Homophily in social networks. Annual Review of Sociology. https://doi.org/10.1146/annurev.soc.27.1.415

Purwandari, B., Ramadhan, A., Phusavat, K., Hidayanto, A.N., Husniyyah, A.F., Faozi, F.H., Wijaya, N.H., Saputra, R.H. (2022). The Effect of Interaction between Followers and Influencers on Intention to Follow Travel Recommendations from Influencers in Indonesia Based on Follower-Influencer Experience and Emotional Dimension. Information (Switzerland). https://doi.org/10.3390/info13080384

Ryu, Sann, Park, Jung Kun. (2020). The effects of benefit-driven commitment on usage of social media for shopping and positive word-of-mouth. Journal of Retailing and Consumer Services. https://doi.org/10.1016/j.jretconser.2020.102094

Song, H.J., Kim, M.C., Choe, Y. (2019). Structural relationships among mega-event experiences, emotional responses, and satisfaction: focused on the 2014 Incheon Asian Games. Current Issues in Tourism. https://doi.org/10.1080/13683500.2018.1462310

Venkatesh, V., James, Y.L., Thong, X.X. (2012). Consumer Acceptance and Use of Information Technology: Extending the Unified Theory of Acceptance and Use of Technology. MIS Quarterly 36, 157–178. https://doi.org/10.2307/41410412

Wang, X.W., Cao, Y.M., Park, C. (2019). The relationships among community experience, community commitment, brand attitude, and purchase intention in social media. International Journal of Information Management. https://doi.org/10.1016/j.ijinfomgt.2019.07.018

Wang, Y., Lu, Z., Cao, P., Chu, J., Wang, H., Wattenhofer, R. (2022). How Live Streaming Changes Shopping Decisions in E-commerce: A Study of Live Streaming Commerce. Computer Supported Cooperative Work: CSCW: An International Journal. https://doi.org/10.1007/s10606-022-09439-2

Wongkitrungrueng, A., Assarut, N. (2020). The role of live streaming in building consumer trust and engagement with social commerce sellers. Journal of Business Research. https://doi.org/10.1016/j.jbusres.2018.08.032

Xu, L., Yan, X., Zhang, Z. (2019). Research on the Causes of the "Tik Tok" App Becoming Popular and the Existing Problems. Journal of Advanced Management Science. https://doi.org/10.18178/joams.7.2.59-63

Xu, P., Cui, B.J., Lyu, B. (2022). Influence of Streamer's Social Capital on Purchase Intention in Live Streaming E-Commerce. Frontiers in Psychology. https://doi.org/10.3389/fpsyg.2021.748172

Xu, X., Wu, J.H., Li, Q. (2020). What drives consumer shopping behavior in live streaming commerce? Journal of Electronic Commerce Research.

Zhang, Wenyao, Zhang, Wei, Daim, Tugrul U., Wang, Ye. (2023). Investigating consumer purchase intention in online social media marketing: A case study of Tiktok. Technology in Society 74. https://doi.org/10.1016/j.techsoc.2023.102289

Zheng, R., Li, Z., Na, S. (2022). How customer engagement in the live-streaming affects purchase intention and customer acquisition, E-tailer's perspective. Journal of Retailing and Consumer Services. https://doi.org/10.1016/j.jretconser.2022.103015

EMOTIONAL ATTACHMENT AND THE PURCHASE INTENTION OF SOCIAL MEDIA BRAND FOLLOWERS: A SOCIO-TECHNICAL APPROACH

Bima Sudarsono Adinsa, Karimah, Samuel Raja Panggabean, Shabiqa Amani,
Zidan Amukti Rajendra and Annisa Monicha Sari
Faculty of Computer Science, Universitas Indonesia
Kampus UI Depok, 16424, Indonesia

ABSTRACT

In the age of social media, brands are constantly seeking ways to engage with and influence followers' behavior. Social media platforms enable brands to create diverse content, affecting followers and potential followers, enabling them to customize marketing strategies and increase engagement. One significant factor in determining followers' purchase intention is the satisfaction of followers and their emotional attachment to social media brands. This study aims to investigate the influence of social media brand followers' emotional attachment and satisfaction on purchase intention using a socio-technical system approach. Data from a survey of 244 followers of a social media brand's account were analyzed using PLS-SEM. The finding indicates that the stronger emotional attachments and follower satisfaction, the more likely the follower's intention to purchase from a social media brand. According to the study's findings, social media brands may benefit by adjusting marketing strategies by focusing on socio and technical characteristics such as the value of information provided, personalization, entertaining content, and brand credibility.

KEYWORDS

Social Media Brand, Socio-Technical System, Emotional Attachment, Satisfaction, Social Commerce, Purchase Intention

1. INTRODUCTION

Social media has become an essential platform for brands to communicate with their followers and advertise their products or services in recent years (Beukeboom, Kerkhof, & Vries, 2015) which enable brands to leverage a diverse range of content various types such as visual, text, and multimedia content, that might affect both current and potential followers (Penttinen, 2023), such as acquiring new follower (Smit, Bronner, & Tolboom, 2007), creating immersive experiences for followers, build a strong image and communicate their values in an engaging way.

Social media allows accounts to follow each other, making it inevitable for a brand to be followed by many individuals. Interactions between a brand and its followers, such as responding to comments, resolving issues, and involving a large user base, enhance their relationship (Hudson, Huang, Roth, & Madden, 2016). As a result, it is critical to understand what factors drive follower participation in social media and the impact it causes (McClure & Seock, 2020). The purpose of this research is to examine how emotional attachment and satisfaction influence followers' purchase intentions towards social media brands using socio-technical system approach.

(Wan, Lu, Wang, & Zhao, 2017) adopted the socio-technical approach to explain users' willingness to donate to social media content creators; (Shen, Zhao, Fan, & Buhalis, 2022) exploring the role emotional attachment on viewers' purchase intention; (C. Y. Li & Fang, 2019) predicting continued intention toward mobile branded apps based on satisfaction and attachment theory; (Santini, Ladeira, & Pinto, 2020) explore follower emotional attachment, which has been demonstrated to offer significant value for firms, directly influencing corporate performance and behavioral intention. However, no research has been conducted to investigate the effect of follower satisfaction and emotional attachment on purchase intention using a socio-technical approach to social media brand. The current study will explore social system (identification, information value, interaction), and technical system (entertainment, personalization, credibility) influence follower' emotional attachment and satisfaction toward purchase intention. Attachment theory helps in understanding the effect of emotional attachment on purchase intention through the technical system. Additionally, follower satisfaction will be examined using a technical system in relation to purchase intention. The findings of this study will contribute to both theoretical and practical implications.

2. THEORETICAL BACKGROUND

2.1 Socio-Technical Approach

An initial objective of the socio-technical approach was to provide a comprehensive understanding of organizations from both a social and technical standpoint (Trist, E.L., Higgin, G.W., Murray, H., Pollock, 1963). It emphasizes that a successful organization is the result of a combination of social and technical factors (Krotov, 2015). A socio-technical approach has been commonly used to study consumer behavior in online communities and social media in recent years (X. Zhang, Wu, & Liu, 2019); social shopping website consumers' purchase intentions were investigated from a socio-technical perspective (X. Hu, Huang, Zhong, Davison, & Zhao, 2016). In their study, both technical and social factors affected the consumers of a social shopping website.

2.2 Attachment Theory

The theory of attachment was developed to explain the interpersonal bonds that form between individuals and specific targets (Bowlby, 1979). When someone forms an attachment to a particular person or object, it influences how they allocate their emotional, cognitive, and behavioral resources towards that target (J.G. Holmes, 2000). Attachment leads to strong motivations and behaviors, such as a desire to maintain physical proximity and a willingness to protect and invest cognitive and financial resources in the attachment target (Whan Park, Maclnnis, Priester, Eisingerich, & Lacobucci, 2010). In early studies on attachment, the desire to form an emotional bond with a specific target was seen as a fundamental need (Mary D. Salter Ainsworth, Mary C. Blehar, 2015). (Wan et al., 2017) and (Fedorikhin, Park, & Thomson, 2008) concur that emotional attachment can result in behaviors that are advantageous for a brand, such as brand loyalty.

3. RESEARCH MODEL AND HYPOTHESIS

In the present study, we examined socio-technical system and attachment theory to explain the effect of followers' engagement on purchase intention of a brand on social media. In Figure 1, our research model is shown. Next, we define the research hypothesis and discuss the constructs' theoretical foundations.

3.1 Social Systems

The social system refers to the relations among people and their characteristics such as attitude, value, and abilities. In this study, we identified three constructs, namely identification, interaction, and information value.

Identification is a cognitive evaluation of the level of similarity between the self and a target group, organization, or person (Wan et al., 2017). Identification with a brand will boost support and commitment to that brand because people tend to pick activities that are consistent with essential components of their identities and support brand that represent those identities (Brown, Barry, Dacin, & Gunst, 2005). The level of social media brand's ability to represent followers' self-images, aspirations, interests, and personalities will be used in this study to explore how identification affects emotional attachment. The more followers feel that their image is represented by the social media brand, the emotional attachment of followers to the social media brand will also increase.

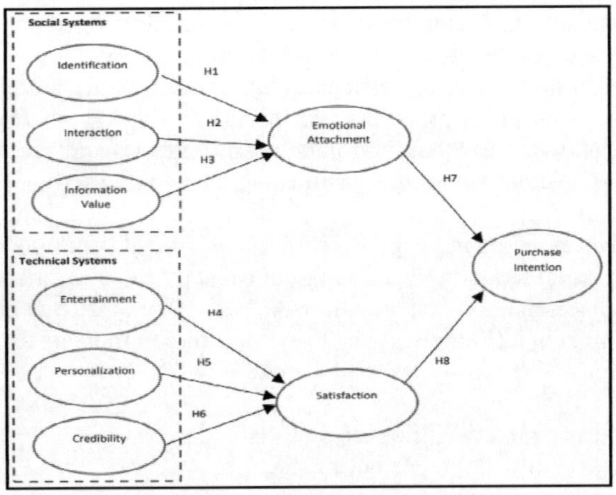

Figure 1. Research Model

Customer-brand interactions can predict consumer commitment to paying high prices and repurchasing goods or services from a brand, as well as help generate brand attachment (Lin, Chen, & Hung, 2011). This study aims to evaluate the impact of social media brand interaction on emotional attachment by examining its ability to make followers feel comfortable. The more followers feel that they can interact with the social media brands and are involved in activities organized by the social media brands, the emotional attachment of followers to the social media brands will also increase.

When researchers examine consumers' or users' choices of a good or service, they often focus on perceived value, a well-established concept. It is one of the most crucial variables in forecasting the attitudes and actions of customers (B. Hu, Liu, & Yan, 2023). Scholars have characterized perceived value in several ways since the construct was first presented, such as a multidimensional construct or a unidimensional construct (Sánchez-Fernández & Iniesta-Bonillo, 2007). According (Sheth, Newman, & Gross, 1991) suggested that the multidimensional perceptive is composed of five dimensions: functional, emotional, social, conditional, and epistemic (Sheth et al., 1991). Information value is a functional value of perceived value involving user perceptions of obtaining knowledge, experience, and services from content on social media (Wan et al., 2017). When followers feel they get high information value from the knowledge or services provided by a content creator, they will follow the content creator and build long-term relationships to improve their experience and get more knowledge, innovative information, or interesting news. The more followers feel they have gained new knowledge, experience and good service from the social media brand, the emotional attachment of followers to the social media brands will also increase.

According to (X. Zhang et al., 2019), the primary predictor of social media use is entertainment, which assesses how much social media can make users feel satisfied and help them pass the time. In this study, the impact of entertainment on satisfaction will be investigated through the extent to which social media brands may bring its users comfort and delight. The amount of satisfaction consumers has with utilizing social media can be influenced by social media's capacity to offer entertainment (Gan & Li, 2018). In the context of this study, as followers become happier and more pleased with a social media brand, their satisfaction with the brand will rise. Therefore, we hypothesize the following:

H1. Identification has a positive influence on emotional attachment.
H2. Interaction has a positive influence on emotional attachment.
H3. Information value has a positive influence on emotional attachment.
H4. Entertainment has a positive influence on satisfaction.

3.2 Technical Systems

The technical system consists of the tools, techniques, procedures, and devices that users utilize to complete activities in social media (Pasmore, Francis, Haldeman, & Shani, 1982). In this study, we identified three constructs, namely entertainment, personalization, and credibility.

Platforms give consumers relevant recommendations that are specifically tailored to meet their unique needs and preferences (Komiak & Benbasat, 2006) in order to leave a positive impression (H. Zhang, Lu, Gupta, & Zhao, 2014). In this study, the efficiency of a social media brands in communicating the unique requirements and preferences of its followers will be used to assess how personalization affects customer satisfaction. The more followers feel that their personal preferences and needs are known by the social media brands, the followers' satisfaction with the social media brands will also increase.

Credibility is a measurement of a message spreader's traits toward the message recipient that have a favorable impact on the degree of message acceptance (Pornpitakpan, 2004). In this study, we analyze the impact of credibility on satisfaction by examining the capacity of social media brands to maintain followers' faith in their commitments, behavior, and attention. A user's level of trust in an online platform can affect how satisfied they are with utilizing it (Pornpitakpan, 2004). The more followers feel social media brands is credible, the followers' satisfaction with the social media brands will also increase. Therefore, we hypothesize the following:

H5. Personalization has a positive influence on satisfaction.

H6. Credibility has a positive influence on satisfaction.

3.3 Followers' Emotional Attachment

Emotional attachment is described as a bond and relationship between followers and social media brand that demonstrates the followers desire to uphold and improve their relationship with the social media brand (Wan et al., 2017). This study investigates the impact of emotional attachment on purchase intention by looking at how social media brands may connect with their followers and encourage them to invest time and money. (Wan et al., 2017) & (Thomson et al., 2005) concur that emotional attachment can result in behaviors that are advantageous for a brand, such as brand loyalty. The more followers feel they have a connection with the social media brands, the purchase intention of followers on the social media brands will also increase.

Satisfaction is characterized as a consumer's emotional evaluation following the purchase of a brand's goods and can be classified as either positive, negative, or neutral (C. Y. Li & Fang, 2019). The level of followers' satisfaction with the experiences and services offered by social media brand to their followers will be used in this study to assess the effect of satisfaction on purchase intention. Users will plan to continue using a product or service when they feel satisfied after utilizing it (C. Y. Li & Fang, 2019). The more satisfied followers are with the social media brands, the more their followers' buying intentions on the social media brands will also increase. Therefore, we hypothesize the following:

H7. Emotional attachment has a positive influence on purchase intention.

H8. Satisfaction has a positive influence on purchase intention.

4. RESEARCH METHODOLOGY

4.1 Data Collection

In the present study, a quantitative technique is applied. A questionnaire and a Likert scale were used to collect data. SEM (Structural equation modeling) is a statistical technique for data processing and analysis.

We collected data social media users in Indonesia who follow a social media brand. A Likert scale of 1 (strongly disagree) to 5 (totally agree) was used to measure participants' agreement or disagreement. To reach respondents widely, the publication was distributed via online media from 12 December 2022 to 21 December 2022. We stopped data collection after obtaining 266 samples, exceeding the 200 samples that are the minimum number of samples required for SEM analysis. After the questionnaire was filled out, the authors interpreted and analyzed the results.

4.2 Demography

To meet study requirements, the authors examined questionnaire respondents if they had a social media account and if they were a follower of a social media brand's account. The authors received 244 respondents valid from 266 respondents based on the outcomes of data collection via a questionnaire on Google Forms.

Table 1. Respondent's characteristics

Characteristic	*Observation*	*Freq.*	*%*	*Characteristic*	*Observation*	*Freq.*	*%*
Age	< 17 Tahun	4	1.6%	Position	Student/college student	154	63.1%
	17 - 25 Tahun	162	66.4%		Private employee	43	17.6%
	26 - 35 Tahun	21	8.6%		Government employee	9	3.7%
	36 - 45 Tahun	9	3.7%		Entrepreneur	16	6.6%
	> 45 Tahun	48	19.7%		Others	22	9%
Gender	Male	100	41%	Monthly income (IDR)	< 1 million	34	13.9%
	Female	144	59%		1 - 5 million	81	33.2%
Education level	Post-secondary and below	8	2%		5 – 10 million	65	26.6%
	Diploma	4	1.6%		10 – 15 million	19	7.8%
	Undergraduate	211	86.5%		15 – 20 million	15	6.1%
	Postgraduate level	18	7.4%		> 20 million	30	12.3%
	Others	3	1.3%				

5. RESULT

5.1 Measurement Model

First, measurement model testing is performed to determine how the theoretical framework and model employed represent the real data, as well as the consistency of the data, to provide correct SEM calculation results. Several criteria for performing the test are indicators of reliability, internal consistency reliability, discriminant validity, and convergent validity (Urbach & Ahlemann, 2010). The loading factor value indicates indicator reliability. The absolute value of the loading factor must be greater than 0.70 (Sleuwaegen, 1992). The values of Cronbach's Alpha (CA), composite reliability (CR), and Average Variance Extracted (AVE) indicate internal consistency. Trustworthy model values of CA> 0.8, 0.9, or 0.7, CR 0.7, and AVE value 0.5 are required. The loading factor and AVE values show convergent validity. Adequate AVE values are more than 0.5 (Urbach & Ahlemann, 2010). The results of AVE, CR and CA calculation for each variable shown in Table 2.

5.2 Hypothesis Testing

In this study, hypothesis is tested using the two-tailed test method by comparing P values at a significance threshold of 0.05, with the hypothesis being rejected if the P value is more than 0.05. Test results shown in Table 3, there are eight hypotheses, all of which are accepted. Aside from that, all the original sample values are positive, and all the P values are less than 0.05, indicating that all pairings of variables have a statistically positive influence.

Table 2. The value of CA, CR, and AVE

	CA	CR (rho_a)	CR (rho_c)	AVE
Credibility	0.812	0.828	0.888	0.725
Emotional Attachment	0.848	0.852	0.908	0.767
Entertainment	0.831	0.834	0.898	0.746
Identification	0.921	0.924	0.944	0.808
Information Value	0.838	0.847	0.902	0.754
Interaction	0.841	0.866	0.903	0.756
Personalization	0.733	0.739	0.848	0.650
Purchase Intention	0.842	0.843	0.894	0.679
Satisfaction	0.825	0.831	0.895	0.740

Figure 2 summarizes the findings. Overall, the explained variances of the dependent variable were quite high (55% for satisfaction, 46% for emotional attachment, and 44% for purchase intention), indicating that the model had adequate predictive ability. Socio-technical systems theory and attachment theory provide useful insights into behavior of a social media brands followers purchase intention.

Table 3. The result of structural testing

Hypothesis & Structural path	Original Sample	T Stat	P values	Result
(H1): Identification -> Emotional Attachment	0,167	3.976	0.000	Accepted
(H2): Interaction -> Emotional Attachment	0,260	6.338	0.000	Accepted
(H3): Information Value -> Emotional Attachment	0,150	3.558	0.000	Accepted
(H4): Entertainment -> Satisfaction	0,106	2.492	0.013	Accepted
(H5): Personalization -> Satisfaction	0,218	5.537	0.000	Accepted
(H6): Credibility -> Satisfaction	0,283	7.294	0.000	Accepted
(H7): Emotional Attachment -> Purchase Intention	0,229	4.802	0.000	Accepted
(H8): Satisfaction -> Purchase Intention	0,285	6.998	0.000	Accepted

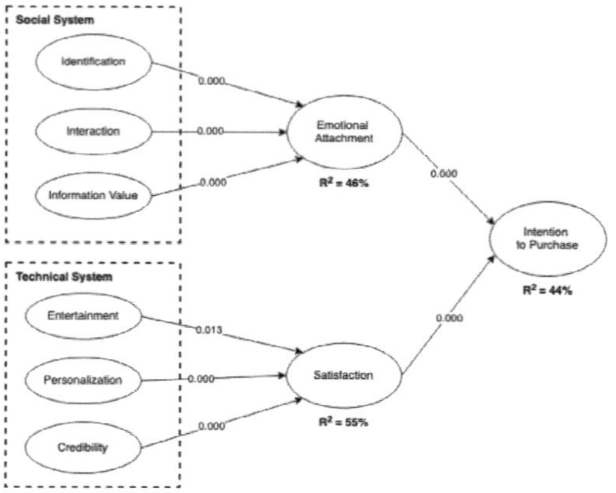

Figure 2. Results for the proposed model

6. DISCUSSION

The SmartPLS study accepted eight hypotheses, indicating the model effectively explains factors influencing purchase intention towards social media brand followers, with interesting findings.

First, we discovered that applying socio-technical system approach to describe follower purchase intention behavior would be beneficial. Second, utilizing attachment theory, we discovered that followers' emotional attachment is dependent on the social system of the social media brand. For example, when followers believe they have something in common with the social media brand they follow (Shen et al., 2022), this affects the follower's long-term relationship with the social media brand (Wan et al., 2017), resulting in followers to become psychologically (emotionally) attached as well as care about the social media brand, and are willing to put in a greater effort, and actively engage with the brand. This has an indirect effect on social media brand followers' purchasing intentions. Social media brands that offer valuable information to their followers increase their emotional attachment, leading to increased emotional attachment and increased intention to make purchases. In addition, interaction between followers and a brand, such as receiving a quick response to a question posed by a follower on the social media brand, will increase the follower's attachment with the social media brands (X. Zhang et al., 2019) and indirectly influence purchase intention on the social media brand that they follow (Wan et al., 2017)

Third, we fill a gap in the study of follower purchase intention on social media brands by investigating follower satisfaction with a social media brand through its technological system. We discovered an intriguing fact: Social media brand content that is entertaining and accessible at any time and location increases followers' satisfaction and indirectly influences their purchase intention towards the brand. (C. Y. Li & Fang, 2019). Furthermore, social media brands that offer personalized information to their followers can enhance their satisfaction and potentially influence their purchase intention. Moreover, brand's credibility, including its ability to deliver on promises, indirectly influences follower satisfaction and purchase intention. A larger brand's credibility leads to more satisfied followers and increased intention to purchase through social media.

7. CONCLUSION AND IMPLICATION

This study offers multiple theoretical and practical contributions. First, earlier research used attachment theory to investigate purchase intention behavior in the context of donations to content creators utilizing a socio-technical system (Wan et al., 2017), short form video addiction (X. Zhang et al., 2019), using attachment theory and satisfaction on continuous intention on mobile branded apps using Expectation confirmation model (C.-Y. Li, 2019), However, a socio-technical approach was not used to examine how satisfied followers are with purchase intention on social media brands. Second, all hypotheses in this study are accepted, which indicates that social media brands must pay attention to social system factors which influence emotional attachment to the brand; and technical system factors which influence follower satisfaction with the brand, to increase purchase intention. The stronger emotional attachments and follower satisfaction, the more likely the follower tends to decide on the purchase on the social media brands. According to the findings of this study, it may be beneficial for social media brands to adjust marketing strategies by focusing on characteristics such as the value of information provided, personalization, content that is both entertaining and accessible to followers at any time, and brand credibility.

8. LIMITATION AND FUTURE WORK

Most of the respondents in this study are students, and it was conducted in Indonesia. Future research could add cross-cultural factors and demography to improve the generalizability of the findings. Other characteristics, such as brand popularity, sociability, and others, might be considered in future study in a socio-technical approach. Third, as the research context, one of the most popular social media brands is chosen. As different social media brand may provide different outcomes, future study should take into consideration other social media brand.

ACKNOWLEDGEMENT

This work was supported by Universitas Indonesia under PUTI Q1 grant No. NKB-293/UN2.RST/HKP.05.00/2023. We gratefully thank Universitas Indonesia for the support.

REFERENCES

Beukeboom, C. J., Kerkhof, P., & Vries, M. De. (2015). ScienceDirect Does a Virtual Like Cause Actual Liking? How Following a Brand ' s Facebook Updates Enhances Brand Evaluations and Purchase Intention. *Journal of Interactive Marketing*, *32*, 26–36. https://doi.org/10.1016/j.intmar.2015.09.003

Bowlby, J. (1979). The Making and Breaking of Affectional Bonds.

Brown, T. J., Barry, T. E., Dacin, P. A., & Gunst, R. F. (2005). Spreading the word: Investigating antecedents of consumers' positive word-of-mouth intentions and behaviors in a retailing context. *Journal of the Academy of Marketing Science*, *33*(2), 123–138. https://doi.org/10.1177/0092070304268417

Fedorikhin, A., Park, C. W., & Thomson, M. (2008). Beyond fit and attitude: The effect of emotional attachment on consumer responses to brand extensions. *Journal of Consumer Psychology*, *18*(4), 281–291. https://doi.org/10.1016/j.jcps.2008.09.006

Gan, C., & Li, H. (2018). Understanding the effects of gratifications on the continuance intention to use WeChat in China: A perspective on uses and gratifications. *Computers in Human Behavior*, *78*, 306–315. https://doi.org/10.1016/j.chb.2017.10.003

Hu, B., Liu, Y. li, & Yan, W. (2023). Should I scan my face? The influence of perceived value and trust on Chinese users' intention to use facial recognition payment. *Telematics and Informatics*, *78*(February). https://doi.org/10.1016/j.tele.2023.101951

Hu, X., Huang, Q., Zhong, X., Davison, R. M., & Zhao, D. (2016). The influence of peer characteristics and technical features of a social shopping website on a consumer's purchase intention. *International Journal of Information Management*, *36*(6), 1218–1230. https://doi.org/10.1016/j.ijinfomgt.2016.08.005

Hudson, S., Huang, L., Roth, M. S., & Madden, T. J. (2016). The influence of social media interactions on consumer-brand relationships: A three-country study of brand perceptions and marketing behaviors. *International Journal of Research in Marketing*, *33*(1), 27–41. https://doi.org/10.1016/j.ijresmar.2015.06.004

Holmes, J.G. (2000). Social relationships: the nature and function of relational schemas,. *European Journal of Social Psychology*.

Komiak, S. Y. X., & Benbasat, I. (2006). ^^ Uldl I C- ^ I l \ f Research Article The Effects of Personalization and Familiarity on Trust and Adoption of Recommendation Agents1. *MIS Quarterly*, *30*(4), 941–960.

Krotov, V. (2015). Critical success factors in m -learning: A socio-technical perspective. *Communications of the Association for Information Systems*, *36*(January 2015), 105–126. https://doi.org/10.17705/1cais.03606

Li, C.-Y. (2019). How social commerce constructs influence customers' social shopping intention? An empirical study of a social commerce website. *Technological Forecasting and Social Change*, *144*, 282–294. https://doi.org/10.1016/j.techfore.2017.11.026

Li, C. Y., & Fang, Y. H. (2019). Predicting continuance intention toward mobile branded apps through satisfaction and attachment. *Telematics and Informatics*, *43*(151), 101248. https://doi.org/10.1016/j.tele.2019.101248

Lin, Y.-T., Chen, S.-C., & Hung, C.-S. (2011). The impacts of brand equity, brand attachment, product involvement and repurchase intention on bicycle users. *African Journal of Business Management*, *5*(14), 5910–5919. https://doi.org/10.5897/AJBM10.862

Mary D. Salter Ainsworth, Mary C. Blehar, E. (2015). *Patterns of attachment: A psychological study of the strange situation*. Pysicology Press.

McClure, C., & Seock, Y. K. (2020). The role of involvement: Investigating the effect of brand's social media pages on consumer purchase intention. *Journal of Retailing and Consumer Services*, *53*(September 2018), 101975. https://doi.org/10.1016/j.jretconser.2019.101975

Pasmore, W., Francis, C., Haldeman, J., & Shani, A. (1982). Sociotechnical Systems: A North American Reflection on Empirical Studies of the Seventies. *Human Relations*, *35*(12), 1179–1204. https://doi.org/10.1177/001872678203501207

Penttinen, V. (2023). Hi, I'm taking over this account! Leveraging social media takeovers in fostering consumer-brand relationships. *Journal of Business Research*, *165*, 114030. https://doi.org/https://doi.org/10.1016/j.jbusres.2023.114030

Pornpitakpan, C. (2004). The Persuasiveness of Source Credibility: A Critical Review of Five Decades' Evidence. *Journal of Applied Social Psychology*, *34*(2), 243–281. https://doi.org/10.1111/j.1559-1816.2004.tb02547.x

Sánchez-Fernández, R., & Iniesta-Bonillo, M. Á. (2007). The concept of perceived value: A systematic review of the research. *Marketing Theory*, *7*(4), 427–451. https://doi.org/10.1177/1470593107083165

Santini, F. D. O., Ladeira, W. J., & Pinto, D. C. (2020). Customer engagement in social media : a framework and meta-analysis, 1211–1228.

Shen, H., Zhao, C., Fan, D. X. F., & Buhalis, D. (2022). International Journal of Hospitality Management The effect of hotel livestreaming on viewers ' purchase intention : Exploring the role of parasocial interaction and emotional engagement. *International Journal of Hospitality Management*, *107*(November 2021), 103348. https://doi.org/10.1016/j.ijhm.2022.103348

Sheth, J. N., Newman, B. I., & Gross, B. L. (1991). Why we buy what we buy: A theory of consumption values. *Journal of Business Research*, *22*(2), 159–170. https://doi.org/https://doi.org/10.1016/0148-2963(91)90050-8

Sleuwaegen, L. (1992). Advances in international marketing. *International Journal of Research in Marketing*, *9*(4), 319–323. https://doi.org/10.1016/0167-8116(92)90003-4

Smit, E., Bronner, F., & Tolboom, M. (2007). Brand relationship quality and its value for personal contact. *Journal of Business Research*, *60*(6), 627–633. https://doi.org/10.1016/j.jbusres.2006.06.012

Trist, E.L., Higgin, G.W., Murray, H., Pollock, A. B. (1963). *Organizational Choice: Capabilities of Groups at the Coal Face under Changing Technologies.* London: Tavistock Publications.

Urbach, N., & Ahlemann, F. (2010). Structural equation modeling in information systems research using partial least squares. *Journal of Information Technology Theory and Application*, *11*(2), 5–40. https://doi.org/10.1037/0021-9010.90.4.710

Wan, J., Lu, Y., Wang, B., & Zhao, L. (2017). How attachment influences user's willingness to donate to content creators in social media : A socio-technical systems perspective. *Information & Management*, *54*(7), 837–850. https://doi.org/10.1016/j.im.2016.12.007

Whan Park, C., Maclnnis, D. J., Priester, J., Eisingerich, A. B., & Lacobucci, D. (2010). Brand attachment and brand attitude strength: Conceptual and empirical differentiation of two critical brand equity drivers. *Journal of Marketing*, *74*(6), 1–17. https://doi.org/10.1509/jmkg.74.6.1

Zhang, H., Lu, Y., Gupta, S., & Zhao, L. (2014). What motivates customers to participate in social commerce? The impact of technological environments and virtual customer experiences. *Information & Management*, *51*(8), 1017–1030. https://doi.org/10.1016/j.im.2014.07.005

Zhang, X., Wu, Y., & Liu, S. (2019). Exploring short-form video application addiction: Socio-technical and attachment perspectives. *Telematics and Informatics*, *42*(April), 101243. https://doi.org/10.1016/j.tele.2019.101243

ETHICAL USE OF ARTIFICIAL INTELLIGENCE (AI) AMONG STUDENTS: DRIVING FACTORS FROM DEONTOLOGICAL AND TELEOLOGICAL PERSPECTIVES

Danang Widyorukmantiyoro Arissetyanto Soehardjo, Steven Samuel Hutapea, Nathanael Horasi, Al Ghifari Enerza Sentanu, Luthfi Alnazhary and Pramitha Dwi Larasati
Faculty of Computer Science, University of Indonesia
Kampus UI depok, Depok, 16418, Indoensia

ABSTRACT

The application of artificial intelligence (AI) in education is growing rapidly and significantly, especially with ChatGPT, an AI-based chatbot system that can interact with humans naturally. ChatGPT is an application that can solve problems users need to be enjoyable and more academic. The use of ChatGPT to add information and assist users is excellent and looks perfect. However, for some fields, especially education, the presence of ChatGPT is considered a threat. With ChatGPT, students can efficiently complete assigned tasks without having to think and do analysis. If the use of ChatGPT is to search for information and increase insight, it improves students' understanding and ability to analyze and solve the problems they face. The presence of ChatGPT makes it easier for students to complete their assignments instantly using ChatGPT's help without having to bother looking for information and carrying out analysis first. This research aims to assess how ethical the use of ChatGPT is among students in completing their assignments. The research method was carried out using qualitative methods by distributing questionnaires. There are nine hypotheses arranged into 30 research instruments. Processing of research instruments was carried out using SmartPLS. There were 308 respondents for this research; after calculations, the results were that moral obligation and justice did not affect subjective norms, perceived behavioral control did not affect the ethical use of AI, and perceived behavioral control did not affect the unethical use of AI intention.

KEYWORDS

Artificial Intelligence, ChatGPT, Ethical of Use Intention, Unethical of Use Intention

1. INTRODUCTION

The development and application of Artificial Intelligence (AI) in education is one of society's technological development. This technology significantly changes various fields, especially in the educational area. Despite the rapid and increasing development of AI, the ethical use of AI in education does not yet have a definite policy and ethics (Becker, 2018). These ethics should align with ethics related to what is available in designing, using, and implementing reliable and trustworthy AI in education (De Cerqueira, 2022). ChatGPT is an artificial intelligence-based software that is currently widely used. ChatGPT itself is a Deep Learning that is used to build a system that answers naturally. This model is based on Natural Language Processing (NLP) technology and uses a transformer architecture to learn human language patterns from existing data. The use of ChatGPT is an exciting topic to discuss. Considering that excitement is widely used as a tool for searching for information and providing solutions to its users' needs. It can be seen since its launch on November 30, 2022. It was recorded that there were up to 1 million users within five days of its launch. This figure continues to increase; in January, there were 100 million users, and the following month, the site was visited more than 1 billion times. The ChatGPT users discussed this time are students who use it to complete their assignments (Reidenbach, 1988). That can happen because this application can be used very quickly and has adequate capabilities to answer the various questions given (Ortiz, 2023).

In the world of ethics, teleology can be interpreted as a moral consideration of the merits and demerits of an action. A significant difference appears between teleology and deontology. We can see this in simple terms from the differences in the two principles. In deontology, we will look at the principle of right and wrong. However, that is not the basis of teleology, but good and evil. When law plays an essential role in deontology, this does not mean that teleology ignores it. Teleology understands what is right and what is wrong, but it is not the final measure (Reidenbach, 1988). Therefore, the author wants to research deontological and teleological perspectives on using ChatGPT by students. This research was carried out to find ethical uses of AI, which are still few to be implemented. Several similar studies that have been carried out include a paper entitled "University Students' Perceptions About Artificial Intelligence" written by Pınar Ural Keleş and Suleyman Aydın (Keles, 2021). The research found that AI has the potential to impact education positively, but there are also concerns about privacy and the ethical use of AI in education. Further research is needed to understand the impact of AI on education fully. From this research, the author will make research more focused on a teleological perspective, with research methods determined according to the research object the author will examine. This way, we can find out whether some benefits or risks can arise from using ChatGPT for use in the world of education (Britannica, 2023).

The following research is entitled "Engineering Education in the Era of ChatGPT: Promise and Pitfalls of Generative AI for Education," written by Junaid Qadir from the Department of Computer Science and Engineering, College of Engineering, Qatar University, Doha, Qatar (Qadir, 2022) This research explores how ChatGPT is used in teaching and learning activities. The analysis starts with a complete simulation of how to use ChatGPT (followed by questions and answers directly from ChatGPT without modification) to the potential that might be obtained from its use. This paper provides several solutions for using ChatGPT, namely using it carefully and having standards and community guidelines for using the chatbot. From this paper, the research team wants to develop ethical use of chatbot technology. This is important because, along with technological developments, students will have unlimited access to make it easier to do their assignments (ChatGPT). Prohibiting students from using chatbots is impossible because, according to the paper above, ChatGPT has a lot of potential to offer to all audiences (this can range from students to teachers, such as lecturers) (Keles, 2021). Therefore, a discussion is needed regarding the ethical actions that students must understand and carry out when using this technology. This aims to ensure students can use or take advantage of these technological developments while upholding ethics and morals in teaching and learning activities.

2. LITERATURE STUDY

This chapter will discuss the theoretical basis of writing, including ChatGPT and the teleological and deontological perspectives used to conduct the research.

2.1 ChatGPT

ChatGPT is a natural language processing tool driven by AI technology. ChatGPT allows you to have human-like conversations and more through the chatbot. Users can access ChatGPT via a browser by visiting chat.openai.com and creating or registering an account first. Once registered, you can immediately chat easily with ChatGPT. There are no fees for using the ChatGPT application (Nav, 2023 & Dilmegani, 2023). The principle of ChatGPT is that this model can predict the words that will be used in a sentence based on context and previous terms. This is done using language modeling techniques, where the model is trained to predict the next word in a ruling based on the earlier comments. The application is to build a chatbot system to conduct conversations with humans naturally and responsively. This chatbot can be used in various fields, such as e-commerce, customer service, and virtual assistants. ChatGPT can, of course, be used in the world of education. Teachers or lecturers can make educational material easier, according to their needs. This can be done by designing the syllabus and assessing the tested material. Teachers or lecturers can also do proofreading, grammar, writing checks, and even provide feedback. Students can also, of course, use ChatGPT in their lives. The most common activity students do is use ChatGPT to help answer questions given by lecturers. Students can also improve their understanding of the concepts and methods provided. Apart from that, students can also improve their writing skills through using ChatGPT. ChatGPT can give feedback on grammatical errors, sentence structure, diction, etc. Learning about new things can also be done using ChatGPT, such as language learning, creating creative ideas, and much more (Dignum, 2018).

2.2 Deontology and Teleology Perspective

The deontological perspective is an ethical theory that focuses on the intrinsic rightness or wrongness of an action without considering the consequences of that action. Several examples of critical ideas can be used in terms of using ChatGPT in college assignments by students. One example that can be related is the doctrine of double impact (The Doctrine of Double Effect). In the context of using ChatGPT for college assignments, this doctrine can mean that using this technology can be justified if the positive effects outweigh the adverse effects. For example, ChatGPT can help students complete assignments more efficiently and quickly, but excessive or unethical use can have negative consequences such as plagiarism (Moores, 2006 & Benjamin, 2021). Apart from that, Ross's Prima Facie Duties theory can also be connected to using ChatGPT in college assignments (Ajzen, 1991). As students, we should respect the authenticity and integrity of scientific work, so using ChatGPT to copy other people's work may conflict with this obligation. While ChatGPT may help write assignments, its use must be responsible and not violate ethical commitments (Moores, 2006).

Finally, rights-based ethics can also be linked to the use of ChatGPT. In the context of coursework, we have the right to academic freedom and fair access to information. Therefore, using ChatGPT to violate these rights may be considered unethical. As users of ChatGPT, we need to ensure that its use does not violate the rights of other students or the rights of the creator of the original work. When using ChatGPT for coursework, it is important to consider ethical aspects and ensure that its use does not violate moral obligations or the rights of others (Benjamins, 2021). Teleology comes from Greek, a combination of telos, "end," and logos, "science." It is a moral theory that takes moral obligations or obligations from what is suitable or desirable as the final goal to be achieved. Contrary to deontology, which argues that the primary standard for a morally correct action does not depend on the good or bad that results (Benjamins, 2021). Teleology is different from consequentialism. Utilitarianism can be formed from these two understandings. The difference between teleology and consequentialism lies in the emphasis of this understanding. Teleology emphasizes the end goal, whereas consequentialism focuses on the consequences of actions (Britannica, 2023). In this discussion, the teleological perspective in using ChatGPT to do college assignments is how AI can provide the final goal students want. By using ChatGPT, students can gain deeper understanding or even complete tasks with the help of ChatGPT.

3. METHODOLOGY AND RESULT

This chapter discusses the methodology used in completing the research. What is discussed is research models, research instruments, data collection, and processing.

3.1 Research Model

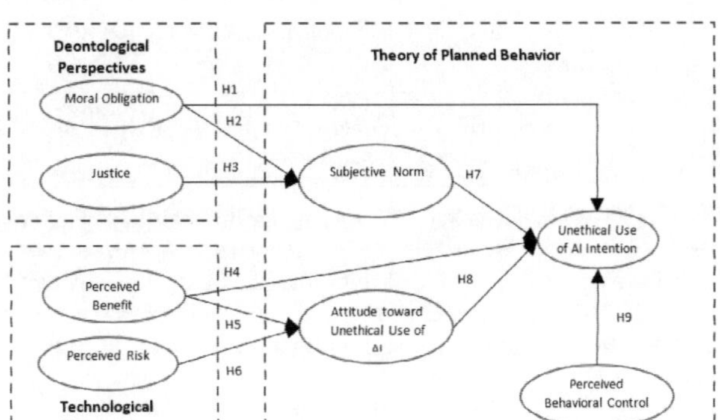

Figure 1. Research model

Figure 1 is the model used in this research. This study has nine hypotheses in total. Using the Moral Duty and Justice factors as part of the Deontological perspective, then in the technology perspective using the Perceived Benefit and Perceived Risk factors. Meanwhile, when using AI for behavior theory, the author uses subjective norms, attitudes, and unethical and behavioral control factors (Terry, 1995; Trafimow, 2002; Stephenson, 2021; Satterfield, 2004)

3.2 Research Instrument

Table 1 below is the instrument used by the author in collecting research data. The variables used include moral obligation, justice, perceived benefit, perceived risk, subjective norm, attitude toward ethical use of AI, perceived behavioral control, and ethical use of AI intention.

Table 1. Research instrument

Variabel	Defintion	Code	Instrument
Moral Obligation	The Responsibility and moral for the ethical use of AI on campus	MO1	I feel guilty if I used ChatGPT to finish my Assignment
		MO2	Using ChatGPT for the benefit of finishing my Assignment is in contradiction with my principle
		MO3	In general, the use of ChatGPT for Taska or Study is eligible.
Justice	The use of ChatGPT is not right for the Assignment	JST1	I feel it unfair to use ChatGPT to finish the Assignment
		JST2	I feel wrong when using ChatGPT to finish Assignment
		JST3	I feel inequitable when using ChatGPT to finish Assignment
Perceived Benefit	The use of ChatGPT makes the task faster	PB1	When I used ChatGPT, my grading increases
		PB2	When I used ChatGPT, my task will be faster
		PB3	When I used ChatGPT, my performance improves
Perceived Risk	Consequences for ChatGPT Used for Assignment	PR1	When I used ChatGPT, it was possible to find out
		PR2	When I used ChatGPT, that was possibly detected as plagiarism
		PR3	When I used ChatGPT, I got a reduced assessment
Subjective Norm	Can choose not to use the ChatGPT for Assignment	SBN1	When I used ChatGPT, most of my friends and lecturers would disagree
		SBN2	Most of my friends and lecturers would look down on me if I used ChatGPT
		SBN3	There is none of my friends and lecturer would be acceptable when I used ChatGPT
		SBN4	My friends think that the behavior of using ChatGPT is wrong.
Attitude Toward Ethical Use of AI	The attitude for using or not using the ChatGPT when finishing the Assignment	ATT1	I think that the behavior of using ChatGPT is not wise
		ATT2	I think that the behavior of using ChatGPT was dangerous
		ATT3	I think that the behavior of using ChatGPT was a bad idea

		ATT4	In general, I will not support the use of AI for Assignment
Perceived Behavioral Control	The behavior to control the intention to use ChatGPT to find the answer	PBC1	I easily used ChatGPT for my Assignment
		PBC2	I know how to use ChatGPT for my Assignment
		PBC3	I am capable of using ChatGPT for my Assignment
		PBC4	Using ChatGPT to do my assignments is within my control
Ethical Use of AI Intention	Intention to use or recommend the ChapGPT to finish the Assignment	ET1	I do not use ChatGPT to finish my Assignment
		ET2	I do not have a plan for using ChatGPT to finish my Assignment
		ET3	I will not recommend using ChatGPT to finish an Assignment

3.3 Data Analysis

The method used in collecting data in this research uses a survey method via an online platform, Google Forms. The questions that have been created are written on the Google Form. This data collection method uses a survey because, considering the convenience of respondents, the Google Form questionnaire is distributed to students at the Faculty of Computer Science, University of Indonesia, who are active in the 2022/2023 academic year and friends from the research team and these students are already familiar with how to fill out Google Forms so that it is easy for respondents to fill out surveys and can avoid errors in data collection. Respondents can use digital devices such as devices or laptops to access Google Forms, which will be saved automatically. This survey is online based, which means that respondents can fill out the survey anywhere and at any time so that the study's distribution is not limited to the nearest location (one area). The time can be carried out until the survey's closing date. The data that has been collected needs to be tested first for its validity and reliability. For this reason, data must be selected to achieve specific values for external loadings, such as Cronbach's alpha, composite reliability, and average variance extracted. Discriminant validity also needs to be checked using the Fornell-Larcker criteria. This check uses the SmartPLS application. With the same application, continue hypothesis testing to accept the null hypothesis, ultimately forming a new model.

4. RESULT AND DISCUSSION

This research discusses the results that have been carried out, as well as discussions related to the results and implications of the research.

4.1 Respondent Demography

Researchers obtained 308 respondents from the data collection process that had been carried out. Of all the respondents, only one person (0.3%) had never used ChatGPT. The respondents comprised 171 women (55.5%) and 137 men (44.5%). Most respondents came from Jabodetabek domiciles, 245 people (79.5%), and the rest lived outside Jabodetabek (20.5%). The age range of respondents is quite diverse. These ages are sorted from the highest to the smallest, namely 116 people aged 19-20 (37.7%), 91 people aged 21-22 (29.5%), and 52 people aged 17-18. (16.9%), Thirty-seven people aged 23-23 years (12%), ten people older than 24 years (3.2%), and at least two people aged under 17 years (0.6%)..Most of these respondents had a bachelor's degree (S1), as many as 256 people (83.1%); the remainder had a Diploma, as many as 30 people (9.7%), and master's (S2), as many as 22 people (7.1%). The field of science taken by most respondents was Social Humanities, namely 162 people (52.8%). Next was the science and technology field with 93 people (30.3%), and the last was the health field with 52 people (16.9%). Almost half of the respondents, namely 157 people (51%), use ChatGPT 3-4 times a week. The second position is 76 respondents (24.7%) using it

1-2 times a week, followed by the 3rd position, namely 52 respondents (16.9%) 5-6 times a week, and the last position is 23 respondents (7.5%) use ChatGPT more than six times a week. However, of the total respondent data, only 236 respondent data was used. This is because some data is dropped when data processing is carried out.

4.2 Hypothesis Test

After carrying out a Measurement model test to prove reliability and validity, we tested nine hypotheses previously defined in the theoretical framework. Hypothesis testing (shown in Table 2 and Table 3) uses a significance level of 0.05 for the two-tailed test. Hypothesis testing using SmartPLS will produce means, standard deviations, t-statistics, and p-values. Thus, the null hypothesis will be rejected when the p-values get a value greater than 0.05, and the idea is accepted when the p-values get a value smaller than or equal to 0.05. The evaluation results show that four hypotheses are rejected, namely H1 (Moral Obligation influences Subjective Norm), H3 (Justice influences Subjective Norm), H6 (Perceived Risk affects Attitude Toward Ethical Use of AI), and H9 (Perceived Behavioral Control influences towards the Ethical Use of AI Intention.

Table 2. Structural model testing result

Hypothesis	Path	Original sample (O)	Sample Mean (M)	Standard Deviation (STDEV)	T Statistics (|O/STDEV|)	P values	Remarks
H1	**MO -> SBN**	0,304	0,27	0,177	1,722	0,085	**Reject**
H2	**MO -> ET**	0,569	0,563	0,061	9,339	0	Accept
H3	**JST -> SBN**	-0,185	-0,135	0,177	1,044	0,297	**Reject**
H4	**PB -> ET**	-0,072	-0,07	0,028	2,543	0,011	Accept
H5	**PB -> ATT**	-0,223	-0,226	0,053	4,194	0	Accept
H6	**PR -> ATT**	-0,093	-0,106	0,065	1,43	0,153	**Reject**
H7	**SBN -> ET**	0,115	0,113	0,028	4,042	0	Accept
H8	**ATT -> ET**	0,351	0,356	0,059	5,993	0	Accept
H9	**PBC -> ET**	-0,004	-0,007	0,034	0,12	0,905	**Reject**

Table 3. Determination Coefficient Testing Result

	R-square	R-square adjusted	Notes
ATT	0,064	0,056	Strong
SBN	0,025	0,017	Poor
ET	0,866	0,863	Strong

4.3 Discussion

This research was conducted to analyze the driving factors from a deontological and teleological perspective for the ethical use of AI by students in lecture assignments. In this research, the statistical technique Variance Structural Equation Modeling (PLS-SEM) was used, and the data was analyzed using the SmartPLS application from the obtained data. The result shows P-values of less than 0.05 indicate that the hypothesis is accepted, while P-values of more than 0.05 suggest that the hypothesis is rejected. These results found that moral obligation and justice do not affect subjective norms, which means H1 and H3 are rejected. This rejection contradicts previous research where moral obligations can influence subjective norms (Gorsuch & Ortberg, 1983; Pomazal & Jaccard, 1976; Schwartz & Tessler, 1972) and contradicts previous research where it was said that justice factors influence the subjective norms of research (Reidenbach and Robin, 1990).

The research results also found that perceived behavioral control does not influence the Ethical Use of AI (ChatGPT). This result also contradicts previous research (Trafimow, Sheeran, Conner, and Finlay, 2002) that perceived behavioral control can influence the Ethical Use of AI. Makes H6 rejected. Another rejection also occurs in H9 with perceived risk, which affects attitude towards behavior, contrary to previous research (Henson, Annou, Cranfield, and Ryks, 2008). The research results show that moral obligations and perceived benefits can influence the Ethical Use of AI (CHatGPT). In the moral obligation variable, because the coefficient value is positive, namely 0.569, this means that the more students are aware of their ethical awareness or distinguishing between what is right and what is wrong, the more they will be aware not to use AI in their lecture assignments, slightly different from before for the variable perceived benefit because the coefficient value is negative, namely -0.072, it can be interpreted that the benefits obtained when using AI (ChatGPT) will make students increasingly use AI in their lecture assignments. Using bootstrap calculations, the p-value of each effect is 0.000, which is smaller than 0.05, so H2 and H4 are accepted. Then, for H5, H7, H8, and H9, it is also acceptable because the calculations that have been carried out provide p-values that are less than 0.05. This indicates that from the theory of planned behavior, only two parameters influence the ethical use of AI (ChatGpt), namely subjective norms and attitude towards the behavior. Then, moral obligation and perceived benefit influence the subjective norm and attitude towards the behavior parameters.

5. IMPLICATION AND CONCLUSION

This research implies that moral obligation and perceived benefit factors influence students in carrying out the Ethical Use of AI (ChatGPT). Then, many students use ChatGPT because many benefits can be obtained and indeed use it based on moral awareness of actions. Based on the results of this research, the University must have an essential role in providing explanations and a better understanding of the ethics of using AI to students. Universities need to carry out stricter supervision over the use of AI in assignments so that unethical use of AI does not occur, and students must also be given training and teaching regarding the ethics of using AI and how to consider the appropriate use of AI in assignments.

This research was identified to analyze factors that influence, from a deontological and teleological perspective, the ethical use of AI among students in carrying out lecture assignments. The research team also concluded that moral obligation and perceived benefit are the factors that influence students to carry out the Ethical Use of AI (Chat GPT) in lecture assignments. However, the research team concluded that several factors, such as moral obligation and justice, do not affect subjective norms, perceived behavioral control does not affect the Ethical Use of AI (Chat GPT), and perceived risk does not affect attitude toward behavior.

From the findings of this research, it is hoped that there will be further research using a larger sample and involving other variables that can influence the Ethical Use of AI (Chat GPT) among students. This research can also include variables such as affecting trust in technology, the tendency to take risks, and other factors that can influence the use of AI in college assignments. The research team also hopes that more extensive research can be carried out at the community and industrial levels to use AI with good ethics and not significantly impact society. The conclusion that can be drawn from this research is that the use of AI in lecture assignments can provide benefits and positively impact students. Still, the research team hopes the University can work together to ensure that students have good ethics and are not hurt completing assignments—student lectures

ACKNOWLEDGEMENT

I would like to acknowledge and give my warmest thanks to my supervisor (prof.nizar) who made this work possible. His/her guidance and advice carried me through all the stages of writing my project. I would also like to thank my student that we can complete this research, thanks to you. Universitas Indonesia for PUTI Q1 grant No. NKB-293/UN2.RST/HKP.05.00/2023.

REFERENCES

Ajzen, I. (1991). *The theory of planned behavior. Organizational Behavior and Human Decision Processes*, 50(2), 179–211. doi:10.1016/0749-5978(91)90020-t

Bauer, H. H., Albrecht, C., Neumann, M. M., & Haber, T. E. (2015). *Enhancing Customer Trust in E-Commerce Through Web Portals*. In Springer eBooks (pp. 57–61). Springer Nature. https://doi.org/10.1007/978-3-319-11761-4_30

Becker, S. A., Brown, M., Dahlstrom, E., Davis, A., DePaul, K., Diaz, V., & Pomerantz, J. (2018). *NMC Horizon Report: 2018 Higher Education Edition*. Educause. https://library.educause.edu/~/media/fles/library/2018/8/2018horizonreport.pdf

Benjamins, R. (2021). *A choices framework for the responsible use of AI. AI And Ethics*, 1(1), 49–53. https://doi.org/10.1007/s43681-020-00012-5

Britannica, T.2023. *Teleological ethics. Encyclopedia Britannica.* https://www.britannica.com/topic/teleological-ethics

De Cerqueira, J. a. S., De Azevedo, A. P., Leão, H. a. T., & Canedo, E. D. (2022). *Guide for Artificial Intelligence Ethical Requirements Elicitation - RE4AI Ethical Guide*. In Proceedings of the . . . Annual Hawaii International Conference on System Sciences. https://doi.org/10.24251/hicss.2022.677

Dignum, V. (2018). *Ethics in artificial intelligence: introduction to the special issue. Ethics and Information Technology*, 20(1), 1–3. https://doi.org/10.1007/s10676-018-9450-z

Dilmegani, C. (2023). *ChatGPT Education Use Cases, Benefits & Challenges in 2023*. AIMultiple. Retrieved April 21, 2023, from https://research.aimultiple.com/chatgpt-education/#:~:text=Providing%20feedback%20to%20students%3A%20ChatGPT,sentence%20structure%2C%20and%20word%20choice.

Henson, S., Annou, M., Cranfield, J., & Ryks, J. (2008). *Understanding Consumer Attitudes Toward Food Technologies in Canada*. Risk Analysis, 28(6), 1601–1617. https://doi.org/10.1111/j.1539-6924.2008.01123.

Keleş, P. U., & Aydın, S. (2021). University Students' Perceptions About Artificial Intelligence. *Shanlax International Journal of Education,* 9(S1), 212-220.

Moores, T.T., & Chang, J.C.J. (2006). *Ethical decision making in software piracy: Initial development and test of a four-component model.* MIS Quarterly, 30(1), 167-180.

Nav, N. (2023). *91 important ChatGPT Statistics & Facts for March 2023 (GPT-4, chatgpt plugins update).* Nerdy Nav. Retrieved April 11, 2023, from https://nerdynav.com/chatgpt-statistics/

Ortiz, S. (2023). *What is ChatGPT and why does it matter? Here's what you need to know*. ZDNET. Retrieved April 20, 2023, from https://www.zdnet.com/article/what-is-chatgpt-and-why-does-it-matter-heres-everything-you-need-to-know/

Qadir, J. (2022). *Engineering education in the era of chatgpt: Promise and pitfalls of Generative AI for Education*. https://doi.org/10.36227/techrxiv.21789434.v1

Reidenbach, R. E. and D. P. Robin. (1988). Some Initial Steps Toward Improving the Measurement of Ethical Evaluations of Marketing Activities. *Journal of Business Ethics* 7(11), 871–879.

Satterfield, T., Mertz, C. K., & Slovic, P. (2004). *Discrimination, Vulnerability, and Justice in the Face of Risk*. Risk Analysis, 24(1), 115–129. https://doi.org/10.1111/j.0272-4332.2004.00416.x

Sedighi, M., Van Splunter, S., Brazier, F. M. T., Van Beers, C., & Lukosch, S. (2016). *Exploration of multi-layered knowledge sharing participation: the roles of perceived benefits and costs*. Journal of Knowledge Management, 20(6), 1247–1267. https://doi.org/10.1108/jkm-01-2016-0044

Stephenson, J. (2021). WHO Offers Guidance on Use of Artificial Intelligence in Medicine. *JAMA Health Forum*, 2(7), e212467. https://doi.org/10.1001/jamahealthforum.2021.2467

Terry, D. J., & O'Leary, J. M. (1995). The theory of planned behaviour: The effects of perceived behavioural control and self-efficacy. *British Journal of Social Psychology,* 34(2), 199–220. https://doi.org/10.1111/j.2044-8309.1995.tb01058.x

The Tech Edvocate. (2018). *7 Roles for Artificial Intelligence in Education*. The Tech Edvocate, https://www.thetechedvocate.org/7-roles-for-artificial-intelligence-in-education/

Trafimow, D., Sheeran, P., Conner, M., & Finlay, K. A. (2002). Evidence that perceived behavioural control is a multidimensional construct: Perceived control and perceived difficulty. *British Journal of Social Psychology*, 41(1), 101–121. https://doi.org/10.1348/014466602165081

E-SOCIETY: A BIBLIOMETRIC PANORAMA

Gustavo Simas da Silva
Federal University of Santa Catarina (UFSC), Brazil
R. Eng. Agronômico Andrei Cristian Ferreira, s/n - Trindade, Florianópolis - SC, Brazil

ABSTRACT

Illustrating a significant growth in scholarly output and collaboration since 1989, with an average growth rate of 6.11% in scientific publications, this paper provides a panoramic bibliometric view of the field of E-Society. Anchored by key themes such as "e-commerce," "e-government," and "information and communication technologies," the research landscape has evolved, with "data privacy" and "network security" emerging as focal areas due to increased digital engagement. The review highlights the importance of advanced computational methods, such as artificial intelligence, which are poised to drive future E-Society innovations. Furthermore, the concentration of certain countries as central nodes of research activity underscores the influence of geopolitical dynamics on scientific collaboration. Despite the dominance of specific regions, there is a clear potential for growth in less represented areas, suggesting opportunities for expanding the digital inclusivity frontier. The article concludes that E-Society research is not only reflective of current societal trends but is also a critical domain for future scholarly pursuit, with the potential to inform and shape the digital transformation of global society.

KEYWORDS

E-Society, Electronic Society, Bibliometric Analysis, Digital Transformation, E-Government, Digital Economy

1. INTRODUCTION

E-Society, a term encompassing e-governance, e-communities, and other electronic elements, has become a focal point of scholarly inquiry in recent years. The concept of e-society refers to a society where e-communities engage in various domains such as e-government, e-democracy, e-business, e-learning, and e-health, utilizing information and communication technologies (ICT) to achieve common interests and goals (Pathak & Pandey, 2021). The development of e-society is reliant on the advancement of ICT to ensure interaction between participants in a more tangible way. The rise of e-society has been facilitated by the sharing economy, which has emerged as an alternative supplier of goods and services traditionally provided by long-established industries.

E-society has also been influenced by the introduction of e-business and global online commerce, representing the virtualization of the economy (Orochovska & Koshetar, 2021). E-governance has been pursued to improve the ability of public actors and institutions to administer and deliver better services to societies and their members. The impact of digitalization at the national level is referred to as the “E-economy” or digital economy, which has both opportunities and threats (Coicaud, 2016; Qiao, 2019).

The development of e-society has had far-reaching effects, including accelerating economic growth and providing more opportunities for businesses, while also creating challenges across numerous domains of society and for policymakers. Moreover, the COVID-19 pandemic has further emphasized the importance of e-society, with online digital transactions being seen as a solution for national economic recovery during the pandemic (Rauf & Thoha, 2022). The pandemic has also led to changes in social communication as a tool of social work under the influence of digitalization, highlighting the complex multilevel system in which modern society operates (Mitchuk et al, 2021).

Within this context, a bibliometric panorama of e-society research can provide a comprehensive understanding of the current knowledge sources and references in this field. Bibliometric analyses, such as those conducted on e-participation (Prastya & Nurmandi, 2021), e-mobility (Desai & Patel, 2023), and digital economy (Xia et al, 2023), offer valuable insights into the trends and critical turns of the development of global research in e-society. These analyses can help identify emerging research areas and guide future research directions. Therefore, to better understand the evolution and thematic landscape of research in this field, this paper undertakes a bibliometric analysis of the literature on E-Society. Using the Scopus database and ("e-society" OR "electronic society") as the search string, limited to conference papers, articles and book chapters, this paper employs methods to draw the current scientific landscape with tools like VOSViewer and RStudio Bibliometrix package. The study aims to map the intellectual structure and scholarly trends within this domain, analyzing citation patterns, keyword frequencies, and co-authorship networks from a multitude of academic databases. This bibliometric review not only provides a macroscopic view of the existing academic discourse but also identifies gaps in the literature, offering insights into potential future research directions.

2. E-SYSTEMS: E-SOCIETY, E-GOVERNMENT, E-ECONOMY

E-society refers to a society that is formed based on new communication technologies. The emergence of e-society has been driven by the development of ICT, which have revolutionized the way information is processed and transmitted. Rooted in the ethos of technological advancement, E-society embodies a complex scenario of virtual communities, e-governance and e-government frameworks, as well as digital economies, presenting both unprecedented opportunities and challenges (Schmid, Stanoevska-Slabeva, & Tschammer, 2001; Jayashree & Marthandan, 2010).

Within this scope, e-governance signifies a fundamental shift in public services and government operations through the integration of digital technology. This transition, marks a move from traditional governance to a more digital form, leading to increased efficiency, transparency, and citizen engagement (Bhatnagar, 2004). Digital platforms have facilitated faster service delivery and improved accessibility to government resources. However, this shift is not without challenges, several authors emphasize the digital divide's role in potentially exacerbating social inequalities, raising concerns about the equitable distribution of digital services (Addo & Senyo, 2021; Dossou et al, 2022; Hustad et al, 2019).

The rise of e-communities has redefined social interactions. Frameworks such as Castells' theory of the Network Society (2011) provide deeper understanding how online communities have transcended physical boundaries, creating spaces for people with shared interests, irrespective of geographical location. Rheingold's concept of "Virtual Communities" (2000) further elucidates how these communities, while offering a sense of belonging and identity, also present challenges in terms of privacy and online behavior norms. Additionally, the concept of AGILE-economy, based on interconnected ideas and principles, is becoming increasingly important in advanced countries, emphasizing the redistribution of investment projects according to established criteria (Voronkova, Nikitenko & Metelenko, 2022).

In essence, the dynamic nature of these "e-systems", encompassing government, community, and economy, presents a rich pool of opportunities and challenges. It invites a nuanced exploration of how digital advancements are reshaping social systems, calling for an inclusive and adaptable approach to harness its potential while mitigating associated risks.

3. THE SCIENTIFIC PANORAMA

A succinct bibliometric summary of research on E-Society from 1989 to 2023 is presented on Figure 1, showcasing a robust annual growth rate of 6.11% and a breadth of involvement with 927 authors contributing to 417 documents across 288 sources. Notably, there's a collaborative spirit in the field, evidenced by an average of 2.56 co-authors per document and a significant 19.18% rate of international co-authorship. Despite a considerable number of single-authored works (114 in total), the community demonstrates interconnectedness through 11135 references and an extensive lexicon of 1220 unique author-supplied keywords. The documents, with an average age of 10.9 years and an average citation count of 8763 per document, reflect both the field's historical depth and its ongoing relevance and influence in academic circles.

There has been a general upward trajectory in publication volume, as seen in Figure 2, punctuated by peaks and troughs, which indicate varying degrees of research activity and interest over time. The increase in publications likely mirrors the growing centrality of E-Society in both academic inquiry and societal relevance, as digital technologies become more ingrained in daily life. Such findings would be substantiated by references to literature that has charted the evolution of digital society and its impacts. Key studies might include Castells' exploration of the network society (Castells, 2011) and Mansell's discussion on digital entitlements (Mansell, 2002), as well as Van Dijk's critique of digital divide research methodologies (Van Dijk, 2006).

Figure 1. Bibliometric summary of research on E-Society.

The bibliometric network in Figure 3 visualizes the interconnectedness and evolution of key themes over time. Central to the network is the term "E-Society," denoting its foundational role, surrounded by prominent related themes like "information technology," "e-government," and "electronic commerce." The varying node sizes suggest the prevalence of each keyword, while the co-occurrence links illustrate the thematic correlations within the literature. The color gradient from blue to yellow reflects the shift in research focus, with recent literature emphasizing emerging concerns such as "data privacy" and "network security." This visualization highlights not only the multidisciplinary nature of E-Society research, drawing from technology, law, and social sciences, but also how recent years have seen a pivot towards the implications of security and privacy in the digital domain.

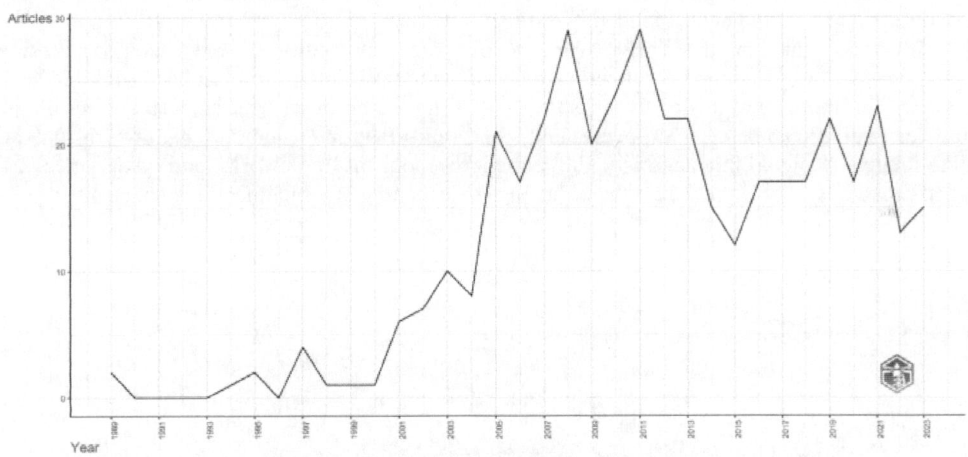

Figure 2. Annual scientific production on E-society research.

Also mapping the co-occurrence of keywords, but this time regarding average normalized citations, with the color coding representing normalized citation counts, Figure 4 presents a similar network. Again, central and large nodes like "e-society," "information technology," "e-government," "world wide web," and "electronic commerce" are indicative of well-established and core areas of E-Society research that have a substantial presence in scholarly discussions. The map indicates that publications with keywords such as “knowledge based systems", “public administration”, “china”, “innovation” and “sustainability” are well cited, revealing a high level of academic interest and recognition in these areas. Specially, the emphasis on "innovation" and "sustainability" indicates a pursuit to align E-Society development with long-term societal goals and responsible technological advancement.

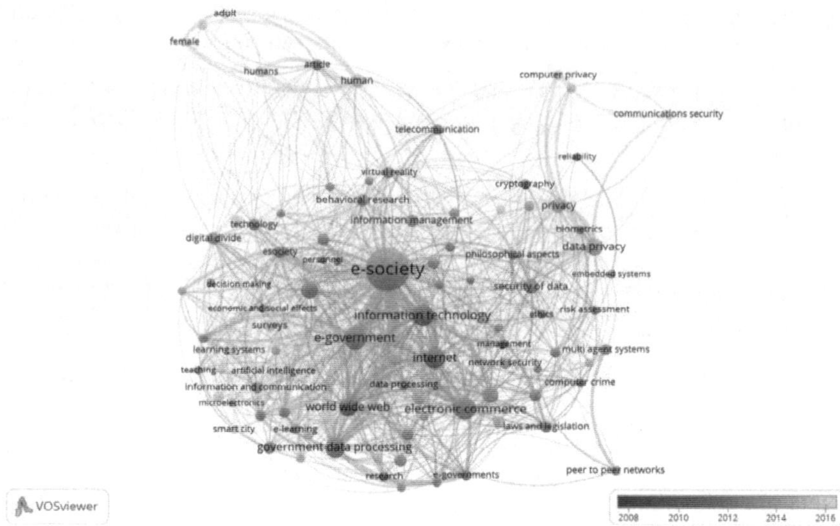

Figure 3. Keywords co-occurrence network coloured by average publication year.

In order to see the thematic evolution across the years, the bubble timeline graph in Figure 5 delineates the relative frequency of specific terms from 1989 to 2023, with the size of each bubble corresponding to the term's prevalence in articles during a given year. This analytical approach offers a narrative on how the focus of E-Society research has shifted and expanded over time.

It is observable that in the early years, terms such as "europe" and "data processing" and “telecommunication” were common, reflecting the foundational role of these technologies in the birth of E-Society. As the timeline progresses towards the 2010’s, there's an observable increase in the frequency of terms like "electronic commerce," "e-government," and "information systems". This growth underscores a broadening interest in digital interactions within commerce, societal frameworks, and governance structures. Such terms' expanding bubbles illustrate the digital age's deepening entrenchment in societal functions.

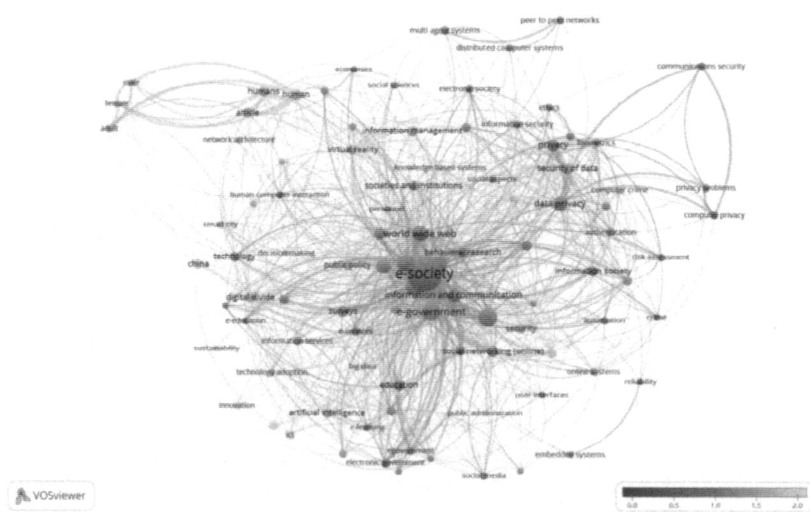

Figure 4. Keywords co-occurrence network coloured by normalized citations.

Simultaneously, the emergence and enlargement of bubbles for "network security," "data privacy," and "computer crime" through the years highlight a parallel and reactive concern with the risks associated with digital expansion, also signifying a shift in academic focus towards addressing the challenges posed by the widespread adoption of digital technologies.

Also, some cutting-edge technologies like "artificial intelligence," "machine learning," and "big data" have become increasingly significant in terms of innovation possibilities. Leveraging advanced computational methods to enhance E-Society's infrastructure and capabilities moves towards a more sophisticated, data-driven future.

Again, the specific mention of "China" as a trending topic suggests a geographical focal point in E-Society research, likely due to the country's rapid technological growth and its impact on global digital practices.

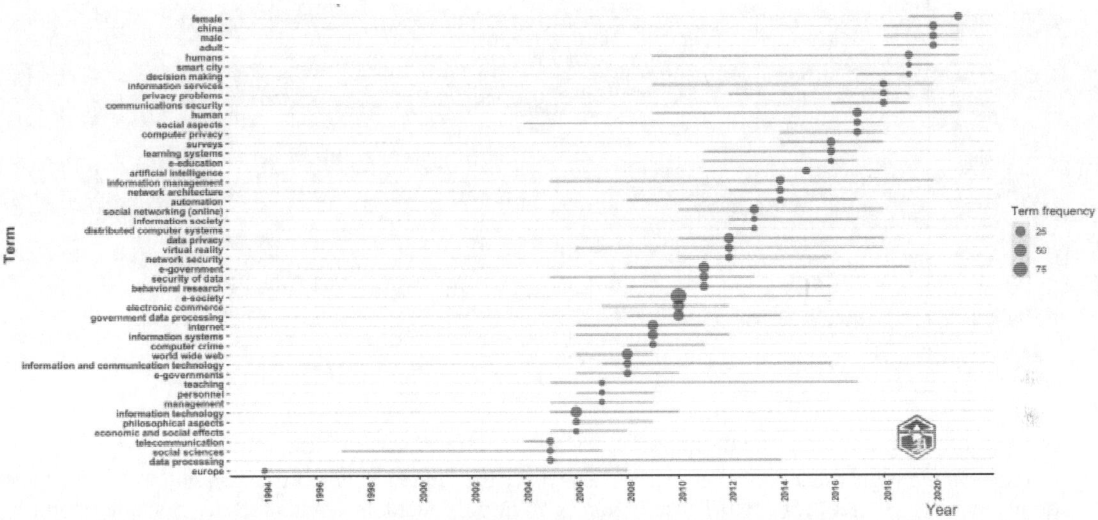

Figure 5. Trending topics associated with e-society across the years.

Using a Walktrap algorithm to classify research themes based on centrality and development, a thematic map from the publications keywords (Keywords Plus) is presented in Figure 6. Central themes, noted for their influence within the field, appear to the right, indicating their role as primary drivers or “Motor Themes” of the E-Society research agenda. Vertically, the density axis represents the internal cohesion and maturity of these themes, with “Niche Themes” at the top, signifying well-developed areas with substantial specialized research.

Motor Themes such as "e-society," "electronic commerce," and "information technology" are positioned as foundational pillars, for their established presence and significant impact on the direction of the field. Meanwhile, Basic Themes including "social networking (online)," "behavioral research," and "artificial intelligence" suggest central, yet still coalescing, domains of study within the scope. These areas are central to the research network but may not have reached the same level of development as the Niche Themes.

Emerging or Declining Themes, located at the lower right quadrant, like "information and communication technology" and the geographic-specific "China," show subjects that are either gaining traction or potentially waning in focus within the scholarly discourse. Conversely, Niche Themes such as "distributed computer systems" and "multi-agent systems" represent areas with a robust body of work and high thematic development, yet these topics may not command the central focus within the broader E-Society research community.

Finally, in terms of co-authorship, the Country Collaboration Map depicts the collaborative links between countries. In the map illustrated in Figure 7, each country's color intensity likely correlates with the volume of E-Society research output it contributes. Darker shades suggest a higher number of publications, indicating that those regions are more actively engaged in E-society research. The lines connecting countries represent collaborative efforts, with the thickness of the lines indicating the strength of the collaboration based on the number of co-authored publications. Such visualizations are crucial for understanding the global dynamics of research, revealing patterns of international cooperation and knowledge exchange.

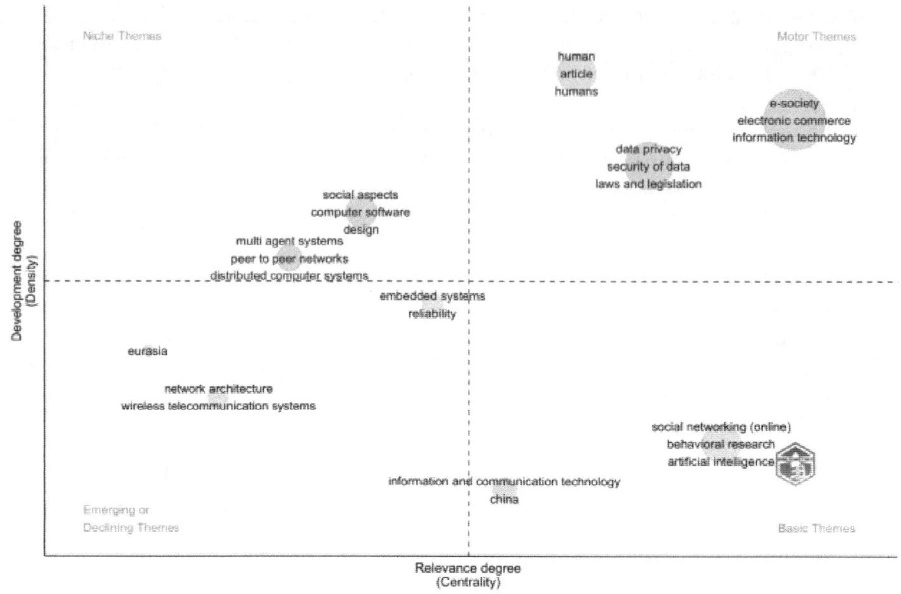

Figure 6. Thematic map on E-society publications.

The map highlights that certain countries, especially the United States, European nations, and China, are key players in E-Society research. These regions do not only yield substantial scientific capital but are also central in international collaboration networks. Clusters of collaboration that indicate regional partnerships or alliances, which could be driven by geographical proximity, shared policy initiatives, or cultural ties.

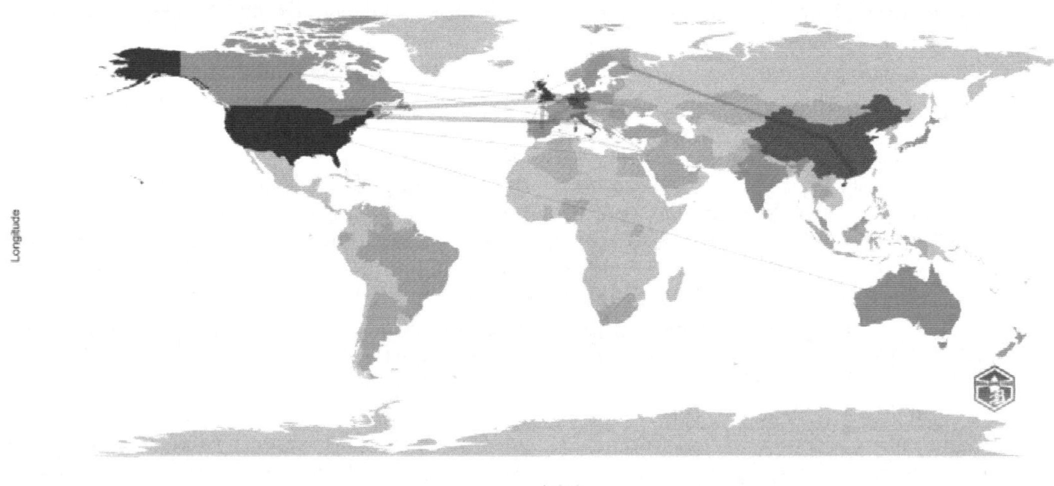

Figure 7. Country collaboration map on E-society publications.

The varying thickness of collaboration evokes Lotka's law of scientific productivity (Sobrino, Caldes & Guerrero, 2009), where a small number of countries are responsible for a large proportion of scientific output. The map might also reflect the "Matthew effect" in science (Perc, 2014), where well-established nations with robust research infrastructures tend to garner more collaboration opportunities, further strengthening their position in the global research network.

Some insights also lie in the subtle ties, the thin lines that connect less prominent nations to the hubs of E-Society research. These represent the undercurrents of scientific endeavor that defy the traditional core-periphery models of scientific collaboration (Wagner et al., 2001). They could be the result of specific international initiatives, like the European Union's Horizon 2020, which fosters research cooperation beyond the EU's borders (Pollex & Lenschow, 2018), or they might arise from the strategic alliances in digital diplomacy and international development programs that aim to bridge digital divides.

Moreover, the absence of international collaborations in certain areas, mainly in South America and Africa, may not denote a lack of activity but could signal potential niches for growth or areas where digital inclusivity is still a frontier. For instance, African nations, often underrepresented in global science networks, are increasingly recognized for their mobile telecommunications research, as they leapfrog traditional infrastructures (Aker & Mbiti, 2010).

4. CONCLUSION

This study has examined the research landscape of E-Society, expliciting the significant expansion and the diverse, interconnected themes underpinning it. The bibliometric analysis, extending from 1989 to 2023, reflects an average annual growth of 6.11% in E-Society publications, marked by a heightened focus on key areas like "e-commerce," "e-government," and more recently, "data privacy" and "network security." These thematic shifts mirror the societal and technological transformations occurring globally.

The thematic map reveals both mature and emerging areas of study, and geographic map pointing regions like the United States, Europe, and China leading in research output and collaboration. However, there is potential for greater inclusivity in global research contributions, particularly from regions like South America and Africa.

This study not only encapsulates the current state of E-Society research but also sets the stage for future explorations, highlighting the need for broader international cooperation and the exploration of new thematic frontiers in the ever-evolving digital landscape.

ACKNOWLEDGEMENT

The present work was carried out with the support of the Coordination for the Improvement of Higher Education Personnel - Brazil (CAPES) - Financing Code 001.

REFERENCES

Addo, A., & Senyo, P. K. (2021). Advancing E-governance for development: Digital identification and its link to socioeconomic inclusion. Government Information Quarterly, 38(2), 101568.

Aker, J. C., & Mbiti, I. M. (2010). Mobile phones and economic development in Africa. Journal of economic Perspectives, 24(3), 207-232.

Bhatnagar, S. (2004). E-government: From vision to implementation-A practical guide with case studies. Sage.

Castells, M. (2011). The rise of the network society. John wiley & sons.

Coicaud, J. M. (2016). Administering and Governing with Technology: The Question of Information Communication Technology and E-Governance. Global Policy, 7(2), 296-300.

Desai, A., & Patel, C. R. (2023). Review of global research on E-mobility: A bibliometric analysis. COMMUNICATIONS, 25(1), A73-A82.

Dossou, T., et al. (2022). Does E-governance reduce income inequality in sub-Saharan Africa? Evidence from a dynamic panel. Evidence From a Dynamic Panel (October 2, 2022). European Xtramile Centre of African Studies WP/22/066.

Hustad, E., et al. (2019). Digital Inequalities: A review of contributing factors and measures for crossing the divide. In Digital Transformation for a Sustainable Society in the 21st Century: 18th IFIP WG 6.11 Conference on e-Business, e-Services, and e-Society, I3E 2019, Trondheim, Norway, September 18–20, 2019, Proceedings 18 (pp. 505-519). Springer International Publishing.

Jayashree, S., & Marthandan, G. (2010). Government to E-government to E-society. Journal of Applied Sciences(Faisalabad), 10(19), 2205-2210.

Mansell, R. (2002). From digital divides to digital entitlements in knowledge societies. Current sociology, 50(3), 407-426.

Mitchuk, O., et al (2021). Changes in social communication as a tool of social work under the influence of digitalization. Studies of Applied Economics, 39(3).

Orochovska, L., & Koshetar, U. (2021). Globalization processes in the sphere of socioeconomic and environmental relations. In E3S Web of Conferences (Vol. 244, p. 10036). EDP Sciences.

Pathak, A. K., & Pandey, R. K. (2021). Emerging Concept of E-Society. Issue 5 Int'l JL Mgmt. & Human., 4, 4.

Perc, M. (2014). The Matthew effect in empirical data. Journal of The Royal Society Interface, 11(98), 20140378.

Pollex, J., & Lenschow, A. (2018). Surrendering to growth? The European Union's goals for research and technology in the Horizon 2020 framework. Journal of Cleaner Production, 197, 1863-1871.

Prastya, D. E., & Nurmandi, A. (2021). A bibliometric analysis of E-democracy on government research. Jurnal Ilmiah Mimbar Demokrasi, 20(2), 71-80.

Qiao, Y. (2019). China’s e-economy: an overview of opportunities and threats. Journal of Asian Development, 5(2), 74.

Rauf, S. A. A., & Thoha, A. M. (2022). Online Digital Transactions as a Solution for National Economic Recovery During the Covid-19 Pandemic. Jurnal Multidisipliner BHARASA, 1(1), 10-19.

Rheingold, H. (2000). The virtual community, revised edition: Homesteading on the electronic frontier. MIT press.

Schmid, B., Stanoevska-Slabeva, K., & Tschammer, V. (Eds.). (2001). Towards the E-Society: E-commerce, E-business, and E-government (Vol. 74). Springer Science & Business Media.

Sobrino, M. I. M., Caldes, A. I. P., & Guerrero, A. P. (2009). Lotka law applied to the scientific production of information science area. Brazilian Journal of Information Science: research trends, 2(1).

Van Dijk, J. A. G. M. (2006). Digital divide research, achievements and shortcomings. Poetics, 34(4-5), 221–235.

Voronkova, V., Nikitenko, V., & Metelenko, N. (2022). AGILE-economy as a factor in improving the digital society. Baltic Journal of Economic Studies, 8(2), 51-58.

Xia, Y., et al (2023). Evolution of digital economy research: A bibliometric analysis. International Review of Economics & Finance, 88, 1151-1172.

THE ROLE OF SOCIAL MEDIA TO NATURAL DISASTER OR CRISIS

Vasilis Kanellopoulos[1], Vassilis Triantafyllou[2], Constantinos Koutsojannis[3] and Efthymis Lekkas[4]

[1]PhD Student at Department of Electrical and Computer Engineering, University of the Peloponnese, Patras, Greece

[2]Professor Department of Electrical and Computer Engineering, University of the Peloponnese, Patras, Greece

[3]Professor, Health Physics & Computational Intelligence Lab, University of Patras, Patras, Greece

[4]Professor Faculty of Geology and Geoenvironment, School of Sciences, National and Kapodistrian University of Athens, Athens, Greece

ABSTRACT

The primary objective of this study is to examine the role of social media in relation to natural disasters, encompassing the periods preceding, during, and following such events. When a disaster occurs, conventional systems collapse (power grids, landlines, electricity, traditional communication channels and computers). Individuals still possess their smartphones equipped with internet access and relevant applications leaving social media networks as the sole means of information exchange. Consequently, the significance of social media has progressively amplified in the realm of disaster preparedness, recovery, and relief efforts. Numerous mobile applications have been developed to help during emergencies. This research aims to explore whether social media platforms can effectively serve as valuable tools, fostering collaborative endeavors between individuals and organizations throughout all phases of emergency management, namely mitigation, preparedness, and response. The investigation draws upon a comprehensive literature review and empirical analysis, examining notable cases across prominent social networks like Facebook, Instagram, Twitter, YouTube, among others.

KEYWORDS

Social Media, IoT, Informatics, Management, Hazard, Natural Disaster

1. INTRODUCTION

In the past, management and response to natural disasters heavily relied on static and predetermined methods. These approaches were based on historical data and predefined plans, lacking the ability to adapt swiftly to rapidly changing situations. However, a significant breakthrough has occurred with the advancement and widespread utilization of real-time data revolutionizing disaster management by providing up-to-the-minute information and insights and empowering decision-makers to respond promptly and flexibly to unfolding events.

By integrating real-time data streams from various sources, such as sensors, satellites, weather stations, and social media, disaster response teams can now receive live updates on the evolving situation. This wealth of dynamic information allows for more accurate assessments of the disaster's scope, magnitude, and impact on affected areas and populations. Real-time data not only enhances situational awareness but also enables better prediction and forecasting, giving authorities the means to anticipate disaster patterns and make informed decisions to protect lives and property. Additionally, it facilitates the coordination of emergency responses, allowing for the deployment of resources precisely where they are most needed at any given moment.

The newfound reliance on dynamic components in disaster management marks a significant paradigm shift from the previous static approaches. It signifies a departure from rigid, pre-established protocols towards adaptive and flexible strategies that can effectively cope with the unpredictable nature of natural disasters. Embracing real-time data has fundamentally transformed the way we perceive, prepare for, and respond to natural calamities, ultimately enhancing our capacity to safeguard communities and minimize the devastating impacts of such events.

This real-time access to information has highlighted the immense value and importance of speed in disseminating information. Considering this change, social media have emerged as a powerful tool for disaster and environmental management. It provides a platform for real-time information sharing and facilitates rapid communication among various stakeholders involved in managing disasters and environmental events. Recognizing the significance of social media in this context, this paper aims to review the existing literature on the role of social media in disaster and environmental management.

Natural disasters are complex phenomena that have far-reaching effects on society, communities, and populations (Hino, M. et al. , 2017). Understanding and assessing the impact of these disasters on the affected population is essential for effective emergency response and relief efforts (Paton, D., & Johnston, D. ,2006; Norris, F. H. et al. ,2008). When natural disasters strike, they often result in significant damage to infrastructure, leading to issues such as lack of clean water, power outages, destruction of homes, and even loss of life (Starbird, K. & Palen, L. ,2011). The people residing in post-disaster areas are particularly vulnerable and require appropriate relief and support from emergency responders, including government agencies and non-governmental organizations. To ensure timely and proportionate rescue and relief operations, it is crucial to gauge the intensity of the population affected by disasters. Although the severity of a disaster's impact on the population is a fundamental concept, it lacks a rigorous definition (Starbird, K. & Palen, L., 2012).

In EU the Public Safety Answering Point 112 was launched 25 years ago and operates alongside national emergency services 24 hours a day, every day of the year. All 112 calls (from a landline or mobile telephone) are routed to the Public Safety Answering Point, providing the general public with information on the emergency situation via various alternative channels and identifying the location of a landline or mobile telephone immediately and securely where the caller is unable to provide their location. Overall, effective management of natural disasters and environmental events relies on understanding their complex impact on communities and populations. By leveraging the power of social media, stakeholders can work together to mitigate the impact of these events and ensure the safety and well-being of affected populations.

2. RELATED WORK

Since disaster happens suddenly, people face a significant challenge to find credible information and take suitable reactions and turn to what they believe is the quickest way to get help. In these cases, and many more, they turned to their preferred new media tool. This same social media technology has spawned numerous volunteer efforts in times of emergency, many of which have been instrumental in adding vital -- and accurate – information used to positive effect by first responders and decision-makers.

Many studies are associated with natural disasters and social media. Social media can be used as a tool by providing information and instructions, with real-time, alerts and warnings and can improve the disaster response by mobilizing online volunteers far away from the epicenter of the crisis to relay information provided by emergency services. Social media can be used to identify both survivors and victims.

Recent disasters have proven the significance of social media for both affected citizens and volunteers alike in the coordination of information and organization of relief activities, often independently of and in addition to the official emergency response. During disasters, social media are widely used by people to share information, opinions, experience, and request for urgent needs.

Here are a few examples of how social media is used in disasters:

Emergency Alerts and Updates: Authorities and relief organizations use social media platforms like Twitter and Facebook to disseminate critical information quickly. They can share evacuation orders, weather updates, road closures, and safety guidelines, helping people stay informed and make informed decisions during a crisis.

Crisis Communication and Coordination: Social media enable real-time communication between emergency responders, government agencies, and affected communities. They help coordinate rescue efforts, allocate resources efficiently, and collaborate with different stakeholders involved in disaster response.

Requesting Help and Reporting Incidents: During disasters, people use social media to ask for help, report incidents, and share their locations. This user-generated information can be valuable for responders to identify areas with the most significant needs and prioritize their efforts accordingly.

Crowdsourcing Information: Individuals share photos, videos, and firsthand accounts of the disaster's impact transforming social media into a powerful crowdsourcing tool, providing valuable insights for responders and help in assessing the extent of the damage.

Fundraising and Donations: Social media platforms facilitate fundraising campaigns for disaster relief efforts. People can quickly share donation links, raise awareness about the situation, and encourage others to contribute to the cause.

Community Support and Mobilization: Those affected by disasters foster a sense of community and solidarity as social media can offer emotional support, share stories of survival and resilience, and provide support for recovery efforts.

Monitoring and Early Warning Systems: Social media data can be monitored and analyzed to detect early warning signs of disasters or rapidly evolving situations. Advanced algorithms can process social media content to identify trends, sentiments, and potential risks.

Connecting Separated Individuals: During disasters that cause displacement, people often get separated from their loved ones. Social media can be used to reconnect family and friends by sharing information about their whereabouts and safety.

Identifying Safe Zones and Resources: People in affected areas can share information about safe locations, available resources, and services like shelter, food distribution centers, and medical facilities through social media finding assistance when needed.

Learning from Past Disasters: Social media data can be analyzed after a disaster to evaluate the effectiveness of response strategies, identify areas for improvement, and gather insights for better preparedness in future events.

Social media have been extensively used during various disasters. Studying both social media and traditional media offers valuable insights to emergency responders during natural disasters. The methodology applied includes sentiment analysis, especially focusing on social media posts from the affected population, in order to achieve a comprehensive analysis of media data.

It's essential to remember that while social media is a valuable tool in disaster response, information shared on these platforms must be verified and corroborated with official sources to avoid the spread of misinformation and potential panic. Therefore, it's crucial to verify information from reliable sources and use social media responsibly during such events.

Some paradigms denote the impact of social media during natural disasters:

The 2013 Central European floods (Kaufhold, M.-A. and Reuter, C. Vernetzte. ,2014). Sentiment analysis was used in order to recognize public opinions and attitudes in specific contexts. Although the term suggests identifying a range of emotions like anger, disgust, fear, happiness, sadness, and surprise, the majority of sentiment analysis methods focus on a simpler task of classifying texts as either positive or negative. The analysis showed a dominant negative sentiment throughout the disaster, which is expected due to the nature of the event. Ongoing work involves investigating temporal patterns and user connections during different disaster phases. Another focus is to link communication patterns to messages of resilience. In the study conducted by Gonçalves et al. (2013), eight state-of-the-art sentiment analysis methods were compared using two English datasets from Online Social Networks messages. The methods under scrutiny were SentiWordNet, SASA, PANAS-t, Emoticons, SentiStrength, LIWC, SenticNet, and Happiness Index.

Hurricane Harvey in August and September of 2017. In the case of Hurricane Harvey, Mayor Turner did an exemplary job of communicating through Twitter but could have included more tweets with inclusive language and more local hashtags earlier in the crisis. The paradigm provided a compelling illustration of how social media, particularly Twitter, can be used in a crisis to provide information, guidance, reassurance and hope to key publics. The analysis in (C.M. Vera-Burgos & D.R. Griffin Padgett, 2020) presents suggestions on how Twitter, and social media in general, can help crisis managers prepare for, communicate during, and move forward following a natural disaster.

The 2019 flood in Polland. In (Dorota Domalewska, 2019) the role of social media platforms, Facebook and Twitter, during the floods that occurred in Poland in May 2019 was presented. The flood resulted from heavy rains and storms, causing severe flooding in parts of eastern and southern Poland and extensive damage. The study analyzed a set of text posts and tweets related to the flood event on social media platforms to understand the sentiments expressed in these online communications and categorized them into three groups: positive, negative, and neutral (objective). The analysis revealed a diverse range of sentiments expressed on social media during the flood event, ranging from positive acknowledgments and compassionate responses to criticism and negativity, including hate speech.

Although Twitter is often referred to as the 'most useful social media tool' particularly for natural disasters it seems that social media is not yet used to its full potential in crisis communications and more research is needed on social media and crisis communication (Eriksson and Olsson, 2016; Spence et al., 2016).

However, the spread of misinformation and disinformation on social media has also become a significant challenge. False or misleading information can circulate rapidly, leading to confusion, panic, and even harm in some cases. Platforms and researchers continue to grapple with developing effective strategies to combat misinformation without infringing on freedom of speech. Another important aspect is the verification of information as there are obvious issues regarding the perceived credibility of social media content in comparison with other media. Information with no clear source, for in-stance, can be implicated in the spread of rumor.

3. CHARACTERISTICS OF NATURAL DISASTERS

Disaster organizations play a crucial role in managing and responding to various types of disasters, whether they are natural calamities like hurricanes, earthquakes, or human-made incidents such as industrial accidents or terrorist attacks. These organizations typically involve various stakeholders, including local government authorities, coordinators, citizens who provide information, and volunteers.

Let's delve deeper into some key players involved in disaster management:

Local Government: Local governments, such as city councils or municipal bodies, are the primary authorities responsible for disaster management within their jurisdiction. They play a vital role in coordinating disaster response and recovery efforts and are responsible:

- The development of comprehensive plans outlining how they will respond to different types of disasters and allocate resources accordingly.
- The collaboration with regional, state, and federal agencies to ensure a coordinated and effective response to disasters.
- The allocation of funds, equipment, and personnel to deal with emergencies.
- Informing citizens about potential risks and the necessary precautions to take during disasters.
- Activation of emergency operations centers during disasters to facilitate communication and decision-making among relevant agencies.

Coordinators: Disaster coordinators are individuals or teams designated to manage disaster response efforts under the guidance of local government or emergency management officials and are responsible for:

- Assessing the scale and impact of the disaster to determine the appropriate response measures.
- Coordinating the deployment of emergency services, personnel, and supplies to affected areas.
- Communicating with various response teams, government agencies, and stakeholders to ensure an integrated approach to disaster management.
- Manage resources with the usage of an Incident Command System (ICS)

Citizens who give information and accept consequences: During a disaster, citizens play a crucial role as both sources of information and active participants in disaster management. They contribute in the following ways:

- Reporting incidents thus providing essential information to emergency services, aiding in faster response times.
- Following instructions: Citizens must be prepared to follow evacuation orders, seek shelter, or take other necessary precautions to protect themselves and their communities.
- Participating in community efforts by volunteering to assist in various tasks.

Volunteers: Volunteers are individuals who selflessly offer their time and skills to support disaster response and recovery efforts. Volunteer role classifications include "helper", "reporter", "retweeter", "repeater" and "reader" (Norris, F. H.et al. ,2008) as well as "information broker", gathering and reporting information. They are a critical asset to disaster organizations and bring various expertise to the table such as:

- Search and rescue: Locate and rescue people trapped in disaster-stricken areas.
- Medical support: Provide essential medical care to the injured.
- Relief operations: Distributing food, water, clothing, etc. to affected communities.

- Psychological support: Counselors, provide emotional support to survivors and affected individuals.
- Reconstruction and recovery: Assist in rebuilding communities and infrastructure after the disaster.

Overall, the effective collaboration and cooperation among these elements are vital for a successful disaster management and response process, as it helps minimize loss of life and property and ensures a quicker recovery for affected communities.

In the context of natural disasters management, moderators are factors or players that can influence the severity of the impact and the effectiveness of disaster response and recovery efforts. Here are some key moderators in natural disasters management:

Preparedness Measures: Preparedness includes having well-designed disaster management plans, early warning systems, evacuation routes, and community education programs.

Government Policies and Regulations: Government policies related to land use, building codes, and zoning regulations can influence the vulnerability of an area to natural disasters.

Community Engagement: Communities that actively engage in disaster planning, response, and recovery efforts tend to fare better during disasters.

Technological Advancements: Advancements in technology, such as satellite-based monitoring systems, early warning systems, and communication tools, play a critical role in disaster management.

International Cooperation: Coordination between countries and international organizations can provide additional resources and expertise to affected regions.

Topography and Geography: The geographical characteristics of an area can influence the impact of certain natural disasters.

Climate Change: Managing the risks associated with climate change is a critical aspect of disaster management.

Economic Development: Wealthier regions may have better infrastructure, healthcare facilities, and financial resources to support recovery efforts.

Media and Public Perception: Accurate and responsible media coverage can help mobilize support and resources, while misinformation or panic can hinder effective management.

Cultural Factors: Cultural beliefs, practices, and traditions can impact disaster management.

Addressing vulnerabilities, enhancing preparedness, and promoting collaboration among stakeholders, disaster management efforts can be more effective in reducing the impact of natural disasters on communities and the environment. Kaufhold & Reuter (2014) suggest "moderators", who establishes supportive platforms for real and virtual activities, mediates offers of and requests for assistance, mobilizes resources and integrates information of various sources.

4. LESSONS LEARNED

A recent 2019 comparison (Sarra Chair et al., 2019) of 18 different platforms revealed some important features applied by the systems:

1. Most platforms work only on Twitter (all except one). Few platforms, however, use both social media and other kinds of input data like Email, SMS, Cell phones, and satellite imagery.
2. Most of the systems indicate organizations as users and only four platforms, indicate citizens as users.
3. Most platforms presented, perform real-time analysis on input data.
4. Only one tool provides real-time recommendations based on data analysis results, which reduces the efficiency of these platforms in helping stakeholders take suitable decisions and save lives during the disaster. This tool also provides input from multiple sources such as social media feeds, multimedia messaging, and citizen reports into alert generation.
5. While most emergency management platforms carry out event detection and data visualization through maps and graphs, few of them, perform sentiment analysis on input data.
6. Some of the systems link remote-sensed data with social media data that are autonomously collected.
7. Social media messages have proven difficult to process using traditional natural language processing algorithms and most success stories in the disaster space have relied on organized crowds of volunteers who process content manually.

8. Almost all approaches have limitations when used by volunteer moderators in disasters: They either demand syntactical requirements from the user; do not provide cross-platform structures, e.g. focus solely on Twitter, or require the use of a new platform and therefore fail to integrate ICT for volunteers into existing networks.

Disaster relief professionals should employ various social media tools and approaches when coordinating disaster relief efforts. This can include devising and executing a specific strategy for each platform, such as using Facebook to share longer information of evacuation instructions for a hurricane, while using Twitter to display immediate information on the hurricane's development itself. The way social media can be used depends on the reach and size of the audience to be addressed to make sure that information reaches as many people as possible.

Social media is constantly evolving, and best practices for its use by emergency officials will change as well since social media play a pivotal role in the realms of disaster and environmental management, acting as a potent instrument for furnishing real-time information and expediting communication between relevant stakeholders. Prominent social media platforms like Twitter and Facebook serve as indispensable conduits to disseminate crucial instructions, evacuation directives, and emergency alerts to affected communities. We must take into account that they are certain limitations and challenges related to the utilization of social media in the context of disaster and environmental management. Currently, most emergency services are only reachable by voice telephone calls, while more and more citizens expect to be able to reach emergency services using alternative ways of communication. In the future, European Emergency Number Association is about integrating these new technologies into emergency services, so that they can receive not just voice, but location information, real-time text, photos, video calls and other data. At the same time social media platforms prove invaluable in mobilizing volunteers and orchestrating concerted response endeavors. One prominent challenge lies in the overwhelming volume of information that officials must contend with, making it arduous to discern authentic and reliable data from falsehoods or deceptive content. Additionally, the usage of social media introduces concerns regarding privacy and legal ramifications that necessitate careful consideration.

5. CONCLUSION

The literature reviewed in this paper suggests that social media can play a critical role in disaster and crisis management, by providing real-time information and facilitating rapid communication among stakeholders. However, it is important to be aware of the limitations and challenges associated with the use of social media and to develop strategies to address these issues. Twitter (C.M. Vera-Burgos & D.R. Griffin Padgett, 2020) is fast becoming a critical source of information about world events large and small. However, it is difficult to translate this information into a format allows users to draw higher-level conclusions. Twitter is a useful tool for crisis management in natural disasters due to several key reasons:

Real-Time Information: Twitter enables real-time communication and information sharing. During a natural disaster, people on the ground, government agencies, and organizations can quickly disseminate critical updates, warnings, evacuation notices, and emergency instructions. This helps to keep the public informed and aware of the latest developments, facilitating prompt action and reducing potential risks.

Rapid Communication: Twitter's platform allows for rapid communication and direct interaction between different stakeholders. Emergency management agencies can quickly respond to queries, address concerns, and provide clarifications.

Wide Reach: Twitter has a vast user base, including individuals, organizations, and news outlets. During a crisis, tweets related to the event often go viral, reaching a large audience. This widespread dissemination of information is crucial for increasing public awareness, mobilizing support, and promoting a sense of solidarity. Moreover, journalists and media professionals often monitor Twitter to gather news, amplifying the reach of crucial updates and emergency messages.

Community Support and Engagement: Twitter fosters community support and engagement during crises. Users can share their experiences, offer help, and organize relief efforts. This enables affected individuals to connect with each other, exchange valuable resources, and provide emotional support. Additionally, Twitter users often collaborate to verify and fact-check information, ensuring the accuracy of shared content and preventing the spread of misinformation.

Data Collection and Analysis: Twitter generates a vast amount of data during natural disasters. This data can be analyzed to gain insights into the impact of the event, assess public sentiment, identify emerging issues, and evaluate the effectiveness of response efforts.

Public Awareness and Education: Twitter can be used by Government agencies, NGOs, and experts to share tips on preparedness, safety precautions, and recovery strategies. This empowers individuals and communities to take proactive measures, increase their resilience, and minimize the impact of future disasters.

It is important to note that while Twitter can be a valuable tool for crisis management, it also has limitations. These include the potential for misinformation to spread quickly, the need for reliable internet access during emergencies, and the challenge of filtering and prioritizing relevant information from the vast volume of tweets. However, when used effectively and in conjunction with other communication channels, Twitter can significantly enhance crisis management efforts during natural disasters.

In essence, the culmination of studies exploring social media's role in disasters has paved the way for an exciting era of data-driven decision-making. The insights drawn from these endeavors can equip researchers and planning entities with the necessary tools to harness the potential of social media as a powerful and agile resource for disseminating critical information, coordinating relief efforts, and mobilizing support during times of crisis. By leveraging the wealth of knowledge gained from these studies, the global community stands poised to achieve greater preparedness, resilience, and effectiveness in managing and responding to disasters of all scales.

6. FUTURE DIRECTIONS

This text emphasizes the need for future research to focus on developing effective strategies for filtering and disseminating information on social media during disasters or environmental events. Additionally, there is a need for more research to determine the best ways to utilize social media in mobilizing volunteers and coordinating response efforts. The text also highlights the importance of conducting research on aerial data as it is expected to present significant big data challenges soon.

Regarding Sentiment Analysis, the authors intend to prioritize creating a specialized vocabulary for disasters based on social media content. This lexicon aims to categorize tweets into precise emotional types, drawing upon the field of disaster psychology.

We intend to design and implement a social media-based platform to enhance disaster detection and communication with citizens, volunteers, and responding organizations before, during, and after a disaster. This platform seeks to involve stakeholders in co-creating security solutions through media coverage and shape citizens' and local communities' perceptions of security. The proposed platform consists of three main functional blocks: a data collection module, a data processing module, and a recommendation module. These modules evaluate data from various sources and deliver them to citizens, volunteers, and responding organizations during a disaster, using "Citizens as Sensors," where citizens contribute data for evaluation and utilization.

To ensure robustness and security, the platform's design and implementation will be based on Web 3.0 and blockchain technologies. Leveraging these technologies aims to enhance data integrity, transparency, and decentralization. Overall, this framework presents a comprehensive approach to using social media and emerging technologies to enhance disaster management, communication, and citizen engagement in security-related processes. Combining Big Data Analytics and Internet of Things technologies can empower disaster management authorities with real-time data, predictive analytics, and advanced decision support systems, ultimately improving response capabilities and coordination among stakeholders, and mitigating the impact of disasters.

While Twitter can be considered a useful tool for sensing natural hazards, some studies reveal that different Twitter behaviors and metrics (such as attention duration, tweet frequency based on vulnerability, proximity, and sentiment) respond differently to various types of natural disasters. It is essential for researchers to recognize that Twitter response patterns for one type of natural hazard may not apply to other types. When evaluating Twitter responses to events like wildfires compared to tornadoes, careful consideration should be given.

Moreover, the social vulnerability of the affected population plays a distinct role in shaping their social media behavior during disasters. Some events have a more extensive impact in terms of geographical distance, may persist for a longer duration, and elicit varying responses among different subgroups of the population.

REFERENCES

Chair Sarra, Charrad, Malika, Narjes Bellamine Ben Saouda. (2019). *Towards A Social Media-Based framework for Disaster Communication*. Procedia Computer Science, Volume 164, 271-278.

Chan, J.C. (2012). *The role of social media in crisis preparedness response and recover*. OECD report. [cited 2014 2/2/2014]

Domalewska Dorota (2019). *The role of social media in emergency management during the 2019 flood in Poland*. 5/2019 vol.27.

Eurostat Articles [30 June 2021]. *Do you participate in social networks? https://ec.europa.eu/eurostat/web/products-eurostat-news/-/edn-20210630-1*

Focus Bari. [January-June 2022]. *FocusOnTechLifeTips. https://focusbari.gr/wp-content/uploads/2022/09/FOCUS-ON-TECH-LIFE_TIPS_22A2_EN.pdf*

Hino, M., Field, C. B., & Mach, K. J. (2017). *Managed retreat as a response to natural hazard risk.* Nature Climate Change, 7(5), 364-370.

Hofmann, M., Betke, H., and Sackmann, S. (2014). *Hands2Help – Ein App-basiertes Konzept zur Koordnation Freiwilliger Helfer. i-com 13*, 1, 29–36.

Hua B. et al. (2015). *Sina Weibo incident monitor and Chinese disaster microblogging classification.* J Digit Inf Manag 13(3):156–161

Kaplan, A.M. and Haenlein, M. (2010). *Users of the world, unite! The challenges and opportunities of Social Media*. Business Horizons 53, 1, 59–68.

Kaufhold, M.-A. & Reuter, C. Vernetzte. (2014). *Selbsthilfe in Sozialen Medien am Beispiel des Hochwassers 2013/ Linked Self-Help in Social Media using the example of the Floods 2013 in Germany. i-com 13"*, 1, 20–28

Marcus, A., Bernstein, M.S., Badar, O., Karger, D.R., Madden, S., and Miller, R.C. (2011). *Twitinfo: aggregating and visualizing microblogs for event exploration*. In Proceedings of the SIGCHI Conference on Human Factors in Computing Systems (CHI '11). ACM, 227–236.

Nabil, A., Eledath J., Mehrotra S. and Venkatasubramanian N. (2012). *Social media alert and response to threats to citizens (SMART-C)*. In Collaborative Computing: Networking, Applications and Worksharing (CollaborateCom), 8th International Conference on IEEE. 181-189).

Norris, F. H., Stevens, S. P., Pfefferbaum, B., Wyche, K. F., & Pfefferbaum, R. L. (2008). *Community resilience as a metaphor, theory, set of capacities, and strategy for disaster readiness.* American Journal of Community Psychology, 41(1-2), 127-150.

Paton, D., & Johnston, D. (2006). *Disaster resilience: An integrated approach*. Charles C. Thomas Publisher.

Quarantelli, E. L. (1984). *Emergent Citizen Groups in Disaster Preparedness and Recovery Activities*.

Reuter, C., Heger, O., and Pipek, V. (2013). *Combining Real and Virtual Volunteers through Social Media.* Proc. ISCRAM. 780-790.

Starbird, K. & Palen, L. (2011). *Voluntweeters: Self-Organizing by Digital Volunteers in Times of Crisis*. In *Proc. CHI.* Vancouver, Canada, 1071-1080.

Starbird, K. & Palen, L. (2012). *How Will the Revolution be Retweeted? Information Diffusion and the 2011 Egyptian Uprising. Proc. CSCW*, 7–16.

Starbird, K. and Stamberger, J. (2010). *Tweak the Tweet: Lever-aging Microblogging Proliferation with a Prescriptive Syntax to Support Citizen Reporting*. Proc. ISCRAM 1-5.

Vera-Burgos, C. M. & Griffin Padgett, D. R. (2020). *Using Twitter for crisis communications in a natural disaster: Hurricane Harvey*. Heliyon, Volume 6, Issue 9, September 2020 e04804.

VIDE GOLD. DIGITIZATION, HETEROGENEITY AND CONVERGENCE ON EIGHT MUSEUMS AND ARCHEOLOGICAL SITES IN THE SOUTH OF ITALY

Dalia Gallico
Università San Raffaele Roma, Italy

ABSTRACT

The incorporation of digital technology in museums can offer a more engaging and interactive experience for visitors. It can also allow to reach a wider audience through resources and online platforms and to provide additional context and information about their collection. However, it is important for museums to consider how to integrate digital technology into their exhibits and ensure that it enriches rather than detracts from the overall visitor experience. By carefully incorporating digital experiences into their museums, they can provide visitors with a more immersive and engaging experience.

Studying the intersection between digital technology and cultural heritage, this thesis aims to explore the potential of digital experiences in the cultural heritage sector and to identify best practices for creating immersive and educational digital experiences that engage and educate users. We will first examine the new technologies at the service of the cultural heritage sector and then move on to market numbers and target users. Through a literature review and successful case studies, we will identify the key factors contributing to the effectiveness of digital experiences applied to cultural heritage and then develop a concrete implementation strategy of these technologies by sector actors. This Project identifies the characteristics of the supplies and services relating to the "Vide Gold" project. The virtual journey continues" promoted by the Regional Directorate of the Museums of Calabria (Italy) with Pon Culture and Development Fesr 2014-20. The entire definitive and executive project is divided into three thematic sections.

- Creation of an infrastructure for WiFi connectivity and Electronic Ticketing System
- Cataloging and Digitization Service of Cultural Heritage
- Communication and Promotion Service of the eight attractors

KEYWORDS

Digital Experience, Cultural Heritage, Virtual Reality (VR), Augmented Reality (AR), Social, Promotion

1. INTRODUCTION

The British Museum launches a big digitization project: the plan is to put the entire collection online. Something like 2.4 million objects, for an investment of £10 million. Finally also in Italy in 2023 we proceed with the digitization of over 600,000 objects including archaeological finds, works of art, drawings and prints of 70 places of national culture, including museums and Italian archaeological areas. The intervention, dedicated to the digitization of Italian museum deposits and intended to enrich, expand and organize the national digital cultural heritage, will align our country with the rest of the world and Europe (with the PSI directive on Open Access), putting over two million new digital resources produced are available to everyone, each accompanied by metadata and available within the national Digital Library.

This Project identifies the characteristics of the supplies and services relating to the "Vide Gold" project. The virtual journey continues" promoted by the Regional Directorate of the Museums of Calabria (Italy) with Pon Culture And Development Fesr 2014-20. The entire definitive and executive project is divided into three thematic sections.

- Creation of an infrastructure for WiFi connectivity and Electronic Ticketing System
- Cataloging and Digitization Service of Cultural Heritage
- Communication and Promotion Service of the eight attractors

The eight attractors subject to intervention are:

1. Museo e Parco archeologico nazionale di Scolacium, Borgia (CZ);
2. Museo e Parco archeologico nazionale della Sibaritide, Cassano allo Ionio (CS)
3. Museo e Parco archeologico nazionale di Locri;
4. Museo e Parco archeologico nazionale di Kaulon, Monasterace (RC);
5. Museo archeologico nazionale di Crotone incluso il Museo di Capo Colonna;
6. La Cattolica, Stilo;
7. Galleria Nazionale di Cosenza;
8. Chiesa di San Francesco di Assisi, Gerace (RC).

2. CREATION OF AN INFRASTRUCTURE FOR WIFI CONNECTIVITY AND ELECTRONIC TICKETING SYSTEM

With this project, the Regional Museums Directorate of Calabria intends to strengthen the Wi-FI technological infrastructure of the museums and archaeological areas related to the attractors.

The objective of:

- Create a WIFI infrastructure, at the service of visitors and employees, which covers the internal environments of the museums of the attractions involved together with the relevant archaeological areas;
- Adopt the most modern technologies in the WIFI network infrastructure in order to guarantee network users safe access;
- Adopt a centralized Hotspot service common to all the Attractors involved, with the aim of simplifying the system management procedures and offering the Visitor the same way of accessing and using the WiFi network.
- Adopt a centralized electronic ticketing system with stations distributed at the museum locations of the 8 Attractors (9 considering the Capo Colonna Museum);
- Use the new network infrastructure also to connect the various ticketing stations to the internet;

The project includes:

1. Supply, configuration, installation and related adaptation works of all the equipment and systems necessary for the creation of the WiFi network (radio and network equipment);

2. Supply, configuration, installation and related adaptation works of a centralized electronic ticketing system for Museums consisting of a physical server and software complete with each lifetime commercial license (i.e. without time limits and without any periodic fee) and at least 9 satellite stations (PC, ticket printer, white tickets, software license if necessary) to be installed at the locations of the eight Attractors.

2.1 Network Architecture

The project involves the creation of a wireless network infrastructure capable of covering both the internal and external areas of the museum premises and the archaeological areas connected to them. Furthermore, a Ticket Office must be installed in each Museum location.

The network systems, in their respective attractors, are created following principles aimed at guaranteeing the security of access to connectivity services based on the intended use. The network system to be created, for each attractor, will have the classic LAN scheme with the star center located in the room where the access point to internet connectivity is present. This Access Point is identified with the device (commonly identified with the name Modem/Router) installed by the internet connectivity service provider.

The Outdoor network system is based on the transmission of connectivity to the various Access Points distributed in the outdoor areas using the PTMP (Point To MultiPoint) scheme. That is, starting from a node of the wired network, located inside the museum building, a cable is laid until it reaches an external point of the building (roof terrace or external facade) where it is installed and electrically powered, a Wireless device called "Base Station". This device will connect, via radio, with a series of further radio devices positioned at different distances, but optically visible to each other, called SUBSCRIBER. Outdoor Access Points are connected to the latter which will distribute the signal to visitors.

2.2 General Project Requirements

The project provides that the network infrastructure must be created in such a way as to be able to:

1. have as a fundamental prerequisite compliance with all current regulations regarding electromagnetic pollution;
2. keep the system status of the WiFi devices under control;
3. have high expandability that allows the expansion of the system in several phases and the potential increase in the number of network devices as well as those that can be used for video surveillance systems, although not foreseen by this project;
4. be subsequently extended to other portions of the territory and/or other types of users without the need to modify the network architecture;
5. accommodate wireless equipment with technologies that in the future would be able to guarantee the improvement of the performance of the network itself;
6. ensure interoperability with any pre-existing wireless networks;
7. operate with a diagnostic system that allows rapid identification of anomalies and provides effective tools for intervention and restoration of normal operations;
8. have extreme ease of use by the operator, who will be able to interact with the system using basic tools known to him;
9. have a notification service that alerts museum operators of a malfunction;
10. use existing infrastructures and enhance the investments already made.
11. manage access to the wireless network.

3. CATALOGING AND DIGITALIZATION SERVICE OF CULTURAL HERITAGE

Reconnaissance services of existing materials in ministerial databases and migration of existing catalog cards into them and implementation of databases with new inventory, cataloging and digitization campaigns of goods relating to the eight attractors exclusively referring to goods on display and not stored in deposits: Museum and National Archaeological Park of Scolacium, Borgia; Sibaritide National Archaeological Park and Museum, Cassano allo Ionio; Museum and National Archaeological Park of Locri, Locri; Kaulon National Archaeological Park and Museum, Monasterace (RC); National archaeological museum of Crotone, Crotone; La Cattolica, Stilo; National Gallery of Cosenza, Cosenza; Church of San Francesco di Assisi, Gerace.

Production of three-dimensional models and data, optimized for web use, aimed at promoting the cultural heritage subject to intervention.

Activity:

- Reconnaissance of existing data in ministerial databases regarding the works and finds exhibited at the eight attractors.
- Computerized inventory and cataloging in the ministerial databases of all the works and finds exhibited at the eight attractors, which are not yet present in the aforementioned ministerial databases;
- All computerized data must always be provided in standard formats and free from any commercial license and, therefore, usable without the need to use proprietary software for which the purchase is necessary;
- All cataloged data, both existing and new, together with the respective files coming from the digitization activities, referred to in the following points, must be inserted into the IT systems that manage the web platform and the mobile APPs
- In detail, computerized cataloging activities are currently divided into the operations specified below, divided by type of cataloging card, in the latest version licensed by the Central Institute for Cataloging and Documentation (hereinafter "ICCD").
- The digitization services include the three-dimensional survey of archaeological sites, using laser scanners and photogrammetric systems, of works of art consisting of sculptures and archaeological finds, using structured light scanners, and of works on paper, using high resolution scanners for Images. The acquired data is processed in order to obtain two-dimensional documents, point and polygonal cloud models, reconstructive models in NURBS;

3.1 Digitization and Data Management Procedures

For each attractor, a digitalisation plan for parts of the buildings, places and artefacts/works on display, with the aim of creating an interoperable 2/3D digital data ecosystem, connected on one hand to the data cataloging and management system , on the other hand to a multilevel platform for access to information for sharing data through a web portal and an app and for the advanced use of the same through on-site devices to support new universal and immersive forms of use of cultural heritage . The digitization procedures are carried out using the most innovative survey technologies, in particular acquisition campaigns are envisaged using drone photogrammetry (where necessary integrated with ground shots); using TOF and/or phase difference laser scanners of the archaeological areas and places deemed relevant for the purposes of the analysis and representation of the eight attractors; using structured light scanners of the works and artefacts on display; using professional scanners for images of works on paper.

3.2 Survey of Archaeological Areas and Buildings

For 3D scanning using a scanner, for a better interpretation of the laser data, the instruments used must use laser beam waveform analysis techniques, in order to obtain correct reflectance parameters independent of the measurement distance. For surveys using photogrammetry, the use of devices with a resolution of no less than 20MP per image is required. The point clouds generated must be complete, aligned, filtered and segmented for the characterization of individual architectural elements, floor plans and vegetation, and must also be textured using suitably balanced high resolution photos. The models must be returned in the form of point clouds and textured polygonal models, within a single global reference system in WGS 84 coordinates. Furthermore, the production of quoted two-dimensional documents, such as plans, elevations, sections and orthophotos on a scale of 1:50, 1:100 and 1:200 depending on the size of the artefacts acquired. The Orthophotos are generated from the models produced by three-dimensional scans, as required by this project. The scales of representation are agreed with the management of the execution of the service during the carrying out of the surveys. The data relating to some buildings are processed according to management protocols for each type of building in order to obtain volumetric reconstructive models in the form of mesh and textured NURBS, also connected to the filing systems of the same. For each artefact, the data management and model production activities are agreed in detail with the management of the execution of the service in order to better optimize data processing times.

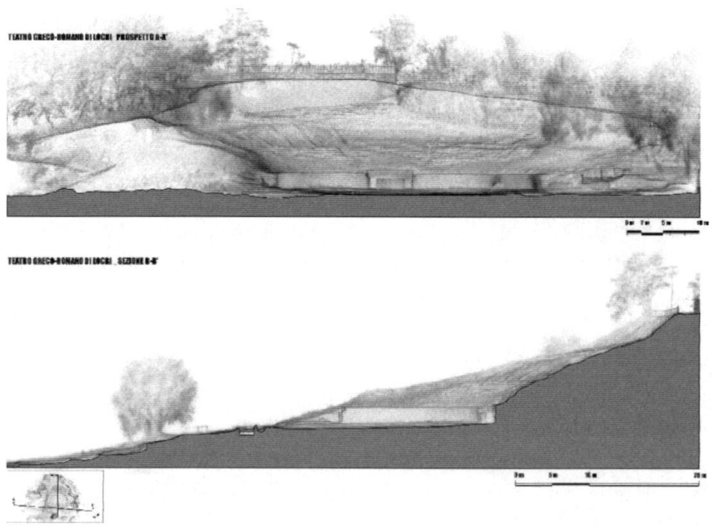

Figure 1. Edited elevation and sections Theatre Locri

3.3 Survey of the Works and Finds on Display

For the three-dimensional survey of medium-sized works of art and finds, the use of structured light scanners with a 3D point precision of no less than 0.1 mm and a resolution of no less than 0.2 mm is required. For the three-dimensional survey of small finds (objects smaller than approximately 300 mm per side), the use of a structured light scanner with 3D point precision of no less than 0.05 mm and resolution of no less than 0.1 mm is required.

The generated point clouds must be complete, aligned, filtered and textured. The models must be returned in the form of point clouds and textured polygonal models, with resolutions equal to 0.2 mm for medium-sized objects and equal to 0.1 mm for small objects.

Template files are delivered in the following formats:

File extension table	**Point clouds**	**Polygonal models**
Structured light laser survey	.ASCII	.OBJ / .PLY / .VRML

File format table for mobile environment	**iOS**	**Android**
Polygonal models from light scanners structured	usdz max 100.000 poligoni max 80mb	gltf max 70.000 poligoni max 30 mb

Figure 2. Two-dimensional drawings Scolacium Theatre

3.4 Digitization of Works on Paper

The digitization of works on paper must be carried out using a professional scanner with a minimum resolution of 1200 DPI. The following formats are provided:

TIFF 6.0 (or later versions) uncompressed with a resolution of no less than 600 optical dpi, color depth of 24 bit RGB for format less than or equal to A4; and with a resolution of no less than 400 optical dpi, color depth of 24 bit RGB for formats larger than A4. This digitization is intended for offline storage and as a backup (master) copy.

The following will subsequently be produced from the master:

JPEG in compressed format at medium resolution, 300 optical dpi and 24 bit RGB color depth.

JPEG in low resolution compressed format, 150 optical dpi, 24 bit RGB color depth.

3.5 Detail of The Monuments Of Which To Produce Volumetric Reconstructive Models

Virtual reconstructive models must be produced in NURNS starting from real-number models from three-dimensional surveys using laser scanners and photogrammetric systems. The models rigorously represent the entire volume of the buildings with levels of detail taking into account the scientific documentation available for each monument.

Figure 3. 3D Model byzantine Basilica Scolacium

4. COMMUNICATION AND PROMOTION SERVICE OF THE EIGHT ATTRACTORS

Thanks to the common thread that conceptually unites the eight stages, the visitor becomes a traveler and, through the kaleidoscope of proposals, draws new perspectives and suggestions from the Calabrian cultural landscape and finds himself immersed in the museum-territory system, the result of the cultural and anthropic stratifications that in the have settled over time. The project perspective is to create an integrated system of communication, promotion and representation of the eight attractors object of the intervention, overcoming the critical issues of fragmentation, indeterminacy, and in some cases the absence, of a coherent univocal communicative message capable of fully represent their cultural value. The architecture of the Project is divided into a transversal line of interventions that will have an impact, with coherence of narrative languages and visual representation, both on Brand Identity actions and promotion of attractors, and on the creation of specific audio/video content of the "immersive" to be installed at the attractors themselves based on the technical indications provided by the Contracting Authority during the execution of the project.

4.1 Description of the Service

Photographic campaign and video footage to support documentary productions: Creation of a photographic campaign (20 photographs for each attractor, for a total of 160) and video footage taken to record places, works and artefacts on display, relating to the eight attractors referred to in this document project. This activity is carried out by adopting a precise narrative and shooting line so that the works produced are distinguishable for the originality of the language and for the cinematographic cut that must be connected with the following point. **Production of documentaries and mini-documentaries.** Production of a series of documentary films that allow us to illustrate and promote the historical-cultural characteristics of the eight attractors, both in individual and aggregate form, referred to in this project. This production, which is divided into different types of works, must be characterized by the ability to generate "empathy" in the viewer with the aim of predisposing him to a more in-depth knowledge of the relevant cultural heritage relating to the eight attractors, within a broader context historical, cultural and landscape. A further objective is to promote the tourist attractiveness of the same eight attractors together with the territories to which they refer. These documentaries must be suitable for subsequent and possible distribution on web channels, social networks, mobile APPs and fixed installations at the attractors' premises. **Multimedia production for video mapping.** Production of audio-visual contributions intended for video projection with the video-mapping technique. At the museum locations of four of the eight attractors, videos must be created which are projected onto architectural surfaces with the aim of increasing the understanding of certain exhibition contexts through the use of hybrid languages between video footage, virtual reconstructions and spatialised three-dimensional sound. The Communication and Promotion Service of the eight Attractors aims to create a single communication system in which expressive languages and narrative solutions are harmoniously integrated into all the tools created for this project. **Video clips.** Video footage at the museums and/or archaeological areas of each of the eight attractors. Cinematic quality shooting, minimum resolution 4k/60 fps, post-production complete with editing, color correction and color grading. Video footage from DRONE at the museums and/or archaeological areas of each of the eight attractors. Cinematic quality shooting, minimum resolution 4k/60 fps, post-production complete with editing, color correction and color grading. **Photographic shooting.** Photographic shooting at the museums and/or archaeological areas of each of the eight attractors. The images must be provided following the post-production and processing phase according to the creative reference requirements present in the General Concept. Files in

RAW and .Jpeg formats must have a minimum size of 30 Megapixels.

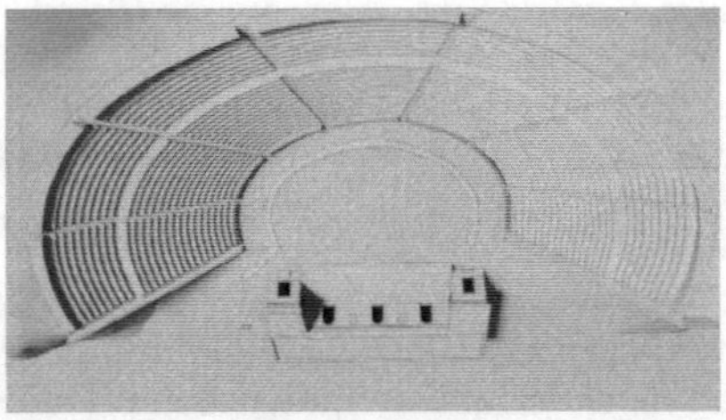

Figure 4-5. Photos and reconstructions of the Greek theater of Locri

The project creates, coordinated with the visual identity system, a communication program capable of integrating traditional exhibition solutions with the most recent technologies for the immersive use of spaces and artefacts. The areas of action are those specific to augmented reality, the result of an immaterial compositional method that characterizes environments and contexts by intervening on elements and surfaces with a technological support apparatus that modifies their spatial and perceptive effects. For each attractor, a multimedia production is created, based on the Video Mapping technique, which can be used for future "immersive" installations.

The multimedia contents must have, on the one hand, a strong didactic value, in order to contribute to the learning of scientific notions by different categories of users with particular regard to students and children, including those with disabilities; on the other hand, they must verify the potential offered by the superposition of narrative layers, rendered through digital languages, on exceptional real contexts.

The project involves the creation of a series of 4 audiovisual productions rendered with the Video-Mapping technique together with the composition of soundscapes rendered using the three-dimensional sound spatialization technique. In the following attractors: Locri Museum, Kaulon Museum and Capo Colonna Museum, video projections must have a minimum resolution of 1920x1200px. For the Kaulon Museum and the Locri Museum the multi-channel audio content must be composed of 4 mono tracks. For the Capo Colonna Museum the multi-channel audio content must be composed of 8 mono tracks. For the National Gallery of Cosenza, the production of 1 video with a minimum size of 3840 x 1200 px and multi-channel sound content consisting of 8 mono tracks is required.

The project involves the production of a series of 2 mini-documentaries which are installed on two video walls (the supply of video walls is not the subject of this tender procedure) positioned in the museum areas of the two attractions Museum of Sibaritide and Museum of Locri The two mini-documentaries, lasting 3 minutes each, must include soundtracks for the video with sound effects and/or original soundtrack, as well as subtitling in dual languages (Italian, English).

All videos are installed on a display with 3840*2160 resolution (4K UHD), therefore video files must have the same resolution.

Creation of documentary videos intended for publication on the project's institutional website. Each documentary video must include voice-overs, in Italian and English, for at least 70% of its duration. Documentaries must provide soundtracks for each video with sound effects and/or original soundtrack, as well as dual language subtitling (Italian, English).

5. CONCLUSION

In conclusion, we can state that, as also revealed by Digital Report 2023, in Italy there is a growing maturity in the use of the digitalization in culture. These tools are used in increasingly diversified ways, above all for the purpose of research, information, sharing and socializing. They offer the possibility of providing cultural products and services adapted to different types of users and users, simplifying their narration, involvement and experientiality, generating consumption practices and proactive learning. Furthermore, they constitute a potentially useful tool for individual growth and intellectual capacity of people, thanks to the vast range of training contents that can be shared and used through the various sharing platforms. This part of the analysis was the basis for the development of a digital strategy defined in two parts: on-site and off-site. For everything that concerns the off-site, therefore the part relating to good practices to be implemented in the digital world to increase brand awareness and interact with the public, we started with support cultural institutions in the creation and promotion of digital content using a platform accessible from mobile or desktop devices. After presenting the Brand Guidelines, we went on to define the aspect and main functions of the application through which all the information on current events and exhibitions is made available together with the digital content created by the institutions. These contents will therefore be available for consultation and above all shareable by the entire community, offering greater visibility to the organizers. Thanks to a fully customizable notification system we will be able to create a totally personalized environment based on the preferences of the individual user, improving the user experience. To complete this first strategic part, we then deepened communication on the web. Starting from the key concepts, such as accessibility and usability and, once understood how indispensable they are in order to be able to create an inclusive virtual environment that responds to the needs of all users, all the tools and best practices to be implemented to respond to these were presented requirements and also to comply with the regulatory framework.. We therefore took advantage of the guidelines provided by WCAG to define the basic principles to follow for the creation of a fully accessible website, also defining the right practices to adopt. Finally, the tools available to verify the accessibility of the institutional website were presented, which can also help to evaluate its usability. As regards the part relating to social networks, we have underlined the importance of how collaboration and co-creation can offer multiple opportunities for improvement and development, if properly studied. Turning now to the on-site strategy, we have defined the positive aspects of phygital contents, emphasizing how the size of the structure and the economic capacity can drastically influence the design choices; Therefore, the comparison with partners in the sector is the right path to follow to bring significant added value to the experience of visiting cultural sites. All this highlights has led to greater awareness and new perspectives for the future, which institutions should consider to facilitate a correct digital transformation of cultural heritage and generate more revenue for museums. The latter should once again become places of cultural production, as well as consumption, creating new art forms and experiences through the support of digital technology. Ultimately, we can state that, despite the growing presence of the Internet and digitization in society, many areas of the Italian cultural and artistic industry are struggling to adapt to these changes, highlighting a persistent gap. It happens that the initiatives promoted by holders of cultural contents do not take into account scientific or commercial innovations. For this reason, cultural institutions need guidance in understanding the importance of developments in digital research and applications in order to meet their innovation needs. The challenges facing every cultural institution include adopting innovative strategies to attract new visitors and make their collections and initiatives more accessible, thus promoting the democratization of knowledge. Digital and the web can be useful development, enhancement and communication tools at various levels, but require specific skills, adequate resources and appropriate investments. However, these actions are particularly complex for small and medium-sized enterprises and emerging realities, which make up a large part of the Italian cultural sector, and represent the subjects most at risk and to be valorised. One of the main challenges of the moment is therefore to ensure that these subjects too have access to the opportunities offered by digital.

REFERENCES

Accessible Resources for Cultural Heritage EcoSystems. (2020). ARCHES project funded by the European call for proposals of the Horizon 2020 programme. https://cordis.europa.eu/article/id/413505-technical-innovations-help-overcome-access-barriers-to-cultural-spaces/it

Bandarin, F., Hosagrahar, J., and Sailer Albernaz, F. (2011). "*Why Development Needs Culture*." Journal of Cultural Heritage Management and Sustainable Development 1 (1): 15–25.

Clarelli M. V. M. (2011). *Il Museo nel mondo contemporaneo*. Carocci editore, Roma

Criconia A. (2011). *L'architettura dei musei.* Carocci editore, Roma

Field Museum https://www.fieldmuseum.org/

Floridi, L. (2017). *La quarta rivoluzione. Come l'infosfera sta trasformando il mondo.* Raffaello Cortina Editore, Milano.

Floridi, L. (2020). *Pensare l'infosfera. La filosofia come design concettuale.* Raffaello Cortina Editore, Milano.

Mandarano, N. (2019). *Musei e media digitali.* Carocci Editore, Roma.

Meschini, A. (2011). *Digital technologies and communication of cultural heritage. State of the art and development prospects: Technologies for the communication of cultural heritage*. https://disegnarecon.unibo.it/article/view/2565/1943

Morace, F. (2018). *Futuro più umano. Quello che l'intelligenza artificiale non potrà mai darci.* Egea, Milano.

MuseumInstaSwap https://www.museuminstaswap.org/

New Museum https://www.newmuseum.org/pages/view/ar-t

SocialMedium https://fryemuseum.org/exhibition/5631/

Symbola, (2022). *I'm Culture 2022.* https://www.symbola.net/ricerca/io-sono-cultura-2022/

HOW MUSEUMS CAN USE THE METAVERSE TO INCREASE AWARENESS

Nikolaos Misirlis and Huong Giang Nguyen
HAN University of Applied Sciences
Arnhem, The Netherlands

ABSTRACT

The study comprehensively evaluates the preparedness of museums and their audiences for transitioning into Metaverse-based interfaces, leveraging the Technology Acceptance Model. It encompasses extensive audience surveys and formulates strategic recommendations for museums, emphasizing the importance of interactive and immersive virtual exhibits. This paper provides a critical analysis of the challenges and opportunities faced by cultural heritage institutions in adopting Metaverse technologies, offering insights into the future of digital engagement in the museum sector. It emphasizes the positive attitude of respondents towards virtual museums and the importance of interactive exhibits in enhancing visitor experiences. The study identifies technological infrastructure, such as VR/AR devices and Metaverse platforms, as key for developing virtual museums. It suggests that despite technological and readiness challenges, the benefits of digitizing collections and engaging audiences in the Metaverse are clear, calling for strategic approaches to improve visitor experiences in virtual museum settings.

KEYWORDS

Metaverse, Virtual Museums, Technology, Digital Transformation, Audience Readiness

1. INTRODUCTION

The term "Metaverse" originated from the prefix "meta" and the word "universe", refers to a "massive virtual environment parallel to the physical world" where people interact through digital avatars (Lee et al., 2021). With the constant changes in technological developments, the Metaverse is expected to become the next wave of computing innovations, promising to bring significant influences in different aspects of human life. It potentially affects how we connect, work, and interact with brands and create shared experiences that might blur physical and digital boundaries (Dwivedi et al., 2022). Although the Metaverse is relatively new to the general public, immersive and interactive online games, such as Second Life, Roblox, or Fortnite, have been available worldwide since the mid-2000s (Dwivedi et al., 2022). Nowadays, the application of the Metaverse can be seen in various fields, from education, finance, and healthcare to entertainment.

Technological innovations and the Metaverse have also transformed our relationship with cultural heritages. Museums, exhibitions, and cultural institutions have begun to explore the Metaverse to bring more ways for the public to engage with their collections. However, the readiness of museums to adopt this digital shift may vary widely. Problems related to technological infrastructure, technological knowledge of organizations' leaders in terms of difficulties and limitations of virtual displays, the cost of new technology, and the audience's readiness towards the Metaverse and virtual museums.

The present study dives into the readiness of museums for this digital transition and the audience's readiness for a Metaverse-based museum experience in the future. It provides insights into the current state of the audience about Metaverse and the related technology, and virtual museums, as well as technological requirements, potential challenges, and digital strategies for museums to enhance their visibility in a virtual world. The second objective is to present findings that help museums assess their readiness for the Metaverse, including technological requirements, challenges, and limitations. When said that, we mean that museums will provide a hybrid experience onsite. Visitors will need to visit the museum and experience the metaverse technologies, while being inside the museums. Ultimately, the researchers develop strategic recommendations for museums to leverage interactive exhibitions and visitors' experiences to improve the museums' global awareness and attract a broader audience.

The researchers will gather and analyze data from various papers and written sources to answer the Main question 1: **How ready are the museums for the Metaverse?**, and six sub-questions, namely:

Sub-question 1: What technology/ infrastructure is required for museums to enter the Metaverse?

Sub-question 2: What are the limitations of digitizing collections for virtual displays?

Sub-question 3: To what extent is the audience aware of the Metaverse concept?

Sub-question 4: What factors can influence the audience's attitudes about virtual museums in the Metaverse?

Sub-question 5: What are the audience's behavioral intentions toward exploring a virtual museum in the Metaverse in the future?

Sub-question 6: What features influence the audience's experience in a Metaverse-based museum?

2. LITERATURE REVIEW

In 1985, Fred Davis created the Technology Acceptance Model – an information system model that examines how users accept and use or reject technology (Patrícia Silva, 1989). The two most important factors of the TAM model are perceived ease of use (PEOU) and perceived usefulness (PU) (Legris et al., 2003) because they directly influence an individual's attitude toward using technology and, eventually, the individual's intention to use the technology (Jang et al., 2021). Besides PEOU and PU, the model also uses attitudes toward technology use (ATU) and behavioral intention (BI) (Davis, 1985). The survey questionnaires were formed according to external variables from the TAM: attitudes towards technology use, perceived ease of use, subjective norms, and behavioral intention. The data will be analyzed to figure out the audience's attitudes towards museums in the Metaverse which will influence their behavioral intention to explore Metaverse-based museums in the future.

Lee et al. (2021) link the Metaverse's virtual environment to the convergence of the Internet, Web technologies, and Extended Reality (XR), which integrates Augmented Reality (AR), Mixed Reality (MR), and Virtual Reality (VR). The technological framework can be tailored for different purposes, such as entertainment, e-commerce, education, etc. (Zhang et al., 2022). Several museums have taken steps into the digitalization journey, such as publishing digital images by Paris Muséees, online exhibitions by Shelburne Museum, etc. However, with the rapid changes in technology innovations, applying metaverse in digital archives still has significant room for improvement. Kang et al. (2022) propose the Virtual Art Museum Education Program (VAMEP) using Roblox Studio, aiming to investigate the effect of virtual art museums on art education using the Metaverse technology. Gao and Braud's study (2023) explores the opportunities VR technologies bring to museums in the Metaverse era, emphasizing recent innovations and developments in digitizing collections in the virtual space. The same research mentions that VR technology can be used as an "auxiliary archiving tool" to improve visitors' experience, and users can access online exhibitions using VR goggles. However, VR devices require modern computers or digital devices to be able to function and are limited by physical limitations and high costs (Gao et al., 2023). Google Art & Culture and Matterport are two of the most well-known VR platforms that allow museums to convert their archives to virtual reality. Research by Phoebe Wu (2022) reviews some digital museums with different approaches and techniques, including the Museums of Contemporary Digital Art (MoCDA), which offers virtual exhibitions based on the museum website; the MEMENTO MINTI exhibition is presented via Decentraland, a virtual social world that allows users to create, experience and monetize content (Decentraland, 2023), gives a similar experience of navigating in a game setting. Longo and Faraci's study discusses the opportunities and challenges of applying metaverse technology to virtual museums, hence providing digital strategies aimed at edutainment (education + entertainment). Hurst, W. (2023) discusses how museums adopted XR to digitize collections and offer remote access, highlighting the role of digital storytelling in creating immersive and adaptive experiences.

Digital Collections

Museums need to digitize their artworks and collections or convert physical objects into high-quality digital assets, making them accessible for preservation, observation, and possibly purchase activities. Hurst et al. (2023), in the case study of developing a 3D art gallery, state that physical artworks can be converted to non-fungible tokens (NFTs). According to Schwiderowski et al. (2023), NFTs are unique, verified, and digitally traceable crypto tokens. In the Metaverse, these tokens will serve as digital representations of its physical items. Besides, VR platforms like Matterport can also be used to create digital versions of collections. Since its collaboration with Meta Ai in 2022, Metaverse's users can create a 3D version of physical items via Matterport platform.

Metaverse Platforms

To be able to enter the Metaverse, it is advisable for cultural organizations to form a partnership with Metaverse's platforms. Roblox has been widely used in developing e-learning environments (Khaled Alhasan et al., 2023), immersive video games, redesigning museum education for the next-level visitor (Savacool C., 2023), or virtual tours (Meier et al., 2020). Besides Roblox, Decentraland is also a platform where museums can consider creating a virtual version of their heritages. Visitors can explore virtual space while making real-time social interactions.

Virtual Reality (VR) and Augmented Reality (AR): Extended reality platforms like Roblox, Decentraland, Second Life, etc can be accessed via VR devices (eg: VR headsets), which allows visitors to enter the virtual museums and walk around the virtual spaces as well as interact with exhibits, AR equipment (eg: AR glasses, smartphones), which allow museums to overlay digital information onto the physical environment, enriching the audience's experience with additional content.

2.1 Methodology

Desk research will use sub-questions as a guideline to search for data from published articles, hence explaining the current concept of the Metaverse, its application across different industries, and how museums can prepare to enter the Metaverse world. All the literature/journals/published research papers were collected from Google Scholar and HAN's database and checked with AAOCC criteria (Authority, Accuracy, Objectivity, Currency, Coverage) (Google Guide, 2022).

In terms of field research, a quantitative survey was used based on previous related studies and the Technology Acceptance Model. The survey's questionnaires aimed to investigate people's attitudes towards museums in the Metaverse and variables that might affect their experience. They were distributed amongst the mass target group (people from 18 to 35 years old). After that, the questions would be coded, and data would be analyzed using SPSS and Google Forms.

Technology Acceptance Model (TAM)

In 1985, Fred Davis created the Technology Acceptance Model – an information system model that examines how users accept and use or reject technology (Patrícia Silva, 1989). The two most important factors of the TAM model are perceived ease of use (PEOU) and perceived usefulness (PU) (Legris et al., 2003) because they directly influence an individual's attitude toward using technology and, eventually, the individual's intention to use the technology (Jang et al., 2021). Besides PEOU and PU, the model also uses attitudes toward technology use (ATU) and behavioral intention (BI) (Davis, 1985).

The survey questionnaires were formed according to external variables from the TAM: attitudes towards technology use, perceived ease of use, subjective norms, and behavioral intention. The data will be analyzed to figure out the audience's attitudes towards museums in the Metaverse which will influence their behavioral intention to explore Metaverse-based museums in the future.

2.2 Findings

The survey questionnaires are designed to support answering the main question. *Is the audience ready for the Metaverse?* and sub-questions (3), (4), (5), (6). The survey was sent and filled in by 442 respondents between 18 and 35 years old. The chart below shows that most respondents are from Vietnam (accounting for 60%) and the Netherlands (accounting for 26.1%).

To what extent is the audience aware of the Metaverse concept?

Figure 2 demonstrates that most respondents are moderately familiar with the Metaverse and have a basic understanding of its concept. However, people from 18 to 22 years old have less knowledge related to the Metaverse than those in the other age groups.

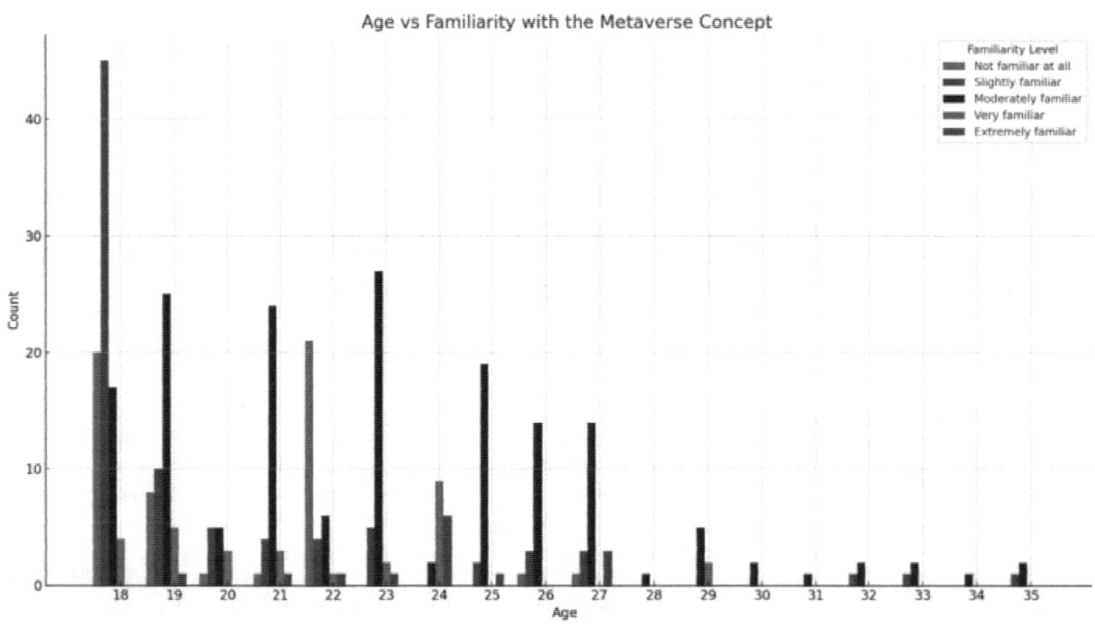

Figure 1. Age & Familiarity with the Metaverse concept

In addition, Figure 2 indicates that the Metaverse concept is more popular among males than females or other genders.

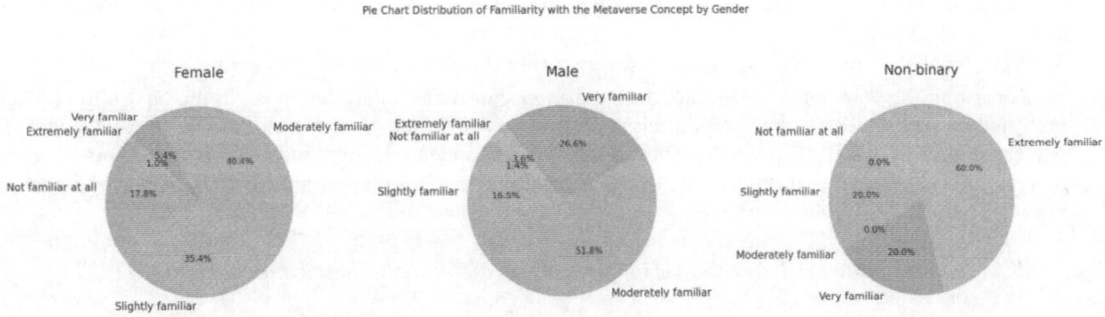

Figure 2. Gender & Familiarity with the Metaverse concept

What factors can influence the audience's attitudes about virtual museums in the Metaverse?

To answer this question, we will look at the relationships between the readiness of the audience and various socioeconomic factors. Overall, 33.9% of respondents are moderately interested, accounting for most of the respondents, and 28.3% are very interested in exploring Metaverse museums.

It can be seen that the majority of respondents either rarely go to a physical museum (only 1 or twice a year) or occasionally (several times a year). People who never visit a physical museum are most likely not interested in exploring a virtual museum, while those who visit several times a year show higher interest.

The chi-square test shows that there is a significant association between an individual's experience in technology utilization and interest in visiting a virtual museum. More specifically, the more familiar and experienced they are with VR/AR technology, the more interested they are in virtual museums.

The result suggests that respondents' perception of how easy or difficult (with 1 being the most difficult and 5 being the easiest) it would be to navigate a virtual museum is associated with their interest in exploring one. People who think it's easy to use tend to show a higher interest in exploring virtual museums, while people who think it's difficult are less interested. It indicates that improving the ease of use may positively influence the public's interest in virtual museums.

In terms of how people's opinions influence the willingness to visit museums in the Metaverse, most answers spread across not influenced (24.9%), slightly influenced (30.8%), and moderately influenced (29.2%) (Figure 3). This suggests that while social factors play a role in the decision-making process, there is still a strong sense of individual preference.

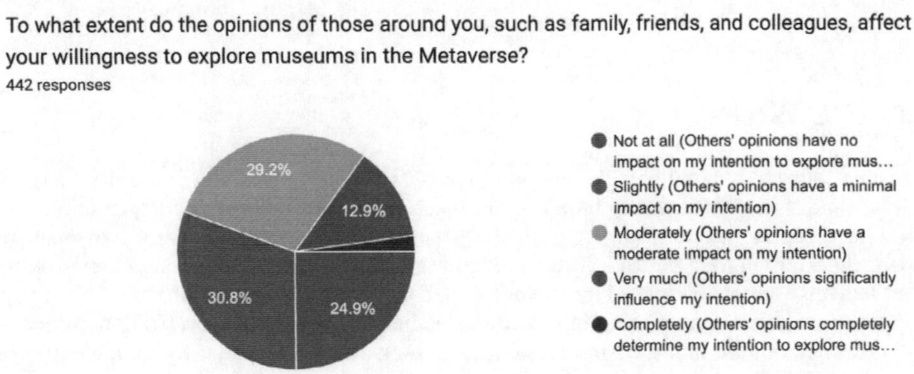

Figure 3. People opinions influence the willingness to explore museums in the Metaverse

What are the audience's behavioral intentions toward exploring a virtual museum in the Metaverse in the future?

Regarding the respondents' likelihood of visiting a museum in the Metaverse in the next 6 months, many respondents are either neutral or unlikely to visit, possibly due to unfamiliarity with the technology or perceived ease of use (Figure 9). However, 36.2% of respondents rated 4 and 5 (meaning that they are likely or very likely to visit), indicating that there is a positive behavioral intention towards exploring museums in the Metaverse.

What features influence the audience's experience in a Metaverse-based museum?

Figure 4 shows that interactive exhibits and the immersive environment heavily influence the audiences' experience of virtual museums in the Metaverse, as these 2 features got the highest "Very Important" rating. Real-time social interactions and Accessibility features are also rated as "Important", demonstrating that users seek socially engaging and inclusive experiences. In contrast, customization, such as customized avatars or personal exhibits, seems to be the least important compared to other features, which shows a lower need for personalization within the experience. Overall, depending on the gathered data above, it is advisable for virtual museums in the Metaverse to prioritize social interactions and interactive exhibits to enhance the audiences' experience.

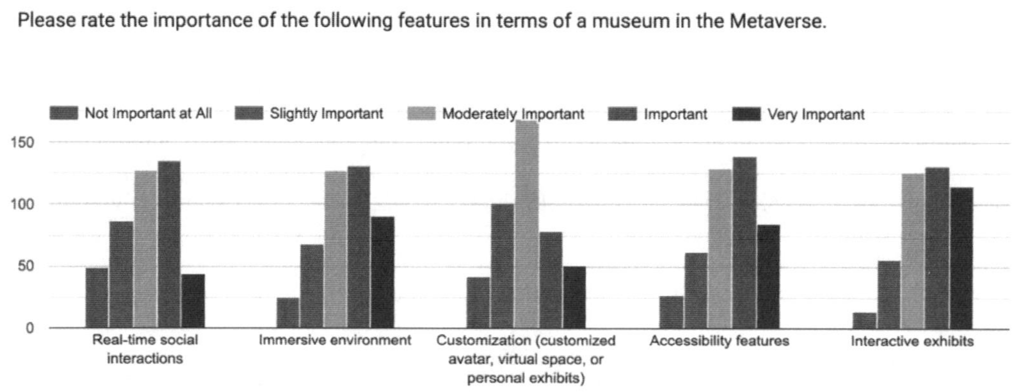

Figure 4. The importance of different features in terms of a museum in the Metaverse

3. CONCLUSION

In conclusion, this study highlights the evolving landscape of museums and cultural heritage in the rapidly advancing Metaverse. This research, based on the Technology Acceptance Model, examines how audiences perceive and accept virtual museums within the Metaverse. The findings reveal two main points: firstly, respondents generally have a positive attitude toward virtual museums, even though they may not be familiar with the Metaverse and its associated technologies. Secondly, the research emphasizes a strong preference for interactive and immersive experiences in virtual museums, distinguishing them from traditional museums.

Museums that venture into the Metaverse need to consider the essential technological infrastructure for this transition, including VR/AR devices, Metaverse platforms, and digital collections. While the potential for enhancing visitor experiences and expanding the audience is significant, museums face challenges such as technological complexity, cost implications, maintenance, authenticity concerns, technology limitations, and varying levels of audience readiness.

Despite these challenges, integrating museums into the Metaverse offers promising benefits. A strategic approach that prioritizes audience education and experience enhancement in Metaverse museums is crucial, along with being prepared technologically.

However, it is important to note that this research is not exhaustive due to constraints on time and resources. Future studies should explore the cost implications of technology adoption, further investigate audience readiness, and examine the dynamics of integrating museums into the Metaverse to gain a more comprehensive understanding of this digital transformation.

In the future, it is recommended that research efforts strive to incorporate a more diverse and extensive sample. This sample should encompass various geographical and demographic segments to ensure that the insights gained are universally applicable. Moreover, conducting longitudinal studies would be beneficial in gaining a deeper understanding of the changing trends in audience attitudes towards virtual museums in the Metaverse. It is essential for cultural institutions considering embarking on this digital journey to thoroughly investigate the economic aspects, such as conducting a cost-benefit analysis of adopting Metaverse technologies. Additionally, it is important to explore potential solutions to the challenges that have been identified. This research endeavor will not only expand our comprehension of the integration of museums into the Metaverse but will also contribute to the development of strategies that effectively bridge the gap between traditional and digital cultural experiences.

REFERENCES

A critical review of the technology acceptance model. Information & Management, 40(3), 191–204. https://doi.org/10.1016/s0378-7206(01)00143-4

Alsharif, A. Y. O., & Owda, M. (2022, April 11). A Technology Acceptance Model Survey of the Metaverse Prospects. ResearchGate; MDPI. https://www.researchgate.net/publication/359893892_A_Technology_Acceptance_Model_Survey_of_the_Metaverse_Prospects

Corona, L. (2023). Digitization: An Overview of the Advantages and Disadvantages. IntechOpen EBooks. https://doi.org/10.5772/intechopen.1002006

Davenport, T., Guha, A., Grewal, D. et al. How artificial intelligence will change the future of marketing. J. of the Acad. Mark. Sci. 48, 24–42 (2020). https://doi.org/10.1007/s11747-019-00696-0

Davis, F. D. (1985). A technology acceptance model for empirically testing new end-user information systems: Theory and results. Massachusetts Institute of Technology. http://hdl.handle.net/1721.1/15192

Dwivedi, Y. K., Hughes, L., Baabdullah, A. M., Ribeiro-Navarrete, S., Mihalis Giannakis, Al-Debei, M. M., Dennehy, D., Metri, B. A., Dimitrios Buhalis, Christy, Conboy, K., Doyle, R., Dubey, R., Dutot, V., Felix, R., Goyal, D. P., Gustafsson, A., Hinsch, C., Ikram Jebabli, & Janssen, M. (2022). Metaverse beyond the hype: Multidisciplinary perspectives on emerging challenges, opportunities, and agenda for research, practice and policy. International Journal of Information Management, 66, 102542–102542. https://doi.org/10.1016/j.ijinfomgt.2022.102542

Gamers in the Museum: A Redesign of Museum Education for the Next Level Visitor - ProQuest. (2023). Proquest.com. https://www.proquest.com/openview/2a3acafc6d3cb328bfd4c6be3076e3bb/1?pq-origsite=gscholar&cbl=18750&diss=y

Gao, Z., Braud, T., & Guljajeva, V. (2023). VR-driven museum opportunities: Digitized archives in the age of the metaverse. In P. Alsina & A. Burbano (Eds.), Possibles (No. 32). Artnodes, UOC. Retrieved dd/mm/aa, from https://doi.org/10.7238/artnodes.v0i32.402462

Google Search Results: Evaluating What You Find - Google Guide. (2022). Googleguide.com. https://www.googleguide.com/evaluating_results.html

Haenlein, M., Kaplan, A., Tan, C.-W & Zhang, P. (2019) Artificial intelligence (AI) and management analytics, Journal of Management Analytics, 6:4, 341-343, DOI: 10.1080/23270012.2019.1699876

Hurst, W., Orestis Spyrou, Bedir Tekinerdogan, & Krampe, C. (2023). Digital Art and the Metaverse: Benefits and Challenges. Future Internet, 15(6), 188–188. https://doi.org/10.3390/fi15060188

Hutson, James and Hutson, Piper, "Museums and the Metaverse: Emerging Technologies to Promote Inclusivity and Engagement" (2023). Faculty Scholarship. 452. https://digitalcommons.lindenwood.edu/faculty-research-papers/452

Jang, J., Ko, Y., Won Sug Shin, & Han, I. (2021). Augmented Reality and Virtual Reality for Learning: An Examination Using an Extended Technology Acceptance Model. IEEE Access, 9, 6798–6809. https://doi.org/10.1109/access.2020.3048708

Kang, D., Choi, H., & Nam, S. (2022). Learning Cultural Spaces: A Collaborative Creation of a Virtual Art Museum Using Roblox. International Journal of Emerging Technologies in Learning (Online), 17(22), 232-245. DOI: 10.3991/ijet.v17i22.33023.

Khaled Alhasan, Khawla Alhasan, & Sama'a Al Hashimi. (2023). Roblox in Higher Education: Opportunities, Challenges, and Future Directions for Multimedia Learning. International Journal of Emerging Technologies in Learning (IJET), 18(19), 32–46. https://www.learntechlib.org/p/223762/

Kim, S., & Ji, Y. (2018, August 22). Gap Analysis. ResearchGate; unknown. https://www.researchgate.net/publication/327879112_Gap_Analysis

Legris, P., Ingham, J., & Collerette, P. (2003). Why do people use information technology?

Meier, C., Saorín, J., Bonnet, A., & Alberto Guerrero Cobos. (2020). Using the Roblox Video Game Engine for Creating Virtual tours and Learning about the Sculptural Heritage. International Journal of Emerging Technologies in Learning (IJET), 15(20), 268–280. https://www.learntechlib.org/p/218337/?nl=1

Misirlis, N., & Munawar, H. B. (2023). An analysis of the technology acceptance model in understanding university students behavioral intention to use metaverse technologies. ArXiv.org. https://arxiv.org/abs/2302.02176

Pan, S., Jung, S., & Suo, S. (2023). Understanding the adoption and usage behaviors of popular and emerging Metaverse platforms: A study based on the extended technology acceptance model. Journal of Broadcasting & Electronic Media, 67(4), 574-595. https://doi.org/10.1080/08838151.2023.2224477

The Museums Took One Step Further: A Study of Digital Museum – 62-830/93-430/830 Spring 2022. (2022). Cmu.edu. https://courses.ideate.cmu.edu/62-830/s2022/?p=783

Welcome to Decentraland. (2023). Decentraland.org. https://decentraland.org/

Zhang, X., Chen, Y., Hu, L., & Wang, Y. (2022). The metaverse in education: Definition, framework, features, potential applications, challenges, and future research topics. Frontiers in Psychology, 13. https://doi.org/10.3389/fpsyg.2022.1016300

CRITICAL THINKING DIGITAL SKILLS AMONG GENERATIONS X, Y, Z

Sabina Lissitsa
Ariel University, Israel

ABSTRACT

Integrating Generational Cohort Theory and Resources and Appropriation Theory the study examines the effects of personal and positional inequalities on critical thinking digital skills (CTDS) among generations X, Y, and Z. The study is based on an online survey of 1495 Israeli Jews aged 18-57. The findings show that CTDS among Gen X were significantly lower, by a large margin, than those of the younger generations, while Gen Z reported the highest level of these skills. Multivariate analysis indicated different effect patterns of personal and positional categorical variables on CTDS. We found that the contribution of personal demographic inequalities (gender, age, ethnicity, religiosity) to the explained variance in CTDS was most pronounced in Gen Y, compared to Gen X and Gen Z. The contribution of Big Five personality traits and positional social inequalities (education, occupational status, language proficiency) to explaining CTDS was similar between Gen X and Gen Y, but among Gen Z these contributions were much less pronounced. Understanding the intergenerational differences in CTDS is crucial for tailoring educational approaches, promoting inclusivity, and harnessing the diverse strengths of each generation to navigate an ever-evolving digital landscape successfully.

KEYWORDS

Critical Thinking Digital Skills, Generational Cohorts, Generation X, Generation Y, Generation Z, Resources and Appropriation Theory

1. INTRODUCTION

The complexities of 21st century work, including non-routine, creative, and interactive tasks, require skilled workers to be independent thinkers, capable of generating and refining their ideas, connecting viewpoints, and also generating new input by engaging in offline and online discussions, i.e., possessing critical thinking skills (Einwiller & Kim, 2020). Furthermore, in these days of fake news, misinformation, and disinformation, critical thinking has become the most important skill for discerning false, incomplete, and outdated information and communication online (Puig et al., 2021). However, systematic analysis of 21st-century digital skills reveals that *critical thinking* is less studied in a digital context compared to other digital skills (Van Laar et al., 2020). Moreover, the majority of articles on 21st-century digital skills describe them on a conceptual level with little evidence of corresponding data. Since the working environment has undergone rapid and significant innovations in recent years, it is important for policy makers to understand how different groups of employees adopt the skills required in the workplace and which factors constitute important predictors of skills in different population groups. As numerous studies have reported salient between-generational differences in various types of skills and different factors responsible for skills acquisition in each generation (Ferreira, 2021), the main purpose of the current study is to evaluate between-generational differences in the effects of individual variables on critical thinking digital skills (hereinafter CTDS).

2. LITERATURE REVIEW

2.1 Digital Inequality and Resources and Appropriation Theory

The approach to defining digital skills has shifted from a technical orientation to a broader perspective that includes content-related or higher-order skills which were recently conceptualized as 21st-century digital skills (Van Laar et al., 2020). The Resources and Appropriation Theory (Van Dijk, 2017) focuses on the distribution and allocation of resources and explains how certain groups or individuals gain access to and exploit these resources to attain power and influence over others. More particularly it examines how both personal and positional inequalities may explain the distribution and control of resources within social systems. Personal categorical inequalities frequently observed in digital inequality research are based on gender, age, race/ethnicity, religiosity and personality traits, whereas positional categorical inequalities pertain to status in the labor market), education and cultural capital characteristics (Elena-Bucea et al., 2021), and urban vs. rural residence. In terms of this theory the CTDS resource has two dimensions – the human resource (the ability to process data judgmentally and analytically) and the technological resource (the ability to use advanced tools, equipment, and technologies).

2.2 Critical Thinking and Critical Thinking Digital Skills

Critical thinking is the cognitive ability to carefully examine events, circumstances or thoughts, and to make informed choices about information and communications received, based on logical reflection and reasoning (Howard et al., 2015). This faculty includes skillful reflection and judgment, which are necessary for, ascertaining the pertinence of information or communication to a given context, and selectively distilling the influx of data as individuals formulate their own autonomous point of view (Dede, 2010). Proficiency in critical thinking enables individuals to construe, comprehend, analyze, and make judicious decisions both in the abstract and in daily actions, and to make reasonable decisions about subsequent courses of action (Warsah et al., 2021). In an age of extensive disinformation, the need for critical assessment of online content is paramount. CSDS enables individuals to gauge online information in terms of its credibility, relevance, and accuracy, thus helping them to make informed decisions and not be led astray by misinformation and fake news. CTDS are essential for 21st century workers who must navigate the digital landscape, extract and interpret valuable information, solve problems, make informed decisions, quickly learn and adapt to new digital tools, software and platforms, foster innovation, and collaborate effectively within digital environments (Van Laar et al., 2020).

2.3 Generational Cohort Theory

Generational cohort theory contends that people who come of age in a given time period are molded by the economic, political, technological and social environment of that period. A generational cohort is often defined as those born in a 20–25 year-period, or in a period that encompasses the birth, maturation and initial child bearing of those in the cohort (Meredith & Schewe, 1994). The focus in the current study is on three generations: X, Y and Z. Gen X (those born between 1964-1980) grew up in a period marked by economic uncertainty and societal uncertainty. Many became independent at a young age because both parents were working or divorced. In terms of their digital orientation, the literature considers Gen X to be 'digital immigrants', whose formative years were not IT intensive. Thus, Gen X members had to devote considerable time and effort to acquire digital skills. In terms of critical thinking, Gen X individuals are alleged to have little tolerance for bureaucracy and rules, but excel in self-reliance (Gursoy et al., 2008) and skepticism, which are considered to be dimensions of critical thinking skills. Generations Y and Z are both considered to be digital natives. However, their formative experiences differ. Individuals born in generation Y (between 1981 and 1994) matured during a period of economic growth. Their characteristics are over-confidence, high achievement orientation, narcissism and a short attention span. Gen Y is depicted as egotistical, flexible, creative, lacking in respect for traditions, and endowed with broad but superficial knowledge. Generation Z (born in and after 1995) faced a world marked by recessions and other financial crises, war and threats of terror, political unrest and the relentless gaze of social media. Gen Z is described as achievement-oriented and pragmatic. They are deficient in consequential thinking, make little effort to make sense of things and seek happiness and pleasure (Klopotan et al., 2020). With diminished problem-solving skills, they do not demonstrate the ability to view a situation, put it in context, analyze it and make a decision.

3. RESEARCH HYPOTHESES

Personal categorical demographic variables. Scholars have found evidence indicating that the development of critical thinking skills is influenced by personal demographic characteristics: age, gender, religiosity and ethnicity. We assumed that technically savvy Gen Z members who have been exposed constantly to disinformation and fake news and have spent their coming-of-age years in societal and economic uncertainty, have developed CTDS unrelated to their demographic background variables. However, this is not the case regarding digital immigrants – Gen X, who should apply their skepticism and self-reliance to the digital environment or Gen Y, who are over-confident and have a short attention span. Thus, we may posit:

H1. Among Gen X and Gen Y, the proportion of variance in CTDS explained by personal categorical demographic variables will be higher than among Gen Z (in terms of change in R^2).

Big Five personality traits. Psychologists claim that personality strongly affects a broad range of cognitive responses (Ajzen, 2005). One of the leading theories of personality is the Five Factor Model (FFM) (McCrae & John, 1992), which includes five constructs: extraversion, conscientiousness, openness to new experience, agreeableness, and neuroticism. Assumedly, the CTDS developed by Gen Z digital natives are less related to their personality traits, compared to older generations. They often demonstrate a high degree of adaptability and flexibility, a preference for teamwork, and a high level of self-directed learning, as reflected in their efforts to seek information online in order to acquire new skills (Klopotan et al., 2020). These traits are essential for developing CTDS and mitigate the importance of personality. In contrast, we may assume that among digital immigrants - Gen X, the application of critical thinking to the digital environment may be related to personality traits, which may promote or suppress this process. The same may be said for the more superficial Gen Y, who experienced the transition from traditional communication methods to digital platforms. Personality traits related to effective communication and collaboration in the digital space can impact the ability of Gen Y to engage in online discussions, share ideas, and collaborate in order to critically process information. Accordingly, we may assume that:

H2: Among Gen X and Gen Y, the proportion of variance in CTDS explained by the Big Five personality traits will be higher than among Gen Z (in terms of change in R^2).

Positional categorical inequalities. Social class or status may be a factor in the development of critical thinking. Due to their economic resources, upper-class families have many structural opportunities such as excellent schools and summer and after-school enrichment programs which facilitate their children's acquisition of educational capital (including critical thinking abilities) (Tsui, 2003). The "habitus" (in Bourdieu's (2003) term) provided by upper-class families tends to promote practices that encourage the exercise of critical thinking. Because higher social classes tend to adopt technological advances more rapidly, they also adjust more quickly and successfully to digital environments. This combination of educational capital and higher-level skills is often associated with higher class urban localities and more respectable vocational avenues. Individuals with greater language proficiency are likely to expend less mental effort on language processing, and their better understanding of language structure increases their ability to engage in critical thinking. As all generations were exposed to structural inequalities (upper-class families in each generation had better opportunities to develop critical thinking ability, compared to those from disadvantaged socio-economic backgrounds), we assume that positional social inequalities will predict CTDS in all generations:

H3: Among all generations the same proportion of variance in CTDS will be explained by positional categorical inequalities (in terms of change in R^2).

4. METHODOLOGY

This study is based on an online survey of Israeli Jews from three generations: Gen X, Gen Y, and Gen Z. The questionnaire included about 35 questions on digital skills, and 20 items on the Big Five personality traits. The study was conducted among the representative sample of 1495 Israeli Jews aged 18-57, of whom 544 respondents (36.4 percent) belong to Gen Z, 485 (32.4 percent) to Gen Y, and 466 (31.2 percent) to Gen X.

Dependent variable - Critical thinking digital skills were measured by nine items, which were based on digital skills instruments (see Van Laar et al., 2018). The respondents were asked: To what extent do you use the Internet to…? Each of these items was measured on a scale of 1 (not at all) to 5 (to a very high extent). The reliability index, Cronbach's alpha, was 0.95.

Independent variables

Demographic variables: age (continuous), gender, ethnicity (immigrants vs. natives) and religiosity (secular, traditional, religious, ultra-orthodox).

Big five personality traits were measured using the reliable 20-item Mini IPIP (Donnellan et al., 2006). Respondents indicated their level of agreement with statements on a five-point Likert scale, ranging from 1 = strongly disagree to 5 = strongly agree.

Positional categorical inequalities: education (less than secondary, secondary, post-secondary, BA, MA, PhD), Hebrew proficiency, English proficiency (scale 1 to 5, 1 – not at all, 5 – to a very high extent), occupational status (managers and respondents who are working in academic occupations vs. other occupations), locality (center vs. periphery).

4.1 Results

Statistical analysis was conducted using SPSS-26 software. In order to explain critical thinking digital skills, a three-step multiple hierarchical regression was conducted separately for the three generations (Table 2). Personal categorical demographic variables (gender, age, religiosity and ethnicity) were entered in the first step, Big five personality traits in the second step and positional categorical inequalities variables in the third step. The multicollinearity assumption was rejected, as the maximal VIF measure of predictors was 1.54 for Generation X, 1.57 for Generation Y and 1.67 for Generation Z. In addition, one-way ANOVA tests with Post Hoc were conducted to examine differences between the generations for the research variables. A significant difference was found between Generation X ($M = 2.93$, $SD = 1.13$), Generation Y ($M=3.59$, $SD = 1.07$) and Generation Z ($M = 3.75$, $SD = 0.98$) in CTDS ($F\ (2;1492) = -11.11$, $p < .001$).

Table 1 is about here

Gen X. The hierarchical regression analysis (Table 1, Model 3) indicated that CTDS among immigrants were lower, compared to natives (beta = -0.09, $p < .05$). The effect of age on CTDS was non-significant. Religiosity and gender did not produce significant results ($p >.05$). The findings show a positive effect of extraversion (beta = 0.18, $p < .001$) on the dependent variable. The effects of openness to experience, conscientiousness and agreeableness were non-significant, while the effect of neuroticism was surprisingly positive (beta = 0.13, $p < .001$). We found a positive association between education and CTDS (beta = 0.16, $p < .001$). Other variables entered in regression Model 3 did not produce significant results ($p > .05$). In all, the independent variables contributed 23.7% to explaining CTDS variance.

Gen Y. We found that CTDS were higher among men, compared to women. (see Table 1, Model 3) (beta = 0.10, $p < .05$). Religiosity and ethnicity did not produce significant results ($p >.05$). We found a significant negative effect of age on CTDS (beta = -0.17, $p < .001$). The findings show a positive effect of conscientiousness (beta = 0.09, $p < .05$) and extraversion (beta = 0.13, $p < .001$) on the dependent variable. The effects of agreeableness and openness to experience were non-significant, while the effect of neuroticism was surprisingly positive (beta = 0.15, $p < .001$). We found a positive association between education and CTDS (beta = 0.11, $p < .001$). CTDS was found to be higher among managers and those who work in academic occupations, compared to others (beta = 0.17, $p < .001$). The independent variables contributed 25.8% to explaining CTDS variance.

Gen Z. We found a negative association between religiosity and CTDS (see Table 1, Model 3) (beta = -0.14, $p < .001$). Gender and ethnicity did not produce significant results ($p >.05$). We found a significant negative effect of age on CTDS (beta = -0.13, p < .001). The effects of openness to experience, conscientiousness, extraversion and agreeableness were non-significant, while the effect of neuroticism was positive (beta = 0.09, p < .05). We found positive associations between education (beta = 0.12, p < .001), English proficiency (beta = 0.19, p < .001) and the dependent variable. In all, the independent variables contributed 12.3% to explaining CTDS variance.

H1 was partially supported by the findings: among Gen Y, the proportion of variance for CTDS explained by the personal categorical demographic variables was higher (ΔR2 = 0.080), than among Gen Z (ΔR2 = 0.043). However, in contrast to H1 we found a similarity between Gen X and Gen Z in the proportion of variance for CTDS explained by the personal categorical demographic variables (among both generations (ΔR2 = 0.043). H2 was fully supported by the findings: among Gen X (ΔR2 = 0.094) and Gen Y (ΔR2 = 0.077) the proportion of variance for CTDS explained by the explained by Big five personality traits was higher than among Gen Z (ΔR2 = 0.025). H3 was partially supported by the findings: in line with this hypothesis, we found a similarity between Gen X and Gen Y in the proportion of variance in CTDS explained by positional categorical inequalities (in both cases close to ΔR2 = 0.100), while in contrast to the hypothesis, among Generation Z this percentage was lower (ΔR2 = 0.055).

5. CONCLUSIONS

The main purpose of the current study was to evaluate between-generational differences in the effects of personal and positional individual variables on critical thinking digital skills. As far as we know this was the first study to attempt to integrate Generational Cohort Theory and Resources and Appropriation Theory in order to reveal which inequalities are likely to challenge the acquisition of one of the most important skills in the 21st-century labour market (Van Laar et al., 2020). Our descriptive findings show that critical thinking digital skills among Gen X were significantly lower, by a large margin, than among the younger generations, while Gen Z reported the highest level of these skills. One possible explanation is that the technological resource (digital skills) is as essential in CTDS as the human resource (the ability to intellectually process, skillfully conceptualize, analyze, synthesize, and evaluate information). Although there is evidence that Gen X invests time and effort to acquire digital skills (Ahn & Jung, 2016), we can assume that transferring their critical thinking literacy into the digital environment was enormously challenging for them. In contrast, for Gen Y and especially for Gen Z the human and technological resources of CTDS, in other words, their cognitive and digital components, are fully integral and inextricable.

The multivariate analysis indicated different patterns of effects of personal and positional categorical variables on CTDS. We found that the contribution of personal demographic inequalities to the explained variance in CTDS was most pronounced in Gen Y. The contribution of personality traits and positional social inequalities was similar between Gen X and Gen Y, but among Gen Z these contributions were much less pronounced. Gen Z was exposed to technology from a very young age, had access to digital tools and resources in educational settings from an early age and integrated it into their daily lives seamlessly. Their shared digital upbringing may diminish the impact of personal and positional inequalities on their digital skills. As a result, Gen Z tends to have a more uniform and advanced level of CTDS compared to previous generations.

Table 1. Summary of hierarchical regression analysis for variables predicting critical thinking digital skills among Gen X (n = 466), Gen Y (N=485) and Gen Z (n = 544)

	Generation X					
	Model 1		Model 2		Model 3	
	B	Beta	B	Beta	B	Beta
(Constant)	4.33**		2.16**		0.90	
Gender (1=male)	0.18*	0.08	0.21*	0.09	0.08	0.04
Religiosity	-0.12*	-0.11	-0.07	-0.06	-0.03	-0.03
Age	-0.02*	-0.10	-0.02	-0.08	-0.01	-0.04
Immigrants	-0.24*	-0.08	-0.22	-0.08	-0.26*	-0.09

Extraversion			0.31**	0.20	0.27**	0.18
Agreeableness			0.07	0.05	0.00	0.00
Consciousness			-0.12	-0.08	-0.08	-0.05
Neuroticism			0.20**	0.16	0.16**	0.13
Openness to experience			0.13*	0.10	0.05	0.04
Education					0.16**	0.16
Hebrew Proficiency					-0.02	-0.01
English proficiency					0.23**	0.22
Locality (1=center_)					0.02	0.01
Occupational status (1=Manager)					0.17	0.07
R^2	0.043		0.137		0.237	
ΔR^2	0.043		0.094		0.100	
			Generation X			
(Constant)	5.64**		3.30**		1.58	
Gender (1=male)	0.01	0.00	0.15	0.07	0.21*	0.10
Religiosity	-0.20**	-0.17	-0.15**	-0.13	-0.09	-0.08
Age	-0.05**	-0.21	-0.04**	-0.17	-0.04**	-0.17
Immigrants	-0.25	-0.07	-0.30*	-0.09	-0.19	-0.06
Extraversion			0.26**	0.19	0.18**	0.13
Agreeableness			0.10	0.08	0.10	0.07
Consciousness			0.14*	0.10	0.13*	0.09
Neuroticism			0.17**	0.15	0.17**	0.15
Openness to experience			-0.09	-0.08	-0.10	-0.09
Education					0.12**	0.11
Hebrew Proficiency					0.13	0.07
English proficiency					0.16**	0.15
Locality (1=center_)					0.10	0.05
Occupational status (1=Manager)					0.37**	0.17
R^2	0.080		0.157		0.258	
ΔR^2	0.080		0.077		0.101	
			Generation Z			
	Model 1		Model 2		Model 3	
	B	Beta	B	Beta	B	Beta
(Constant)	4.96**		3.93**		2.94**	
Gender (1=male)	0.04	0.02	0.09	0.05	0.08	0.04

Religiosity	-0.18**	-0.18	-0.17**	-0.17	-0.15**	-0.14
Age	-0.04*	-0.08	-0.03	-0.08	-0.06**	-0.13
Immigrants	0.14	0.04	0.13	0.04	0.08	0.02
Extraversion			0.07	0.06	0.06	0.05
Agreeableness			0.14*	0.11	0.09	0.07
Consciousness			-0.05	-0.04	-0.07	-0.06
Neuroticism			0.10*	0.10	0.09*	0.09
Openness to experience			0.01	0.01	-0.02	-0.02
Education					0.12**	0.12
Hebrew Proficiency					0.19	0.08
English proficiency					0.18**	0.19
Locality (1=center_)					0.01	0.01
Occupational status (1=Manager)					0.07	0.02
R^2	0.043		0.068		0.123	
ΔR^2	0.043		0.025		0.055	

#p<.1; *p < .05; **p < .001

The consequences of lower critical thinking digital skills among disadvantaged social groups, especially among Gen X, can be significant and multifaceted, affecting various aspects of their lives. It may reduce their labor market opportunities, job security, career advancement and income parity, perpetuating the cycle of socioeconomic disadvantage for their children. The potential outcomes may include disadvantages that start at the individual level but afterwards have consequences for society as a whole: social exclusion of individuals and groups, health disparities, reduced civic engagement or, contrarily, joining extreme political movements or sects. Addressing the consequences of lower CTDS among disadvantaged social groups requires a multifaceted approach. It involves investing in digital literacy training and education programs tailored to the specific needs of these communities, providing equitable access to technology and digital resources, and addressing systemic barriers that perpetuate social inequalities. By empowering disadvantaged groups through digital skills, societies can foster inclusion, bridge the digital divide, and work towards more equitable opportunities and outcomes for all. Understanding the intergenerational differences in CTDS is crucial for tailoring educational approaches, promoting inclusivity, and harnessing the diverse strengths of each generation for successful navigation of an ever-evolving digital landscape.

REFERENCES

Ajzen, I. (2005). Attitudes, personality, and behavior, McGraw-Hill Education (UK).

Bourdieu, P. (2003). Cultural reproduction and social reproduction. Culture: Critical concepts in sociology, 3, 63-99.

Dede, C. (2010). Comparing frameworks for 21st century skills. 21st century skills: Rethinking how students learn, 20, 51-76.

Donnellan, M. B., Oswald, F. L., Baurd, B. M. & Lucas, R. E. (2006). The mini-IPIP scales: tiny-yet-effective measures of the Big Five factors of personality. Psychological assessment, 18, 192.

Einwiller, S. A. & Kim, S. (2020). How online content providers moderate user-generated content to prevent harmful online communication: An analysis of policies and their implementation. Policy & Internet, 12, 184-206.

Elena-Bucea, A., Cruz-Jesus, F., Oliveira, T. & Coelho, P. S. (2021). Assessing the role of age, education, gender and income on the digital divide: Evidence for the European Union. Information Systems Frontiers, 23, 1007-1021.

Ferreira, N. (2021). Positive Coping Skills, Thriving and Social Connectedness: Are There Generational Differences in the Digital Workplace? Agile coping in the digital workplace: emerging issues for research and practice. Springer.

Gursov, D., Maier, T. A. & Chi, C. G. (2008). Generational differences: An examination of work values and generational gaps in the hospitality workforce. International Journal of Hospitality Management, 27, 448-458.

Howard, L. W., Tang, T. L.-P. & Jill Austin, M. (2015). Teaching critical thinking skills: Ability, motivation, intervention, and the Pygmalion effect. Journal of Business Ethics, 128, 133-147.

Klopotan, I., Alekcic, A. & Vinkivic, N. (2020). Do business ethics and ethical decision making still matter: Perspective of different generational cohorts. Business Systems Research: International journal of the Society for Advancing Innovation and Research in Economy, 11, 31-43.

Mccrae, R. R. & John, O. P. (1992). An introduction to the five-factor model and its applications. Journal of personality, 60, 175-215.

Meredith, G. & Schewe, C. (1994). The power of cohorts: Americans who shared powerful experiences as young adults, such as the hardship of the great depression, fall into six cohorts. American Demographics, 16, 22-22.

Tsui, L. (2003). Reproducing social inequalities through higher education: Critical thinking as valued capital. Journal of Negro Education, 318-332.

Van Dijk, J. A. G. M. (2017). Digital divide: Impact of access. The international encyclopedia of media effects, 1-11.

Van Laar, E., Van Deursen, A. J. A. M., Van Dijk, J. A. G. M. & De HaanN, J. (2020). Determinants of 21st-century skills and 21st-century digital skills for workers: A systematic literature review. Sage Open, 10, 2158244019900176.

Warsah, I., Morganna, R., Uyun, M., Afandi, M. & Hamengkubuwono, H. (2021). The impact of collaborative learning on learners' critical thinking skills. International Journal of Instruction, 14, 443-460.

A NON-INTRUSIVE TOOL FOR GLOBAL NAVIGATION SATELLITE SYSTEM MODULE INSPECTION

Antoine Bossard
Graduate School of Science, Kanagawa University, 3-27-1 Rokkakubashi, Kanagawa, Yokohama 221-8686, Japan

ABSTRACT

Geolocation has become ubiquitous in our daily lives: not only is it used to facilitate our trips, which is the main purpose of, for instance, a car navigation system, but a variety of applications rely on it, ranging from marketing (advertisement) to military via entertainment (video games, such as Niantic's Pokémon Go). Geo-positioning and the data inferred from it is also at the centre of multiple privacy issues. The COVID-19 pandemic has also shown several usages of this positioning technology for health and epidemiology matters. Although it is clear that georeferencing enables various important scenarios, hence its ubiquity, geolocation operations stay mostly invisible to users. In this paper, we propose a non-intrusive tool designed to provide users with information regarding satellite communications made by their devices. In other words, this proposal aims at inspecting global navigation satellite system (GNSS) communications via the corresponding modules embedded in electronic devices. It should be noted that not only do we propose such a prototype, but we also investigate the applicability of its principle.

KEYWORDS

GNSS, GPS, Georeferencing, Geolocation, Tracking, IoT

1. INTRODUCTION

Geolocation is about determining the geographical position of the user. It is made possible by several techniques and technologies. For instance, mobile phone carriers can rely on their network of cell towers to locate a cell phone user. The IP address of an Internet user can also reveal significant information regarding the user's geographical position. In addition, this is precisely the purpose of the global navigation satellite system (GNSS), which consists of several, distinct actors: the global positioning system (GPS) is the American GNSS, Galileo the European one, BeiDou the Chinese one and GLONASS the Russian one. (The Japanese GNSS, called QZSS, is currently based on the American GPS.)

Given the numerous potential applications involved, geo-positioning technology has rapidly convinced investors: it is now part of our lives in various forms, such as car navigation systems, mobile phones' applications (e.g. weather forecasting) and entertainment with video games like Niantic's Pokémon Go (Colley et al., 2017). And this is without mentioning military applications, which did come first (Lachow, 1995). The populations of several of our countries have also experienced applications of geo-positioning during the COVID-19 pandemic.

Nevertheless, given that georeferencing operations are most of the time background tasks, users generally stay unaware of the information used. One of the rare encounters of users with georeferencing operations is when an application requests permission for access to geolocation information as provided by the GNSS module of the device, typically of the smartphone. Hence may arise privacy concerns.

Aiming at addressing this issue, we describe in this paper a non-intrusive tool for the inspection of global navigation satellite system modules, importantly including their debugging *in situ* (Bossard, 2021). Such modules are in charge of communicating with the satellite system and provide the user device with relevant information, including, but not restricted to, location information (Betke, 2001). This proposal is deemed non-intrusive in that it requires minimum tempering with the device that is to be inspected. Furthermore, the general cost of the proposed solution, for both hardware and software, is kept at a minimum as well. Finally, we investigate the applicability of the proposal's principle.

Regarding related works, previous research has focused on GNSS module precision analysis (Li et al., 2015) and error measurement (Williams, 2004), two subjects that are however more related to geophysics than computer science and engineering. Applicative research of geo-positioning is by far the most frequent in the engineering field, for instance with autonomous vehicles (Milanés et al., 2008) and tracking systems (Lee et al., 2014). Related to the security issue, attempts at detecting GNSS spoofing have also been made (Lee et al., 2013). Furthermore, a tool for GNSS receptivity analysis has been proposed by Sinivee (2009).

It can also be noted that there exist GNSS analysis solutions for smartphones: for instance and most notably, Google has released the GnssLogger App (Google, 2023) to collect and display various location data from the GNSS module embedded into an Android smartphone. Being official Google software, this application incidentally somehow shows the relevance of this research: it is meaningful to be able to provide users with such GNSS data. This is also made clear by the Android OS API with the `android.location` package and the newer `com.google.android.gms.location` package. However, although such a reporting tool is available for Android smartphones, it is not applicable to the Internet of things (IoT) devices as these are minimalistic devices incomparable to a smartphone in terms of features, performance and cost. Which is why we focus in this research on IoT devices. (The case of a smartphone is however further discussed in the validation section of this paper.)

The rest of this paper is organised as follows: the proposal is presented in detail in Section 2. Then, the obtained results are discussed in Section 3. The validity of our proposal is further analysed in Section 4. Finally, Section 5 concludes this paper.

2. METHODOLOGY

In this section, we describe in detail the non-intrusive tool proposed for the inspection of modules in charge of communicating with global navigation satellite systems.

2.1 Hardware

The prototype of our proposal is based on an ATmega328P microcontroller (Microchip, 2020), powered and interfaced via an Arduino Nano board.

Communication between the ATmega328P microcontroller of the prototype and the target GNSS module is conducted with the Universal asynchronous receiver-transmitter (UART) device (serial communication). To this end, the transmit line (TX) of the GNSS module is derived and connected to the receive line (RX) of the prototype microcontroller. Such serial communication is conducted at a precise baud rate, which has to be that of the target GNSS module, obviously. Hence, our proposal provides users with several selectable baud rates (this is further detailed in the next section). The currently selected baud rate is made visible to the user with a LED array included within the prototype. Technically, baud rate selection is realised with a switch (i.e. a mechanical push-button) which emits when pressed a signal to the microcontroller so as to trigger baud rate adjustment of its UART device. Precisely an external interrupt (INT0) is triggered on a low to high change of the state of the corresponding line (i.e. port pin).

Regarding the I/O ports of the microcontroller used by the prototype, the RX line of its UART device is obviously required (i.e. pin 0 of port D). In addition, we have used four pins for the LEDs that indicate communication with a particular satellite system (pins 0 to 3 of port C; see Table 1). Another five pins are used to control the LED array which shows the selected baud rate to the user of the prototype (pins 3 to 7 of port D). Finally, the pin corresponding to the external interrupt INT0 (i.e. pin 2 of port D) is connected to the baud rate selection switch mentioned previously.

Table 1. A summary of the connections at port C of the proposed prototype

Pin name	GNSS name	GNSS origin	LED colour
PC0	GPS	USA	red
PC1	BeiDou	China	green
PC2	GLONASS	Russia	yellow
PC3	Galileo	European Union	blue

A simplified schematic of the circuit of the proposed device is given in Figure 1a and a photograph of its implementation in Figure 1b. The line labelled "to TX" in the former is to be connected to the transmitter line (TX) of the GNSS module.

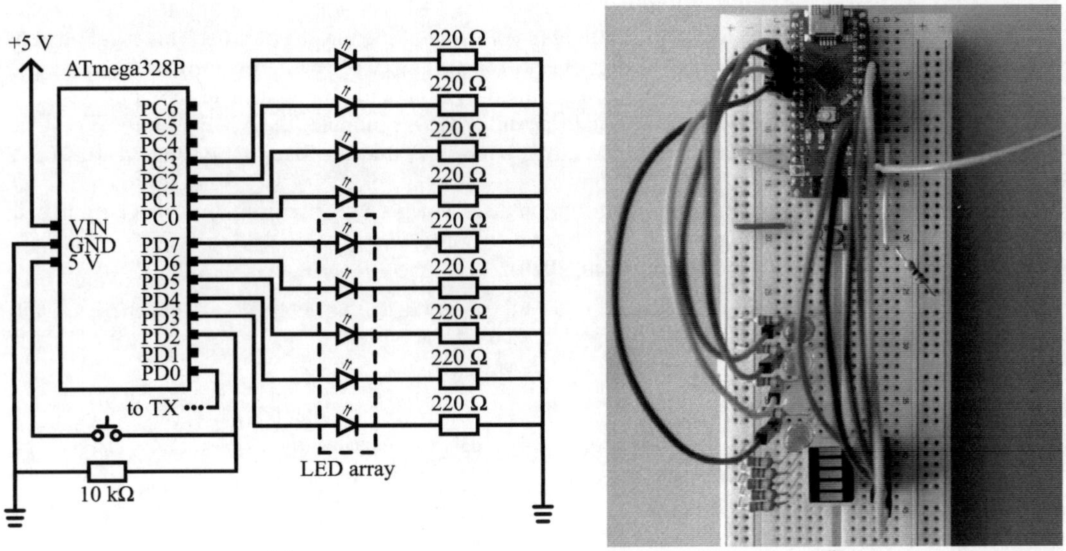

(a) (b)

Figure 1. (a) A simplified schematic of the circuit of the proposed device; (b) a photograph of its implementation

2.2 Software

In order to minimise the memory footprint of the proposal, we have directly relied on the assembly programming language to control the microcontroller that is at the core of the prototype as described in the previous section (cf. Bossard, 2022). As a result, the UART device of the prototype microcontroller that is used for serial data transfers between the prototype and the GNSS module is directly controlled with its special-purpose registers (Microchip, 2020).

In this program, we activate interrupts so as to catch external interrupts (at INT0) which are used to detect requests by the user of the prototype to adjust the baud rate. In practice, five baud rates (standard rates: 4800 bps, 9600 bps, 19200 bps, 57600 bps and 115200 bps) are predefined in the program. One of these is then selected by reading the baud rate index, which is managed by the program. The default baud rate of the prototype is set at 9600 bps (cf. Section 4).

An overview of the execution flow of the microcontroller program that is running on the prototype is given in Figure 2.

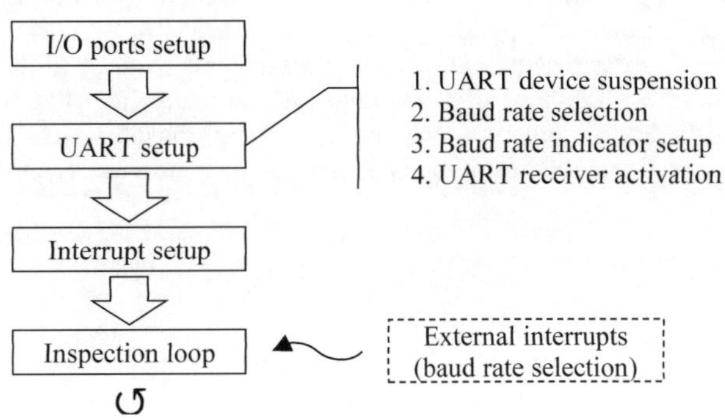

Figure 2. An overview of the execution flow of the microcontroller program running on the prototype. External interrupts can be received for baud rate selection

As soon as the inspection loop starts, the NMEA protocol sentences (Betke, 2001; Transistor Gijutsu Editorial Board, 2009) are received and analysed by the prototype microcontroller. For each sentence, the corresponding satellite system (e.g. GPS, Galileo, BeiDou) is deduced form the talker identifier included at the beginning of the sentence and the state of the corresponding LED is toggled by setting to 1 the corresponding bit of the PINC register (i.e. the register used to read the value of the pins of port C). This toggling behaviour of the PINC register is documented in the data sheet of the ATmega328P microcontroller (Microchip, 2020). The prototype user can thus check the operation of the GNSS module by looking at the blinking state of the LEDs: this enables verification of both the baud rate of the GNSS module (the NMEA protocol sentences are not correctly received in the case of a mismatching baud rate) and the satellite systems it uses (e.g. GPS, GLONASS).

An excerpt of the microcontroller program run on the ATmega328P, precisely the UART setup code with the predefined baud rates, is shown in Listing 1. Each baud rate is expressed in the form of an integer, calculated function of the processor frequency (Microchip, 2020).

Listing 1. An excerpt of the prototype microcontroller program, written in assembly: the UART setup code with the predefined baud rates

```
baud_rates:
.byte 207, 103, 51, 16, 8, 0 ; 4800, 9600,
19200, 57600, 115200 bps (and null)

; Stop UART before setting it up
ldi r16, 0b00000000
sts 0xC1, r16 ; UCSR0B

; Setup the baud rate
ldi r30, lo8(baud_rates)
ldi r31, hi8(baud_rates)
add r30, r25 ; r25: current baud rate index
clr r0 ; r0 <- 0 (does not modify Carry flag)
adc r31, r0
lpm r1, Z ; r1 now contains the baud rate code
sts 0xC4, r1 ; UBRR0L
```

```
; (code continued)

; Light the corresponding LED
ldi r16, 0b00000100 ; it will be shifted left
mov r1, r25 ; r1 <- baud rate index
inc r1 ; r1 <- baud rate index + 1
loop_shift:
lsl r16
dec r1
brne loop_shift
out PORTD, r16

; Finally, activate the UART receiver
ldi r16, 0b00010000 ; RXEN0 bit set
sts 0xC1, r16 ; UCSR0B
ret
```

3. RESULTS AND DISCUSSION

In this section, after describing the experimental conditions, we review the experimental results obtained from our implementation of the proposal.

3.1 Experimental Setup

In addition to the proposed prototype, we have realised a target device which consists of an ATmega32U4 microcontroller (hosted by an Arduino Micro board) connected to a GNSS module: a Quectel L76K chip (Quectel, 2021) mounted on the corresponding WaveShare board (SKU 23721).

A photograph of this entire experimental setup, except its power source (a PC), is shown in Figure 3: at the top the Quectel L76K GNSS module, in the middle the target device that is based on an ATmega32U4 microcontroller and at the bottom our implementation of the proposal. In this figure, the whole system is in operation: it can be observed that the prototype is operating at a baud rate of 9600 bps – the second LED of the array is lit – and that at least the LED that corresponds to the BeiDou satellite system is blinking.

Figure 3. A photograph of the entire, and operating, experimental setup (only the power source, a PC, is not shown): from top to bottom, the Quectel L76K GNSS module, the target device based on an ATmega32U4 microcontroller and the proposed prototype

3.2 On GNSS-Related Capabilities of the Proposal

When the GNSS module is configured for communication with the two satellite systems GPS and BeiDou only, which is the default for the GNSS module used in this experiment, the corresponding two LEDs blink (the red and green LEDs). When GLONASS is added by emitting the corresponding proprietary sentence (command) to our GNSS module: "`$PCAS04,7`" (Quectel, 2021), the corresponding three LEDs of the prototype blink (the red, green and yellow LEDs).

In addition, because the QZSS satellite system is based on the American positioning system (i.e. GPS), the proposed prototype cannot distinguish between QZSS and GPS communications. Furthermore, since the GNSS module used in this experiment supports only the GPS (with QZSS), BeiDou and GLONASS satellite systems, no communication with the European Galileo GNSS is detected (the blue LED is never lit).

3.3 On Hardware Requirements of the Proposal

In this section, we discuss hardware facts and measure the various hardware costs that are induced by the proposal.

First and foremost, we have confirmed that the proposal does not disturb the operation of the main device (i.e. the operation of the device, like an IoT device, whose GNSS module is being inspected), which is obviously crucial.

Second, as explained, the prototype is based on an ATmega328P microcontroller hosted by an Arduino Nano board (SKU: A000005), whose cost is, at the time of writing, USD 24.90. The price of the other electronic components can be reasonably estimated at a maximum of USD 10.00.

Third, the machine code of the program that controls the prototype takes only 167 bytes of program memory. The data memory space (precisely, the internal SRAM) is not used: only physical registers are. As a result, the cost of the proposal, both components and memory, stays low.

3.4 Possible Improvements

We have noticed during our experiments a slight chatter effect (i.e. contact bounce) at the switch used for baud rate selection on the prototype. Concretely, shifting between the predefined baud rates, which is triggered by pressing the corresponding switch (push-button), can at times happen unexpectedly fast. This behaviour is infrequent enough though and does not hamper normal operation of the prototype. Improvement of this minor issue is part of future works.

4. VALIDATION

In this section, we show the applicability of the proposal by considering the compatibility issue with several GNSS modules and devices. To this end, we review some of their essential features.

We have summarised in Table 2 several properties and features of various GNSS modules, and from various manufacturers, currently (or until recently) available on the market. These data have been obtained directly from the product specifications and data sheets provided by manufacturers. Even if not exhaustive, these data at least show that GNSS modules of various manufacturers from different countries support the UART interface (possibly among other communication interfaces, such as Philips' I^2C bus) together with the NMEA protocol, and that at the baud rates supported by our proposal. Therefore, the system described in this paper is thus compatible with these GNSS modules. (Additional products, albeit significantly older, are reviewed in Transistor Gijutsu Editorial Board, 2009: one can note that some older GNSS modules such as Garmin's GPS15-W (USA) and SPA's イオ 111wUDB9s (Japan) only support a baud rate of 4800 bps, which is however also supported by our proposed inspection system.)

Table 2. A summary of several properties and features of GNSS modules currently (or until recently) on the market; data taken from the product specifications and data sheets provided by manufacturers

Manufacturer	Country	GNSS module	UART	Default baud rate (bps)	NMEA protocol
EBYTE	China	E108-GN02	yes	9600	yes
Position	Japan	GPS-54	yes	9600	yes
Position	Japan	GSU-151	yes	115200	yes
Quectel	China	L76K	yes	9600	yes
Quectel	China	L26K	yes	9600	yes
Quectel	China	LC76F	yes	9600	yes
Quectel	China	LC29H	yes	115200	yes
u-blox	Switzerland	MAX-M10S	yes	9600	yes
u-blox	Switzerland	NEO-M8	yes	9600	yes
YIC	Taiwan	GT-502	yes	9600	yes

Next, we mention that although smartphones can rely on an application such as Google's GnssLogger as explained in introduction, they can in some special circumstances acquire GNSS data *even when positioning is disabled*. This is for instance the case for emergency calls and texts (e.g. refer to Android OS 12 positioning settings and the corresponding documentation; see Android Help, 2023). This shows that even when positioning is disabled on the smartphone, and thus the GNSS reporting application unusable (the GnssLogger application requires positioning permission; see Google, 2023), our system could be used to track GNSS communication.

So, we in addition show that our proposal is also applicable to the smartphone scenario. Let us consider to this end the PinePhone from Pine64 since it is an open design smartphone with thus hardware information easily available. As mentioned in its hardware schematics (Pine64, 2020), the PinePhone relies on a Quectel EG25-G chip for GNSS needs, chip which supports the NMEA protocol and features a UART interface at a default baud rate of 115200 bps, and which thus provides the UART TX line required by our proposal (Quectel, 2020). Hence, assuming that the PinePhone replicates a conventional smartphone design (it is based on a Quad-Core Cortex-A53 ARM CPU), our proposal could be applied to smartphones in general.

5. CONCLUSIONS

Georeferencing is nowadays part of our lives: entertainment (video games), navigation, natural disaster management and relief as well as military applications are numerous. Although ubiquitous, from a user point of view, geo-positioning remains however largely invisible: it is typically a background task. Which can be an issue as far as privacy is concerned. We have described in this paper a non-intrusive tool for GNSS module inspection, including debugging, such as those used with IoT, thus enabling feedback for users of such satellite communication devices, in other words most of us. The experimental results obtained have been discussed and the validity of our approach has been shown by reviewing various GNSS modules of several mainstream manufacturers currently (or until recently) on the market. Applicability to smartphones has also been investigated.

Regarding future works, currently the proposed prototype requires deriving the TX line of the GNSS module, which may be difficult in some situations. Investigating further this issue is obviously a meaningful objective. In addition, elimination of contact bounces, that is debouncing, for baud rate selection is yet another possible future task. And GNSS spoofing detection (Lee et al., 2013) could also be another future development of our proposal.

ACKNOWLEDGEMENTS

The author is sincerely grateful to the four reviewers for their insightful comments and suggestions which helped improve this paper.

REFERENCES

Android Help, (2023). *Manage your Android device's location settings.* https://support.google.com/android/answer/3467281. Accessed on 2 November 2023.

Betke, K., (2001). *The NMEA 0183 Protocol*. Revised edition.

Bossard A., (2022). Memory optimisation on AVR microcontrollers for IoT devices' minimalistic displays. *Chips*, Vol. 1, No. 1, pp. 2-13. https://doi.org/10.3390/chips1010002

Bossard, A., (2021). Autonomous on-chip debugging for sensors based on AVR microcontrollers. *Journal of Sensor Technology*, Vol. 11, No. 2, pp. 19-38. https://doi.org/10.4236/jst.2021.112002

Colley, A. et al., (2017). The geography of Pokémon GO: beneficial and problematic effects on places and movement. In *Proceedings of the CHI Conference on Human Factors in Computing Systems*. Denver, Colorado, USA, pp. 1179-1192. https://doi.org/10.1145/3025453.3025495

Google, (2023). *GnssLogger App*. https://play.google.com/store/apps/details?id=com.google.android.apps.location.gps.gnsslogger. Accessed on 2 November 2023.

Lachow, I., (1995). The GPS dilemma: balancing military risks and economic benefits. *International Security*, Vol. 20, No. 1, pp. 126-148.

Lee, D.-K. et al., (2020). Detection of GNSS spoofing using NMEA messages. In *Proceedings of the European Navigation Conference*. Dresden, Germany, 2020, pp. 1-10. https://doi.org/10.23919/ENC48637.2020.9317470

Lee, S. et al., (2014). Design and implementation of vehicle tracking system using GPS/GSM/GPRS technology and smartphone application, In *Proceedings of the IEEE World Forum on Internet of Things*. Seoul, Korea, pp. 353-358. https://doi.org/10.1109/WF-IoT.2014.6803187

Li, X. et al., (2015(. Accuracy and reliability of multi-GNSS real-time precise positioning: GPS, GLONASS, BeiDou, and Galileo. *Journal of Geodesy*, Vol. 89, No. 6, pp. 607-635. https://doi.org/10.1007/s00190-015-0802-8

Microchip Technology, (2020). *ATmega48A/PA/88A/PA/168A/PA/328/P – megaAVR data sheet*. DS40002061B.

Milanés, V., et al., 2008. Autonomous vehicle based in cooperative GPS and inertial systems. *Robotica*, Vol. 26, No. 5, pp. 627-633. https://doi.org/10.1017/S0263574708004232

Pine64, (2020). *PinePhone v1.2b Released Schematic*. Revision 1.2b (11 October 2020).

Quectel Wireless Solutions, (2020). *LTE Standard Module Series – EG25-G Hardware Design*. Version 1.4 (21 September 2020).

Quectel Wireless Solutions, (2021). *L76K GNSS Protocol Specification*. Version 1.1 (16 December 2021).

Sinivee, V., (2010). Simple yet efficient NMEA sentence generator for testing GPS reception firmware and hardware. In: Sobh, T., Elleithy, K., Mahmood, A. (eds) *Novel Algorithms and Techniques in Telecommunications and Networking*. https://doi.org/10.1007/978-90-481-3662-9_35

Transistor Gijutsu Editorial Board, (2009). *GPS のしくみと応用技術* (in Japanese). CQ Publishing, Tokyo, Japan.

Williams, S. D. P. et al., (2004). Error analysis of continuous GPS position time series, *Journal of Geophysical Research*, Vol. 109, No. B3, pp. B03412:1- B03412:19, https://doi.org/10.1029/2003JB002741

OPPORTUNITIES AND LIMITS OF AI-SUPPORTED GENERATION OF PRODUCT DESCRIPTIONS

Gino Bernardini, Marek Opuszko and Meena Stöbesand
Ernst-Abbe-University of Applied Sciences Jena, Germany

ABSTRACT

The abundance of products available in e-commerce demands effective product descriptions to enhance customer engagement and drive sales. However, manually crafting comprehensive descriptions for each product can be a time-consuming and labor-intensive task. To address this challenge, this research investigates the potential of artificial intelligence (AI) to automate product description generation. A prototype system utilizing the GPT-3.5 large language model is proposed, capable of generating product descriptions from product data of an existing online shop. The system's architecture, evaluation methodology, and findings are detailed, demonstrating its ability to produce high-quality, human-like descriptions that effectively convey product attributes and benefits. Ultimately, this work highlights the transformative power of AI in streamlining product description creation and advancing e-commerce efficiency.

KEYWORDS

e-Commerce, Artificial Intelligence, Open AI, Prestashop, ChatGPT

1. INTRODUCTION

The rapid growth of e-commerce has revolutionized the way consumers shop, offering a vast selection of products from the comfort of their homes. However, the sheer volume of available products can make it difficult for customers to locate the items they seek. This is where effective product descriptions play a crucial role in guiding consumer decisions and driving sales. Manually creating comprehensive product descriptions for each item can be a time-consuming and resource-intensive task, often requiring specialized expertise. This manual process can hinder e-commerce businesses' ability to keep up with the ever-increasing product catalog and maintain competitive market positions. Artificial intelligence (AI) presents a promising solution to automate product description generation, streamlining the process and freeing up resources for other crucial tasks. AI language models, such as GPT-3.5, have demonstrated their ability to generate human-quality text, including product descriptions that accurately represent product features and benefits.

This research aims to explore the potential of AI in automating product description generation for e-commerce platforms. A prototype system using the GPT-3.5 language model is developed, capable of generating product descriptions from structured product data. The system's architecture, evaluation methodology, and findings are presented, highlighting its ability to produce high-quality, informative descriptions that enhance customer engagement and contribute to increased sales.

2. AI IN E-COMMERCE

AI now holds a significant role in various segments and processes of e-commerce business enterprises as it might improve business performance on many levels (Huang and Rust 2018; Canhoto and Clear 2020). Bawack et al. (2022) showed, that research on AI in e-commerce has been steadily increasing since its inception in 1991, showing an annual growth rate of 10.45% in publications. This trend is particularly notable since 2013. Since numerous applications emerged, AI in market research analyzes vast data for hidden trends, aiding in opportunity identification, product development, and targeted marketing (Syam & Sharma 2018; Stone et al. 2020). In customer marketing, AI personalizes messages and recommendations based on individual preferences learned through data analysis and even automates message generation (Jarek et al. 2019). For CRM, AI automates negotiation through chatbots, suggests deals based on past data (Reynolds 2017; Krasadakis 2017), and handles customer inquiries (Lo & Campos 2018).

In order management, AI automates tasks like order verification, matching, and personalized confirmations (Bock et al. 2020). It optimizes picking, packing, and shipping, prioritizing based on urgency and efficiency (Stone et al. 2020). AI also tackles billing/payment by automating customer billing, fraud detection, and payment collection, improving cash flow and cost reduction (Bajpai 2020). For scheduling/fulfillment, AI streamlines the process by optimizing routes, scheduling deliveries, and automating order fulfillment (Lam et al. 2015; Paschen et al. 2019).

In terms of content creation using AI, Wu and colleagues (Wu et al. 2023) discussed the efficiency and scalability of AI-generated content (AIGC), highlighting its advantages over traditional human writing in terms of speed, language localization, and the ability to generate personalized social media posts. They emphasized AIGC's rapid content production capabilities, which can produce articles in minutes compared to the longer time required by human writers, and its utility in language localization and personalized content creation across various websites by analyzing users' online data. In the realm of e-commerce, AI-generated content significantly enhances operational efficiency with platforms like JD.com (Zhang et al. 2019) and Taobao (Gong et al. 2019) employing algorithms for generating product titles and descriptions and utilizing intelligent customer service systems. However, there is a notable gap in comprehensive quality studies that assess the impact and effectiveness of these AI-driven approaches on consumer engagement and sales performance.

3. CONCEPT - PROTOTYPE

This chapter presents the architecture of the prototype system, which consists of a Python application, a PrestaShop installation, and an OpenAI API connection (Prestashop 2023, OpenAI 2023). The Python application serves as the system's core, responsible for communicating with the OpenAI API and generating product descriptions as well as communicating with the API of Prestashop to retrieve the base data of each product.

3.1 Python Application

The Python application acts as the system's central component, handling the generation of product descriptions based on input from the PrestaShop API where base data of products are stored in the shop system's database. It employs the GPT language model to process product data and generate descriptions that should accurately reflect product features and benefits.

The application's primary functionality includes:

- Data Extraction: Extract product data from the PrestaShop database, including product titles, attributes, and other relevant information.
- Preprocessing: Preprocessing the extracted product data to ensure it is in a format compatible with the GPT-3.5 language model. This may involve cleaning, formatting, and structuring the data.
- Description Generation: Utilizing the GPT-3.5 language model to generate product descriptions based on the preprocessed data.
- Description Formatting: Formatting the generated product descriptions to ensure they adhere to the PrestaShop platform's requirements. This may involve adjusting text styles, adding product links, and ensuring compatibility with the platform's HTML structure.
- Description Submission: Submit the generated product descriptions to the PrestaShop database, replacing existing descriptions or inserting new ones as needed.

3.2 PrestaShop API

The PrestaShop RESTful API serves as the interface between the Python application and the PrestaShop e-commerce platform. It enables the system to interact with product data, receive requests for new product descriptions, and submit generated descriptions to the PrestaShop database.

The key functionalities include:

- Product Data Access: Providing the Python application with access to product data stored in the PrestaShop database. This allows the application to retrieve the necessary information for generating product descriptions.
- Description Submission: Submitting generated product descriptions to the PrestaShop database from the Python application. This ensures that the new descriptions are reflected in the platform's product pages.

3.3 OpenAI API Integration

The OpenAI API serves as the primary interface for the Python application to interact with the GPT-3.5 language model. It allows the application to send text prompts and receive generated text responses.

The API integration enables the following interaction:

- Text Prompt Submission: The Python application submits text prompts to the OpenAI API, providing concise descriptions of the products for which descriptions are required.
- Generated Response Retrieval: The Python application receives generated text responses from the OpenAI API, which are then processed and formatted for submission to the PrestaShop database.

3.4 System Integration

The overall system integration involves the coordinated operation of the Python application, the PrestaShop API, and the OpenAI API. The Python application initiates the process by sending requests to the PrestaShop API for product data. The application processes the base data and generates product descriptions using a prompt, which is then formatted and sent back to the PrestaShop API. The Prestashop API inserts the new descriptions into the PrestaShop database, effectively updating the product pages with the generated descriptions. The seamless integration of these components would allow for the automated generation of product descriptions directly within the PrestaShop platform, streamlining the process and enhancing the overall e-commerce experience for both customers and businesses.

4. PRODUCT DESCRIPTION GENERATION

This section provides a detailed analysis of the results from the generation of product descriptions, as described in the previous section. The products were categorized into three main groups: Clothing (Youth Fashion), Music, and Electronic Products. The assessment was conducted separately for each category to compare the specific challenges and characteristics within each. This approach allowed for a holistic analysis of the generated product descriptions across all categories. The quality and coherence of the generated texts were examined for differences between product categories. It also helped identify specific patterns and trends in the generated product descriptions, allowing for the evaluation of text generation quality across different product categories. The evaluation of AI-generated content requires a clear input prompt. However, it became evident, that generating all product descriptions with a single, universal input prompt was not effective due to its complexity and challenges. A one-size-fits-all prompt for generating product descriptions failed because diverse product categories like music and clothes demand unique approaches. Generic prompts lead to inaccurate and generic descriptions with low quality, highlighting the need for tailored prompts specific to each category. This led to the need to develop differentiated and tailored input prompts to align the precision and quality of generated product descriptions with the specific requirements of each category and the shop operator.

4.1 Prestashop Product Data

We used 3 sample products in 3 different categories: music, youth fashion, and electronics.

- Youth Fashion:
  - Adidas sandals
  - A women's body top from Wasted Paris
  - Levi's jeans
- Electronics:
  - iPhone 12 Mini by Apple
  - JCM 800 guitar amplifier by Marshall
  - WH-CH520 headphones by Sony
- Music:
  - Album System of a Down by System of a Down
  - Album Loud by Rihanna
  - Album We Aimed for the Stars by Amelie Tobien

The product data in the PrestaShop database was limited to base data. For example, for music products, this included record name, record label, release year, and artist. For clothes, this included size, color, fit, and material. For consumer electronics, this included manufacturer, name, type, color, and some technical details like the frequency range of headphones.

Base data examples of a music product:

- Record name: "System of a Down"
- Record label: Sony Music Entertainment
- Release year: 1998
- Artist: System of a Down
- Duration: 40 Minutes

4.2 Model Parameters

The GPT-3.5 language model has several parameters that can be used to control the quality and creativity of the text it generates. These parameters include:

- Temperature: This controls the creativity of the text. Higher values lead to more creative, but less coherent, text. Lower values lead to more coherent, but less creative, text.
- Max tokens: This limits the length of the generated text.
- Top-p: This controls the probability that the model will select the most likely next word. Higher values lead to more predictable text. Lower values lead to more creative text.
- Frequency penalty: This penalizes the repetition of certain words or phrases.
- Presence penalty: This penalizes the use of certain patterns of words or phrases.

The prototype system used in this research used the following parameter settings:

- Temperature: 1
- Max tokens: 550
- Top-p: 0.7
- Frequency penalty: 0.6
- Presence penalty: 0.4

These settings were chosen to achieve a balance between creativity and coherence, as well as to limit the length of the generated text and avoid frequent repetitions of words or phrases. The following are some specific examples of how these parameters can affect the generated text:

- Temperature: A higher temperature would lead to text that is more creative, but might also be less accurate or relevant.
- Max tokens: A higher value would allow the model to generate longer text, but might also lead to less concise or informative text.
- Top-p: A higher value would lead to text that is more predictable, but might also be less creative.
- Frequency penalty: A higher value would lead to text that is less repetitive, but might also be less informative.
- Presence penalty: A higher value would lead to text that is less patterned, but might also be less creative.
- The choice of parameter settings will depend on the specific application of the text generation system.

4.3 Results in the Category Music

The following prompt was used to create a product description: "*create a truthful and appealing product description, with everything you can find about the band or artist and the album, including a tracklist (as an HTML list) and with the following properties (please select only relevant properties for a product description):*", followed by the products' base data. The results of the analysis of the generated product descriptions for music products are mixed. In some cases, the descriptions are accurate, relevant, and grammatically correct. In other cases, they contain errors or inaccuracies. The AI was able to generate accurate and informative descriptions of the artists and albums. However, it sometimes struggled to convey the emotional impact of the music. The tracklists were often inaccurate, with either completely false information or partially false information in the form of fictional song titles or titles from other albums by the artist. The AI was more accurate for well-known artists, such as Rihanna. However, it struggled more with less well-known artists, such as Amelie Tobien.

Example of generated product description for product "Loud" from artist "Rihanna": "*Rihanna, one of the most successful and innovative artists of our time, presents "Loud", an album that has taken the music world by storm. With her unique voice and impressive talent, Rihanna has once again proven why she is one of the biggest stars in pop music.*". The AI-generated product description effectively showcases extensive knowledge about Rihanna, highlighting her immense fame and pop music genre. The description is highly readable, well-structured, and free of grammatical errors. The track list (not shown above) is mostly accurate, presenting songs in the correct order and with correct names, but it omits one, listing only eleven out of twelve tracks on the album.

4.4 Results in the Category Youth Fashion

The following prompt was used to create a product description: "Create an appealing product description in youth language. Use only noteworthy features of this product from the following features (features do not have to be used verbatim):", followed by the products' base data. The AI proficiently produces grammatically correct and pertinent descriptions in an informal, youthful style, effectively utilizing and enhancing all relevant product features. The accuracy is maintained with no significant deficiencies noted. During testing, the AI-generated descriptions for diverse items including an Adidas sandal, a Wasted Paris women's body top, and Levi's jeans, all of which are viable for e-commerce integration without further editing. A minor critique is the AI's occasional over-precision in feature inclusion, leading to a somewhat uneven narrative flow, despite instructions to avoid verbatim feature replication. Example of a generated product text for the product "sandals" from "Adidas": "*Hey everyone, check out these fresh Shmoofoil sandals from Adidas! They're really the bomb and have everything you need. The molded footbed provides mega comfort and makes your feet feel like they're floating on clouds. And the strap is also totally dope, it's woven and looks ultra stylish. These sandals are perfect for summer or just lounging on the beach. Whether you rock them with swim trunks or jeans, they always look fresh in black. You'll definitely turn heads! So what are you waiting for? [...]*".

4.5 Results in the Category Electronics

This section reviews the generated product descriptions in the area of technology. Three different technical products were reviewed: the iPhone 12 Mini from Apple, the JCM 800 guitar amplifier from Marshall, and the WH-CH520 headphones from Sony. The generated texts were again analyzed based on four criteria (accuracy, relevance, grammar, and coherence). This prompt is used to generate descriptions: "*Please write an accurate and attractive product description for a technical product, using all available technical details that you are aware of. The description should include the following features of the product (please choose only relevant features that are necessary for a meaningful product description):*", followed by the products' base data.

In a similar way to the youth fashion sector, AI demonstrates an extremely competent performance. The AI integrates the product features extremely skillfully with its own information in the product description. It carefully selects all relevant details and completes the description in a convincing, sales-promoting language, providing precise details about the product features. Furthermore, the texts produced are characterized by their high relevance, as they highlight the essential features and characteristics of each product and do not tend to explain unimportant terms, as was done in the case of youth fashion. Repetitions or irrelevant mentions are rare. The grammatical structure of the texts produced was almost flawless. Here is an example of a text generated by GPT 3.5 concerning the JCM 800 guitar amplifier from Marshall: "*The JCM 800 from Marshall is a high-quality guitar amplifier that offers everything you need for the perfect sound with its 100 watts of power and one channel. With its numerous controls - presence, bass, mids, treble, master volume, and preamp volume - you can adjust your sound down to the smallest detail. The JCM 800 features a serial effects loop that allows you to seamlessly integrate your favorite effects into your setup. The two speaker outputs [...]*".

5. EVALUATION

The evaluation of the generated product descriptions focuses on four key criteria:

- **Accuracy** forms the backbone of this assessment and has the highest weighting of 40%. It is crucial to ensure that the descriptions generated correspond to the actual properties and features of the products to the greatest possible extent.
- **Relevance** follows with a weighting of 30%. It assesses how well the generated descriptions meet the needs and requirements of the target group and ensures that they are informative and targeted.
- **Grammar**, with a weighting of 15%, helps to ensure that the generated content is linguistically correct and understandable to ensure readability.
- **Coherence**, with a weighting of 15%, refers to the structure and logic of the information within the product descriptions. Although less weighted, it still contributes to the overall user experience by ensuring that the information is presented in a meaningful context.

Table 1. Evaluation System

Points	Explanation	Weighted Points
	Accuracy (40%)	
0.0	numerous incorrect information or claims	0.0
1.0	contains some false information, but also correct aspects	4.0
3.0	occasional errors or inaccuracies > Generally correct	12.0
5.0	precise, error-free, and accurate information	20.0
	Relevance: (30%)	
0.0	contains no relevant information	0.0
1.0	contains some information, but mainly irrelevant	3.0
3.0	contains both relevant and irrelevant information	9.0
5.0	contains mainly relevant information	15.0
	Grammar: (15%)	
0.0	> 5 errors	0.0
1.0	3-5 errors	1.5

3.0	1-2 errors	4.5
5.0	no errors	7.5
	Coherence / Structure: (15%)	
0.0	no clear structure or logic, information scattered	0.0
1.0	limited structure -> information difficult to follow	1.5
3.0	recognizable structure -> some sections well organized	4.5
5.0	well-structured, fluent, and logical with a clear presentation of content	7.5
	TOTAL	**50.0**

We used a human expert rater with a background in e-commerce to evaluate the quality of each product description. The raters score each description on a scale of 1 to 5 for each dimension, as shown in Table 1. The overall quality of each description is then calculated as the sum for each category with a total maximum of 50 points. The results in Table 2 show that the music category received the worst rating. This is mainly due to a lack of accuracy. The AI often generated incorrect or misleading information in this category, e.g. incorrect tracklists or inaccurate artist or album information. The fashion and technology categories received better ratings. In these categories, the product descriptions generated were generally more accurate and relevant. However, there were also some minor shortcomings here, e.g. in the relevance of the information in the youth fashion category. When comparing the three categories, it is noticeable that the category with the fewest product features, in this case, music has the highest error rate. This is due to the fact that the AI has to rely more on its own knowledge base in such cases. If this knowledge base contains little or no information about the products, the AI tends to generate inaccurate or misleading statements. On the other hand, for products with comprehensive product features, as is the case with technology products, the AI generates more accurate and relevant product descriptions.

Table 2. Evaluation Results

Music	Accuracy	Relevance	Grammar	Coherence	Total Points
Loud	12	15	7.5	7.5	42
System of a Down	12	9	7.5	7.5	36
We aimed for the Stars	4	3	7.5	7.5	22
Fashion	Accuracy	Relevance	Grammar	Coherence	Total Points
Sandals	20	9	7.5	7.5	44
Body-Top	20	9	7.5	7.5	44
Jeans	20	9	7.5	7.5	44
Electronics	Accuracy	Relevance	Grammar	Coherence	Total Points
Headphones	20	15	7.5	7.5	50
Guitar Amplifier	20	15	7.5	7.5	50
Mobile Phone	20	9	7.5	7.5	44

The music category has the worst rating, as the AI often generates incorrect or misleading information here. The fashion and technology categories have better ratings, but there were also some minor shortcomings here. Interestingly, in the dimension grammar and coherence, the AI-generated prompts were flawless and showed no errors, leading to an identical scoring for each category. While AI product descriptions face category-specific challenges, their consistent grammaticality and coherence offer a valuable foundation for accurate and compelling content creation.

6. CONCLUSION

The study highlights the significant potential of Artificial Intelligence (AI) in automating the generation of product descriptions in e-commerce, particularly for businesses managing large catalogs of products. The use of language models demonstrates a promising avenue to increase productivity and reduce costs associated with manually creating product descriptions. This automation becomes increasingly crucial as the number of products in e-commerce platforms expands, where manual handling becomes impractical and resource-intensive. However, the research also underscores the necessity of manual oversight and control in this process. While AI can produce high-quality descriptions in many instances, its performance varies significantly across different product categories. Particularly in categories with less structured or standardized information, such as music, the AI-generated descriptions exhibited inaccuracies and inconsistencies. This necessitates a hybrid approach, where AI-generated content is supplemented and verified through human intervention.

REFERENCES

Bajpai, K. (2020). Artificial Intelligence in billing and invoice processing: The future is here! [online https://www.elorus.com/blog/artificial-intelligence-billing-invoice-processing/ (Accessed 16 May 2020).

Bawack, R. E., Wamba, S. F., Carillo, K. D. A. et al. (2022). Artificial intelligence in E-Commerce: a bibliometric study and literature review, in: *Electron Markets,* vol. 32, no. 1, pp. 297–338, [online]: https://doi.org/10.1007/s12525-022-00537-z

Bock, D. E., Wolter, J. S., Ferrell, O. C. (2020). Artificial intelligence: disrupting what we know about services, in: *Journal of Services Marketing*, vol. 34, no. 3, pp. 317–334, [online] doi:10.1108/jsm-01-2019-0047

Canhoto, A. I., Clear, F. (2020). Artificial intelligence and machine learning as business tools: A framework for diagnosing value destruction potential. in: *Business Horizons*, vol. 63, no. 2, pp. 183–193, [online] doi:10.1016/j.bushor.2019.11.003

Gong, Y., Luo, X., Zhu, K. Q., Ou, W., Li, Z. & Duan, L. (2019). Automatic generation of Chinese short product titles for mobile display. In AAAI Conference on Artificial Intelligence, pp. 9460-9465.

Huang, M., Rust, R. T. (2018). Artificial Intelligence in Service, in: *Journal of Service Research*, vol. 21, no. 2, pp. 155–172, [online] doi:10.1177/1094670517752459

Jarek, K., Kozminskiego, A. L., Mazurek, G. (2019). Marketing and Artificial intelligence, in: *Central European Business Review*, vol. 8, no. 2, pp. 46–55, [online] doi:10.18267/j.cebr.213

Krasadakis, G. (2017). AI Buyer/Seller Negotiation agents - The Innovation Machine - Medium, in: *Medium*, 24.06.2019, [online] https://medium.com/innovation-machine/artificial-intelligence-negotiation-agents-49d666cd9952 (Accessed 16 Mai 2020).

Lam, H. Y., Choy, K. L., Ho, G. T. S., et al. (2015). A knowledge-based logistics operations planning system for mitigating risk in warehouse order fulfillment, in: *International Journal of Production Economics*, vol. 170, pp. 763–779, [online] doi:10.1016/j.ijpe.2015.01.005

Lo, F. Y, and Campos, N. (2018). Blending Internet-of-Things (IoT) solutions into relationship marketing strategies, in: *Technological Forecasting and Social Change*, vol. 137, pp. 10–18, [online] doi:10.1016/j.techfore.2018.09.029

OpenAI, o.J. API Reference - OpenAI API. Platform OpenAI. [online] https://platform.openai.com/docs/api-reference (Accessed 4 Oct. 2023).

Paschen, J., Kietzmann, J., Kietzmann, T. C. (2019). "Artificial intelligence (AI) and its implications for market knowledge in B2B marketing", *Journal of Business & Industrial Marketing*, vol. 34, no. 7, pp. 1410–1419, [online] doi:10.1108/jbim-10-2018-0295

PrestaShop, o.J. About PrestaShop, the open source e-commerce software. PrestaShop. [online] https://prestashop.com/about-us/ (Accessed 27 Sept. 2023).

Reynolds, M. (2017). Chatbots learn how to negotiate and drive a hard bargain. *New Scientist*, vol. 234, no. 3130, p. 7, [online] doi:10.1016/s0262-4079(17)31142-9

Stone, M., Aravopoulou, E., Ekinci, Y., et al. (2020). Artificial intelligence (AI) in strategic marketing decision-making: a research agenda, in: *The Bottom Line: Managing Library Finances*, vol. 33, no. 2, pp. 183–200, [online] doi:10.1108/bl-03-2020-0022

Syam, N., and Sharma, A. (2018). Waiting for a sales renaissance in the fourth industrial revolution: Machine learning and artificial intelligence in sales research and practice, in: *Industrial Marketing Management*, vol. 69, pp. 135–146, [online] doi:10.1016/j.indmarman.2017.12.019

Wu, J., Gan, W., Chen, Z., Wan, S. & Lin, H. (2023). Ai-generated content (AIGC): A survey. arXiv preprint arXiv:2304.06632.

Zhang, T., Zhang, J., Huo, C. & Ren, W. (2019). Automatic generation of pattern-controlled product description in e-commerce. In The World Wide Web Conference, pp. 2355-2365.

BARRIERS TO STAKEHOLDER INVOLVEMENT IN THE DIGITALISATION OF THE UNITED KINGDOM CONSTRUCTION INDUSTRY

Boroto Hwabamungu
University of Bath
Claverton Down, Bath BA2 7YA United Kingdom

ABSTRACT

This study explored the UK construction industry's digitalisation complexities with a focus on barriers to stakeholder involvement. Past literature was firstly reviewed to identify reported trends. A qualitative interpretive study was then conducted using semi-structured interviews to collect data. A thematic analysis followed and identified six categories of barriers to stakeholder involvement namely digitalisation complexity and ubiquitous change, digitalisation leadership and management approach, organisational context and culture, poor stakeholder involvement strategic planning, poor digitalisation stakeholder landscape management and communication challenges. The authors are in the process of developing this research further to identify mitigating strategies and best practice processes for stakeholder involvement best practice in digitalisation.

KEYWORDS

Stakeholder, Digitalisation, Stakeholder Involvement Barrier, Digital Technology Adoption, Digital Transformation, Construction Industry

1. INTRODUCTION

The discourse on digitalisation and digital transformation highlights the breadth of the digital technology landscape, and the need for the construction industry to catch up with other industries and sectors (Olanipekun and Sutrisna, 2021). In the context of the construction industry in the UK, the achievement of digital transformation objectives requires an understanding of success factors such as stakeholder involvement with the aim of positively impacting digitalisation in the industry. To capitalise on the opportunities that digital technologies provide, the UK government has embarked on major digitalisation and digital transformation initiatives (Kavuri et al., 2020). Many organisations in the industry have subsequently been implementing digital technologies to improve efficiencies.

While there are established benefits of adopting digital technologies in the construction industry (Olanipekun and Sutrisna, 2021), digital transformation remains a challenging undertaking. For example Prebanic and Vukomanovic (2021) argue that the industry lags behind other sectors and that digitalisation projects are affected by the tri-dimensional complexity of construction projects, digital transformation initiatives and stakeholders' risks. Stakeholder influence has been examined by scholars such as Yang et al. (2014) who highlight the interplay between stakeholder factors and construction projects' life cycle. Similarly, Xia et al. (2018) argue for good stakeholder management practices, given the peculiarities of construction projects and the need to manage risks related to construction projects' risks related to stakeholder involvement.

While the role of multiple stakeholders and the need for good stakeholder management practice are emphasized in the literature (Xia et al., 2018), few studies have explored the barriers to stakeholder involvement in the adoption of digital technologies in the construction sector. Given their complexity, the need for improved efficiencies in the industry, the roles of different stakeholders involved, and the need to strategically tackle related risk elements, this study therefore addresses this important gap.

The remainder of this paper is organized as follows: firstly, an overview of digitalisation and stakeholder involvement in the construction industry is provided in the background section. Then the research methodology used in the study and the study findings are described. The findings of the study are then discussed. Lastly, the study's relevance and implications for further research are presented in the concluding section.

2. BACKGROUND

The construction industry is one of the UK's largest GDP contributors, employing approximately 9% of its workforce (Alaloul et al., 2022). It has faced historic challenges in delivering quality project outputs on time and budget (Oyegoke et al., 2010). The industry has been undergoing major digital transformation, driven by the need to improve efficiencies. In recent years, and following global economic and technological trends, organisations in the industry have had to embrace disruptive digital technologies to maximising the benefits of their adoption (Woodhead et al., 2018). Such technologies include, but are not limited to, Building Information Modelling (BIM), Common Data Environment (CDE), unmanned aerial systems, cloud-based project management, augmented and virtual reality, artificial intelligence, cybersecurity, big data and analytics, blockchain and laser scanning (Forcael et al., 2020). They can be classified into three technological support clusters spanning technologies that support smart construction sites, simulation and virtualisation (Osunsanmi et al., 2020). In comparison to other industries construction has been lagging in the adoption of these innovative technologies (Arifin et al., 2022, Shojaei and Burgess, 2022).

To ensure successful adoption, it is crucial to address the many challenges that affect digitalisation in the construction industry. In the context of the UK, Shojaei and Burgess (2022) identify six digitalisation challenge dimensions: people, culture, procedure, technology, goals and infrastructure. They reiterate the need for research on stakeholder involvement and the adoption of digital technologies. Projects in the industry are characterised by the involvement of various stakeholders with different roles and interests (Xia et al., 2018). Good stakeholder management practice and the need for adequate tools and guidelines on how stakeholders should be involved are essential for successful construction projects in general (Storvang and Clarke, 2014), and digitalisation projects in the UK construction industry in particular.

Guidelines and approaches from the general management literature (Walker et al., 2008) are a useful starting point. However, they must be adapted to the specific context of the UK construction sector. Stakeholder theory concepts and stakeholder management guidelines have received greater attention across sectors and industries (Zarewa, 2019). These concepts can provide guiding capabilities in the construction industry digitalisation process regarding stakeholder landscape, influence, engagement strategies and involvement to improve digitalisation outcome. Defined as "any group or individual who can affect or is affected by the achievement of the organisation's objectives" (Freeman, 1984), stakeholders influence digitalisation in different ways (Brunetti et al., 2020).

While existing literature covers stakeholder management guidelines and approaches, there exist barriers to stakeholder involvement in different organisational and industry contexts. This study explored the barriers to stakeholder involvement in the digitalisation of the UK construction industry.

3. RESEARCH METHOD

The research presented here is a qualitative interpretive study (Myers, 2009) following a case study approach (Yin, 2009). Data was collected through semi-structured interviews, a technique that allows the collection of detailed information from participants and the development of a good understanding of social and cultural contexts (Myers, 2009). A total of nineteen Interviews were carried out between January and June 2023. They involved participants across seven construction companies, who spanned the full range of seniority including directors, digital team leads, BIM managers, digital solutions providers, architects, engineers. The interviews were conducted online via MS Teams and then transcribed into text. A thematic analysis was them carried out in a multiple iteration process where Activity Analysis and Development (ActAD) framework, an enhance Activity Theory (AT) adaptation (Mursu et al., 2007), was used as the guiding theoretical framework. This study is part of ongoing research investigating the impact of stakeholder involvement on the adoption of digital technologies in both the construction industry and the health care sector of the UK.

Table 1. Summary of conducted interviews

Participant types	Number of participants interviewed
Director	3
Programme/ Digitalisation lead	2
BIM/project manager	3
Associate partner	2
Architect	4
Engineer	2
Sales and marketing executive	3
TOTAL	**19**

4. FINDINGS

The iterative thematic analysis identified eighteen initial themes, which were coded and then grouped into six major themes. In the coding the acronym BC (Barrier in Construction) followed by a first digit indicating the level of grouping and a second digit identifying each theme withing the grouping is used. The final themes are digitalisation complexity and ubiquitous change, digitalisation leadership and management approach, organisation context and culture, poor stakeholder involvement strategic planning, poor digitalisation stakeholder landscape management, and communication challenges as summarised in Table 2 below. The barriers identified are not in order of importance but are rather intertwined and interdependent as illustrated in Figure 1. It was observed that communication challenges impacted all the identified barriers as highlighted by the thicker full lines. Similarly, it emerged that there was a relationship between digitalisation leadership and management approach, poor stakeholder involvement strategic planning and poor digitalisation stakeholder landscape management, as illustrated by the thicker dashed lines. Further investigation is being undertaken to explore the interdependencies between these barriers.

Table 2. Summary of thematic analysis outcome

Preliminary themes	Final themes
Complexity and scope of digitalisation project **[BC2.16]**	**Digitalisation complexity and ubiquitous change**
Partner company liquidation **[BC2.7]**	
Technological innovation and choice of technologies' providers **[BC2.18]**	
Project scope and costs underestimation **[BC2.12]**	
Managerial and leadership approach **[BC2.2]**	**Digitalisation leadership and management approach**
Management and leadership lack of understanding project details **[BC2.17]**	
Digital team formation dynamics **[BC2.15]**	
Organisational culture **[BC2.1]**	**Organisational context and culture**
Partner companies' protectionism **[BC2.8]**	
Organisation size, regional differences, and lost communication **[BC2.14]**	
Industry male-dominated characteristic **[BC2.6]**	
Lack of stakeholder involvement plan **[BC2.1]**	**Poor stakeholder involvement strategic planning**
Tensions emanating from Stakeholder groups hierarchical roles **[BC2.11]**	
Lack of clarity on digitalisation project ownership **[BC2.4]**	
Lack of accountability for project success **[BC2.5]**	**Poor digitalisation stakeholder landscape management**
Lack of commitment to common project goal **[BC2.9]**	
Management and leadership lack of understanding of project details **[BC2.17]**	
Lack of adequate communication mechanisms, Organisation size, regional differences, and lost communication **[BC2.14]**	**Communication challenges**
Miscommunication and misunderstandings regarding project scope and costs estimated **[BC2.13]**	

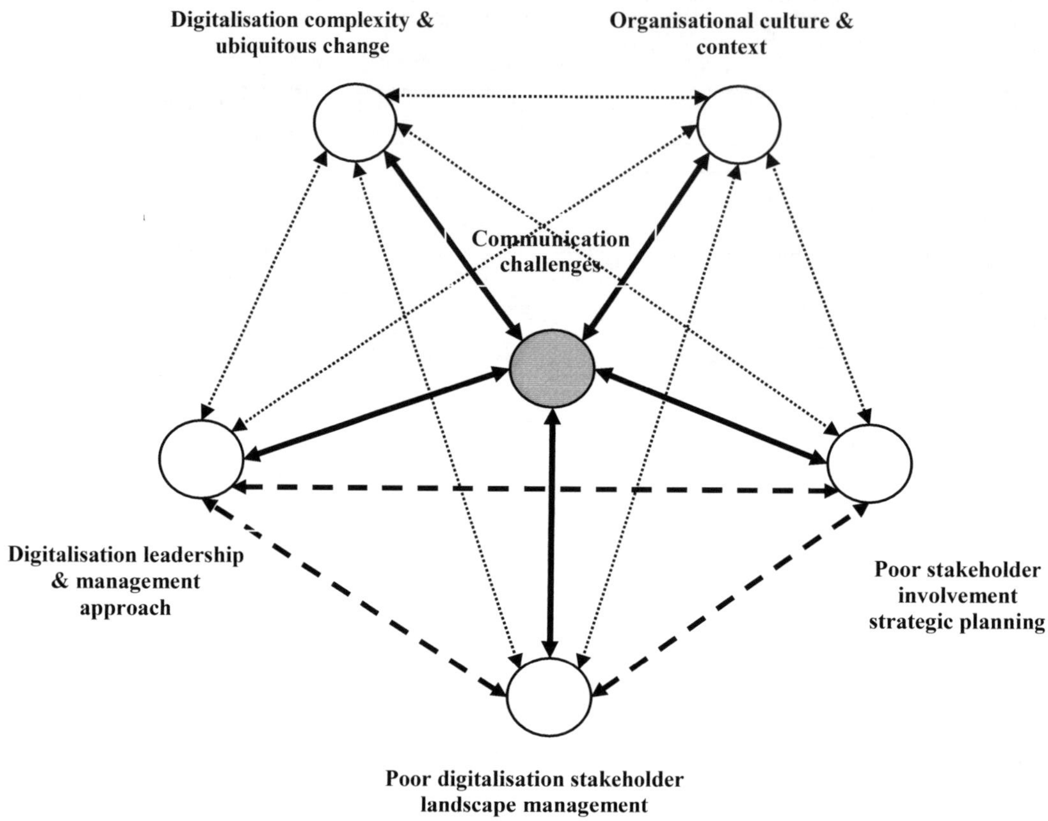

Figure 1. Barriers to stakeholders' involvement interdependence

4.1 Digitalisation Complexity and Ubiquitous Change

The complexity of digitalisation projects coupled with ubiquitous change are a barrier to the involvement of stakeholders throughout digitalisation project lifecycles. From inception, it is difficult to identify all the stakeholders that will be critical to success. Digitalisation projects are long-term in nature, and, over time, there are constant multi-dimensional changes at different levels of the digital transformation process that have implications on stakeholder involvement. These changes include the pace of innovation and related digital technological change, changes in project and team dynamics, changes in partnerships and changes in the stakeholder landscape. Over time it therefore becomes harder to effectively involve all relevant stakeholders and to have the right digitalisation team, as illustrated by the following participant observation:

> *"So it's not as straightforward... people say technology is nice and easy and makes our life better...It's not true. It involves a whole different level of complexity, and this complexity needs us to have specific teams that are experienced in this discipline".* ***(Participant C7)***

4.2 Digitalisation Leadership and Management Approach

Leadership and management approaches negatively affected how stakeholders were involved in digitalisation projects, particularly building the right digitalisation team. In this regard, two participants made the following observations:

*"There were challenges with digital leaders who were fairly new to the business. Because we're such a big machine it takes some time to actually understand all the ins and outs of the business. And it takes time to build up the right team around you". **(Participant C5)***

*"When we come together to deliver projects, good project managers really should be bringing the team together and bringing everyone in together to accomplish a common goal. And I don't think we do that particularly well within the industry". **(Participant C10)***

Leadership and management approaches are not only essential for successful digitalisation projects, they are critical for the identification and involvement of relevant stakeholders which, in turn contribute towards better digitalisation outcome.

4.3 Organisation Context and Culture

The multi-faceted complexities such as the nature of construction projects, the roles of various partnering organisations, and peculiar organisational practices that characterise the industry, dictate how projects are delivered. Practices that are ingrained in day-to-day organisational operations hinder the involvement of stakeholders during the digitalisation process. The intricacies around construction project delivery, and individual organisations' focus on completing their respective tasks with little involvement of other partnering organisations has debilitating consequences to the project, as highlighted in the following observation.

*"I think there's a lot of that blame culture if something goes wrong within the company. If something goes wrong on site, the site team will blame the design team or the commercial team. If something is not built correctly then the designers will blame the site team and then the site team will blame the suppliers or someone else. There's a lot of that and it's not good". **(Participant C10)***

4.4 Poor Stakeholder Involvement Strategic Planning

The industry is characterised by reactive and not proactive stakeholder involvement practices, which are a consequence of poor strategic planning. It was noted that in various cases, the need to involve certain stakeholder groups was identified very late in the project lifecycle, leading to major digitalisation challenges. This is directly related to digitalisation projects' leadership and management approaches in the industry (Section 4.2). Adequate project management is essential in this regard as highlighted by this participant.

*"A key part of robust project management is having a clear stakeholder plan and clear accountabilities. And none of that is particularly complicated. But there's a difference between not really doing it and doing it well... As part of a robust project management approach, you need to have adequate focus on the stakeholder engagement strategy and plan first. And then a core part of that, be very clear from the outset who's the accountable owner and who are the responsible parties. Without those two things, it will never get off the ground". **(Participant C15)***

4.5 Poor Digitalisation Stakeholder Landscape Management

Directly linked to poor stakeholder involvement strategic planning is poor digitalisation stakeholder landscape management. The inability to plan how stakeholders will be involved in the digitalisation process can lead to challenges in stakeholder identification, involvement, and management. This has implications regarding accountability for the success or failure of a project, as highlighted by one participant:

*"I think there can be challenges in who is accountable for the project... so if we're talking about a digital system, you can only have one person who is accountable for its success. Likewise, if we're not clear on individual's responsibilities we can have more than one person responsible for the digital solution. If they're not clear on the responsibilities and the accountabilities, you've got no chance of getting it owned in the business and getting it sustained". **(Participant C15)***

It is therefore imperative that organisations in the construction industry adhere to good stakeholder management practices, to ensure clarity on responsibilities and digitalisation success accountability.

4.6 Communication Challenges

Communication challenges are another barrier to stakeholder involvement. This is central to the manifestation of all the identified barriers, as the impact of the lack of adequate communication mechanisms spreads across all dimensions, with vertical (between different hierarchical and seniority levels) and horizontal (at the same hierarchical and seniority levels) communication challenges identified at different stages of the digitalisation process. Given the complexity of digitalisation projects and the implications of communication challenges on stakeholder involvement and digitalisation project success or failure, participants made the following observations:

> *"I think with construction and engineering technology, it's a little bit more complicated and sometimes you need to share more detail with people in different teams globally...Between global business and what's happening in specific countries or regions... So now when the Managing Director sees the report, he/she sees two different sets of reports, one saying it's on hold, the other one's saying it's in progress. So which one is the correct one? So you can automatically see there's a breakdown in communication"* ***(Participant C10)***
>
> *"If you look on a project level, I think a lot of the engagement between teams is like between disciplines and exchanging information. I think that really depends on the project and the teams involved. I think sometimes that can be really difficult".* ***(Participant C9)***

5. DISCUSSION

The digitalisation of UK construction is an organisational transformation process that will enable the industry to take advantage of innovative digital technologies. This is critical in an age when digital technologies have been widely adopted across other sectors. The industry's digital transformation journey is prone to various challenges including barriers to stakeholder involvement. These barriers need to be strategically resolved to achieve better digitalisation outcomes. As argued by Brunetti et al. (2020), embarking on a digitalisation and digital transformation journey is a necessary complex organisational undertaking with unavoidable organisational process redesign within an ever-changing technological ecosystem where innovation is constant. They reiterate the need to develop adequate strategies to address the many challenges of digitalisation. This is critical for the construction industry, where multiple-stakeholder complexities can be hard to navigate.

The slow adoption of digital technologies in the construction industry is particularly associated with the complex construction environment within which digitalisation is undertaken. Complexity is attributed not only to the industry, but also to the nature of construction and digitalisation projects in an industry where resistance to change is a prevalent and predominant culture (Zulu and Saad, 2023). This complexity is exacerbated by the challenge of managing the relevant stakeholders. In this regard, Yang et al. (2014) argue that the construction industry's digitalisation stakeholder landscape is broad and necessitates good management to effectively address stakeholder attributes such as power, legitimacy, urgency and proximity. In the case of multifarious infrastructure projects with multiple stakeholder groups and role players, Zarewa (2019) identified that inadequate and ineffective stakeholder management practices negatively affect the successful delivery of construction projects.

The effects of poor stakeholder involvement strategic planning and poor digitalisation stakeholder landscape management highlight the challenges of implementing stakeholder management guidelines in the industry. In this regard Ebiloma and Rimtip (2019) argue for better adoption and adaptation of good management principles and tools such as the project management body of knowledge (PMBOK) in the construction industry of the UK. Basic principle and guidelines provided in the PMBOK suggest four essential stakeholder management processes: identification of project stakeholders, planning of stakeholder engagement, management of stakeholder engagement and monitoring, and control of stakeholder engagement (Project Management Institute, 2013). These would provide better outcomes if adopted and adapted for the construction industry. Similarly, Faraji et al. (2022) reiterate the relevance of adopting and adapting the PMBOK's eight performance domains to the construction industry context: stakeholders, teams, lifecycle, planning, project work, delivery, measurement and uncertainty.

Appropriate digitalisation leadership, a robust management approach and adequate communication strategies can be catalytic to addressing stakeholder involvement barriers and achieving digitalisation benefits in the UK construction industry. Digitalisation leaders and managers need attributes that are conducive to successful digitalisation. Zulu and Khosrowshahi (2021) identify the following six types of digital leadership: proactive and forward-thinking, supportive, uncoordinated, cautious, resistant and visionless, and undriven leaders. Johari and Hendra (2023) on the other hand suggest four digital leadership dimensions: competency of digital leaders, capacity of digital leaders, organisation structure, and organisation strategy. These digital leadership attributes and dimensions have implications for the manifestation of stakeholder involvement barriers and the success of digitalisation projects in the industry. Digitalisation leaders and managers therefore need appropriate leadership styles and the necessary digital leadership attributes for successful digitalisation and digital transformation.

6. CONCLUSION

This study has provided insight into the barriers to the involvement of stakeholders in the digitalisation and adoption of digital technologies in the UK construction industry. It identified six barriers: organisational context and culture, digitalisation leadership and management approach, poor stakeholder involvement strategic planning, communication challenges, poor digitalisation stakeholders' landscape management and, digitalisation complexity and ubiquitous change. It is therefore imperative that managers and leaders be aware of these barriers when they undertake the implementation of digital technologies. This insight is essential in the quest for successful digital technologies' adoption at a time when the construction industry is undergoing digitalisation and digital transformation to improve efficiencies and to derive the benefits that other industries have already achieved through successful digitalisation.

The findings indicate that while stakeholder involvement is an enabler for successful digitalisation, there are barriers that hinder its success. The study contributes to the body of knowledge on stakeholder theory, stakeholder management and digital technology adoption by highlighting the influence of contextual parameters on barriers to stakeholder management practice in digitalisation. The barriers highlight the need to adapt stakeholder management practice and digitalisation principles to the specific context of the construction industry of the UK. This brings to fore the need to further explore the extent to which each of these barriers affect digitalisation. Further research is being undertaken by the authors to investigate the interdependencies between these barriers and the similarities and differences in other sectors.

ACKNOWLEDGEMENT

The work reported in this paper was undertaken as part of the Made Smarter Innovation: Centre for People-Led Digitalisation, at the University of Bath. The project is funded by the Engineering and Physical Sciences Research Council (EPSRC) Grant EP/V062042/1.

REFERENCES

Alaloul, W. S. et al, (2022). Assessment of economic sustainability in the construction sector: evidence from three developed countries (the USA, China and the UK). *Sustainability,* Vol. 14, paper 6326.

Arifin, J. et al, (2022). A literature review of digital transformation in the construction industry. *Proceeding of the 3rd South American international industrial engineering and operations management conference*, July 19-21 Asuncion, Paraguay.

Brunetti, F. et al, (2020). Digital transformation challenges: strateges emercing from a multi-stakeholder approach. *The TQM journal,* Vol. 32, pp. 697-724.

Ebiloma, D. O. and Rimtip, M. N., (2019). Factors affecting the success or failure of project management methologies (PPM) usage in the UK and Nigerian Construction industry. *International journal of innovation and sustainability,* Vol. 3, pp. 17-28.

Faraji, A.,et al, (2022). Applicability-Compatibility Analysis of PMBOK Seventh Edition from the Perspective of the Construction Industry Distinctive Peculiarities. *Buildings,* Vol. 12, paper 210.

Forcael, E.et al, (2020). Construction 4.0: a literature review. *Sustainability,* Vol. 12, paper 9755.

Freeman, R. E. (1984). *Strategic management: a stakeholder approach,* Boston, Pitman.

Project management institute. (2013). *A Guide to the Project Management Body of Knowledge (PMBOK®Guide),* Newtown Square, USA, Project Mangement Institute.

Johari, S. and Hendra, S., (2023). An overview of digitalisation leadership dimensions in construction industry. *International journal of business and technology management,* Vol. 5, pp. 49-66.

Kavuri, A. S. et al, (2020). Scenarios for the digitalisation of the construction industry. *In:* Scott, L. and Neilson, C. J., eds. The 36th annual ARCOM conference, 7-8 September, UK. Association of researchers in construction management, 425-434.

Mursu, A. et al, (2007). Activity theory in information systems research and practice: theoretical underpinning for an information systems development model. *Information research* 12, Paper 311.

Myers, M. D. (2009). *Qualitative resarch in business management,* London, Sage publications.

Olanipekun, A. O. and Sutrisna, M., (2021). Facilitating digital transformation in construction: a systematic review of the current state of the art. *Frontiers in built environment,* 7, 660758.

Osunsanmi, T. O. et al, (2020). Appraisal of stakeholders' willingness to adopt construction 4.0 technologies for construction projects. *Built environment project and asset management,* Vol. 10, pp. 547 - 565.

Oyegoke, A. S.et al, (2010). The myth behind integration in the UK construction industry. *International journal of procurement management,* Vol. 3, pp. 247-264.

Prebanic, K. R. and Vukomanovic, M., (2021). Realizing the need for digial transformation of stakeholder management: a systematic review in the construction industry. *Sustainability,* Vol. 13, paper 12690.

Shojaei, R. S. and Burgess, G., (2022). Non-technical inhibitors: exploring the adoption of digital innovation in the UK construction industry. *Technology forecasting & social change,* Vol. 185, paper 122036.

Storvang, P. and Clarke, A. H., (2014). How to create a space for stakeholder involvement in construction. *Construction management and economics,* Vol. 32, pp. 1166-1182.

Walker, D. H. T. et al, (2008). Influence, stakeholder mapping and visualization. *Construction managment and economics,* Vol. 26, pp. 645-658.

Woodhead, R. et al, (2018). Digital construction: from point solutions to IoT. *Automation in construction,* Vol. 93, pp. 35-46.

Xia, N. et al, (2018). Towards integrating construction risk management and stakeholder management: a systematic review and future research agendas. *International journal of project management,* Vol. 36, pp. 701-715.

Yang, R. J. et al, (2014). Stakeholders' Attributes, Behaviors, and Decision-Making Strategies in Construction Projects: Importance and Correlations in Practice. *Project Management Journal,* Vol 45, pp. 74-90.

Yin, R. K. (2009). *Case study research: design and methods,* London, Sage publications.

Zarewa, G. A. (2019). Barriers to effective stakehoder management in the delivery of multifarious infratructure projects. *Journal of Engineering, Project, and Production Management,* Vol. 9, pp. 85-96.

Zulu, S. L. and Khosrowshahi, F., (2021). A taxonomy of digital leadership in the construction industry. *Construction management and economics,* Vol. 39, pp. 565-578.

Zulu, S. L. and Saad, A. M., (2023). A sensemaking perspective of digitalisation in construction organisations. *Sustainability,* Vol. 15, Paper 2344.

STRATEGIC DIGITAL ENVIRONMENT ASSESSMENT VIS-À-VIS A REGIONAL STRATEGIC DIGITAL GOVERNMENT FRAMEWORK. APPLICATION TO OECD DIGITAL GOVERNMENT POLICY FRAMEWORK IN ESTONIA

Sara Halim and Bouchaib Bounabat
ALQUALSADI Team, ENSIAS, Mohammed V University in Rabat, Morocco

ABSTRACT

In today's world, the adoption of digital technologies varies across different countries and regions due to factors such as infrastructure, education, and cultural differences. A digital transformation strategy must therefore be tailored to each country's unique context, in addition to the regional strategies applied in the region. This article introduces a methodology that evaluates the digital transformation readiness of the environment, taking into account national and regional limitations. Transformational issues are discussed in this article: the analysis of regional strategic digital government frameworks and the study of the link between these frameworks and a country's environmental assessment.

KEYWORDS

Digital Government, Regional Environment, Strategic Planning

1. INTRODUCTION

Digital transformation is a complex process that varies across different countries and regions. As such, developing effective digital government strategies requires a deep understanding of the unique national and regional contexts in which they are implemented. Faced with these constraints, the Digital Government Strategy Environment (DGSE) aims to assess the digital environment of the country to set appropriate future objectives. However, it raises the query: to what extent can the DGSE addresses the regional constraints?

The contribution of this article is to present a methodological approach that assesses the level of readiness of the environment for digital transformation while considering both national and regional constraints and to illustrate this approach with an application to the OECD Digital Government Policy Framework in Estonia.

This paper is organized as follows. Section 2 presents the Regional Strategic Digital Government Framework (RSDGF) as a strategic model that aims to guide and support the development of digital government initiatives within a specific region or group of countries, followed by a subsequent attention to the OECD Digital Government Policy Framework. In Section 3, the link between DGSE assessment and the RSDGF will be established, and the proposed methodological approach for assessing the level of environmental readiness will be introduced. Finally, Sections 4 and 5 will detail the application of this methodological approach to the OECD Digital Government Policy Framework in Estonia.

2. REGIONAL STRATEGIC DIGITAL GOVERNMENT FRAMEWORK

2.1 Definitions:

Regional Strategic Digital Government Framework (RSDGF) is an approach that provides a set of guidelines for the effective use of digital technologies in the governance processes of a specific region. Successful e-government requires a deep understanding of the specific context in which it is being implemented, including the political, economic, social, and cultural factors that shape the governance landscape of a particular country or region. (United Nations, 2018). Governments must take into account these regional constraints and tailor their strategies accordingly. Janssen and Kuk (2016) argue that effective digital government initiatives must take into account the specific social, economic, and political factors that influence the use of technology in a given context. Similarly, Jaeger, and Grimes (2010) suggest that successful e-government initiatives require an understanding of the cultural and political contexts in which they are implemented.

2.2 Examples:

Several RSDGF have been created in the world with the aim of addressing regional constraints and targeting a digital transformation that is equitable, and sustainable. Some notable examples include:

- The Digital Compass 2030 (EC, 2021) adopted by the European Commission aims to guide Europe's digital transformation with four main goals: to ensure that all Europeans have access to reliable digital infrastructure, to make Europe a leader in digital technologies and innovation, to promote a fair and competitive digital economy, and to enhance digital skills and education for all.
- The ASEAN Digital Masterplan 2025 (ASEAN, 2015) launched by the Association of Southeast Asian Nations aims to promote the development of a digital economy in the region. It includes initiatives to improve digital infrastructure, promote cross-border e-commerce, and enhance digital skills and literacy.
- The OECD Digital Government Policy Framework (DGPF)(OECD, 2020) is a policy instrument designed to help governments all over the world identify key determinants for effective design and implementation of strategic approaches for the transition towards digital maturity of their public sectors.
- The United States-Mexico-Canada Agreement (USMCA, 2020) digital trade chapter aims to facilitate cross-border data flows and promote the development of digital trade in North America. It includes provisions related to: (i) Prohibition of data localization requirements; (ii) Prohibition of customs duties on digital products; (iii) Promotion of interoperability between digital trade systems; (iv) Protection of personal information, and (v) Promotion of cybersecurity cooperation between the three countries.

2.3 OECD Digital Government Policy Framework

The OECD Digital Government Policy Framework aims at advancing the maturity of the 6 dimensions, by emphasizing levers, that help overcome bureaucratic legacies, verticality and silos, and fosters horizontality, integration, co-ordination and synergies across government. It is also applied in peer reviews and frames the methodology and survey design of the OECD Digital Government Index (DGI) which measures countries' digital government maturity across the six dimensions (OECD, 2018)(OECD, 2020).

- **Digital by design:** Government approaches “digital” with an understanding of the strategic activities involved with long-lasting transformation. Digital technologies are leveraged in order to rethink government to deliver an efficient public services. In particular, digital by design governments focus on: End-to-End digitalization process, Simplification, and Innovation.
- **Data-driven:** Government recognizes data as a strategic asset and foundational enabler for the public sector to work together, forecast needs, understand performance, and respond to change. A data-driven government focuses on applying data to generate public value through these activities: Anticipation and planning, Delivery and Evaluation and monitoring.
- **Open by default:** Government is committed to disclosing data in open formats, collaborating across organizational boundaries and involving those outside of government in line with the principles of the Council on Open Gov (OECD, 2017b). It encompasses: Participation; transparency and; Inclusiveness
- **User-driven administration**, providing ways for citizens to communicate their needs and for government to include, and be led by, them when developing policies and public services. A government is user-driven when it provides users: the accessibility to appropriate channels; service Design and Delivery to easily identify the needed services; and compliance as services are more aligned on users.
- **Government as a platform**: Governments build supportive ecosystems that support and equip public servants to design effective policy and deliver quality services, and to enable collaboration with and between users to harness their creativity, knowledge and skills. This dimension is then achieved through the main activities: Support ecosystem, public services Marketplace and collaborative government.

- **Proactive policy making and service delivery**: Governments can anticipate, and rapidly respond to, the needs of their citizens. They also release data as open data rather than reacting to a request for access to public sector information. Proactive government focus on: the users' need for anticipation, the prior experiences exploitation and the agility of government processes.

3. STRATEGIC DIGITAL ENVIRONMENT ASSESSMENT

3.1 Digital Government Strategy Environment

Digital Government Strategy (DGS) is a governance tool which provides a vision statement to guide the government's digitalization with the aim of improving service quality and increasing competitiveness. A DGS is set through the definition of multiple Strategic Objectives (SOs) which are in turn composed by Sub-Strategic Objectives (SSOs) that focus on meeting customer needs through digital government services. Based on the digital trends, governments select the technical foundations (FTs) necessary to achieve DGS strategic objectives that will support their strategy and respond to their growing need for innovation. SOs' achievement is supported by the Digital Government Strategic Environment, which embraces six dimensions:

- **Governance**: refers to the way in which digital technologies are used to improve governance processes. Effective governance in the digital era requires a comprehensive strategy that includes the development of appropriate policies, regulations, and infrastructure to support the use of technology in government.
- **Legal:** refers to the laws, policies and regulations that govern the use of digital technologies in the public sector. It encompasses laws related to data privacy, intellectual property rights, and access to information. It also refers to the creation of a legal framework that supports the effective and responsible use of technology by government agencies, while protecting the rights and interests of citizens.
- **Organizational:** refers to creating a structure that supports the effective use of technology, streamlines administrative processes, and clarifies roles and responsibilities to increase efficiency.
- **Human:** refers to the consideration of the human factor involved in the implementation of digital technologies within government systems. It encompasses the development of digital skills and digital literacy among citizens, and the provision of appropriate training for the adoption of digital tools.
- **Financial:** involves the allocation and management of financial resources to support digital initiatives. It encompasses identifying funding sources, allocating budgets, and monitoring financial performance. It also involves developing new funding models and establishing governance structures to ensure accountability and transparency in the use of public funds.
- **Technical:** refers to the development and deployment of digital technologies to support the delivery of public services and improve citizen engagement. It involves the use of disruptive technologies to foster innovation and the infrastructure access and sharing capacities to ensure accessibility.

3.2 Link Between DGSE Assessment and RSDGF

The DGSE framework emphasizes the importance of assessing a specific country's digital environment to identify barriers and develop a digital strategy that meets the needs of both citizens and the government.

However, a successful digital transformation strategy must be tailored to each country's context but also the regional challenges that affect the adoption of digital technologies. In fact, without coordinated and comprehensive intervention, countries are at risk of further widening the digital innovation divide. (ITU, 2021) Equally important is donor coordination at the global, regional, and national levels to ensure inclusive oversight and concerted global action (Worldbank, 2016). Adopting the RSDGF allows governments to tailor their strategy in order to address regional constraints such as regional regulations and policies, regional collaboration, and economic factors. Therefore, it is necessary to align the DGSE with the requirements imposed by the RSDGF. The Digital Enablers perspective should include the Foundational Technologies (FT) required for the realization of Strategic Objective (SO) specific to the country, based on an assessment of the environment, as well as the SOs brought by the RSDGF.

3.3 Proposed Methodological Approach

The methodological approach proposed for the assessment of the level of environmental readiness are based on 4 steps: SOs and SSOs Identification, FT Importance Evaluation, Government Strategic Environment (GSE) Readiness Level Evaluation, and Maturity Levels Identification.

- **SOs and SSOs Identification,** based on needs identified following the environment assessment or based on the RSDGF principles. An SO can responds to the administration and/or the customer needs. Each SO is broken down into several SSOs that represent measurable steps necessary for achieving the overall SO.
- **FT importance Evaluation (Weights Fixation),** consisting in defining how much a FT contributes to reach a specific SO. These weights can be identified based on qualitative analytical scrutiny of specialized and proven reports and best practices in Government digital transformation domain, and calculated according to the importance of each FT and the benefits that are derived from its use.
- **GSE Readiness Level Evaluation,** done through the study of the digital environment based on the six key dimensions (governance, technical, legal, organizational, human and financial), as described in (Halim and Bounabat, 2023). Each dimension is broken down into key factors, whose readiness level indicates each factor capacity to support the FTs implementation.
- **Maturity Levels Identification,** describing the maturity of the environment in achieving SSO, providing valuable insight into the progress of digital transformation in government. Its calculation is based on both the FT weight and the GSE Readiness Level Evaluation.

4. APPLICATION TO OECD DGPF

4.1 DGPF Dimensions as Strategic Objectives

For the OECD, a digital government that presents higher levels of maturity across the six-dimensions is better placed not only to achieve internal efficiencies and transparency, but also to deliver public services that match and potentially exceed people's expectations. Therefore, each dimension can be classified as a strategic objective and decomposed in its turn into a set of adequate specific SSO (See Table 1).

Table 1. Decomposition of the six OCDE dimensions into SSO

Strategic Obj.	Strategic Sub- Objective	Signifiance
User Driven	Needs Compliance	Making designed and developped services more aligned on users views, needs and aspirations
	Accessibility	Allowing the user to access to appropriate channels to communicate with the government
	Service Design and Delivery	Allowing the user to easily identify the needed services through the most convenient channel
Open By Default	Transparency	Making core government processes more accountable
	Inclusiveness	Making core government processes more inclusive
	Participation	All the ways in which Stakeholders can be involved in service design and delivery
Proactivness	Users Needs Anticipation	Ensuring that users needs have been anticipated and appropriately addressed
	Prior experience exploitation	Providing users with a seamless and satisfactory experience when using services
	Agility	Making core government processes more agile
Digital By Design	Simplification	Rethink and re-engineer business processes and internal operations
	End-to-End Service	Deliver a complete service, without needing a human intervention
	Innovation	Mobilizing emerging technologies and data to innovate public services
Data Driven	Anticipation and planning	Using data in the anticipation of possible change and the forecasting of needs
	Delivery	Using data to inform and improve policy implementation and the responsiveness of gov.
	Evaluation and monitoring	Using data to measure impact, audit decisions and monitor performance
Government as a Platform	Support Ecosystem	Supporting and equipping services to meet the users' needs
	Public Services Marketplace	Existing foundation for multiple actors to contribute to the provision of public services
	Collaborative Government	Ensuring that users' needs have been anticipated and appropriately addressed

4.2 FTs Weights for SSOs (FT importance Evaluation)

The study of the SSO's achievement level related to the OECD SOs is out based on several reports and articles published on governments digital transformation (World Bank, 2015; 2016; 2018; 2020) (ILO, 2021; 2022) (Jelenic, M., 2018) (OECD, 2020) (Margetts, H. and Naumann, A., 2016) (Denise Feldner, 2020). The weights presented below are generated via data analytics tool Dedoose (https://www.dedoose.com). Regarding the analysis of the weight, the first step is to create, the code tree concerning the different FTs and SSOs. Then, excerpts are created by highlighting paragraphs and attaching them to the codes that the snippet refers to. Once all the excerpts created, the Code Co-Occurrence Table was used to present the frequencies for which all code pairings were applied to the same excerpt and, by default, overlapping excerpts.

Table 2. Dedoose Analysis results related to FT weights vis-à-vis SSOs

	Digital Enablers Perpsective	Data management	Digital Identity	Emerging Technologies	Interoperab ility	Multi-channels Digital Services	One-Stop-Shop Portal
Open by default	Inclusiveness	0,133	0,333	0,067	0,200	0,200	0,067
	Participation	0,154	0,154	0,077	0,077	0,385	0,154
	Transparency	0,083	0,250	0,083	0,333	0,083	0,167
Data Driven	Anticipation and planning	0,417	0,083	0,167	0,167	0,083	0,083
	Delivery	0,294	0,118	0,176	0,235	0,118	0,059
	Evaluation and monitoring	0,563	0,063	0,188	0,063	0,063	0,063
Digital by design	End-to-End service	0,125	0,125	0,063	0,563	0,063	0,063
	Innovation	0,214	0,071	0,357	0,214	0,071	0,071
	Simplification	0,048	0,333	0,048	0,143	0,143	0,286
Gov as a platform	Collaborative Government	0,059	0,118	0,059	0,412	0,294	0,059
	Public Services Marketplace	0,167	0,056	0,111	0,333	0,167	0,167
	Support Ecosystem	0,136	0,136	0,136	0,364	0,136	0,091
Proactivness	Agility	0,095	0,238	0,143	0,190	0,190	0,143
	Prior Experiences Exploitation	0,450	0,050	0,300	0,100	0,050	0,050
	User needs anticipation	0,462	0,077	0,231	0,077	0,077	0,077
Use driven	Accessibility	0,043	0,391	0,043	0,174	0,217	0,130
	Needs Compliance	0,071	0,286	0,143	0,357	0,071	0,071
	Service Design and Delivery	0,118	0,118	0,118	0,353	0,176	0,118

5. STRATEGIC DIGITAL ENVIRONMENT READINESS ASSESSMENT

5.1 Strategic Digital Environment Readiness Assessment - Estonia Use Case

5.1.1 Theoretical Part

The Digital Government Environment perspective describes how the environment dimensions combine to support FTs implementation. The calculation of each FT Preparedness Level (PL) relies on public agencies maturity model described in (Halim and Bounabat, 2023) and inspired by (Gonzalo & al., 2011).

$$\mathbf{Value(dim_{jk}) = (\sum RL(Factor_{jkp}) / NF_k)} \quad \text{(I)}$$

NF_k : Number of Factors composing the dimension$_k$, and $RL(Factor_{jkp})$: Readiness Level of the Factor$_p$, $RL_{jkp} \in \{1,2..5\}$

$$\mathbf{PL(FT_j) = (\sum Value(dim_{jk})) / ND\_DGE} \quad \text{(II)}$$

Where ND_DGE: Number of DGE dimensions

The readiness level (RL) of each factor measures the state of readiness that support the implementation of each FT. It is estimated through specific questionnaire and has to be defined between the level 1 and 5 where each level' signification is detailed in Table 3.

Table 3. Readiness level signification

Readiness Level	Signification
1	Government is aware of the considered factor importance vis-à-vis a specific FT
2	Government starts implementing dedicated actions to reinforce the factor role to set-up the FT
3	Government starts developing dedicated and planned actions to reinforce the factor role to set-up the FT.
4	Dedicated strategic action plans and policies are regularly measured
5	Dedicated strategic plans are regularly updated and continually improved to respond to changes.

5.1.2 Estonia Use Case

This use case aims to define the maturity of Estonia's digital environment based on several articles (Worldbank, 2016, 2018; Heller, 2017; Goede, 2019; Feldner, 2020; Bharosa and al., 2020; OECD, 2020a; ILO, 2021; Salumaa-Lepik and al., 2021; Ehin and al., 2022). The first step is to define the readiness level of each factor. Then, using the equations (I) and (II), the value of each dimension composing the digital environment perspective can be calculated (see Table 4). The focus is on theses six FTs:

Table 4. Estonia's dimensions' values

Env. Dimensions	Factors	Data Management	Digital Identity	Emerging Technologies	Interoper ability	Multi-channels' Services	One-Stop-Shop
Governance	Strong Political leadership	4	4	3	4	3	4
	Governance structure strategy	5	4	4	4	4	5
	Clear IT Governance	4	4	4	4	4	4
	Governance Value	**4,33**	**4,00**	**3,67**	**4,00**	**3,67**	**4,33**
Human	Internal human IT Skills	4	5	5	5	4	5
	Cultural aspects	3	4	4	4	4	4
	Citizen digital readiness	4	4	4	4	4	4
	Human Value	**3,67**	**4,33**	**4,33**	**4,33**	**4,00**	**4,33**
Financial	D-Gov initiatives Funding	5	5	4	4	4	5
	Investment Promotion	4	4	4	4	4	4
	Institution of awards schemes	4	3	4	3	3	4
	Public procurement management	3	4	3	4	4	4
	Financial Value	**4,00**	**4,00**	**3,75**	**3,75**	**3,75**	**4,25**
Organizational	Simplified admin. procedures	4	5	5	5	5	5
	Clear definition of internal roles	3	4	4	5	4	4
	IT acquisition policies	5	3	3	4	4	4
	Organizational Value	4,00	4,00	4,00	4,67	4,33	4,33
Technical	Persistence of a heavy IS legacy	3	5	3	5	4	4
	Infrastructure Access sharing	4	5	3	5	5	4
	Converged networks & services	4	3	4	4	3	3
	Disruptive IT adoption	5	4	5	3	4	4
	Technical Value	4,00	4,25	3,75	4,25	4,00	3,75
Legal	Citizen protection	5	5	5	5	4	5
	Coverage legal framework	4	4	4	4	4	4
	Quality of IT regulation	4	5	4	4	4	4
	Intellectual Property protection	4	4	3	4	3	3
	Legal Value	4,25	4,50	4,00	4,25	3,75	4,00
PL-Value(FT)		**4,04**	**4,18**	**3,92**	**4,21**	**3,92**	**4,17**

Estonia is among the leading countries in the world in the field of e-governance (Kerikmäe & Nyman Metcalf, 2020b; Salumaa-Lepik, Kerikmäe & Nisu, 2021). The financial risks have been well managed by Estonian public administration as Estonia's approach has been to finance its digital infrastructure and digital innovation through small steps. (ILO, 2021) The country also has a well-educated workforce as children are learning programming in primary school—solving technical problems, as well as building and controlling robots. (Feldner, 2020) Estonia is widely credited with being a pioneer in e-governance (Goede, 2019). Therefore, an e-governance academy has been created to capture and distribute the knowledge (Heller,2017). The country has established a number of different agencies and organizations that are responsible for different aspects of e-governance such as the Information System Authority who coordinates the development and administration of the state's information system. (https://www.ria.ee/en/)(Bharosa, and al, 2020) Estonia has implemented a number of laws and regulations that support the use of technology in government: the Population Register Act and the Personal Data Protection Act regulate the use of data recorded in the Population Register (Ehin, 2022), the "once only rule": Under Estonian law, government agencies should not ask people for data that any other agency holds. (Feldner, 2020) For the technical dimension, Estonia is often cited as a leader in the field of digital readiness, due in large part to its successful implementation of e-services such as e-ID, e-tax, e-health, e-education, and e-voting. One of the biggest Estonia's technical asset is X-ROAD which is an interoperability system that allows data exchange for residents, public institutions, and private companies. (Bharosa, and al, 2020) (Goede, 2019)

5.2 Maturity Levels Identification – Estonia Use Case

5.2.1 Theoretical Part

The Digital Enablers perspective encompasses FTs necessary to an SSO achievement, accordingly to their importance rate or weight. The Achievement Indicator (AI) of an SSO, according to (Halim, Bounabat, 2023) and (Gonzalo & al., 2011), is the weighted average of the weighted Preparedness Level (PL) of its associated FTs, as shown in Eq. (III).

$$\mathbf{AI(SSO_i) = \sum (Weight_{ij} * PL(FT_j)), \text{ where } \Sigma\ Weight_{ij} = 1} \qquad \text{(III)}$$

Based on Readiness Levels presented in Table 4, the definition of the maturity levels listed in Table 5 are inspired by (Valdés, et al., 2011) capability levels, and (CMU/SEI, 2010) Capacity Maturity Model.

Table 5. Maturity level of sub-strategic objectives

Maturity level	AI(SSO)	Signifiance : The environment necessary to achieve the SSO is
0 - Initial	[0,1[	limited, and its development process is unpredictable
1 - Developing	[1,2[	implemented by dedicated projects, and its development process is frequently reactive
2 - Defined	[2,3[	implemented through planned projects, and its development process is more proactive
3 - Managed	[3,4[	implemented by proactive and regularly measured strategic action plans and policies
4 - Integrated	[4,5[	implemented by dedicated measured and continually improved

5.2.2 Estonia Use Case

The AI of an SSO is the weighted average of the weighted Preparedness Level (PL) of its associated FTs, as shown in Eq. (III). Based on the PL for each FT calculated in section 4.2 and the weights generated through Dedoose (Table 2), the achievement indicator for each SSO can be deducted (Table 6).

Table 6. The Maturity Level of OECD SSOs

	Digital Enablers Perpsective	Achievement Indicator	Maturity Level
Open by default	Inclusiveness	4,096	4-Integrated
	Participation	4,037	4-Integrated
	Transparency	4,132	4-Integrated
Data Driven	Anticipation and planning	4,060	4-Integrated
	Delivery	4,068	4-Integrated
	Evaluation and monitoring	4,037	4-Integrated
Digital by design	End-to-End service	4,145	4-Integrated
	Innovation	4,043	4-Integrated
	Simplification	4,124	4-Integrated
Gov as a platform	Collaborative Government	4,090	4-Integrated
	Public Services Marketplace	4,091	4-Integrated
	Support Ecosystem	4,098	4-Integrated
Proactivness	Agility	4,083	4-Integrated
	Prior Experiences Exploitation	4,028	4-Integrated
	User needs anticipation	4,036	4-Integrated
User driven	Accessibility	4,109	4-Integrated
	Needs Compliance	4,123	4-Integrated
	Service Design and Delivery	4,095	4-Integrated

The SSOs reach the highest maturity level (Integrated) as the different OECD dimensions in Estonia are fully implemented and continually updated. Estonia is described as "open by default" as it has taken a transparent approach to sharing information with its citizens. This has helped to build trust and engagement with the government. Estonia's digital government is data-driven as it places a strong emphasis on using data and analytics to inform and improve its policies and services. It collects and aggregates data from various sources to inform decision-making and improve the design and delivery of government services. Estonia's digital government is often described as digital-by-design because its government has digitized its processes and services with the goal of creating a more efficient, and accessible government. This has been reflected in the development of a wide range of digital services, that meet the needs and expectations of its citizens, such as electronic ID systems, online voting, and digital signatures. In order to reach the "government as a platform" strategic objective, Estonia provides a digital infrastructure that allows citizens to access government services and information efficiently, and enables businesses and organizations to build their own digital services and applications on top of the government's platform. Estonia is described as "proactive" because it has taken a forward-looking and innovative approach to using technology to enhance and transform the way its government operates. It is always seeking new ways to better serve its citizens like through the exploitation of prior experiences. Estonia is described as "user-driven" as it places a strong emphasis on co-creation with citizens in order to ensure that the digital services provided are effective and meet the needs of its users.

6. CONCLUSION

This paper underscores the role of digital transformation in governments and emphasizes the importance in the formulation of successful strategies of considering both national constraints following the DGSE framework and regional constraints imposed by the Regional Strategic Digital Government Framework. The contribution of this article is to present a methodological approach that assesses the level of readiness of the environment for digital transformation and help governments develop an effective digital transformation strategy. It is outlined in four steps: (i) SOs Identification based on the country and RSDGF objectives; (ii) FT importance Evaluation; (iii) GSE Readiness Level Evaluation; (iv) Maturity Levels Identification.

Applying this approach to Estonia based on the OECD Digital Government Policy Framework has defined Estonia's digital transformation maturity level based on the core SOs imposed to the OECD members. While the use case serves as an example, the methodological approach can be applied to any government. The approach can be especially beneficial for governments seeking to improve their level of digitalization, as well as for countries that are part of a union and need to implement strategies that align with their individual country goals, as well as the goals of the union as a whole. This article can lead to future work such as defining approaches to improve the level of maturity of digital governments based on strategic planning, or strategies based on trend predictions toward digital transformation.

REFERENCES

ASEAN. (2015). *ASEAN Digital Masterplan 2025. The Association of Southeast Asian Nations.* Available at: https://asean.org/wp-content/uploads/2021/09/ASEAN-Digital-Masterplan-EDITED.pdf

EC. (2021). *2030 Digital Compass: The European way for the Digital Decade*. European Commission, Brussels. eufordigital.eu/wp-content/uploads/2021/03/2030-Digital-Compass-the-European-way-for-the-Digital-Decade.pdf

Ehin P., Solvak M., Willemson J., Vinkel P. (2022). *Internet voting in Estonia 2005–2019: Evidence from eleven elections.*

Feldner D. (2020). *E-Estonia – "Europe's Silicon Valley" or a New "1984" ?. Redisigning Organizations: Concepts for the Connected Society*. Chapter 16. Pp 215-228

Goede M. (2019). *E-Estonia: The e-government cases of Estonia, Singapore, and Curaçao*. Archives of Business 7(2)

Halim and Bounabat. (2023). *A conceptual framework for assessment of digital Government strategy environment. Application to digital Government development in Africa*. E-Society and Mobile Learning. Lisbon, Portugal 11-13.

Heller, N. (2017). *Estonia, the Digital Republic*. [online] The New Yorker. Available at: https://www.newyorker.com/magazine/2017/12/18/estonia-the-digital-republic [Accessed 30 Nov. 2018].

ILO. (2021). *E-formalization case study. E-Estonia: A digital society for the transition to formality.*

ILO. (2022). *The digital transformation of apprenticeships: Emerging opportunities and barriers.* Flanders.

ITU. (2021). *Regional Good Practices: Accelerating innovation entrepreneurship and digital transformation in Europe.*

Jelenic, M. (2018). *From theory to Practice. Open Government Data, Accountability and service Delivery*. World Bank

Kerikmäe, T. & Nyman-Metcalf, K. (2020b), '*The rule of law and the protection of fundamental human rights in an era of automation,*' in J.-S. Gordon (ed.) Smart Technologies and Fundamental Rights, Philosophy and Human Rights, Leiden: Brill, pp. 221–239. https://doi.org/10.1163/9789004437876_011

Margetts, H. and Naumann, A. (2016). *Government as a Platform: What can Estonia show the world.* Oxford Internet Institute, University of Oxford.

Nitesh Bharosa, Silvia Lips , and Dirk Draheim. (2020). *Making e-Government Work: Learning from the Netherlands and Estonia*. Electronic Participation pp 41- 53.

OECD. (2018), *Digital Government Review of Brazil: Towards the Digital Transformation of the Public Sector*, doi.org/10.1787/9789264307636-en, based on the OECD (forthcoming c), The Digital Government Framework.

OECD. (2020a). *Education Policy Outlook: ESTONIA.*

OECD. (2020b). *The OECD Digital Government Policy Framework: Six dimensions of a Digital Government*. https://www.oecd.org/gov/the-oecd-digital-government-policy-framework-f64fed2a-en.htm

Pachidi, S., Spruit, M., & Van De Weerd, I. (2014). *Understanding users' behavior with software operation data mining*. Computers in Human Behavior, 30, 583–594.

Salumaa-Lepik, K.; Kerikmäe, T. & Nisu, N. (2021), '*Data protection in Estonia,*'. Data Protection around The World. Privacy Laws in Action, The Information Technology and Law Series, 33, Cham: Springer, pp. 23–57.

Steinfeld, N. (2016). "*I agree to the terms and conditions": (how) do users read privacy policies online? An eye-tracking experiment*. Computers in Human Behavior, 55, 992–1000.

United Nations. (2018). *E-government survey 2018: Gearing e-government to support transformation towards sustainable and resilient societies*. United Nations Publications.

USMCA. (2020). *United States-Mexico-Canada Agreement (USMCA).* Implementing Instructions June 30, 2020. CBP Publication Number 1118-0620. U.S Customs and Border Protection.

World Bank. (2015). *Estonia: A successfully integrated population-registration and identity management system.*

World Bank. (2016). *Estonian e-Government Ecosystem: Foundation, Applications, Outcomes.*

World Bank. (2018). *Privacy by design: Current Practices in Estonia, India and Austria.*

World Bank. (2020). *Digital Government Readiness Assessment (DGRA) Toolkit* V.31.

HORIZONTALLY INTEGRATED IOT SYSTEMS AND THEIR LIMITATIONS

Richard Dabels, Marvin Davieds, Frank Russow and Thomas Mundt
Department of Computer Science, University of Rostock, Rostock, Germany

ABSTRACT

The Internet of Things (IoT) has become commonplace in many areas of work and life. Many technologies have been developed that cover a wide range of applications. However, this has made the IoT landscape extremely fragmented. Many times it is not even in the interest of the developers of such technologies to open them up to outside use. However, as it is in our interest as end users and society to process the data generated in a wide variety of smart environments, work is already underway on the *horizontal integration* of the fragmented IoT landscape. Often though, the limitations of the underlying technologies are not sufficiently addressed. Using the example of an integration of Smart Home to Smart City, this paper examines the problems that would arise in a practical implementation of horizontal integration. To this end, various application scenarios are presented to enable a qualitative assessment of feasibility.

KEYWORDS

Horizontal Integration, LoRa, ZigBee, Smart Environments

1. INTRODUCTION

The horizontal integration of smart environments is a major problem of the Internet of Things (IoT) (Al-Fuqaha et al., 2015; Filipponi et al., 2010; Prazeres and Serrano, 2016; Noura et al., 2019; Dabels, 2023). IoT as a term itself is also hard to define. Miorandi et al. refer to the IoT as a dynamic and distributed network of smart objects, also called things, that provide or consume data related to the physical world. Things are entities that have (1) certain physical characteristics (like shape and size), (2) communication functionalities, (3) a unique identifier, (4) a human-readable name that describes the object as well as a machine-readable address used to communicate with the object, (5) the ability to perform basic or even more advanced computational task, and finally are (6) able to sense or influence the physical reality around them (Miorandi et al., 2012). Here IoT is, among other things, characterized by its heterogeneity in terms of the devices taking part in the systems as well as their computational and communication capabilities that necessitate bespoke architectures and protocols. Depending on the intended use, for example as a smart home, smart hospital, smart city, or other smart environment, a wide variety of technologies is used.

The fact that the term IoT is as complex as its users means that its landscape is extremely fragmented. This can be seen from the fact that each technology has its protocols, APIs, devices, and platforms, which are often incompatible with one another (Noura et al., 2019). By the horizontal integration of these smart environments, we mean overcoming this fragmentation and making the IoT systems more compatible with each other.

Related to IoT and horizontal integration is the topic of Society 5.0, which as a concept has been gaining traction over the last couple of years (Fukuyama, 2018; Deguchi et al., 2020; Mishra et al., 2022). It describes an iteration of concepts already known, like data collected from sensors – the "real world" as described by Deguchi et al. – being used and processed by computers. The difference with Society 5.0 is the impact this automated data processing has on society, actively guiding the decisions of its participants by "merging the physical space and cyberspace" (Deguchi et al., 2020).

But still, there is the problem of interoperability and fragmentation of IoT systems. Mishra et al. describe a smart city architecture consisting of four layers: The Sensing Layer, Data Management Layer, Transmission Layer, and Application Layer (Mishra et al., 2022). Of particular interest for this work are the Sensing and the Transmission Layer, since here the conflict of horizontal integration plays out. Both are responsible for accessing diverse technologies which creates a myriad of problems, some of which are addressed within this paper.

There are many approaches to solving this interoperability problem in the literature that implement middlewares with publish/subscribe mechanisms (Prazeres and Serrano, 2016; Filipponi et al., 2010; Collina et al., 2012; Dave et al., 2020). The Message Queuing Telemetry Transport protocol (MQTT) is often used and the projects are usually oriented towards the upper layer of the OSI model. There are also proposals on the opposite side, such as the use of software-defined radios, which can be used to implement a wide variety of technologies on the same hardware (Gavrila et al., 2018; Lin et al., 2013).

Another problem in the literature is that the definition of smart environments is very vague. In (Dabels, 2023), the term *Smart X* is introduced, which defines smart environments based on their technological characteristics. A smart home and a smart city thus differ in terms of the technologies and requirements placed on them and can therefore be considered distinct Smart X.

This paper examines the extent to which LoRa, a technology for Long Range communication within smart cities, can be suitable as a tunnel technology for ZigBee networks, which are commonly used in smart home systems. Since the smart city and smart home are understood as Smart X, the considerations should in principle also apply to other technologies in the respective areas.

In doing so, problems of the respective technology are addressed which, to the authors' knowledge, have received little attention in the literature to date. As soon as integrations are developed for the smart city, problems arise about the data throughput, latency, or the respective duty cycle. The latter in particular is a concept that is not generally known in conventional computer networks but represents a significant limitation in technologies such as LoRa (Adelantado et al., 2017).

Using network traffic from an existing ZigBee network, calculations are made to determine the feasibility of a ZigBee network that internally uses a LoRa bridge to overcome longer distances. Solutions are postulated for the associated problems as to how this bridging can be improved in the future. Limitations of the technologies that will inevitably arise when implementing a concept such as the horizontal integration of such fundamentally different technologies are also highlighted.

2. RELATED WORK

The problem of interoperability in IoT networks is by no means new. There are several approaches in the literature that deal with the problems of connecting distinct smart environments. This is often referred to as the horizontal integration of *vertices* or *horizontal markets* (Al-Fuqaha et al., 2015; Filipponi et al., 2010; Prazeres and Serrano, 2016; Noura et al., 2019; Dabels, 2023). An attempt to categorize smart environments is made in (Dabels, 2023), where the term *Smart X* is used to point out the technological differences between the various smart environments. The integration of such Smart X is intended to simplify and more precisely define the problem of horizontal integration.

To enable horizontal integration, middleware architectures are often used to implement a compatibility layer between the various networks and technologies. In (Prazeres and Serrano, 2016), for example, the concept of *fog computing* is applied to the Internet of Things. Here, the computing power of a network is shifted to its edge and closer to the information sources. This results in a platform called SOFT-IoT with a paradigm that Prazeres and Serrano call *Fog of Things*. The devices are connected via an MQTT middleware, while interfaces to other protocols and services are established via so-called *FoT gateways*.

Another project is *SOFIA*, which was developed as an *Event Driven Architecture* for the monitoring and management of smart cities (Filipponi et al., 2010). Here, networks consist of so-called *Semantic Information Brokers* (SIB) and *Knowledge Processors* (KP), which each implement publish/subscribe mechanisms and are responsible for the generation and utilization of information. Together they form a core network of SIBs, with the KPs representing the interface to the network. Among the smart environments mentioned are Smart Personal Spaces, Smart Indoor Spaces, and Smart City Spaces.

Another system for improving interoperability is the QUEST broker (Collina et al., 2012). This broker supports multiple protocols and stores data in its own format. Publish/subscribe mechanisms are supported by an MQTT server on each instance. The QUEST broker from Collina et al. also extends the MQTT server with a Representational State Transfer (REST) interface on which the most recently published values are provided.

Dave et al. have developed another broker called PONTE to improve interoperability. The focus of this project is on interoperability at the application layer, especially between MQTT, Constrained Application Protocol (CoAP), and HTTP (Dave et al., 2020). As PONTE is a further development of the aforementioned QEST broker (Collina et al., 2012), data persistence and an HTTP interface are supported in addition to the MQTT publish/subscribe capabilities. The enhancements compared to QEST essentially lie in the implementation of a CoAP server and other data storage engines such as MongoDB, LevelDB, and Redis.

The architectures just mentioned are just a small selection of the middleware solutions developed in the literature. According to (Derhamy et al., 2017), having a large selection of solutions creates a new problem: middlewares also need translation mechanisms to be compatible with each other. The compatibility problem is therefore not solved but merely shifted to a more abstract level. Instead, a service-oriented translator is proposed by (Derhamy et al., 2017), with the help of which the integration competence is shifted to a participant of the in-house *Arrowhead* framework[1]. Among other things, it is worth mentioning that an intermediate data format is used for the translation process, and protocols are not translated directly into each other.

Interoperability is also established when specialized solutions are developed for the interconnection of two specific protocols. For example, Shi et al. shows how certain ZigBee control commands can be transmitted via LoRa (Shi et al., 2019). This works by selecting the LoRa user data in such a way that it is interpreted by ZigBee devices as valid signals (payload encoding). In this way, a direct connection between devices can be established without routing via the mesh network.

However, solutions on lower layers of the network stack are also possible. Software-defined radios are theoretically capable of being configured for a wide range of IoT protocols. Universal network devices that can be dynamically expanded to include new radio technologies are therefore conceivable. Projects on this topic have already been developed, for example, (Gavrila et al., 2018) and (Lin et al., 2013).

Finally, protocol convergence is also a possibility for the future of the IoT. For this consideration, Derhamy et al. compares the development of the IoT with that of the Internet, where convergence towards the Internet Protocol has taken place (Derhamy et al., 2017). However, it is also noted that beyond TCP and UDP, there are still many protocols that are not compatible with each other.

3. SMART HOME TO SMART CITY

The test scenario described in this paper represents the integration between Smart Home and Smart City. Smart Home and Smart City are Smart X as described by (Dabels, 2023). This means that the research presented here can, in principle, also be translated to other Smart Home and Smart City technologies. The test setup consists of an existing Smart Home ZigBee network and the study is strictly theoretical. The data recorded will be used to determine the extent to which LoRa is suitable for tunneling ZigBee traffic between two networks.

A realistic scenario for such a test setup would be, for example, a flood or irrigation sensor in a secondary ZigBee setup that notifies the user of the system in their home of an incident in a poorly connected location via the primary ZigBee network. This can be seen in Figure 1. Please also note that in this scenario, we do not have two independent networks, but one network which is extended by a LoRa tunnel.

However, this general test setup itself leaves many implementation details open, which will affect the network parameters discussed below. For example, LoRa is usually only used in so-called LoRaWANs. This means that sensor data is not transmitted directly between two end devices but is first sent via a LoRaWAN network with gateways, network, and application servers. Although point-to-point connections are possible with LoRa, they are not representative of a realistic application scenario.

[1] https://arrowhead.eu

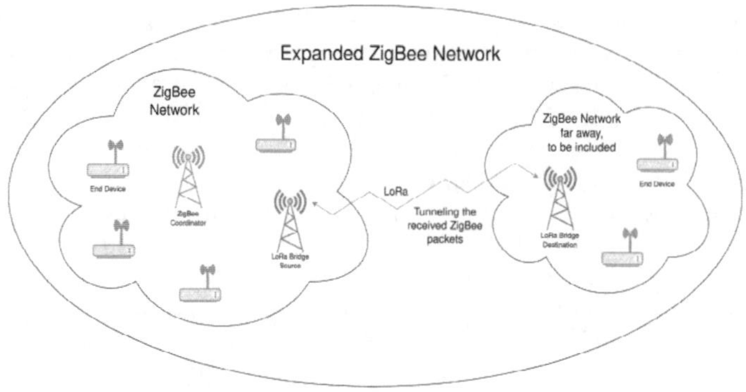

Figure 1. Extended ZigBee network

There is also the question of how the ZigBee sensor is connected to an actuator. Most of the literature describes middleware architectures that can be used very flexibly (Prazeres and Serrano, 2016; Filipponi et al., 2010; Collina et al., 2012; Dave et al., 2020). However, it is also theoretically possible to tunnel ZigBee devices via a technology such as LoRa and thus establish a direct connection between sensors and actuators. In the application scenario of Figure 1, this is even possible without using sequence numbers such as in TCP to reestablish order, as the maximum size of a LoRa telegram is greater than that of ZigBee (IEEE Computer Society, 2009; Semtech Corporation, 2019).

Where possible, such special features are addressed and presented within this paper. Nevertheless, it cannot be guaranteed that the scenario described here is equivalent to a real application of the technologies. Many possibilities for optimizing such a mechanism for data compression are also deliberately omitted.

For the experiments presented here, no ZigBee tunnel was implemented via LoRa. Instead, representative ZigBee data streams were recorded, and calculations were performed with the help of the respective documentation (IEEE Computer Society, 2009; Semtech Corporation, 2020; Semtech Corporation, 2019) as well as other sources. With the help of these calculations, we can make qualitative statements about the methods of the LoRa tunnel.

4. EXPERIMENTAL SETUP

The test setup consists of an existing ZigBee network. A Conbee 2 with the ZSHARK sniffing firmware from dresden elektronik[2] was used to record the data. With this firmware, it is possible to read and save the ZigBee network traffic in Wireshark, a tool commonly used in network analysis. The ZigBee network key known in advance was stored in Wireshark to be able to analyze the data traffic in plain text. Additionally, a SONOFF ZigBee 3.0 USB Dongle Plus is used as a coordinator for the existing ZigBee network. For the Smart Home system, an instance of Home Assistant was used, whereby ZigBee2MQTT is used to manage the network.

From the recorded data traffic, only the sections that are representative of one of the following three scenarios are generated with the help of filters. These scenarios are intended to show the applications for which a ZigBee tunnel via LoRa would be suitable in a real scenario and are as follows:

1. *RFD Join:* The join process is essential for a functional ZigBee tunnel – if no join can be performed via it, devices can only be integrated into the network by physically transporting them to the coordinator's network. The abbreviation RFD stands for *Reduced Function Device*, which is a device class in ZigBee alongside the *Full Function Device*. The main difference between these classes is whether the devices are battery-operated and therefore not routing-capable. The packets that are required for a successful join process are selected by a suitable filter within Wireshark. This includes the *Beacon Request* and *Association Request* of the RFD, the *Beacon* of the router to which the RFD has connected, the *Association Response* with which the RFD is assigned a network address and all subsequent packets in which the RFD appears as the source or destination address. The latter are sent out for further configuration and to read out the capabilities of the new device. As no assumptions should be made in this work about the relevance of individual broadcasts for the

[2] https://www.dresden-elektronik.com/wireless/software/zshark.html

RFD, all broadcasts in the ZigBee network are also transmitted via the tunnel as soon as a short address has been assigned.

2. *Single Device:* Only the data traffic of a single RFD device is considered in this scenario. It is representative of the setup shown in Figure 1 – for example, a flooding or temperature sensor that is to be connected to a ZigBee home network over a greater distance using LoRa. Of all three scenarios described, the lowest traffic volume is to be expected in this scenario, as only one device and the coordinator are involved in the communication. All broadcast messages are also included here for a worst-case estimate.

3. *No Filters*: This scenario shows how the LoRa tunnel would react under the total traffic volume of a ZigBee network in a small apartment with 13 FFDs and 11 RFDs. This is a worst-case scenario insofar as the entire traffic of an apartment's network is transmitted via the tunnel.

5. PERCEIVED PROBLEMS

In this section, various problems are determined that can occur under the test setup proposed in Figure 1. Values from the official standards for maximum packet sizes and from the literature are used for the calculations. Examples of this can be maximum packet sizes or an expected runtime for protocol translation.

5.1 Latency

Latency is probably one of the most noticeable problems for the end user. It is not only the line-up latency in complex integrated networks that is a problem, but also the translation of protocols into each other. How long the input delay can be depends largely on the user and the usage environment. Residents of a Smart Home will generally have certain expectations on the speed at which their input is executed. Mozilla states that input latency should be less than 100 ms for websites[3]. As smart homes are a completely different concept, this is only a guideline. Realistically, input delays of up to 200ms should also be acceptable, although this also depends on the application. This value is also recommended by Google for the smart home sector[4].

However, the requirements for other smart environments, such as Smart Grids, are much more significant. Changes in the power grid must be responded to within a very short time, which is a major challenge, especially in times of the energy transition. In comparison with the Smart Home, however, the line-up latency of the individual nodes of the Smart Grid must be taken into account, as more communication participants are to be expected between the transmitter and receiver than in Smart Homes. A Smart Grid with a network structure comparable to a smart home should generate significantly lower latencies.

Admittedly, the latency for a use case such as in Figure 1 is not particularly important: For a flood warning, it is not relevant to a resident whether they are notified within one or ten seconds. For the general use case, however, a relatively low latency is desirable. The reason for this is that the horizontal integration of smart environments should not be considered based on individual cases, but universally applicable concepts should be developed. A solution that promises latencies of less than 10 seconds will not be sufficient for many smart environments. An extreme case occurs when the duty cycle of such a system is exceeded. This is discussed in more detail in Section 5.4.

In Section 4 an experimental setup is described in which two LoRa nodes communicate directly with each other. It was also mentioned that this is not a common application for LoRa, as this is normally used within a WAN in LoRaWAN. Potsch and Hammer also deal in detail with the problem of latency in LoRaWAN networks (Potsch and Hammer, 2019). It turns out that the latency in LoRaWAN networks is mainly dependent on the spreading factor (SF) and the frequency used. Even the transmission of just a few bytes (8) with a high SF (12) at 125 kHz generates latencies of more than one second for the airtime of the telegram alone. With 50 bytes and SF 12, this is already around 2.5 seconds. In a LoRaWAN network, on the other hand, latencies of less than one second from one node directly to another cannot be achieved even under optimum conditions.

---

[3] https://developer.mozilla.org/en-US/docs/Web/Performance/How_long_is_too_long
[4] https://developers.home.google.com/cloud-to-cloud/support/faq#response-latency

Potsch and Hammer conclude that LoRaWAN is not suitable for Industrial IoT (IIoT) scenarios if processes must be carried out in real-time. Instead, it is explicitly pointed out that less time-critical processes such as smart metering and building automation are feasible. For the test setup shown in Section 4, the delays mentioned are acceptable.

5.2 Protocol Interoperability

For different protocols to be translated to each other, there must be a cross-system semantic understanding of the communicated data. In (Rahman and Hussain, 2020), various problems associated with semantic interoperability in the IoT are highlighted. However, it is proving very difficult to find a universally valid standard that can be applied across the board. Works such as those by (Dave et al., 2020) and (Collina et al., 2012) even define middleware architectures that deal with the problem of interoperability. However, the numerous middleware solutions that already exist in the literature do not so much solve the actual problem of interoperability as shift it to interoperability between the individual middlewares (Derhamy et al., 2017).

This paper does not propose a universal solution. The use of ZigBee and LoRa results in some special features that cannot be transferred to other interoperability problems. For example, if two ZigBee networks are to be connected, the protocols do not necessarily have to be translated. A ZigBee packet is up to 127 bytes in size (IEEE Computer Society, 2009), while the maximum size of a LoRa packet is 255 bytes (Semtech Corporation, 2019). This makes it possible to tunnel ZigBee traffic through LoRa traffic, even if other approaches could be more efficient.

5.3 Data Throughput

Establishing an end-to-end connection via a tunnel or similar method is only one prerequisite for successful communication. If an overload occurs in conventional IP networks, there are various ways of throttling the data rate. These include, for example, dropping packets, which reduces the window size in TCP and thus the data rate. Overloads occur when a participant in the network traffic can no longer process all packets in real-time.

Although the tunneling of ZigBee packets via LoRa can work, data throughput is a major problem. The bit transmission rate depends on the frequency used and the Spreading Factor (SF), of which there are six (SF7-SF12) to choose from. One disadvantage of using a low SF is that the distance over which the technology can be used to communicate is reduced. The upside however is that the data rate is much greater using a low SF.

Depending on these parameters, data rates of 0.3 kbit/s to 27 kbit/s are possible (Adelantado et al., 2017). However, this does not refer to the usable data rate, but to the gross or raw data rate. Only 0.3 kbit/s can be achieved if SF12 and a frequency of 125 kHz are set. The highest possible data rate of 27 kbit/s can be achieved when transmitting under SF7 at 500 kHz. According to (Goursaud and Gorce, 2015), the following formula can be used to calculate the data rates:

$$R = SF \cdot \frac{BW}{2^{SF}}$$

As a frequency of 500 kHz is not permitted in Europe according to (ETSI, 2018), 250 kHz is used for the following calculations. SF7 is also assumed to represent the best-case scenario for LoRa. Even under these assumptions, data transmission with LoRa is many times lower than in ZigBee. At full capacity, a LoRa network will therefore never be able to tunnel the entire network traffic of ZigBee.

RF Join: The entire pairing process took 19.6 seconds in the test setup from Section 4 and according to Wireshark, 10,297 bytes (82,376 bits) were transmitted. The effective transmission rate of 4.2 kbit/s is far below the maximum and far above the minimum data rate of LoRa. Under the right conditions, the data rate for pairing should therefore not be problematic. The cutoff is, for example, at SF9 and 250 kHz (4.4 kbit/s) or SF7 and 125 kHz (6.8 kbit/s). However, as the transmission time of LoRa and the retransmission of ZigBee traffic on the other side of the tunnel must be added together, timing problems may occur during pairing. In a realistic deployment scenario with LoRaWAN, this line-up latency accounts for a large part of the overall latency (Potsch and Hammer, 2019). The concerns regarding successful pairing processes can neither be dispelled nor confirmed by the purely theoretical consideration of this process.

Single Device: The device selected in this experiment can measure three data points. Depending on the time or sufficiently large value change, these are sent individually or summarized in Report Attributes commands from the sensor. Seven such packets with an average size of 65 bytes were captured during a recording which took place in the morning between 6:00 and 7:30 and lasted 5739 seconds to represent a typical morning routine. This corresponds to a data transmission rate of 0.6 bit/s, which can even be achieved under the worst-case conditions for LoRa (SF12 with 125 kHz, 0.37 kbit/s). It should therefore be possible to tunnel individual devices.

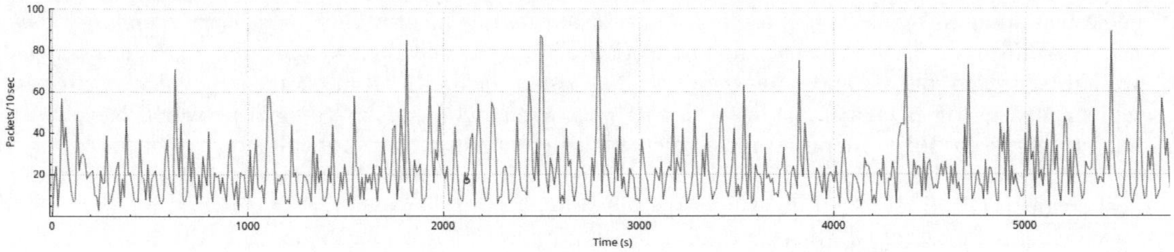

Figure 2. Wireshark I/O Graph for non-filtered data

No Filters: A total of 737,008 bytes (5,896,064 bits) were transmitted in the same duration, which corresponds to a data transmission rate of 1.027 kbit/s. This value is also far below the maximum, but still above the minimum data transmission rate of LoRa and could even be achieved with SF10 at 125 kHz (1.2 kbit/s) or SF11 at 250 kHz (1.3 kbit/s). However, problems could occur if the data rates in a smaller time window are higher than the average data rate over the entire period under consideration. In Figure 2 it can be seen that the use of the ZigBee network was relatively even over the recording window and no particular load peaks occurred. In principle, however, the combined use of smart home functions may generate data volumes that temporarily overload the data rates enabled by LoRa. This was already the case in RF Join, for example. Theoretically, however, the data transmission rate should only pose a problem under the most unfavorable conditions possible.

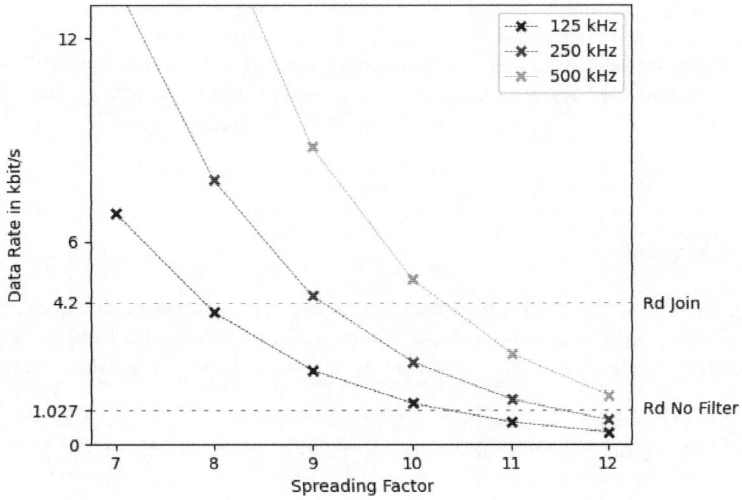

Figure 3. LoRa data rate depending on the spreading factor and bandwidth

We can conclude that the sufficiency of the data rate is highly dependent on the parameters of LoRa as well as the workload of the bridged ZigBee network. Figure 3 shows those parameters for each of the scenarios mentioned. If peaks like in the RFD Join scenario appear, most setups fail to deliver a sufficient data rate. In case no such peaks appear during regular traffic, the data rate is not enough under very high SF and 125 kHz. A tunnel for only a single device although has such low requirements (0.6 bit/s), that we chose not to render it within Figure 3.

5.4 Duty Cycle

Duty cycles are a mechanism that primarily occurs in IoT networks and is used to regulate data traffic in media that are used by many participants. They define the so-called *relative frequency occupancy time* and thus determine how long the devices in a network are allowed to send packets within a certain time window. An alternative to duty cycles are the so-called *listen before talk* mechanisms, which are often not implemented in IoT networks due to the higher energy restrictions. Conventional networks based on IEEE 802.3 (Ethernet) or IEEE 802.11 (WiFi) implement different mechanisms for collision avoidance.

The duty cycle for LoRa is defined in the ETSI standard EN 300 220-2 and is set at < 1 % per hour for most channels (ETSI, 2018). If this value is reached by transmissions within the network, the corresponding device must not make any further transmissions. In normal use, it is rare for the duty cycle to be reached in LoRaWAN networks. However, the tunneling of packets through LoRa is also not an intended use of the technology and may very well exceed this value.

The Things Network provides an online tool for calculating airtime[5]. For the best-case scenario, this means that 222 bytes of user data can be transferred in 184 ms. This average value is then used to calculate the airtime and duty cycle.

RF Join: During pairing, 10,297 bytes were transmitted in 247 packets under the conditions specified in Section 4. With an average airtime of 43.65 ms per data packet at SF 7 and 250 kHz, this means that the airtime of the entire process amounts to 10.78 seconds. Of the maximum 36 seconds of the duty cycle, 29.95 % is therefore used. This means that 3 paring processes can take place per hour under optimum conditions.

Single Device: As described above, we recorded seven data packets with an average payload size of 65 bytes for the selected RFD. This results in a total average airtime of $61.57\ ms \cdot 7 = 430.99\ ms = 0.43\ s$, which is well below the maximum airtime of 36 s at < 1 % channel utilization. Accordingly, individual RFDs with a low transmission frequency are suitable for tunneling via LoRa.

No Filters: Over the entire recording interval of 5739 seconds, 737,008 bytes of data were transmitted in 12471 messages during normal operation. This means that the packets have an average payload size of 59 bytes. If this network traffic were transmitted via LoRa, the average airtime per data packet would be 56.4 ms and the total airtime for all data packets recorded and tunneled via LoRa would be 703,3644 s. Since only 36 s of airtime can be allocated for a duty cycle of < 1 %, this amount of data cannot be transmitted in 1.5 h under any circumstances. It is therefore clear that an average ZigBee network cannot be completely tunneled in practice.

6. CONCLUSION

We have shown several different problems that occur when integrating Smart Home and Smart City technologies. The protocols in question were ZigBee and LoRa - both of which are currently used within real application scenarios. Integrating these technologies may well be a relevant problem within the topic of horizontal integration (and in extension Society 5.0), in which we try to overcome the technological boundaries of different Smart X.

To this account, we have shown the limits of the technologies in question and examined four different concrete problems in view of an experimental setup which has been described in Section 4. The perceived problems mentioned in Section 5 are latency, protocol interoperability, data throughput, and duty cycle. We conclude that overcoming and addressing these problems is highly dependent on the technologies to be integrated and the parameters of their operation.

[5] https://www.thethingsnetwork.org/airtime-calculator/

LoRa as an exemplary technology for Smart City alone shows how a system's suitability for integration purposes can vary based on its mode of operation. Figure 3 in particular shows that there is not one answer to whether these two technologies can be horizontally integrated, but that it depends on multiple factors and the respective operational scenario. Moving forward, such parameters must be put into consideration when the question integrated smart environments arises.

This work shows only a selection of problems that can occur in horizontally integrated environments and approaches them theoretically. We fully expect more problems to arise when implementing concrete and low-level solutions to protocol interoperability and integration. Considering existing solutions mainly focus on a high-level approach to solving interoperability within smart environments, this can be considered an attempt to steer the discussion towards the inherent properties associated with technologies such as ZigBee, LoRa and many more.

7. FUTURE RESEARCH

The concept presented in this paper does not claim to integrate Smart X Smart Home and Smart City in a significantly efficient way. Rather, it aims to show how two disparate technologies can be transparently connected without the use of middleware. It has been shown that this is often not possible without compromise.

In Section 5.4, for example, no transmission of the entire network traffic is possible. Pairing is possible, but three times per hour at most. This may be sufficient for connecting a few sensors, however, failed attempts have an even greater negative effect. One reason for the rapid exhaustion of the duty cycle is that ZigBee data packets are transmitted in their entirety.

One solution is to aggregate the data before transmission. For example, a temperature sensor could only transmit an average value every 10 minutes rather than every minute. The data volume of individual connections could thus be optimized.

We see further potential for optimization in filtering the packets to be transmitted through the tunnel. For example, broadcasts such as *Permit Join Request* or *Device Announcement* could be aggregated again by routers and thus only routed through the tunnel once. If there are no routers on the side of the tunnel that is not home to the coordinator, packets relevant for routing could be filtered.

Another solution would be to encode and transmit the user data more efficiently. This would require an intermediate representation, which has already been developed in various projects. The disadvantage of such a solution would be that the complete transparency of the approach presented here would be lost.

The main problem in Section 5.3 is also the amount of data that must be transmitted via the slower LoRa tunnel. If the transmissions accumulate, this can lead to unexpected behavior in the communication. This may need to be investigated more closely in an implementation of the approach. In principle, both approaches mentioned above are also suitable for reducing the problem of data throughput.

To maintain the duty cycle, it would be possible to switch frequencies when a frequency is exhausted. A similar process is already used in Bluetooth under the name *frequency hopping*. Here, however, it is used more to avoid interference in the 2.4 GHz band than to use duty cycles multiple times. Such approaches are also conceivable in LoRa (Adelantado et al., 2017).

The combination of many heterogeneous technologies also raises questions about how such complex systems can be maintained. Auditing IoT networks is often a difficult process due to the focus on the energy efficiency of the sensors. In an integrated IoT landscape, this process becomes very difficult if it is made up of an extremely large number of subsystems.

Finally, solutions should also be developed for problems such as packet loss. LoRa already offers protection mechanisms if transmissions fail through the use of acknowledgments. However, the existence of such procedures cannot be assumed for every technology. For this reason, these and other problems addressed in this section should be considered in further work.

REFERENCES

Adelantado, F. et al. (2017). Understanding the Limits of LoRaWAN. *In IEEE Communications Magazine*, Vol. 55, No. 9, pp. 34-40

Al-Fuqaha, A. et al. (2015). Internet of Things: A Survey on Enabling Technologies, Protocols, and Applications. *In IEEE Communications Surveys & Tutorials*, Vol. 17, No. 4, pp. 2347-2376

Collina, M. et al. (2012). Introducing the QEST broker: Scaling the IoT by bridging MQTT and REST. *2012 IEEE 23rd International Symposium on Personal, Indoor and Mobile Radio Communications - (PIMRC)*, Sydney, Australia, pp. 36-41

Dabels, R. (2023). Smart X: A Description for Smart Environments. *e-Society 2023*. Lisbon, Portugal, pp. 1-8

Dave, M. et al. (2020). Ponte Message Broker Bridge Configuration Using MQTT and CoAP Protocol for Interoperability of IoT. *First International Conference, COMS2 2020*. Gujarat, India, pp. 184-195

Deguchi et al. *(2020). Society 5.0: A people-centric super-smart society*. Springer Singapore, Singapore.

Derhamy, H. et al. (2017). IoT Interoperability—On-Demand and Low Latency Transparent Multiprotocol Translator. *In IEEE Internet of Things Journal*, Vol. 5, No. 4, pp. 1754-1763

European Telecommunications Standards Institute. (2018). EN 300 220-2, V3.2.1

Filipponi, L. et al. (2010). Smart City: An Event Driven Architecture for Monitoring Public Spaces with Heterogeneous Sensors. *2010 Fourth International Conference on Sensor Technologies and Applications (SENSORCOMM)*. Venice, Italy, pp. 281-286

Fokuyama, M. (2018). Society 5.0: Aiming for a New Human-Centered Society. *In Japan Spotlight*, Vol. 27, No. 5, pp. 47-50

Gavrila, C. et al. (2018), Reconfigurable IoT Gateway Based on a SDR Platform. *2018 International Conference on Communications (COMM)*. Bucharest, Romania, pp. 345-348

Goursaud, C. and Gorce, J. M. (2015). Dedicated networks for IoT: PHY / MAC state of the art and challenges. *In EAI Endorsed Transactions on Internet of Things*, Vol. 1, No. 1, pp. 1-11

IEEE Computer Society. (2009). IEEE Std 802.15.4™-2015, IEEE Standard for Low-Rate Wireless Networks

Lin, Y. et al. (2013). Wireless IoT Platform Based on SDR Technology. *2013 IEEE International Conference on Green Computing and Communications and IEEE Internet of Things and IEEE Cyber, Physical and Social Computing*. Beijing, China, pp. 2245-2246

Miorandi, D. et al. (2012). Internet of things: Vision, applications and research challenges. *In Ad Hoc Networks*, Vol. 10, No. 7, pp. 1497-1516

Mishra, P., Thakur, P. and Singh, G. (2022). Sustainable Smart City to Society 5.0: State-of-the-Art and Research Challenges. *In SAIEE Africa Research Journal*, Vol. 113, No. 4, pp. 152-164.

Noura, M. at al. (2019). Interoperability in Internet of Things: Taxonomies and Open Challenges. *Mobile Networks and Applications*, Vol. 24, No. 3, pp. 796-809

Potsch, A. and Hammer, F. (2019). Towards End-to-End Latency of LoRaWAN: Experimental Analysis and IIoT Applicability. *2019 15th IEEE International Workshop on Factory Communication Systems (WFCS)*. Sundsvall, Sweden, pp. 1-4

Prazeres, C. and Serrano, M. (2016). SOFT-IoT: Self-Organizing FOG of Things. *2016 30th International Conference on Advanced Information Networking and Applications Workshops (WAINA)*. Crans-Montana, Switzerland, pp. 803-808

Rahman, H. and Hussain, Md. I. (2020). A comprehensive survey on semantic interoperability for Internet of Things: State-of-the-art and research challenges. *In Transactions on Emerging Telecommunications Technologies*, Vol. 31, No. 12, pp. 1-25

Semtech Corporation. (2019). LoRa and LoRaWAN: A Technical Overview

Semtech Corporation. (2020). SX1276/77/78/79 - 137 MHz to 1020 MHz Low Power Long Range Transceiver

Shi, J., Mu, D. and Sha M. (2019). LoRaBee: Cross-Technology Communication from LoRa to ZigBee via Payload Encoding. *2019 IEEE 27th International Conference on Network Protocols (ICNP)*. Chicago, IL, USA, pp. 1-11

HARDWARE AND SOFTWARE INVENTORY BEST PRACTICES APPLIED TO GOVERNMENT COMPUTER NETWORK AND SYSTEMS

Welber Santos de Oliveira[1], Felipe Barreto de Oliveira[1], Fábio Lúcio Lopes de Mendonça[1], Luiz Augusto dos Santos Pires[1], Renato José da Silva Camões[2], Robson de Oliveira Alburquerque[1] and Georges Daniel Amvame Nze[1]

[1]*Electrical Engineering Department, University of Brasilia - Brasília, Federal District 70910-900, Brazil*

[2]*LATITUDE/UNB decision-making technology laboratory - University of Brasilia - Brasília, Federal District 70910-900, Brazil*

ABSTRACT

Security of computer environments is one of the main topics in the last decade. Adopting best practices is also important because it provides parameters to evaluate systems and networks in terms of use and security related to hardware and software inventory. Considering such aspects, this paper presents management best practices for information systems and computer networks related to hardware and software inventory using open-source solutions, pointing at security and asset monitoring applied to the environment of the Brazilian General Attorney of the National Treasury (PGFN). The adopted methodology presents strategies for good results in evaluating asset monitoring and management processes related to the inventory of hardware and software used in the PGFN computer network.

KEYWORDS

Hardware Inventory, Software Inventory, Best Practices, Network Security

1. INTRODUCTION

This paper considers the adoption of best practices allied to open-source software to provide solutions for hardware and software inventory of computer networks used in the environment of the Brazilian General Attorney of the National Treasury (PGFN) to help computer management and computer security controls to reduce security risks.

Companies of different sizes are aware of the risks and give significant focus to the efforts of their information technology (IT) and security teams to prevent attacks on their computer systems by malicious actors. To accomplish this, companies establish robust safeguards that include individuals, processes, and technology to defend against cyber-security threats. Even though these defenses, at some point, are good, providing some security controls against threats, it might be surprising to acknowledge that they are sometimes being built on quicksand (Smyth, 2015). Also, the first two controls from the SANS Critical Security Controls (SANS, 2021) emphasize the need to inventory, track, and rectify hardware devices to allow access only for those authorized. This is important because attackers seek to exploit unprotected systems attached to the network, such as outdated software versions.

According to (Hughes, 2022), over 75% of organizations have increased their use of open-source tools, recognizing their growing dependence, while the 2020 crisis led 68% of companies to adopt open-source solutions to cut costs (Germain, 2021). (Ruffin & Ebert, 2004) highlights the legal aspects of open-source software, allowing use, modification, and distribution under certain conditions. Proprietary products contrast in terms of flexibility and costs. Embracing open source implies adjusting support and implementing best practices, even without being the owner.

This paper presents the methodology supported by management best practices for information systems and computer networks related to hardware and software inventory using open-source software. The main idea is to reduce risks while providing good security to hardware and software assets' visibility and monitoring in the

PGFN. The adopted methodology shows that adopting best practices allied to open-source software brings satisfactory results in evaluating asset monitoring and management processes related to the inventory of hardware and software used in the computer network of PGFN.

This paper is organized as follows. After this introduction, section 2 provides some related work considering the adoption of best practices, followed by section 3, where the methodology adopted in this work is presented and explained. Chapter 4 provides a case study and the corresponding results. Section 5 concludes this paper and provides some ideas for future works.

2. RELATED WORKS

Several studies have proposed the implementation of best practices in software inventory usage. Some of these will be mentioned in this section.

In work by Muyumba & Phiri (2017) was presented a model for efficient management of spare parts inventory for the Zambian Air Force (ZAF) equipment was proposed. The aim was to develop an architecture capable of preventing human errors (such as inventory duplication) that could arise from manual controls. To achieve this, a cloud-based architecture was developed, leveraging barcode technology. The outcome was an automated inventory control system that significantly improved speed and reduced susceptibility to errors.

The study conducted by Silva & Pinto (2019) aims to propose a review of asset management in a microenterprise in Bragança Paulista. To achieve this, defined steps were implemented, encompassing the generation of business value from the solution. They installed OCS Inventory NG and performed a Network Inventory, deploying software agents on each asset in the park. As a practical outcome, the authors obtained reports with an environmental analysis that facilitates decision-making.

In the work presented by Labanda-Jaramillo et al. (2019), research was conducted to enhance the IT management processes at the National University of Loja. For this purpose, the study was divided into several stages, one focusing on administering network asset configurations. As a result, using the OCS Inventory proved efficient in identifying the characteristics of the university's asset configurations, thereby assisting in identifying obsolete systems or hardware.

In the study proposed by Shackleton (2017), one of the objectives was to assess the applicability of the OCS Inventory in the NIST 800-53 framework (Joint Task Force Transformation Initiative, 2013). To achieve this, a Proof of Concept (PoC) was developed, configuring Windows 10 servers, a collection of servers from 2008 R2 to 2012 R2, and 5 Ubuntu 16.04 LTS servers. As a result, the author concluded that the following controls are implemented in the OCS Inventory: ID CM-8 (1), ID CM-8 (2), and ID CM-8 (7). The controls ID CM-8 and ID CM-8 (4) were partially covered. However, the remaining controls (ID CM-8 (3), ID CM-8 (3)(a), ID CM-8 (6), and ID CM-8 (8)) were not implemented.

3. METHODOLOGY AND PROCESSES

The methodology elaborated for the PGFN includes the description of the methods and processes developed during the research, establishing techniques that were used to elaborate the solution for knowledge management and security controls.

3.1 Methods Employed

To execute the proposed objectives, 10 phases were elaborated for implementing the software and hardware inventory management system in the PGFN. Figure 1 indicates the phases considered, and table 1 resumes each phase. These practices are related to the key points of best practices expressed in the work of Olson & Weins (2009).

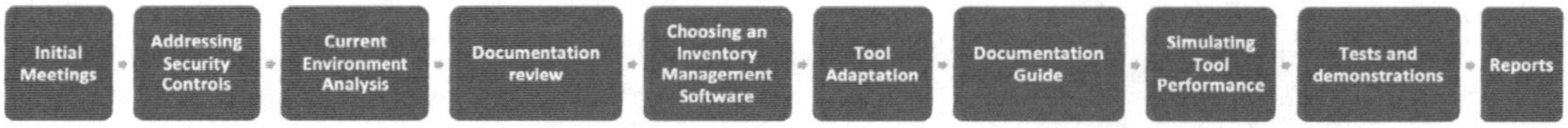

Figure 1. Methodology phases applied to hardware and software inventory for the PGFN

Table 1. Phases resume

Phase	Description
Initial Meetings	To meet the needs of the PGFN, meetings were conducted with managers and technicians to understand the organization's demands. Technical issues were identified in PGFN's environment to enhance management and motivate the specific needs of the management team. Reference to key point "Executive Sponsorship" presented by Olson & Weins (2009).
Addressing Security Controls	Exploring the issues identified in the initial meetings, as well as the concerns raised by the PGFN team itself, the need to prioritize efforts toward implementing hardware and software inventory management was emphasized. As it discusses the priorities and how the organization should handle inventory software, this item is related to the key point of "Open-Source Policy" in the work of Olson & Weins (2009).
Current Environment Analysis	To define the tool that best fits the scenario found, it was also necessary to have a greater notion not only of the existing problems but also of the plans and objectives with inventory management, in addition to understanding the size of the computational park and its organization in the different units of the PGFN.
Documentation review	Practice is necessary for understanding the environment, customizing the tool, and adapting to the established strategy and previous steps. Important to identify sources of research, communities, support, and websites. It can be referred to as the key point of "Provisioning" in the work of Olson & Weins (2009).
Choosing an Inventory Management Software	An analysis and comparison of various open-source software, including GLPi, OCS Inventory, Zabbix Inventory, and CITSmart, were conducted. The tools were presented to the management team, highlighting their strengths and weaknesses. Additionally, the computational requirements were assessed. Based on this analysis, the adoption and implementation of OCS Inventory was proposed as the suitable solution to meet the identified demands. As this item is analyzing the conditions of the software and choosing the best solution based on the software's capabilities that attends best to the organization's policy, it is related to the key point "Open-Source Policy" in the work of Olson & Weins (2009).
Tool Adaptation	Regardless of the extent of tool coverage, each topology and technological park present variations between companies, which justifies the need for customization in using these tools. For this, a customized script was created, ensuring the full operation of the tool. This practice referred to the key point, "Open-Source Policy," in the work of Olson & Weins (2009).
Documentation Guide	An OCS Inventory installation script was established, including the script created. Reference can be made to the key point "Requests and Approvals" in the work of Olson &Weins (2009
Simulating Tool Performance	An implementation and simulation within a controlled environment were executed, employing a Virtual Machine to execute the installation and the tool's efficacy was examined. This action can be related to the key point "Operationalizing Open-Source Policies," as highlighted in the work of Olson & Weins (2009).
Tests and demonstrations	Practice responsible for the tests, demonstrations, and audit analysis of the proposed environment, verifying its adequate functioning. This step is like the key point, "Auditing," presented in the work of Olson & Weins (2009).
Reports	Practice is presented to generate reports on the steps performed as well as the results obtained during the process, this practice being like the key point "Reporting" described by Olson & Weins (2009).

3.2 Processes Used

To assist the implementation of the new tool, a process model was designed according to the Business Process Management Notation (BPMN) (Figure 2), which expresses the actions performed by each of the actors present in the process, thus presenting an equal and general view of the best practices applied.

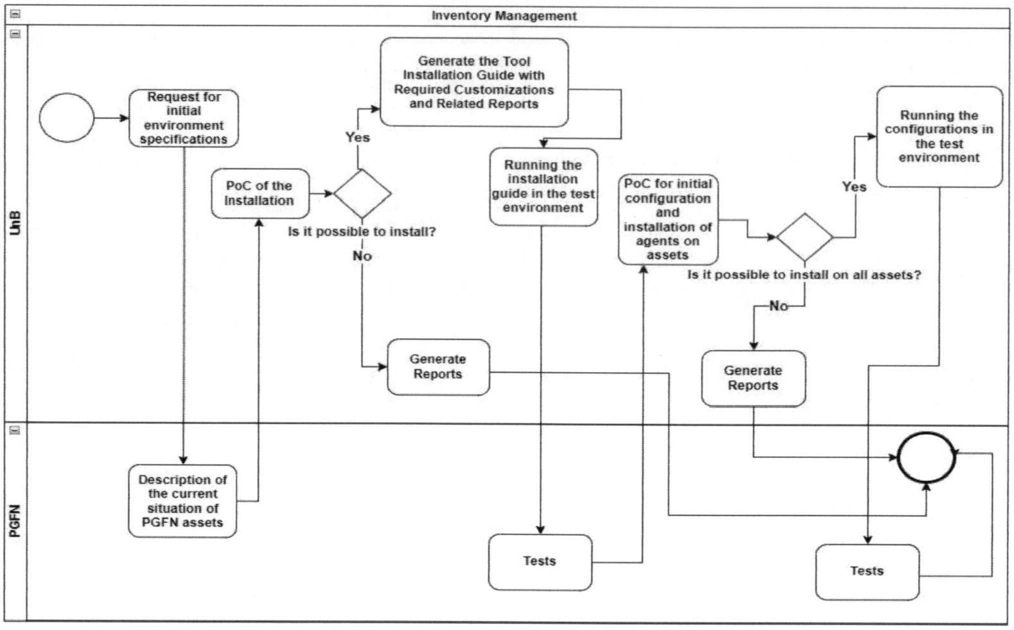

Figure 2. BPMN Model

To execute this process, a case study was created, which initially required a detailed description of the initial scenario of the structure. After the survey, it was necessary to formulate and create test scenarios, where several forms of updating were tested to build and update the installation guide. Finally, the improvements achieved were presented.

4. CASE STUDY AND RESULTS

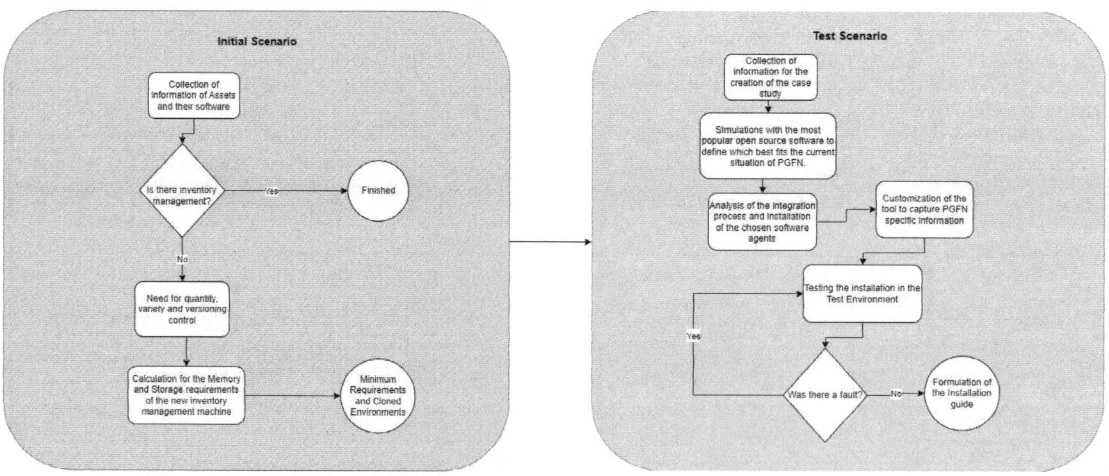

Figure 3. Flows used to structure and apply defined best practices

As a guide for the case study, 2 flowcharts were described (Figure 3), showing the steps followed in each scenario where the first scenario describes how to verify the actual situation in the company, using special strategies to know the specifications. The second scenario explains how to adapt the open-source solutions for the different proposed specifications. Each scenario will be presented with more details in the following.

4.1 Initial Scenarios and Test Considerations

The PGFN has extensive hardware and software assets and needs a tool to manage this inventory as optimally as possible. First, it was necessary to understand what the inventory being requested covered, to align the expectations of the parties, and to investigate the history of inventory management in the agency. To this end, meetings were held where real cases were presented and the main problems to be solved were detailed, to determine the mandatory requirements of the software to be implemented.

The decision was reached that open-source management software would be the most viable option for solving this demand, as it would be free of financial costs. Based on the research, the research team determined the reasons for keeping track of inventory and defining software and hardware inventory. Having a discovery and inventory system that can track assets by hardware, operating system, applications, and versions is important when it comes to keeping track of computers and which users are using them, thus discovering unknown and unauthorized devices on the network and determining the heterogeneity of the computer park and thus making decisions about when to update or not update any network assets. The hardware inventory includes everything connected to the network, with people, or that generates information. This class includes devices such as laptops, cell phones, tablets, desktops, printers, servers, routers, etc. Software inventory is a specialist program that detects operating systems, licenses, versions, manufacturers, developers, drivers, complementary devices, libraries, registry keys, and APIs. This inventory involves collecting information on all the software used in the company, cross-referencing the information, and then making decisions.

After comparing open-source software inventory management solutions and presenting the pros and cons to the PGFN team, one specific issue became relevant. In addition to the comparative criteria established, a list of requirements was given that the inventory solution must manage to satisfy the needs of PGFN's inventory management model, these being: Machine name, IP and MAC address; Vendor; Model; CPF (Brazilian Person ID Number); Status; Software (Name and version); Last capture (Last login register); Group (Region); Location.

Several options that would meet the needs mapped at PGFN were analyzed to determine the best choice among those studied: OCS Inventory, Zabbix Inventory, CITSmart, and GLPi. The first three were presented to the PGFN; a description is attached to this report. After further synchronous virtual meetings, expectations were aligned, and the steps to be taken by the team were determined.

Therefore, in addition to presenting the chosen inventory software in a comparative manner, it was necessary to demonstrate each by collecting all the data presented in the previous section.

4.2 Comparison of Best Solutions

OCS Inventory was recommended following a comparative study carried out by the research infrastructure team, which was then presented to PGNF. The study evaluated five key criteria: documentation, updates, community, usability, functionality, and robustness, as shown in Table 2.

Table 2. Criteria Evaluation

Phase	Description
Documentation	both tools offer comprehensive resources, with GLPI exhibiting a finer granularity by categorizing its documentation into distinct levels: administrator, user, and developer.
Updates	GLPI's updates are more recent than those of OCS. Nevertheless, this disparity doesn't wield substantial significance in the comparison, as both tools adhere to an identical server update schedule. The notable divergence is primarily evident in the version intervals concerning agent updates.
Community	While GLPI boasts a larger community of contributors, OCS maintains a more vibrant presence on the GLPI subreddit. It's essential to underscore that both tools have thriving communities, and various deployment solutions are accessible for each.
Usability	When considering usability, it's important to mention that both tools support the Portuguese language. However, OCS distinguishes itself with a simpler and more intuitive interface, in contrast to GLPI's interface, which offers many configuration options that can occasionally lead to complexities in navigation.
Functionality	GLPI not only maintains an asset inventory but also offers features like ticket management, problem tracking, resource reservation, maintenance planning, and much more. It's used to facilitate efficient management of IT assets and improve process organization. An interface is utilized to manage the

Phase	Description
	inventory of computers, peripherals, printers, and related components, employing inventory tools like Fusion Inventory or OCS Inventory; Managing warranties and financial data, including purchase orders, warranties, and extensions; Data Center Infrastructure Management (DCIM); Knowledge base and Frequently Asked Questions (FAQ); Managing the lifecycle of items and overseeing contracts, contacts, and documentation pertaining to inventory items; Incident, request, problem, and change management; Supports numerous plugins that provide additional features. OCS Inventory performs automatic device discovery on the network, gathers information, and maintains an up-to-date inventory. It is designed to provide accurate and real-time information about hardware and software assets within an organization. Relevant inventory information; Network discovery; Cutting-edge broadcast system for deploying software, executing scripts, and issuing commands on computers, all while avoiding network overload; SOAP-accessible Web service; Intuitive web interface for ease of use; Plugin support through APIs; Support for multiple operating systems, including Microsoft Windows, Linux, BSD, Sun Solaris, IBM AIX, HP-UX, MacOS X, Android; N-tier architecture utilizing common standards, HTTP/HTTPS protocols, and XML data formatting
Robustness	The device attributes that OCS can capture are the operating system version, installed software and their versions, equipment serial number, hardware component model and features, and more. The agent's IP Discover functionality enables the discovery of all computers and devices on the network, streamlining inventory item registration. The sole requirement to receive information from a computer is that the OCS Inventory client program, the agent, is installed. Once installed, the agent itself transmits the data to the server. For inventorying data from a device with an embedded system, where agent installation isn't feasible, collection must occur via SNMP protocol. Moreover, even smartphones with Android can be inventoried through the OCS Inventory app.

4.3 Tools Adaptations

In general, it is common for inventory solutions to record practically all this information, but two of them became a temporary obstacle in the execution of the project. The Group and Locality fields do not exactly depend on information present on the machine, as they are related to external factors and, therefore, cannot be automatically cataloged by the inventory software. A machine's Locality is determined by its IP address, where each locality corresponds to a different IP range determined by PGFN. The Group (Region) obeys a domain restriction of 5 items, and its value for each device obeys a logic involving its Locality.

The primary solution presented, which allowed this information to be mapped, was to use the TAG field (a free field for entering any information), which can be filled in during the configuration of the inventory solution agent so that it would be possible to add the equipment's Locality so that it could be used as a query parameter during the generation of reports and inventory management.

However, the need for this manual work to fill in the Locality and Group fields made the proposed alternative unfeasible, so the challenge became how to register the Locality and Group in an automated way.

Studying the criteria that establish the Locality field, we saw that the IP range that characterizes each locality could be used as a search parameter in the inventory database, allowing us to locate all the equipment that belongs to a specific IP range. However, with this query, it would still not be possible to separate the elements if the range is not defined by an entire octet. To solve this problem, the possibility of using Regular Expressions in the query was explored, as this feature will allow for a much more specific query.

After a careful analysis, PGFN asked for some clarifications on the organization of some data, including two pieces of information that depended on factors external to the information stored in the asset: the group, which indicates the region in the country where an item is located, and the location, which is determined by a predetermined IP mask that represents the PGFN unit where the item is located.

4.4 Comparison and Discussions

Table 3 compares the results of the studies related to the proposed work. The following sections describe the importance of the results obtained.

Table 3. Comparison between related work and the proposal presented

Heading level	Definition of Best Practices	Process Model and Flowcharts	Generalization	Improving control and monitoring
(Ruffin & Ebert, 2004)	-	-	X	-
(Muyumba & Phiri, 2017)	-	-	-	-
(Olson & Weins, 2009)	-	-	X	-
(Arsan et al., 2013)	X	-	X	X
This research	X	X	X	-

4.4.1 Discussions

Regarding improving software optimization and updates, the license updates for OCS involve upgrading the system. They can be associated with improvements in functionality and increased security, among other aspects. Keeping the OCS (Open Computers and Software Inventory) software updated is crucial for various reasons, but two stand out. A) Security: Frequent updates include security patches that help protect the system against known vulnerabilities. By keeping the OCS updated, PGFN reduces the risk of cyber-attacks and potential invasions. B) Compatibility: As new technologies and operating systems are released, OCS updates can ensure compatibility with these new platforms, ensuring the software functions seamlessly in updated environments. Updating OCS is essential to ensure security, stability, performance, compatibility, access to new features, and adequate technical support.

Regarding vulnerability prevention, security tests, and assessments should be conducted to identify potential weaknesses in the system and address them before attackers exploit them. Within this scope, it's crucial to implement robust authentication methods such as strong passwords, two-factor authentication, or integration with secure authentication systems to prevent unauthorized access. Another critical factor is ensuring that data transmitted and stored by the OCS is encrypted, preventing unauthorized third-party access to confidential information. Lastly, stringent access control to the system's functionalities is important to prevent vulnerabilities, allowing only authorized users access to specific areas and resources.

Regarding asset control and monitoring, as per the OCS implementation documentation mentioned in (Olson & Weins, 2009), it's possible to enhance control by focusing on the following aspects. A) Data Centralization: Enhancing OCS's capability to gather and store precise asset information, ensuring all relevant data is centralized and easily accessible. B) Process Automation: Implementing automation for asset data collection and updates, reducing manual errors, and ensuring real-time updated records. C) Management Policies: Establishing clear asset management policies to standardize procedures, assign responsibilities, and ensure compliance with regulations. D) Proactive Monitoring: Integrating continuous monitoring systems to swiftly identify and respond to asset changes, such as software updates, hardware modifications, or device movements within the network. E) Reporting and Analysis: Enhancing reporting and analysis capabilities to provide valuable insights into the asset status, aiding in strategic decision-making. F) Integration with Other Tools: Integrating with other management tools, such as help desk systems or security solutions, creates a comprehensive view of assets and enables more efficient actions.

Regarding aggregating the institution's management process, the OCS evidently contributes to PGNF's hardware and software asset management and control, maintaining an updated and detailed inventory. Additionally, it's instrumental in providing information about installed software versions and status, streamlining the planning of future updates and maintenance within PGNF. In most organizations, the OCS not only aids in compliance and audits but also significantly streamlines technical support by enabling swift identification of system issues and providing crucial maintenance-related information.

5. CONCLUSION

PGFN increased its visibility to assets with the proposed methods, processes, and best practices. Although there is no significant advantage, one must consider the limitations of capabilities and personnel that affect government institutions.

Considering all the important steps it may take, it is important to mention the absence of a correct management process regarding hardware and inventory. Without hardware and software inventory, the organization is blind to the number of risks with outdated hardware and software in their computer network. Only this is enough security risk for the management team to review its practices and solutions.

In this sense, this research proposed a corresponding methodology followed by processes and the support of best practices to increase environmental security and apply better security controls, thus reducing the attack surface and increasing visibility and monitoring of the computer network. It applied a 10-phase methodology with the main objective to increase the quality of the security controls. The results show how best practices allied to good open-source management solutions increase the security of the environment in terms of visibility, monitoring, and helping decision-making processes supported by security risk facts in the environment when considering hardware and software inventory solutions.

As future work, it is the intention of this research to evaluate new scenarios as the needs of PFGN evolve; besides creating a robust plan for decision-making regarding the security risks of dealing with outdated hardware and software in a government environment, indicating what main advantages, limitations, and possible applications it may be considered.

ACKNOWLEDGEMENTS

This work is supported by the Office of the Attorney General of the National Treasury (No. PGFN 23106.148934/2019-67). It is also partially funded by CNPq – National Council for Scientific and Technological Development (PQ-2 312180/2019-5 in Cybersecurity and 465741/2014-2), in part by the National Department of Audit of the Unified Health System (SUS) - DENASUS (23106.118410/2020-85), in part by the Ministry of Economy of Brazil (DIPLA 005/2016 and ENAP 083/2016), partly by the Administrative Council for Economic Defense (CADE 08700.000047/2019-14), partly by the Office of the Solicitor General (AGU 697.935/2019), and partly by the Foundation for Research Support of the Federal District – FAPD.

REFERENCES

Arsan, T., Başkan, E., Ar, E. and Bozkuş, Z. (2013). A software architecture for inventory management system. *In Innovations and Advances in Computer, Information, Systems Sciences, and Engineering* (pp. 15-27). Springer New York.

Da Silva, S. F. and Pinto, J. D. S. (2019). Análise da importância da gestão de ativos de TI no ambiente de micro e pequenas empresas. *Revista Científica e-Locução*, 1(15), pp. 18-18.

Germain, J. M. (2021). The rise of open source: Pandemic, economy, efficiency, trust. Available at: https://www.linuxinsider.com/story/the-rise-of-open-source-pandemic-economy-efficiency-trust-87057.html (Accessed 28 December 2023).

Hughes, O. (2022). Open source is more important than ever, say developers. here's what's driving adoption. Available at: https://www.zdnet.com/article/open-source-is-more-important-than-ever-say-developers-heres-why/ (Accessed 28 December 2023).

Joint Task Force Transformation Initiative. (2013). NIST SP 800-53 Rev. 4. Available at: https://csrc.nist.gov/pubs/sp/800/53/r4/upd3/final (Accessed 28 December 2023).

Labanda-Jaramillo, M., Chamba-Eras, L., Coronel-Romero, E., Granda, J. L., Quezada-Sarmiento, P.A. and Roman-Sanchez, M. (2019). June. Proposal for the Reengineering of Processes in the Management of Information and Communication Technology. *In 2019 14th Iberian Conference on Information Systems and Technologies (CISTI)* (pp. 1-5). IEEE.

Muyumba, T. and Phiri, J. (2017). A Web based Inventory Control System using Cloud Architecture and Barcode Technology for Zambia Air Force. *International Journal of Advanced Computer Science and Applications*, 8(11).

Olson, G. and Weins, K. (2009). Ten key elements of open source governance in the enterprise. Available at: https://pt.slideshare.net/RogueWaveSoftware/openlogic-ten-elements-of-open-source-governance (Accessed 28 December 2023).

Ruffin, C. and Ebert, C. (2004). Using open source software in product development: A primer. *IEEE software*, 21(1), pp. 82-86.

SANS. (2021). CIS Critical Security Controls Version 8. Available at: https://www.cisecurity.org/controls/v8 (Accessed 08 January 2024).

Shackleton, B. M. (2017). Towards Collection of Cost-Effective Technologies in Support of the NIST Cybersecurity Framework.

Smyth, V. (2015). Cyber-security fortresses built on quicksand. *Network Security*, 2015(8), pp. 5-8.

SOCIAL MEDIA USE AND NEGATIVE EMOTIONS: A SURVEY OF UNIVERSITY STUDENTS

Vanessa P. Dennen[1] and Yasin Yalçin[2]
[1]*Florida State University*
Tallahassee, FL, USA
[2]*Recep Tayyip Erdogan University*
Rize, Turkey

ABSTRACT

This study examines how university students experience negative emotions due to social media use and also provides initial validation of the Social Media Negative Emotion Questionnaire. Findings show that the degree to which this population experiences negative emotions during social media use varies widely, but most college students report an experience that is in the middle. The platforms most associated with negative emotions were dating apps, Instagram, Snapchat, and TikTok, and the activities most associated with negative emotions involved dating and posting and reading posts among one's peer group. Statistically significant differences were found by gender, with male university students reporting lower degrees of negative emotions attached to social media use in general. When examined by platform, these significant differences were found among Instagram, TikTok, and dating app users.

KEYWORDS

Emotion, Social Media, Embarrassment, Shame, Guilt

1. INTRODUCTION

Shame, guilt, and embarrassment are closely related negative emotions that occur in social contexts (Tangney et al., 1996). Social media is one context where these emotions can occur, through phenomena like unhealthy social comparison (Alfasi, 2019), and discomfort due to awkward, unplanned interactions (Loh & Walsh, 2021) that create context collapse (Davis & Jurgenson, 2014). Research on emotions and social media has primarily focused on how they are expressed in social media content (Rout et al., 2018) and people's reactions to specific social media content (Panger, 2017; Wheaton et al., 2021). This study seeks to identify platforms and activities that are most associated with negative emotions and, in recognition of well-established gendered differences in how youth use social media, it explores the relationship between gender, social media use, and negative emotions.

2. LITERATURE REVIEW

Social media use can be a contradictory activity. People use social media knowing that it comes with some risk of discomfort, but finding that personal benefits outweigh that risk (Dennen, 2009; Lieber, 2010). Youth find ways to distance themselves from negative experiences, such as the drama that is inherent in having online connections to peer groups (Dennen et al., 2017), in order to maintain a presence in these social spaces that are heavily intertwined with their school experiences (Dennen et al., 2020; Rutledge et al., 2019) and their in-person social experiences (Dredge & Schreurs, 2020). For youth, achieving separation between online and offline worlds can be difficult and may not be desirable.

The reasons why youth use social media are complex, and their corresponding feelings about their social media use are equally complex. Emotions like guilt have been associated with concerns about time spent on social media (Panek, 2014), level of messaging activity (Halfmann et al., 2021), and conflicts arising with friends and family due to social media use (Luqman et al., 2020). For contemporary youth, the diverse activities that they engage in online can lead to equally diverse emotions, creating a "see-saw" effect in which any particular use might trigger both positive and negative reactions (Weinstein, 2018). Although some youth may find social media to be a social panacea, and other may perceive it as a toxic digital wasteland, for most its use is assumed as a part of navigating contemporary life.

Because of its ubiquitous presence and well-documented incidents with negative behaviors, how youth use social media is of interest to researchers and practitioners across diverse disciplines (Greenhow et al., 2019). Researchers have sought to better understand the relationship between social media use and social relationships, wellbeing, and mental health. For example, a study that used experience sampling to study adolescent reactions to passive social media use found that sense of well-being varies across the population (Beyens et al., 2020). Similarly, adolescent reasons for using social media platforms like Instagram have been studied, finding that they vary based on personal need for feedback, levels of social comparison, and intensity of use (Sanchez-Hernandez et al., 2022). Across this body of literature, it becomes apparent that social media users navigate both positive and negative elements of the medium and make personal choices in order to achieve their desired outcomes.

3. CONTEXT AND RESEARCH QUESTIONS

In this study, we investigate the role negative emotions play in social media use, focusing on use by university students. Developmentally, university is a time of transition for many students. Those who attend shortly after completing high school use social media to assist with various informational, informal learning, and social needs during that transition (Dennen et al., 2023). Their social media use is less monitored than it is during the high school years (Dennen et al., 2019), and university students are expected to be more mature social media users than their slightly younger peers. Of course, this does not make them immune to negative emotions when using social media.

In this study, social media is broadly defined to include not only popular social networking sites, but also other online platforms through which social networking and sharing occur such as watch party and messaging applications. The questions guiding this study are:

1. To what degree do university students experience negative emotions when using social media?
2. What platforms are most associated with negative emotions on social media?
3. What activities are most associated with negative emotions on social media?
4. Are there gendered differences related to social media use and negative emotions?

These questions are addressed via data collected from a cross-sectional survey of university students.

4. METHOD

Participants in this study were 404 undergraduate students at a large public university in the United States. Participants' age ranged between 18 and 36 with a mean of 20.37 and a standard deviation of 1.92. There were 113 male (28.0%), 285 female (70.5%), and 6 non-binary (1.5%) participants among the sample. In terms of school year, there were 42 freshman (11.9%), 82 sophomore (20.3%), 143 junior (35.4%), and 131 senior (32.4%) students. University students, while a convenient sample, are an appropriate population for doing initial work in this area. Their age group is known to be heavy social media users and to be affected by Internet and social media use in both positive and negative ways.

The survey used in the study was a subset of a larger survey, and included demographics items, 21 items about negative emotions experienced when using different platforms, 16 items about negative emotions experienced when engaged in different social media activities, and the Social Media Negative Emotion Questionnaire (SMNEQ). SMNEQ is an 18-item scale designed by the researchers for this study and based on the Brief Shame and Guilt Questionnaire (BSGQ; Novin & Rieffe, 2015). Specifically, it uses the same items format, scale, and scoring procedure. However, the items focus on social media scenarios and rather than using two sub-scales to measure shame and guilt, the SMNEQ asks about scenarios that may lead to feelings shame, guilt, or embarrassment as a single scale. SMNEQ and other survey items were developed via a focus group and pilot testing process with undergraduate students.

Each item of SMNEQ presents participants with a scenario related to social media use. These situations are associated with behaviors that could lead to negative emotions such as shame (negative emotions based on one's social media actions and how others might perceive them), guilt (negative emotions based on outcomes of one's social media actions), or embarrassment (negative emotions based on how one is portrayed on social media). The scale asks participants to indicate to what extent they would experience negative emotions if they were to encounter the situation. The items are scored on a scale consisting of 1*: Not at all, 2: A little,* and *3: A lot*. The SMNEQ scale showed good internal consistency reliability with a coefficient alpha value of a = .873, which is similar to the reliability of the BSGQ (Broekhof et al., 2020; Novin & Rieffe, 2015). The study was approved by the researchers' Institutional Review Board and participants consented prior to participating. Data collection occurred via an online survey using the Qualtrics online survey platform.

Data analysis entailed using descriptive statistics to answer the first three research questions. Independent sample's *t*-tests were conducted to investigate mean differences between male and female students to answer the fourth research question.

5. FINDINGS

5.1 Negative Emotions on Social Media Platforms

To answer the first research question, individual items of the SMNEQ were analyzed descriptively. Scores ranged from a low of 18 (n = 16), meaning that the participant reported no negative emotions related to social media use to a high of 54 (n = 2), meaning that the participant reported a likelihood of experiencing negative emotions on each item. The mean was close to the midpoint for possible scores (M = 32.06, SD = 6.99), and the median and mode were 32 and 36, respectively. These findings suggest that most participants associate certain situations with negative emotions, although not every situation is likely to create a strong degree of negative emotion and some participants are free of negative emotions altogether in this context. Table 1 presents descriptive statistics for the individual SMNEQ items in a descending order of the mean values.

5.2 Social Media Platforms Associated with Negative Emotions

The second research question addressed social media platforms associated with negative emotions. Participants were asked to indicate the degree to which they experienced negative emotions like shame, guilt, or embarrassment when using these platforms. The responses were scored on a 3-point Likert scale which consisted of *1: Not at all, 2: A little,* and *3: A lot*. The results are presented in Table 2. The platforms that were most associated with negative emotions were dating apps, Instagram, TikTok, and Snapchat. Platforms that were least likely to be associated with negative emotions were watching party apps, payment applications, Twitch, Pinterest, and streaming video services.

5.3 Social Media Activities Associated with Negative Emotions

The second research question addressed social media activities associated with negative emotions. Participants were asked to indicate the degree to which they experienced negative emotions like shame, guilt, or embarrassment when engaging in these activities. The responses were scored on a 3-point Likert scale which consisted of *1: Not at all, 2: A little,* and *3: A lot*. The results are presented in Table 3. The activities that were most associated with negative emotions were searching for dates, viewing or reading what peers posted, posting photos to social media, posting updates to social media, following celebrities on social media, and interacting with peers on social media. Although posting updates to one's social media accounts in the form of photos and updates was potentially associated with negative emotions for around 45% of the sample, those rates drop to less than 30% when asked about posting memes or links to one's profile or documenting one's life for personal consumption. Activities that were least likely to generate negative emotions were playing a networked game, supporting hobbies and interests, sharing links to social media profiles, exploring future, and supporting health and wellness.

Table 1. Descriptive Statistics for the Social Media Negative Emotion Questionnaire

	Mean	SD
You have a big assignment due tomorrow, but you spend 30 minutes scrolling through your social media feed. You feel guilty.	2.25	.663
You post a new photo to your profile. You think you look very attractive in this photo. No one likes or comments on it. You feel embarrassed.	2.11	.723
You had an unfortunate event happen while you were with a friend. The friend writes a post about your misfortune and tags you in the post. You feel embarrassed.	2.09	.781
Your best friend gets sloppy drunk and starts posting random and out of character things to Instagram. You could try to stop them, but you don't because the posts are funny. You feel guilty.	2.05	.720
Your friend borrows your phone to look something up while you go pick up some coffee. Suddenly you realize your friend could access your search history. Recently you were searching for information on a topic you consider private. You feel ashamed.	2.01	.740
You screenshot an embarrassing post from an acquaintance's private account so you can share it with a friend and then message it to the friend. You feel guilty.	1.98	.770
You post a photo from your birthday party even though your best friend thinks they look bad in that photo. You feel guilty.	1.91	.655
Your mom posts photos of you at your most awkward point during your tween years and tags you. You feel embarrassed.	1.88	.759
You want to share a photo but feel it is unflattering so you edit it before posting it. You feel ashamed.	1.86	.729
You share a post to your account and a friend comments that it is fake news. You feel embarrassed.	1.83	.739
You get your weekly screentime report on your phone and see that your time on social media increased last week. You feel ashamed.	1.81	.754
You're at a special family event, but checking social media on your phone when you hope no one is looking. A family member notices and gives you a look. You feel guilty.	1.79	.721
You post about your recent activities with friends but restrict the posts so your family can't see them. You feel guilty.	1.46	.638
You are out to dinner with a group of people who start discussing how many social media followers they have. You realize you have fewer than anyone else there. You feel embarrassed.	1.45	.630
You download a new app to check it out. Some of your friends have said the app is for losers, but you like it. You bury the app in a folder on your phone so no one else is likely to see it. You feel ashamed.	1.44	.601
Your friend comments that they noticed you are following a somewhat cringey celebrity online. You feel embarrassed.	1.41	.580
You meet someone at a party, go home, and stalk their online profiles. You feel ashamed.	1.39	.586
You are curious about a topic that you're not comfortable discussing with friends. You investigate it online. You feel ashamed.	1.35	.568

Table 2. Social Media Platforms and Negative Emotions

	N	Mean	SD
Dating apps	191	1.76	.707
Instagram	403	1.69	.672
TikTok	361	1.57	.688
Snapchat	400	1.57	.634
Yik Yak	152	1.34	.575
Facebook	355	1.27	.509
Twitter [platform name since changed to X]	355	1.25	.510
Reddit	152	1.24	.498
Networked online gaming	148	1.21	.484
YouTube	391	1.18	.426
Messaging Apps	357	1.15	.414
Discord	122	1.15	.400
Video Conferencing	390	1.14	.372
Streaming Video Services	394	1.11	.376
Pinterest	288	1.10	.341
Payment Applications	389	1.07	.291
Watching Party	137	1.07	.312

NOTE: N represents active users. Only platforms with 100 or more active users reported.

Table 3. Social Media Activities and Negative Emotions

	N	Mean	SD
Search for dates online	188	1.65	.703
View/read what peers have posted to their social media profiles	397	1.50	.673
Post photos from my life to my social media profiles	391	1.50	.559
Post updates about my life to my social media profiles	362	1.46	.551
Follow celebrities on social media	367	1.38	.579
Interact with peers on their social media profiles	400	1.36	.584
Read news posted to social media	378	1.36	.585
Document my life/memories	378	1.31	.509
Post memes to my social media profiles	267	1.30	.536
Exchange direct messages (DMs) with my friends	399	1.29	.540
Make creative work to share online	249	1.28	.483
Support health and wellness	372	1.27	.548
Explore my future	372	1.25	.519
Share links to my social media profiles	260	1.23	.455
Support hobbies and interests	375	1.21	.475
Play a networked game	250	1.18	.402

5.4 Gender and Social Media Use and Emotions

The fourth research question addressed gendered differences related to social media use and negative emotions. To answer the research question, we conducted an independent sample's *t*-test and investigated the mean difference between male and female students on the SMNEQ total scores. The *t*-test found that male students ($M = 29.81$, $SD = 7.64$) experienced significantly lower levels of negative social media emotions compared to female students ($M = 33.07$, $SD = 6.49$), $t(396) = -4.279$, $p < .001$.Moreover, we conducted a series of independent samples *t*-tests to investigate differences between male and female students on their negative emotions associated with social media platforms and activities. In terms of social media platforms, *t*-test results revealed that male students experienced significantly lower levels of negative emotions on Instagram ($t(395) = -3.551, p < .001, M_{male} = 1.51, M_{female} = 1.77$, Cohen's $d = .664$), TikTok ($t(355) = -2.453$, $p = .015$, $M_{male} = 1.43$, $M_{female} = 1.63$, Cohen's $d = .685$), and dating apps ($t(185) = -3.139$, $p = .002$, $M_{male} = 1.52$, $M_{female} = 1.86$, Cohen's $d = .688$). Furthermore, in terms of social media activities, *t*-test results revealed that male students experienced significantly lower levels of negative emotions when engaging in posting updates about their lives ($t(197.491) = -2.990$, $p = .003$, $M_{male} = 1.32$, $M_{female} = 1.50$, Cohen's $d = .547$), documenting life or memories ($t(207.489) = -2.170$, $p = .031$, $M_{male} = 1.23$, $M_{female} = 1.35$, Cohen's $d = .508$), and following celebrities ($t(205.620) = -2.038$, $p = .043$, $M_{male} = 1.29$, $M_{female} = 1.42$, Cohen's $d = .578$). What these findings do not account for, however, are individuals who opt out of a platform or activity. Participants only reported negative emotions based on platforms that they currently use and activities in which they currently engage. It is possible that some participants decline to use platforms or engage in activities because they associate the platforms and activities with a risk of experiencing negative emotions.

6. DISCUSSION AND IMPLICATIONS

The findings show that university students experience are diverse in their experience of negative emotions when using social media. The variance in how this population feels about social media is not surprising, and is similar to the findings of Beyens et al. (2020), which stressed the individualized nature of how adolescents experience social media and wellbeing. Most students reported negative emotions at a moderate level, meaning that they only had mild negative emotions or strong negative emotions were limited to just a few situations. Viewed in light of findings from other studies, such as the limited effect of social media use on self-esteem (Valkenburg et al., 2021), it appears likely that social media users find ways to mitigate or minimize their individual negative experiences on social media. This would, in turn, allow them to use social media in ways that result in perceived benefits and positive outcomes.

Findings show that platforms and activities most heavily associated with peer social interaction and self-disclosure were most likely to yield negative emotions. These findings provide some initial insights into the specific everyday activities that lead to negative emotions when using social media, and the degree of those experiences. For example, getting positive attention such as likes on social media are connected to self-esteem (Marengo et al., 2021). It is not surprising, then, to see that for some social media users a dearth of attention could lead to negative emotions. Our findings about platforms and activities reinforce findings from earlier studies about the diverse nature of social media use (Weinstein, 2018) and confirm that passive social media use does not inherently have deleterious effects (Valkenburg et al., 2022).

Many of SMNEQ items that were most likely to result in negative emotions related to online identity, which further aligns with the platform and activity findings. Online identity appears to be an area of fragility. It is comprised of both one's identity performance and relational activity (Cover, 2012). University students are concerned about how they are perceived and how they are portrayed. Although this study did not ask about experiences of positive emotions, it seems likely that the experiences that trigger negative emotions also have the capability of leading to positive outcomes.

Prior studies can be used to explain the significant differences found between male and female participants. Others studies have found that females are more engaged in online social support than males (Tifferet, 2020), and this increased interpersonal element could make them more vulnerable to negative experiences. Females have also been found to have greater privacy concerns (Tifferet, 2019), which also may connect to this same sense of vulnerability, exacerbated by situations in which privacy may be risked for social rewards (Hallam & Zanella, 2017).

7. CONCLUSION

Based on these findings, we conclude that many university students use social media despite the potential that doing so will lead to some level of negative emotion. Further, when their social media use focuses on identity and relationship issues, the corresponding vulnerability leads to associations with negative emotions. These findings do not mean that social media is inherently bad when used for such purposes. Rather, one might consider the virtual social realm as an extension of the physical social realm, opening up users to similar vulnerabilities and the potential for triggering negative emotions.

This study has several limitations. It did not explore the full range of negative emotions or negative scenarios that individuals might experience, and focuses narrowly on a specific subset of youth, undergraduate university students. The findings from this population should not be generalized to other youth populations (e.g., high school students and young adults who have not attended university), and should also be considered in terms of the cultural context of the sample. The study did not consider positive emotions, and the survey only asked participants to rate platforms they actively used, potentially overlooking individuals who have chosen not to use specific platforms due to corresponding negative emotions.

This study has implications for people who work with youth and for researchers who study social media use. By understanding which platforms and activities are most associated with negative emotions, we can seek ways to help youth navigate their social media use and even avoid some negative experiences. Additionally, the SMNEQ provides a helpful way to measure one's propensity to experience negative emotions when using social media. Future research should be done to further refine and validate the SMNEQ, to consider the role of positive emotions, and to expand this line of inquiry to other populations. Additionally, as this line of research evolves, it might include an exploration of how individual differences factor into one's experience of social media.

REFERENCES

Alfasi, Y. (2019). The grass is always greener on my Friends' profiles: The effect of Facebook social comparison on state self-esteem and depression. Personality and Individual Differences, 147, 111-117. https://doi.org/10.1016/j.paid.2019.04.032

Beyens, I., Pouwels, J. L., van, D., II, Keijsers, L., & Valkenburg, P. M. (2020). The effect of social media on well-being differs from adolescent to adolescent. Scientific Reports, 10(1), 10763. https://doi.org/10.1038/s41598-020-67727-7

Broekhof, E., Kouwenberg, M., Oosterveld, P., Frijns, J. H. M., & Rieffe, C. (2020). Use of the brief shame and guilt questionnaire to deaf and hard of hearing children and adolescents. Assessment, 27(1), 194-205. https://doi.org/10.1177/1073191117725169

Cover, R. (2012). Performing and undoing identity online: Social networking, identity theories and the incompatibility of online profiles and friendship regimes. Convergence-the International Journal of Research into New Media Technologies, 18(2), 177-193. https://doi.org/10.1177/1354856511433684

Davis, J. L., & Jurgenson, N. (2014). Context collapse: Theorizing context collusions and collisions. Information, Communication & Society, 17(4), 476-485. https://doi.org/10.1080/1369118x.2014.888458

Dennen, V. P. (2009). Constructing academic alter-egos: Identity issues in a blog-based community. Identity in the Information Society, 2(1), 23-38.

Dennen, V. P., He, D., Shi, H., & Adolfson, D. (2023). College students, networked knowledge activities, and digital competence: Implications for online instructors. Online Learning, 27(4). https://doi.org/10.24059/olj.v27i4.4046

Dennen, V. P., Rutledge, S. A., & Bagdy, L. M. (2019). Social media use in high school settings: Rules, outcomes, and educational opportunities. In Proceedings of the 10th International Conference on Social Media and Society (pp. 205-213). ACM. https://doi.org/10.1145/3328529.3328561

Dennen, V. P., Rutledge, S. A., & Bagdy, L. M. (2020). (Dis)connected: The role of social networking sites in the high school setting. American Journal of Education, 127(1), 107-136. https://doi.org/10.1086/711016

Dennen, V. P., Rutledge, S. A., Bagdy, L. M., Rowlett, J. T., Burnick, S., & Joyce, S. (2017). Context collapse and student social media networks: Where life and high school collide. Proceedings of the 8th International Conference on Social Media & Society, Article 32. https://doi.org/10.1145/3097286.3097318

Dredge, R., & Schreurs, L. (2020). Social media use and offline interpersonal outcomes during youth: A systematic literature review. Mass Communication and Society, 23(6), 885-911. https://doi.org/10.1080/15205436.2020.1810277

Greenhow, C., Cho, V., Dennen, V. P., & Fishman, B. J. (2019). Education and social media: Research directions to guide a growing field. Teachers College Record, 121(14). https://doi.org/10.1177/016146811912101413

Halfmann, A., Meier, A., & Reinecke, L. (2021). Too much or too little messaging? Situational determinants of guilt about mobile messaging. Journal of Computer-Mediated Communication, 26(2), 72-90. https://doi.org/10.1093/jcmc/zmaa018

Hallam, C., & Zanella, G. (2017). Online self-disclosure: The privacy paradox explained as a temporally discounted balance between concerns and rewards. Computers in Human Behavior, 68, 217-227. https://doi.org/10.1016/j.chb.2016.11.033

Lieber, A. (2010). A virtual veibershul: Blogging and the blurring of public and private among orthodox Jewish women. College English, 72(6), 621-637.

Loh, J., & Walsh, M. J. (2021). Social media context collapse: The consequential differences between context collusion versus context collision. Social Media+ Society, 7(3), 20563051211041646.

Luqman, A., Masood, A., Weng, Q., Ali, A., & Rasheed, M. I. (2020). Linking excessive SNS use, technological friction, strain, and discontinuance: The moderating role of guilt. Information Systems Management, 37(2), 94-112. https://doi.org/10.1080/10580530.2020.1732527

Marengo, D., Montag, C., Sindermann, C., Elhai, J. D., & Settanni, M. (2021). Examining the links between active Facebook use, received likes, self-esteem and happiness: A study using objective social media data. Telematics and Informatics, 58. https://doi.org/10.1016/j.tele.2020.101523

Novin, S., & Rieffe, C. (2015). Validation of the brief shame and guilt questionnaire for children. Personality and Individual Differences, 85, 56-59. https://doi.org/10.1016/j.paid.2015.04.028

Panek, E. (2014). Left to their own devices: College students' "guilty pleasure" media use and time management. Communication Research, 41(4), 561-577. https://doi.org/10.1177/0093650213499657

Panger, G. T. (2017). Emotion in social media (Publication Number 10283129) [Ph.D., University of California, Berkeley]. ProQuest Dissertations & Theses Global. Ann Arbor.

Rout, J. K., Choo, K.-K. R., Dash, A. K., Bakshi, S., Jena, S. K., & Williams, K. L. (2018). A model for sentiment and emotion analysis of unstructured social media text. Electronic Commerce Research, 18(1), 181-199.

Rutledge, S. A., Dennen, V. P., Bagdy, L. M., Rowlett, J. T., & Burnick, S. (2019). Exploring adolescent social media use in a high school: Tweeting teens in a bell schedule world. Teachers College Record Yearbook, 121(14).

Sanchez-Hernandez, M. D., Herrera, M. C., & Exposito, F. (2022). Does the number of likes affect adolescents' emotions? The moderating role of social comparison and feedback-seeking on Instagram. The Journal of Psychology, 156(3), 200-223. https://doi.org/10.1080/00223980.2021.2024120

Tangney, J. P., Miller, R. S., Flicker, L., & Barlow, D. H. (1996). Are shame, guilt, and embarrassment distinct emotions? Journal of personality and social psychology, 70(6), 1256.

Tifferet, S. (2019). Gender differences in privacy tendencies on social network sites: A meta-analysis. Computers in Human Behavior, 93, 1-12. https://doi.org/10.1016/j.chb.2018.11.046

Tifferet, S. (2020). Gender differences in social support on social network sites: A meta-analysis. Cyberpsychology, Behavior and Social Networking., 23(4), 199-209. https://doi.org/10.1089/cyber.2019.0516

Valkenburg, P. M., Beyens, I., Pouwels, J. L., van Driel, I. I., & Keijsers, L. (2022). Social media browsing and adolescent well-being: Challenging the "passive social media use hypothesis". Journal of Computer-Mediated Communication, 27(1), zmab015. https://doi.org/10.1093/jcmc/zmab015

Valkenburg, P., Beyens, I., Pouwels, J. L., van Driel, I. I., & Keijsers, L. (2021). Social media use and adolescents' self-esteem: Heading for a person-specific media effects paradigm. Journal of communication, 71(1), 56-78. https://doi.org/10.1093/joc/jqaa039

Weinstein, E. (2018). The social media see-saw: Positive and negative influences on adolescents' affective well-being. New media & society., 20(10), 3597-3623. https://doi.org/10.1177/1461444818755634

Wheaton, M. G., Prikhidko, A., & Messner, G. R. (2021). Is fear of COVID-19 contagious? The effects of emotion contagion and social media use on anxiety in response to the coronavirus pandemic. Frontiers in Psychology, 11, 3594.

THE BALANCE OF PUBLIC AND PRIVATE INTERESTS IN THE USE OF DIGITAL TECHNOLOGIES IN LAW ENFORCEMENT (LEGAL-COMPARATIVE STUDY)

Marina L. Davydova[1*], Evgeny A. Mamay[2] and Ekaterina D. Smagina[2]
[1]*Volgograd State University, Russia*
[2]*HSE University (Nizhny Novgorod), Russia*

ABSTRACT

The article examines the use of digital technologies in law enforcement and the balance between public and private interests in that relevance. The text analyses the system of legal regulations and law enforcement practice. The authors study legal acts that regulate relations in the sphere of ICT. The empirical bases of the paper consist of the more than 30 decisions adopted by various judicial instances in Russia, as well as more than 20 decisions of the European Court of Human Rights. The authors compared the legislation and practice of the USA, the United Kingdom of Great Britain and Northern Ireland, France, and the European Union as the whole. The conclusion determined the current level of regulation of digital legal relations in terms of balancing the interests of individuals, society, and the State to achieve private as well as public interests. The study identified gaps and imbalances in the regulation of the area under consideration, as well as key directions for improvement in the legislative and law enforcement activity.

KEYWORDS

Private Life, Electronic Data, Database, Balance, Law Enforcement, Competing Public and Private Interests, European Court of Human Rights, Constitutional Court of the Russian Federation

1. THEORETICAL BACKGROUND, HYPOTHESES, OBJECTIVES AND METHODOLOGY OF RESEARCH

With the universal digitalization and development of information and communication technologies (ICT), the boundary between privacy and publicity is gradually becoming less distinct. The Internet and modern technologies have a significant positive potential, but at the same time also create numerous vulnerabilities and channels for information leaks, which can lead to invasion of privacy, violation of personal and family privacy, and compromise the inviolability of personal correspondence and messages.

American lawyers Louis Brandeis and Samuel Warren (1890) were the first to draw attention to the importance of ensuring the privacy of each person and predicted the threats of violation due to the development of mass media. The development of ICT has led to numerous scientific studies on the conflict between universal digitalization and privacy. The first group of studies (Winkler, T., Rinner, B., 2011; Wicker S., Schrader D., 2011; McKee H.A., 2011) focus on privacy protection systems and technological solutions. The second group is constituted by social studies, focusing on the behavioral characteristics of participants in digital communication, perception of privacy (Amos C. et al., 2014), digital security training (Barnard-Wills D., 2012), and the impact of digital literacy on changing behavioral stereotypes (Preibusch S., 2015). Finally, legal studies encompass a significant field that concentrates on the legislative regulation of privacy protection, digital rights of citizens (Champion A., 2007) digital methods of personal identification (Beck E., 2015), the storage and use of personal data (Mantelero A., 2014), the legality of mass surveillance (Desai D., 2014). The Russian jurisprudence tends to follow general trends in legal scholarship (Odnoshevin I., 2018; Omelin V., 2019; Hovavko S., 2016).

[*]Corresponding author email: davidovaml@volsu.ru

It is important to note that the inviolability of private life is guaranteed by the Universal Declaration of Human Rights (Article 12), the International Covenant on Civil and Political Rights (Article 17), and the European Convention for the Protection of Human Rights and Fundamental Freedoms (Article 8, hereinafter referred to as 'the Convention'). Without taking into account the specifics exactly of the digital sphere, article 23 of the Constitution of Russia guarantees the protection of privacy. At the same time the Russian Constitution defines the permissible purposes for restricting human rights and freedoms necessary to protect the foundations of the constitutional order, morality, health, rights and legitimate interests of others, as well as to ensure national defense and state security (Part 3 of Article 55). Indeed, in certain circumstances, it may be necessary to invade the privacy in order to maintain public order, ensure state security, prevent crimes, detect criminals, identify missing persons, etc. Thus, the protection of private life becomes a point of conflict between privacy and public interests that requires finding a proper balance between these two groups of interests.

The Russian legislation has incorporated numerous privacy protection standards from international law, foreign legislation, and the judicial practice of international courts. Therefore, the Russian legal system has long been aligned with the practices of the European Court of Human Rights (referred to as the ECHR hereafter). Announcing the intention to withdraw from the Council of Europe the Russian Minister of Foreign Affairs Sergey Lavrov (2022) stated that the rights and freedoms of the Russian citizens will not be affected. From his point of view, the Constitution of Russia provides the same level as the European Convention on Human Rights guarantees, and the Russian legislation incorporates the legal provisions of the main Council of Europe documents.

This study is based on two interrelated assumptions. First of all, the Russian legislator's long-term orientation towards the legal standards of ensuring human rights in leading countries worldwide has affected the conceptual essence of legislation that affects various aspects of the digital sphere of society. The laws are supposed to reflect certain guarantees and the law enforcement agencies are supposed to implement the relevant norms. Contrary, the State, with its wide range of legal and organizational resources, can build a mechanism of interaction with society that benefits itself but may be detrimental to privacy and the preservation of private life.

The study focuses on the lawful combination of public and private interests and the legislative criteria for law enforcement restrictions in the ICT sphere implemented at the regulatory level and developed in reference to law enforcement (including judicial) practice. This study will use the terms 'digital legal relations' and 'legal relations in the sphere of ICT' interchangeably. These terms refer to social relations that are regulated by legal norms and mediated by computers and other ICTs, including the Internet. Regarding the aforementioned subject area, we will use the term 'privacy' to refer to all private interests that come with the use of ICT.

The aim of this study is to create a model for balancing private and public interests in digital legal relations. To achieve this, the following tasks will be undertaken: 1) to identify the legal guarantees of privacy in legislation, and 2) to assess the extent to which these guarantees are reflected in subordinate normative rules and their practical implementation in relation to the use of technology.

The research methodology is based on the formal-legal (dogmatic) method of scientific cognition. It includes the study of doctrinal sources, systemic and comparative legal analysis, technical-legal analysis and content analysis of domestic and foreign legislation and materials of law enforcement practice. As part of the research, the authors analyzed more than 25 normative legal acts in the sphere of ICT, more than 50 decisions adopted by the ECHR, the Constitutional Court of Russia (hereinafter referred to as the CC of Russia) and the Supreme Court of the Russian Federation and various other courts in Russia. The authors obtained comparative legal material by studying the legislation of foreign countries, including the United States, the United Kingdom of Great Britain and Northern Ireland, France, and the European Union as a whole. In addition, during the studying we conducted a survey of more than 30 law enforcement officers who use the ICT in their professional activities.

The provided information was analyzed in order to identify and generalize the criteria for a lawful restriction of privacy, which is the only legal way to strike a proper balance between private and public interests.

2. RESEARCH RESULTS

In law enforcement, ICTs are primarily used as direct sources of legally relevant information, as well as means and methods of obtaining, storing and processing such information.

The legal regulation of these areas raises a question that combines ethical and legal issues: 'What is more important - public or private interests?' The state and society have a shared interest in public security against internal and external threats, maintaining public order, preventing crimes and other offences, preserving morality, and creating suitable conditions for societal existence and development. Individuals have a wide range of private interests, including personal identification, inviolability of personal and family secrets, confidentiality of correspondence, telephone conversations, postal, telegraphic and other communications, freedom of speech and self-expression in the digital space.

The study of doctrinal, normative, and law enforcement sources enabled us to formulate the conditions (criteria) for the lawful combination of public and private interests.

These criteria can be divided into three groups:

— Criteria of lawfulness *ante factum*, which precede the imposition of restrictions in the sphere of digital relations. Any measures, such as detective activities or investigative actions, that aim to restrict the constitutional rights of citizens, should be accompanied by clear legislative regulations. These regulations have to include a preliminary determination of the scope of application of restrictions, their duration, and the circle of persons to whom they should be applied.

— Criteria for legality *in ipso actu* are met when restrictions are imposed. It is mandatory to obtain preliminary judicial legalization or permission to conduct any actions, which restrict personal rights and freedoms. The conducting activities also requires the subsequent judicial control, if there are grounds to suspect violations of current legislation.

— Criteria for *post-factum* lawfulness are the guarantees for the protection of privacy that remain in place after restrictions and prohibitions have been imposed. To ensure the protection of citizens' privacy, it is necessary to limit the duration of data storage in state data bases and information systems. Additionally, a regulated procedure for automatic deletion of information upon official request of a citizen should be established. It is also important to provide citizens with the ability to be informed about the availability of personal information in state data bases.

2.1 Ante Factum – Legislative Regulation

Proper legislative regulation is fundamental to the lawful introduction of restrictions and prohibitions in the digital sphere, including establishing legal and factual grounds for the measures, defining the objects of state influence, specifying the subject matter of the restrictions imposed, identifying the public bodies or officials vested with the relevant powers, providing safeguards to prevent abuse of power by law enforcement officers, and outlining the procedures that should accompany the restrictions imposed.

In the sphere of digital relations, the legality of restrictions is typically determined by whether acts committed by individuals can be attributed to a specific category of offences. Such categories are usually established by legislation, often National Criminal Codes, which prescribe a particular type and amount of punishment. For example, the CC of Russia in its Decision dated 14 July 1998 mentioned that legislation allows restrictions on privacy only at reference to crimes (criminal offences), and the detective actions or operational-search activity which are relevant to a different type of offences must be terminated.

In both Russian and international judicial practice, inadequate normative regulation has led to questions about the possible illegality of actions taken by public authorities. Examples of such situations include cases “S. and Marper v. United Kingdom” (2004), “Shimovolos v. Russia” (2009), and “Ben Faiza v. France” (2012). For instance, in the case of Ben Faiza v. France, the ECHR considered the situation of wiretapping and surveillance of a person suspected of drug trafficking, founding that the French legislation in 2010 did not clearly limit the discretionary powers of the authorities.

It is important to note that legal restrictions on constitutional rights should be implemented through both legislative and subordinate normative regulation. This may require addressing the issue of preserving state secrets. In Russia, the Criminal Procedure Code of the Russian Federation dated December 18, 2001 and the Law “On Operational-Search Activity” dated August 12, 1995 (hereinafter referred to as the Law on ORD) prescribe the mechanism for transforming information obtained during detective-search activities (such as detecting signs of a crime or the results of such unlawful acts) into information that holds evidentiary and criminal procedural value. Interdepartmental instructions also provide guidance on these proceedings.

In the regulation of the imposition of prohibitions and restrictions on the use of ICTs, it is crucial to specify the scope, duration and applicability of these restrictions to a particular group of people. The primary question in determining the essence of legal regulation in this case is who should be subject to state control: all individuals involved in digital communication, whether voluntarily or involuntarily, or only specific categories of individuals whose activities pose a threat to the legally protected interests of the state, society, and individuals.

Currently, legal guarantees are applied to all citizens, but legislative regulation pays special attention to protecting the legal status of individuals who play a significant role in civil society, such as human rights defenders, journalists, and lawyers. Although legislation and practice in different countries have some contradictions in granting them such status, it is important to ensure equal protection under the law for all individuals.

The ECHR established a strict standard for identifying cases of politically motivated persecution of human rights defenders in the case of Azerbaijani human rights defender Rasul Jafarov (March, 2016). However, some countries that claim to be liberal-democratic use available technologies to protect their interests from human rights defenders deemed to be 'wrong' (Cases of Catt v. the United Kingdom, 2015; Félix Dagregorio and Alain Mosconi v. France, 2011). Despite the political regime in a particular country, the general conclusion regarding the current practice of protecting human rights defenders is the uncertainty of their status. As a rule, the legal protection is provided by national laws and judicial procedures as long as human rights activity is symbolic in nature and does not mean interference in the authority or political processes.

In contradistinction to human rights activists, strict safeguards against unlawful interference in private lives protect journalists, advocates and judges, because the exercise of their professional powers is impossible without limiting outside influence on their activities.

At the same time, judicial practice reveals deviations from the general rule. For example, in the case of Nagla v. Latvia (2010), the ECHR analyzed the police seize of digital media from the journalist, who published materials obtained from illegally accessed tax database. The ECHR emphasized that a journalist's right to not disclose their sources should be viewed as an integral part of the right to information, which must be treated with the utmost care.

Experts note that there is inadequate procedural safeguarding of journalistic secrecy in Russia (BFM, 2018). The Law "On Mass Media" dated December 27, 1991 requires the editorial office of a media outlet to keep the source of information confidential, unless a court order is received in connection with a pending case. While journalists are not exempt from being questioned as witnesses under the Code of Criminal Procedure of Russia, law enforcement officials may involve journalists as witnesses to bypass the legal prohibition on questioning members of the media. In contrast to the above category, advocates, defense counsels and judges enjoy significantly greater legal safeguards.

The Russian legislature grants a special legal protection to advocates. According to part 3 of article 8 of the Federal Law "On Advocacy and Advocates in the Russian Federation" dated May 31, 2002, detective activities and investigative actions against advocates are only permitted with a court decision. As noted by the CC of Russia (Decision № 629-O-O of March 22, 2012), judicial legalization of detective search and investigative actions against a lawyer action relates only to the sphere of his actual attorney-like activity, but not to the criminal act he (or she) himself (or herself) commits, as incompatible with the status of an advocate. At the same time, existing judicial practice shows that courts of first instance often violate the requirements of criminal procedure legislation. Thus, in the case 'Kolesnichenko v. Russia' (2004), the ECHR found violations of the Convention in the fact that the court allowed the investigative body to conduct searches in the home and office of a lawyer who was not suspected of committing any crime, but was the defender of the accused in a criminal case.

Law protects judges from unlawful interference in their lives. The practice has developed a mechanism for complying, on the one hand, with established guarantees of independence of judges, and on the other hand, avoidance of corporate environment influence and the concealment of crimes committed by colleagues within the judicial community. For instance, if there are signs of a particularly serious crime conducted by a judge, the law enforcement bodies can obtain decision of superior court allowed to limit the judge immunity including the secrecy of telephone and other communications, the inviolability of his office and residential premises, office and personal vehicles (Decision of the CC of Russia № 12-P dated June 9, 2011).

One issue that requires particular attention due to the new possibilities arising from the development of ICTs is the databases that contain information about individuals. In contemporary society, there is a widespread debate regarding the use of ICT and big data collection for indirect identification of individuals, even if the rules of automatic information processing are not formally violated. Databases in the hands of Information Service Providers (ISPs), Communication Service Providers (CSPs) and Telecom Operators currently do not have comprehensive legal regulation, remaining a 'gray' area of contact between public and private interests. Even data encryption alone cannot mitigate all potential threats due to the technical principle that 'anything that is encrypted can be decrypted'.

Only genomic and fingerprint registration have more or less proper legislative regulation. Thanks to the development of ICT, they are gradually merging into a general standard of forensic registration, becoming important tools in the hands of law enforcement agencies. At the same time genomic and fingerprint registration are often becoming the subject of legal disputes (S. and Marper v. the United Kingdom, 2004; M.K. v. France, 2009; Gaughran v. the United Kingdom, 2015).

State fingerprint registration in the Russian Federation has a fairly long history, and is currently carried out on the basis of the Federal Law "On State Fingerprint Registration in the Russian Federation" dated June 25, 1998. This law contains a list of thirty-five categories of persons to whom it applies mandatory fingerprinting, including those suspected, accused or convicted of committing a crime. The maintaining of fingerprint database regulated by acts of the Government of the Russian Federation, dozens of ministerial regulations, as well as joint orders at the interministerial level, which determine the order of information exchange. The coverage of fingerprint record database in Russia is approximately 34 million fingerprint cards (Mihajlov M., 2015, p. 293), which accounts for approximately 25% of the country's total population. For comparison, the British database IDENT1 contained 26,298,205 fingerprints relating to 8,397,761 individuals, which is approximately 12.5% of the population (FINDS, 2022).

Although fingerprint records currently receive significant attention, it is expected that over time they will gradually become less important in forensic registration, as genomic records take precedence. As of 1 January 2020, the All-Russian database of genomic information contained genomic data for 0.6% of the total population of the Russian Federation (Explanatory note to the Bill No. 1048800-7, 2020). In comparison, the National DNA Database (NDNAD) in the United Kingdom, established in 1995, contained 6,568,035 profiles of individuals as of March 31, 2020, representing approximately 9.8% of the population (NDNAD_Strategy_Board, 2020). It should be noted that the United Kingdom has legalised the collection of genetic identifiers for arrestees, as well as for detainees falling under the so-called 'serious' status (murder, rape, terrorism, robbery, theft, etc.). In the USA genomic registration is highly fragmented, however, the DNA Identification Act of 1994 (34 U.S. Code § 12592) authorized the creation of the National DNA Index at the federal level. It contains over 14,836,490 criminal profiles, 4,513,955 arrestee profiles, and 1,144,255 samples (as of October 2021) recovered from crime scenes (CODIS - NDIS Statistics, 2021), accounting for only approximately 4.4% of the total US population, including convicted offenders, arrestees, detainees, unidentified human remains, missing persons, and relatives of missing persons.

The genomic registration in Russia is regulated by the Federal Law "On State Genomic Registration in the Russian Federation" dated December 3, 2008. On January 25, 2023, the Parliament of Russia adopted the Law, that expanded the list of obligatory registered persons including all individuals who are suspected of committing crimes, accused of committing crimes, and those who are subjected to administrative arrest.

2.2 In Ipso Actu – Judicial Control

Researchers have found that over 50% of the complaints received by the CC of Russia regarding operational-search activities using technical means question the legality of their conduct without a court decision (Chernyh A., 2019, p. 17). The Law on ORD stipulates that the bodies carrying out detective search must obtain court decisions for conducting activities that restrict constitutional rights such as the secrecy of correspondence, telephone conversations, postal, telegraphic and other messages transmitted via electronic and postal communication networks.

A crucial requirement for the judicial legalization of lawful restrictions on the constitutional rights of citizens is obtaining them in advance. The case of Trabajo Rueda v. Spain, considered by the ECHR in 2017, is a striking example of a violation of this requirement. The applicant left his computer in a workshop for technical work. During the check, the technician discovered files containing child pornography and immediately reported to the police station. The officers examined the contents of the computer, initiated an investigation, and subsequently arrested the applicant, remanded him in custody. After examining the case, the ECHR concluded that the police's seizure of the computer and inspection of its files without prior judicial authorization violated Article 8 (right to respect for private life) of the Convention. The court found that this action was not proportionate to the legitimate aims pursued and was not necessary in a democratic society.

The legislation and law enforcement practice consider an urgent situation as justified exception to the general rule of prior judicial legalization (Omelin V., 2019). According to the Law on ORD, such cases include those that may lead to the commission of a grave crime, as well as situations where there is data on events and actions (or inaction) that pose a threat to the state security. Detective-search action may be carried out, but only with mandatory notification of the court within 24 hours and receipt of a court decision within 48 hours. If the act of judicial legalization within the specified period is not received, the action must be terminated.

During the expert survey, we identified some nuances in the implementation of this legal mechanism. Firstly, in some cases, judges interpret the urgency of the action in a limited way. For example, if the detective-search action can be conducted during working hours, judge may not consider it urgent. Additionally, for many regions of Russia, preliminary judicial legalization is often unfeasible due to the distance between the relevant police bodies and courts. The resolution of these difficulties can be achieved by introducing stable and secure videoconferencing channels.

Judicial review also plays a crucial role in overseeing mechanisms for mass and targeted data collection in the digital space. The ECHR has considered this issue in several cases, including Big Brother Watch and Others v. the United Kingdom (2013, 2014, 2015), Szabó and Vissy v. Hungary (2014). In these cases the ECHR concluded that, due to the many threats that states face in the modern world, the use of a mass interception regime in itself does not violate the Convention. Once in place, this regime would have been subject to "end-to-end safeguards", which underscores the importance of assessing the measures introduced in terms of the necessity and proportionality of such actions at each stage of the process. Finally, mass interception must be subject to independent oversight, both from the outset, when the purpose and scope of the operation are determined, and to independent review after the fact. The court must decide the specific search queries and messages that are subject to verification, the specific conditions for searching for information, for example, personal identifiers, email addresses, etc.

The point of view of Russian law enforcement practice was expressed in the positions of the CC of Russia (Decisions № 8-P dated May 20, 1997; № 8-P dated March 11, 1998; № 9-P dated July 16, 2008). According to these judgments, the mere adoption of a decision by public authorities with a guarantee of subsequent judicial control does not contradict the requirements of the Constitution of the Russian Federation, since it allows you to correct violations by appealing them in the prescribed manner in competent court.

2.3 Post Factum – Retention, Destruction of Information Received and Reporting of its Existence

The ECHR and national courts have developed a clear understanding of the reasonable duration for both the application of restrictive measures in the digital sphere (as previously discussed) and the storage of collected data in state information systems.

The ECHR determines that the duration of data retention should be based on the severity of the offence, the level of public danger posed by the offender, and the purpose of collecting information, which is to prevent the commission of new offences. Therefore, the seriousness of the offence committed should determine how long the information identifying a person should be kept. The ECHR considers indefinite retention of information to be exceptional. For example, in the cases of 'B.B. v. France', 'Gardel v. France' and 'M.B. v. France' the ECHR found that the length of retention of the information – a maximum of 30 years – was consistent with the purpose of the Sex Offender Database, since the applicants had been convicted of raping 15-year-old minors while in a position of authority.

Guided by the above criteria, it is important to note that the Russian legislation and law enforcement practices in Russia differ significantly from the standards developed by the ECHR. For instance, the Russian Law "On State Fingerprint Registration in the Russian Federation" dated June 25, 1998 stipulates that such information must be stored until the registered persons reach the age of 100 years or their death is confirmed. The Federal Law "On State Genomic Registration in the Russian Federation" dated December 3, 2008 defines the period of storage of this data until the death of registered individuals is confirmed. In the absence of such information, the data will be stored until the individual would have turned 100 years old.

In connection with the above-mentioned criteria of the legality of storing information in the information systems it is natural to establish a regulated procedure for deleting information from state registers and databases. In general, it can be carried out either on the basis of a person's application, if his/her registration was voluntary (as a rule, this procedure does not provide for any formal difficulties). Automatic deletion made upon expiry of the time limits for storage of the relevant information (in Russia - practically indefinitely), or in connection with the termination of the circumstances that served as a basis for entering the relevant information into the system. The latter mechanism requires a separate discussion.

Disproportionate interference with privacy can occur when data is stored on individuals who are legally defined as having little or no public danger. The ECHR has established that any data collected and stored on particular person must be deleted, if that person is acquitted, criminal proceedings against him have been refused, or the case has been terminated (Case 'M.K. v. France', 2009).

The legislation of the Russian Federation regarding this matter is simplified and does not have complex differentiation in the grounds for registering and storing information. Among the foreign legislations we have studied, the registration requirements in France are the most complex and differentiated. For instance, the period of storage of genomic information in the FNAEG database varies depending on the age of the person to be registered (adult/juvenile), procedural status, and category of offence (FNAEG, n.d.).

The establishment of a regulated procedure for informing citizens of the availability of information about them in state registers and databases is crucial to ensuring the legal guarantees mentioned above. The case of Youth Initiative For Human Rights v. Serbia (2006) raised this issue in the ECHR practice.

The Russian legislation currently provides at least two mechanisms for appealing to public authorities to obtain information about oneself: the general procedure for consideration of citizens' appeals and a special procedure provided for by the Law on ORD. It is important to acknowledge that although laws provide formal legal guarantees, the implementation of mechanisms to protect citizens' rights is often limited. The CC of Russia has stated that unclassified detective-search measures cannot be presented in open court proceedings as it would render the operational-search activity meaningless. Assessing the legality and validity of the actions of law enforcement agencies that refuse to disclose information that has become known during the operational investigation process is the prerogative of the relevant prosecutorial authorities and courts of general jurisdiction (Decision of the CC of Russia № 375-O dated October 20, 2005).

3. CONCLUSION

Based on the conducted research, it is concluded that the Russian legislation incorporates advanced legal guarantees developed at the international level and in the national legislation of foreign countries. The ECHR has repeatedly emphasized that the use of modern scientific methods in the criminal justice system must be carefully assessed to balance the potential benefits against the privacy interests of individuals. This is particularly relevant in cases involving the use of digital technologies. Any state claiming to be a pioneer in the development of new technologies has a special responsibility to find the right balance.

In Russia, legislative regulations on restrictions and prohibitions in the digital sphere are based on the general principles of ensuring privacy and respecting the constitutional rights of individuals. Compared to the British and American legislative regulation of privacy restrictions studied by the authors, the Russian legislation is more clearly structured. The main guarantees are introduced in federal legislation, rather than being relegated to the executive branch, which is a characteristic of the legislation of some the US states. Meanwhile, in France in contrast to Russia, the existing practice of the ECHR is reflected in a more detailed and nuanced regulation of specific issues related to state intrusion into citizens' private lives.

The Russian legislation has a bias towards prioritizing public interests over private interests. This is in line with international trends and is justified by the need to effectively combat crimes and other offences. The authors' study of judicial and law enforcement practices suggests that Russian law enforcement agencies often neglect the guarantees established by legislation, resulting in legal disputes arising from the violation of citizens' privacy rights. In accordance with the decisions of higher courts and the legal positions of the CC of Russia, appropriate amendments are made to the legislation. This leads to a gradual change in Russian law enforcement practice, which aims to achieve a balance between private and public interests.

ACKNOWLEDGEMENT

The study is financially supported by the Russian Science Foundation, project № 23-78-10175, https://rscf.ru/project/23-78-10175/

REFERENCES

Affaire Ben Faiza c. France (Requête № 31446/12). Available online: https://hudoc.echr.coe.int/eng?i=001-180657 [Accessed: 23.11.2023]

Affaire Félix Dagregorio et Alain Mosconi c. France (Requête № 65714/11). Available online: https://hudoc.echr.coe.int/rus?i=001-175036 [Accessed: 24.10.2023]

Affaire Trabajo Rueda c. Espagne (Requête № 32600/12). Available online: https://hudoc.echr.coe.int/eng?i=001-173787 [Accessed: 23.11.2023]

Amos, C. et al, (2014). Investigating Privacy Perception and Behavior on Weibo. *Journal of Organizational and End User Computing.* 26(4). P. 43–56.

Barnard-Wills D., (2012). E-safety education: Young people, surveillance and responsibility. *Criminology & Criminal Justice.* 12(3). P. 239–255.

Beck E.N., (2015). The Invisible Digital Identity: Assemblages in Digital Networks. Computers and Composition. 2015. 35. P. 125–140.

BFM, (2018). Obysk u zhurnalista kak sposob raskryt' ego istochniki. Available online: https://www.bfm.ru/news/376395 [Accessed: 24.10.2023] (In Russian)

Brandeis L., Warren S., (1890). The right to privacy. *Harvard Law Review*. vol. IV. NQ 5.

Case of Big Brother Watch and others v. The United Kingdom (Applications №№ 58170/13, 62322/14 and 24960/15). Available online: https://hudoc.echr.coe.int/eng?i=001-210077 [Accessed: 23.11.2023]

Case of Catt v. the United Kingdom (Application № 43514/15). Available online: https://hudoc.echr.coe.int/rus?i=001-189424 [Accessed: 24.10.2023]

Case of Gaughran v. The United Kingdom (Application № 45245/15) Available online: https://hudoc.echr.coe.int/rus?i=001-200817 [Accessed: 17.12.2023]

Case of Kolesnichenko v. Russia (Application № 19856/04). Available online: https://hudoc.echr.coe.int/eng?i=001-92147 [Accessed: 23.11.2023]

Case of M.K. v. France (Application № 19522/09). Available online: https://hudoc.echr.coe.int/eng?i=001-119075 [Accessed: 17.12.2023]

Case of Nagla v. Latvia (Application № 73469/10). Available online: https://hudoc.echr.coe.int/eng?i=001-122374 [Accessed: 24.10.2023]

Case of S. and Marper v. United Kingdom (Applications № 30562/04 and 30566/04). Available online: https://hudoc.echr.coe.int/eng-press?i=003-2571936-2784147 [Accessed: 23.11.2023]

Case of Shimovolos v. Russia (Application № 30194/09). Available online: https://hudoc.echr.coe.int/eng-press?i=003-3581541-4053078 [Accessed: 23.11.2023]

Case of Szabó and Vissy v. Hungary (Application № 37138/14). Available online: https://hudoc.echr.coe.int/eng?i=001-160020 [Accessed: 23.11.2023]

Case of Youth Initiative for Human Rights v. Serbia (Application № 48135/06). Available online: https://hudoc.echr.coe.int/eng?i=001-120955 [Accessed: 17.12.2023]

Chamber Judgments B.B., Gardel, M.B. v. France, (2009). Available online: https://hudoc.echr.coe.int/fre-press?i=003-4480954-5400075 [Accessed: 17.12.2023]

Champion A., (2007). *Trusted Computing and Digital Rights Management.* Clearinghouse. 2007. Available online: https://www.researchgate.net/publication/34658680_Trusted_Computing_and_Digital_Rights_Management_Clearinghouse [Accessed: 24.10.2023]

Chernyh, A.A., (2019). Podhody Konstitucionnogo Suda Rossijskoj Federacii k voprosu o neobhodimosti polucheniya sudebnyh reshenij pri provedenii operativno-rozysknyh meropriyatij s ispol'zovaniem tekhnicheskih sredstv. *Vestnik Sibirskogo yuridicheskogo instituta MVD Rossii.* №. 2 (35). P. 16–24. (In Russian)

CODIS - NDIS Statistics, (2021). Available online: https://www.fbi.gov/services/ laboratory/biometric-analysis/codis/ndis-statistics [Accessed: 23.11.2023]

Delo Rasula Dzhafarova protiv Azerbajdzhana (Zayavlenie № 69981/14). Available online: https://hudoc.echr.coe.int/rus?i=001-165559_[Accessed: 24.10.2023] (In Russian)

Desai, D.R., (2014) Constitutional Limits on Surveillance: Associational Freedom in The Age of Data Hoarding. *Notre Dame Law Review.* 90(2). P. 579–632.

Explanatory note to the Bill No. 1048800-7, (2020). Available online: https://sozd.duma.gov.ru/bill/1048800-7 [Accessed: 23.11.2023] (In Russian)

FINDS (Forensic Information Databases Service). 22/09/22. Available online: https://assets.publishing.service.gov.uk/government/uploads/system/uploads/attachment_data/file/1052529/FIND_Strategy_Board_Policy_Access_and_Use.pdf [Accessed: 23.11.2023]

FNAEG (Fichier national automatisé des empreintes génétiques). Available online: https://www.service-public.fr/particuliers/vosdroits/F34834 [Accessed: 17.12.2023]

Grodzinsky, F.S., Tavani, H.T., (2005). P2P Networks and the Verizon v. RIAA Case: Implications for Personal Privacy and Intellectual Property. *Ethics and Information Technology*. 7(4). P. 243–250.

Hovavko, S.M., (2016). Pravovye garantii soblyudeniya konstitucionnyh prav cheloveka i grazhdanina pri provedenii operativno-rozysknyh meropriyatij. *Obshchestvo i pravo.* 4(58). P. 131–136. (In Russian)

Lavrov, S., (2022). Zayavlenie MID Rossii o zapuske procedury vyhoda iz Soveta Evropy 15 marta 2022 goda. Available online: https://www.mid.ru/ru/press_service/spokesman/official_statement/1804379/ [Accessed: 16.03.2022)

Mantelero, A., (2014). The future of consumer data protection in the EU Re-thinking the «notice and consent» paradigm in the new era of predictive analytics. *Computer Law & Security Review.* 30(6). P. 643–660.

McKee, H.A., (2011). Policy Matters Now and in the Future: Net Neutrality, Corporate Data Mining, and Government Surveillance. *Computers and Composition*. 28(4). P. 276–291.

Mihajlov, M.A., (2015). Sovershenstvovanie sistemy daktiloskopicheskoj registracii: konferenciya v gosudarstvennoj dume. *Uchenye zapiski Krymskogo federal'nogo universiteta imeni V.I. Vernadskogo*. 1. P. 292–305. (In Russian)

NDNAD_Strategy_Board, (2020). Available online: https://assets.publishing.service.gov.uk/government/uploads/system/uploads/attachment_data/file/913011/NDNAD_Strategy_Board_AR_2018-2020_Web_Accessible.pdf [Accessed: 23.11.2023]

Odnoshevin, I.A., (2018). Sudebnyj kontrol' - garantiya konstitucionnyh prav grazhdan, vovlechennyh v sferu operativno-rozysknoj deyatel'nosti. *Yurist - Pravoved.* 4(87). P. 187-192. (In Russian)

Omelin, V.N., (2019). O provedenii operativno-rozysknyh meropriyatij v sluchayah, ne terpyashchih otlagatel'stva. *Zakon i pravo*. 3. P. 112–114. (In Russian)

Preibusch, S., (2015). Privacy behaviors after Snowden. *Communications of the ACM.* 58(5). P. 48–55.

Wicker, S., Schrader, D., (2011). Privacy-Aware Design Principles for Information Networks. *Proceedings of the IEEE.* 2011. 99. P. 330–350.

Winkler, T., Rinner, B., (2011). Securing Embedded Smart Cameras with Trusted Computing. *Eurasip Journal on Wireless Communications and Networking*. DOI: 10.1155/2011/530354

EMPOWERING RURAL AND REMOTE HEALTH PROFESSIONALS TRAINING: A COST-EFFECTIVE SKIN SUTURING SIMULATOR FOR MOBILE LEARNING IN CLINICAL SKILLS ACQUISITION

Rebecca Mosaad[1], Julia Micallef [1], Aliyat Olatinwo[1], Gordon Brock[2] and Adam Dubrowski[1]
[1]Ontario Tech University, Ontario, Canada
[2]Society for Rural Physicians of Canada, Quebec, Canada

ABSTRACT

Introduction: This study aimed to develop a cost-effective suturing and knot typing simulator that aligns with the expectations of experts, addressing the need for affordable yet high-quality medical training tools. The focus was on assessing the efficacy of a silicone skin suture task trainer, created through a 3D printed mold, for use in mobile learning, specifically in rural and remote contexts.
Methods: Rural and remote trainees participating in a skills acquisition workshop, engaged in a 90-minute suturing simulation station. They received minimal feedback from physician educators to simulate independent practice. After the practice, they completed a survey assessing the acceptability and feasibility of the simulator for the intended training purpose, as well as providing feedback for future improvements.
Results: Results from quantitative data revealed the simulator's potential to develop competence (4.2 out of 5) and confidence (4.1 out of 5). Participants expressed a readiness to practice suturing independently using the simulator (4.3 out of 5). Notably, the realism of the simulator was identified as an area for improvement in terms of anatomical correctness (3.6 out of 5) and accuracy (3.4 out of 5), while durability scored high (4 out of 5). Participants found the simulator easy to use (4.4 out of 5) and well-suited for developing cognitive (4.4 out of 5) and psychomotor skills (4.2 out of 5) related to suturing and knot typing. Several improvements were noted, especially in the areas of anatomical representativeness, material selection, and interactions between the simulator and clinical tools.
Conclusions: This paper outlines the acceptability and feasibility of the simulator, designed to complement an online learning management system for hands-on clinical skill learning within the mobile learning paradigm. Despite high self-efficacy and educational value scores, concerns about realism suggest a need for a hybrid design approach that balances costs and anatomical fidelity in simulator development.

KEYWORDS

Simulation-Based Education, Mobile Learning, Additive Manufacturing, Rural and Remote Education, Suturing Techniques, Clinical Education

1. INTRODUCTION

The rising popularity of Simulation-Based Education (SBE) in healthcare training stems from its ability to offer a platform for healthcare professionals to master essential procedural skills before applying them to real patients (Kothari et al., 2017). Typically, situated in simulation laboratories, most SBE activities facilitate the teaching and learning of crucial competencies and skills necessary for healthcare professionals (Al-Elq, 2010). These simulated environments serve as experiential classrooms, providing nursing students with a practical, clinical-like setting without jeopardizing patient safety. This instructional model is known as the Centralized Model of Simulation-Based Education (Ce-SBE), where learners convene at a simulation lab to practice skills using commercially available simulators under supervision and expert feedback (Barth et al., 2022).

A notable feature of SBE is its adaptability to mobile learning, enabling learners to practice hands-on clinical skills beyond the confines of simulation laboratories, from the comfort of their homes or other locations. This approach is termed the Decentralized Model of Simulation-Based Education (De-SBE) (Barth et al., 2022). To implement De-SBE successfully, two technological prerequisites are essential: a dedicated Learning Management System (LMS), and an affordable, flexible, and portable simulator (Barth et al., 2022).

In previous work, we proposed a theoretical, evidence-based model for structuring remote, online psychomotor skills acquisition through LMS (Dubrowski et al., 2021). This system comprises four main components aligned with the elements of deliberate practice, encompassing: a) opportunities for hands-on repetition; b) mechanisms to enhance motivation and consistency in LMS usage; and c) provision of accurate feedback. Hands-on practice is a key component to distinguish remote and online LMSs for psychomotor skills acquisition from those designed for cognitive and affective skills. Various methods, from take-home task trainer simulators, to off-the-shelf solutions, to DIY (do it yourself) approaches can enable facilitation.

Building on our prior work with additive manufacturing (AM) (Clarke et al., 2022; Micallef et al., 2022), we have developed an inexpensive simulator suitable for De-SBE, specifically targeting suturing and knot-tying skills. These fundamental procedural clinical skills necessitate ongoing manual practice to foster the required hand-eye coordination and dexterity. Medical students, nurses, and paramedics stand to benefit from the opportunity to hone these skills wherever and whenever they find convenient (Barth et al., 2022).

The objective of this study was to produce an inexpensive suturing and knot typing simulator that met the quality and functionality expectations of experts (Micallef et al., 2021). Thus, this study aimed to assess the perceived efficacy of a cost-effective silicone skin suture task trainer, crafted from a 3D printed mold, for use in De-SBE.

2. MATERIALS & METHODS

Participants: A total of fourteen junior rural and remote physicians participated in one, two-hour workshop. This was hosted during the 30th Annual Rural and Remote Medicine Course hosted by the Society of Rural Physicians of Canada (SRPC) in Niagara Falls, Ontario in April 2023. They practiced the suturing skills using the suturing simulator developed, as well as animal models (porcine feet), under limited supervision (two tutors who answered questions). This participant group was selected as they practice in rural and remote areas and therefore they understand the context in which wheel simulators are intended to be used.

Simulator development: The development of the simulator was done through a two-step process. The mold was designed through the Fusion360™ software application. It was then printed using an Ultimaker S5 3D printer using Ecotough™ filament material. The silicone skin was made using the two-part Ecoflex™ 00-20 FAST, mixed with Silc-Pig™ colouring for pigmentation. The assembly was done in a three-steps: 1) a layer of silicone was poured to cover half the volume of the mold and left to cure; 2) then a layer of mesh was placed on the cured silicone, followed by a second layer of silicone poured on top; 3) finally, the simulator was left at room temperature to cure in the mold for 60 minutes before it was removed. Both the 3D printed mold and the silicone skin suture task trainer were designed and manufactured in the Ontario Tech University, maxSIMhealth laboratory

Data collection setup: Each participant was provided with a needle driver, suturing scissors, sutures (4-0), surgical tape, anesthetic (lidocaine), skin forceps, latex gloves, 18-gauge needle, syringe, (right), as well as the suturing simulator (left).

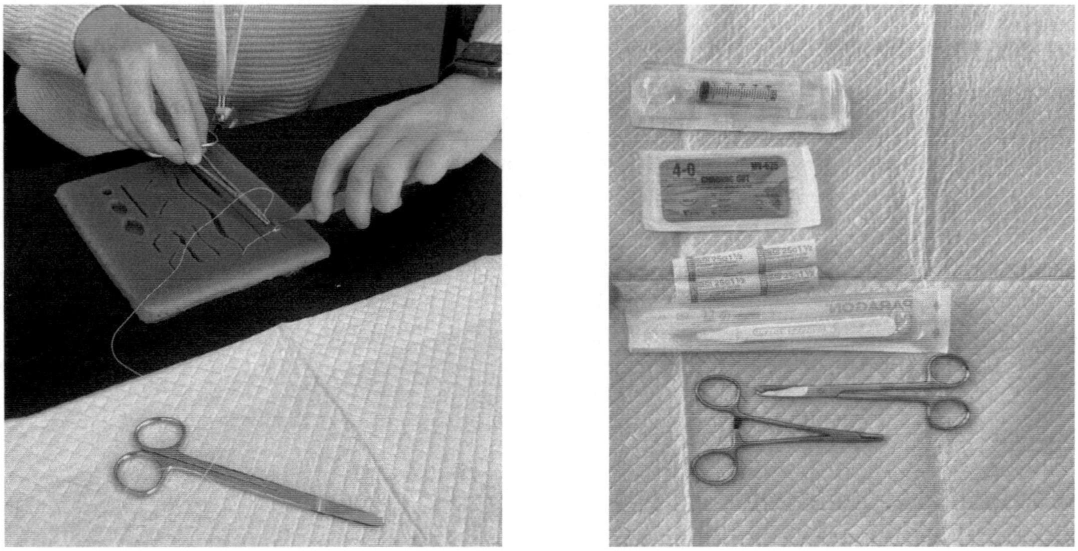

Figure 1. Experimental set up that was used for data collection. Left panel: Tools provided to the participants during the workshop; right panel: skin suture simulator

Procedure: Before each skill development session, all participants were asked to complete a consent form and were provided time to raise any questions or concerns about the study. Each participant then completed a 90-minute suturing stimulation station during the conference workshop, where they received approximately 10 minutes of instruction from a physician educator followed by time to practice their suturing technique independently. The two physician educators circulated during this time and were available for additional assistance if the students required it. The educators were instructed to provide minimal feedback in order to simulate independent practice. The last 5 minutes of the session were designated for participants to complete workshop evaluation forms.

3. DATA COLLECTION INSTRUMENT AND ANALYSES

Quantitative data: At the end of the two-hour workshop, all participants were asked to fill out workshop evaluation forms. In addition to standard educational quality improvement evaluation forms collected routinely by SRPC (which were not used for this study) a short survey questionnaire that evaluated the simulator was distributed to participants. The survey, following a modified version of the Michigan Standard Simulation Experience Scale (MiSSES) template, was used to assess the fidelity, functionality, and the teaching quality of the simulator (Seagull & Rooney, 2014). There were three main sections to the survey: (1) self-efficacy; (2) realism and; (3) educational value and overall rating. In total, there were nine, 5-point Likert scale questions. The survey was developed as a Google Forms, but a printed version was provided to the participants.

Qualitative data: The survey also included five open-ended prompting questions designed to elicit qualitative responses from participants: (1) Please comment on how the simulator may improve your self-efficacy; (2) Please comment on how the simulator's realism could be improved; (3) Please suggest any changes you would make to the simulator; (4) Please suggest specific ways to improve your learning experience; (5) Provide alternative simulators that you may have used to train this skill in the past, and how does it compare to the current simulator. These comments were transferred verbatim into a single Google Sheet document for analysis.

To enhance the rigor of the thematic analysis, two researchers were involved in the coding process. Each researcher independently read through every comment, identifying and developing initial coding themes. Following this initial coding phase, the researchers engaged in a collaborative session during which they compared their independently generated themes. Through an hour-long online discussion, the researchers aligned their coding themes, identifying overarching themes that were common across the comments (Braun & Clarke, 2006).

Subsequently, each researcher independently reviewed all the comments using the newly established codebook based on the agreed-upon themes. The thematic analysis was conducted using Google Sheets, providing a structured and collaborative platform for organizing and synthesizing the data. In the final step of the analysis, the agreed-upon themes were synthesized, and supporting comments were selected to illustrate each theme.

4. RESULTS

Quantitative data: The survey data were considered ordinal data and are presented as mean and standard deviations (SDs) for each question (Jamieson, 2004; Norman, 2010). This was chosen as our participant numbers were low and the objective of the analysis was to inform the design rather than to provide evidence of validity. The results from the survey are broken down into quantitative data and qualitative data.

The results for the quantitative data (Figure 2) indicate that the simulator has the potential to develop competence (4.2 out of 5) and confidence (4.1 out of 5), and the participants expressed that they would be able to practice the suturing skills independently with this simulator (4.3 out of 5). The realism of the simulator appeared to be its weakest point in terms of the overall anatomical correctness (3.6 out of 5) and accuracy (3.4 out of 5), while the durability was scored high (4 out of 5). Finally, the participants perceived the simulator to be easy to use (4.4 out of 5), and well suited for independent development of both cognitive (4.4 out of 5) and psychomotor skills (4.2 out of 5) related to suturing and knot typing.

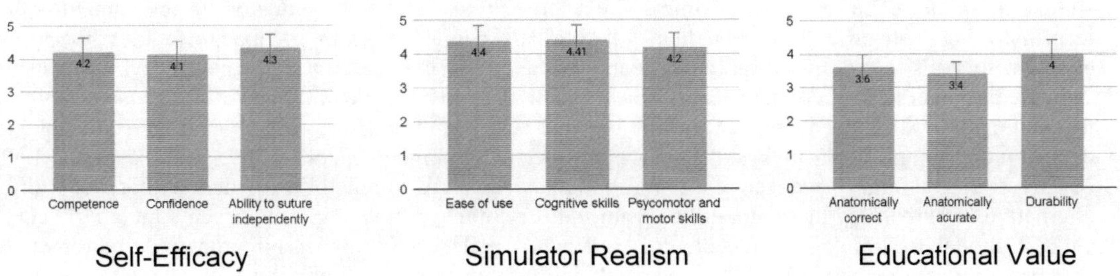

Figure 2. Averages and standard deviations were obtained from the surveys on the 5-point Likert scale in the areas of self-efficacy, the simulator's realism, and the educational value of the simulator

Qualitative data: The participants provided a total of 21 short-answer comments, evenly distributed among the four prompting questions. Through an hour-long online discussion, the researchers aligned their coding themes, identifying four overarching themes that were common across the comments. These were:

Simulator Realism: One of the comments suggested uncertainty about the simulator's superiority over other training methods. Issues like flatness, lack of mimicry of skin layers, and the need for increased tensile strength in plastic suggests a focus on making the simulator more realistic to enhance training. "The simulator worked but not sure it would have been better than other ways" (Participant 3).

Material Properties: Comments about the simulator being too rubbery, the need for layers, and the influence of glue in silicone highlight the importance of the materials used in the simulator. Improving these properties could contribute to a more authentic training experience. Furthermore, a number of participants described issues with the thread ripping through the silicone too easily which suggests that more attention needs to be paid to the interaction between medical tools and the simulator. "Still quite rubbery. Does not mimic the layers of skin well." (Participant 8). "Thread ripped threw the simulator too easily and gripped the needle/ thread too strongly" (Participant 10).

Cost and Alternatives: Comparisons between pig skin, foam, plastic models, and orange peel highlight considerations of cost, fidelity, and ethical concerns (as in the case of using animals). That is, although the simulator was developed to be a cost-effective ($5.00 USD) alternative, non-standardized simulators such as animal and plant-based ones were perceived as cheaper yet effective simulators that can be used in low-stakes De-SBE training. "Orange was better. Pig skin is more pliable" (Participant 10).

Skill Level and Background Knowledge: The need to clarify the skill level or background knowledge required for advanced levels suggests consideration for tailoring the simulator to different proficiency levels in surgical training. "Clarify skill level/ideal background knowledge needed to do advance level" (Participant 8).

5. DISCUSSION

This idea of using online LMS technology geared toward mobile learning, such as the one described here and referred to as De-SBE, for health professions training in psychomotor, and clinical skills was tested in the past (Habti et al., 2021). However, this mobile learning model was tested in a major urban center and with a group of highly specialized trainees. Specifically, the participants, senior surgical trainees, learned a hand-sewn bowel anastomosis procedure, using a custom-designed online, LMS with the results indicating that the surgical residents liked this training platform and found that it helped improve their understanding of the technique (Habti et al., 2021). Because the De-SBE paradigm requires both a dedicated LMS to provide information, guidance, and feedback (Dubrowski et al., 2021), as well as cost-effective simulators accessible to the learners where they are. This ensures they are suitable for deployment in rural and remote contexts and used for generalists training. The principle of mobile learning, and the multidimensional aspects of education, present ample opportunity for the integration of simulators through the learning management system. The current project tested the acceptability and feasibility of such simulators, as well as sought end-point users' feedback on how the simulator could be improved to deliver the desired learning outcomes.

The rural and remote learners expressed high self-efficacy scores after practicing the suturing skills on the simulator. In the realm of learning clinical skills through cost-effective simulators in the context of mobile learning, a high self-efficacy score indicates individuals' confidence in their capacity to adeptly acquire and apply these skills in real life situations on patients. Self-efficacy, as defined in psychology, encapsulates an individual's belief in their competence to execute such skills (Micallef et al., 2023). These results suggest that the simulator was deemed both an acceptable and feasible option, affording the individual learners the opportunity to hone in on their skills in a controlled environment. Additionally, because of the lightway construction and highly reduced costs of manufacturing, the simulator provided a more cost-effective alternative to purchasing these simulators from industry, and/ or traveling to an urban simulation center, i.e. Ce-SBE model, for training (Siraj et al., 2021). When considering mobile learning for rural and remote health care provider's training, the flexibility and accessibility of our solution highlights the potential impact on skill development, without the need to travel and leaving patients unattended (Doucet et al., 2017).

Furthermore, the simulator received very high scores (4.2 out of 5) on the educational value it carried. In the realm of contemporary health professionals' education, especially in the context of rural and remote training, a high score on the educational value of a simulator signifies a recognition among learners of the simulator's effectiveness as a pedagogical instrument (Micallef et al., 2023). This recognition extends beyond the mere utilization of simulation technology, encompassing its potential to enhance the learning experience and foster skill acquisition. The amalgamation of clinical skill acquisition and cost-effective simulators, coupled with online learning technologies underscores the dynamic evolution of health professionals' education methodologies. The positive relationship between a high educational value score and the integration of mobile learning suggests that learners acknowledge the transformative impact of ubiquitous access to educational resources. This alignment reflects a paradigm shift in health professionals' education, where learners increasingly recognize the versatility and convenience of mobile learning in conjunction with hands-on simulation experiences (Guérard-Poirie et. al., 2023; Blouin et. al., 2023; Pelletier et. al., 2023). Future iterations of this simulator's implementation, and data collection should consider a larger sample size.

Although the learners reported high self-efficacy and high educational value of the simulator, they also highlighted areas for improvement of the physical and anatomical features of the simulator. The feedback gathered revealed several areas for improvement, primarily centered around simulator realism. Participants expressed uncertainty regarding the simulator's superiority compared to other training methods, citing issues such as flatness, a lack of mimicry of skin layers, and a need for increased tensile strength in the plastic components. To enhance the training experience, there is a clear call for improvements in simulator realism, ensuring that it more accurately mirrors the complexities of human anatomy (Hamstra & Dubrowksi, 2005). One participant remarked, "The simulator worked, but not sure it would have been better than other ways", emphasizing the importance of addressing these concerns with realism to establish the simulator as a preferred and effective training tool.

Another critical aspect for refinement lies in the material properties of the simulator. Participants noted that the simulator felt too rubbery, lacked layers, and exhibited issues with the thread ripping through the silicone too easily. These comments underscore the significance of selecting and refining materials to create a more authentic training experience (Habti et al., 2021). Attention to detail in the interaction between medical tools and the simulator has also been identified as a critical, necessitating adjustments to material properties to better simulate the tactile and structural aspects of real tissue. Furthermore, considerations around cost-effectiveness and alternatives emerged, with participants comparing the simulator to various materials such as pig skin, foam, plastic models, and even orange peels. While the simulator was designed to be cost-effective the participants perceived alternatives, such as animal and plant-based simulators, as potentially cheaper and effective options for low-stakes training. Balancing cost, fidelity, and ethical concerns becomes paramount in refining the simulator's design to meet the diverse needs of surgical training (Siraj et al., 2021). Lastly, participants highlighted the importance of clarifying the skill level or background knowledge required for advanced levels of training, emphasizing the need to tailor the simulator to different proficiency levels in surgical training to maximize its educational impact.

In conclusion, the suturing simulator was considered a functional and cost-effective simulator with a cost of approximately $5.00 USD. This is because it was designed and produced following a design-to-cost approach, meaning cost was the most important constraint taken into consideration throughout the process (Siraj et al., 2021). Because of the cost-effective nature of the simulator, and its overall acceptability as a training tool, this simulator is ideal for use in the De-SBE context, especially when combined with a dedicated LMS (Wahab & Dubrowski, 2022).

6. CONCLUSION

This paper described the acceptability and feasibility of a simulator designed to complement an online learning management system to provide hands-on learning of clinical skills within the mobile learning paradigm. The simulator was an acceptable and feasible learning tool, as evidenced by high self-efficacy and educational value scores. However, the participants also expressed concerns about the realism of the simulator, suggesting a hybrid design approach, which places equal attention on costs and realism.

ACKNOWLEDGMENT

This work was supported by the Canada Research Chair and Canadian Foundation for Innovation: the John R. Evans Leaders Fund (JELF) to Adam Dubrowski and the Canada Graduate Scholarships-Masters program awarded to Julia Micallef through the Natural Sciences and Engineering Research Council of Canada (NSERC).

REFERENCES

Al-Elq, A. H. (2010). Simulation-based medical teaching and learning. *Journal of family & community medicine, 17*(1), 35–40. https://www.ncbi.nlm.nih.gov/pmc/articles/PMC3195067/

Barth, B., Arutiunian, A., Micallef, J., Sivanathan, M., Wang, Z., Chorney, D., Salmers, E., McCabe, J., & Dubrowski, A. (2022). From Centralized to Decentralized Model of Simulation-Based Education: Curricular Integration of Take-Home Simulators in Nursing Education. *Cureus.* 14(6), e26373. https://doi.org/10.7759/cureus.26373

Blouin, V., Bénard, F., Pelletier, F., Abdo, S., Meloche-Dumas, L., Kapralos. B., Dubrowski, A., & Patocskai, E. (2023) Optimizing the Learner's Role in Feedback: Development of a Feedback-Preparedness Online Application for Medical Students in the Clinical Setting. *Cureus*. 15(5):e38722. https://doi.org/10.7759%2Fcureus.38722

Braun, V. & Clarke, V. (2006). Using thematic analysis in psychology. *Qualitative Research in Psychology*, 3 (2). pp. 77-101. http://dx.doi.org/10.1191/1478088706qp063oa

Clarke, K. M., Micallef, J., Jolly, A. K., Sivanathan, M., Siraj, S., Button, D., Patey, C., & Dubrowski, A. (2022). Hacking Intraosseous Infusion Skills Training With 3D Printing: maxSIMIO Drilling System. *Cureus*. 14(11), e31272. https://doi.org/10.7759/cureus.31272

Doucet, G., Ryan, S., Bartellas, M., Parsons, M., Dubrowski, A., & Renouf, T. (2017) Modelling and Manufacturing of a 3D Printed Trachea for Cricothyroidotomy Simulation. *Cureus*. 18;9(8):e1575. https://pubmed.ncbi.nlm.nih.gov/29057187/

Dubrowski, A., Kapralos, B., Peisachovich, E., Da Silva, C., & Torres, A. (2021). A Model for an Online Learning Management System for Simulation-Based Acquisition of Psychomotor Skills in Health Professions Education. *Cureus, 13*(3), e14055. https://doi.org/10.7759/cureus.14055

Guérard-Poirier, N., Meloche-Dumas, L., Beniey, M., Torres, A., Kapralos, B., Dhane, M., Mercier, F., Younan, R., Dubrowski, A., & Patocskai, E. (2023) The exploration of remote simulation strategies for the acquisition of psychomotor skills in medicine: a pilot randomized controlled trial. *Cureus*. 288:372-382. https://doi.org/10.7759/cureus.14055

Habti, M., Bénard, F., Arutiunian, A., Bérubé, S., Cadoret, D., Meloche-Dumas, L., Torres, A., Kapralos, B., Mercier, F., Dubrowski, A., & Patocskai, E. (2021). Development and Learner-Based Assessment of a Novel, Customized, 3D Printed Small Bowel Simulator for Hand-Sewn Anastomosis Training. *Cureus*. 13(12), e20536. https://doi.org/10.7759/cureus.20536

Hamstra, SJ., & Dubrowski, A. (2005). Effective Training and Assessment of Surgical Skills, and the Correlates of Performance. *Surgical Innovation*. https://doi.org/10.1177/155335060501200110

Jamieson S. (2004). Likert scales: how to (ab)use them. *Medical education, 38*(12), 1217–1218. https://doi.org/10.1111/j.1365-2929.2004.02012.x

Kothari, L. G., Shah, K., & Barach, P. (2017). Simulation based medical education in graduate medical education training and assessment programs. *Progress in Pediatric Cardiology*. 44, 33-42. https://www.sciencedirect.com/science/article/abs/pii/S1058981317300097?via%3Dihub

Micallef, J., Arutiunian, A., Hiley, J., Benson, A., & Dubrowski, A. (2021). The Development of a Cost-Effective Infant Intraosseous Infusion Simulator for Neonatal Resuscitation Program Training. *Cureus*. 13(10), e18824. https://doi.org/10.7759/cureus.18824

Micallef, J., Broekhuyse, A., Vuyyuru, S., Wax, R., Sridhar, S. K., Heath, J., Clarke, S., & Dubrowski, A. (2022). Application of 3D Printing in Training Health Care Providers; the Development of Diverse Facial Overlays for Simulation-Based Medical Training. *Cureus*. 14(7), e26637. https://doi.org/10.7759/cureus.26637

Micallef, J., Button, D., Uribe Quevedo, A., McClatchey, C., King, L., & Dubrowski, A. (2023). The Perceived Effectiveness of Various Forms of Feedback on the Acquisition of Technical Skills by Advanced Learners in Simulation-Based Health Professions Education. *Cureus*. 15(8), e44279. https://doi.org/10.7759/cureus.44279

Norman G. (2010). Likert scales, levels of measurement and the "laws" of statistics. *Advances In Health Sciences Education: Theory And Practice*. 15(5), 625–632. https://doi.org/10.1007/s10459-010-9222-y

Pelletier, F., Torres, A., Meloche-Dumas, L., Guérard-Poirier, N., Kaviani, A., Kapralos, B., Mercier, F., Dubrowski, A., & Patocskai, E. (2023) The Role of Collaborative Observational Practice and Feedback-Discourse to Promote Remote Acquisition of Technical Surgical Skills. *Journal of Surgical Research*. https://www.journalofsurgicalresearch.com/article/S0022-4804(23)00049-5/fulltext

Seagull, F. J., & Rooney, D. M. (2014). Filling a void: developing a standard subjective assessment tool for surgical simulation through focused review of current practices. *Surgery*. 156(3), 718–722. https://www.surgjournal.com/article/S0039-6060(14)00218-9/fulltext

Siraj, S., Sivanathan, M., Abdo, S., Micallef, J., Gino, B., Buttu, D., Clarke, K. M., Mnaymneh, M., Torres, A., Brock, G., Pereira, C., & Dubrowski, A. (2022). Hands-On Practice on Sustainable Simulators in the Context of Training for Rural and Remote Practice Through a Fundamental Skills Workshop. *Cureus*. 14(9), e28840. https://doi.org/10.7759/cureus.28840

Wahab, S., & Dubrowski, A. (2022) Adapting the Gamified Educational Networking (GEN) Learning Management System to Deliver a Virtual Simulation Training Module to Determine the Enhancement of Learning and Performance Outcomes. *Cureus*. 14(6): e26332. https://doi.org/10.7759/cureus.26332

GEOGEBRA APPLETS FOR FOSTERING CONCEPTUAL UNDERSTANDING IN ALGEBRA

Ma. Louise Antonette N. De Las Peñas[1], Mark Anthony C. Tolentino[1], Maria Alva Q. Aberin[1], Agnes D. Garciano[1], Juan Carlo F. Mallari[1], Jumela F. Sarmiento[†,1] and Debbie Marie B. Verzosa[2]
[1]*Department of Mathematics, Ateneo De Manila University, Philippines*
[2]*Department of Mathematics and Statistics, University of Southern Mindanao, Philippines*

ABSTRACT

This paper discusses two *GeoGebra* applets, *Radical* and *Parabola*, that are designed to strengthen the conceptual understanding of specific topics in algebra. The design and pedagogical basis of the applets are presented. The integration of the applets in teaching Grade 9 mathematics in a partner high school in the Philippines is then discussed. Finally, we report feedback gathered from students and teachers during this integration. Their feedback indicates the potential of these applets for improving students' learning of algebra.

KEYWORDS

Mobile Technology in Teaching Mathematics, Mathematical Applets, *Geogebra* Applets, Algebra Applets

1. INTRODUCTION

In the time of the COVID-19 pandemic in the Philippines, the Department of Education (DepEd) has called for the blended learning modality in schools (DepEd Memo 012, 2020). This introduced several challenges in the teaching and learning of mathematics. Due to the limited time for DepEd to prepare printed materials in lieu of face-to-face classes, there was a need to prepare more instructional materials to help teachers address the Most Essential Learning Competencies (MELCs) prescribed by DepEd's curriculum (DepEd 2020). Under projects funded by the Philippine government (De Las Peñas et al, 2023, De Las Peñas et al 2022), the authors collaborated with particular DepEd School Division Offices to design and create mathematical applications (apps) accompanied with teaching guides and instructional videos to provide teachers with alternative means to teach mathematics. These apps are also being recommended for use in the new normal under the DepEd's *Basic Education Learning Recovery Plan* in which schools are directed towards addressing learning gaps brought about by the pandemic (DepEd Memo 664, 2022).

This short paper contributes to the literature on mathematical learning and the role of technology during the time of COVID-19 and the new normal. In particular, we present two mathematical applets, namely *Radical* and *Parabola*, that were created under the aforementioned government projects and that were designed for Grade 9 students in algebra. We focus on these two applets that give students opportunities to interact with mathematical concepts in a dynamic geometry environment (DGE). These were created using the open-access software *GeoGebra* (https://www.geogebra.org/), making these easily accessible through contemporary technologies such as tablets and mobile phones.

The applets highlight different instructional design features that can be provided with digital tools to support the teaching and learning of mathematics. The *Radical* applet employs the immediate feedback feature that supports practice, where students get the opportunity to strengthen content knowledge previously acquired by practicing at their own pace, and repeatedly, as often as needed (Hillmayr et al., 2020). The *Parabola* applet, on the other hand, makes use of the dragging mode of a DGE to arrive at dynamic families of graphs and to observe relationships among various elements such as the graphs and their corresponding equations. This makes the applet a potential tool for students to engage in conjecture making (Baccaglini-Frank & Marrioti, 2011). Through these features, the two applets aim to add to the large repository of applets that are available online and demonstrate how educators can enhance existing applets with additional instructional design features. For example, while the GeoGebra repository contains many applets on radicals, few if any offer prompts or hints. Similarly, it includes many applets on parabolas, but there appears to be no applet that simultaneously displays the vertex and standard form of a parabola together with its discriminant.

The interested reader can access the applets discussed in this paper and the other mathematical apps of the aforementioned projects from the website https://mathplusresources.wordpress.com/.

2. DESCRIPTION OF THE APPLETS

Two of the mathematical apps that we have designed are applets created with the algebra/geometry software *GeoGebra*. Existing studies around the world point towards the affordances in using *GeoGebra* in mathematics education (Antonini & Lisarelli, 2021; Azizah et al., 2021; Tong et al, 2021; Mudaly et al., 2019; Wassie & Zergaw, 2019; Shadaan et al., 2013). In our case, we found that *GeoGebra* applets are appropriate for the Philippine setting as they can provide wider accessibility for teachers and students since these can run on mobile technologies (both Android and iOS). Moreover, *GeoGebra* allows for the creation of content that can be exported as interactive and dynamic worksheets published as applets. This made it easy for us to create instructional materials on topics that were needed immediately based on the requests of teachers in our partner schools during the time of COVID-19. The applets are straightforward to use via *GeoGebra*'s tools that are intuitive and easy to manipulate. Advantageous to teachers was *GeoGebra*'s "construction protocol bar," through which they gathered insights on the processes used to create the applets. This allowed them to create their own applets for other topics and was helpful given their limited time for teaching preparations.

2.1 The *Radicals* Applet

The *Radicals* applet is designed to address one of the learning competencies for Grade 9 mathematics under the content strand algebra, which is "simplifying radical expressions using the law of radicals" (DepEd, 2016). The objective of the app is to strengthen the student's conceptual understanding of simplifying radicals, particularly breaking down the radicand into perfect and non-perfect *n*th powers and applying the property $\sqrt[n]{ab} = \sqrt[n]{a}\,\sqrt[n]{b}$. The students are guided to solve each question provided by the applet (Figure 1(a)). Students can verify their answer using the applet and get appropriate feedback (Figure 1(a)-(b)). Afterwards, the students proceed to the next question. Note that the applet randomizes the questions, so the questions vary per student.

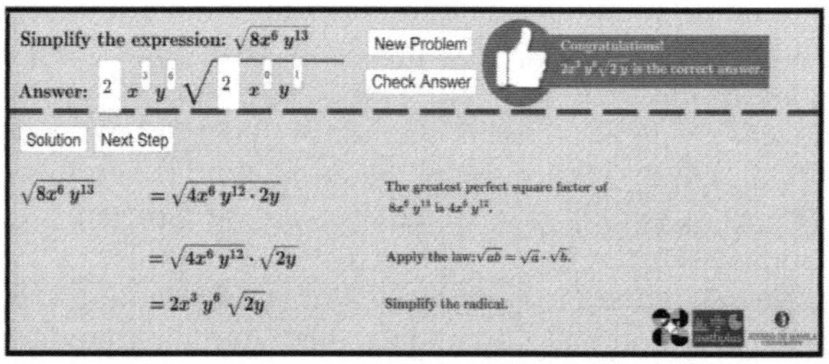

(a)

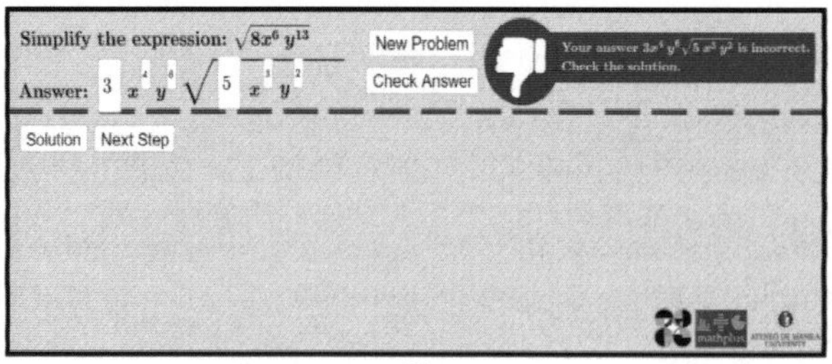

(b)

Figure 1. Screenshots from the *Radical* app showing: (a) step-by-step solution and feedback on a correct answer; and (b) feedback on a wrong answer

2.2 The *Parabola* Applet

The *Parabola* applet addresses the following Grade 9 learning competencies: graphs a quadratic function of the form $y = a(x - h)^2 + k$ (domain, range, intercepts, axis of symmetry, vertex, direction of opening of the parabola). The applet allows the student to analyze the effects of changing the values of a, h, and k in the quadratic function $y = a(x - h)^2 + k$ on its graph. Sliders are provided so students can experiment on the values of a, h, k (See Fig. 2). It also gives the value of the discriminant, so students can explore its connection to other properties of its graph, such as its x-intercepts.

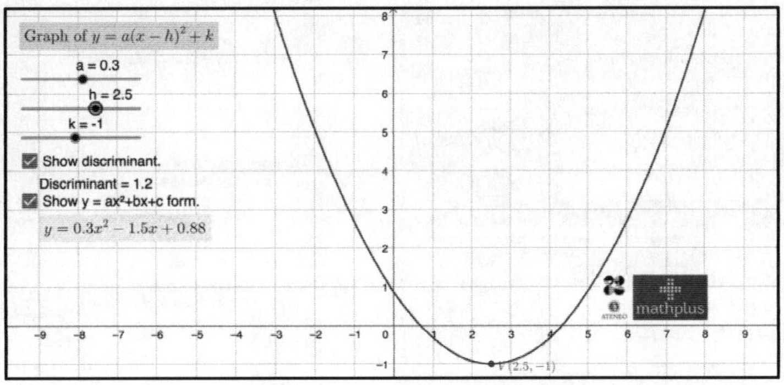

Figure 2. A screenshot of the *Parabola* applet showing the sliders on the values a, h, and k

3. PEDAGOGICAL BASIS OF THE APPLETS

The *Radicals* applet is an example of the use of technology to support "practicing," where repeated use of technology deepens and develops skills that foster understanding of mathematical concepts and strengthens content knowledge (Thurm & Barzel, 2021; Hillmayr et al., 2020). The repetitive feature of the applet allows for deliberate practice, which can modify and enhance previously learned skills and build advanced skills in addition to pre-existing ones (Ericsson, 2016; Garciano et al., 2023). The design of incorporating a feedback mechanism in the applet is crucial so that students engage in a process of practice when working independently without the aid of the teacher (Bokhove, 2011).

The *Parabola* applet is anchored on the framework that technology helps in the teaching and learning of geometry through dynamic interactive graphical representations (Laborde et al., 2006). For example, exploring the graphs of $y = a(x - h)^2 + k$ and using sliders for a, h, and k gives students the opportunity to test, conjecture, and generalize effects of the changing values for a, h, and k. The sliders serve as a dragging mechanism. The dragging feature in a dynamic geometry environment (DGE) illustrates the transformation technology can bring in the representations of mathematical objects, the family of graphs in this case, representing invariant relationships with each of a, h, k (Laborde & Laborde, 2014). The graphs are no longer static objects and are now dynamic objects.

4. INTEGRATION AND USE OF THE APPLETS

In this section we discuss how the *Radical* and *Parabola* applets were used in the teaching and learning of Grade 9 mathematics in a high school in Quezon City, Philippines in school years 2021-2022 and 2022-2023.

For 2021-2022, DepEd implemented a blended-modality form of instruction, so there were synchronous and asynchronous classes. Modules and instructional materials, prescribed by DepEd for the students, were distributed by the school administrators to the parents. During this time, teachers met their students at least once a week through Google Classroom. Written works were required from the students on a regular basis, which were to be done asynchronously. In the synchronous classes, the applets were used to introduce the lesson (Figure 3(a)-(b)). Follow-through sessions were done asynchronously by asking the students to use the applets for exploration and to answer exercises (Figure 4(a)-(b)).

For 2022-2023, DepEd resumed face-to-face classes in schools. The applets were used in the classroom for the lessons, and for assigned homework.

We were able to gather feedback from teachers and students based on the integration of the two applets in school years 2021-2022 and 2022-2023. We discuss these feedback below.

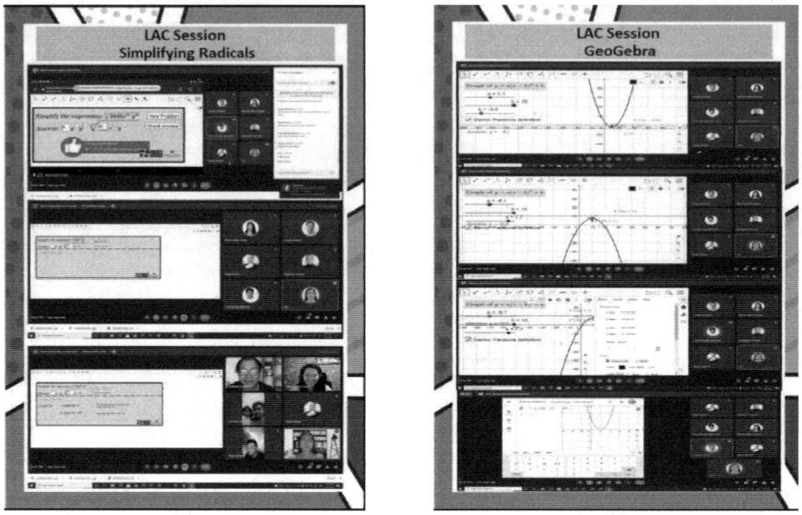

(a) (b)

Figure 3. Screenshots of the use of the a) *Radical* applet and b) *Parabola* applet in Google classroom

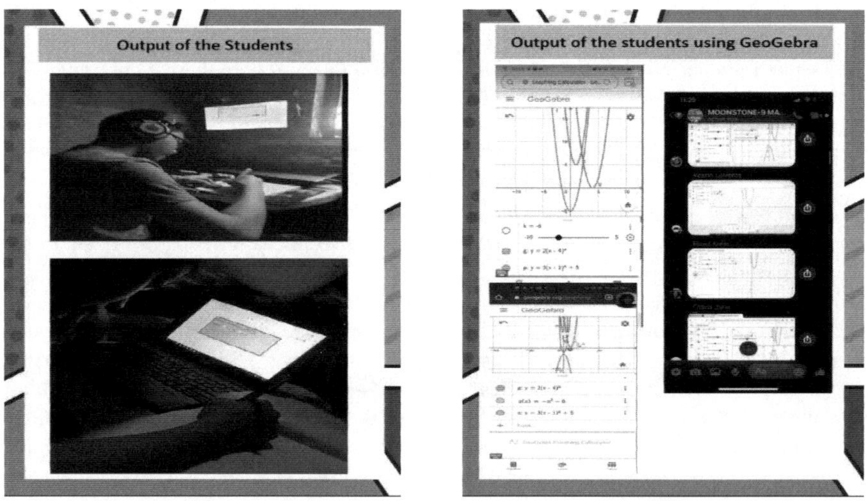

(a) (b)

Figure 4. Screenshots of the work of the students carried out asynchronously

a) *Radical* applet: We were able to get qualitative feedback from teachers and students on the use of the applet during the blended modality of instruction in 2021-2022. First, specific instructions were given by the teachers to the students on how to use the *GeoGebra* applets, including downloading instructions (Figure 5(a)). The applet was used in the synchronous sessions for teaching the concept. Then students were asked to answer exercises given by the applet asynchronously. For each radical expression, they were first asked to record their solutions in their notebooks. Then afterwards, they were asked to check their solutions versus the detailed solution provided by the applet. They submitted snapshots of their work through Messenger to their teachers (Figure 5(b)).

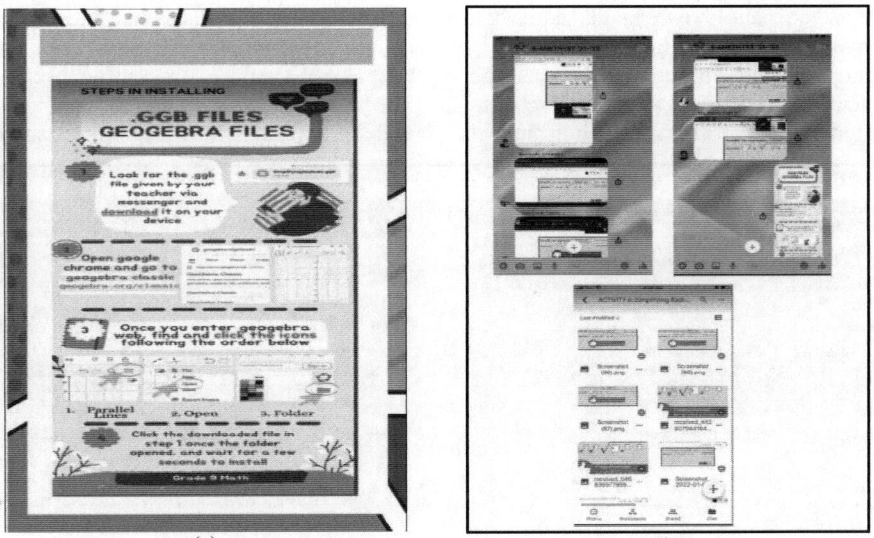

(a) (b)

Figure 5. (a) Instructions on the *GeoGebra* files; (b) screenshots of sample solutions on simplifying radicals sent through messenger app to the algebra teacher

During an online Program Implementation Review (PIR) a few months after the use of the *Radical* applet, the teachers reported the experiences in their classes. Parents also gave comments with regards to the experiences of their children. In general, the applet helped the students understand the simplification of radical expressions through constant practice. It was useful that the applet was able to generate various types of expressions, and the students did not only rely on the exercises given by the teacher or those provided in the modules. This was also useful for the teachers, because of the limited opportunities they had to create as many exercises as possible for the students. The teachers shared the following during the PIR: The students remarked that being able to see the detailed solutions with the reasoning of each step from the applet was helpful. They liked that they were able to identify their mistakes from the solution provided by the applet since they were not always with their teachers. Working with the applet kept them interested in doing the exercises.

b) *Parabola* applet: In 2022-2023, during the first year of implementation of face-to face classes after the pandemic, we were able to obtain an initial quantitative assessment on the use of the applet. While teaching the lesson on quadratic functions, four Grade 9 sections were randomly selected to form two pairs of experimental and control classes in such a way that each pair (experimental and control) of classes are taught by the same teacher; thus, two teachers are involved. Pretests and posttests were administered to the four classes.

The experimental classes used the *Parabola* applet. Each student had a tablet where the applet was installed. The worksheets (Figure. 6(a)-(b)) were answered by the students individually on different days. One worksheet (Figure. 6(a)) dealt with exploring the graph $y = a(x - h)^2 + k$ and using sliders for a, h, and k. The students were first asked to explore the effects of changing the values of a, h, and k on the graphs and write their observations. Then they were asked to make conjectures on properties of the graphs such as the coordinates of the vertex, equation of the axis of symmetry, opening of the graph, and domain and range of $f(x) = a(x - h)^2 + k$. For the second worksheet (Figure. 6(b)), one type of questioning involved giving specific equations (e.g., $y = -2(x + 1)^2 +7$), and students were asked to provide the vertex, x- and y-intercepts, domain, and range. Another type of question involved giving properties of the graph of the parabola and the student was asked to give a possible equation for the parabola that satisfied the properties.

The control sections employed the traditional approach, where the teachers taught the lesson without the *Parabola* applet and the worksheets.

Based on the data shown in the table below, for one pair of experimental and control classes, the experimental class showed a higher level of improvement from their pretest to posttest scores when compared to the control. On the other hand, the other pair of classes only exhibited little difference in their levels of improvement. Thus, these results indicate that the use of the *Parabola* applet and other related resources (teaching guide, student worksheets) may have the potential to affect students' learning positively.

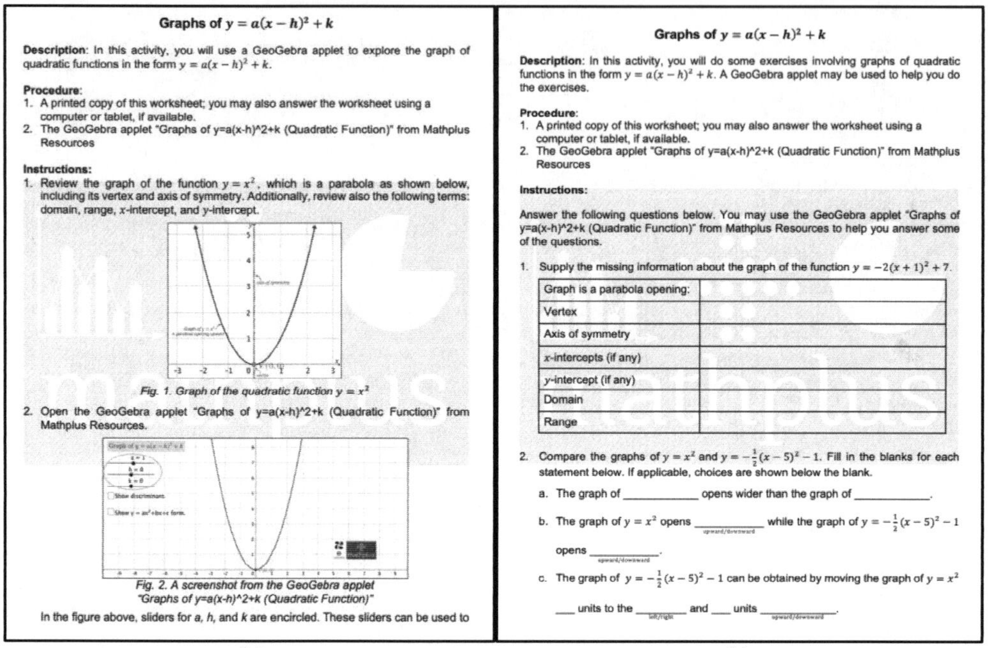

Graphs of $y = a(x-h)^2 + k$

Description: In this activity, you will use a GeoGebra applet to explore the graph of quadratic functions in the form $y = a(x-h)^2 + k$.

Procedure:
1. A printed copy of this worksheet; you may also answer the worksheet using a computer or tablet, if available.
2. The GeoGebra applet "Graphs of y=a(x-h)^2+k (Quadratic Function)" from Mathplus Resources

Instructions:
1. Review the graph of the function $y = x^2$, which is a parabola as shown below, including its vertex and axis of symmetry. Additionally, review also the following terms: domain, range, x-intercept, and y-intercept.

Fig. 1. Graph of the quadratic function $y = x^2$

2. Open the GeoGebra applet "Graphs of y=a(x-h)^2+k (Quadratic Function)" from Mathplus Resources.

Fig. 2. A screenshot from the GeoGebra applet "Graphs of y=a(x-h)^2+k (Quadratic Function)"

In the figure above, sliders for *a*, *h*, and *k* are encircled. These sliders can be used to

(a)

Graphs of $y = a(x-h)^2 + k$

Description: In this activity, you will do some exercises involving graphs of quadratic functions in the form $y = a(x-h)^2 + k$. A GeoGebra applet may be used to help you do the exercises.

Procedure:
1. A printed copy of this worksheet; you may also answer the worksheet using a computer or tablet, if available.
2. The GeoGebra applet "Graphs of y=a(x-h)^2+k (Quadratic Function)" from Mathplus Resources

Instructions:

Answer the following questions below. You may use the GeoGebra applet "Graphs of y=a(x-h)^2+k (Quadratic Function)" from Mathplus Resources to help you answer some of the questions.

1. Supply the missing information about the graph of the function $y = -2(x+1)^2 + 7$.

Graph is a parabola opening:	
Vertex	
Axis of symmetry	
x-intercepts (if any)	
y-intercept (if any)	
Domain	
Range	

2. Compare the graphs of $y = x^2$ and $y = -\frac{1}{2}(x-5)^2 - 1$. Fill in the blanks for each statement below. If applicable, choices are shown below the blank.
   a. The graph of ____________ opens wider than the graph of ____________.
   b. The graph of $y = x^2$ opens ____________ (upward/downward) while the graph of $y = -\frac{1}{2}(x-5)^2 - 1$ opens ____________ (upward/downward).
   c. The graph of $y = -\frac{1}{2}(x-5)^2 - 1$ can be obtained by moving the graph of $y = x^2$ ___ units to the ________ (left/right) and ___ units ____________ (upward/downward).

(b)

Figure 6. Worksheets for the experimental class

Table 1. Mean pretest, gain, and posttest scores for the two pairs of experimental and control classes

	Teacher A		Teacher B	
	Experimental A	Control A	Experimental B	Control B
Number of Students	36	28	31	31
Mean Pretest Scores	20.24%	22.70%	22.58%	22.81%
Mean Gain Scores	31.15%	11.73%	13.36%	15.21%
Mean Posttest Scores	51.39%	34.44%	35.94%	38.02%

However, assessing the effectiveness of the applet and complementary resources more accurately will require further studies. As evident in Table 1, all four classes involved in the study had relatively similar mean pretest scores. The mean gain scores then indicate that all four classes actually received low mean posttest scores, with only Experimental A receiving a mean posttest score (i.e., 51.39%) above 50%. The performance of these classes indicates that there has been a *learning gap* in mathematics that might have transpired even before (aside from during) the integration of the resources. Considering this, further studies on assessing the effectiveness of the aforementioned resources will need to carefully consider the possible presence of such learning gaps.

6. CONCLUSION AND OUTLOOK

In this paper, we discussed two *GeoGebra* applets *Radicals* and *Parabola* that were designed and developed to support the teaching and learning of algebra, especially in the context of the COVID-19 pandemic and the new normal in the Philippines. Capitalizing on sound pedagogy and the affordances of mobile technology, the two applets demonstrate how educators can enhance existing apps with additional instructional design features. These two applets were integrated into Grade 9 classes in one of our partner high schools in the Philippines. Based on feedback gathered from teachers and students during this integration, the applets, as well as some complementary resources, can ease teachers' work and have the potential to improve students' learning of algebra topics.

However, various factors such as learning gaps in mathematics or given the possibly extraordinary education situation brought about by the pandemic, further studies are needed to accurately assess the effectiveness of these applets. In the near future, additional experimental studies employing a pretest-posttest design will be conducted. This will involve the inclusion of more classes, thereby expanding the overall sample size for a comprehensive analysis. Given their potential, however, it is also important to continue the development and improvement of such resources.

ACKNOWLEDGEMENT

This paper is one of the outputs of the Ateneo Mathplus Resources Laboratory housed at the Department of Mathematics, School of Science and Engineering, Ateneo de Manila University. The authors thank the Department of Science and Technology-Philippine Council for Industry, Energy, and Emerging Technology Research and Development (DOST-PCIEERD) and the University Research Council (URC), Ateneo de Manila University for the support of the development of the mathematical resources for Grades 1 to 11 Mathematics. Much appreciation is extended to our DepEd partners particularly DepEd School Division Quezon City, Dr Joel Feliciano, Ms. Gina Acosta and Ms. Nora Villalobos and the other teachers and administrators of our partner schools.

REFERENCES

Antonini, S. and Lisarelli, G. (2021). Designing tasks for introducing functions and graphs within dynamic interactive environments. *Mathematics*, Vol. 9, No. 5, 572.

Azizah, A. N. et al. (2021). The effectiveness of GeoGebra to improve visual representation ability. *Journal of Physics: Conference Series*, Vol. 1808, 012059.

Baccaglini-Frank, A. and Mariotti, M. A. (2011). Conjecture-generation through dragging and abduction in dynamic geometry. In Méndez-Vila, A., (Ed.), *Education in a Technological World: Communicating Current and Emerging Research and Technological Efforts* (pp. 100-107).

Bokhove, C.,9 (2011). *Use of ICT for acquiring, practicing and assessing algebraic expertise*, Dissertation, Utrecht University.

De Las Peñas, M. L. A. N. et al. (2022). *Technology Interventions for Mathematical Reasoning, Statistical Thinking and Assessment, DOST-PCIEERD Terminal Report.*

De Las Peñas, M. L. A. N. et al. (2023). *Mathematical Resources for Distance Learning Utilizing Community LTE Networks and Television Frequencies DOST-PCIEERD Terminal Report.*

Department of Education (DepEd), (2016). *K to 12 Curriculum Guide: Mathematics*. Retrieved September 17, 2023, from https://www.deped.gov.ph/wp-content/uploads/2019/01/Math-CG_with-tagged-math-equipment.pdf

Department of Education (DepEd), (2020). *K to 12 Most Essential Learning Competencies with Corresponding CG Codes*. Retrieved September 17, 2023, from https://commons.deped.gov.ph/K-to-12-MELCS-with-CG-Codes.pdf

Department of Education (DepEd), *DepEd Order No. O12, s.(2020): Adoption of the Basic Education Learning Continuity Plan for SY 2020-2021 in light of the COVID 19 Public Health Emergency.* Retrieved September 19, 2023, from https://authdocs.deped.gov.ph/deped-order/do_s2020_012-adoption-of-the-be-lcp-sy-2020-2021/

Department of Education (DepEd) Region I, (2022). *Regional Memorandum No. 664, s. 2022: Basic Education Learning Recovery Plan in light of the COVID 19 Pandemic*. Retrieved September 19, 2023, from https://depedro1.com/wp-content/uploads/2022/06/ rm0664s2022.pdf

Ericsson, K.A. (2016). Summing up hours of any type of practice versus identifying optimal practice activities: commentary on Macnamara, Moreau, & Hambric. *Perspectives on Psychological Science*, Vol. 11, No. 3, pp. 351-354.

Garciano, A.D. et al. (2023). Practice through play using mobile technology. In P. Kommers, I. Arnedillo Sánchez, & P. Isaías (Eds.), *Proceedings of the International Conferences on E-society 2023 and Mobile Learning 2023* (pp. 351-358). International Association for the Development of the Information Society.

Hillmayr, D. et al. (2020). The potential of digital tools to enhance mathematics and science learning in secondary schools: a context-specific meta-analysis. *Computers & Education*, Vol. 153, 103897.

Laborde, C. and Laborde, J.M. (2014). Dynamic and tangible representations in mathematics education, In S. Rezat, M. Hattermann, & A. Peter-Koop (Eds.), *Transformation – A Fundamental Idea of Mathematics Education: A New Approach* (pp. 187-202).

Laborde, C. et al. (2006). Teaching and learning geometry with technology, In A. Gutiérrez & P. Boero (Eds.), *Handbook of Research on the Psychology of Mathematics Education: Past, Present and Future* (pp. 275-304).

Mudaly, V. and Fletcher, T. (2019). The effectiveness of GeoGebra when teaching linear functions using the iPad. *Problems of Education in the 21st Century*, Vol. 77, No. 1, pp. 55-81.

Shadaan, P. and Leong, K. E. (2013). Effectiveness of using GeoGebra on students' understanding in learning circles. *Online Journal of Educational Technology*, Vol. 1, No. 4, pp. 1-11.

Thurm, D. and Barzel, B. (2022). Teaching mathematics with technology: a multidimensional analysis of teacher beliefs. *Educational Studies in Mathematics*, Vol. 109, pp. 41-63.

Tong, D. H. et al. (2021). The effectiveness of using GeoGebra software in mathematics classrooms: a case study of teaching continuous functions in high schools. *Journal of Hunan University*, Vol. 48, No. 9, pp. 256-268.

Wassie, Y. S. and Zergaw, G. A. (2019). Some of the potential affordances, challenges and limitations of using GeoGebra in mathematics education. *EURASIA Journal of Mathematics, Science and Technology Education*, Vol. 15, No. 8, em1734.

THE FEELING OF SELF-EFFICACY AND ITS IMPACT ON PERFORMANCE ON A MOBILE LEARNING APPLICATION

Nicolas Loiseau, Adrien Bruni, Pierre Puigpinos and Jean-Christophe Sakdavong
CLLE CNRS UMR 5263, University of Toulouse, 5 allée Antonio Machado, Toulouse, France

ABSTRACT

This paper explores the concept of self-efficacy and its impact on individual performance on a mobile learning application. Self-efficacy refers to one's belief in their ability to achieve their goals and is a key factor in everyday life. To investigate the relationship between self-efficacy and performance, we conducted an experiment with 104 participants, which consisted of two parts. First, we evaluated their self-efficacy levels using a survey designed to assess their perceived self-efficacy levels before and after their tests. Second, we asked participants to pilot a drone in a virtual environment and complete a series of races as quickly as possible. Our findings demonstrate that self-efficacy does indeed affect the individual performance, as we observed a clear correlation between self-efficacy levels and task completion times.

KEYWORDS

Self-Efficacy, Learning Performance, HLCE, Mobile Learning

1. INTRODUCTION

Self-efficacy can be likened to a tool, a confidence that guides an individual to be influenced by their actions and the resulting outcomes. This article explores the impact of various forms of assistance on learners' self-efficacy with the uniqueness of this study lying in its experimental framework.

Specifically, we aim to analyze the effect of self-efficacy in a computerized learning environment (known as HLCE) on e-learning activities and tasks. In the first section, we will define the different concepts through a literature review. Then, we sought to see if there is a link between self-efficacy and performance in a computer-based environment. To do so, we measure three values, which are the self-efficacy before learning, the self-efficacy after learning, and the participant's performance at the end of the lesson. Finally, this will lead to a discussion on our experiment, analysis of the obtained results, and a conclusion.

2. LITERATURE REVIEW

2.1 State of The Art

2.1.1 Self-Efficacy Concept

Although there are numerous theories on self-efficacy, the theory most commonly used is Bandura's (1986, 2012) theory of self-efficacy. In this state of art, we will first define Bandura's theory before presenting other theories that challenge it. These alternative perspectives are relevant and necessary to provide a second point of view.

Bandura (1986) is among the most cited authors in his field, and his theories enjoy widespread acceptance among his peers. Although he engages in discussions on the concept of self-efficacy, it is an integral component of Social Cognitive Theory (SCT) (Bandura, 1986), which represents an interpretation of human actions and behaviors. According to this theory, behavior is shaped by intra-personal influences that intersect and form a part of the determining conditions governing the environment and life of each individual. In a sense, each person is considered the master of their destiny or, at the very least, of their influence on themselves, albeit unconsciously.

The sense of self-efficacy is one of the influences within these intra-personal factors. It is defined as a trait that both influences and is influenced by our goals and environment throughout our lifespan, and it is believed to impact our achievements. For instance, an individual who has developed a strong sense of self-efficacy in academic settings may be more inclined to undertake intellectual challenges and persevere in the face of obstacles. According to Bandura (2012), self-efficacy is an amalgamation of various elements, including mastery of personal experience, social modeling, social pressure, and physiological and emotional states. For example, social modeling could be illustrated by the observation that an individual, witnessing a role model succeed in a specific task despite challenges, may enhance their own belief in the capacity to overcome similar difficulties. These elements converge to shape an individual's sense of efficacy, which, in turn, influences our motivation and efforts.

2.1.2 How Does One Build Its Self-Efficacy

Albert Bandura (2004) identified four sources of self-efficacy: mastery experiences, vicarious experiences, verbal persuasion, and physiological and emotional states. Mastery experiences, the most significant source of self-efficacy, are heavily influenced by past successes and failures in a specific domain. Small successes can build up an individual's sense of self-efficacy over time.

Vicarious experiences, or observing the successes or failures of others, can also impact an individual's self-efficacy. However, comparing oneself to others can also lead to negative effects, so it's important to focus on progress and improvement.

Verbal persuasion, or receiving feedback from significant others, can be helpful in increasing self-efficacy if it's specific, respectful, non-attributive, and accompanied by recommendations for improvement.

Finally, physiological and emotional states can impact an individual's sense of self-efficacy, but techniques such as mood mapping or meditation can help regulate emotions and improve self-efficacy. Being aware of these sources can help individuals stay motivated and increase their chances of success in achieving their goals.

2.1.3 Consequences of Self-Efficacy on Other Variables

Bandura highlights the importance of social and self-evaluative consequences, where an individual judges their efficacy and the result they expect to obtain when thinking about performing an action.

Self-efficacy has multiple repercussions through one-self, its motivations and influences and finally the results obtained. In this schematic, two elements in particular play a crucial role: self-efficacy and result expectation.

People thus become their own active agents who shape their outcomes. It's no longer an external influence or even their personality traits (such as envy, shyness, etc.), but their own feelings that influence them: A group of persons is more likely to succeed in a task if it believes more in its ability compared to another group, despite both groups having similar abilities for this task (Bandura, 2012). This difference is the result of high self-efficacy, where individuals systematically identify their environment that will positively influence (in this case) their actions and therefore performances.

The effects of self-efficacy on other variables have been largely studied and Bandura's hypothetis have been confirmed in most of the works as confirm meta-analysis like (Honden et al., 1990) or more recent studies like (Brown, 2012) confirming self-efficacy has a positive effect on problem solving.

2.1.4 Effects of Self-Efficacy in Hlces/Mobile Learning

A Human Learning Computer Environment (HLCE) is a set of systems designed to facilitate the learning of users (learners). They are often used to facilitate the acquisition of skills or knowledge, guided by the HLCE to varying degrees. According to Balacheff and al. (1996), HLCE encompasses education and training methods in all areas where knowledge transfer is desired. This implies that a computer-based learning environment encompasses various agents that interact in various ways, including human agents such as learners and teachers and artificial agents such as robots, accessing learning resources locally or via computer networks.

An HLCE can serve as a tool for information presentation and processing or as a means of communication between humans and machines or between humans through the machine. Koper (2001) describes an HLCE as a social system that facilitates interaction between human and artificial agents to form a cohesive unit with the primary goal of human learning. It includes all the objects, contexts, and behaviors of agents that play an important role in learning, matching computer-based learning environments to pedagogical environments.

Research has shown that the use of HLCEs can have many benefits, such as improving learning outcomes, engagement, and motivation (Bailey, 2014; Healy and al., 2017; Van Leeuwen & Janssen, 2019). Additionally, HLCEs can offer more personalized learning experiences by adapting to individual needs and preferences (Feng and al., 2018). With the growing demand for online and remote learning, HLCEs have become increasingly important tools in education and training.

Mobile learning is regarded as an instructional strategy that enables students to continue their learning activities outside of the traditional classroom by using digital devices like tablets and mobile phones (Crompton, 2013). Mobile learning can only exist thanks to an HLCE.

Lukuman (2023) has studied self-efficacy in this context explaining that mobile learning is essential to achieving continuous learning outside of the classroom. Their study has shown the importance of self-efficacy in order to achieve mobile learning.

Gloria (2016) has shown how important was the training to increase self-efficacy during mobile learning because they think that self-efficacy is important in order to achieve the learning goals. From our site, we aim to study this last part.

Haeng-Nam and al. (2015) have found, in the context of mobile learning, that higher level of self-efficacy results in higher levels of performance expectancy, social influence, and effort expectancy.

As we are more interested in effective performance, we will now review some studies about the link between self-efficacy and effective performance

2.1.5 Recent Experiments on The Link Between Self-Efficacy and Performance

We have found several experiments conducted on self-efficacy and performance on learning tasks provided by HLCEs but nearly nothing conducted with mobile learning.

* Bicen and Kocakoyun (2014) studied the effect of self-efficacy on student engagement in an online learning environment. The researchers recruited 132 university students enrolled in online courses, who completed questionnaires to assess their level of self-efficacy and engagement in learning.

The results showed that students with high self-efficacy were significantly more engaged in their learning than those with low self-efficacy. Furthermore, the researchers found that students with high self-efficacy had a greater sense of control over their learning and were more willing to take on challenging tasks. These findings suggest that self-efficacy may play an important role in promoting student engagement and success in online learning environments.

Moreover, the study highlights the importance of providing students with opportunities to develop and improve their self-efficacy. The researchers suggested that online instructors can foster self-efficacy by providing positive feedback and creating a supportive learning environment. By doing so, students may feel more confident in their abilities to learn and engage with course content, which can ultimately lead to better academic performance.

* Wang and al. (2013) aimed to explore the impact of self-efficacy on student motivation in an online learning environment. The researchers recruited 320 university students who were taking online courses at a Chinese university. The participants completed questionnaires to assess their level of self-efficacy and motivation to learn.

The results showed that students with high self-efficacy were significantly more motivated than those with low self-efficacy. Additionally, students with high self-efficacy showed greater persistence in their online learning, meaning they were more likely to continue studying even in the face of difficulties. These findings suggest that self-efficacy may play an important role in student motivation and perseverance in online learning.

The study also highlights the importance of the learning environment for the development of self-efficacy. The researchers found that students who had access to high-quality educational resources and frequent online interactions with teachers were more likely to develop strong self-efficacy.

2.2 Retained Hypothesis

Bandura has demonstrated that self-efficacy has effects on various variables, including learning and learning performances. Bican and Kocakoyun (2014) and Wang et al. (2013) have shown that self-efficacy influences positively performance. Haeng-Nam and al. (2015) have shown that it is also true in a mobile learning context for "expectancy".

Therefore, we propose the following hypothesis: **A positive evolution of self-efficacy has a significant positive impact on performance in a mobile learning application.**

The hypothesis suggests that there may be a relationship between the changes in an individual's self-efficacy and their subsequent performance outcomes.

3. METHODOLOGY

During this experiment, we aim to verify whether a change in self-efficacy has an impact on actual performance.

To do so, we measure three values, which are the self-efficacy before learning, the self-efficacy after learning, and the participant's performance at the end of the lesson. Performance is evaluated by the time needed to complete their tasks, while we're using surveys to evaluate their self-efficacy.

3.1 Participants

To conduct this experiment, we collected various data through two forms and a mobile drone piloting learning application. A total of 104 people signed up. The forms were collected with Qualtrics Europe which respects GDRP regulations.

The data obtained with the forms were collected between May 2022 and July 2022, and the drone piloting learning application was developed with Unity by the nonprofit AD2RV association.

All collected data is anonymous and has not been used for any purpose other than that of the experiment conducted within the scope of our hypothesis.

3.2 Experimentation Setup

The experiment consists of three parts. In the first part, the participant is asked to complete a survey to gather some information about themselves, such as their age and gender. After this, the participant receives a unique one-time-use code by email, which allows them to move on to the second stage of the experiment, which involves learning to pilot a drone.

In the second part of the experiment, the participant uses a smartphone android application on a personal smartphone (figure 1). The participant receives a brief explanatory video showing the final obstacle race they will have to complete. At the end of the video, the participant is asked to rate their degree of confidence in completing the race in less than 50 seconds on a scale of 1 to 100 (first measure of self-efficacy). After this question, the participant goes through seven different challenges of increasing difficulty to learn how to pilot the drone. The main goal of the participants is to learn piloting in order to complete the course in the shortest possible time. Before each of the 7 steps (lessons), the participant can decide to request assistance, which includes aids to facilitate their progress and a simple aid where an image shows how to direct the drone.

Figure 1. Illustration of the application.

At the end of the learning phase, the participant is asked to once again evaluate their ability to complete the final course within in less than 50 seconds (second measure of self-efficacy). Then the participant has to complete the final course with measurement of his performance. Finally, after completing the test, the participant is asked to fill out a final survey to gather information on difficulties they encountered.

4. RESULTS

4.1 Sample

Of the 104 participants approached, 44 people completed the experiment. 25 women and 19 men were remaining.

4.2 Descriptive Processing of Data

In the context of this experiment, 3 metrics were collected and used to create our measures of evolution and performance. The evolution of self-efficacy is represented by the difference between the self-efficacy after learning (metric 1) and the one before (metric 2). Therefore, the evolution will be positive if the participant feels more confident than at the beginning, and negative in the opposite case.

In addition, we use another value which is the time to complete the course in seconds (metrics 3). The lower this measure, the greater the participant's performance will be. Table 1 presents the descriptive statistics about our two main resulting variables.

Table 1. Descriptive statistics

	Self-Efficacy evolution	Final Performance
Minimum	-100	35.30
1st Quantile	-12	40.16
Median	0	49.91
Mean	-0.9512	79.88
3rd Quantile	11	83.01
Maximum	66	256.57

4.3 Inferential Statistics

To be able to evaluate and validate our hypothesis, we need to verify whether the evolution of our self-efficacy allows for an improvement in user performance. With two continuous variables at our disposal, it is therefore more appropriate to seek an answer through regression methods.

At first, we tried to use the raw data as it is to perform a linear regression. Unfortunately, the test of the normality of residuals was not conclusive. In turn, we attempted to apply transformations to our explanatory variables with the aim of discovering a new relationship or enhancing our results.

To try to reduce the range of our performance, we apply the following transformation:

$$y = \log10(performance - 35.2)$$

log10 function is used to reduce the range of our values, while the -35.2 centers performances around the minimum. Since the log10(x) function is not defined at 0, the minimum is slightly higher. As expected, the range of our data has been reduced (figure 2).

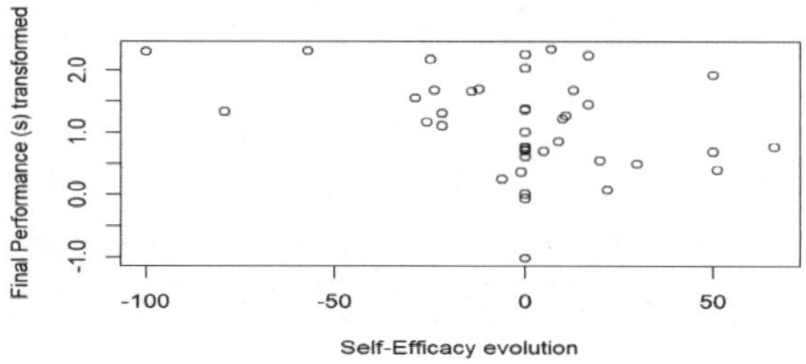

Figure 2. Graph of self-efficacy evolution by final performance transformed

Then, we calculate the coefficients of the regression line with our transformation:

$$y = -0.0085 * x + 1.1194.$$

To validate these results, we must first show that the model coefficients are non-zero. By setting:

-H0: The coefficient is equal to 0.

-H1: The coefficient is different from 0.

Choosing alpha equal to 5%, we reject H0 ($p=0.0281$) and validate the non-nullity of the coefficients at the alpha threshold of 5%.

In the second step, we need to verify that the residuals of our model (figure 3) follow a normal distribution, meaning that the residuals are not correlated with each other.

With the help of the *Shapiro-Wilk* hypothesis test, with the following hypotheses:

-H0: the data follows a normal distribution with mean 0 and standard deviation 1.

-H1: the data does not follow a normal distribution.

The null hypothesis H0 is accepted at the 5% significance level ($p=0.348$). Our residuals (figure 3) do follow a centered and reduced normal distribution, and we can accept the previous results.

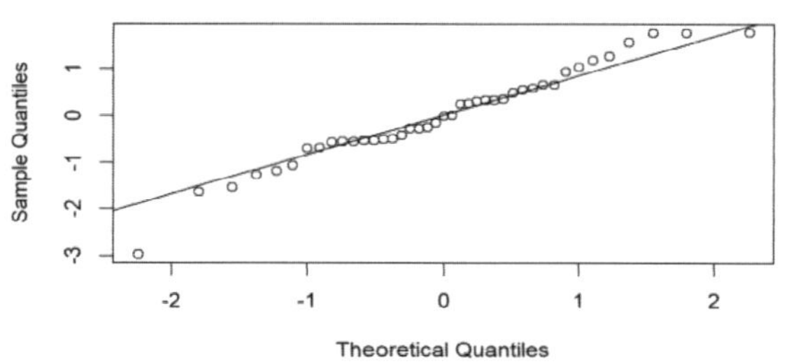

Figure 3. Representation of the residuals distribution with the performances transformed

Through the process of transformation, we can highlight a non-linear relationship between our variables.

By performing the inverse operation associated with our initial transformation on our regression line, we can visualize a new curve that corresponds to the same line in the original space, as seen below in the figure 4. The inverse transformation associated with y is: $x = 10^y+35.2$

This function between self-efficacy evolution and final performance confirms that our main hypothesis is verified.

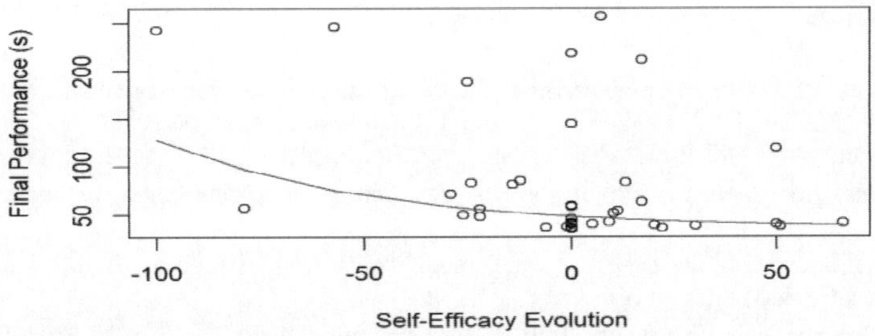

Figure 4. Final regression of self-efficacy over performance

5. DISCUSSION

The study aimed to analyze the relationship between learners' self-efficacy evolution and their performance in a learning task. The sample consisted of 44 participants, 25 females and 19 males, who completed the experiment. Four measures were collected: self-efficacy before and after learning, the time required to complete the task, and the final performance.

Firstly, the data was analyzed descriptively. The results showed that self-efficacy evolution was generally negative, although some participants showed significant improvement. Final performance was also highly variable, with completion times ranging from 35 to 256 seconds.

With these results, we tried to prove that the evolution of self-efficacy has a positive impact on performance. To do so, we conducted a linear regression with a transformation of the original variable, resulting in a verified non-linear relation between self-efficacy and performance. In addition, the original slope of the regression is lower than 0, showing a negative correlation: The higher the evolution of the self-efficacy is, the lower the performance (in our case, the unit for performance is the second).

In conclusion, this study shows that self-efficacy evolution has a positive effect on final performance in a learning task which also matches with (Haeng-Nam and al., 2015) results about performance expectancy.

In the specific context of CBLEs and mobile learning, the result is even more interesting because it is possible to automatize the intervention process such as with positive feedback (Peifer, 2020). We are currently doing a study to check if positive feedback could help to improve self-efficacy. Moreover, this study has broader implications for our understanding of human performance and achievement. The findings suggest that self-efficacy plays a crucial role in determining individual performance, and that self-belief is a key factor in achieving success. As such, it is critical to understand the role that self-efficacy plays in shaping individual outcomes and to develop strategies that help individuals cultivate a sense of self-efficacy to improve their performance.

As an opening question, it would be interesting to ask if the relationship between self-efficacy and performance is influenced by other factors, such as motivation, previous experience, or individual learning preferences. Future research could explore the effectiveness of self-efficacy interventions in different settings and with larger sample sizes.

6. CONCLUSION

In conclusion, this study, which has been conducted though a mobile learning application, provides insights into the relationship between self-efficacy and performance: A positive evolution of self-efficacy has a significant positive impact on performance in a mobile learning application. The main application of this result is that educators/CBLE/Mobile learning application designers should try to do their best in order to improve learner's self-efficacy by digital means like positive feedback.

REFERENCES

Balacheff, N., Kaput, J.J. (1996). Computer-Based Learning Environments in Mathematics. In: Bishop, A.J., Clements, K., Keitel, C., Kilpatrick, J., Laborde, C. (eds) International Handbook of Mathematics Education. Kluwer International Handbooks of Education, vol 4. Springer, Dordrecht.

Bandura, A. (1986). Social foundation of thought and action: A social cognitive theory. Englewood Cliffs, NJ: Prentice-Hall.

Bandura, A. (2004). Social Cognitive Theory for Personal and Social Change by Enabling Media. In A. Singhal, M. J. Cody, E. M. Rogers, & M. Sabido (Eds.).

Bandura, A. (2012). Social cognitive theory. In P. A. M. Van Lange, A. W. Kruglanski, & E. T. Higgins (Eds.).

Peifer, C., Schönfeld, P., Wolters, G., Aust, F., Margraf, J. (2020). Well Done! Effects of Positive Feedback on Perceived Self-Efficacy, Flow and Performance in a Mental Arithmetic Task. Frontiers in Psychology. 11. 10.3389/fpsyg.2020.01008.

Bicen, H., & Kocakoyun, S. (2018). Perceptions of Students for Gamification Approach: Kahoot as a Case Study. International Journal of Emerging Technologies in Learning (iJET).

Brown, A.D., Dorfman, M.L., Marmar, C.R., Bryant, R.A.. The impact of perceived self-efficacy on mental time travel and social problem solving. Conscious Cogn. 2012 Mar;21(1):299-306. doi: 10.1016/j.concog.2011.09.023. Epub 2011 Oct 21. PMID: 22019214.

Crompton, H. (2013). A historical overview of mobile learning: Toward learner-centered education. In Z. L. Berge & L. Y. Muilenburg (Eds.), Handbook of mobile learning. Florence.

Haeng-Nam, S., Dae-Yul, J., Yeon-Su, J., Jae-Ik, S. (2015). The Relationship among Self-Efficacy, Social Influence, Performance Expectancy, Effort Expectancy, and Behavioral Intention in Mobile Learning Service. International Journal of u- and e- Service, Science and Technology. 8. 197-206.

Hashemi, M., Azizinezhad, M., Najafi, V., & Nesari, A. J. (2011). What is mobile learning? challenges and capabilities. Procedia-Social and Behavioural Sciences, 30, 2477-2481.

Holden G, Moncher MS, Schinke SP, Barker KM. Self-efficacy of children and adolescents: a meta-analysis. Psychol Rep. 1990 Jun;66(3 Pt 1):1044-6. doi: 10.2466/pr0.1990.66.3.1044. PMID: 2143028.

Koper, R. (2001). Modeling units of study from a pedagogical perspective. The pedagogical metamodel behind EML.

Lukuman, K. (2022). Examining students'readiness for mobile learning: Effects of mobile phone self-efficacy and internet self-efficacy. NOUN Journal of Education. Vol 8, 2022, pp. 96-110.

Wang, Chuang & Schwab, Götz & Fenn, Pete & Chang, Mei. (2013). Self-Efficacy and Self-Regulated Learning Strategies for English Language Learners: Comparison between Chinese and German College Students. Journal of Educational and Developmental Psychology.

SPART – AN AFFORDABLE MOBILE AUGMENTED REALITY ALTERNATIVE TO INTERACTIVE TABLETOPS IN EDUCATION

Sebastian Simon, Iza Marfisi-Schottman and Sébastien George
LIUM, Le Mans Université, 72085 Le Mans, Cedex 9, France

ABSTRACT

Technology to support collaborative learning has come a long way. Interactive tabletops support collaboration when correctly integrated in activity design. While these devices can now, in principle, be purchased by the general public, wide adoption in schools is hindered by their high cost and lack of mobility. In this paper, we analyze the potential technologies that could replace such devices. After developing a dozen prototypes to further test the potential of the most promising technologies, we found one robust, affordable and accurate solution: SPART (on-Surface Positioning for Augmented RealiTy) allows augmenting any flat surface (images etc.) with tablets or smartphones, addressing both affordability and mobility. This paper focuses on the technological innovations that were designed for SPART.

KEYWORDS

Mobile Computer Supported Collaborative Learning, Augmented Reality, Peephole Interaction

1. INTRODUCTION

Computer-supported collaboration has been found to positively impact learning (Dillenbourg, 2000). The design of appropriate software and hardware has long been a challenge in itself. In the 2000s, several custom interactive tabletop devices, that display dynamic information and allow user input, were designed and experimented for research purposes (Mateescu et al., 2019). In the following years, large touchscreen technology, as used for interactive tabletops, has rendered obsolete these custom setups and this technology has now widely proven its potential for collaborative learning. However, this technology is rarely used in educational contexts because of its high costs and lack of mobility, even though it could support new collaborative teaching paradigms (Aslan and Reigeluth, 2013).

Indeed, large interactive tabletops remain a non-negligible investment (2 000 € and above) for educational institutions such as schools. In addition, situated learning and alternative setups to classic configurations of one teacher – many students have evolved, alongside remote learning (Maqsood et al., 2021). Situated learning, during field trips in particular, calls for mobile collaborative devices that can be used outside classroom settings. This is not the case of current tabletops that weigh more than 100 kg and rely on an external power supply. Researchers are therefore turning to Augmented Reality (AR), which can be used through smartphones or tablets to display digital information on surfaces (such as traditional tables). However, classic, camera-based AR technology is not without issues for collaboration.

Firstly, if an image is augmented (*e.g.* a map of the world), the camera has to capture a critical portion of the image used as AR marker, which requires users to stand at sufficient distance and hold the device appropriately. This is not feasible over a long period of time with large smartphones or tablets, due to muscle fatigue (Pereira et al., 2013). Holding the device (especially with two hands for children) also makes interactions with virtual or physical objects difficult. Another issue is its interpersonal use within a group: If only one person is holding the device, other group members have to huddle around this person to see the augmentation. An alternate solution is for all members to use individual devices to work in the augmented space, but the focus on devices decreases awareness of what other group members or the teacher is doing, which is a major component of collaboration (Brudy et al., 2018).

These issues could be prevented if mobile devices were directly placed on the to-be-augmented surface (map, image, plan etc.). As shown in figure 1, this configuration, very similar to the one of an interactive tabletop, provides a common focal point for group attention and allows all group members to view augmentations while maintaining awareness on other group members' actions and keeping hands free. Furthermore, the mobile device serves as a convenient input method since its horizontal position on the surface allows for stability and is accessible from all angles.

Figure 1. SPART: on-Surface Positioning for Augmented RealiTy

While screen size is not directly proportional to collaboration quality (Zagermann et al., 2016), tablets still provide less screen space (typically 10") then tabletops (80" and above) to interact with. We therefore propose a peephole-type interaction that requires users to slide the device on the surface to see and interact with augmentations beyond the device's display. We call this setup SPART for on-Surface Positioning for Augmented RealiTy. It allows to augment static surfaces by sliding the device on it. It is suitable for use in schools being mobile and inexpensive (compatible with any available tablet or smartphone).

There is little research on such a setup which cannot be achieved with classic AR technology (the camera is obstructed as the device is lying on its back). A vertical augmentation prototype of a whiteboard has been developed by Sanneblad and Holmquist (2006) but has entailed issues with muscle fatigue and fear of breaking the tablet while holding it. To the best of our knowledge, no technology supports a horizontal peephole setup.

In this paper, we address the question whether it is possible to develop an affordable and mobile alternative to interactive tabletops and what type of technology is available and appropriate. Therefore, we initially identify the requirements of a potential device for teaching in classrooms and during field trips. We then review the possible technologies and evaluate them against these requirements. Technologies that fulfilled the most requirements resulted in prototypes. SPART-ME is currently the only prototype that fulfils all the requirements and is thus presented in detail in the second half of this paper. We then conclude with possible use cases for such a tool and future development perspectives for the presented prototype.

2. STATE OF THE ART

The peephole interaction described above requires the device's (smartphone or tablet) ability to accurately determine its position, relative to the surface it is placed on. In the following subsections we present the different technologies in modern mobile devices that exhibit the potential to do so. We also discuss their compatibility with the constraints related to supporting collaborative learning and using such technology in schools and outdoor settings (to support situated learning). Whenever a technology had the potential to satisfy these constraints, we developed prototypes to verify and test information on requirement satisfaction previously estimated during the review. All prototypes carry the name "SPART" with a suffix that identifies the used technology. More than 10 prototypes were created before SPART-ME, the variant presented in section 3.

2.1 Requirements

To guarantee an ergonomic user experience and a future use in the educational field and situated setting we identified the following requirements:

- **Accuracy**: The technology allows to retrieve the device's position with an accuracy of one centimeter or better. This assures that the user can easily associate the screen content with its underlying surface and that the virtual content is close to the real position of its static counterpart.
- **Fluidity**: When the device is slid on the surface, the technology allows for as little delay as possible when updating the image. The requirement to achieve a good reactivity is therefore estimated at minimum 10 position updates per second.
- **Minimum operating range**: A standard size for printed media in Europe is the A3 format, a surface of 29,7 x 42 cm. The technology should thus cover at least these dimensions.
- **Mobility:** Situated learning often uses learning contexts that mirror the educational content, such as field trips (*e.g.* for biology). The technology should therefore be portable: lighter than 500 g and not exceed dimensions of a notebook (A4).
- **Robustness:** The technology should function independently of outside conditions, such as sunlight, wind or ambient noise.
- **Affordability**: Potential use in educative setups depends on the possibility to deploy the technology in sufficient numbers. Thus, the device price should not exceed 50 € per unit.
- **DIY & Reparability:** Ideally, the technology should not require high skills in any specialized area and the production and assembly of a prototype should be within the range of educators or students. Components should be easily available; assembly should not require specialized tools or take long.
- **Multi-device support:** The technology should allow multiple devices to be located simultaneously to allow for multi-device scenarios (at least two).

For each evaluated technology, we verified if it could be excluded based on existent studies and using our requirements. When a requirement is met, it is marked with a "+", when there was evidence that criteria could not be met, it is highlighted with a "-" in Table 1. When unsure, a "?" marks the uncertainty aspect.

2.2 Localization Techniques

The localization techniques are presented in three categories, along with the possible technologies that can support them. The results are summarized in Table 1.

2.2.1 Dead Reckoning Techniques

Dead reckoning refers to localization techniques using object movement relative to its environment (speed, angle etc.). Those measurements allow to estimate device positions from an initial reference point.

Smartphones embark sensors in their Inertial Measurement Unit (IMU), some of which can be used to estimate the direction (gyroscope) and distance (accelerometer) from a known starting point. However, due to noise and required double integration in order to obtain a distance vector from an acceleration, this method is highly unreliable. We measured a 10 cm drift error after 10 cm distance from a reference point when used for positioning with small accelerations due to a high noise to signal ratio (*-accuracy, -robustness*).

Computer mice can be used to perform optical dead reckoning. However, the cumulating error builds up very quickly. In addition, uneven ground or imperfections in the surface increase the error (*-robustness)*. Another drawback of this approach is mouse drift since the rotation of the mouse cannot be distinguished from a translation and consequently is considered as the latter. Setups with two mice and external cameras can reach a maximum of 4 cm accuracy (*-accuracy*) (Sekimori and Miyazaki, 2007).

We also developed a hybrid prototype based on a **Magnetic Dead-reckoning technique**. A grid of small magnets attached to the surface allows the smartphone's magnetometer to sense a repeating pattern and count transitions between fields. If one or more movements are erroneous, the setup requires recalibration. In order for this technique to work, high sensor measurement frequency and precision are necessary. However, magnetometer modules in smartphones typically do not exceed read frequencies of more than 30 Hz (which is insufficient for moderate movements across thin field lines) (*-accuracy*). Hall-sensors can provide higher frequency readings but would require stronger (thus bigger) magnets, which decreases affordability and robustness as strong magnets attached to surfaces such as paper will easily stick together and damage it (*-affordability -robustness*).

2.2.2 Fingerprinting Techniques

Fingerprinting is a technique that relies on sensors within the device to measure unique values of its environment at every position, or inversely an environment capable of sensing the device (*e.g.* a touchscreen)

Switch grids can be used to implement this technique. In its most basic form, a keyboard is a fingerprinting device, localizing finger position with an accuracy of about 2-3 cm (and associating the position to a symbol or letter) by physically closing a circuit in a grid of switches. For such localization approaches to work, the device must reliably trigger switches sufficiently small to provide an accuracy above 1 cm. While theoretically possible, the number of switches (1260 to cover an A3 sheet) required for 1 cm accuracy requires extensive wiring (*-DIY*) and is costly (*-affordability*). **Capacitive grids** suffer a similar issue, since a high number of electrodes must be wired. Additionally, a device can't be distinguished from another (*-multi-device*).

NFC tags can be used to create an artificial environment for the NFC reader of a mobile phone to read location information off those tags. The SPART-NFC prototype was developed with an NFC grid. Each tag has absolute position information stored that can be read by a smartphone placed on a tag. This prototype was abandoned due to an accuracy of less than 2 cm (NFC antenna range and size) and a read frequency of less than 10 Hz leading to a high rate of missed NFC tags (*-accuracy*, *-fluidity*).

Magnetic fingerprinting can be used with magnetometers in tablets and smartphones which have the capacity of measuring magnetic fields in three dimensions. By creating artificial magnetic fields with Neodymium magnets, the smartphone can fingerprint the field and use a mapping (position per field value triple) of the field to determine its position. We developed SPART-MA-F, a high-accuracy prototype limited to a surface of 20x20 cm due to the rapidly declining magnet field strength (*-range*). Creating an equally heterogeneous field with multiple magnets to overcome size limitations was tested but did not prove reliable (*-robustness*) due to variation in field strength and symmetry in commercially available magnets.

Similarly, fingerprinting can also be used with wave-based technologies such as **Wifi, Bluetooth or acoustic waves**. These waves have a signal strength that decreases with distance. It is therefore possible to read the signal strength of waves from different emitters for known locations. However, due to reflection and overlapping, accuracy beyond four centimeters is not possible (*-accuracy, -robustness*) (Wang, Yang and Sun, 2018). Driver software and operating systems also limit frequency of signal strength readings *(-fluidity).*

Infrared ink codes are a recent technology developed in educational speaking pens. This technology relies on a small infrared camera, integrated into the top of the pen, which reads a code, printed with infrared ink on the page of a book, invisible to humans. While it would be possible to print codes with distinct location information codes on a surface and attach such a small and cheap CMOS camera with a microcontroller to a smartphone, position could only be retrieved in slow movements or when the device is at rest (*-fluidity*). In addition, the special ink is not widely available (*-DIY)* and the longevity of the ink under environmental influences such as sunlight is uncertain (*?robustness*).

Computer vision is another optic passive fingerprinting technology. Visual tracking technologies are used for Augmented Reality by detecting the position of an object within the field of a camera in order to add object-dependent information to its position on the screen. An implementation with a smartphone displaying a marker and another smartphone running tracking software would work best for high angles. However, the additional smartphone increases cost (*-affordability*) and would require an apparatus to hold it at a minimum height (*-mobility*). The technology is also prone to variable light conditions and occlusion from a hand moving the smartphone (*-robustness*).

An active **sonar** technology with an accuracy of 1 cm has been developed under the project name "FingerIO" (Nandakumar et al., 2016). Any device with two microphones and a speaker can localize fingers or other objects around a smartwatch or a similar device. Therefore, we deduct a possible implementation in a smartphone that locates itself in reference to a small object on which the emitted sound waves get reflected. This technology is, however, not available since it is currently commercialized and thus disclosed. It also seems unfeasible to distinguish different objects, making the use of multiple devices unlikely (*-multi-device*). Also, the noise of a sliding phone would likely interfere with measurements and position could only be retrieved at rest (*-fluidity, -robustness*).

Radar and LIDAR cannot achieve accuracy beyond 10 cm (in the case of commercially available LIDAR sensors) due to the speed of light with which their emitter waves propagate (*-accuracy*).

2.2.3 Triangulation and Trilateration Techniques

The use of geometry to respectively use either angle or distance to known points in space is a widely used localization technique.

GPS, Wi-Fi and Bluetooth wave-based localization techniques are particularly well studied and initially seemed promising. Indeed, modern smartphones include communication modules for various wavelengths: Bluetooth and Wi-Fi (2.4 & 5 GHz), GSM (900Mhz) and GPS (1600Mhz). However, these are not accurate enough for our use case (< 1cm). GPS can reach up to 30 cm at best (Moore, 2017) but depends on a variety of factors and cannot be used in buildings. Bluetooth or Wi-Fi accuracy does not exceed one meter while GSM triangulation is limited to 500 m (*-accuracy*). UWB is a recent development of a sensor capable of emitting bursts of electromagnetic waves of different wave lengths to detect objects at close proximity but the accuracy does not exceed 10 cm (*-accuracy*). Internal GPS, Wi-Fi and Bluetooth modules also do not provide sufficient reading speeds (scans containing wifi strength information) to obtain adequate fluidity (*-fluidity*).

Smartphones also contain **acoustic** receiver and transmitter modules (microphone and speaker). Sub-centimeter accuracy has been achieved for example by Qi (2017) in an indoor setting with specialized hardware (*+accuracy*). However, sound is reflected by obstacles and signals of emitters must be filtered from ambient noise, reducing accuracy when used with a conventional smartphone, therefore increasing computational complexity and requiring hardware with costs above 100 € (*-affordability*).

Light triangulation consists of a laser (point or line) and a camera located above or beneath the laser at a given angle. Where the laser hits an object, the camera can filter the point/line of the laser and the position can be retrieved by taking into account the angle of the camera and the position of the laser within the field of the camera. Xiao and Scavella have managed sub-centimeter accuracy in a DIY 3D scanner project (Scavella, 2020). They noted however difficulties with different types of object materials, reflecting or dispersing laser light (*-robustness*). The approach has its limitations in the angle of view of the camera (similarly to fiducial markers) and requires at least an embedded system such as a Raspberry Pi and a camera (*-cost*).

Mechanical trilateration techniques can also be used by attaching physical strings to the device and measuring their length. Sensors such as potentiometers are accurate (*+accuracy*), widely available (*+DIY* & reparability) and measurements can be read at high speeds (>10 kHz) (*+fluidity*). However, space is required to house reels for the strings and a rigid support is required, reducing mobility (*-Mobility*).

Table 1. A summary of the technology review and (*) prototypes

Technique	Technology	Requirements							
		Accuracy	Fluidity	Range	Mobility	Robustness	Affordability	DIY	Multi-device
Dead reckoning	Smartphone dead reck.*	-	+	+	+	-	+	+	+
	Computer mice	-	+	+	+	-	-	+	+
	Magnetic dead-reckoning*	-	+	+	+	-	-	+	+
Fingerprinting	Switch grids	+	+	+	+	+	-	-	+
	Capacitive grid	+	+	+	+	+	-	-	-
	NFC tag grid*	-	-	+	+	+	+	+	+
	Magnetic fingerprinting*	+	+	-	+	-	+	+	+
	Wifi/Bluetooth/Acoustic	-	-	+	+	-	+	+	+
	Infrared ink	+	-	+	+	?	+	-	+
	Computer vision	+	+	+	+	-	-	+	+
	Sonar (FingerIO)	+	-	+	+	-	+	+	-
	Radar and Lidar	-	+	+	+	+	+	+	+
Triangulation/ Trilateration	GPS/WIFI/Bluetooth	-	-	+	+	-	+	+	+
	Acoustic trilateration*	+	+	+	+	+	-	+	+
	Light triangulation	+	+	+	+	-	-	+	+
	Mechanical trilateration*	+	+	+	-	+	+	+	+

Review Conclusion. Our literature review, experimental developments and tests are summarized in Table 1. Accuracy is an issue for any dead reckoning technique. These technologies also share a lack of robustness. For passive fingerprinting techniques to work, some artificial layer for the device's sensors is necessary, which generally entails issues of robustness or complexity. The creation of a reliable overlay (in the case of magnetic fingerprinting and NFC) which doesn't get distorted by environmental conditions is a challenge. Active fingerprinting methods are less prone to environmental variability due to the use of an emitting signal but either lack accuracy or are costly. Finally, the triangulation and trilateration techniques seem the most promising, especially the ones based on acoustic and mechanical trilateration. Thus, we focused on the development of the SPART-AC and SPART-ME prototypes. SPART-AC could not provide its theoretical accuracy at the time of writing. Even though simulations predict sub-centimeter accuracy, the use of the prototype in real contexts shows accuracy issues due to ambient noise and objects (hands) that the acoustic waves bounce off of. The SPART-ME prototype, developed to test mechanical trilateration was the most successful in living up to the predictions from the technology review. We present this prototype in the next section.

3. SPART-ME

SPART-ME uses two string potentiometers to implement a MEchanical trilateration technique that relies on the length of the unwound strings between the object and two known points in the 2D plane (see Figure 2). The smartphone (1) is held within a custom plastic frame (2). To this frame is attached a metal ring (3) on which the ends of the potentiometer strings (4) can slide when the smartphone (1) is moved.

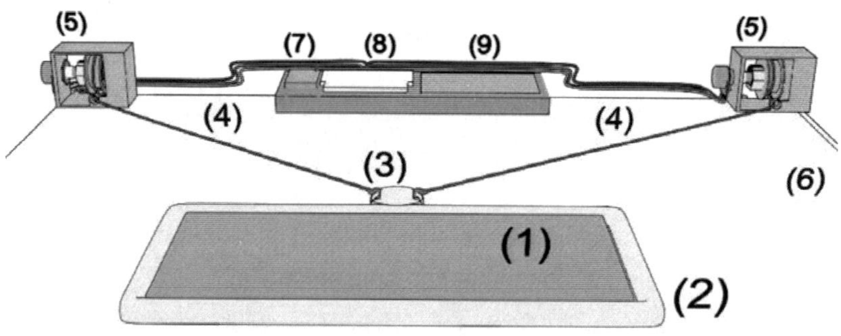

Figure 2. SPART-ME: Two 3D-printed string potentiometers (5) linked to an ADC (7) providing 15 Bit precision of the measured length connect to a microcontroller (8) sending data via a Bluetooth interface to the smartphone (1)

Mechanical parts of the string potentiometers and housing of electronics can be printed with conventional fused deposition modelling 3D printers. The two string potentiometers (5) are attached to a support (6) and their voltage divider pin is connected to a dedicated analog-to-digital converter (7). Both analog-to-digital converter and potentiometers are powered from the 3,3V pin of a microcontroller (8). The microcontroller (8) and analog-to-digital converter (7) are connected via a four line I2C connection. The microcontroller (8) is powered by a battery pack (9) or an external power supply.

3.1 Performance

Accuracy. To assess the accuracy of the prototype, we compared the real position and calculated position on 81 positions on a 9x9 grid (at positions every 5 cm, covering an area of 45x45cm) The mean error for the current prototype is 0,4 cm. The error increases with distance (but also very close) to the potentiometers and especially in the center of the x-axis. It fulfills the accuracy requirement of an average error below 1 cm.

Fluidity. Currently, the refresh rate is set to 15 positions per second. It can be increased by setting the communication speed between the device and the microcontroller. The current speed was chosen to reduce power consumption.

Minimum operating range. The current prototype can effectively cover a surface of an A2 sheet, limited by the strings' length, the reels' diameter and the potentiometers' limitation to 10 turns. Increasing the wheels' diameter and strings' length allows to increase the operational range but will reduce accuracy.

Mobility, Robustness, Affordability & Reparability. In terms of mobility, the weight of the battery-powered prototype is acceptable (700 g) but it is cumbersome to transport because the potentiometers have to be attached to a rigid support. The prototype is robust since it is immune to sunlight and noise. The entire prototype is affordable since it can be produced for 80 € as a mobile version or 50 € for a version that has to be connected to a power supply: Two 10 turn potentiometers can be purchased for 30 €, keychain holders are available for 2 €, an ADS1115 analog to digital converter for 5 €, a microcontroller with Bluetooth (e.g. Seeed XIAO NRF52840) for 10 € and the remaining parts can be printed with a standard 3D printer for under 2 € filament cost. Finally, the assembly of the prototype requires soldering skills and is accessible to most DIY hobbyists. A detailed guide still needs to be tested with the local technology school teachers.

3.2 User Software

Several applications have been developed for SPART-ME. A first application was designed to augment the map of a city. It allows the user to see icons for important buildings and to click on them to open an information window. In addition, we implemented six buttons to change the layers shown on the map (satellite humidity images of different years to show the impact of climate change on a local scale). The buttons are also sketched on the paper map (and are therefore visible at all times) demonstrating the use of static interfaces that become interactive when the device is slid on the interface.

Another application was developed for and tested with students in middle-school. It features virtual overlays with seismic data on an A3 world map and access to vertical depth position of earthquakes at predefined positions. Students had to identify tectonic plate limits and relative movement types (*e.g.* subduction) in this activity. The activity was structured in a coloring, classification and hypothesis building task. The prototype was promptly adopted by students who reported a positive user experience. Results point to low cognitive load in the use of the unfamiliar interaction type and the movement of the tablet seemed to support spatial reflections by students as well as collaborative coupling styles. Indeed, in a later interview, a student stated that even when not actively engaged with his peers, the tablet was a good visual indicator on what his peers were working on, thus allowing him to visually keep track of the group activity while reflecting on a related problem. In another instance, students engaged in lengthy off-topic conversations and picked up their peer's work without transition after having regularly checked the tablets position on the table from a distance. The prototype operated flawlessly throughout the accumulated nine hours of use.

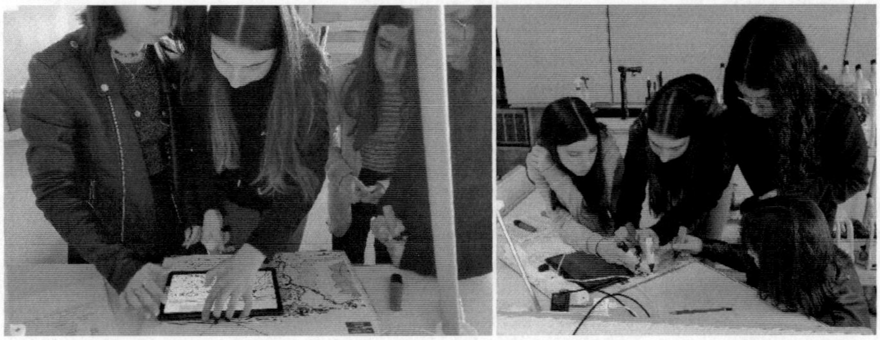

Figure 3. A group of students using SPART-ME to augment a tectonic map

In a recent development, the system has been modified to use weights for retraction of strings and 3D printed hall-sensor based rotary encoders. This effectively removes the space limit and reduces part costs to 20€ per unit. This variation can be used to create affordable smartboards (in conjunction with a projector) and augment large wall mounted maps. Strings and weights configured to counterbalance the weight of the attached device mitigate muscle fatigue or fear of breaking the device as in the experiment of Sanneblad and Holmquist (2006).

4. CONCLUSION

In this paper we reviewed localization technology and techniques under the angle of eight requirements typical for use in classrooms and during school trips. This review provided insights on promising, available technology to create accurate, fluid, robust, affordable, easy to maintain and multi-device compatible prototypes. Consequently, we presented SPART-ME, a prototype to investigate the interest of peephole interactions for mobile computer-supported collaborative learning to mimic a mobile interactive tabletop. The prototype fulfills all requirements with a variety of applications and a positive outlook for improved affordability and mobility. While the benefits for collaborative learning still have to be confirmed by large scale user studies, the technology has already been successfully used in an in-classroom study pointing towards benefits for collaborative learning. We can thus answer positively the question whether the hypothesized device can be developed and that the most accessible technology seems to be a mechanical trilateration. Finally, SPART is not restricted to educational applications: affordable interactive museum panels, augmented annotation tools (for plans), decision-making tools for team meetings are possible

ACKNOWLEDGEMENTS

This work is part of the SituLearn project, supported by the French National Agency for Research, reference ANR-20-CE38-0012. Thanks, Guy Theard, for testing this and consequent prototypes with your students.

REFERENCES

Aslan, S. and Reigeluth, C.M. (2013). 'Educational Technologists: Leading Change for a New Paradigm of Education', *TechTrends*, Vol. 57, No. 5, pp. 18–24.

Brudy, F. et al. (2018). 'Investigating the Role of an Overview Device in Multi-Device Collaboration', *Proceedings of the 2018 CHI Conference on Human Factors in Computing Systems*. New York, NY, USA, pp. 1–13.

Dai, S., He and He, L. (2020): Autonomous WiFi Fingerprinting for Indoor Localization. *2020 ACM/IEEE 11th International Conference on Cyber-Physical Systems (ICCPS)*, Sydney, NSW, Australia, pp. 141-150.

Dillenbourg, P. (2000). *Collaborative-learning: Cognitive and Computational Approaches*. Elsevier, Oxford, UK.

Maqsood, A. et al. (2021). 'The paradigm shift for educational system continuance in the advent of COVID-19 pandemic: Mental health challenges and reflections', *Current Research in Behavioral Sciences*, Vol. 2, p. 100011.

Mateescu et al. (2019). 'Collaboration on large interactive displays: a systematic review', *Human-Computer Interaction*, Volume 36, pp. 1–35.

Moore, S. (2017). Superaccurate GPS Chips Coming to Smartphones in 2018. *IEEE Spectrum*. Available at: https://spectrum.ieee.org/superaccurate-gps-chips-coming-to-smartphones-in-2018 (Accessed: 18th January 2023).

Nandakumar, R. et al. (2016) 'FingerIO: Using Active Sonar for Fine-Grained Finger Tracking', *Proceedings of the 2016 CHI Conference on Human Factors in Computing Systems*. San Jose California USA, pp. 1515–1525.

Pereira, A. et al. (2013). 'Holding a tablet computer with one hand: effect of tablet design features on biomechanics and subjective usability among users with small hands', *In: Ergonomics*, Vol. 56, No. 9, pp. 1363–1375.

Qi, J. (2017). A Robust High-Accuracy Ultrasound Indoor Positioning System Based on a Wireless Sensor Network. In *Sensors, Vol. 17, No. 11, p. 2554.*

Sanneblad, J. and Holmquist, L. (2006). 'Ubiquitous Graphics: Combining hand-held and wall-size displays to interact with large images'. *Proceedings of the working conference on Advanced visual interfaces,* pp. 373–377.

Scavella, M.X. and T. (2020). Laser 3D Scanner Uses Raspberry Pi. *Circuit Cellar*. Available at: https://circuitcellar.com/research-design-hub/laser-3d-scanner-uses-raspberry-pi/ (Accessed: 5 July 2023).

Sekimori, D. and Miyazaki, F. (2007). 'Precise Dead-Reckoning for Mobile Robots using Multiple Optical Mouse Sensors', Filipe, J., Ferrier, J.-L., Cetto, J. A. and Carvalho, M. (eds.) *Informatics in Control, Automation and Robotics II*. Dordrecht: Springer Netherlands, pp. 145–151.

Wang, S. et al. (2018). 'Fingerprinting Acoustic Localization Indoor Based on Cluster Analysis and Iterative Interpolation', *Applied Sciences (Switzerland)*, 8(10), p. 1862.

Zagermann, J. et al. (2016) 'When Tablets meet Tabletops: The Effect of Tabletop Size on Around-the-Table Collaboration with Personal Tablets', *Proceedings of the 2016 CHI Conference on Human Factors in Computing Systems*. New York, NY, USA, pp. 5470–5481.

THE CONVERGENT VALIDITY OF MOBILE LEARNING APPS' USABILITY EVALUATION BY POPULAR GENERATIVE ARTIFICIAL INTELLIGENCE (AI) ROBOTS

Victor K. Y. Chan
Macao Polytechnic University
Rua de Luís Gonzaga Gomes, Macao SAR, China

ABSTRACT

This article seeks to explore the convergent validity of (and thus the consistency between) a few popular generative artificial intelligence (AI) robots in evaluating popular mobile learning apps' usability. The three robots adopted in the study were Microsoft Copilot, Google PaLM, and Meta Llama, which were individually instructed to accord rating scores to the eight major usability dimensions, namely, (1) content/course quality, (2) pedagogical design, (3) learner support, (4) technology infrastructure, (5) social interaction, (6) learner engagement, (7) instructor support, and (8) cost-effectiveness of 17 currently most popular mobile learning apps. For each of the three robots, the minimum, the maximum, the range, and the standard deviation of the rating scores for each of the eight dimensions were computed across all the mobile learning apps. The rating score difference for each of the eight dimensions between any pair of the above three robots was calculated for each app. The mean of the absolute value, the minimum, the maximum, the range, and the standard deviation of the differences for each dimensions between each pair of robots were calculated across all the apps. A paired sample *t*-test was then applied to each dimension for the rating score difference between each robot pair over all the apps. Finally, Cronbach's coefficient alpha of the rating scores was computed for each of the eight dimensions between all the three robots across all the apps. The computational results were to reveal whether the three robots awarded discrimination in evaluating each dimension across the apps, whether each robot, with respect to any other robot, erratically and/or systematically overrate or underrate any dimension over the apps, and whether there was high convergent validity of (and thus consistency between) the three robots in evaluating each dimension across the apps. Among other auxiliary results, it was revealed that the convergent validity of (and the consistency between) the three robots was marginally acceptable only in evaluating mobile learning apps' dimension of (1) content/course quality but not at all in the dimensions (2) pedagogical design, (3) learner support, (4) technology infrastructure, (5) social interaction, (6) learner engagement, (7) instructor support, and (8) cost-effectiveness.

KEYWORDS

Convergent Validity, Mobile Learning Apps, Usability, Generative Artificial Intelligence (AI)

1. INTRODUCTION

Mobile learning apps have become increasingly popular in recent years, with the number of adoptions ever soaring (Camilleri and Camilleri, 2020; Fan and Wang, 2020). As a result, there is a growing need to evaluate the usability of mobile learning apps to ensure that they are effective and user-friendly (Nielsen, 1994) and for users to select mobile learning apps from the market. For such evaluation, traditionally, usability testing has been conducted through manual methods such as questionnaire surveys, interviews, and focus groups (Maramba et al, 2019). However, these methods may be time-consuming, expensive, and subjective.

Generative artificial intelligence (AI) may be a promising alternative to traditional methods of evaluating mobile learning apps' usability. Generative AI refers to a category of AI algorithms that generate new outputs based on the data that they have been trained on. Unlike traditional AI systems that are designed to recognize patterns and make predictions, generative AI creates new content in the form of images, text, audio, and more. (Baidoo-Anu and Ansah, 2023; Gartner, 2023; World Economic Forum, 2023)

Albeit nascent, generative AI, and AI in general, in the context of education has already been extensively examined in extant literature. Macroscopically, for example, Gligorea et al (2023) is a compendious literature review of major AI categories' application to education and learning. More specifically, Leiker et al (2023) addressed the gap concerning the impact of using generative AI to create learning videos with synthetic virtual instructors. In the experiment with $n = 83$ adult learners, those in both the experimental group (adopting an AI-generated learning video with a synthetic virtual instructor) and the control group (employing a traditionally produced instructor video) demonstrated significant improvement from pre- to post-learning ($p < .001$), with no significant differences in gains between the two groups ($p = .80$), and with no qualitative differences in the perceived learning experience. These findings suggest that AI-generated learning videos have the potential to be a viable substitute for videos produced via traditional methods in online educational settings, making high quality educational content more accessible across the globe.

Ilieva et al (2023) spearheaded another application domain. The authors explored and compared the main characteristics of existing educational chatbots leveraging generative AI. They further proposed a new theoretical framework for blended learning with intelligent chatbots integration enabling students to interact online and instructors to create and manage their courses using generative AI tools. The advantages of the proposed framework are as follows: (1) it provides a comprehensive understanding of the transformative potential of AI chatbots in education and facilitates their effective implementation; (2) it offers a holistic methodology to enhance the overall educational experience; and (3) it unifies the applications of intelligent chatbots in teaching–learning activities within universities.

Regrettably, the author is not aware of any existing literature head-on evaluating mobile learning apps' usability by means of generative AI robots. This is exactly the gap that this article is to fill. In particular, this article is to utilize multiple popular generative AI robots to evaluate the various usability dimensions or perspectives of an appreciable number of popular mobile learning apps on the market, drawing on global users' comments on the apps' dimensions as appear on the web. The ultimate purpose is to determine whether the evaluations by the robots are consistent as gauged by the convergent validity of such evaluations. In fact, it is almost impractical to define the superiority of any particular robot's evaluation over others in view of the non-existence of any "yardstick" of evaluation as the paramount reference for any robot's evaluation to benchmark against. All one can do to decide which evaluation to be regarded as reliable is to measure the consistency between multiple evaluations. If a set of evaluations turn out to be consistent, it will be likely, if not absolutely, that all of them are reliable. This is exactly the concept of convergent validity of an operationalized instrument or scale to measure an abstract construct in most social or behavioral sciences. This article seeks to explore such convergent validity of and thus consistency between a few popular generative AI robots in evaluating popular mobile learning apps' usability.

2. METHODOLOGY

2.1 Data and Materials

The present study experimented with three very popular generative AI robots, namely Microsoft Copilot (Cambon et al, 2023), Google PaLM, (Anil, 2023), and Meta Llama (Oxford Analytica, 2023) as candidates for the evaluation of mobile learning apps' usability, the first being bundled with the Microsoft Edge browser and the other two being accessible through the AI portal poe.com. Eight major dimensions to evaluate a mobile learning app's usability were adopted (Albelbisi, 2020; Hew and Cheung, 2014; Khalil and Ebner, 2014; Kizilcec et al., 2013; Liyanagunawardena et al., 2013), they being (1) content/course quality, (2) pedagogical design, (3) learner support, (4) technology infrastructure, (5) social interaction, (6) learner engagement, (7) instructor support, and (8) cost-effectiveness, which were rated by each of the above robots. Content/course quality measures the overall quality and relevance of the course content, including the course design, instructional strategies, and assessment methods. It is essential to ensure that the course content is up-to-date, accurate, and relevant to the learners' needs. The quality of the mobile learning app's content is a critical factor that affects learners' satisfaction with the course. Pedagogical design refers to the design of the courses, including the teaching methods, assessment strategies, and learning outcomes. It is essential to ensure that the courses are designed in a way that encourages active learning and promotes learner engagement. The pedagogical design of a mobile learning app's courses is a critical factor that affects learners' engagement and motivation. Learner support includes the support provided to learners throughout the courses on the mobile learning app. It is essential to ensure that learners have access to adequate support, including technical support and academic support. Learner support is a critical factor that affects learners' completion rates and overall satisfaction with a mobile learning app's courses. Technology infrastructure measures the technological capabilities of the mobile learning app, including its ability to deliver course content, interact with learners, and manage learner data as well as how user-friendly, accessible, and reliable it is. Technology infrastructure may be assessed by metrics like a mobile learning app's uptime, speed of content delivery, compatibility with different devices, and security measures. Social interaction refers to the opportunities for learners to interact with each other and with the instructors. It is essential to ensure that learners have opportunities to collaborate, discuss, and share ideas with each other. Social interaction is a critical factor that affects learners' engagement and satisfaction with a mobile learning app's courses. Learner engagement measures the level of interaction between learners and the course content. Engagement is a crucial factor in determining the effectiveness of a mobile learning app as it affects the learning outcomes of learners. It can be appraised by such metrics as the average time spent on the course content, the number of interactions with the course materials, the number of forum posts and comments by learners, and the average completion rate of the mobile learning app's courses. Instructor support measures the level of support provided to learners by the instructors. Instructor support is important because it fosters a sense of community and increases learner engagement. It can be gauged by metrics such as the response time to learners' queries, the quality of responses to learners' queries, the availability of instructors during course hours, and the frequency of instructor-led sessions. Cost-effectiveness measures the cost of delivering the course content and the benefits derived from it. Cost-effectiveness is important because it determines the viability of a mobile learning app as a mode of delivering education. It can be translated into metrics, namely, the cost per learner, the return on investment of the mobile learning app, the cost savings compared to traditional modes of education delivery, and the revenue generated by the mobile learning app. (Chan, 2023)

The data collection commenced by searching for some popular mobile learning apps through specifying the keywords "mobile learning apps" for the Google search engine, which enumerated 18 apps below:

"Khan Academy, Quizlet, Photomath, EdApp, Kahoot!, iSpring Learn, Adobe Learning Manager, Connecteam-All-In-One, Dayforce, 360Learning, TalentCards, Adobe Connect, Moodle, Socrative Student, TalentLMS, LearnUpon, Trainual, BrainPOP Jr," referring to them as "Applications / M-Learning: From sources across the web." It is noteworthy that the search above effectively "commissioned" the Google search engine to shortlist currently popular mobile learning apps.

Then, the following request, explicitly spelling out the above 18 apps, was submitted to Copilot, PaLM, and Llama individually:

> "For each of the eight dimensions (1) content/course quality, (2) pedagogical design, (3) learner support, (4) technology infrastructure, (5) social interaction, (6) learner engagement, (7) instructor support, and (8) cost-effectiveness, please give a rating score to each of the popular mobile learning apps (namely, Khan Academy, Quizlet, Photomath, EdApp, Kahoot!, iSpring Learn, Adobe Learning Manager, Connecteam-All-In-One, Dayforce, 360Learning, TalentCards, Adobe Connect, Moodle, Socrative Student, TalentLMS, LearnUpon, Trainual, BrainPOP Jr. or as large a subset of them as you like) based on a scale of 1 to 10 (1 being the worst and 10 the best). Please derive your scores from global users' textual comments on these eight dimensions of these platforms as appear all around the web. It would be nice if you put your scores in a table form."

All the three robots replied with the rating scores in all the eight dimensions for all the 18 apps above. It is worth noting that the request above accentuated "...derive your scores from global users' textual comments on these eight dimensions of these platforms as appear all around the web." In order words, the robots were instructed to derive their scores from global users' textual comments appearing all around the web instead of echoing any analogous scores already published somewhere on the web or elsewhere. Also, in view of BrianPOP Jr. targeting the children's market (BrainPOP Educators, 2023) as opposed to the general education market of the remaining 17 apps, the former was excluded from further analysis.

It is noteworthy that all generative AI robots' outputs are dependent on the data on which they were trained, and such training data were inevitably updated up to a certain cutoff date. Any outputs are thus reflective of what the world was as of the cutoff date. By submitting to the three robots a simple question about their training data cutoff dates, it was revealed that Copilot, PaLM, and Llama of this study were trained on data up to somewhere around the end of 2023, September 2021, and September 2022, respectively. In other words, these three robots' rating scores relate to the 17 apps as of these three dates respectively. Equally noteworthy is that this study aimed to examine the convergent validity of (and thus the consistency between) these three robots in evaluating these 17 apps' eight usability dimensions, so its original scope did not include (and, as a matter of fact, its research resources were far insufficient to support) microscopically and technically discerning the way these three robots interpreted, comprehended, and measured each dimension of these 17 apps when being evaluated. Rather, such microscopic and technical (or even algorithmic) details were treated as black boxes such that this study focused on the ultimate evaluation results in the form of rating scores as what they were and on the convergent validity of (and thus the consistency between) these three robots' rating scores awarded to each dimension of the 17 apps irrespective of such microscopic and technical details.

2.2 Analysis

For each of the three robots, the minimum, the maximum, the range, and the standard deviation of the rating scores awarded by the particular robot for each of the eight dimensions were computed across all the 17 mobile learning apps. An appreciable range and standard deviation for a particular dimension signifies that the robot concerned accords discrimination in rating the dimension across the apps.

Then, the rating score difference for each of the eight dimensions between any pair of robots was calculated for each app. The mean of the absolute values, the minimum, the maximum, the range, and the standard deviation of the differences for each dimension between each pair of robots were calculated across all the 17 apps. If the mean of the absolute values, the range, and the standard deviation are sufficiently small for a particular dimension, it is indicated that the robots in the pair neither overrate nor underrate erratically with respect to each other the dimension across the apps. A paired sample t-test was then applied to each dimension for the rating score differences between each robot pair over all the 17 apps. If the t-test is significant for a particular dimension and the corresponding mean difference is positive (negative), it is implied that the first robot in the pair systematically overrates (underrates) the dimension with respect to the second robot.

Finally, for more statistically rigorous confirmation of the consistency between all the three robots' evaluation, Cronbach's coefficient alpha (DeVellis, 2005) of the rating scores was computed for each of the eight dimensions between all the three robots across all the apps. If Cronbach's coefficient alpha is high, for instance, over 0.5 or 0.6 (Ling et al, 2021; Nunnally, 1967) for a particular dimension, it is revealed that there is consistency between all the three robots in rating the dimension across the apps. Stated differently, the corresponding convergent validity of all the three robots in rating the dimension across the apps is high.

3. RESULTS

Table 1 enumerates the minimum, the maximum, the range, and the standard deviation of the rating scores as rated by each of the three robots for each of the eight dimensions across all the 17 mobile learning apps. Whereas all the three robots rated with considerable discrimination, Copilot did more so than the other two robots, especially, in the three dimensions learner support, social interaction, and instructor support as manifested by the disparity between the ranges and the standard deviations of these three dimensions' scores as rated by Copilot and those of other dimensions as also rated by Copilot and between the ranges and the standard deviations of most dimensions' scores as rated by Copilot and those as rated by the other two robots. By the same token, Llama rated the dimension learner support with less discrimination than it rated other dimensions and than the other two robots rated all the eight dimensions.

Table 1. The minimum, the maximum, the range, and the standard deviation of the rating scores as rated by each of the three robots for each of the eight dimensions across all the 17 mobile learning apps

Robot (sample size n)	Minimum/ maximum/ range/ standard deviation	Content/ course quality	Pedagogical design	Learner support	Technology infrastructure	Social interaction	Learner engagement	Instructor support	Cost-effectiveness
Copilot ($n = 17$)	Minimum	6	6	5	6	4	6	5	7
	Maximum	9	9	9	9	9	9	9	10
	Range	3	3	4	3	5	3	4	3
	Standard	0.9583	0.9785	1.2274	0.9984	1.4246	0.9583	1.1991	1.0847

	deviation								
PaLM (*n* = 17)	Minimum	7	7	7	7	6	7	7	8
	Maximum	9	9	9	9	8	9	9	10
	Range	2	2	2	2	2	2	2	2
	Standard deviation	0.6157	0.6157	0.6157	0.6157	0.6860	0.6077	0.6157	0.6157
Llama (*n* = 17)	Minimum	6	5	7	6	5	4	3	6
	Maximum	9	8	8	9	8	7	6	8
	Range	3	3	1	3	3	3	3	2
	Standard deviation	0.6691	0.6691	0.4609	0.6468	0.7838	0.6691	0.6691	0.6391

Table 2 lists the mean of the absolute values, the minimum, the maximum, the range, and the standard deviation of the rating score differences for each of the eight dimensions across all the 17 mobile learning apps between any pair of robots. Relative to PaLM, Copilot appeared to have overrated or underrated erratically the dimension social interaction in view of the corresponding mean of the absolute values, the corresponding range, and the corresponding standard deviation of the differences being greater than or equal to those for all the other seven dimensions. Likewise, in comparison with Llama, Copilot seemed to have overrated or underrated erratically the dimension social interaction as demonstrated by the corresponding range and standard deviation of the differences being greater than those for the remaining seven dimension.

Table 2. The mean of the absolute values, the minimum, the maximum, the range, and the standard deviation of the rating score differences for each of the eight dimension across all the 17 mobile learning apps between each pair of robots

Robot pair (sample size *n*)	Mean of the absolute values/ minimum/ maximum/ range/ standard deviation of the differences	Content/ course quality	Pedagogical design	Learner support	Technology infrastructure	Social interaction	Learner engagement	Instructor support	Cost-effectiveness
Copilot – PaLM (*n* = 17)	Mean of the absolute values	0.6111	0.9444	1.0556	1.0556	1.1667	0.8889	1.1111	0.8889
	Minimum	-2	-2	-3	-2	-2	-2	-2	-2
	Maximum	2	2	2	2	3	2	2	2
	Range	4	4	5	4	5	4	4	4
	Standard deviation	1.0432	1.1618	1.4061	1.2433	1.4818	1.0626	1.4142	1.2042
Copilot – Llama (*n* = 17)	Mean of the absolute values	0.8889	1.5556	1.1111	1.2778	1.3889	2.4444	3.2778	1.6111
	Minimum	-2	-1	-3	-2	-3	0	0	-1
	Maximum	2	3	2	2	3	4	5	4
	Range	4	4	5	4	6	4	5	5
	Standard deviation	1.0966	1.3284	1.4552	1.3198	1.8875	1.3525	1.7017	1.4127
PaLM – Llama (*n* = 17)	Mean of the absolute values	0.3889	1.2778	0.3889	0.4444	0.5556	2.3333	3.2778	1.6111
	Minimum	-1	0	-1	-1	-1	1	2	1
	Maximum	1	2	2	1	2	3	4	3
	Range	2	2	3	2	3	2	2	2
	Standard deviation	0.5745	0.5745	0.6691	0.5941	0.8085	0.5941	0.5745	0.6978

Table 3 depicts the paired sample *t*-tests of the rating score differences for each of the eight dimensions between each pair of robots over all the 17 mobile learning apps. Vis-à-vis Llama, Copilot tended to systematically overrate the five dimensions pedagogical design (at the 1% significance level or $p < 0.01$), technology infrastructure ($p < 0.05$), learner engagement ($p < 0.01$), instructor support ($p < 0.01$), and

cost-effectiveness ($p < 0.01$) whilst PaLM inclined to systematically overrate the four dimensions pedagogical design, learner engagement, instructor support, and cost-effectiveness, all at the 1% significance level
($p < 0.01$). Otherwise, with respect to each other, the three robots neither overrated nor underrated systematically any other dimensions.

Table 3. The paired sample *t*-test of the rating score differences for each of the eight dimensions between each pair of robots over all the 17 mobile learning apps

Differences (sample size *n*)	Dimension	Mean difference / [95% confidence interval]	*t* (*p*-value) / degrees of freedom
	Content/course quality	.059 / [-.438, .556]	.251 (.805) / 16
	Pedagogical design	.000 / [-.603, .603]	.000 (1.000) / 16
	Learner support	-.294 / [-1.038, .450]	-.838 (.415) / 16
Copilot – PaLM	Technology infrastructure	.353 / [-.301, 1.007]	1.144 (.269) / 16
(*n* = 17)	Social interaction	.118 / [-.629, .865]	.334 (.743) / 16
	Learner engagement	.000 / [-.545, .545]	.000 (1.000) / 16
	Instructor support	.059 / [-.656, .774]	.174 (.864) / 16
	Cost-effectiveness	-.176 / [-.786, .433]	-.614 (.548) / 16
	Content/course quality	.353 / [-.191, .896]	1.376 (.188) / 16
	Pedagogical design	1.294 / [.596, 1.993]	3.928 (.001**) / 16
	Learner support	.000 / [-.771, .771]	.000 (1.000) / 16
Copilot – Llama	Technology infrastructure	.706 / [.007, 1.404]	2.142 (.048*) / 16
(*n* = 17)	Social interaction	.353 / [-.591, 1.296]	.793 (.439) / 16
	Learner engagement	2.353 / [1.674, 3.032]	7.349 (.000**) / 16
	Instructor support	3.353 / [2.501, 4.204]	8.348 (.000**) / 16
	Cost-effectiveness	1.471 / [.741, 2.200]	4.272 (.001**) / 16
	Content/course quality	.294 / [-.008, .596]	2.063 (.056) / 16
	Pedagogical design	1.294 / [.992, 1.596]	9.077 (.000**) / 16
	Learner support	.294 / [-.059, .647]	1.768 (.096) / 16
PaLM – Llama	Technology infrastructure	.353 / [.041, .665]	2.400 (.029) / 16
(*n* = 17)	Social interaction	.235 / [-.192, .663]	1.167 (.260) / 16
	Learner engagement	2.353 / [2.041, 2.665]	16.000 (.000**) / 16
	Instructor support	3.294 / [2.992, 3.596]	23.104 (.000**) / 16
	Cost-effectiveness	1.647 / [1.286, 2.008]	9.675 (.000**) / 16

** $p < 0.05$; ** $p < 0.01$

Table 4 delineates Cronbach's coefficient alpha of the rating scores for each of the eight dimensions between all the three robots over all the 17 mobile learning apps. Of all the eight dimensions, only the dimension content/course quality rendered a value of Cronbach's coefficient alpha marginally high enough (Nunnally, 1967) to indicate consistency between the three robots in evaluating the dimension. The values of Cronbach's coefficient alpha for the dimensions learner support, technology infrastructure, instructor support, and cost-effectiveness were found unavailable, implying sublimely inconsistency between the three robots. Likewise, those for the dimensions pedagogical design, social interaction, and learner engagement were all less than .15, uncovering similar inconsistency probably to a lesser extent. In summary, on the one hand, the convergent validity of the three robots was marginally acceptable for the dimension content/course quality, and thus the three robots may be rather reliable in evaluating this dimension of mobile learning apps' usability. On the other hand, the convergent validity of all the remaining seven dimensions was far from practicality, and thus one is better off refraining from evaluating these dimensions of mobile learning apps' usability by these three robots at least in the way adopted in this study.

Table 4. Cronbach's coefficient alpha of the rating scores for each of the eight dimensions between all the three robots over all the 17 mobile learning apps

Sample size *n*	Content/ course quality	Pedagogical design	Learner support	Technology infrastructure	Social interaction	Learner engagement	Instructor support	Cost-effectiveness
17	.566	.115	Nil [a]	Nil [a]	.149	.141	Nil [a]	Nil [a]

[a] In violation of the assumptions underlying Cronbach's coefficient alpha due to a negative average covariance among the rating scores accorded by the three robots.

4. CONCLUSION

There are quite some factors underlying inconsistency between generative AI robots in the evaluation of mobile learning apps or electronic learning platforms in general (or, in fact, anything under the sun). Albeit generative AI robots are promising as a new-fangled method to incisively analyze global users' textual comments at scale and to rate the multifaceted dimensions of each mobile learning app based on such comments, robots are beset by a number weaknesses. Inconsistency between different robots may be ascribed to the weaknesses as illuminated by Chan's (2023) study on MOOC platforms, which are tangentially comparable to mobile learning apps, and adaptively outlined below:

1. Textual user comments on mobile learning apps hinge on the content/courses experienced by the users concerned. Even for the same app, user comments may differ owning to the different content/courses studied.
2. Textual user comments are subjective and susceptible to bias or variation to the extent that even for the same mobile learning app, user comments may vary substantially across particular users.
3. Given profuse disparate user comments, a particular robot's ratings for a particular mobile learning app are very specific to the sample of user comments included in the robot's training. Therefore, it comes as no surprise to uncover discrepancy between two or more robots' ratings for the same app while the robots were presumably trained on different samples of user comments.
4. On the one hand, generative AI robots (inclusive of the three in this study) are powered by language models of considerably varied technologies and scales (Cambon et al, 2023; Anil, 2023; Oxford Analytica, 2023). For example, the number of parameters in the robots and the volumes of training data may differ tremendously. On the other hand, mobile learning apps (for example, the 17 ones in this study) may target disparate market niches and thus feature differently functionalities. In particular, the user interface, the gamification level, the multimedia content support, etc. may differ drastically across the apps. When different robots evaluate different apps, there may be a second degree of variation, precipitating inconsistency between the robots. The inconsistencies manifested in Tables 1 to 3 may have resulted as such.

One intriguing point in contrast with Chan's (2023) study on MOOC platforms is that the consistency found in the current study is far lower than that in Chan's. Whether this is due to the inherent nature of mobile learning apps versus that of MOOC platforms or due to the algorithms in the robots is beyond the scope of the current study and could be a subject of further research.

Also, this study itself is not without its critics. First, only three generative AI robots Copilot, PaLM, and Llama were experimented with in this study against the backdrop of myriad robots in operation worldwide. Second, these three robots were trained on data up to some cutoff dates, so even the rating scores generated by them today cannot catch up with the latest mobile learning apps and their versions. Therefore, it is invaluable to further extend the range of generative AI robots, in particular, those having incorporated the most current data in their training. Third, the disparity between the 17 apps regarding the volumes of global users' textual comments on them may have biased the evaluation by the three robots. Whereas this disparity is beyond the control of the author, this study tended to "absorb" such disparity and focused on the ultimate evaluation results in the form of rating scores as what they were and on the convergent validity of (and thus the consistency between) these three robots' rating scores awarded to each dimension of the 17 apps. In case of high convergent validity, all the three robots would theoretically be trustworthy to an extent even if such disparity existed.

Notwithstanding the relatively low convergent validity identified in this study and the other limitations above, generative AI robots are undeniably poised to be a major means of evaluation of opinions whether in academia or industry and whether in the domain of mobile learning apps or otherwise. Such evaluation is way less time-consuming, less expensive, less subjective, and broader in the coverage of more opinions from more users of more geographic locales worldwide than evaluation by humans.

REFERENCES

Albelbisi, N. A., (2020). Development and Validation of the MOOC Success Scale (MOOC-SS). *In Education and Information Technologies*, Vol. 25, No. 5, pp. 4535-4555. Accessed December 29, 2023 at https://doi.org/10.1007/s10639-020-10186-4

Anil, R., (2023). PaLM 2 Technical Report. *arXiv:2305.10403v3*. Accessed December 13, 2023 at https://doi.org/10.48550/arXiv.2305.10403

Baidoo-Anu, D. and Ansah, L. O., (2023). Education in the Era of Generative Artificial Intelligence (AI): Understanding the Potential Benefits of ChatGPT in Promoting Teaching and Learning. *Journal of AI*, Vol.:7, No. 1, pp. 52-62. Accessed December 12, 2023 at https://dergipark.org.tr/en/pub/jai/issue/77844/1337500.

BrainPOP Educators, (2023). BrianPOP Jr. Accessed December 14, 2023 at https://educators.brainpop.com/contact-us

Cambon, A. et al., (2023). Early LLM-based Tools for Enterprise Information Workers Likely Provide Meaningful Boosts to Productivity. Accessed December 13, 2023 at https://www.microsoft.com/en-us/research/uploads/prod/2023/12/AI-and-Productivity-Report-First-Edition.pdf

Camilleri, M.A. and Camilleri, A.C., (2020). The Students' Readiness to Engage with Mobile Learning Apps. *In Interactive Technology and Smart Education*, Vol. 17, No. 1, pp. 28-38. Accessed December 12, 2023 at https://doi.org/10.1108/ITSE-06-2019-0027

Chan, V. K. Y., (2023). Evaluating Popular MOOC Platforms by Generative Artificial Intelligence (AI) Robots: How Consistent are the Robots? *Proceedings of 20th International Conference on Cognition and Exploratory Learning in Digital Age 2023 (CELDA 2023)*. Madeira Island, Portugal, pp. 329-336.

DeVellis, R. F., (2005). Inter-rater reliability. In Kempf-Leonard, K., *Encyclopedia of Social Measurement*. Elesvier.

Fan, J. and Wang, Z., (2020). The Impact of Gamified Interaction on Mobile Learning APP Users' Learning Performance: the Moderating Effect of Users' Learning Style. *In Behaviour & Information Technology*, pp. 1-14.

Gartner, (2023). Gartner Experts Answer the Top Generative AI Questions for Your Enterprise: Generative AI isn't just a Technology or a Business Case — it is a Key Part of a Society in Which People and Machines Work Together. Accessed December 12, 2023 at https://www.gartner.com/en/topics/generative-ai

Gligorea, I. et al, (2023). Adaptive Learning Using Artificial Intelligence in e-Learning: A Literature Review. *Education Sciences*, Vol 13, No. 12, pp. 1216. Accessed December 12, 2023 at https://doi.org/10.3390/educsci13121216

Hew, K. F. and Cheung, W. S., (2014). Students' and Instructors' Use of Massive Open Online Courses (MOOCs): Motivations and Challenges. *In Educational Research Review*, Vol. 12, pp. 45-58. doi: 10.1016/j.edurev.2014.05.001

Ilieva, G. et al, (2023). Effects of Generative Chatbots in Higher Education. *Information*, Vol. 14, No. 9, pp. 492. Accessed December 12, 2023 at https://doi.org/10.3390/info14090492

Khalil, H. and Ebner, M., (2014). MOOCs Completion Rates and Possible Methods to Improve Retention - A Literature Review. *Proceedings of EdMedia 2014--World Conference on Educational Media and Technology*. pp. 1305-1313.

Kizilcec, R. F. et al, (2013). Deconstructing Disengagement: Analyzing Learner Subpopulations in Massive Open Online Courses. *Proceedings of the Third ACM International Conference on Learning Analytics and Knowledge*. pp. 170-179. doi: 10.1145/2460296.2460330

Leiker, D. et al, (2023). Generative AI for Learning: Investigating the Potential of Learning Videos with Synthetic Virtual Instructors. In Wang, N. et al (eds), Artificial Intelligence in Education. Posters and Late Breaking Results, Workshops and Tutorials, Industry and Innovation Tracks, Practitioners, Doctoral Consortium and Blue Sky. AIED 2023. *Communications in Computer and Information Science*, Vol 1831. Accessed December 12, 2023 at https://doi.org/10.1007/978-3-031-36336-8_81

Ling, H.-C. et al, (2021). Exploring the factors affecting customers' intention to purchase a smart speaker. *In Journal of Retailing and Consumer Services*, Vol. 59.

Liyanagunawardena, T. R. et al, (2013). MOOCs: A Systematic Study of the Published Literature 2008-2012. *In The International Review of Research in Open and Distributed Learning*, Vol. 14, No. 3, pp. 202-227. doi: 10.19173/irrodl.v14i3.1455

Maramba, I. et al, (2019). Methods of Usability Testing in the Development of eHealth Applications: A Scoping Review. *In International Journal of Medical Informatics*, Vol. 126, pp. 95-104. Accessed December 12, 2023 at https://doi.org/10.1016/j.ijmedinf.2019.03.018.

Nielsen, J., (1994). *Usability Engineering*. Morgan Kaufmann Publishers, San Francisco, USA.

Nunnally, J. C., (1967). *Psychometric Theory*. McGraw-Hill, New York, USA.

Oxford Analytica, (2023). Meta LLaMa leak raises risk of AI-linked harms. *Expert Briefings*. Accessed December 13, 2023 at https://doi.org/10.1108/OXAN-ES276597

World Economic Forum, (2023). What is Generative AI? An AI Explains Accessed December 12, 2023 at https://www.weforum.org/agenda/2023/02/generative-ai-explain-algorithms-work/

EDUCITY, A PROJECT FOR A SUSTAINABLE SMART LEARNING CITY ENVIRONMENT – PRELIMINARY RESULTS

Rita Rodrigues[1,2], João Ferreira-Santos[2], Julia Draghi[2], Margarida M. Marques[2] and Lúcia Pombo[2]
[1]*Research Center on Didactics and Technology in the Education of Trainers*
[2]*(CIDTFF), Department of Education and Psychology (DEP), University of Aveiro, Portugal*

ABSTRACT

To drive effective change towards sustainable development, several courses of action have been devised, and education was pointed as a way to attain this goal. Recognizing the impact of learning in context, it is essentialto develop innovative educational proposals that bring schools into other social contexts. This study aims to present, albeit preliminarily, the potential of the EduCITY smart learning city environment for Education for Sustainable Development. The research explores mixed methods to analyse students' perceptions of one component of the smart learning city environment, the EduCITY app, which supports mobile educational games, and its potential to promote learning about sustainable development. To this end, an analysis of data collected during five educational game activities supported by this app was conducted. Data was collected anonymously through a post-game questionnaire, and through automatic app logs of game performance. Participating students recognised the value of the EduCITY app in promoting education for sustainable development. There was also a positive trend in promoting learning about sustainability through the scores andnumber of correct and incorrect answers per game. This article presents indicators of the value of the EduCITY project in promoting sustainable smart learning city environments, specifically through the use of the EduCITYapp and its multimedia resources. Future work includes the co-creation of games with students, teachers and citizens towards education for sustainability to gather data to assess whether the EduCITY smart learning cityenvironment can promote changes in citizens to empower them towards sustainable development.

KEYWORDS

Education for Sustainable Development, Mobile Learning, Game-Based Learning, Augmented Reality, Smart Learning City Environment

1. INTRODUCTION

The current era faces significant change and challenges in social, cultural, technological, and environmental domains (UN, 2015). Responding to these multiple challenges, various players and international organizations are turning to Education as an agent of transformation (Morin, 2002).

Technological advances have brought new potentialities to Education (OECD, 2022), as, e.g., the use of mobile devices is blurring the spatial boundaries of schools (Scavarelli et al., 2021), and capitalizing on new learning dynamics (UNESCO, 2021). One highlighted focus areas is the field of Education for Sustainable Development (UNESCO, 2021). This emphasis stems from the urgent need to change habits, and raise awareness of the emergent issues. Alongside formal activities in Citizenship Education and informal educative awareness-raising, bringing the school closer to students, and their families, daily lives has proved to be a fundamental change factor (UNESCO, 2021). The development of new educational strategies that take place outside the school environment makes Education closer to reality and involve those contexts in new dynamics (Pombo & Marques, 2019; Sebastián-López & González, 2020). These new dynamics are based not only on new trans- and interdisciplinary conceptions of curriculum development but also on new learning approaches, such as Game-based Learning (Pombo, 2022). By adding other technological possibilities, namely Augmented Reality (AR) resources, it is possible to develop educational solutions that are both engaging and innovative.

Building on EduPARK success (funded by FEDER and FCT), which won the prestigious 2018 Team Award for Innovation in Teaching & Learning from the European Consortium of Innovative Universities (ECIU), the

EduCITY aims to promote sustainable cities via a smart learning city environment supported by a mobile app featuring AR and challenge-based location games. The app is fed by a game creation web platform for users without programming skills. Games validated by the EduCITY team become available to all. This innovative pedagogy fosters "learning by doing", where AR mobile games enable environmental awareness in the city (Pombo, 2022). This work focuses on the app component. It allows the exploration of AR content deployed through image-based markers, such as natural markers (e.g., tiles) or markers in plaques installed for that purpose (Pombo, 2022). This AR technology and other multimedia content, such as 3D objects, videos, or images are supported by mobile devices, which are accessible and have high potential for educational purposes (Schaal & Lude, 2015; Sung et al., 2016). The EduCITY app relies on games that employ cross-subjects questions gradually revealed along previously planned paths. This approach potentially promotes engagement and motivation, considering the main factors that impact student performance during the learning process (Fatih, Kumalija & Sun, 2018). Mobile AR and other multimedia content serve as effective pedagogical tools for Education for Sustainable Development, enabling students to learn and reflect on their behaviour through games. Anonymous data collection on game performance, combined with the results of the anonymous questionnaires offer insights of, e.g., participants' awareness and behaviours change towards sustainable development. Although the EduCITY smart learning city environment is still in development, game playing activities with the app prototype have already been carried out with students from different educational levels, which are presented in the following sections.

The aim of this article is to analyse, albeit preliminarily, the potential of the smart learning city environment, created under the EduCITY project, for Education for Sustainable Development. It is organized into four sections. The first, the Introduction, contextualizes and introduces the aim of study, briefly showing the links between the different analysed themes and introducing one of the smart learning city environment components, the EduCITY app. The second section is focused on the methodological options, presenting data collection and analysis processes and tools. This section also deepens the research context, including the EduCITY app, the games implemented with students, and the multimedia resources integrated into the games. The third section presents the preliminary results and their discussion, using graphics to facilitate the reading and interpretation of data. Analysing preliminary data makes it possible to evaluate, validate, and improve the app's features and games. The fourth section focuses on the conclusions, with special emphasis on the value of the EduCITY app. Proposals for future research are also presented, based on the development of the app and new games.

2. MATERIALS AND METHODS

This paper reports a mixed methods study that aims to analyze students' perceptions regarding the EduCITY app and its potential to promote learning about sustainable development. To answer the research question "What are the students' perceptions about the value of the activity to promote sustainable development after playing with the EduCITY app?", the research team organized five activities for students to play a game in April and May 2023. These activities involved 132 students (from school-year 7 to 11), from four different schools located in Aveiro, Vila Real, Porto, and Cinfães. In each activity, students were organized in groups of 2-5 elements, according to the availability of adults to accompany the students in the activities. Three different games were used in the five activities, depending on the age of the students: "EduCITY on the UA campus", "UA Informa" and "Recursos Naturais por Aveiro" [Natural Resources in Aveiro]. All the games and multimedia resources were developed by the EduCITY team, except the "Recursos Naturais por Aveiro game. This later game was co-created by an 8th-grade class under the supervised teaching practice of the Master's course in "Teaching Biology and Geology in the 3rd Cycle of Basic Education and Secondary Teaching" at the University of Aveiro. In each game, a path in Aveiro city was defined, questions and answers were formulated, and associated multimedia resources were produced.

The games were played by 132 participant-students and all agreed to participate in this study. According to the defined exclusion criteria, 24 questionnaires were excluded and a total of 108 questionnaires were considered valid. The exclusion criteria were: questionnaires answered incompletely; questionnaires with the same answer selected to all the sentences, questionnaires with several answers to the same sentence. Regardless of the chosen game, each group played the game for an average of one hour using a smartphone of the project, as the app was not available in the stores yet. The games were previously downloaded to mobile devices and no internet connection was required to play *in situ*.

This section comprises three subsections: i) a description of the EduCITY app and the games implemented; ii) a description of the types of multimedia resources integrated into the EduCITY app; and iii) data collectionand analysis approaches and tools.

2.1 EduCITY App

Having as the main challenge the promotion of smart and sustainable cities, the EduCITY project (https://educity.web.ua.pt/) creates a disruptive smart learning city environment. The most visible component is the mobile app that supports active location games with challenges and multimedia resources. This app is available in Portuguese and English, and it is one of the main outputs of the project (Pombo, 2022).

Designed for user-friendliness, the app is fed with co-created games and multimedia resources to be explored while touring the city. These games are co-created by educational stakeholders (teachers and students of all levels, from Basic to Higher Education) and the wider community in training courses and workshops. Any interested user can create a game in the web-platform that is immediately available to be tested in the app through a specific code. To be publicly available, games are submitted for validation by the EduCITY team. The platform collects anonymous game logs for the game creators to be able to analyse and decide on eventual improvements to conduct (Pombo, 2022).

This innovative pedagogy uses real-world pervasive and mobile devices for "learning by doing", where the AR games allow environmental awareness in the city, which becomes a living laboratory of experimentation, and citizens act as "active scientists" and agents in sustainable changes (Pombo & Marques, 2019).

The app features a mascot, "Mr. Pinky" the flamingo, guiding players through the game journey. "Mr. Pinky" directs players to the points of interest in the city, gives access to multimedia content, and supports players' in answering multiple-choice questions. In the EduCITY app, multimedia resources serve various purposes, such as, to contextualize the players, provide information, and visualization of difficult concepts.

It is important to highlight that for this study, three different games integrated into the EduCITY app were considered. The "EduCITY on the UA campus" game (see Figure 1) was the first one to be tested by students. In this activity, 27 secondary teaching students from Aveiro explored the UA Campus, visited nine points of interest, and answered 24 questions. All students agreed to participate in this study and answered the questionnaire, but 2 questionnaires were excluded. After this first activity, some corrections were made, such as the improvement of the questions itself for increased clarity, and the enhancement of the multimedia resources. The revised game was implemented again with 35 students from Vila Real. Once more, all students agreed to participate in this study and answered the questionnaire, but 10 questionnaires were excluded. This game was also played by 32 students from Porto. Again, all students agreed to participate in this study, but 4 questionnaires were excluded. This game was played by 94 participating students, but only 78 questionnaires were considered for this study.

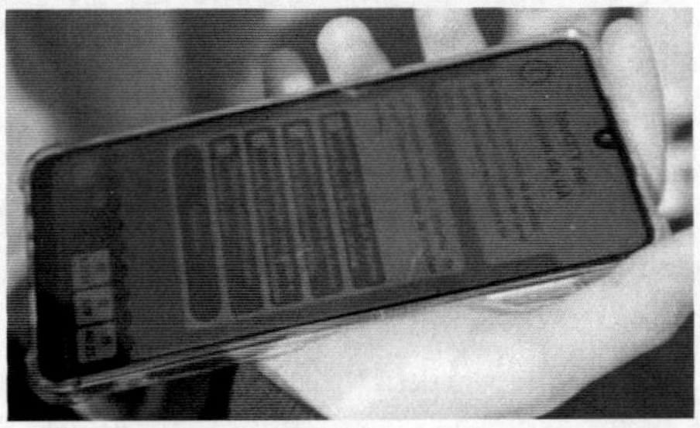

Figure 1. Students playing the "EduCITY on the UA campus" game

The "UA Informa" game was developed in collaboration with the UA Informa project (https://www.ua.pt/pt/uainforma). Thus, all the resources developed by UA Informa were integrated into the EduCITY app. This game follows a path through the UA Campus with 11 points of interest and 33 questions on the multimedia resources or the local context of each point of interest. This game was implemented with the smallest group, consisting of 10 students from Cinfães. One of the questionnaires was excluded.

The "Recursos Naturais por Aveiro" game was co-developed by 28 students from an 8th-grade class and 2 future-teachers under their Masters' Teacher Education course. The aim was to promote the 8th-grade student's ability to question, work collaboratively, and learn about natural resources and their sustainable exploitation.

All students participated in this study, but 7 questionnaires were excluded.

All games integrate challenges and multiple-choice questions aiming to promote learning related to the following topics: recycling, renewable energies, food waste, and ocean plastic pollution, articulating curricular contents of Science, Mathematics, Education for Citizenship, and cultural aspects of Aveiro city. Players always get immediate constructive feedback to their answers, after selecting the correct or incorrect answer(s). The feedback is developed to explain the correct answer or to give further information on the topic.

AR integrates virtual information that complements the observable reality in some specific locations and multimedia resources (images, videos, and audio) that are conceived to support students in answering correctly the questions, in an appealing way (Pombo & Marques, 2019). Immediately after finishing the game, symbolic EduCITY prizes were given to the teams with the best performance and the students participating in this study voluntarily answered an evaluation questionnaire.

2.2 Multimedia Resources Integrated into the EduCITY App

Depending on their purpose, multimedia resources can take different formats including image, video, audio,and in the case of AR, 3D models. Multimedia resources are used to motivate students to learn about sustainable development, and games become more attractive with virtual elements combined with the real elements of the city. The images, videos, and audio are associated to the questions' introduction and/or feedback. For the development of these resources, a bibliographical search is made, and reliable information websites are consulted, to guarantee the quality of the content.

During the game path, the students have to search for AR markers that contain information that supports the answer to specific questions. The AR markers can be natural, or they can be installed on EduCITY information plaques. The natural markers are, typically, photographs of cultural heritage (e.g., tiles), of city signals (e.g., information signals at the entrance of museums), among others. They give access to a variety of content, usually based on text and images. The AR markers installed on plaques include information about plant species. All plaques have the same content layout – AR Book – but the information in each one varies according to the plant species, such as the scientific and common names, the information about the plant, leaf, flower, and fruit, its family (in biological classification), its origin and some curiosities (Figure 2). These plaques are installed at the University of Aveiro and across Aveiro city.

Figure 2. An example of a plant species AR Book content, triggered through 2D marker detection

In more detail, when selecting the "Plant" button information about the plant is displayed, such as its height and the trunk. The "Leaf" button displays a description of the leaf, including its morphology. It can also contain a photograph or a 3D model of the leaf. The same applies to the flower and the fruit. To produce the 3D models of the leaves, each was photographed from both sides without zooming and on a white base. Then the model was assembled using the Blender program. Furthermore, the 3D models of the flowers and fruits (Figure 3) were made with the Polycam Pro app, a 3D capture app (Figure 3). On the right side of the board, the "Origin" button indicates the origin of the species plant, mentioning whether it is a native or exotic species. This information is supported by a map with the respective distribution highlighted. The "Ecology" button presents the habitat and the months in which the species is in the flowering or fructifying states, with illustrative photographs. The "Curiosities" button contains a variety of information, including the meaning of the scientific and common names, and other facts, e.g., its medicinal use.

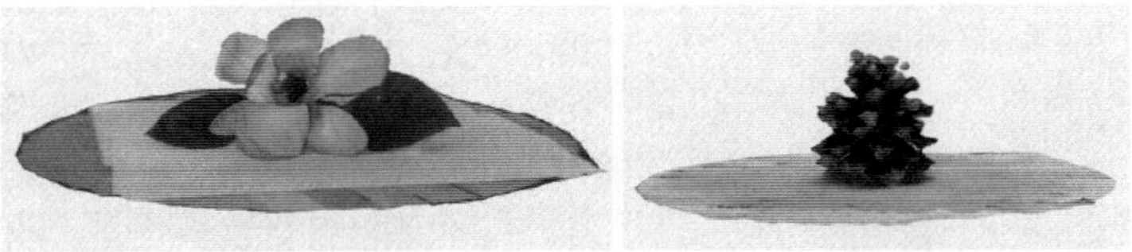

Figure 3. Examples of 3D capture using the Polycam Pro app

The AR multimedia resources can be created by the EduCITY team and also by other users, such as teachers and students without programming skills, for project sustainability after the funding period.

2.3 Data Collection and Analysis

Data was collected anonymously through a post-game questionnaire and automatic game performance logsof the following games: "EduCITY on the UA Campus", "UA Informa" and "Recursos Naturais por Aveiro". Due to the nature of these activities, it was not possible to arrange a pre-test date.

The questionnaire was divided into four sections: A. Value of the activity in promoting learning about sustainable development; B. Evaluation of the EduCITY application; C. Global appreciation of the activity; and D. Profile of the respondents. This study focuses on section A, which requires students to select one option from a 5-point Likert scale of their level of agreement (strongly disagree, disagree, neutral, agree, strongly agree) with eight statements. The sentences collect data on: knowledge, skills, values and attitudes towards sustainability. The sentences are antagonistically worded, i.e., each topic has one sentence positively worded and the other negatively worded, to support the identification of a lack of seriousness in completing the questionnaire.

Game performance logs included scores, the number of correct and incorrect answers for each question, and the playing time. This data was collected directly from the app in an anonymous manner and provides indicators of the game's ability to support learning. This quantitative data was analyzed using descriptive statistics and presented in graphs. The results of both data collection methods were triangulated to analyze the value of this game (Creswell & Creswell, 2023) in promoting conservation attitudes. The results are presentedand analyzed in the following section.

3. PRELIMINARY RESULTS AND DISCUSSION

At the time of the activity, students were attending grades 7 to 11 in the Portuguese Education System: 7.40% in grade seven; 59.25% in grade eight; 1.85% in grade nine; 23.15% in grade ten, and 8.33% in grade eleven.

Graphic 1 reveals the student's opinion about the value of the activity to promote Sustainable Development learning. In the sentence "Through this activity, I had access to real-world information, and I learnt about sustainability", 48.1% of the students agreed, 43.5% strongly agreed, 7.4% had a neutral answer, and 0.9% disagreed. No student strongly disagreed with this sentence. The associated sentence, about whether the activityprovides information about sustainability in a way that was difficult to understand, 38.0% of students disagreed, 32.4% strongly disagreed, 14.8% agreed, 10.2% had a neutral answer, and 4.6% strongly agreed. Overall, the majority of the students (strongly) agreed with the positive formulated sentence and (strongly) disagreed withthe negative one, indicating that the activity supported knowledge learning on sustainability.

In the sentence "I feel more confident about environmental sustainability issues", 47.2% of the students agreed, 26.9% strongly agreed, 23.1% had a neutral answer, 1.9% strongly disagreed and 0.9% disagreed. In the opposite sentence, regarding the activity not promoting skills in environmental sustainability, 65,7% of the students strongly disagreed, 13.9% disagreed, 8.3% agreed, 6.5% had a neutral answer, and 5.6% strongly agreed. These results reveal a smaller tendency of students acknowledging the activity's power to promote sustainability skills.

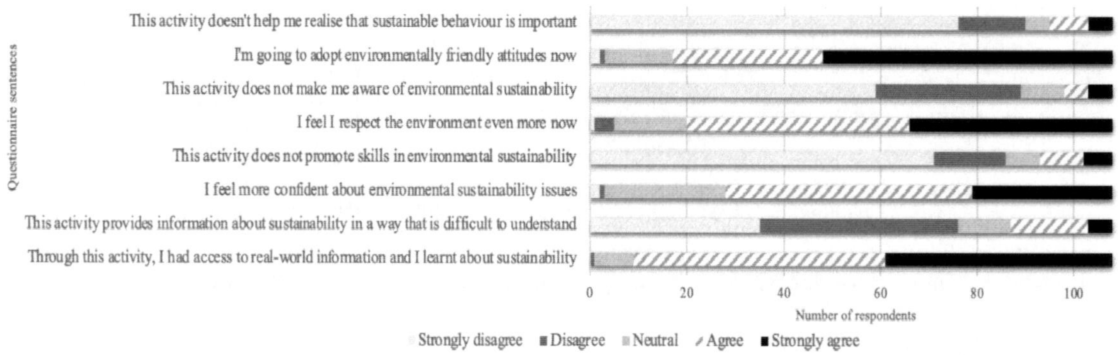

Graphic 1. Students' opinion about the value of the activity to promote sustainable development learning

In the sentence "I feel I respect the environment even more now", 42.6% of students agreed, 38.9% strongly agreed, 13.9% had a neutral answer, 3.7% disagreed, and 0.9% strongly disagreed. On the associated sentence, about the activity's incapacity to make students aware of environmental sustainability, 54.6% of students strongly disagreed, 27.8% disagreed, 8.3% had a neutral answer, 4.6% agreed, and 4.6% strongly agreed. These results reveal a tendency for students to consider that the activity promotes sustainability-related values.

In the sentence "I'm going to adopt environmentally friendly attitudes now", 55.6% of the students strongly agreed, 28.7% agreed, 13.0% had a neutral answer, 1.9% strongly disagreed, and 0.9% disagreed. In the related sentence, regarding the activity not supporting awareness on the importance of sustainable behavior, 70.4% of students strongly disagreed, 13.0% disagreed, 7.4% agreed, 4.6% had a neutral answer, and 4,6% strongly agreed. These results reveal a positive perception regarding the awareness power of the game playing activity of environmental sustainability attitudes.

Considering the analysis of game logs, three different graphics were developed, corresponding to the three played games. Graphic 2 represents the game logs of the 18 groups that played the "EduCITY on UA Campus"game, showing the correct and incorrect answers, per group. The collected data reveal, overall, that students were aware or were able to learn about the game Sustainable topics, since all groups answered mostly correctly,except one group (group 6), whose correct and incorrect answers were in the same number (12).

Related to the "UA Informa" game, Graphic 3 presents the results of the 3 groups of students that played thegame. The data shows that the 3 groups achieved a good game performance considering the number of correctanswers. Although all the groups demonstrated good performance, the group with the highest number of incorrect answers selected 8 incorrect answers in a total of 33 (group 1).

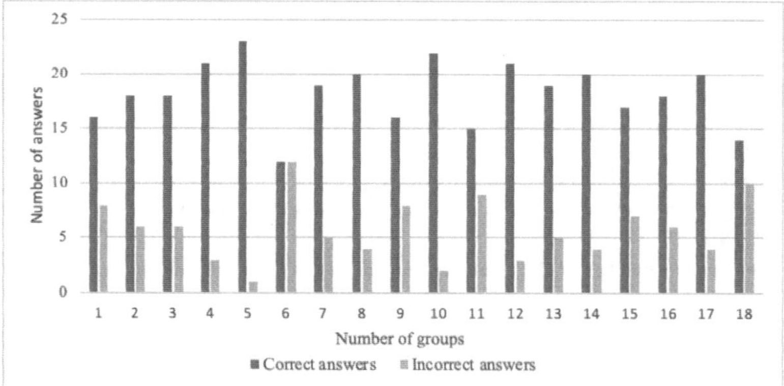

Graphic 2. Summary of student's game results of "EduCITY on the UA campus"

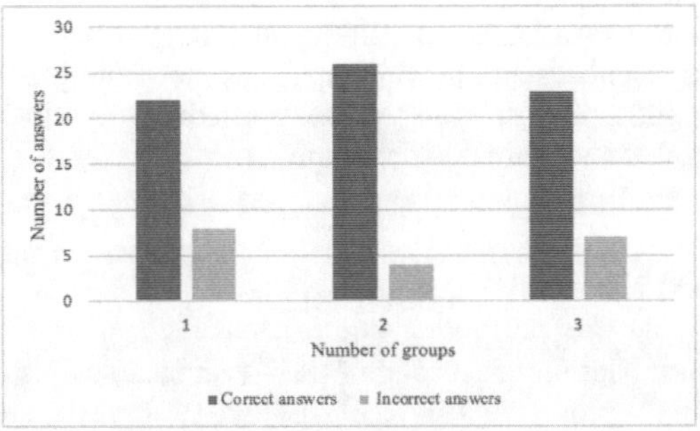

Graphic 3. Summary of student's game results of "UA Informa"

Graphic 4 reveals the game logs considering "Recursos Naturais por Aveiro". Once more, results indicate that students had a good performance based on the high number of the right answers. It is important to highlight that this game was co-created and played by the same students.

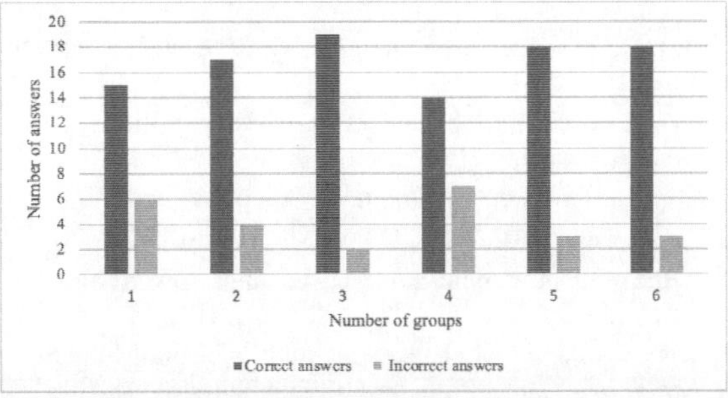

Graphic 4. Summary of student's game results of "Recursos Naturais por Aveiro"

4. CONCLUSION

The results of this study, although preliminary, support the assertion that the EduCITY smart learning city environment, through the exploration of the app and games, enables dynamic learning approaches and brings real context to learning purposes. This is related to the arguments described by Scavarelli et al. (2021), which implies the importance of bringing educational activities into outdoor environments, an issue also highlighted by UNESCO (2021). In addition, it can be shown that the app and its games empower students on Sustainable Development issues, namely, the adoption of new environmentally friendly attitudes. It is also understandable that the positive results may be related to the engagement shown by the students, e.g., when exploring AR resources and visualising videos and images. This is demonstrated by the fact that some questions can only be answered correctly after learning the information on the multimedia resources, e.g., "How long does it take for a plastic bottle to decompose?". Therefore, exploring the EduCITY app allows the exploration of Sustainable Development issues from different digital contents, such as AR. This feature adds new layers of information to reality, and can be used as a pedagogical tool, bringing innovation, richness, and variety of content that can be used through an interdisciplinary and holistic process (Morin, 2002). The design and development of the paths, the selection of the points of interest, and the questions make it possible to enhance these characteristics. In terms of the research question, the five activities developed within the EduCITY app for the collection of data that shows a positive trend about the features of the app itself and the EduCITY project, specifically in terms of Education for Sustainable Development. By using accessible technology, this app brings citizens closer to the development of smart learning city environments. And, since one of the objectives of EduCITY is to promote Sustainable Development, it can be assumed that this objective is being achieved.The results also demonstrate the importance of educational apps, such as EduCITY, in providing innovation and engagement in sustainable development learning.

Future work includes the organization and development of several activities with different co-created games involving different partners, such as schools, municipalities, and enterprises. During this phase, data will be systematically collected to gather information to assess whether the EduCITY app can promote changes in citizens to empower them towards sustainable development.

ACKNOWLEDGEMENT

This work is financed by Portuguese funds through FCT – Fundação para a Ciência e a Tecnologia, I.P. within the framework of the EduCITY project "PTDC/CED-EDG/0197/2021". The first author's work is funded by FCT with a research grant (BI/UI57/8275/2022); the second author work is funded by FCT with a research grant (2023.00257.BD); the forth author work is funded FCT under the Scientific Employment Stimulus - Individual Call (2022.02153.CEECIND).

REFERENCES

Creswell, J. W., & Creswell, J. D. (2023). *Research DeCsign: Qualitative, Quantitative, and Mixed Methods Approaches* (6th ed.). SAGE Publications, Inc.

Fatih, Y., Kumalija, J. & Sun, Y. (2018). 'Mobile learning-based gamification in a history learning context', in *14h International Conference Mobile Learning 2018*, Lisboa, pp. 143–147.

Morin, E. (2002). *Os sete saberes para a educação do futuro*. Edições Piaget.

OECD. (2022). *Trends Shaping Education 2022*. OECD Publishing. https://doi.org/10.1787/6ae8771a-en.

Pombo, L. (2022). Exploring the role of mobile game-based apps towards a smart learning city environment – the innovation of EduCITY. *Education and Training*. https://doi.org/10.1108/ET-06-2022-0238

Pombo, L., & Marques, M. (2019). An app that changes mentalities about Mobile Learning – the EduPARK Augmented Reality Activity. *Computers*, *8(2)*(37). https://doi.org/10.3390/computers8020037

Scavarelli, A., Arya, A., & Teather, R. J. (2021). Virtual reality and augmented reality in social learning spaces: a literature review. *Virtual Reality*, *25*, 257–277. https://doi.org/10.1007/s10055-020-00444-8

Schaal, S., & Lude, A. (2015). Using Mobile Devices in Environmental Education and Education for Sustainable Development - Comparing Theory and Practice in a Nation Wide Survey. *Sustainability (Switzerland)*, *7*(8), 10153– 10170. https://doi.org/10.3390/su70810153

Sebastián-López, M., & González, R. de M. (2020). Mobile Learning for Sustainable Development and Environmental Teacher Education. *Sustainability*, *12*(9757), 1–13. https://doi.org/10.3390/su12229757

Sung, Y. T., Chang, K. E., & Liu, T. C. (2016). The effects of integrating mobile devices with teaching and learning on students' learning performance: A meta-analysis and research synthesis. *Computers and Education*, *94*, 252–275. https://doi.org/10.1016/j.compedu.2015.11.008

UN. (2015). *Transforming our world: the 2030 Agenda for Sustainable Development (A/RES/70/1)*. UN General Assembly. https://doi.org/10.1163/15718093-12341375

UNESCO. (2021). *Reimagining Our Futures Together: A New Social Contract for Education.* https://en.unesco.org/futuresofeducation/

Short Papers

THE USE OF GENERATIVE AI IN MEDICINE: A COMPARISON OF DIFFERENT LLMS ASSISTING WITH WOMEN'S FERTILITY INQUIRIES

Mona Khadem Sameni
Department of Economics, James Madison University
Harrisonburg, Virginia, USA

ABSTRACT

Large Language Models such as ChatGPT, Bard, or Claude, can serve as a novel method for assisting patients receiving medical services. These models that are using deep learning techniques to comprehend natural language and produce human-like responses instantaneously, are especially useful when patients do not have immediate access to their clinicians' inputs. The main goal of this research is to conduct a comparative evaluation of three AI-powered Large Language Models in their ability to assist women seeking information about fertility-related matters. By identifying the strengths and limitations of these Large Language Models (LLMs), we can contribute to the development of more effective AI-driven diagnostic and support systems. This, in turn, can lead to improved patient care within the fields of fertility and endocrinology. Furthermore, it has the potential to lower the strain on specialized healthcare services that experience high patient volumes. This shift can allow healthcare professionals to focus more on the most critical treatments, potentially resulting in a cost-effective channel for patients to access accurate information about their condition. The findings of this research show that overall, ChatGPT4 seems a better choice for patients to receive a timely response to their fertility-related questions. It provides quick, organized, and more complete information and typically guides the patients along the correct path. Although there are occasions where Bard and Claude outperform GPT4 in delivering precise timelines or citing specific references, the data is not compelling enough to challenge ChatGPT4's leading position.

KEYWORDS

LLM, Chatgpt, AI, Women's Health, Fertility

1. INTRODUCTION

Large Language Models (LLMs), a form of artificial intelligence, have recently seen an explosive surge in utilization across various sectors. These natural language models that primarily use transformer models, utilize massive datasets to recognize, translate, and create content. When these technologies are applied to healthcare, they hold a great potential to reshape the dynamic between patients and their healthcare providers and enable both parties to reduce the information asymmetry between them and enables them to make more informed decisions. Recent research, such as that by Balas and Ing (2023) and Santoshi and Noguchi (2023), indicates that since its introduction in late 2022, ChatGPT, one leading AI platform, has been effectively leveraged in healthcare such as to suggest preventive actions in clinical environments. El Dahdah et al. (2023) also highlight the capability of ChatGPT to serve as a "triage" tool during medical emergencies.

The field of obstetrics and gynecology, especially within infertility and endocrinology, is not immune to recent trends. Grunebaum et al. (2023) delve into the promising capabilities of ChatGPT in this realm. They highlight that while ChatGPT offers articulate and insightful responses to obstetrics and gynecological queries, it sometimes falls short in offering the most recent data and proper fact referencing. On a similar note, Sengupta et al. (2023) contrast the performance of ChatGPT3.5, ChatGPT4, and other Large Language Models (LLMs) in augmenting research in gynecology and infertility. Their findings point to challenges like deployment expenses, interpretation difficulties, processing times, and the risk of overfitting. Building on this, Chervenak et al. (2023) investigate the expanding opportunities offered by ChatGPT, taking a set of fertility-related queries from the CDC as a reference. While they acknowledge the significance and pertinence of the information

ChatGPT provides, they also underscore potential improvements, such as specialized training for specific domains and the inclusion of dependable source citations.

This study's primary objective is to expand on existing research, assessing the efficacy of three LLMs—ChatGPT4, Bard, and Claude—in addressing patient queries related to fertility and offering pertinent support. To my awareness, this is the first study, as of October 2023, that evaluates the capacity of these state-of-the-art LLMs to deliver timely insights and possibly, relief, to individuals navigating the complex path of fertility challenges. My core emphasis lies in determining how well these AI systems respond to patient questions, which platform excels in presenting scientifically supported information, which conveys details in a more lucid, structured fashion, and which can transcend basic informational tasks to provide emotional reassurance to couples facing fertility hurdles.

2. AI PLATFORMS AND METHODS

This study offers a comparative analysis of three prominent Large Language Models in offering insights on women's fertility and gynecological concerns. The platforms under examination are ChatGPT4, Bard, and Claude. ChatGPT4, a superior and subscription-based successor of GPT-3, was first introduced to the public in March 2023. This platform, distinct from GPT-3 in its subscription-based access, also offers a free version for the public limited to 10 queries daily. The creator of this advanced language model characterizes it as superior in terms of creativity, visual recognition, and contextual depth.

On the other hand, Bard's waitlist was launched by Alphabet, Google's parent company, in March 2023, following the debut of ChatGPT. Later in May 2023, the waitlist was removed, and people could start using it in more than 180 countries.[1] While its foundational architecture echoes ChatGPT, its main feature is its capability to gather real-time data from the internet. This means users can inquire about weather updates or the latest news headlines. Finally, Claude, Anthropic's chatbot is another next-generation AI assistant that has been designed to provide useful, honest, and helpful information for the users. The architects claim that users have been reporting less harmful output, a more user-friendly platform, and a more personable interaction with the platform.[2]

For this research, I compiled information and rewrote questions posed by members of various publicly available fertility support groups online. These online community members are either undergoing fertility treatments or have previously completed their journey. An initial analysis of the members' inquiries identifies three distinct categories. The first entails medical questions, delving into the specifics of procedures, conditions, and treatments. The second revolves around community and support, aiming to offer encouragement, uplifting anecdotes, and feedback. Lastly, the third category encompasses organizational and administrative queries, including topics like insurance, financing treatment options at the clinics, and communication with the medical and nursing staff.

The primary focus of this research is on clinical and medical queries. To begin, I chose 10 clinical questions at random, which were posted by online community members in the summer and fall of 2023. I then posed these queries to the three AI platforms mentioned earlier, recording the contextual depth and breadth of their answers, and contrasting them with the original responses from the online communities. Additionally, I selected three community and support questions at random to assess how effectively these AI chatbots can offer crucial support during one's fertility journey. Lastly, I selected three administrative questions to determine the proficiency of these LLM platforms in delivering valuable and timely information.

---

[1] https://www.techtarget.com/searchenterpriseai/definition/Google-Bard#:~:text=On%20March%2021%2C%202023%2C%20Google,with%20a%20vague%20release%20date.

[2] https://www.anthropic.com/index/introducing-claude

3. RESULTS

Table 1 displays the questions and answers produced by the three AI systems described earlier. It can be seen that most inquiries revolve around clinical aspects related to fertility and advice on increasing its chances of success. The first column of the table entails the subjects of these queries, covering medication rationales, diagnostic evaluations, optimal timing for pregnancy tests, recommended treatment methods, medication adjustments, physical activities during an IVF cycle, strategies for a successful embryo transfer, alcohol intake while trying to conceive, and the suggested activity intensity post-treatment. Columns 2-5 provide a summarized/itemized version of responses from ChatGPT4, Bard, Claude, and actual feedback from support group members.

Upon initial observation, ChatGPT4 appears to be the most thorough and consistent platform, offering complete and detailed answers to every question. Moreover, it excels in segmenting the discussed topics into smaller sections and delving deeper into each. As an example, in question 1 when prompted to provide the purpose of adding aspirin and pred(nisolone) or blood thinner to an FET (Fresh Embryo Transfer), it breaks the topic down into reasons for aspirin, reasons for prednisolone and reasons for blood thinners. Each medication's benefits are elaborated in more depth compared to the information offered by Bard or Claude. In addition, the information given by any of these platforms, was much more complete than any real-world answers provided by the community members. However, in this very particular case, Bard provides some better background information and offers some research findings. Overall, on question 1, Claude has the weakest performance, with only offering some general reasoning and very broad non-specific context.

Questions 2 and 3 seek timelines for specific diagnostics or pregnancy tests. In response to inquiries about the optimal times for signs or symptoms of pregnancy and initiating tests, ChatGPT4 gives a broad timeframe while highlighting unique situations and individual differences. In contrast, Bard offers a more precise timeline, underscoring that each patient's journey is distinct. A consistent theme across these platforms' replies is their focus on delivering basic advice and urging the patients to seek detailed guidance from their medical team. This advice is of paramount clinical value because the path of pregnancy and fertility is filled with intense stress, influencing potential outcomes and lack of proper support might result in lack of interest in continuing treatments.

Questions 4 and 6, interestingly, received no responses from the online communities. This underscores another potential value of AI platforms in providing sought-after information to patients. A standout feature of ChatGPT4 emerges in its answer to question 6, about a robust medicated protocol. It proficiently presents five varied choices, elaborating on the risks and expenses of each, laying the groundwork for well-informed decisions by patients.

Questions 7-10 ask for guidance on the suitable amount of physical activity while trying for natural conception or post-FET. They also request user recommendations for a fruitful transfer and necessary lifestyle changes, such as refraining from alcohol, as one waits for pregnancy test results. Notably, for question 7, Bard and Claude offer more hands-on and day-to-day suggestions, especially concerning yoga during and post-FET. When inquired about tips for a successful FET, ChatGPT4 lists various strategies, highlighting recommended supplements and environmental hazards to steer clear of. For questions 9 and 10, while all platforms deliver valuable insights, ChatGPT-4 stands out by reinforcing its suggestions with up-to-date scientific references.

Table 1. Provisional Diagnosis/tips/guidelines formulated by Different Generative AI Platforms

Queries	ChatGPT-4	Bard	Claude	Actual User Responses
1) What is the purpose of adding aspirin and pred or blood thinners to a FET ?	Aspirin: 3 reasons Prednisolone: 3 reasons Blood Thinners: 3 reasons General Information: Basic	Aspirin: 4 reasons Prednisolone: 2 reasons Blood Thinners: 2 reasons General Information: -Relevant research cited. -Risks of taking medication mentioned.	A total of 5 reasons mentioned. -Information not classified. -No relevant research cited.	* User answers were mentioned by all three platforms.
2) Is there a particular day in your cycle that you have to get the ERA and Receptiva tests?	ERA: 3 facts Receptiva Dx: 2 facts General Information: -Mention of special circumstances -Warnings given	ERA: 1 fact Receptiva Dx: -Exact timeline given General Information: -Description of tests provided -Warnings given	-Brief Description of both tests. General Information: -Warnings given	*Very incomplete user response.
3) How many days after ovulation did you test positive?	-Complete explanation of early stages of pregnancy. -Mention of approximate timeline -Mention of Variation	-Mention of very broad timeline	-Mention of a very detailed timeline and chances of testing positive.	*User responses were mentioned by all three platforms.
4) Does anybody have experience with being diagnosed with anything other than blocked tubes during HSG procedure?	-Mention of 9 conditions -Categories defined. -Extraordinary situations discussed.	-Mention of 5 conditions -No categories defined.	- Mention of 7 conditions -No categories defined.	*No user responses.
5) what protocol did you do for endo that suppressed endo and gave you success for your ER and FET without laparoscopy?	-Mention of 8 different solutions. -Categories defined.	-Mention of a very broad approach -No categories defined.	-Mention of 6 different protocols. -No categories.	*One user response *Answer discussed by Claude and GPT4
6) Does anyone recommend a more aggressive medication for timed intercourse besides l3traz0l3 and 0vidr3l?	-Mention of 5 alternatives. -Discussion of risks. -Discussion of costs	-Mention of 4 alternatives -No categories defined. -Additional information provided.	-Mention of 7 alternatives. -No categories defined. -Warnings given.	*No user responses.
7)Fertility yoga during stims or after?	-Yoga during each of fertility	-Yoga during and after stims discussed.	-Yoga during each stage of IVF discussed.	*User tips were also discussed by Bard.

	treatments discussed. -Mention of risks	-Tips for Yoga given -Poses recommended.	-Tips for healthy Yoga provided.	
8) Any tips to help make my embryo stick?	-12 tips discussed. -Mention of medications, supplements, and environmental toxins.	-10 tips discussed. -No mention of toxins.	-9 tips discussed. -Mention of mental health and emotional support.	*User tips only discussed stress reduction, discussed by all AI platforms.
9) Should alcohol be avoided when doing fertility treatment?	-Answer: yes. -7 potential risks discussed. -research cited.	Answer: Yes. -4 potential risks discussed. -research cited. -Answers not properly categorized.	Answer: Yes. -6 potential risks discussed. -No mention of research.	*User responses ranged from no drinking to moderate drinking.
10) Talk to me about activity level after transfer.	-Immediate and following days activities discussed. -Additional tips provided.	-Immediate tips provided. -Alternative activities discussed.	-Detailed day-by-day tips provided. -Alternative activities discussed.	*User responses provided by all platforms.

Table 2 highlights various questions on topics that often draw patients to online communities, such as success stories, encouragement, and reassurance. Here, the AI platforms seem to fall short in meeting users' needs. The responses from these platforms are typically either overly broad or entirely made up. For these and other questions categorized earlier as "administrative," the LLMs perform inadequately when retrieving information from the internet or their latest database update, struggling to emulate a genuine human interaction. As of October 2023, it seems Meta AI has tried to address this gap in the market by launching real-time AI assistants3 modeled after celebrities, aiming for a more human-centric experience. Yet, Meta has not released any medical AI assistants, making them unrelated to the objectives of this research.

Table 2. Real-world personal stories

Case	ChatGPT-4	Bard	Claude	Actual User Responses
First time Fresh transfer success stories ? Please share…	-Mention of a few success stories that appear to be fabricated.	Mention of a few success stories that appear to be fabricated.	-Tips for a successful transfer provided.	*Personal stories shared.
Anyone experience late ovulation the cycle after Ivf stims or a failed transfer ?	-Various reasons explained. -Tips offered.	-Only 1 reason explained. -Tips offered.	-Various reasons explained. -Tips offered.	*Personal stories shared.
Has anyone had a positive test with minimal symptoms after transfer?	-Mention of 5 reasons why tests might be positive with no symptoms. - Broad real-world examples discussed.	-No mention of reasons why no symptoms are present. -Coping tips offered.	-Mention of 5 reasons why tests might be positive with no symptoms. -No real world examples. -Coping tips offered.	*Women with no symptoms responded.

[3] https://about.fb.com/news/2023/09/introducing-ai-powered-assistants-characters-and-creative-tools/

4. CONCLUSION

Although joining online communities while trying to conceive can serve as an outlet for women grappling with fertility challenges to share their personal experiences, the information shared often lacks completeness, accuracy, consistency, or even veracity. In such cases, particularly when dealing with medical inquiries, Large Language Models (LLMs) can be invaluable. This is especially crucial for women undergoing time-sensitive treatments, who might not always have immediate access to their physicians or medical teams, especially during weekends or holidays.

This study draws on inquiries and information from publicly available online communities with members who are all undergoing fertility treatments. The research evaluates the performance of three different AI platforms based on 10 commonly asked medical/scientific and 3 community/support questions. Overall, these platforms offer more comprehensive responses to patient medical queries than those provided by the online community members. Notably, ChatGPT4 consistently stands out by delivering more thorough, well-organized answers. It also provides valuable tips, coping strategies, risk warnings, and encourages patients to seek advice from medical professionals.

Between Bard and Claude, Claude demonstrates superior information categorization and offers more useful insights regarding medical inquiries. Furthermore, it excels in providing accurate guidance through various post-treatment steps. However, none of these platforms effectively create a sense of community and support, which can be crucial for alleviating the stress and addressing the mental health needs of women on the journey to conceive. While Meta has embarked on the path of providing a more human-like experience, the current versions of its AI assistants seem to have a long way to go in bridging this much-needed gap.

REFERENCES

Balas, M., & Ing, E. B. (2023). Conversational AI models for ophthalmic diagnosis: Comparison of ChatGPT and the Isabel Pro Differential Diagnosis Generator. *JFO Open Ophthalmology*, 1, 100005.

Chervenak, J., Lieman, H., Blanco-Breindel, M., & Jindal, S. (2023). The promise and peril of using a large language model to obtain clinical information: ChatGPT performs strongly as a fertility counseling tool with limitations. *Fertility and Sterility*, 120(3), 575-583.

El Dahdah, J., Kassab, J., El Helou, M. C., Gaballa, A., Sayles III, S., & Phelan, M. P. (2023). ChatGPT: A valuable tool for emergency medical assistance. *Annals of Emergency Medicine*, 82(3), 411-413.

Grünebaum, A., Chervenak, J., Pollet, S. L. Esq, Katz, A., & Chervenak, F. A. (2023). The Exciting Potential for ChatGPT in Obstetrics and Gynecology. *American Journal of Obstetrics and Gynecology*, 228(6), 696-705.

Honda, S., & Noguchi, T. (2023). Promise and Pitfalls of ChatGPT for Patient Education on Coronary Angiogram. *Annals of the Academy of Medicine*, Singapore, 52(7), 338-339.

Sengupta, P., Dutta, S., Chakravarthi, S., Jegasothy, R., Jeganathan, R., & Pichumani, A. (2023). Comparative Efficacy of ChatGPT 3.5, ChatGPT 4, and other Large Language Models (LLMs) in gynecology and infertility research. *Gynecology and Obstetrics Clinical Medicine*, September 2023.

IDENTIFICATION OF PROSTATE CANCER RISK FACTORS USING THE PROSTATE, LUNG, COLORECTAL AND OVARIAN (PLCO) TRIAL DATA

Alexander Chen,[1] Jeffrey Wang,[1] Davis Zhang,[2] Zhiming Yang[3] and Yulong Gu[4]
[1]*Conestoga High School, 200 Irish Road, Berwyn, PA 19312, USA*
[2]*Chatham High School, 255 Lafayette Avenue, Chatham, NJ 07928, USA*
[3]*MidLantic Urology, 211 S Gulph Rd, King of Prussia, PA, 19406, USA*
[4]*Stockton University, 101 Vera King Farris Drive, Galloway, NJ 08205, USA*

ABSTRACT

Prostate cancer constitutes a substantial public health concern, characterized by a high incidence rate and a significant impact on mortality. Extensive employment of statistical models has been a cornerstone in the analysis of prostate cancer data, with a keen focus on crucial variables, including serum prostate specific antigen levels, Gleason score, age, family history, race/ethnicity, medical history, diet, physical activities, and more. These models serve as indispensable tools for risk assessment, facilitating treatment decisions, and offering valuable insights into survival analysis. In this ongoing study, we propose to use logistic regression and Cox proportional hazard regression models to dissect the Prostate, Lung, Colorectal, and Ovarian (PLCO) Cancer Screening Trial dataset. Our primary objectives include identifying factors associated with (1) prostate cancer development and (2) with prostate cancer-specific mortality. At this stage, our study primarily focuses on exploring PLCO data, selecting relevant variables, and outlining the model description.

KEYWORDS

Prostate Cancer, PLCO Trial, Survival Analysis, Risk Factors, Cox Proportional Hazards Regression Model, Logistic Regression

1. INTRODUCTION

Prostate cancer represents a pressing public health challenge, ranking as the most prevalent cancer diagnosis among American men, other than skin cancer (American Cancer Society 2023a, Siegel 2022). In 2023, projections indicated around 288,300 new cases of prostate cancer, underscoring the urgency of early detection and effective risk evaluation (American Cancer Society 2023b). Statistical models have emerged as pivotal tools in addressing this issue, with a specific focus on pertinent factors including serum prostate specific antigen (PSA) levels, Gleason score, age, family history, and racial/ethnic backgrounds (Adamy 2011, Bratt 2002, Epstein 1994, Kupelian 1997, Moul 1996). These models provide invaluable insights into risk forecasting, aiding treatment decisions, and facilitating survival analysis (Chase 2022, Mohler 2010).

Risk stratification within the realm of prostate cancer carries significant clinical implications notwithstanding complexity. For instance, individuals undergoing radical prostatectomy who have low-risk tumors identified pathologically have <1% chance of subsequent prostate cancer-specific mortality, but up to 33% of such cases are upstaged or upgraded to intermediate risk or high-risk disease with higher mortality risk (Busch 2014, Eggener 2011, Filson 2015, Mullins 2012). Louie's (2015) review of risk prediction models accentuates the need for precise risk assessment, as some of those patients classified as low-risk patients may develop aggressive diseases. Enikeev's (2020) study revealed inferior cancer-specific survival rates among intermediate-risk patients compared to their low-risk counterparts after 10 and 15 years, with no substantial difference in overall survival at 5 years, but a worsening trend for intermediate-risk patients after a decade. Baboudjian's (2022) review of 25 studies involving 29,673 intermediate-risk patients illuminated the divergent survival rates and significantly elevated risks of metastasis, prostate cancer-related deaths, and all-cause mortality within this group. These findings advocate for a judicious inclusion of intermediate-risk patients in active surveillance, with particular attention to those with low-volume Grade Group 2 tumor.

Beyond the aforementioned factors, additional variables such as dietary habits, caffeine and alcohol intake, physical activity, medication usage, and personal medical histories have also garnered attention in the analysis of prostate cancer data (Chen 2021, Freedland 2004, Gupta 2022, Hong 2020, McTiernan 2019, Shephard 2017). Statistical models, ranging from logistic regression and decision trees to machine learning algorithms like Random Forest and Support Vector Machines (SVM), have been employed to facilitate the development of clinical decision support systems, screening tools, and risk assessment calculators, which aim to enhance diagnosis and management of prostate cancer. On the other hand, fundamental challenges remain within the field, including enhancing the precision of risk prediction, comprehending the genetic and environmental factors influencing prostate cancer, and refining treatment recommendations.

The Prostate, Lung, Colorectal, and Ovarian (PLCO) Cancer Screening Trial is an important resource for prostate cancer research. It enrolled 76,678 healthy men aged 55-74 between 1993 and 2001, with a median follow-up of 12 years. The PLCO dataset includes information regarding prostate cancer screening, diagnostic procedures, treatments, baseline diet and drug usage questionnaires, as well as prostate cancer incidence by 2009 and mortality data by 2018, providing a rich dataset free to researchers worldwide. Initially designed to assess the efficacy of cancer screening tests, one key finding was that routine screening employing PSA testing and digital rectal examination did not bring about a significant reduction in prostate cancer mortality (Andriole 2009, Andriole 2012). Numerous studies have harnessed PLCO dataset for diverse research objectives, encompassing the examination of the long-term consequences of screening, the exploration of the impact of prostate cancer screening on quality of life, and the refinement of risk models pertaining to prostate cancer.

Our ongoing study using PLCO data aims to develop further understanding on what risk factors may contribute (1) to the development of prostate cancer and (2) to prostate cancer-specific mortality, respectively.

2. METHODOLOGY

Survival analysis is a statistical method used to analyze time-to-event data, often applied in medical research to understand the time it takes for an event of interest to occur, such as death, disease progression, or other outcomes. It provides insights into factors affecting the probability and timing of events. The Cox Proportional Hazard (Cox PH) model, is a survival analysis technique used to evaluate the influence of multiple predictor variables on the time-to-event outcome. It assumes that the hazard (the risk of an event occurring) for a subject is proportional to the hazard of a reference group, with the proportionality represented by hazard ratios.

Logistic regression is a statistical model used to analyze the relationship between a binary/multilevel categorical dependent variable (e.g., presence or absence of an event) and one or more independent variables. It estimates the probability of the categorical outcome based on a linear combination of predictor variables.

This ongoing study focuses on identifying significant risk factors among a diverse set of factors in the PLCO data, such as age, race/ethnicity, marital status, personal and family medical history, body mass index, lifestyle choices (e.g., smoking, diet, physical activity), education levels, and clinical and pathological data. By utilizing logistic regression and Cox PH model, we aim to unravel the relationships between these factors and health outcomes, providing insights into prostate cancer risk and its implications for mortality. We identify prostate cancer incidence by PLCO diagnosis data (if it was diagnosed) or, among those undiagnosed cases, cause-of-death data (as 'due to prostate cancer'). Prostate cancer specific mortality is identified using the cause-of-death data. We use Python analysis packages such as lifelines and statsmodels in the study analysis.

3. PRELIMINARY RESULTS

A total of 76678 men (Mean age at baseline = 62.7, 85% non-Hispanic White) were included in the PLCO trial with complete data and are all included in our analysis of risk factors associated with prostate cancer development. As shown in Table 1, 4.4% participants are non-Hispanic Black and most affected by prostate cancer with an incidence rate of 15.5%. Groups such as Asian, Hispanic, Pacific Islander, and American Indian exhibit lower incidence rates (8-11%) than non-Hispanic Black and non-Hispanic White (11.9%).

Table 1. Race/ethnicity distribution in PLCO data

Race/ethnicity	PLCO trial male participants		Prostate cancer (PC) patients		
	#	%	#	% among all PC patients	% among PLCO male participants by race
Non-Hispanic White	65177	85.0%	7764	86.2%	11.9%
Non-Hispanic Black	3370	4.4%	524	5.8%	15.5%
Asian	3008	3.9%	241	2.7%	8.0%
Hispanic	1603	2.1%	158	1.8%	9.9%
Pacific Islander	464	0.6%	48	0.5%	10.3%
American Indian	187	0.2%	20	0.2%	10.7%
Unknown	2869	3.7%	255	2.8%	8.9%
Total	**76678**	**100.0%**	**9010**	**100.0%**	**11.8%**

The overall risk of developing prostate cancer among all PLCO trial male participants was 11.8%, with elevated risks (17.6%) among those having a family history of the disease (see Table 2).

Table 2. Prostate cancer incidence rates grouped by family history

Family history status of prostate cancer	PLCO trial male participants		Prostate cancer (PC) patients		
	#	%	#	% among PC patients	% among PLCO male participants by family history
No family history	66654	86.9%	7621	84.6%	11.4%
Has family history – Immediate family member	5326	6.9%	937	10.4%	17.6%
Possible family history – Relative or unclear cancer type	1217	1.6%	139	1.5%	11.4%
Unknown status	3481	4.5%	313	3.5%	9.0%
Total	**76678**	**100.0%**	**9010**	**100.0%**	**11.8%**

We are currently selecting covariate variables for our statistical models by exploring a comprehensive array of variables within the PLCO dataset. Our first goal is to gain a thorough understanding of the risk factors contributing to the development of prostate cancer. For this purpose, we are utilizing the complete dataset from PLCO's main dataset into the Cox PH model with prostate cancer incidence as the primary event. To achieve our second objective, which is to identify risk factors for prostate cancer-specific mortality, we plan to employ logistic regression models on a filtered dataset consisting of individuals who have been diagnosed with prostate cancer and those who have passed away due to prostate cancer. This filtered dataset comprises 9,010 men.

4. CONCLUSION

The PLCO trial (including 76,678 men aged 55-74) is a valuable and extensive resource for prostate cancer research, offering a wealth of diverse features and data. Our preliminary findings identified an overall 12% incidence rate with African Americans and those with family history mostly affected. We plan to use Cox proportional hazard model and logistic regression to better understand the risk factors for developing prostate cancer and for prostate cancer specific mortality, which may lead to more accurate risk assessment for prostate cancer. This, in turn, may assist clinicians in identifying individuals at higher risk and tailoring screening and preventive strategies accordingly. Understanding the factors associated with prostate cancer development and mortality may provide valuable insights for treatment decisions. Physicians may make more informed choices regarding the management of prostate cancer patients, potentially leading to improved outcomes.

ACKNOWLEDGEMENT

We thank the Cancer Data Access System at the National Cancer Institute for providing the PLCO dataset.

REFERENCES

Adamy A. et al, (2011). Role of prostate specific antigen and immediate confirmatory biopsy in predicting progression during active surveillance for low risk prostate cancer. *Journal of Urology*, Vol. 185, No. 2, pp. 477-482.

American Cancer Society, (2023a). *Key Statistics for Prostate Cancer*. Available at: https://www.cancer.org/cancer/types/prostate-cancer/about/key-statistics.html (Accessed: 20 Oct 2023).

American Cancer Society, (2023b). *2023 Estimates*. Available at: https://cancerstatisticscenter.cancer.org/ (Accessed: 20 Oct 2023).

Andriole G. et al, (2009). Mortality results from a randomized prostate-cancer screening trial. *N. Engl. J. Med.*, Vol. 360, No. 13, pp. 1310-1319.

Andriole G. et al, (2012). Prostate cancer screening in the randomized Prostate, Lung, Colorectal, and Ovarian Cancer Screening Trial: mortality results after 13 years of follow-up. *J. Natl. Cancer Inst.*, Vol. 104, No. 2, pp. 125-132.

Baboudjian M. et al, (2022). Active Surveillance for Intermediate-risk Prostate Cancer: A Systematic Review, Meta-analysis, and Meta Regression. *Eur Urol Oncol.*, Vol. 5, No. 6, pp. 617-627.

Bratt O. et al, (2002). Hereditary prostate cancer: clinical characteristics and survival. *Journal of Urology*, Vol. 167, No. 6, pp. 2423-2426.

Busch J. et al, (2014). Higher rates of upgrading and upstaging in older patients undergoing radical prostatectomy and qualifying for active surveillance. *BJU Int.*, Vol. 114, No. 4, pp. 517-521.

Chase E. et al, (2022). Development and validation of a life expectancy calculator for US patients with prostate cancer. *BJU Int.*, Vol. 130, No. 4, pp. 496-506.

Chen X. et al, (2021). Coffee consumption and risk of prostate cancer: a systematic review and meta-analysis. *BMJ Open*, Vol. 11, No. 2, pp. e038902.

Eggener S. et al, (2011). Predicting 15-year prostate cancer specific mortality after radical prostatectomy. *Journal of Urology*, Vol. 185, No. 3, pp. 869-875.

Enikeev D. et al, (2020). Active Surveillance for Intermediate-Risk Prostate Cancer: Systematic Review and Meta-analysis of Current Protocols and Outcomes. *Clin Genitourin Cancer*, Vol. 18, No. 6, pp. e739-e753.

Epstein J. et al, (1994). Pathologic and clinical findings to predict tumor extent of nonpalpable (stage T1c) prostate cancer. *JAMA*, Vol. 271, No. 5, pp. 368-374.

Filson C. et al, (2015). Expectant management for men with early stage prostate cancer. *CA: A Cancer Journal for Clinicians*, Vol. 65, No. 4, pp. 265-282.

Freedland S. et al, (2004). Impact of obesity on biochemical control after radical prostatectomy for clinically localized prostate cancer: a report by the Shared Equal Access Regional Cancer Hospital database study group. *Journal of Clinical Oncology*, Vol. 22, No. 3, pp. 446-453.

Gupta N. et al, (2022). Systematic review of the impact of a plant-based diet on prostate cancer incidence and outcomes. *Prostate Cancer Prostatic Dis.*, Vol. 25, No. 3, pp. 444-452.

Hong S. et al, (2020). Alcohol Consumption and the Risk of Prostate Cancer: A Dose-Response Meta-Analysis. *Nutrients*, Vol. 12, No. 8, pp. 2188.

Kupelian P. et al, (1997). Family history of prostate cancer in patients with localized prostate cancer: an independent predictor of treatment outcome. *Journal of Clinical Oncology*, Vol. 15, No. 4, pp. 1478-1480.

Louie K. et al, (2015). Do prostate cancer risk models improve the predictive accuracy of PSA screening? A meta-analysis. *Annals of Oncology, the journal of the European Society for Medical Oncology*, Vol. 26, No. 5, pp. 848-864.

McTiernan A. et al, (2019). Physical Activity in Cancer Prevention and Survival: A Systematic Review. *Med Sci Sports Exerc.*, Vol. 51, No. 6, pp. 1252-1261.

Mohler J. et al, (2010). NCCN clinical practice guidelines in oncology: prostate cancer. *Journal of the National Comprehensive Cancer Network: JNCCN*, Vol. 8, No. 2, pp. 162-200.

Moul J. et al, (1996). Black race is an adverse prognostic factor for prostate cancer recurrence following radical prostatectomy in an equal access health care setting. *Journal of Urology*, Vol. 155, No. 5, pp. 1667-1673.

Mullins J. et al, (2012). Radical prostatectomy outcome in men 65 years old or older with low risk prostate cancer. *Journal of Urology*, Vol. 187, No. 5, pp 1620-1625.

Shephard R. (2017). Physical Activity and Prostate Cancer: An Updated Review. *Sports Med.*, Vol. 47, No. 6, pp. 1055-1073.

Siegel R. et al, (2022). Cancer statistics, 2022. *CA: A Cancer Journal for Clinicians*, Vol. 71, No. 1, pp. 7-33.

ONLINE TRANSDIAGNOSTIC INTERVENTION FOR EMOTIONAL, TRAUMA- AND STRESSOR-RELATED DISORDERS IN THE MEXICAN POPULATION

Anabel de la Rosa Gómez[1], Lorena Alejandra Flores Plata[1], Raquel García Flores[1,2], Pablo Valencia[3], Dulce Díaz Sosa[3] and Alejandrina Hernández Posadas[3]
[1]Faculty of Higher Studies Iztacala, SUAYED, National Autonomous University of Mexico, Mexico
[2]Sonora Technological Institute, Mexico
[3]Faculty of Higher Studies Iztacala, National Autonomous University of Mexico, Mexico

ABSTRACT

Anxiety, depressive, and trauma- and stressor-related disorders occur at high levels of prevalence in the Mexican population. Likewise, treatments based on transdiagnostic cognitive-behavioral therapy have demonstrated high effectiveness when applied with telepsychology. The aim was to evaluate the suitability, clinical utility, and acceptance/satisfaction of an online transdiagnostic intervention delivered by an Internet-based intervention for emotional and trauma-related disorders and stressors. Participants who met the inclusion criteria (n=225) between 18 and 70 years old were randomly assigned to one of the three arms of the study: a) Internet-guided transdiagnostic intervention with synchronous assistance (n=74), b) Internet-guided transdiagnostic intervention (n=74), c) waiting list group (n=77). It was observed that, in all the outcome variables, the group without treatment presented non-significant differences between the pre- and post-test. On the other hand, in both treatment groups, statistically significant differences were observed in all outcome variables, (depression, anxiety, post-traumatic stress, general symptoms and emotional dysregulation) in each of the experimental conditions (without treatment, self-management only treatment and self-management treatment with therapeutic support), except emotional dysregulation. This variable showed a significant change only in the group that included support from a therapist (but not in the completely self-managed treatment).
Data showed significant improvement in clinical measures of depression, anxiety, and emotional regulation in the two treatment groups. Significant differences were reached between treatment groups vs WL. And it obtained a good acceptance/satisfaction index reported by the participants in both treatment groups. The discussion considers the findings of the study and its relevance in the Mexican context, as well as the feasibility of conducting studies.

KEYWORDS

Emotional, Transdiagnostic, Randomized Pilot Trial

1. INTRODUCTION

Transdiagnostic treatments have demonstrated efficacy in addressing the challenges associated with comorbidity between disorders. These treatments target common or shared risk factors, including underlying mechanisms, psychological processes (cognitive, behavioral, and physiological), and the maintenance of overlapping symptoms (attentional biases, negative thinking, avoidance, etc.). This approach relies on a convergent and integrative scientific perspective (Mansell et al., 2012). Barlow et al. (2004) propose a Unified Transdiagnostic Behavioral Cognitive Protocol (Unified Protocol, UP), designed for the treatment of Emotional Disorders (ED), emphasizing emotional regulation. The UP has proven effective not only in reducing anxiety and/or depression symptoms, but also in increasing attendance at therapeutic sessions compared to conventional psychological interventions (Păsărelu et al., 2017).

While there are limited studies on the efficacy of internet-based treatment for trauma and stress-related disorders, the existing evidence is promising. Studies on war veterans with Posttraumatic Stress Disorder (PTSD) suggest the effectiveness of Transdiagnostic therapy in cognitive emotion regulation, avoidance, and symptom reduction compared between experimental and control groups (Varkovitzky et al., 2018). Gutner et al. (2022) reported substantial improvement over time in trauma-exposed veterans across conditions (UP, present-centered therapy, or treatment as usual), with large effect sizes (range: -2.15 to -3.32), with the UP demonstrating the largest change. In terms of suitability, clinical utility, and acceptability, the UP has shown promise for improving efficiency, satisfaction, and the personalizing of mental healthcare (Gutner et al., 2019). Meyer et al. (2022) administered UP over the Internet to treat stress symptoms, obtaining a significant reduction in self-reported PTSD symptoms after treatment and improvements in effect size.

Emotion-focused transdiagnostic interventions delivered via the Internet can enhance the reach and impact of programs in psychological treatment focused on trauma and emotional disorders (Gonález-Robles, 2020; Hadjistavropoulos et al., 2021). However, there is a scarcity of controlled clinical studies investigating the effects of transdiagnostic treatment via the Internet for ED adapted to the context and culture in Latin America (De la Rosa et al., 2022).

The general objective of this study was to determine the indicators of suitability, clinical utility, and satisfaction of a transdiagnostic online intervention for the treatment of emotional disorders and those derived from stress and trauma in a Mexican community sample.

2. METHOD

The design of a controlled, randomized superiority clinical trial was implemented with parallel groups and three arms, involving repeated measurements at four moments: pretest, posttest, follow-up at three, six and 12 months. Participants, aged between 18 and 70 years, were randomly assigned in a 1:1:1 to one of the three arms of the study: a) Internet-guided transdiagnostic intervention with synchronous assistance, b) Internet-guided transdiagnostic intervention, c) waiting list group. This study adheres to the CONSORT statement and SPIRIT guidelines. The trial is registered under ClinicalTrials.gov with the identifier NCT05225701.

Participants

The eligibility evaluation consisted of the application of self-administered questionnaires online via the following webpage: https://e-motion.iztacala.unam.mx/. Inclusion criteria comprised: a) age 18 or older; b) voluntarily participation in the study; c) meeting at least two of the following criteria: moderate general symptomatology measured by the SCL-90-R, mild or moderate anxiety measured by the BAI, mild or moderate depression measured by the BDI-II; d) access to computer equipment with an internet connection; e) valid email address; f) basic digital skills in the use of an operating system and internet navigation. Individuals meeting these initial criteria were invited to an individual videoconference session to assess comorbidities with psychiatric disorders, alcohol and drug abuse, serious medical illnesses, or suicidal behaviors. The interview was conducted by supervised trainee therapists using the Mini International Neuropsychiatric Interview.

Exclusion criteria included: a) current or past psychotic disorder; b) alcohol and drug abuse or dependence; c) moderate or severe risk of suicide; d) undergoing psychological and/or pharmacological treatment during the study. Criteria for elimination encompassed: a) not-acceptance of the conditions of informed consent, and b) missing three consecutive treatment sessions.

Evaluations

Diagnostic interview: International Neuropsychiatric Interview, version 5.0.0 (MINI), covering major psychiatric disorders of DSM-IV-R and ICD-10. Symptom Checklist (SCL-90). (Sheehan et al., 2006).

Primary outcome measures: Beck Anxiety Inventory (BAI) (Beck et al., 1998; Robles et al., 2001). Beck Depression Inventory (BDI-II) (Beck et al., 1988; González et al., 2015).

Secondary outcome measures: Difficulties in Emotional Regulation Scale (DERS) (Gratz and Roemer, 2008), validated in the Mexican population by De la Rosa et al. (2021).

Opinion measures: Acceptability was assessed with three questions on a 1 to 10 scale regarding appropriateness, usefulness, and applicability of the treatment for other psychological problems. Appropriateness measured with two questions on a 1 to 10 scale regarding interest and understanding of the activities. Satisfaction assessed with two questions on a 6-point Likert scale.

Randomization and Blinding

Randomization was conducted by an independent investigator through the web system with a 1:1:1 ratio for block saturation per condition. Participants were assigned randomly to one of the three arms:

a) Internet-guided transdiagnostic intervention with synchronous assistance, b) Internet-guided transdiagnostic intervention, c) waiting list group. This study adheres to CONSORT statement and SPIRIT guidelines, with a trial registration number of ClinicalTrials.gov NCT05225701. Participants retained the right to withdraw from treatment at any time. The assessor, participant and investigator were blinded. The individual who administered the initial assessments remained blind to the treatment group of the patients. This evaluator was different from the one who administered the treatment throughout the study.

Interventions

Experimental Condition. The online Transdiagnostic intervention was implemented through a self-implemented web system based on the Unified Protocol (Barlow et al., 2016), comprising eight modules, called "stations". Each module, designed to be covered weekly, the intervention platform was called E-motion, with 24/7 access. Psychological counseling was carried out in eight individual 60-minute sessions, one for each station, conducted weekly via videoconference. Each psychotherapist had a designated supervisor, an expert in the intervention. Responsible for monitoring compliance and protocol application.

2.1 Results

A screening process was initially conducted to determine eligibility for assessment. Out of a total of 3,593 people who accessed the page, 2,969 people completed the scales, and 978 underwent the MINI Mental Interview. Of the participants evaluated, 225 ware assigned as follows: a) 74 participants to the Internet-guided transdiagnostic intervention with synchronous assistance, b) 74 participants to the Internet-based self-guided Transdiagnostic intervention, c) 77 participants to the waiting list group.

The comparison of pre- and post-test scores for each outcome variables (depression, anxiety, post-traumatic stress, general symptoms, and emotional dysregulation) was conducted in each experimental conditions (no treatment, self-care treatment only and self-care treatment with therapeutic support). It was observed that, in all outcome variables, the group without treatment presented non-significant differences between the pre- and post-test, aligning with expectations. However, in both treatment groups, statistically significant differences were observed in all outcome variables except emotional dysregulation, which showed a significant change only in the group that included support from a therapist (but not in the entirely self-managed treatment). To quantify the observed differences, the standardized mean difference (*d*) was estimated, with absolute values interpreted as follows: insignificant difference ($d < 0.20$), small difference ($0.20 < d < 0.50$), medium difference ($0.50 < d < 0.80$) and large difference ($d > 0.80$). According to this criterion, the most significant changes between the pre- and post-test were observed in the depression and general symptomatology variables, wherein large differences were noted, especially in the group that included therapeutic support.

Table 1. Average pre- and post-test scores

Group	Depression (0–63)				Anxiety (0–60)				Pstraumatic Stress (0–80)			
	Pre	Post	*p*	*d*	Pre	Post	*p*	*d*	Pre	Post	*p*	*d*
No treatment				-				-				-
	28.60	26.10	.272	0.37	17.10	14.30	.386	0.29	30.10	29.80	.953	0.02
Self-managed				-				-				-
	20.38	12.75	.009	1.26	14.50	7.25	.008	1.31	30.38	14.38	.012	1.19
Self-management +				-				-				-
Therapist	23.86	9.50	<.001	1.51	16.14	9.95	.002	0.75	37.86	20.73	<.001	1.02

Note. The p-value corresponds to a paired t-test. *d* = standardized mean difference.

The results demonstrated a superiority in the intervention groups compared to the WL group. Additionally, both treatment groups reported a high acceptance and satisfaction index among participants. These findings suggest a potential for equally effective use of the Unified Protocol (UP) in treating comorbid cases.

3. CONCLUSION

The results obtained agree with the reviewed literature (e.g., Osma et al., 2018) by showing that the treatment through a psychological program applied via the Internet was efficacious in reducing the anxious and depressive symptoms of the participants. In both treatment conditions, a significant decrease was observed compared to the pretest.

The transdiagnostic model can be successfully applied to telepsychology to treat symptoms of anxiety, depression, and trauma-related disorders in Mexicans. The online delivery of the unified protocol (UP) reduces depression, emotional dysregulation, anxiety, intolerance of uncertainty, and psychological distress. Although more research is needed. Among the limitations, it is important to consider the absence of follow-ups to find out the maintenance of the improvement achieved in the clinical indicators, or to find out if a long-term difference is achieved between the treatment groups. These follow-ups are currently being carried out.

ACKNOWLEDGEMENT

This work was supported by the CONACYT-FORDECYT-PRONACES/1401/2021. The funding institution had no role in the design of the study or in the collection, analysis, and interpretation of the data, and had no role in the writing of the manuscript.

REFERENCES

Barlow, D. H., Allen, L. B., & Choate, M. L., (2016). Toward a unified treatment for emotional disorders. *Behavior Therapy*, Vol. 47, No. 6, 838-853. https://doi.org/10.1016/j.beth.2016.11.005

Barlow, D. H., Allen, L. B. & Choate, M. L., (2004). Toward a unified treatment for emotional disorders. *Behaviour Therapy*, Vol. 35, No. 2, pp. 205–230. https://doi.org10.1016/S0005-7894(04)80036-4

Beck, A. T., Epstein, N., Brown, G., & Steer, R. (1998). Beck Anxiety Inventory. *APA PsycTests*. https://doi.org/10.1037/t02025-000

Beck, A. T., Steer, R. A. & Carbin, G. M., (1988). Psychometric properties of the Beck Depression Inventory: twenty-five years of evaluation. *Clinical Psychology Review*, Vol. 8, No. 1, 77-100. https://doi.org/10.1016/0272-7358(88)90050-5

De la Rosa-Gómez, A., Flores-Plata, L. A., Esquivel-Santoveña, E. E., Santillán Torres Torija, C., García-Flores, R., Dominguez-Rodriguez, A., Arenas-Landgrave, P., Castellanos-Vargas, R. O., Berra-Ruiz, E., Silvestre-Ramírez, R., Miranda-Díaz, G. A., Díaz-Sosa, D. M., Hernández-Posadas, A., Flores-Elvira, A. I., Valencia, P. D., & Vázquez-Sánchez, M. F., (2022). Efficacy of a transdiagnostic guided internet-delivered intervention for emotional, trauma and stress-related disorders in Mexican population: study protocol for a randomized controlled trial. *BMC Psychiatry*, Vol. 22, No. 1, pp. 537. https://doi.org/10.1186/s12888-022-04132-6

De la Rosa-Gómez, A., Hernández-Posadas, A., Valencia, P. & Guajardo-Garcini, D., (2021). Análisis dimensional de la Escala de Dificultades en la Regulación Emocional (DERS-15) en universitarios mexicanos. *Revista Evaluar*, Vol. 21, No. 2, 80-97. https://doi.org/10.35670/1667-4545.v21.n2.34401

González, D., Reséndiz, A. & Reyes-Lagunes, I. (2015). Adaptation of the BDI-II in Mexico. *Salud Mental*, Vol. 38, No. 4, 237-244. https://doi.org/10.17711/sm.0185-3325.2015.033

González-Robles, A., Díaz-García, A., García-Palacios, A., Roca, P., Ramos-Quiroga, J. A., & Botella, C., (2020). Effectiveness of a Transdiagnostic Guided Internet-Delivered Protocol for Emotional Disorders Versus Treatment as Usual in Specialized Care: Randomized Controlled Trial. *J Med Internet Res*, Vol. 22, No. 7, e18220. doi: 10.2196/18220.

Gratz, K. L. & Roemer, L., (2008). Multidimensional assessment of emotion regulation and dysregulation: development, factor structure, and initial validation of the difficulties in emotion regulation scale. *Journal of Psychopathology and Behavioral Assessment*, Vol. 30, No. 315. https://doi.org/10.1007/s10862-008-9102-4

Gutner, C. A., Canale, C. A., Vento, S. A., & Wiltsey Stirman, S., (2019). Stakeholder Preferences on Transdiagnostic Psychosocial Treatment for Trauma-Exposed Veterans. *Administration and policy in mental health*, Vol. 46, No. 5, pp. 660–669. https://doi.org/10.1007/s10488-019-00948-9

Hadjistavropoulos, H. D., McCall, H. C., Thiessen, D. L., Huang, Z., Carleton, R. N., Dear, B. F., & Titov, N., (2021). Initial Outcomes of Transdiagnostic Internet-Delivered Cognitive Behavioral Therapy Tailored to Public Safety Personnel: Longitudinal Observational Study. *Journal of Medical Internet Research,* Vol. 23, No. 5, e27610. https://doi.org/10.2196/27610

Mansell, W., Harvey, A., Watkins, E., & Shafran, R., 2009. Conceptual foundations of the transdiagnostic approach to CBT. *Journal of Cognitive Psychotherapy: An International Quarterly*, Vol. 23, No. 1, pp. 6-19. https://doi.org/10.1891/0889-8391.23.1.6

Mayer, E., Coe, E., Pennington, M., Cammarata, C., Kimbrel, N., Ostiguy, W., Leto, F. & Gulliver, S., 2022. The Unified Protocol for Transdiagnostic Treatment of Emotional Disorders Delivered to Firefighters via Videoconferencing: Pilot Outcomes Highlighting Improvements in Alcohol Use Disorder and Posttraumatic Stress Disorder Symptoms. *Cognitive and Behavioral Practice*. (en línea). https://doi.org/10.1016/j.cbpra.2022.08.004

Osma, J., Suso-Ribera, C., García-Palacios, A., Crespo-Delgado, E., Robert-Flor, C., Sánchez-Guerrero, A., Ferreres-Galan, V., Pérez-Ayerra, L., Malea-Fernández, A., & Torres-Alfosea, M. Á., (2018). Efficacy of the unified protocol for the treatment of emotional disorders in the Spanish public mental health system using a group format: study protocol for a multicenter, randomized, non-inferiority-controlled trial. *Health and quality of life outcomes*, Vol. 16, No. 1, pp.46. https://doi.org/10.1186/s12955-018-0866-2

Păsărelu, C. R., Andersson, G., Bergman-Nordgren, L. & Dobrean, A., (2017). Internet delivered transdiagnostic and tailored cognitive behavioral therapy for anxiety and depression: a systematic review and meta-analysis of randomized controlled trials. *Cognitive Behaviour Therapy*, Vol. 46, No. 1, pp. 1–28. http://dx.doi.org/10.1080/16506073.2016.1231219.

Robles, R., Varela, R., Jurado, S. & Páez, F., (2001). Versión mexicana del Inventario de Ansiedad de Beck: Propiedades psicométricas. *Revista Mexicana de Psicología*, Vol. 18, No. 2, 211-218

Sheehan, D., Janvas, J., Baker, R., Harnett-Sheehan, K., Knapp, E., & Sheehan, M., (2006). Mini international neuropsychiatric interview.

Varkovitzky, R. L., Sherrill, A. M., & Reger, G. M., (2018). Effectiveness of the Unified Protocol for Transdiagnostic Treatment of Emotional Disorders Among Veterans With Posttraumatic Stress Disorder: A Pilot Study. *Behavior modification*, Vol. 42, No. 2, pp. 210–230. https://doi.org/10.1177/0145445517724539.

TOWARDS A MORE ENGAGED DEMOCRACY: USING STATISTICAL METHODS TO DETECT ELECTION FRAUD IN THE 2022 PHILIPPINE NATIONAL ELECTIONS

Juan Miguel Cardaño, Bryan Patrick Mande, Seth William Tionko, Aldrich Ellis Asuncion and Jeric Briones

Department of Mathematics, Ateneo de Manila University,
Katipunan Avenue, Loyola Heights, Quezon City, Philippines 1108

ABSTRACT

This paper aims to show how citizens can further participate in the elections, aside from just voting. Given the accusations of fraud, this study demonstrates how existing election fraud detection methods can be used in the 2022 Philippine National Elections (PNE) context. Specifically, histograms known as *2D vote turnout distributions* were first utilized to model the frequency of the winner's percentage of votes based on the voter turnout in each electoral unit, with key parameters introduced to detect fraud. Vote turnout distributions were then simulated using parametric models involving the aforementioned fraud parameters, with the goal of replicating the actual election fingerprints. Using provincial election data for the presidential elections, initial results showed that the presidential election data in the 2022 PNE proved to be inconclusive for some aggregate levels. That is, compared to other countries, fraud cannot be detected on a large scale, but rather on a smaller scale. For example, in one town in the country, the fraud parameters indicated the possibility of fraudulent mechanisms present in the election data. Thus, using statistical tools for electoral fraud detection can empower the citizens to be more vigilant and engaged in their country's democratic processes.

KEYWORDS

National Elections, Fraud Detection, Statistical Models, Voting Irregularities, Engaged Citizenry

1. INTRODUCTION

There are several statistical concepts and methods that could be utilized for fraud detection. Some of them include using *Benford's Law* (Mebane, 2006) and vote-shares-based analysis through kernel densities (Rozenas, 2017) to detect fraud. However, problems also arise as one needs to establish a basis for the expected values for fair elections and it is also possible to have false positive errors as large amounts of data can show irregularities despite being fair.

Allegations of fraud are inevitable in every election, with the 2022 Philippine national elections (PNE) being no exemption. There were doubts in the candidates' victory due to several reasons, ranging from power outages in some areas of the country, to malfunctioning election machines – fueling skepticism about the transparency and fairness of the election and possible roots of election fraud (Mercado, 2022). Some of these claims include specific vote ratios and allegations substantiated through anecdotal means (supplied by media or election watchdogs) (Cabristante, 2022; Mendoza, 2022). However, the potential existence of fraud using quantitative and/or, statistical methods in the 2022 PNE had not been extensively investigated.

Thus, the study takes into consideration the method used in Klimek et al. (2012) where they showed that statistical tools can be used in election fraud detection through the use of parametric generative models. While traditional election forensics methods like *Benford's Law* and *Integer Percentage* focus on identifying individual anomalies in vote counts or turnout, the Klimek et al. approach takes a more comprehensive view. Lacasa and Fernandez-Gracia (2018) discussed that unlike *Benford's Law*, which analyzes the distribution of single digits in vote counts, or *Integer Percentage*, which flags suspiciously round vote shares or turnouts, Klimek et al. delves into the relationship between the votes and turnout for each party. This allows them to simultaneously detect two types of fraud: incremental fraud (where vote counts are subtly manipulated in proportion to turnout to inflate a specific party's vote share without raising obvious red flags), and extreme fraud (where dramatic alterations to vote counts and turnout create spikes or dips in the data, indicating blatant manipulation). By plotting two-dimensional histograms, Klimek et al. visually reveal the patterns associated with both types of fraud. This provides a richer picture of potential irregularities compared to simpler methods that rely solely on single-dimensional analysis or statistical tests. Therefore, while traditional methods can identify suspicious data points, Klimek et al.'s approach offers a more nuanced understanding of the interplay between votes and turnout, potentially uncovering subtler forms of manipulation and providing a more powerful tool for identifying electoral fraud.

Utilizing the parametric model of Klimek, Asuncion, et al. (2022) tried to detect election fraud in the 2022 PNE. They applied the said model to the election data aggregated at the national level. However, their results were inconclusive as the values of the fraud parameters were inconsistent compared to the values determined in Klimek et al. They were not able to clearly conclude if fraud is present or not. They then suggested that further analysis be performed at lower-level election data.

Therefore, this study aims to explore if a systematic and replicable means to understand election events can be applied in the 2022 PNE context. Specifically, this study builds on the work of Asuncion, et al. by comparing vote distributions and values of the fraud parameters at the lower level using data aggregated from precincts. This will ideally allow the study to identify potential election fraud, if any, in the 2022 PNE. By leveraging statistical tools and using deeper aggregation levels, this study hopes to fortify democratic processes in the country and empower the citizens to use statistical methods for a more engaged democracy.

2. METHODOLOGY

We present a brief overview of the methodology utilized by Klimek et al. Election data (number of eligible persons to vote, valid votes, and votes for the winning party/candidate) in each precinct is collated. Then, a histogram known as the *2D vote turnout distributions* or *fingerprints* is constructed. This histogram determines the frequency of the winner's percentage of votes based on the voter turnout in each electoral unit. A key characteristic being looked at in fingerprints is its smearing at the upper right which signifies that practically everyone who voted supported the winning party. This smearing is one of the primary indicators that there is a possibility of fraud. The fingerprint modality is another sign that reveals questionable voting activity. This suggests that the voters' preference is unclear. Klimek et al. identified three sample fraudulent elections—Uganda and Russia (2011 and 2012)—in their study that exhibit both smearing to the upper right side and bimodal characteristics (see Figure 1).

The main idea behind the study is to replicate the fingerprints generated from the actual data using a generative model that includes fraud parameters (see Figure 1). These parameters, incremental fraud f_i and extreme fraud f_e, indicate the probability of fraud. The former indicates the probability that either a fraction of the oppositions' votes and/or votes of the non-voters are added to the total winner's votes, while the latter is for the probability that votes for the opposition/s taken away are added to the winning party's total votes. Then, the fraud parameters f_i and f_e are estimated by fitting their corresponding generative model to the actual voter turnout distribution. That is, for each realization m, we find the parameters f_i and f_e that minimizes the statistic

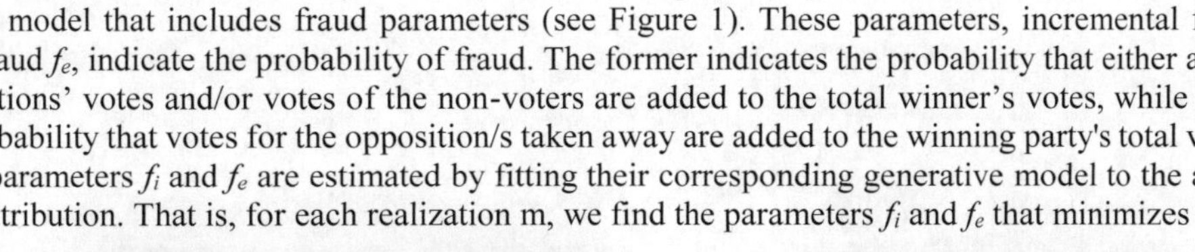

Figure 1. Actual sample (left) and simulated (right) fingerprints from the study of Klimek et al. Voter turnout is shown by the *x*-axis, while the winner's percentage of the total votes is represented by the *y*-axis

$$S = \sum_{i=1}^{n} \left(\frac{f(v_i) - f\left(v_i{}^{(m)}\right)}{f(v_i)} \right)^2,$$

where $f(v_i)$ is the probability distribution function (pdf) of the actual votes and $f(v_i^{(m)})$ is the pdf of the model. This allows the use of the goodness-of-fit test concept in replicating the fingerprint generated from the actual data and identifying fraud parameters f_i and f_e.

In this study, the presidential election data for each lower-level unit was gathered and analyzed independently. The total number of votes and voter turnout in each province and the fraction of valid votes of the winning party was identified to create a 2D histogram. Values of the fraud parameters f_i and f_e were then estimated using the generative model, represented visually through boxplots to observe its range and spread.

3. PRELIMINARY RESULTS AND DISCUSSION

Based on the resulting fingerprints for each of the provinces in the Philippines, five provinces were selected to have their boxplot of values of f_i and f_e boxplot generated. Two of the five provinces were chosen due to their bimodal characteristics and smearing at the upper right, and the other three provinces were selected for their approximate normality.

Among the five provinces, one province, labeled **P1** for brevity, was explored more thoroughly. Because of the large standard deviation of its values of f_i (mean = 0.09, sd = 0.104) and f_e (mean = 0.4508, sd = 0.283), the election data appeared to be inconclusive (see Figure 2). Fair elections in Klimek et al. had f_i and f_e values near zero, and a standard deviation of less than 0.005 and 0.01, respectively. In **P1's** case, its f_i was low (not greater than 0.3 which is the value determined by Klimek et al.) compared to those of fraudulent elections. However, its f_e was also high (not less than 0.3). Furthermore, the sd values of f_i and f_e were also greater than 0.005 and 0.01, respectively, allowing the values to be one to three standard deviations away from zero. Thus, unlike the election results analyzed by Klimek, et al., the model parameters provided no strong indication that the election was fair nor fraudulent.

Thus, the other four provinces, specifically their parameter boxplots, were also examined (see Figure 3). From the boxplots, it can be noticed that the values of f_e also had large standard deviations. Except for one province, the values of f_i were also small, with one province having a value of 0.0013 only. This suggests that the obtained model parameters from the election data, at its current aggregation level, was not a strong indication that the election was fair nor fraudulent.

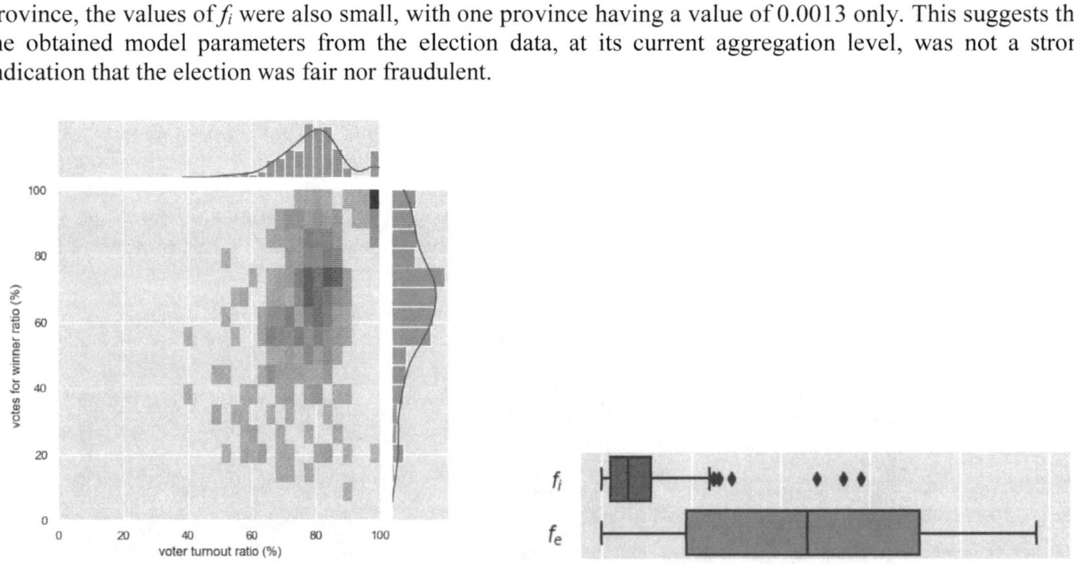

Figure 2. Fingerprint and empirical distributions, and the parameter boxplots for the province **P1**

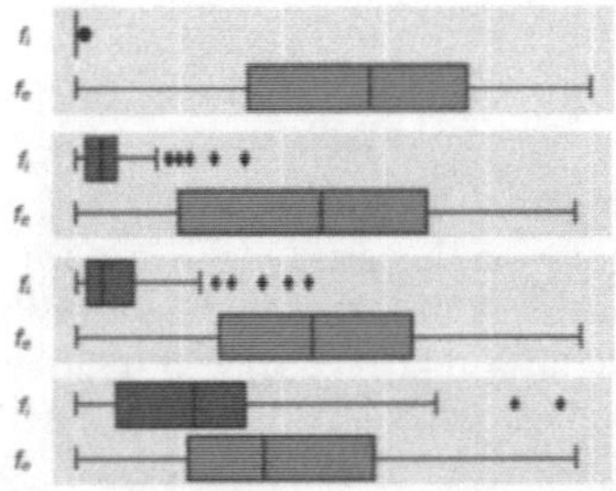

Figure 3. Boxplots of values for f_i and f_e for remaining four out of five selected provinces

3.1 Further Level Analysis

The analysis probed further to the municipal level to investigate if the reason behind the large standard deviation for the values of f_i and f_e is due to the aggregation level. The various municipalities under **P1** were analyzed to determine the values of f_i and f_e, and to possibly identify which ones contributed to the province having high standard deviation, if ever that was the case.

In the province **P1**, six municipalities were selected based on population. The boxplot of values for f_i and f_e of five out of six municipalities appeared to have a large standard deviation (see left of Figure 4), similar to province **P1**, and so yield an inconclusive outcome as well. However, one municipality, labeled **M1** for brevity, was interesting due to its boxplots of values of f_i and f_e having a low standard deviation (see right of Figure 4). Its values of f_i (mean = 0.8222, sd = 0.1006) and f_i (mean = 0.0822, sd = 0.0753) resemble the conditions of a fraudulent election described by Klimek, et al., as well as its large standard deviation values for f_i and f_e.

Since there was still the issue of having large standard deviations for the values of f_i and f_e, another municipality, labeled **M2** for brevity, was chosen (specifically the municipality with the largest population). Here, the analysis delved further into the barangay level using the two barangays having the largest and the median populations, respectively. From the results, it was seen that the election data is still inconclusive and had a similar boxplot of values compared to their municipal counterpart (see Figure 5).

Compared to Asuncion et al.'s values of f_i and f_e of 0.1267 and 0.3943, respectively, for the national data, the boxplots of values of f_i and f_e for the selected provinces and municipalities also seemed to be inconclusive. That is, the election data was not a strong indication that the election was fair since the parameters were greater than zero. Yet, the election data was also not a strong indication that the election was fraudulent since the parameters were not as large compared to those of sample fraudulent elections in Klimek et al. Only the boxplots of values of f_i and f_e of municipality **M1** seemed to provide conclusive results, and indicate the possibility of fraudulent mechanisms present in the election data.

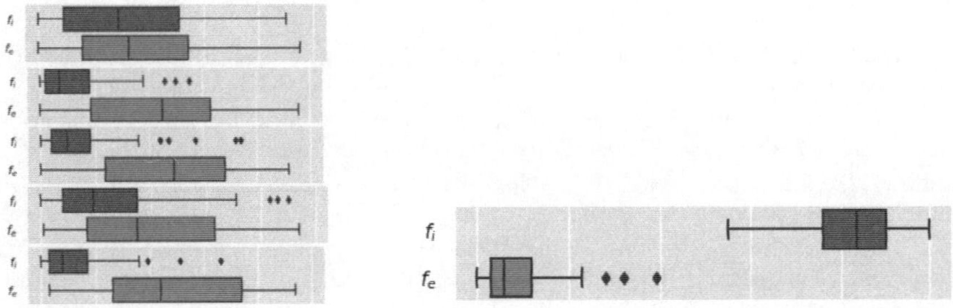

Figure 4. Boxplot of values for f_i and f_e of five out of six municipalities in **P1** (left), and of municipality **M1** (right)

Figure 5. Boxplot of values for f_i and f_e of two barangays in municipality **M2** in province **P1**

4. CONCLUSION

In this paper, we applied an existing statistical framework to detect election fraud in the Philippine election context. To be specific, using statistical tools, an election can be classified as not fair if there is a substantial value of fraud parameter f_e in favor of a single party. Moreover, irregular voting behavior can also be inferred from the value of f_i, which were greater than zero on all aggregation levels. In this study, we observed that while Klimek et al.'s parametric generative model can detect fraud in other countries, the model had limitations in the Philippine election context. To be specific, we noted that fraud in the 2022 PNE cannot be detected on a big scale (i.e., national) but rather, possibly, on a smaller scale (i.e., municipal). The fraud parameters generally had large standard deviation, rendering them mostly inconclusive when applied to high-level election data. However, after using lower-level election data, the statistical tool worked as intended. To further substantiate this preliminary observation, we intend to eventually apply and extend the analysis we employed to our selected province **P1** and municipality **M1** to other provinces and its municipalities and barangays to have a better idea of the reach of the systemic fraud, if it exists, in the country's election data.

While the paper mostly showed how statistical tools can be used for election fraud detection, it also actually showcased how these tools can be used by ordinary citizens to better engage and safeguard their country's democratic processes. Using systematic and replicable means to understand election events that transpired is actually something not fully explored by the citizens in the past. This study can be a foundational resource that complements the works of experts and researchers who are well-versed in the local political system. The quantitative analysis could supplement existing researches involving the political, social, and historical context of each electoral area. This research also serves as an additional tool by providing a standardized framework based on statistical analysis, which, when supplemented with the contextual insights of local experts, can verify allegations of fraud. As Abdelzadeh and Ekman (2012) put it, "*attentive critical citizens*" are an asset, and are thus important, to have a vivid democracy. Thus, being able to use the tools readily available in our information society can empower citizens to be a more proactive member of the democracy, to collaborate with people from different fields, and thereby pushing our society towards a more engaged democracy.

ACKNOWLEDGEMENT

The authors would like to thank the Parish Pastoral Council for Responsible Voting, the Ateneo de Manila University Mathematics Department, and Dr. William Emmanuel Yu, Dr. Eden Delight Miro, and Mr. Arjan Aguirre of Ateneo de Manila University for their assistance.

REFERENCES

Abdelzadeh, A. and Ekman, J. (2012). Understanding Critical Citizenship and Other Forms of Public Dissatisfaction: An Alternative Framework. *Politics, Culture and Socialization*, Vol 3, No. 1-2, pp. 177–194.

Asuncion, A. et al, [forthcoming], Detecting Localized Systematic Fraud in the 2022 Philippine National Elections. *Proceedings of the 6th International Conference on Mathematics and Mathematics Education*.

Cabristante, R. (2022). Geek news: A look into the 'constant 47% ratio' between Marcos' and Robredo's votes. *ABS-CBN News*. https://news.abs-cbn.com/spotlight/05/12/22/a-look-into-the-constant-47-ratio-in-marcos-vs-robredo-votes

Klimek P. et al. (2012). Statistical detection of systematic election irregularities. *Proceedings of the National Academy of Sciences*, Vol. 109, No. 41, pp. 16469-16473.

Lacasa, L., & Fernández-Gracia, J. (2018). Election Forensics: Quantitative methods for electoral fraud detection. *Forensic Science International*, 294, e19-e22.

Mebane, W. (2006). *Election Forensics: Vote Counts and Benford's Law*, Technical Report.

Mendoza, J. E. (2022). Comelec cites fastest transmission of election returns. *Inquirer*. https://newsinfo.inquirer.net/1595276/comelec-cites-fastest-transmission-of-election-returns

Mercado, N. A. (2022). Long queues, faulty VCMs, power outages hound opening of 2022 polls. *Inquirer*. https://newsinfo.inquirer.net/1594331/long-queues-faulty-vcms-power-outages-hound-opening-of-2022-polls

Rozenas, A. (2017). Detecting election fraud from irregularities in vote-share distributions. *Political Analysis*, Vol 25, No. 1, pp. 41-56.

FACETS OF CYBERCRIME ENCOUNTERED UNDER COVID PANDEMIC: THE MANIFOLD LANDSCAPE AND LESSONS TO BE LEARNED

Ameema Miftha, Marc Conrad and Marcia Gibson
Institute For Research in Applicable Computing
The University of Bedfordshire, University Square, Luton, Bedfordshire, UK

ABSTRACT

This paper explores the profound impact of COVID-19 pandemic on the landscape of cybercrime. The paper discusses the various ways in which the pandemic has influenced cybercriminal activities, cybersecurity challenges and the strategies being employed by the cybercriminals. It has been found that Covid-19 pandemic has had a significant impact on cybercrime. The cybercriminals have exploited the fear and uncertainty surrounding the pandemic to launch phishing attacks. These attacks have disrupted the production and distribution of essential goods, causing significant economic impact. This sets the platform for organizations to think and adapt to this evolving threat landscape.

KEYWORDS

COVID-19, Cybercrime, Cybersecurity, Pandemic, Remote Work, Phishing, Ransomware, Digital Transformation

1. INTRODUCTION

Covid-19 can be considered the biggest opportunity for Black-Hat Hackers who used the pandemic to gain greater prominence in the cybercrime world. Investigation firms have shown evidence that cybercrimes increased by over 300% in a span of six months from January 2020 to May 2020. FBI reported that cybercrimes increased by a few hundred to five thousand a day in this span (Fully verified, 2023). Already, over one-third of cybercrimes use healthcare organizations and banks as their soft targets, and which increased massively in the post-covid scenario. Reportedly, cyber-attacks in healthcare organizations increased by 240% in the last 2 years (Fully verified, 2023). A recent example is of the Brno University Hospital where the cyber-attack brought the entire hospital system down. Emergency care was put on hold and seriously ill patients had to be instantly transferred to other facilities (Swiss info, 2020). One can clearly imagine the loss of 'personal data' of the patients and how the cyber-attackers can exploit this data for more such security breaches.

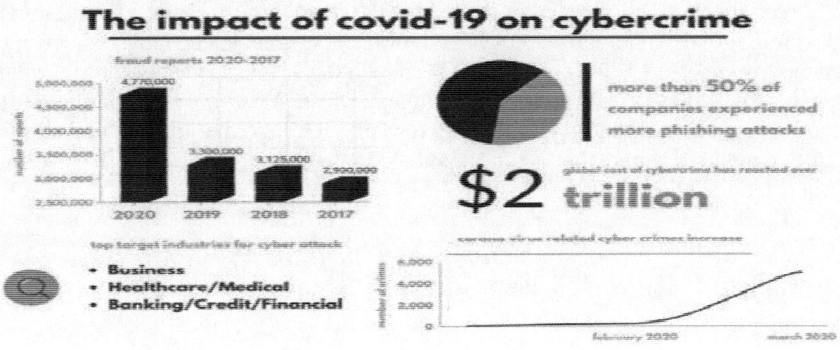

Figure 1. Impact of covid-19 on cybercrime, sourced from (Fully verified, 2023)

2. METHODOLOGY

This research comprises desk-based secondary research, exploring existing public domain data. The information pertaining to prevalence of cyberattacks and their rise during and after the Covid scenario has been gathered and linked to the 'possible' causes that led to this trend. The 'data' provided a solid argument for keeping it argumentative and elaborating a line of thought based on statistical evidence and interpretive analysis. The primary goal was to gather and evaluate existing information to support the research objectives, rather than collecting new data. This involved collection of both quantitative and qualitative data from across a wide range of sources such as historical records, government publications, market data and academic research.

3. HOW COVID 19 HAS CHANGED THE CYBER THREAT LANDSCAPE

3.1 Identity Theft

Covid-19 has been widely associated with mass confusion and fear among the people (Swiss info, 2020). A lot of cyber-attacks used this as the ground for unethically sourcing key personal data. Fraudsters, impersonating medical personnel, contacted members of the public and secured confidential information in the name of coronavirus testing or health services (Reuters, 2021). In fact, these are not the only cases of identity theft. Across the European Union, smugglers and human traffickers used the migration crisis for building a repository of forged documents. These stolen identities are now being used to gain masked entries into the otherwise secure network of hospitals or banks. Reportedly, the migration crisis during the pandemic period led to high cases of forged citizenship throughout Europe. Today, cyber-attackers have a greatly enhanced bank of forged driving licenses, credit cards, ID cards and passports providing easier authentication and access to systems requiring such documents as proof of identity. Reportedly, $3.3 billion was lost during the year 2020 due to identity fraud. The scenario has been no different in emerging countries like India where '*business offers and schemes' have resulted in 600% rise in cybercrime during Covid-19 pandemic*' (Kshetri & Sharma, 2021).

3.2 Vulnerabilities of New Normal

Another emergent contributory factor that has added to the woes of cybercrime in the Covid-19 scenario is the 'new normal'. Given government restrictions in all the countries, the culture of Work from Home (WFH) became the new normal. Even after the restrictions have been removed, companies are still finding the model cost-economic and less capital intensive. However, the problem is that cyber-security is highly neglected in the backdrop of the new normal. Most organizations still do not provide cyber-safe remote working environment. The evidence illustrates a remarkable shift in the reported cases on direct attack to companies, fraudulent malware transfer and phishing. In Switzerland, the National Cyber Security Centre (NCSC) reported 350 cases of direct attack on companies in the year 2020, compared to below 100 cases for the same period last year (Swiss info, 2020). Later the studies linked these cyber-attacks the lack of deterrent measures/inherent protection on the computers of WFH employees (Reuters, 2021). This aspect of 'new normal' has led to greater exposure to cyber-risks. Statistical reports have indicated that 47% of WFH employees become victims of phishing attacks (Tessian W., 2020). The rise has further been linked with high spread of 'fake' information on Coronavirus / pandemic, where the factor of panic led to increased likelihood to click these malicious links. It has been found that an average of $137,000 is lost for every cyber-security breach on a remote working site (Actionfraud, 2021).

3.3 Irresponsible Cyber-Behavior during Stress

One in seven WFH employees faced a cyber-attack during the Corona period (www.swissinfo.ch, 2019). It is interesting to note that the majority of data breaches happen due to human error. Reportedly, the hackers know how to maneuver people into clicking a malicious link, known as phishing. The fear and confusion resulting from the Covid-19 pandemic helped create abundant opportunities to conduct social engineering against individuals (Statista, 2021). In countries like India, where internet penetration is still not as per global levels, there has been a rise of 37% in cyber-attacks during the first quarter of 2020 i.e. immediately when the Coronavirus pandemic began.

In fact, the scope of cybercrime in Covid and post-Covid scenario has had a similar effect on cyber-violence and cyber-stalking cases. This global rise has been consistent across countries like the United States, Australia, India and Philippines (Wangnelsy & Affoum, 2021). Violence against Women (VAW), a designated human rights violation, has increased exponentially because of the Covid-19 pandemic. Reportedly, stalking and harassment rose by 20% during the 2020 Covid lockdowns, but as the pandemic restrictions were eased, the crime went up by 31% compared to the pre-pandemic period (Bussu, 2023).

In fact, it has now manifested in more and different unprecedented forms (Bracewell, Hargreaves, & Stanley, 2020). For example, reduced opportunities for physical surveillance of their victims forced the stalkers to escalate other methods of stalking. UK based studies mentioned how the stalkers used tracking devices to keep track of their victims (Bracewell, Hargreaves, & Stanley, 2020). Similarly, Cyberstalker used malicious reports to get into the system of one of his victims. Due to Covid-19, there was a dramatic rise in the use of social media platforms so that the people could lessen their feelings of isolation. The Cyberstalker used this to intensify their activities (Singh, 2020).

4. HOW COVID-19 HAS MADE WORKPLACE EXPOSED TO CYBER CRIME

Arguably, WFH routine is something that provides cyber-attackers an opportunity to exploit the weaknesses of an under-protected system. During the period February 2020 to May 2020, more than half a million people faced data-breaches during video-conferencing services (Deloitte, 2021). The personal data was sold on the dark web by the hackers. OpenBullet, a tool for hacking, was found to have been used extensively for the cybercrime. Reportedly, video-conferencing services suffered a vulnerability where attackers could access both present and previously used passwords and usernames to make illegitimate entries into other systems as well. The stolen data allowed the hackers to easily identify the passwords and login ids of millions of individuals.

One of the major problems with high incidences of cyber-attacks is because businesses did not take appropriate preventive measures, especially against phishing attacks. Despite all the losses and increased frequency of hacking, the businesses still work on Bring Your Own Device (BYOD) approach in place of Corporate Owned Personally Enable (COPE) approach. One can easily presume the fact that BYOD approach makes the system highly vulnerable to external attacks are there is no standardization being followed. There is only a very small number of WFH systems which run on anti-malware or antivirus tools (go.cynet.com, 2021). Moreover, the pandemic also made the cyber-attackers more sophisticated in their approach. Reportedly, 35% of malware is 'state-of-art' kind and built on highly effective platforms (go.cynet.com, 2021). The new forms of Artificial Intelligence (AI) and machine learning have added more potency to phishing attacks. The new forms of ransomware attacks were advanced phishing attacks that used the information around vaccine development and vaccination scheduling for spreading malware (Deloitte, 2021). There are only a handful of companies that have thought about antivirus protection, cyber-security awareness, phishing awareness, home-network security, use of VPN, identifying weak spots, developing crisis plans and fixing the leaks (Tessian, 2020).

5. SCENARIO OF HUMAN HACKING DURING THE PANDEMIC

The problem is that 'stress' has been a major contributor to people falling victim to phishing attacks during the Covid-19 period. Empirical studies have shown that over half of the cyber-crime victims agreed that they were in stress when they clicked the malicious link (Tessian, 2020). Especially during the Covid-19 pandemic, this became more visible. Google recorded over 18 million email scams on a weekly basis during Covid-19 pandemic, which was 215% of what was recorded a year later (Lyons, 2020). It has been reported that 240million spam messages on coronavirus are being distributed daily over Google. These are different subject lines but same email in different words. Google has responded that hackers are using phishing attacks and scams to use both financial incentives and fear to create an urgency to manipulate users to respond. The studies that examined the link between stress and phishing have shown that higher stress and anxiety are positively linked to inappropriate cyber behaviour. The studies have shown how stress would disrupt neurons in the prefrontal cortex of the brain to take intelligible decisions (Park, 2016). It has been claimed that, 'anxiety evokes hypofrontality and disrupts rule-relevant encoding by dorsomedial prefrontal cortex neurons'. Similarly, anxiety would prompt people to take hasty decisions without really considering the negative outcomes. Hackers seem to be smart enough to make use of such scientific information to their benefit.

The pandemic of Covid-19 led to total lockdown in almost every country, and which subsequently led to confinement of people in their homes. What this eventually led to was despair and anxiety among many people. Cybercriminals capitalised on the fears and anxieties among the masses. One can see this with the use of Black Net Rat and Corona anti-virus software that claims to prevent the user's Smartphone from coronavirus. Some people fell for these scam sand exposed their digital devices to data breaches (Europol, 2021). In fact, a great number of fake corona-detection devices and unethical drugs were sold unscrupulously by illegal entities during the time. Malicious links and fake emails were the means through which the trafficking of counterfeit products took place. Similarly, many links surfaced which claimed to endorse crowd-funding campaigns for pooling money for building oxygen-banks and new hospitals to treat Coronavirus. It was later found that many of the fake links/websites diverted funds to alternative criminal pockets (Actionfraud, 2021). There have been instances where fake emails constructed to appear to be sent on behalf of governmentally introduced grant schemes at the time, led to downloaded ransomware and stolen money (UNECA, 2021). The ransomware software 'Maze' affected the software company Cognizant, the overall cost to regain access to data and systems was reportedly in the millions (Reuters, 2021).

Cybercriminals used the pandemic for exploiting people's curiosity and their search for information on the digital medium. Confined to their homes, many people had no other option but to depend on any piece of information that they could get during that time. This was an unprecedented situation, and cyber criminals used it to serve their malicious intent. The European General Data Protection Regulation (GDPR) puts it clearly – the Covid-19 pandemic offers an opportunity to deliberately exploit people' sense of insecurity, curiosity, and their need for information for criminal or malicious activities (Tasheva, 2017).

6. LESSONS FOR THE FUTURE

The COVID-19 pandemic has sped up digitalization and made it easier for companies, government officials, and end users to comprehend the significance of cybersecurity in creating a digital future that is sustainable (Bussu, 2023). Although the pandemic is no longer ongoing, the WFH culture persists either in full or with increased numbers of 'hybrid' roles. It is imperative that businesses prioritize cybersecurity and take action in a number of policy areas if they are to meet the high standards of security required in the industrialized society and take part in the expanding cyber economy.

Major weaknesses exist in the areas of risk and compliance management, application security, security analysis and investigation, and cloud computing security (Statista., 2021). Online collaborative work styles, such as WFH, are large-scale, reasonably priced, state-of-the-art, but cybersecurity training programs for professionals and practitioners need to be addressed by the commercial sector (Tasheva, 2017).

Also, by definition, cybercrime is a transnational crime, but its ecosystem lacks the strong laws, organizations, and operational coordination necessary to effectively combat the trespassing. Since 2013, there has been progress in creating common cybersecurity institutions, with ENISA being given a more robust mandate to boost cybersecurity capabilities, construction and consciousness (Verizon, 2021). Still, in order to combat cybercrime collectively, businesses must widen the circle and include additional member states and third-country allies. Increasing the resilience of cybersecurity will not only safeguard global cybersecurity but also promote its growth. Businesses may benefit from the expertise in establishing internationally acclaimed standards, such as worldwide regulation on the General Data Protection.

7. CONCLUSION

The Covid-19 pandemic has had a significant impact on cybercrime. First of all, Cybercriminals exploited the fear and uncertainty surrounding the pandemic to launch phishing attacks. They sent fake emails and messages claiming to provide information, safety tips, or government stimulus packages. These messages often contained malware or links to malicious websites. Also, with the shift to remote work, organizations had to quickly adapt their cyber-security measures. A majority of these were unprepared which left the remote workers and their companies vulnerable to attacks. Cybercriminals targeted remote work infrastructure and exploited security gaps in remote access solutions. This is reflected into high incidences of ransomware attacks the frequency of which increased during the pandemic, these affected healthcare organizations, municipalities and various businesses. Criminals recognized the importance of healthcare data during the pandemic, and some even pledged not to attack healthcare facilities. Cybercriminals also targeted supply chains and critical infrastructure to exploit weaknesses in organizations. These attacks disrupted the production and distribution of essential goods, causing significant economic impact.

Covid-19 also exposed the online arena to increased scams. As more people turned to online shopping, cybercriminals launched scams related to fake e-commerce websites, fraudulent products, and counterfeit Covid-19-related items. This contributed to financial losses and identity theft. In the healthcare segment, the increased use of tele-health services exposed vulnerabilities in healthcare systems. This led to privacy breaches and data leaks. Cybercriminals took advantage of these weaknesses. The pandemic also saw a surge in disinformation and misinformation spread through various online channels. Some cybercriminals used these tactics to manipulate public opinion, promote scams and to spread fear.

Covid-19 led to a new mode of working in the regime of new normal. Notably, remote work and online meetings became more prevalent with the spread. This raised concerns about the security and privacy of video conferencing apps. Incidents of "Zoom bombing" and other security issues highlighted the need for better security practices. Clearly, the pandemic disrupted the cyber-security workforce and made it difficult for organizations to hire and retain skilled professionals. This shortage of cyber-security experts exacerbated security risks.

Given the legal and regulatory changes, some governments introduced new regulations and laws to address cyber threats during the pandemic. These changes aimed to bolster cyber-security and protect critical infrastructure. Organizations and individuals have to adapt by enhancing their cyber-security measures, increase awareness, and being more cautious about online activities. The pandemic underscored the importance of robust cyber-security practices and highlighted the need for ongoing vigilance in an increasingly digital world.

In the future, in order to combat cybercrime collectively, organizations need to widen the circle and include additional member states and third-country allies. Increasing the resilience of each-other's cybersecurity will not only safeguard global cybersecurity but also promote its growth. Individual nations will benefit from each-other's expertise in establishing internationally developed standards.

REFERENCES

Actionfraud. (2021). COVID-19 related scams - news and resources. Retrieved from www.actionfraud.police.uk: https://www.actionfraud.police.uk/covid19

Bracewell, K., Hargreaves, P., & Stanley, N. (2020). The Consequences of the COVID-19 Lockdown. Journal of Family Violence (2022) 37:951–957.

Bussu, A. (2023). Exploring the impact of cyberbullying and cyberstalking on victims' behavioral changes in higher education during COVID-19: A case study. International Journal of Law, Crime and Justice.

Deloitte. (2021). Impact of COVID-19 on Cybersecurity. Retrieved from https://www2.deloitte.com: https://www2.deloitte.com/ch/en/pages/risk/articles/impact-covid-cybersecurity.html

Europol. (2021). Rise-of-fake-corona-cures-revealed-in-global-counterfeit-medicine-operation. Retrieved from www.europol.europa.eu: https://www.europol.europa.eu/newsroom/news/rise-of-fake-%E2%80%98corona-cures%E2%80%99-revealed-in-global-counterfeit-medicine-operation

Fully verified. (2023). The impact of covid-19 on cybercrime. Retrieved from fully-verified.com: https://fully-verified.com/the-impact-of-covid-19-on-cybercrime/#:~:text=Coronavirus%20–%20the%20biggest%20threat%20to%20cybersecurity&text=Already%20at%20the%20beginning%20of,crimes%20have%20increased%20by%20300%25.

go.cynet.com. (2021). Covid19 Cyberattack Analysis. Retrieved from https://go.cynet.com/covid-19-cyberattack-analysis?utm_source=thn.

Kshetri, N., & Sharma, A. (2021). A review and analysis of online crime in pre and post COVID scenario with respective counter measures and security strategies. Journal of Engineering, Computing and Architecture · December 2021.

Lyons, K. (2020). Google saw more than 18 million daily malware and phishing emails related to COVID-19 last week. Retrieved from www.theverge.com: https://www.theverge.com/2020/4/16/21223800/google-malware-phishing-covid-19-coronavirus-scams

Park, J. (2016). Anxiety Evokes Hypo frontality and Disrupts Rule-Relevant Encoding by Dorsomedial Prefrontal Cortex Neurons. Journal of Neuroscience 16 March 2016, 36 (11) 3322-3335; DOI: https://doi.org/10.1523/JNEUROSCI.4250-15.2016.

Reuters. (2021). Hacking-against-corporations-surges-as-workers-take-computers-home. Retrieved from www.reuters.com: https://www.reuters.com/article/us-health-coronavirus-cyber-corporations/hacking-against-corporations-surges-as-workers-take-computers-home-idUSKBN21Z0Y6

Singh, D. (2020). Lockdown effect: No rules of social distancing apply here. Retrieved from The Financial Express.

Statista. (2021). Cybercrime in India – statistics and facts. Retrieved from Published by: Sandhya Keelery: https://www.statista.com/topics/5054/cyber-crime-in-india/#dossierKeyfigures

Statista. (2021). Areas with biggest shortage of cybersecurity skills within organizations worldwide in 2021. technology category.

Swiss info. (2020). Jump in cyber-attacks during Covid-19 confinement. Retrieved from www.swissinfo.ch: https://www.swissinfo.ch/eng/jump-in-cyber-attacks-during-covid-19-confinement/45818794

Tasheva, I. (2017). European cybersecurity policy: Trends and prospects. EPC Policy Brief, 8.

Tessian. (2020). Why We Click: The Psychology Behind Phishing Scams and How to Avoid Being Hacked. Retrieved from www.tessian.com: https://www.tessian.com/blog/why-we-click-on-phishing-scams/#:~:text=In%20a%20recent%20survey%20conducted,a%20phishing%20email%20at%20work

Tessian, W. (2020). Why We Click: The Psychology Behind Phishing Scams and How to Avoid Being Hacked. Retrieved from www.tessian.com: https://www.tessian.com/blog/why-we-click-on-phishing-scams/#:~:text=In%20a%20recent%20survey%20conducted,a%20phishing%20email%20at%20work

UNECA. (2021). UN health agency warns against coronavirus COVID-19 criminal scams. Retrieved from www.uneca.org: https://www.uneca.org/stories/un-health-agency-warns-against-coronavirus-covid-19-criminal-scams

Verizon. (2021). Data breach investigations report. Results and analysis.

Wangnelsy, S., & Affoum, A. (2021). Cyber harassment: A growing concern in the age of COVID. Retrieved from https://blogs.worldbank.org/developmenttalk/cyber-harassment-growing-concern-age-covid

www.swissinfo.ch. (2019). One in seven Swiss residents hit by cyber-attacks. Retrieved from https://www.swissinfo.ch: https://www.swissinfo.ch/eng/internet-security_one-in-seven-swiss-residents-hit-by-cyber-attacks/44858084

PRIVACY AND DIGITAL GOVERNMENT: PERSPECTIVES FROM PUBLIC ORGANIZATIONS IN BRAZIL

Manuella Maia Ribeiro and Luciana Portilho
Brazilian Network Information Center (NIC.br)
Avenida das Nações Unidas , 11541, 7th floor, Sao Paulo - SP, Brazil

ABSTRACT

Government organizations' increasing adoption of digital technologies is associated with more actions to avoid risks related to privacy and data protection violations. Protecting people's data can also positively impact trust in government and digital government initiatives. In this context, this paper aims to analyze Brazilian public organizations based on data surveys related to implementing privacy and data protection actions in the public sector. Among the results from national surveys, Brazilian government organizations are still in the initial phase regarding implementing actions to improve citizens' privacy and data protection rights.

KEYWORDS

Privacy, Data Protection, Digital Government, Trust, Public Policies

1. INTRODUCTION

Digital technologies have enabled improved provision of information, services, and public policies for society (United Nations Department of Economic and Social Affairs [UN DESA], 2020). In this context, Brazil has been undergoing a digital transformation in the public sector, expanding the use of data analysis for decision-making and the adoption of information and communication technologies (ICT) for delivering public services (Brazilian Internet Steering Committee [CGI.br], 2022). However, the increase in collection, storage, and analysis of people's data has raised concerns about potential risks to privacy and data protection for citizens due to the public sector's access and use of Big Data and other data-driven technologies (Bleeker, 2020). In response, international organizations have issued recommendations on the use of citizen data. The United Nations Development Programme (UNDP) emphasizes the importance of governments adopting general standards or, if not available, regional or international reference frameworks for data protection (UNDP, 2020).

For public policies, as in the healthcare sector, the expansion of digital health has led to rapid growth in the volume and variety of patient information available in electronic format, increasing and diversifying access possibilities. However, these data can reveal certain vulnerabilities, and their uncontrolled use can violate the fundamental rights of individuals, especially those related to privacy, equality, intimacy, and human dignity (Botelho & Camargo, 2021). In this sense, the Pan American Health Organization (PAHO) recognizes trust and information security in the digital healthcare environment as one of the eight principles of digital transformation in Latin America and the Caribbean countries (PAHO, 2021).

In the context of education, safeguarding the privacy of students, mainly children, is a crucial aspect of their digital rights, which must be protected through appropriate means in their best interests. For this protection, the United Nations launched Global General Comment No. 25 on the rights of the child in the digital environment, which extends the scope of the Convention on the Rights of the Child to digital spaces. The Child Online Protection Act (COPPA) and the General Data Protection Regulation (GDPR) also emphasize the importance of children's privacy, security, and data protection in digital environments.

Thus, it is crucial to adopt measures to ensure the protection and privacy of citizens' data in order to build trust in the government and its digital initiatives. In the case of Brazil, the General Data Protection Law, enacted in 2018, regulates the guidelines for processing personal data in both physical and digital forms by individuals and organizations, including the public sector. In addition to general requirements, there is a specific chapter with rules for public organizations. In addition to defining principles and limits, it also addresses the use of personal data for improving services and public policies for society.

Certain sectors such as healthcare and education are subject to special legal protection from LGPD because of the significant risks involved if this type of personal data is mishandled or widely disclosed. It is worth highlighting that the collection and processing of personal data of children and health information are considered sensitive data. According to the LGPD, sensitive data needs greater caution regarding data processing.

Therefore, with the enactment of the LGPD, carrying out actions to protect data and privacy have become one of the main challenges for public organizations in Brazil. These concerns are especially relevant when implementing public policies, where a balance must be struck between processing personal data to improve public sector performance and the potential risks to citizens such as data leaks, automated systems leading to discriminatory decisions, surveillance, among others. Given this context, this paper aims to provide an overview of data protection initiatives in the Brazilian public sector, including the adoption of practices by government organizations in general, public healthcare facilities, and public schools.

Data from three national surveys, namely ICT in Health 2021 (CGI.br, 2021b), ICT in Education 2020 (CGI.br, 2021a), and ICT Electronic Government 2021 (CGI.br, 2022), were used for the analysis. These surveys were conducted through computer-assisted telephone interviews (CATI) and were stratified sample studies. The primary focus of these studies was to gather information on different aspects related to the use of technology by public organizations, which included questions about measures taken to ensure data protection and privacy. The ICT in Health survey covered all Brazilian healthcare facilities, both public and private. In the 2021 edition, 1,524 managers were interviewed, representing 112,075 healthcare facilities. The ICT in Education survey was conducted in public and private Basic Education schools in urban and rural areas. It included 3,678 schools in 2020, representing 127,171 educational institutions in Brazil. The ICT Electronic Government survey, in 2021, interviewed 580 Brazilian federal and state government organizations and 3,543 local governments.

2. DATA PROTECTION IN BRAZILIAN PUBLIC ORGANIZATIONS

This section of the paper demonstrates how different Brazilian public sector institutions, administrative organizations, public health facilities, and public schools have dealt with data protection and privacy of citizens' after the LGPD. The following section will present data from government organizations about federal and state levels of government, including the Executive, Legislative, and Judiciary branches and the Public Prosecutor's office. At the local level, only the Executive was analyzed. Then, results from public healthcare facilities and public schools will be presented, focusing on initiatives about measures for data protection and privacy of patients and students.

2.1 Public Organizations from Federal, State and Local Governments

Concerning the implementation of the Brazilian General Data Protection Law, federal government organizations tend to comply more with the law than state and local government ones. According to the ICT Electronic Government survey (2022), 81% of federal organizations mentioned appointing a person responsible for processing personal data, compared to only 33% of state government organizations. It was also found that the Judiciary organizations (81%) and the Public Prosecutor's Office (73%) were more likely to cite this appointment than the Legislative (40%) and Executive (34%) government organizations. At the local level, only 14% of local governments had defined the person responsible for processing personal data. The proportion was higher among capitals and cities, with more than half million inhabitants (42% and 41%, respectively).

The Brazilian General Data Protection Law (LGPD) emphasizes the importance of transparency in processing personal data, ensuring that data subjects can access clear, precise, and easily accessible information, preferably through the Internet. However, the research reveals that 65% of federal and 34% of state government organizations provided Internet service channels for this purpose. Judiciary organizations were again in a better situation, with three out of four offering this type of channel. In contrast, less than a third of local governments had Internet service channels for citizens to address concerns about their personal data, even among those with more than 500,000 inhabitants, where only 36% provided this type of service.

The survey results underscore the need for digital channels prepared to receive such demands. The research also investigated the provision of LGPD training or qualification for public employees. The study revealed that among federal and state agencies with an IT department, 91% of Judiciary and 82% of Public Prosecutor's Officers organizations offered training on the LGPD to at least one employee. While half of the Legislative and Executive organizations offered this type of training (49% and 50%, respectively), only a quarter of local governments in the countryside provided courses or training on the LGPD for employees in the technology sector, compared to 63% of capitals.

2.2 Public Healthcare Facilities

According to the ICT in Health survey (CGI.br, 2021b), in 2021, only 21% of public healthcare facilities and 38% of private facilities had a document defining an information security policy. Furthermore, there has been no significant variation in public facilities over the past few years, indicating that, despite the existence of the LGPD, little has been done to establish an information security policy. In the case of private healthcare facilities, there is a trend of adopting information security policies in recent years according to the survey data.

Regarding actions related to compliance with LGPD, the law stipulates that the processing of personal data must be based on a legitimate, specific, explicit, and informed purpose for patients. Despite this, only 26% of public facilities surveyed personal data, classified their purposes and legal bases, while 35% in private ones. The provision of contact channels ensures greater transparency in operations and data processing, but only 33% of public healthcare facilities made these channels available.

Another issue is that 21% of public facilities published a privacy policy on the facilities' or health department's website, In this case, this percentage is not very different from private ones. It should also establish a transparent relationship and ensure mechanisms for the data subject's participation. Additionally, less than one-fifth of public facilities implemented processes to anonymize personal data and 16% implemented an incident response plan. Private ones were 39% and 33%, respectively.

Finally, 23% of public and 40% of private facilities conducted an awareness campaign about LGPD for their employees. Such training contributes to healthcare professionals' better understanding of the risks associated with information availability in a virtual environment and raises awareness of the importance of data confidentiality and integrity. Lack of awareness on this topic can facilitate data breaches, cyberattacks, and other threats that compromise both patient and healthcare establishment security.

2.3 Public Schools

Regarding the storage of personal data, the ICT in Education survey (CGI.br, 2021a) showed that 85% of public schools recorded or accessed students' registration data, such as name, address, phone number, and date of birth. Additionally, 43% of public schools recorded or accessed electronically formatted information about students' physical conditions, such as weight, height, allergies, and more.

Another focus of collecting information about children and adolescents is through the apps used by schools. One-quarter of schools had their institution-specific app. In 12% of schools, the app allowed for the tracking of students' daily activities, such as meals, behavior, mood, and participation.

During the COVID-19 pandemic, schools were closed due to necessary social distancing measures. This led to a significant increase in the use of digital platforms, environments, apps, and networks in Basic Education. As a result, 59% of public schools conducted distance learning through video conferencing platforms as a strategy to maintain pedagogical activities during the pandemic. Furthermore, the use of social networks and instant messaging apps reached an adoption rate of 90%.

Even after the pandemic, the use of virtual platforms, networks, and environments for teaching and learning continues to grow. However, this increased usage also implies an increase in associated risks with these tools. To mitigate these risks, some measures have been adopted, such as organizing debates and lectures in 56% of public schools and implementing training programs for teachers (38%) and students (26%). These actions aim to raise awareness about the importance of protecting privacy and personal data when using devices and the internet. Given the context presented, it is fundamental for schools to have well-defined data protection and information security policies. However, in the case of public schools, only 37% possessed such a document, while in private schools, the proportion was 60% in 2020.

3. CONCLUSION

According to the survey results analyzed for this paper, Brazilian public organizations are still in the early stages of adapting to the LGPD legislation, with only a part of the organizations focused on actions to promote the measured actions regarding privacy and data protection.

Among the branches, the judiciary is leading the way, with most institutional structures and actions related to the LGPD already in progress. Federal government organizations had more initiatives on this theme than state and local governments, showing disparities among different levels of government in Brazil. The public healthcare sector also faces significant challenges adapting to the LGPD requirements. Finally, public primary schools have vast student information in the education sector, including data generated through activity monitoring applications, such as images of children and adolescents. However, less than half of primary public schools have a document defining a data protection and information security policy. In this context, failure to comply with LGPD can result in financial penalties and data collection rights suspension, which can make complex governments' activities.

In recent years, the digital transformation of the healthcare sector in Brazil has advanced through the expansion of information and communication technology (ICT) infrastructure, the development of applications by both the public and private sectors, and their adoption by healthcare professionals. As a result, a large amount of patient information has been used in tools such as electronic health records, telehealth, and information exchange between healthcare facilities and institutions, highlighting the urgent need for standardization and regulation to ensure the correct and secure use of the generated data. Despite these advancements, few healthcare facilities, especially public ones, have taken more effective actions to ensure the protection of patients' personal data, as recommended by LGPD. The importance of having this policy is that it should outline internal processes and policies that ensure compliance with regulations and best practices related to the protection of personal data.

The protection of data and privacy of children and adolescents in schools is one of the main challenges in the education sector, primarily due to the various forms of collecting personal data. These forms go beyond what is consciously shared by children, adolescents, and their guardians and extend to information collected in their online practices. In the case of public schools, this challenge becomes even greater, as the responsibility for data collection and protection is shared with government agencies.

Based on this scenario, there are still several challenges in adapting public institutions to the requirements of the LGPD. There is a need for the public sector to develop plans with rules of good practice and privacy and data protection governance that map personal data used by its various institutions and determine how these data should be processed, particularly sensitive data.

REFERENCES

Botelho, M. C., & Camargo, E. P. do A., (2021). *A aplicação da Lei Geral de Proteção de Dados na saúde. Revista de Direito Sanitário*, 21(e0021). https://doi.org/10.11606/issn.2316-9044. rdisan.2021.168023

Brazilian Internet Steering Committee, (2021a). *Survey on the use of information and communication technologies in Brazilian schools: ICT in Education 2020 (COVID-19 edition — Adapted methodology).* https://www.cetic.br/media/docs/publicacoes/2/20211124200326/ tic_educacao_2020_livro_eletronico.pdf

Brazilian Internet Steering Committee, (2021b). *Survey on the use of information and communication technologies in Brazilian healthcare facilities: ICT in Health 2021 (COVID-19 edition — Adapted methodology).* https://cetic.br/media/docs/publicacoes/2/20211124123911/ tic_saude_2021_livro_eletronico.pdf

Brazilian Internet Steering Committee, (2022). *Survey on the use of information and communication technologies in the Brazilian public sector: ICT Electronic Government 2021.* https://cetic.br/media/docs/publicacoes/2/20220725170710/ t ic_governo_el e tronico_2021_ l ivro_ eletronico.pdf

Pan American Health Organization, (2021). *Eight guiding principles of digital transformation of the health sector: A call to Pan American actio*n. https://iris.paho.org/handle/10665.2/54256

United Nations Department of Economic and Social Affairs, (2020). E-*government survey 2020: Digital government in the decade of action for sustainable development: With addendum on COVID-19 response.* https://publicadministration.un.org/egovkb/ Portals/egovkb/Documents/un/2020- Survey/2020%20UN%20E-Government%20 Survey%20(Full%20Report).pdf

United Nations Development Programme, (2020). *Guidance to UNDP country offices on the privacy, data protection and broader human rights dimensions of using digital technologies to combat COVID-19.* https://www.sdg16hub.org/content/covid-19-guidance-undp-country-offices-privacy-data-protection-and-digital-technologies

WHAT IS THE TRUTH AND CURRENT SITUATION OF THE METAVERSE? CONSUMERS POINT OF VIEW

Sonia San-Martín[1] and Cristina Torrego[2]
[1]*Professor of Marketing*
[2]*Degree project student*
Facultad de CC. Económicas, C/ Parralillos 09001, Universidad de Burgos, Spain

ABSTRACT

The Metaverse can be regarded as a new virtual space that uses technology to extend the physical world through augmented and virtual reality, and offers an opportunity for businesses and users to interact with each other in both real and simulated environments through avatars and holograms (Dwivedi, 2022). The aim of this exploratory work is to investigate consumers' knowledge, perceptions and emotions related to this virtual world. The methodology followed in this study is a survey of a sample of 152 Spanish consumers. Results show there is still little comprehension, confusion and use of metaverse for shopping and branding impact.

KEYWORDS

Metaverse, Marketing, Virtual, Consumers, Challenges

1. INTRODUCTION

Metaverse is gaining great relevance, an immersive virtual space based on Virtual Reality, which aims to combine with the physical world to enhance user experiences (Khatri, 2022, p. 1). The significant advancement of technology is enabling a more interactive and immersive creation of experiences inside this virtual world (Leveau & Camus, 2023). For this reason, both large and small companies are adapting (or at least trying to) their business models to this new world (Dwivedi, 2022, p. 2). The evolution of the metaverse seems unstoppable. In June 2022, the consulting firm McKinsey and Company published a report estimating the potential economic value of this virtual world at 5 trillion dollars by 2030, as it is shaping up to be the biggest growth for several industries in the coming years. However, the concept of the metaverse has been evolving for almost two decades through platforms such as Second Life, Roblox, Fortnite or Decentraland (2020). Statista (2021) conducted a survey with 200 executives, presidents, CEOs, and members of the Board of Directors from companies in Belgium, Germany, Spain, France, the UK and USA that were already investing in the metaverse. This survey revealed that nearly 70% believe that this virtual space will be highly successful in the next five years. See Figure 1 for companies' opinions.

It is necessary to know the opinions of early adopters of metaverse and the knowledge, perceived experience and emotions that this virtual space inspires in people to advise companies about its use for marketing purposes and debate about its future. Therefore, this work aims to address three research questions. RQ1: do consumers know what Metaverse is? RQ2: What are the user's perceived experience and emotions generated by Metaverse? RQ3: Is there a buying intention to buy brands that appear in Metaverse? An empirical studied was performed, which consisted of a survey carried out on a sample of 152 Spanish consumers through social media.

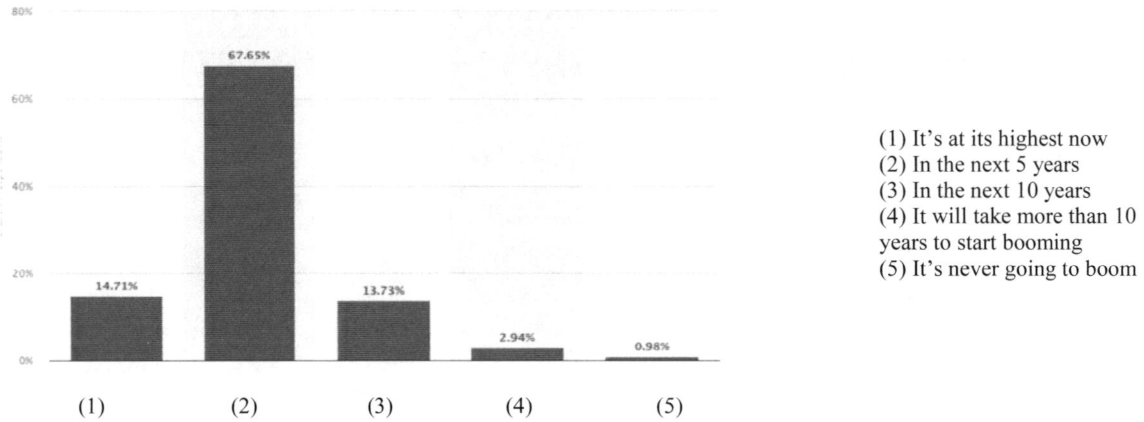

Figure 1. Metaverse boom expectation business according to companies worldwide (Statista, 2022)

2. THE METAVERSE. CONCEPTUALIZATION AND CHALLENGES

What is the Metaverse? Even though this word has gained significant relevance in recent months and, seemingly, appears to be an easy question, its answer is actually quite complicated as it is still in an early phase and there is no global consensus on its meaning or description due to the lack of its full conceptualization (see a revision by Dwivedi, 2022, p. 23). Kotler et al. (2021) provide their own definition of this new marketing space, considering it as "the application of technologies that mimic human beings to create, communicate, deliver, and enhance value along the customer journey" (Kotler et al., 2021, pp. 19-20).

Following Wang et al. (2023), metaverse marketing has the characteristics of perception, interactivity, and interest, which positively affect consumers' purchase intention. Leveau & Camus (2023) base on experiential marketing study to examine the effects of body position and embodiment in shaping consumer intentions mediated by immersion and enjoyment during a virtual reality experience. Experience and emotions felt during and after navigating the Metaverse can be a key for this virtual space to be adopted for branding and even for shopping.

The Metaverse face various challenges. One challenge is the interoperability between virtual worlds, as the ideal scenario would allow users, through their avatars, to move from one world to another with their belongings, as well as share assets and data across multiple platforms and networks (Horta, 2021). Additionally, there is the risk of personal data being stolen due to the large amount of information collected by XR technologies, needing a robust security network to promote user trust. Besides, there is also the inconvenience derived from the lack of an economic, tax, and legal regulation, which prevents from knowing and claiming for penalties or reaching a successful resolution.

Another challenge is related to the psychological impact that is likely to result from the possible addiction to the Metaverse, as it happens in other fields, such as with videogames. While the exact effects on health are not yet known, it can be imagined that they will be significant, given the current growing addiction to technology in general. Lastly, more closely tied to marketing, there is the drawback of "a lack of stability and standards that hinders the planning and execution of companies' marketing campaigns" (Bushell, 2022, p. 4). Additionally, there is intense competition among companies advocating for the Metaverse, as they aim to be the first to attract customers, secure a market share, and gain customer loyalty.

3. EMPIRICAL STUDY

Quantitative methods were employed in data analyses through a survey answered by a sample of the population. The questionnaire was created using Google Forms and distributed via social media using a non-probabilistic sampling of consumers. The sample size consisted of 152 participants of different age intervals (18-26 years old 55,3%; 27-41 years old 9,9%; 42-57 years old 21,6%; 58-76 years old 13,2%) and genders (males 33,6% and females 66,4%). Firstly, participants were asked about the time they spend on the Internet and their understanding of the Metaverse. The percentage of participants who spend less than 4 hours online was 41.4%, between 4 and 7 hours was 44.8%, and more than 7 hours was 13.8%. As for the primary activity each person engages in while being online, it is clear that entertainment predominates above all else (with 46.7% of responses), followed by information search (19.7%) and communication with others (15.1%). However, it is worth noting that nearly 15% of respondents affirmed that they spend their time online working or studying, which has gained great significance since the global pandemic in 2020.

Regarding RQ1, although the majority of respondents have heard of the Metaverse, many do not know how to define it or have a vague idea of its meaning. Among the 113 participants who affirmed to have heard of it, 46% define it only as a digital universe, a parallel world, or a virtual space, while 27% provided a more elaborate definition (some more than others, and some more accurate than others). Some of these definitions include: "an improved new version of the Internet, evolving into a more physical part, transforming work, entertainment, it's a new way of life using technology"; "experiences that connect the real world with the virtual world, and people can interact and transition online"; "a parallel virtual world where you can have a job, buy objects to use in that world... Other definitions given by our sample are: "a virtual world that you can enter through the Internet and Virtual Reality, and in which you can do things like play, shop, interact with others"; or "a virtual world (there can be as many as decided) for virtual meetings, online classes, virtual offices, video games, fantasy worlds". The remaining respondents admit to knowing little and are unable to define it. Next, they were asked to rate, on a scale from 1 (little) to 5 (much), their understanding of the Metaverse. More than a half consider that they barely know or understand the Metaverse. In contrast, only one person rates themselves as an expert in the field.

Only 6.6% of respondents have accessed it, compared to 93.4% who have not entered this world. Here we can observe the current lack of knowledge about what this virtual space really is and represents, indicating that there is still a long way to go for this new world concept to be firmly established in people's minds. That 6.6% have university studies. As for RQ2, 70% out of the ones that have accessed Metaverse belong to Generation Z (between 18 and 26 years old), and they all express curiosity about the Metaverse. In contrast, the Millennials (between 27 and 41 years old) who have accessed it express distrust. See Figure 2 for all emotions reported by the sample.

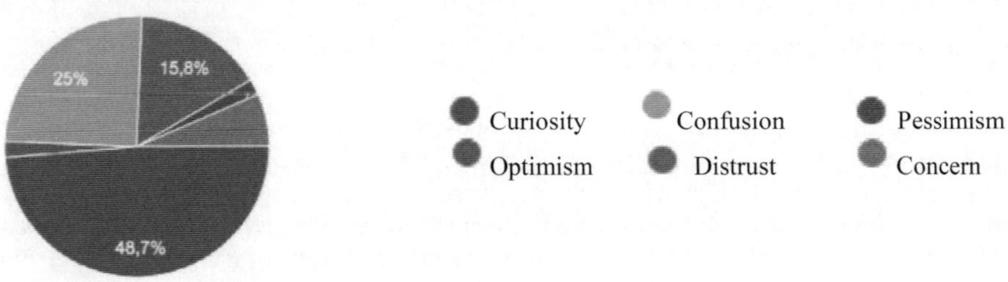

Figure 2. Emotions that Metaverse generate in sample users

There is also a diversity of opinions among these individuals who have accessed the Metaverse regarding the experience it offers and its implications for brands (Figure 3). They were asked about the advantage for brands that include metaverse in their business strategy, as well as the potential risks involved. As such, 90% perceive it as implying a more interactive relationship between seller and buyer, and as a tool for obtaining better experiences. However, they are not as certain about the risks, with one participant even stating that everything related to the Metaverse is currently a challenge.

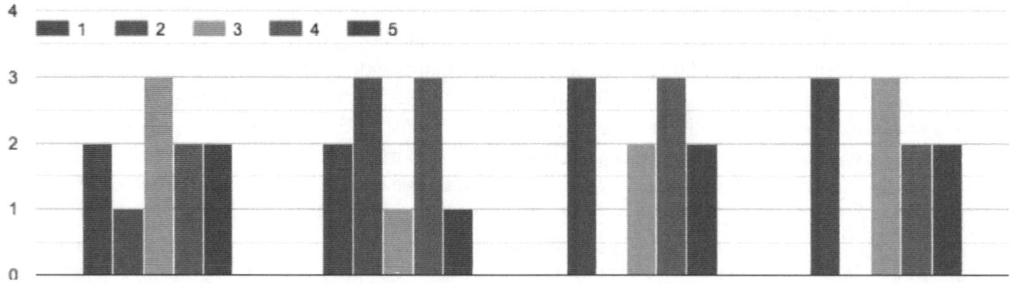

This virtual world offers an entertaining experience.

Experience in metaverse is satisfying.

Firms should use metaverse for advertising and marketing.

Brands can contact now more with consumers thanks to metaverse.

Figure 3. Interviewees' opinions who have accessed the Metaverse

Finally and addressing RQ3, they were asked if they find it more likely that they will purchase products from a company present in metaverse. Of the 152 respondents, 78.9% stated that their acquisition of products or services is not depending on the brand being or not in metaverse. 48% of the ones that would buy certain brands if they are in metaverse responded that they find it more likely to buy from companies already established in metaverse because it is the future; 38.5% emphasize that there are products and services that can only be acquired in that virtual world as they are not sold physically. On the other hand, among the reasons why respondents said they would not buy from companies present in metaverse, the most chosen option (66.7%) corresponded to the fact that they prefer to physically consume those products and services, and not have their avatar doing it. Additionally, many of them stated that they are not familiar with this concept or that it inspires distrust.

4. FINAL CONSIDERATIONS

This study contributes to a gap in the literature in which there is an absence of Spanish empirical studies similar to this one on metaverse, considering conceptualization, perceived experience and emotions. Thanks to the emergence of new virtual spaces like the metaverse, brands will be able to position their products and services in ways they have never done before, providing immersive experiences. We could say that companies that do not invest part of their time and resources using the metaverse for marketing and advertising purposes may be at a disadvantage compared to their competitors, potentially losing potential customers by not interacting with them widely.

According to the empirical study conducted in this work, while the majority of the population has heard the word metaverse, more than a half do not understand its meaning because they are unable to give a consistent definition, showing the lack of consensus that Dwivedi (2022) pointed out. Our results align with the analysis by Kanterman and Naidu (2021), which shows that the largest increase in revenue will correspond to entertainment. Companies must consider this virtual world in their business model in one way or another. This does not mean that each one should create its own digital space, but rather that all should be willing to investigate and learn in which direction it can help to expand their business. Some will indeed create their own one because they have enough resources and human capital to allocate part of it to metaverse, but other companies will form alliances with those that already have their own virtual world to reduce costs, or simply use existing collaborative virtual spaces (such as Decentraland or Roblox). It will also be necessary to train employees and hire younger profiles that are already educated in VR or AI, so that the firm as a whole understands how metaverse works and can convey this to its target. In fact, there are already companies with positions like Chief Metaverse Officer, such as Movistar.

As far as emotions are concerned, most people are curious about this virtual space or feel confused about it. For these two reasons, it is necessary to expand education and information about this virtual world. This can be done by companies that are already using it and are also making it known through advertising and massive events that do not always clarify concepts, but rather create confusion in people's minds. It would be advisable to overcome the fear and distrust of many consumers when thinking about buying on the metaverse, implementing training activities that can inform about the benefits of this virtual space and that appeal to enjoying, gamification and positive emotions. Companies should segment their target according to the emotions they want that their customers feel when navigating the Metaverse.

Furthermore, our study indicates that the presence of a brand in the Metaverse does not necessarily influence purchasing decisions; the surveyed consumers are not swayed by something they do not yet fully understand. However, companies can consider this new channel for omnichannel branding to develop integrated experiences.

Regarding the limitations of this exploratory work, not all companies are at the same point regarding the use and presence in the Metaverse and conceptualizations of the metaverse vary among the population, sometimes even leading to confusion of terms given the early stage of this disruptive innovation. In the empirical study, the surveyed population was convenience-based and mostly comprises young consumers, as it was sent to contacts through social media, implying that these individuals are already familiar with digitalization. As further research, it would be interesting to develop a structural model to know the antecedents of buying in metaverse. Besides, we could implement a cross-cultural analysis to find out if cultural and technological differences among users from different countries can have an impact (i.e. Chinese studied in Wang et al. (2023) vs Spanish market studied here).

ACKNOWLEDGEMENT

The authors thank the support of the Junta of Castilla and León (Spain) and the European Regional Development Fund (ERDF) (project reference VA219P20).

REFERENCES

Bushell, C. (2022). The Impact of Metaverse on Branding and Marketing, Available at *https://ssrn.com/abstract=4144628*

Dwivedi, Y. (2022). Metaverse beyond the hype: Multidisciplinary perspectives on emerging challenges, opportunities, and agenda for research, practice and policy. *International Journal of Information Management,* 66, 102542.

Horta, M. (2021). Marketing en el metaverso. *Rebujito marketing.* Available at: *https://rebujitomarketing.com/empresas/marketing-y-metaverso*

Kanterman, M. & Naidu, N. (2021). Metaverse may be $800 billion market, next tech platform, *Bloomberg Intelligence,* Available at *https://www.bloomberg.com/professional/blog/metaverse-may-be-800-billion-market-next-tech-platform/*

Khatri, M. (2022). Revamping the Marketing World with Metaverse – The Future of Marketing. *International Journal of Computer Applications* (0975 – 8887), 184 (29), September, 975-8887.

Kotler et al. (2021). Marketing 5.0: Tecnología para la Humanidad. John Wiley & Sons, Inc.

Leveau, P-H. & Camus, S. (2023). Embodiment, immersion, and enjoyment in virtual reality marketing experiences, *Psychology &Marketing*, 40 (7), 1329-1343.

McKinsey and Company (2022). Value creation in the metaverse: The real business of the virtual world. Available at *https://www.mckinsey.com/capabilities/growth-marketing-and-sales/our-insights/value-creation-in-the-metaverse*

Statista (2021). ¿Cuántas horas al día pasamos conectados a Internet? Available at *https://es.statista.com/grafico/22701/tiempo-medio-de-uso-diario-de-internet/.*

Statista (2022). Metaverse boom according to companies worldwide 2022. Available at *https://www.statista.com/statistics/1302240/metaverse-business-boom/#:~:text=Metaverse%20boom%20according%20to%20companies%20worldwide%202022&text=According%20to%20a%20March%202022,in%20the%20next%20five%20years.*

Wang, J.; Du, B. & Cao, X. (2023). A Study of the Impact of Metaverse Marketing Characteristics on Consumers' Purchase Intention, *Digitalization and Management Innovation II,* R.J. Dwyer (Ed.), 26, 106-119.

ENHANCING PURCHASE INTENTIONS THROUGH LIVE STREAMING: AN INVESTIGATION OF SHOPEE'S LIVE-STREAMING

Ahmad Rafiuddin, Alfred Prasetio, Azhar Addzikri, Mirza Faisal, Shehaanmakya Reksohaminoto and Ika Chandra Hapsari
Faculty of Computer Science, Universitas Indonesia
Kampus Universitas Indonesia, Depok, 16424

ABSTRACT

Live streaming was mainly used by organizations for things like broadcasting sports events, music performances, interviews, and conferences. Nowadays, in e-commerce industry, more people started using live streaming for various reasons, from promoting products to having interactive entertainment with their audience. In Indonesia, live streaming for online shopping has become very popular, especially on platforms like Shopee. On Shopee's live streaming, it's not just about showcasing products; it's also about encouraging people to buy during the live broadcasts. Our study applies a previously established adaptation of the Innovation Diffusion Theory (IDT) that incorporates 'Gratification' from the Uses and Gratification Theory (UGT) to explore its impact on purchase intentions in the realm of live streaming technologies. We conducted an analysis using data from 216 participants, employing Partial Least Squares Structural Equation Modeling (PLS SEM) to assess the influence of this combined theoretical model. Our research findings indicate that variables such as innovation diffusion, the level of satisfaction obtained, authentic experience, subjective well-being, and compatibility significantly influence consumers' purchase intentions during Shopee live streaming sessions. This means that companies, like Shopee, should keep working on making their live streaming better, as it makes people more likely to want to buy things.

KEYWORDS

Shopee Live-Streaming, Uses and Gratification, Innovation Diffusion, Purchase Intention

1. INTRODUCTION

Live streaming services have gained popularity in recent years, particularly in e-commerce, as they allow for real-time interaction and engagement with users. Live streaming services not only enable users to attend and witness events in real-time but also offer opportunities for direct interaction with live streamers and fellow users through chat and comment features. Research by Chen et al. (2020) reveals that contemporary audiences now favour watching live video content on e-commerce platforms over reading textual content.

In Indonesia, the rise of live streaming is evident through the increasing number of apps offering these services, such as Shopee Live, which enables sellers to showcase their products directly to viewers. According to a survey conducted by Jajak Pendapat on June 5, 2022, involving 2,712 respondents, it was revealed that 83.7% of the Indonesian population had watched online shopping through live-streaming features (Annur, 2022).

Several studies have been conducted to investigate user intentions and acceptance of live streaming services, incorporating theories such as the Uses and Gratification Theory (UGT) and the Technology Acceptance Model (TAM). Study by Hua & Chiu, 2022 aimed to analyse the purchase intentions of young people in China regarding the live-streaming service provided by the TikTok application. This study integrated the Technology Acceptance Model (TAM) and the Uses and Gratification Theory (UGT), incorporating several variables, namely perceived ease of use, perceived usefulness, ritualised use, instrumental use, attitude towards live-streaming, and purchase intention. The results of Hua & Chiu (2022)'s research demonstrated that all variables significantly influenced the purchase intentions of young people in China using the TikTok live-streaming service, with perceived ease of use being particularly influential. However, while UGT and

TAM provide valuable frameworks for understanding certain aspects of technology adoption and use, the multifaceted nature of modern technological innovation and its impacts on consumer behaviour demand more comprehensive and dynamic theoretical models.

The research by Kim et al. (2020) that combines Uses and Gratifications Theory (UGT) with Innovation Diffusion Theory (IDT) in the context of virtual reality (VR) in tourism has yielded significant findings. Their study revealed that attributes of innovation diffusion such as simplicity, benefit, and compatibility are closely related to authentic experiences and subjective well-being. Additionally, attributes of UGT like informativeness, social interactivity, and playfulness were found to positively influence authentic experiences and subjective well-being.

Building upon these insights, our research aims to modify and adapt Kim et al.(2020)'s model to a different context, specifically live streaming on the Shopee platform. Given the substantial contextual differences, we plan to adjust the variables influencing IDT and the variables affecting gratification. The goal is to explore how these attributes interact and influence user experiences and subjective well-being in the context of online shopping live streaming. This will allow us to gain a deeper understanding of the factors that motivate and influence user behaviour in this evolving and new digital context.

This research is significant in the Indonesian context, where Indonesia has a large population and Shopee leads the live streaming landscape. Investigating the factors influencing consumer behaviour can provide valuable insights for businesses operating in similar markets and inform strategies for online shopping through live streaming.

2. THEORETICAL BACKGROUND

This research incorporates a blend of several theoretical frameworks, including the Innovation Diffusion Theory, the Uses and Gratification Theory (UGT), as well as concepts of Authentic Experience and Subjective Well-Being, to provide a comprehensive analysis. The Innovation Diffusion Theory explains the factors that influence an individual's decision to adopt or use a specific technology, such as complexity, relative advantage, and compatibility (Karahanna et al., 1999; Chiang, 2013). This theory is essential for examining users' acceptance of innovations introduced by Shopee as a live streaming service provider. The Uses and Gratification Theory (UGT) explains that individuals use media or services to satisfy specific desires and needs, and can describe why someone chooses one service over another (Ruggiero, 2000; Cheung et al., 2011). This theory is used to evaluate the extent to which user satisfaction influences purchase decisions, with variables such as social interactions, enjoyment, and informativeness (Hsu & Lin, 2023; Kim et al., 2020; Gan & Li, 2018). Authentic Experience refers to users' perception of the authenticity of their experience with a product (Smith, 2009). In this study, we aim to examine how authentic experiences, resulting from the combination of innovation and gratification variables, influence users' purchase intentions. Subjective Well-Being refers to feeling happy, including satisfaction and positive affect while consuming a product (Kim et al., 2020). This study explores the extent to which subjective well-being, resulting from the combination of innovation and gratification variables, influences users' purchase intentions.

3. CONCEPTUAL MODEL

This study explores the relationship between innovation diffusion and user gratification in live-streaming services. Innovation diffusion is analyzed through simplicity, relative advantage, and compatibility. Simplicity indicates the platform's ease of use, while relative advantage includes benefits like convenience and access to unique content. Compatibility assesses the platform's fit with users' existing preferences and experiences. These factors help understand the impact of innovations on user behavior in e-commerce live streaming.

Subsequently, we will examine the influence of innovation diffusion and gratification on the authentic experience and subjective well-being perceived by users. When a technology provider keeps introducing relevant innovations and enhancing features, users are more likely to feel engaged and satisfied with the platform (Kim et al., 2020). Therefore, we propose:

H1: Innovation diffusion significantly influences users' authentic experience.

H2: Innovation diffusion significantly influences subjective well-being.

H3: Gratification significantly influences authentic experience.

H4: Gratification significantly influences subjective well-being.

The relationship between authentic experience and purchase intention in the context of live-streaming services can be explained as a closely intertwined connection. Authentic experience establishes a solid foundation for users' purchase intent (Kim et al., 2020). Therefore, we propose:

H5: Authentic experience significantly influences purchase intention.

When users feel satisfied with their shopping experience through live-streaming, it positively influences their subjective well-being. This satisfaction can motivate them to take concrete actions in the form of purchases. Thus, high subjective well-being often has a positive impact on purchase intention. Therefore, we propose:

H6: Subjective well-being significantly influences purchase intention.

Our propose research model is shown in Figure 1.

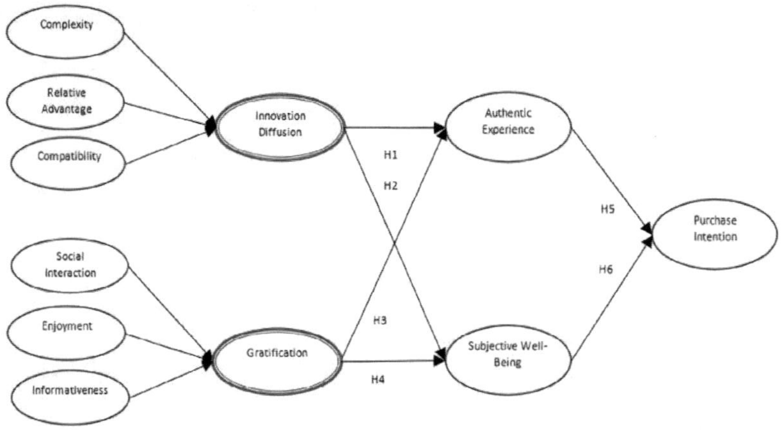

Figure 1. Research model (Note: Figure created by author)

4. METHODOLOGY

Our team conducted research using an online survey targeting Shopee customers who have previously used Shopee live-streaming services as sellers, buyers, or viewers. Respondents who have never used the live-streaming feature were not included in the study. The questionnaire had two parts: demographics and statements related to the research topic, adapted from prior studies Kim et al., (2020), and Chiang (2013). Respondents provided feedback on these statements using a 5-point Likert scale. Data was collected from 258 respondents, with 216 valid responses included in the final dataset. We used Structural Equation Modelling Partial Least Squares (SEM PLS) for data analysis due to its suitability for handling complex relationships and smaller sample sizes (Hair et al., 2019).

5. RESULT AND ANALYSIS

The data analysis process has two main stages: measurement model testing and structural model testing. In the first stage, we assess the accuracy of the instruments used in the study, ensuring they reliably measure the underlying concepts. In the second stage, we examine the relationships between the measured variables and test the research hypotheses. During measurement model testing, we use rule of thumb criteria to determine reliability and convergent validity. Reliability is assessed using Cronbach's Alpha (CA) and Composite Reliability (CR), aiming for values of 0.7 or higher. Convergent validity is evaluated using Factor Loadings and Average Variance Extracted (AVE), with variables ideally having Factor Loadings 0.7 or higher and AVE values of 0.5 or higher (Hair, 2009). All variables in this study exceed these criteria, ensuring data reliability and validity.

This research encompasses the structural model testing phase with the objective of validating hypotheses using the partial least squares algorithm. The testing is carried out at a significance level of 0.05. Consequently, if any p-values exceed 0.05, the corresponding hypotheses will be rejected.

Table 1. Hypothesis testing (author's analysis)

Hypothesis	Parameter	Original Sample	T-Statistics	P Values	Result
H1	ID-> AE	0.225	3.438	0.000	Accepted
H2	ID-> SW	0.397	5.952	0.000	Accepted
H3	GR -> AE	0.549	8.881	0.000	Accepted
H4	GR -> SW	0.387	5.881	0.000	Accepted
H5	AE -> PI	0.251	4.162	0.000	Accepted
H6	SW -> PI	0.567	9.52	0.000	Accepted

From Table 1 above, it can be observed that all the previously formulated hypotheses regarding the positive effects between the variables are supported. As shown in Table 1, both innovation diffusion and gratification have a positive influence on authentic experience and subjective well-being, similarly, authentic experience and subjective well-being positively affect users' purchase intentions.

6. DISCUSSION

The results of this research indicate that Innovation Diffusion has a significant positive influence on Authentic Experience and Subjective Well-Being. This implies that as live-streaming service providers introduce more innovations, users will experience a higher level of authenticity and subjective well-being. This aligns with the Innovation Diffusion Theory, which suggests that innovations positively accepted by users will have a favourable impact on their experiences (Kim et al., 2020). Consequently, Shopee can understand that continuously enhancing innovation in their live-streaming platform will significantly benefit the authenticity of user experiences and their subjective well-being. This could involve developing new features, improving broadcast quality, and enhancing user-friendliness. Through ongoing innovation, Shopee can retain and attract more users.

Furthermore, the research demonstrates that Gratification has a significant positive influence on Authentic Experience and Subjective Well-Being. Therefore, efforts to improve innovation and gratification should be considered by companies to enhance purchase intention. This is consistent with the principles of the Uses and Gratification Theory (UGT), which suggest that users seek satisfaction from media use, and this satisfaction can influence user perceptions and behaviour (Ruggiero, 2000). In the context of Shopee Live, users who find satisfaction in the live-streaming service tend to experience more positive outcomes and heightened subjective well-being, which in turn, likely enhances their inclination to make purchases. Therefore, it is essential for companies like Shopee to recognize the significant impact of user satisfaction in shaping their experiences and influencing their buying decisions. An effective strategy to elevate this satisfaction is to offer exclusive discounts to viewers during live shopping events, thereby boosting user engagement and gratification.

The implications of this research for Shopee are that the company should concentrate its efforts on creating authentic shopping experiences and enhancing users' subjective well-being. One concrete step that Shopee can take is to improve the quality of its live-streaming services, including video and audio stability and image clarity. Moreover, content innovation is crucial, involving the presentation of more engaging, informative, and entertaining content for users. User interaction during live streaming should also be improved by providing features such as direct questions and comments to sellers or streamers. The development of new features that make live streaming more engaging and beneficial for users can also be an effective strategy.

Additionally, Shopee needs to enhance the product information provided during live-streaming and regularly analyse data while listening to user feedback. Providing training and support for sellers or streamers using their live-streaming platform is also essential. By implementing these measures, Shopee can create a better and more satisfying live-streaming environment for users. In the long run, this will influence users' purchase intentions, enhance Shopee's business sustainability, and strengthen customer loyalty.

7. CONCLUSION AND FUTURE RESEARCH

This study investigates innovation diffusion and user gratification in live-streaming services, with a focus on simplicity, relative advantage, and compatibility of platforms. It also assesses user satisfaction, incorporating informativeness, social interactivity, and enjoyment in the context of Shopee's live streaming. The methodology and findings offer a framework that can be replicated in similar research, particularly in studies exploring the use of live streaming in various contexts, making it a valuable reference for future studies in this rapidly evolving field.

ACKNOWLEDGEMENT

This research is supported and funded by the Universitas Indonesia through the PUTI Q1 grant, No. NKB-293/UN2.RST/HKP.05.00/2023.

REFERENCES

Annur, C. M. (2022). Survei Jakpat: Shopee Rajai Penggunaan Live Shopping di Indonesia | Databoks—Databoks.katadata.co.id. https://databoks.katadata.co.id/datapublish/2022/07/06/survei-jakpat-shopee-rajai-penggunaan-live-shopping-di-indonesia

Chen, Y., Lu, F., & Zheng, S. (2020). A Study on the Influence of E-Commerce Live Streaming on Consumer Repurchase Intentions. International Journal of Marketing Studies, 12, 48. https://doi.org/10.5539/ijms.v12n4p48

Cheung, C. M. K., Chiu, P.-Y., & Lee, M. K. O. (2011). Online social networks: Why do students use facebook? Computers in Human Behavior, 27(4), 1337–1343. https://doi.org/10.1016/j.chb.2010.07.028

Chiang, H.-S. (2013). Continuous usage of social networking sites: The effect of innovation and gratification attributes. Online Information Review, 37(6), 851–871. https://doi.org/10.1108/OIR-08-2012-0133

Gan, C., & Li, H. (2018). Understanding the effects of gratifications on the continuance intention to use WeChat in China: A perspective on uses and gratifications. Computers in Human Behavior, 78, 306–315. https://doi.org/10.1016/j.chb.2017.10.003

Hair, J. F. (2009). Multivariate data analysis.

Hair, J. F., Risher, J. J., Sarstedt, M., & Ringle, C. M. (2019). When to use and how to report the results of PLS-SEM. European Business Review, 31(1), 2–24. https://doi.org/10.1108/ebr-11-2018-0203

Hsu, C. L., & Lin, J. C.-C. (2023). The effects of gratifications, flow and satisfaction on the usage of livestreaming services. Library Hi Tech, 41(3), 729–748. https://doi.org/10.1108/LHT-02-2021-0069

Hua, Q., & Chiu, C. L. (2022). Analysis of Young Chinese Purchase Intention on TikTok Live Streaming. Management Review: An International Journal, 17(1), 65–99.

Karahanna, E., Straub, D., & Chervany, N. (1999). Information Technology Adoption Across Time: A Cross-Sectional Comparison of Pre-Adoption and Post-Adoption Beliefs. MIS Quarterly, 23, 183–213. https://doi.org/10.2307/249751

Kim, M. J., Lee, C.-K., & Preis, M. W. (2020). The impact of innovation and gratification on authentic experience, subjective well-being, and behavioral intention in tourism virtual reality: The moderating role of technology readiness. Telematics and Informatics, 49, 101349. https://doi.org/10.1016/j.tele.2020.101349

Ruggiero, T. E. (2000). Uses and Gratifications Theory in the 21st Century. Mass Communication and Society, 3(1), 3–37. https://doi.org/10.1207/S15327825MCS0301_02

PRIVACY AND DIGITAL LITERACY IN THE INTERNET OF THINGS

Nelson Vieira and Mary Barreto
University of Madeira, Faculty of Exact Sciences and Engineering
University Campus of Penteada, 9020-105, Funchal, Portugal

ABSTRACT

The advent of ubiquitous computing has resulted in the widespread use of Internet of Things (IoT) devices, which are expected to control every aspect of our everyday live with a prevalence in the billions. These devices open up new avenues for the collection and exploitation of user and non-user personal data. Most end users are not even aware or have little control over the information that is being collected about them by these systems. This work took a rounded approach to this problem by first compiling current solutions and future research opportunities in the literature. Then a survey was conducted to learn more about the general knowledge of individuals about privacy, IoT and online habits. Survey responses revealed that participants, even though lacked knowledge of IoT privacy, valued having access to more information about privacy related terminology.

KEYWORDS

Privacy, Internet of Things, Ubiquitous Computing, Digital Literacy

1. INTRODUCTION

Privacy in the way we know it now is a fairly recent concept (Vincent, 2016), it has historically been regarded as a luxury rather than a necessity, although privacy is recognized as a human right, as stated in article 12 of the Universal Declaration of Human Rights (Roosevelt *et al.*, 1948): "No one shall be subjected to arbitrary interference with his privacy, family, home or correspondence, nor to attacks upon his honour and reputation. Everyone has the right to the protection of the law against such interference or attacks".

Privacy can be defined (Spiekermann and Cranor, 2009) as the right to govern how personal information and data is collected and used. This definition can cause some confusion with security (HIV.gov, 2018), the key difference between security and privacy is that security deals with the protection of data from potential threats, whereas privacy deals with personal information and how users want it used and maintained.

Internet of Things is a term that first appeared in the 1990s, and it can be linked to Mark Weiser's paper on ubiquitous computing (Weiser, 1991), the first use of the term was in 1999 by Kevin Ashton (Ashton, 2009) to describe a system in which items may be connected to the internet by sensors.

Given the importance of digital literacy on the decision making of users, the questionnaire conducted for this work aimed to gather the general privacy concerns of individuals and their interactions with IoT devices. The questionnaire was the structured to address the following research question (RQ):

RQ1: What are the perceptions of individuals on digital privacy, and does it match with their actions?

2. STATE OF THE ART

2.1 Privacy Paradox

The use of a variety of digital devices has numerous advantages, but they also bring the ubiquity of data capturing equipment, therefore, it is understandable why users have serious concerns about the privacy of their personal data. The privacy paradox happens when the opinions stated by the users are radically different from their actions. There have been multiple papers written on this subject (Williams, Nurse and Creese, 2017; Gerber, Gerber and Volkamer, 2018), some papers attempt a theoretical explanation while others attempt an empirical one. There has been very different interpretations or explanations of this paradox, from individual choice behaviour (Wakefield, 2013) to illusion of control (Brandimarte, Acquisti and Loewenstein, 2013).

This paradox has been proven to be debased by a number of empirical studies (Sannon, Bazarova and Cosley, 2018; Xie and Karan, 2019), online privacy practices are founded on separate privacy mindsets and so they are not inherently paradoxical.

2.2 Approaches to Privacy in IoT

There have been a number of SLRs (Gupta and Ghanavati, 2022; Kühtreiber, Pak and Reinhardt, 2022) and systematic mapping reviews (Porras *et al.*, 2018; Ahmed *et al.*, 2019) done to study privacy and security issues in IoT.

(Sicari *et al.*, 2015) examined research and activities that focused on IoT privacy and security solutions. The authors started by describing the requirements for IoT privacy and security, such as access control, confidentiality, and authentication, then they conducted a literature study in connection to these three requirements and concluded that IoT privacy issues have only been partially examined and that further attention is required. The study has some shortcomings: the prior research analysis focuses primarily on security requirements while ignoring privacy considerations.

The research conducted by (Tzafestas, 2018) focuses on an overview of broad ethical questions, ideas, and theories that can be applied in the IoT, security, privacy, and trust elements, and the role of governments. Privacy protection, security, usability, user experience, trust, and safety have been identified as the primary ethical problems in IoT. The author concludes that to address sophisticated and tricky unethical and illegal behaviour across the IoT, more specific IoT legislation and ethical norms for IoT need to be devised and constantly updated.

2.3 Proposed Solutions

An interactive theatre experience was developed by (Skirpan *et al.*, 2022) as a case study of an innovative approach to gather user awareness about their online behaviour regarding privacy. This was created to try to prove that a simulated experience with a credible privacy problem may encourage people to act before encountering a breach. The authors noted that after contacting people months after the initial interviews that they did not really changed their behaviour regarding their privacy.

Some papers seek to improve legislation (Weber, 2015; Fabiano, 2017), these authors defend that without the express agreement of the individual concerned, private information obtained by IoT devices must not be retained or processed in any form, and necessary procedures must be taken to guarantee that the data collected is not that of an unrelated individual.

(Colnago *et al.*, 2020) designed a personalized privacy assistant (PPA) and conducted interviews to examine user perceptions of hypothetical PPA implementations. The authors found that the participants' attitudes regarding the various implementations were generally favourable, although they also voiced worries, which varied depending on the degree of automation. After the design phase, a privacy assistant (Feng, Yao and Sadeh, 2021) was developed using a notice and choice approach. The application is not capable of identifying new IoT devices, users have to add new devices on a webpage (Das *et al.*, 2018).

3. METHODOLOGY

This work consisted on compiling the state of the art on the most relevant topics from which the main privacy concepts were selected to be explored on the questionnaire with the aim to collect user perceptions of privacy.

3.1 User Perceptions

The questionnaire consisted of 86 questions divided into 7 sections to gauge users' digital literacy, the first section being about general privacy questions, then about the predisposition to data sharing, to concerns with privacy then about daily digital routines, then about profile identification, subsequently about IoT general knowledge before a final part about non-identifiable demographic data. The scale utilized is based on the work of Philip K. Masur (Masur, 2018), it was chosen because it provides a more nuanced understanding of the knowledge of participants. This survey was partially based in a study done by the government of the Philippines in the context of their privacy act of 2012 (Survey and Center, 2022) and by (Alves, 2021), which was about Portuguese citizen's perception about privacy in the wake of GDPR.

There were 45 participants when the questionnaire was available. Several online survey dissemination services were used, as well as social networks and personally to close acquaintances, to acquire participants but there was no financial incentive for completing the survey.

From the respondents, 47% are male and 51% are female, while 2% do not identify as neither. 40% of the participants are younger than 25 years old, 31.11% are aged between 26 and 35.9% are between 36 and 45 years old, 18% are older than 46 but younger than 65 and 2% have more than 65 years. 66.67% of the respondents have a bachelor's degree, 17.78% have only finished high school, 2.22% only have a basic education, 11.11% have a master's degree and 2.22% have a doctorate. Most survey participants, 60%, are from Portugal, 20% are from the USA, 4.44% from the UK while 15.66% are divided between the following countries: Germany, Australia, Sweden, Netherlands, China, Indonesia and Canada.

The sample of participants is random, but because of the dissemination process (mostly online platforms) there might have been some selection bias. The survey was arranged in a way to minimize response bias which include leading questions. When gathering the survey results some bias might have creeped up since different cultural and socio-economic backgrounds were not considered to have an impact, the dissemination process along with globalization makes these aspects not very relevant to this particular study.

4. RESULTS

Most participants agreed that data privacy is important to them and as such should be protected. Most also have some knowledge of behaviours or techniques to do in an online environment, be it connected to the internet or on some local network. When asked to define digital privacy, most participants did not know how to properly define it, only approximately 16% of participants supplied a concrete answer. Curiously, no one mentioned security, which contradicts with the responses regarding privacy and security being synonymous in which 53.33% of participants believe it to be.

Participants have some digital literacy of IT terms, as shown on Figure 1, most know the more popular terms such as wi-fi and cookies, but as the terms become more esoteric the general knowledge starts to drop.

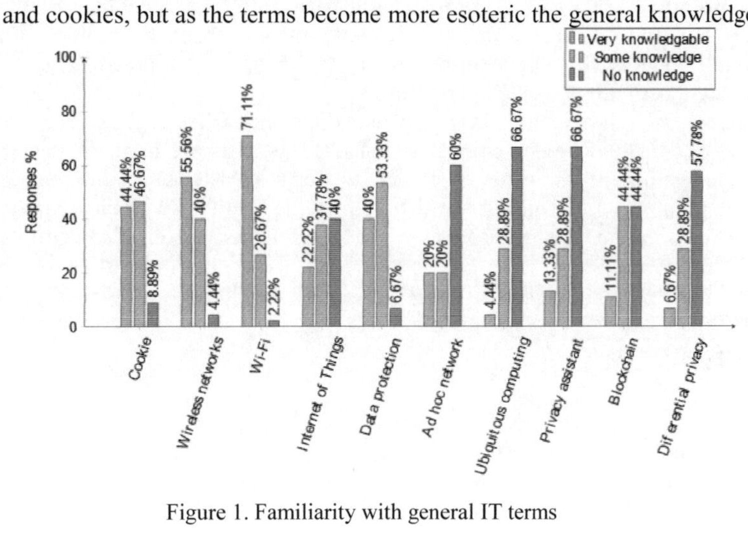

Figure 1. Familiarity with general IT terms

Regarding users' online habits, all participants have, or have access to, a smartphone and they use it in their daily lives, most participants concede that they spend a lot of their daily time using it and are somewhat worried but do not actively try to protect their data privacy, which goes against their earlier responses regarding their worry of personal data privacy.

Regarding participants' attitudes toward regulations, most participants are aware of regulations related to digital privacy, like GDPR or CCPA, but it is not clear to them what they represent, and they do not show a clear interest in knowing more about these regulations.

Participants are interested in knowing how their data is used by organizations, and privacy notices are one way to convey such information, 53.33% are not familiar with the reason data is collected but are still curious. Most participants agree that lengthy texts and font size, 86.67% and 77.78% respectively, affect their willingness to read them, 71.11% confess to agreeing to the notices just to use the service due to a fear of missing out.

Most participants are unaware of the flow of digital data, as 82.22% state being unfamiliar with data brokers. But they are aware of the fact that organisations collect their private data and use it in various ways, even without knowing exactly what they do with the data according to previous responses.

In terms of IoT usage and literacy, about 2/3 of the participants have interacted in some way with a device, and from those only 35.56% have a device in their homes. Even though most participants have interacted with an IoT device they had trouble explaining what the Internet of Things is. When asked to describe it, 48% of the participants wrote some kind of "do not know" variation, from the other 52% that gave a more elaborate answer 70% gave a generic answer that could be applied to several concepts. Only two participants managed to describe IoT accurately.

Familiarity with IoT devices does not imply understanding of IoT systems or the majority of IoT related concepts or terms, the most recognized terms are the ones who have more visibility in everyday life like smart home, smart vehicle or fully autonomous car. Esoteric terms like the ones describing networks or protocols are mostly unknown to most respondents.

5. DISCUSSION

There are two main ways to provide privacy in IoT systems, through security or providing in some way user awareness like the in the case of using privacy notices, other ways like through legislation or usage of a framework/architecture that provides privacy mainly fall into one these two categories. Literature that addresses any AI field (Zhao *et al.*, 2020) or blockchain (Ali, Dolui and Antonelli, 2017) also fall under privacy through security. Most of the literature assumes that security and privacy are synonyms, for example (Fabiano, 2017; Opara *et al.*, 2022), and so most of the proposed solutions fall under privacy through security. The proposed solutions that use privacy notices, like (Feng, Yao and Sadeh, 2021), are implemented in a way that use other devices like smartphones that provide the notices themselves, it is hard to provide privacy notices on the IoT devices themselves because many of these devices do not have a screen. Because there are still no standards for implementing privacy notices, and best practices are scattered throughout the literature, they are mostly implemented haphazardly.

To answer the research question **RQ1**, the questionnaire makes it clear that there is a general lack of digital literacy, especially when it comes to IoT. This still being a new technology and only quickly expanding on the last decade, the people that have the most knowledge are the ones working in areas related to IT or technology in general. This survey also helps to demystify the privacy paradox. Participants seemed eager to learn more about IoT, many had no knowledge of the term, even if some of them knew some devices that belong to the IoT.

6. FUTURE WORK

Privacy literacy is an underdeveloped research field in IoT systems, while privacy is explored along with security and other adjacent fields, this aspect of IoT is still in its infancy, but should be further researched as there is a clear lack of knowledge by most individuals. This situation prevents them from forming decisions that benefit them in the long term. Organizations already exploit this fact and bad actors can also take advantage of this, as has already happened.

7. CONCLUSION

This work aimed to do an exploratory analysis of privacy in IoT systems. A survey was conducted to better understand user's knowledge on this subject, it portrays a majority viewpoint from Portuguese people, since 60% of participants were Portuguese. According to the literature review and user responses, there is a significant knowledge gap regarding IoT privacy, particularly for individuals who have a general lack of technological literacy. Hopefully, the work conducted will be useful in supporting researchers going forward.

REFERENCES

Ahmed, B.S. *et al.* (2019). 'Aspects of quality in Internet of Things (IoT) solutions: A systematic mapping study', *IEEE Access*, 7, pp. 13758–13780.

Ali, M.S., Dolui, K. and Antonelli, F. (2017). 'IoT Data Privacy via Blockchains and IPFS', in *Proceedings of the Seventh International Conference on the Internet of Things*. New York, NY, USA: Association for Computing Machinery (IoT '17). Available at: https://doi.org/10.1145/3131542.3131563.

Alves, M.H. da S. (2021). *GDPR in Portugal: Analysis of citizens' perception about privacy*. Master's Thesis. NOVA Information Management School.

Ashton, K. (2009). *That "Internet of Things" thing*. Available at: https://www.rfidjournal.com/that-internet-of-things-thing.

Brandimarte, L., Acquisti, A. and Loewenstein, G. (2013). 'Misplaced confidences: Privacy and the control paradox', *Social psychological and personality science*, 4(3), pp. 340–347.

Colnago, J. *et al.* (2020). 'Informing the Design of a Personalized Privacy Assistant for the Internet of Things', in *Proceedings of the 2020 CHI Conference on Human Factors in Computing Systems*. New York, NY, USA: Association for Computing Machinery (CHI '20), pp. 1–13. Available at: https://doi.org/10.1145/3313831.3376389.

Das, A. *et al.* (2018). 'Personalized Privacy Assistants for the Internet of Things: Providing Users with Notice and Choice', *IEEE Pervasive Computing*, 17, pp. 35–46. Available at: https://doi.org/10.1109/MPRV.2018.03367733.

Fabiano, N. (2017). 'Internet of Things and Blockchain: Legal Issues and Privacy. The Challenge for a Privacy Standard', in *2017 IEEE International Conference on Internet of Things (iThings) and IEEE Green Computing and Communications (GreenCom) and IEEE Cyber, Physical and Social Computing (CPSCom) and IEEE Smart Data (SmartData)*, pp. 727–734. Available at: https://doi.org/10.1109/iThings-GreenCom-CPSCom-SmartData.2017.112.

Feng, Y., Yao, Y. and Sadeh, N. (2021). 'A Design Space for Privacy Choices: Towards Meaningful Privacy Control in the Internet of Things', in *Proceedings of the 2021 CHI Conference on Human Factors in Computing Systems*. New York, NY, USA: Association for Computing Machinery (CHI '21). Available at: https://doi.org/10.1145/3411764.3445148.

Gerber, N., Gerber, P. and Volkamer, M. (2018). 'Explaining the privacy paradox: A systematic review of literature investigating privacy attitude and behavior', *Computers & security*, 77, pp. 226–261.

Gupta, S. and Ghanavati, S. (2022). 'Privacy in the Internet of Things: Where do We Stand? A Systematic Literature Review'. Available at: https://doi.org/10.36227/techrxiv.19874329.v1.

HIV.gov (2018). *The Difference between Security and Privacy and Why It Matters to Your Program*. Available at: https://www.hiv.gov/blog/difference-between-security-and-privacy-and-why-it-matters-your-program.

Kühtreiber, P., Pak, V. and Reinhardt, D. (2022). 'A survey on solutions to support developers in privacy-preserving IoT development', *Pervasive and Mobile Computing*, 85, p. 101656. Available at: https://doi.org/10.1016/j.pmcj.2022.101656.

Masur, P.K. (2018). *Situational privacy and self-disclosure: Communication processes in online environments*. Cham, Switzerland: Springer.

Opara, A. *et al.* (2022). 'A framework for representing internet of things security and privacy policies and detecting potential problems', in *Proceedings of the 37th ACM/SIGAPP Symposium on Applied Computing*, pp. 198–201.

Porras, J. *et al.* (2018). 'Security in the internet of things - a systematic mapping study'.

Roosevelt, E. *et al.* (1948). *Universal Declaration of Human Rights*. Available at: https://www.un.org/en/about-us/universal-declaration-of-human-rights.

Sannon, S., Bazarova, N.N. and Cosley, D. (2018). 'Privacy lies: Understanding how, when, and why people lie to protect their privacy in multiple online contexts', in *Proceedings of the 2018 CHI Conference on Human Factors in Computing Systems*, pp. 1–13.

Sicari, S. *et al.* (2015). 'Security, privacy and trust in Internet of Things: The road ahead', *Computer Networks*, 76, pp. 146–164. Available at: https://doi.org/10.1016/j.comnet.2014.11.008.

Skirpan, M. *et al.* (2022). 'Is a Privacy Crisis Experienced, a Privacy Crisis Avoided?', *Commun. ACM*, 65(3), pp. 26–29. Available at: https://doi.org/10.1145/3512325.

Spiekermann, S. and Cranor, L.F. (2009). 'Engineering Privacy', *IEEE Transactions on Software Engineering*, 35(1), pp. 67–82. Available at: https://doi.org/10.1109/TSE.2008.88.

Survey, P. and Center, R. (2022). *Conduct of Privacy Survey*. Available at: https://www.privacy.gov.ph/wp-content/uploads/2022/01/CONDUCT-OF-PRIVACY-SURVEY-Final-Report-v3.pdf.

Tzafestas, S.G. (2018). 'Ethics and law in the internet of things world', *Smart cities*, 1(1), pp. 98–120.

Vincent, D. (2016). *Privacy: A short history*. Cambridge: Polity Press.

Wakefield, R. (2013). 'The influence of user affect in online information disclosure', *The Journal of Strategic Information Systems*, 22(2), pp. 157–174.

Weber, R.H. (2015). 'Internet of things: Privacy issues revisited', *Computer Law & Security Review*, 31(5), pp. 618–627. Available at: https://doi.org/10.1016/j.clsr.2015.07.002.

Weiser, M. (1991). 'The Computer for the 21st Century', *Scientific American*, 265(3), pp. 94–105.

Williams, M., Nurse, J.R.C. and Creese, S. (2017). 'Privacy is the Boring Bit: User Perceptions and Behaviour in the Internet-of-Things', in *2017 15th Annual Conference on Privacy, Security and Trust (PST)*, pp. 181–18109. Available at: https://doi.org/10.1109/PST.2017.00029.

Xie, W. and Karan, K. (2019). 'Consumers' privacy concern and privacy protection on social network sites in the era of big data: empirical evidence from college students', *Journal of Interactive Advertising*, 19(3), pp. 187–201.

Zhao, Y. *et al.* (2020). 'Local differential privacy-based federated learning for internet of things', *IEEE Internet of Things Journal*, 8(11), pp. 8836–8853.

IMPLEMENTING A SMART CITY DIGITAL TWIN USING THE RAPIDS ARCHITECTURE

Atul Suresh[1], Varun V. Valapel[1], Roy George[2] and Khalil Shujaee[2]
[1]*IVA Pvt. Ltd.*
Technopark, Trivandrum, India
[2]*Department of Cyber-Physical Systems*
Atlanta, GA 30314, USA

ABSTRACT

The application of Digital Twin (DTs) technology towards the Smart City paradigm promises to revolutionize the planning, and management of the city infrastructure and services. The DT can integrate data streams from different sources, including Internet of Things (IoT) sensors, traffic cameras, weather reports, and social media activity, supported by physics-based, simulation, and analytical models to create a virtual representation of the different facets of a city's operations. The DT technology is used to optimize urban services, resource allocation, and infrastructure management thereby improving the quality of life for city residents. The cost of developing the Smart City DT depends on the complexity of the project, data acquisition and storage, infrastructure, software development, and personnel costs. This research project seeks to mitigate these costs through the design and development of a unified, implementation platform, the Real-Time Advanced Platform for Industrial Digitization System (RAPIDS) that may be used to create application specific DTs incurring lower costs, by exploiting reusability of workflows, and eliminating data silos. RAPIDS uses micro-services to implement its functional components enhancing the resilience and robustness of the model. From the user standpoint RAPIDS environment is a low-code environment, that enables experimentation with different design models and configurations, facilitating the reusability of functional components and workflows. We describe the use of RAPIDS for a Visual Analytics application in a city traffic monitoring scenario.

KEYWORDS

Smart City, Digital Twin, Micro-Services Architecture, Visual Analytics, IoT

1. INTRODUCTION

The widespread and affordable access to automation building blocks has made the concept of the Smart City increasingly feasible. The Smart City has been promoted as a informational mechanism in reducing the cost of providing city services and promoting environmental sustainability and enhancing the quality of life of citizens. Urban planning, physical infrastructure, information and communications technology infrastructure, and the implementation of smart solutions are identified as key components of a smart city (Kumar,2020). Accelerating the development of the Smart City is the affordable access to cyber-physical system infrastructure that includes cameras, sensors, mobile computing infrastructure, and advances in Artificial Intelligence. The Smart City Digital Twin (SCDT) is a intended to ultimately virtualize the processes and systems of the city on a digital platform by integrating data from different sources, including Internet of Things (IoT) sensors, traffic cameras, weather reports, and social media activity, supported by physics-based, simulation, and analytical models to enable in-depth monitoring, and support rapid and timely decision support. The cost of developing an SCDT is significant, and critically dependent on the complexity of the project. Cost components include the data acquisition and storage, the computational and enabling infrastructure, software development including system/process modeling and simulations, and the personnel resources. We introduce the Real-Time Advanced Platform for Industrial Digitization System (RAPIDS), which we have developed as a generalized implementation platform for the design and development of Digital Twins. There are several advantages to this system- 1. RAPIDS is a low-code environment that incorporates a drag and drop functionality that reduces the cost of creating application-specific SCDTs; 2. The platform model permits the sharing of information across city applications and functions, permitting the reusability of functions, workflow and data products, 3. It provides an scalable platform that permits integration of additional software functionalities and sensors seamlessly using the concept of micro-services, making the system resilient and fault tolerant. Several parts of the system have been implemented including the AI/Machine Learning, and the Visual Analytics component and have found application in the Smart City and Aerospace domains (Manuja, 2023). The paper is organized as follows: Section 2 outlines the system architecture of the RAPIDS platform and Section 3 describes a SCDT traffic monitoring application of RAPIDS. Section 4 concludes the paper.

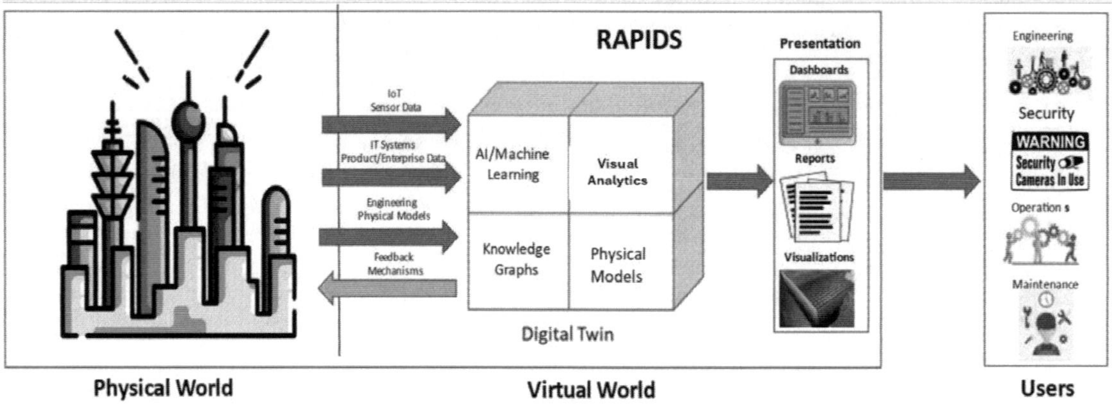

Figure 1. System Architecture of RAPIDS

2. THE RAPIDS PLATFORM

The digital twin is a virtual representation that replicates the structure, context, and behavior of a physical entity [Digital Twin AIAA]. The digital twin acquires, correlates, analyzes and performs decision making on the data, delivering an assessment of the corresponding physical entity. The digital twin expedites the processes of evaluation, diagnosis, and prediction compared to conventional methods. Across industry segments the adoption of digital twins, has been propelled by advancements in Artificial Intelligence, the Internet of Things (IoT), and cloud infrastructure. The notion of the digital twin concept is credited to Michael Grieves, particularly in the context of Product Lifecycle Management (PLM) (Grieves, 2016)., NASA and the U.S. Air Force were early pioneers in the application of digital twin technology, developing numerous aerospace-related applications. In recent years, numerous research organizations and companies have risen to the challenge of extending the theory and practical applications of this technology to diverse industry sectors including Smart Cities (DaSilva, 2022; Austin, 2020; Jafari, 2023; Weil, 2023). The design, development and evaluation of the SCDT is performed using the Real-Time Advanced Platform for Industrial Digitization System (RAPIDS) platform developed by the authors for industrial digitization (Manuja, 2023). The platform is a web-based tool for visualizing, analyzing, and processing the large data sets generated in such applications. Figure 1 shows the abstract RAPIDS architecture applied to City functions and the downstream Smart City applications in the Engineering, Security, Operations, and Maintenance.

3. A SMART CITY VIDEO ANALYTICS USE CASE

Video analytics (VA) uses techniques from artificial intelligence (AI) and computer vision (CV) to capture patterns, objects, movements, and anomalies from video automatically. In the context of a Smart City, the ability to process large amounts of video data rapidly, in conjunction with Internet of Things (IoT) sensors, makes video analytics a useful tool for real-time monitoring and decision making, making cities efficient, safe, and responsive. Traffic management is an application of video analytics in Smart Cities, where the video analytics system detects congestion, accidents, or traffic violations (Zhang, 2023). Other applications include the improvement of traffic flow by optimizing traffic signals and rerouting traffic; and improving pedestrian safety. VA is being applied to public safety, by identifying incidents of vandalism, theft, or suspicious behavior; crowd management; and generating automatic alerts for law enforcement that enable timely intervention. Environmental monitoring is another area of application for VA, used to assess air quality, detect pollution sources, and monitor wildlife in urban areas to promote a cleaner and more sustainable city. In the urban planning setting VA may be used to optimize urban design, and resource allocation helping city managers to make decisions on infrastructure improvements. In summary, VA is an essential component of the Smart City, promoting data-driven decision making that can enable equitable, healthy, sustainable urban environments.

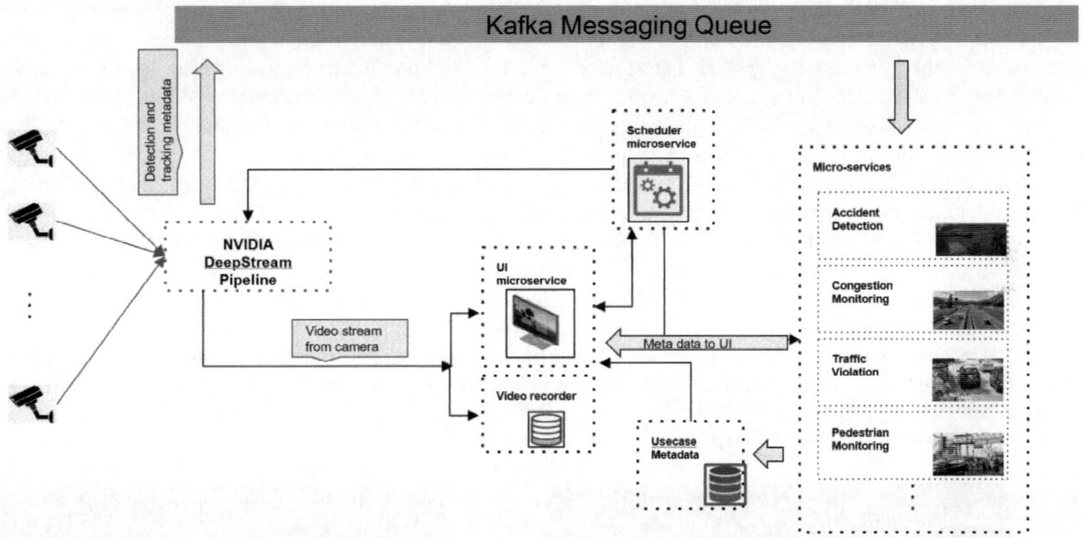

Figure 2. Micro-Services Architecture of SCDT Visual Analytics Component

In this project we implement a micro-services architecture to develop the VA component of the Smart City Digital Twin. The microservices architecture is a software development methodology developed to address the challenges of building large, complex applications by breaking them down into smaller components. Applications are structured as a collection of small, independent services, each focused on a specific function or business capability. These services are loosely coupled and communicate with each other via well-defined APIs. This architectural approach results in the development of VA components that are scalable, modular, and resilient. The resulting system can incorporate both new and legacy components and is resilient to failure. However, development of a micro-services architecture could be more complex due to many service components, services communication and orchestration challenges, and additional performance monitoring overhead. Figure 2 shows the micro-services architecture of the VA component of the SCDT.

The RAPIDS VA component is implemented using the NVIDIA DeepStream pipeline, a streaming analytic toolkit designed for constructing AI-driven applications. DeepStream is used to ingest streaming data from different sources such as USB/CSI cameras, video files, or RTSP streams. The DeepStream applies GPU-driven deep learning techniques to extract application-based abstractions from low-level video pixel data. The DeepStream SDK serves as a foundational layer for a range of video micro-service solutions for SCDT traffic applications such as accident detection, congestion monitoring, pedestrian analysis, etc. The DeepStream pipeline is flexible and permits multiple deep learning frameworks with multiple streams, and with the ability to create ensembles of learning models. Apache Kafka provides a high-speed, scalable, and fault-tolerant publish-subscribe messaging system that is the backbone of the VA component. It provides the basis for the distributed VA applications by handling both persistent and on-demand consumers. Kafka provides resilience and automated recovery in the face of failures facilitating communication and seamless integration of the VA micro-services. The VA component provides archiving of the video stream and also of the meta-data associated with each micro-service. The User Interface (UI) of each application is managed independently by the corresponding micro-service. The distributed architecture of the VA component makes it inherently scalable permitting the addition of sensors (cameras) and data sources on demand, and the addition of new micro-services without reference to the existing applications.

4. RESULTS

Within the framework of the smart city digital twin RAPIDS architecture, a Proof of Concept (PoC) was developed to emphasize the application of Visual Analytics for the monitoring of traffic dynamics. Figure 3 captures a snapshot of the system, to showcasing the analysis of an accident scene through the overlay of distinct software functionalities on an *exemplar* video stream. The PoC has two primary features, which are used by functional micro-services that provide additional knowledge regarding the scene. First the, PoC comprehends the accident scene itself, offering a detailed representation crucial for situational awareness and analysis; and second, the system identifies objects that contribute to a comprehensive understanding of the elements involved in the incident. Using these capabilities as primitives, we are able to derive several elements that provide more knowledge regarding the scene, the actors involved in the accident (motorcycle and rider), the number of bystanders who congregate (crowd enumeration), traffic violations (illegal parking), stray animals on road (anticipated application), etc. These knowledge components are computed by microservices which use raw video to perform scene recognition and generate higher abstractions. Note that our objective in the paper is not to show the Video Analytics capability, but rather to demonstrate the showcase the RAPIDS architecture, and show how the Video Analytics component may be applied to SCD. RAPIDS ensures the seamless integration of additional hardware components and supports the incorporation of additional ML functionalities as required by applications thereby enabling adaptability to evolving needs. The scalable and multifaceted architecture enables RAPIDS as an innovative and robust platform for integrating the functionalities and services required of a Smart City.

Figure 3. Street Scene Video Capture with Micro-service Situational Annotation

5. CONCLUSION

The Smart City Digital Twin (SCDT) is aimed at digitally transforming city processes and systems by integrating diverse data sources, including IoT sensors, traffic cameras, weather reports, and social media activity. This integration is facilitated by physics-based models, simulations, and analytical tools to enable thorough monitoring and provide timely decision support. The development cost of an SCDT is varies based on project complexity and includes the costs of data acquisition, storage, computational infrastructure, software development, and personnel resources. The Real-Time Advanced Platform for Industrial Digitization System (RAPIDS) is introduced as an adaptable platform for designing SCDTs. RAPIDS offers several advantages, including a low-code environment, information sharing across city functions, creation of executable models deployable on various hardware, scalability through micro-services, and a resilient, fault-tolerant architecture. This paper outlines the RAPIDS architecture and describes a Proof-of-Concept traffic monitoring video analytics application using RAPIDS in the SCDT context. The use of micro-services based architecture provides city administrators with a low-cost approach to digitizing and monitoring city applications. Additional sensors and off-the-shelf software components are easily integrated into the architecture as needed. The system is robust against the failure of individual services and is limited only by the hardware of the individual servers needed to handle the load. Additional scalability may be added in the form of distributed servers that provide additional services. There is a trade-off between the flexibility and the resulting complexity of system maintenance and updates in real scenarios. We are currently applying RAPIDS to different SCDT monitoring and security applications including pedestrian and crowd monitoring.

ACKNOWLEDGEMENT

This research is funded in part by NSF Grants No. FAIN-1901150, NSF 1926806, and DOEd Grant P116Z220008 (1). Any opinions, findings, and conclusions expressed here are those of the author(s) and do not reflect the views of the sponsor(s).

REFERENCES

Austin, M., et al., Architecting smart city digital twins: Combined semantic model and machine learning approach. *Journal of Management in Engineering*. 2020, 36

DaSilva Mendonça, Rafael, et al., Digital twin applications: A survey of recent advances and challenges. *Processes* 10.4 (2022): 744

Deng, T., et al. A systematic review of a digital twin city: A new pattern of urban governance toward smart cities, Journal of Management Science and Engineering, Volume 6, Issue 2, 2021, Pages 125-134

Digital Twin: Definitions &Value, AIAA and AIA Position Paper, December 2020

Grieves, M., Origins of the Digital Twin Concept .2016. Available online: https://www.researchgate.net/publication/307509727_ (Retrieved 25 September2023)

Jafari, M., Kavousi-Fard, A., Chen, T. and Karimi, " M., A Review on Digital Twin Technology in Smart Grid, Transportation System and Smart City: Challenges and Future, *IEEE Access*, vol. 11, pp. 17471-17484, 2023, doi: 10.1109/ACCESS.2023.3241588.

Kumar, H., et al., Moving towards smart cities: Solutions that lead to the Smart City Transformation Framework, *Technological Forecasting and Social Change,* 2020, 153, 119281.

Manuja, A., Saurav, A., Varun, V.V., Mathew, A., George, R., Multi-Sensor Failure Recovery in Aero-Engines Using a Digital Twin Platform: A Case Study, *Computing Conference 2023*, July 22-23, 2023, London, UK

Nam, T.; Pardo, T.A. Conceptualizing smart city with dimensions of technology, people, and institutions. *Proceedings of the 12th Annual International Digital Government Research Conference: Digital Government Innovation in Challenging Times*. 2011, 282–291.

Ruohomäki T, Airaksinen E, Huuska P, Kesäniemi O, Martikka M, Suomisto J. Smart city platform enabling digital twin. *2018 International Conference on Intelligent Systems,* 2018, 155-161.

Weil, C., Bibri, S. E., Longchamp, R., Golay, F., Alahi, A., Urban Digital Twin Challenges: A Systematic Review and Perspectives for Sustainable Smart Cities, *Sustainable Cities and Society*, Volume 99, 2023, 104862, ISSN 2210-6707, https://doi.org/10.1016/j.scs.2023.104862.

Zhang, Y., Wang, H. & Wang, X. Research on the improvement of transportation efficiency of smart city by traffic visualization based on pattern recognition, *Neural Comput & Applic*, 35, 2211–2224, 2023. https://doi.org/10.1007/s00521-022-07222-4

PROPOSAL ON DISTRIBUTED MQTT BROKERS ARCHITECTURE

Kazuhiro Kosaka[1], Masaki Mitsuuchi[1], Tetsuya Yokotani[2] and Koichi Ishibashi[3]
[1]*The Graduate School of Electrical Engineering and Electronics, Kanazawa Institute of Technology, Nonoichi, Ishikawa, Japan*
[2]*Department of Electrical and Electronic Engineering, College of Engineering, Kanazawa Institute of Technology, Nonoichi, Ishikawa, Japan*
[3]*Department of Information and Computer Science, College of Engineering, Kanazawa Institute of Technology, Hakusan, Ishikawa, Japan*

ABSTRACT

Message Queue Telemetry Transport (MQTT) is a popular communication protocol for IoT, in which Publishers and Subscribers communicate through a single broker. Therefore, a distributed broker is necessary to accommodate multiple Publishers and Subscribers at multiple locations. Previous studies have used a method in which multiple brokers are connected in a ring to share information. However, in this method, the processing delay time increases as the number of brokers and Hops increases. In this study, we propose a direct connection method between distributed brokers that reduces the processing delay time. We also use an Analytic Hierarchy Process (AHP) to determine the communication protocol used to connect brokers. Next, partial prototyping was performed to estimate the latency.

KEYWORDS

IoT, MQTT, Distributed Brokers, DDS

1. INTRODUCTION

Currently, IoT services are being deployed in various fields (Al-Fuqaha, et.al, 2015), and the number of IoT devices is expected to increase to 32.4 billion in 2022 and 44 billion by 2025, according to forecasts (MIC, Information and Communication in Japan White Paper, 2023). Given these factors, implementing IoT services over the current Internet is inefficient because of the increase in control information and consumption of network resources (Yokotani and Sasaki, 2016). The most widely used and efficient communication protocol for IoT is Message Queue Telemetry Transport (MQTT) (Yassein, et.al, 2017). MQTT is lightweight, with a header size of 2 Bytes. However, MQTT requires a distributed broker to accommodate numerous Publishers and Subscribers among multiple locations because Publishers and Subscribers communicate through a single broker. This study proposes a new distributed broker coordination scheme in which an Analytic Hierarchy Process (AHP) is used to determine the communication protocol to be used to connect brokers. Next, partial prototyping is performed to estimate the latency.

2. RELATED WORKS

In previous studies, cooperation has been achieved by connecting distributed brokers in a ring (Ohno, et.al, 2021) (Yokotani, et.al, 2021). In this method, the MQTT brokers are connected in a virtual ring constructed using VLANs. Each broker has an Access Control block and a Shared Memory block. The Access Control block handles the information transfer and loop prevention. The Shared Memory block is a table that manages topics and their information.

The processing delay with this scheme is 44.51[ms] to 44.39[ms] (Ohno, et.al, 2021). The processing delay time increases as the number of collaborating brokers increases, making it impossible to support use cases that require low latency, such as factories. Therefore, the author proposes a method for achieving low-latency communication by directly connecting distributed brokers.

3. PROTOCOL SELECTION BY AHP

A communication protocol is selected for direct connection between brokers. An Analytic Hierarchy Process (AHP) (Saaty, 1988) (Aziz, et.al, 2016) was used for selection. The purpose was to "select the communication protocol used to connect brokers directly." The nine evaluation criteria were scalability, compatibility with existing transports, throughput, latency, IP dependence, reliability, lightweight, route control, and OAM functionality. In addition, seven alternative protocols were selected: MQTT, DDS, AMQP, XMPP, CoAP, HTTP, and WebSocket. A questionnaire was administered to six people.

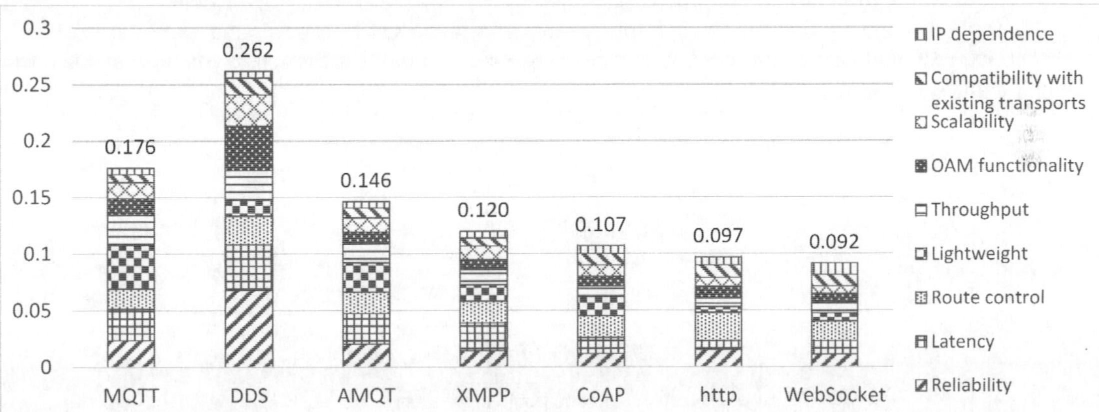

Figure 1. Evaluation results using AHP

Based on the evaluation results shown in Figure 1, the most suitable protocol was DDS. It received the highest evaluation scores for reliability, latency, route control, OAM functionality, scalability, and compatibility with existing transports. Therefore, DDS is used as the communication protocol used to connect brokers directly.

4. PROPOSED METHOD

DDS is used as a protocol to connect brokers directly. DDS is a Publish/Subscribe type topic-based communication protocol. Three methods have been proposed for inter-broker connection using DDS. Methods 1–3 are illustrated in Figures. 2 to 4.

In method 1, the broker that acquires information from MQTT constructs a Topic Table that indicates the broker to which the topic is transferred. As the broker determines the forwarding destination broker according to the Topic Table, it is necessary to implement a coordination function between the DDS and the lower layer (IP and/or MAC). Generally, topics are tied to IoT services; therefore, constructing a topic table for information transfer on a service-by-service basis is relatively easy.

In Method 2, a Default Broker (DB) was set up to centrally manage the Topic Table of Method 1. In this case, if the destination broker for the information acquired from MQTT using Method 1 is not in the Topic Table within the broker or if the destination broker cannot be detected, the information is transferred to the DB.

In this case, the number of brokers passing through the DDS will increase, and it will be necessary to implement an interworking function between the DDS; however, it will be easier to implement regular brokers, and the processing load will be reduced. In addition, depending on the operation, it is possible to define DB as a Rendezvous Point and ensure the consistency of Publish/Subscribe messages. This is expected to reduce the amount of traffic.

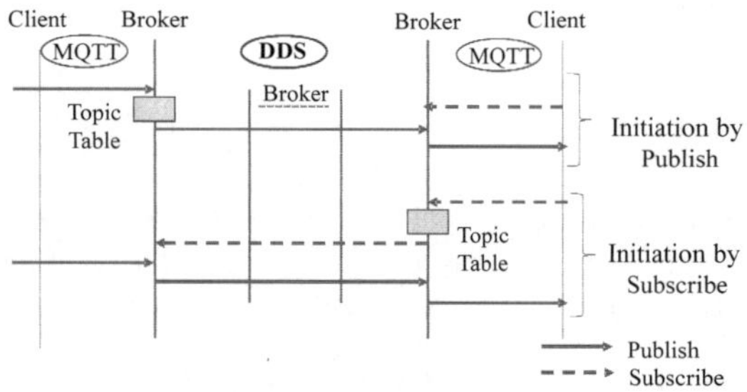

Figure 2. Proposed method 1

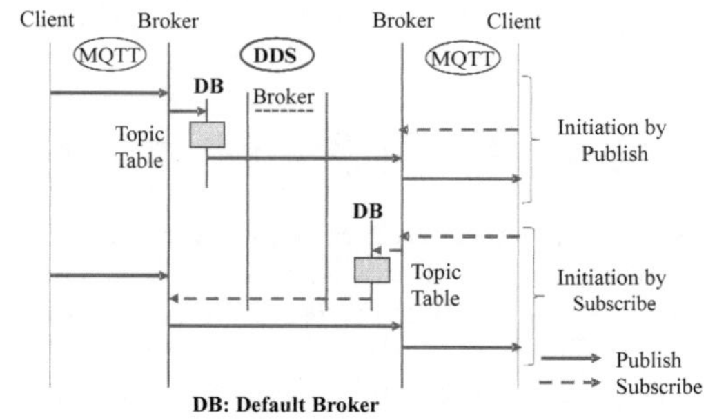

Figure 3. Proposed method 2

In Method 3, the broker that obtains information from the MQTT forwards the DDS messages to each broker using IP multicast. In this case, it is necessary to create a multicast group in advance, and cooperation with the Internet is required.

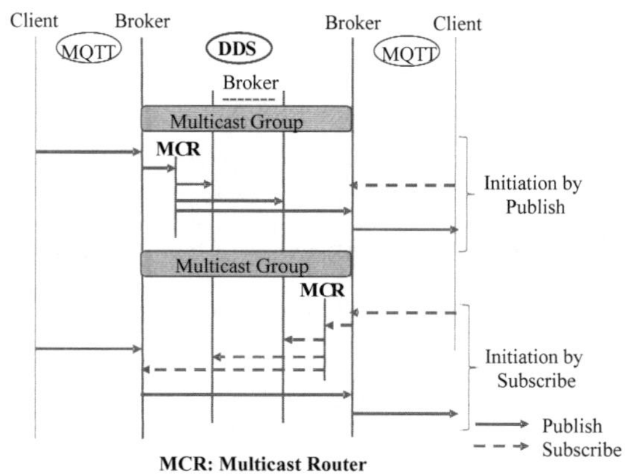

Figure 4. Proposed method 3

5. PROTOTYPING

We created a prototype of Method 1 in two parts and estimated the end-to-end processing delay time. Part 1 eliminates the Topic Table function in the broker of Method 1 and creates a function to transfer only between specific brokers. Part 2 creates a function to search the destination broker from the Topic Table as a separate program. By adding these two processing delays, we obtain the processing delay for Method 1.

The configuration of the MQTT and DDS conversion function in Part 1 is shown in Figure 5. For implementation, the RTI Connext RTI Routing Service (RTI Routing Service) was used as a base. MQTT and DDS adapters were created in Routing Service to enable MQTT and DDS communication. The information obtained from the MQTT was specified to match the DDS format.

The operation illustrated in Figure 5 is as follows: ①Routing Service subscribes to the MQTT broker. ② Routing Service converts MQTT Topic, ID, QoS, message, etc. to DDS format. ③Routing Service published with DDS. ④Subscribe Routing Service with DDS. ⑤Routing Service converts DDS data into MQTT message format. ⑥Publish Routing Service to MQTT broker.

The function to search the transfer destination BROKER from the Topic Table in Part 2 was created in C language. Inside the Topic Table, I created a structure with a pair of Topic and destination brokers and created an array of this structure.

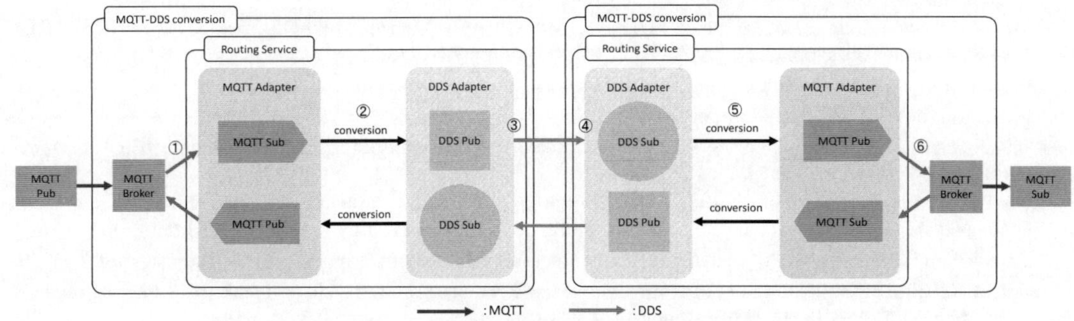

Figure 5. Configuration of MQTT-DDS conversion

6. PERFORMANCE EVALUATION

The experimental configuration of part 1 is shown in Figure 5. The processing delay time measures the time from when the MQTT Pub sends information to when the MQTT Sub receives information. The amount of data to be sent was 10 bytes, and the measurements were performed 1000 times.

The results are summarized in Table 1. For the measured processing delay time, the maximum value was 4.272[ms], and the minimum value was 4.200[ms] within the 99% confidence interval.

In Part 2, we used a binary search to search for the destination broker in the Topic Table and measured the processing delay time. A total of 100,000 topics were set in the Topic Table. In the search, we searched all 100,000 topics and measured the maximum and average processing times. The results are summarized in Table 2. As a result of measuring the processing time, the maximum was 100.7[μs], and the average was 1.7[μs].

Adding the results of Parts 1 and 2 and estimating the processing delay time of Method 1 results in Table 3. The maximum value was used for the processing time of part 2. As shown in Table 3, the processing delay of Method 1 increased from 4.301 [ms] to 4.373 [ms], indicating that the response performance was better than that in previous research.

Table 1. Confidence interval for part 1

Maximum[ms]	Minimum[ms]
4.272	4.200

Table 2. Processing time for part 2

Maximum[μs]	Average[μs]
100.7	1.7

Table 3. Estimated delay processing time for method 1

Maximum[ms]	Minimum[ms]
4.373	4.301

7. CONCLUSIONS

In this paper, the author introduced previous research on distributed broker federation methods in MQTT and described the issues. The author then proposed a new distributed broker coordination scheme that solves these issues and estimated its performance. The results were estimated to prove to be effective. In the future, the author will create prototypes of other methods and evaluate their performances.

REFERENCES

Al-Fuqaha, A., et.al (2015). Internet of Things: A Survey on Enabling Technologies, Protocols, and Applications. IEEE Communications Surveys & Tutorials, vol. 17, no. 4, pp. 2347-2376.

Aziz, N. F., Sorooshian, S., & Mahmud, F., (2016). MCDM-AHP METHOD IN DECISION MAKINGS. ARPN Journal of Engineering and Applied Sciences, VOL. 11, NO. 11, pp.7217-7220.

Ministry of Internal Affairs and Communications, Information and Communication in Japan White Paper (2023).

MQTT.org. (nd). MQTT. http://mqtt.org/.

Ohno, S., et.al (2021). Distributed MQTT broker architecture using ring topology and its prototype. IEICE Communications Express, Volume 10 Issue 8 Pages 582-586.

Real-Time Innovations, Inc. (nd). RTI Routing Service, https://community.rti.com/static/documentation/connext-dds/6.1.0/doc/manuals/connext_dds_professional/services/routing_service/index.html.

Saaty, T. L., (1988). What is the analytic hierarchy process?. Mathematical models for decision support, pp. 109-121.

Yassein, M. B., et.al (2017). Internet of Things: Survey and open issues of MQTT protocol. 2017 International Conference on Engineering & MIS (ICEMIS), Monastir, Tunisia, pp. 1-6.

Yokotani, T., & Sasaki, Y., (2016). Comparison with HTTP and MQTT on required network resources for IoT. International Conference on Control, Electronics, Renewable Energy and Communications (ICCEREC), Bandung, Indonesia, pp. 1-6.

Yokotani, T., et.al. (2021). IoT platform with distributed brokers on MQTT. International Journal of Future Computer and Communication, vol. 10, no. 1, pp. 7–12.

CAN'T WE JUST USE COMPUTERS? INITIAL EFFORTS ON TECHNOLOGY-ENHANCED LEARNING OF OPERATIONS RESEARCH IN A PHILIPPINE UNIVERSITY

Lester C. Hao[1], Jeric C. Briones[1,2] and Mark Anthony C. Tolentino[1]
[1]Department of Mathematics, Ateneo de Manila University,
[2]Department of Finance and Accounting, Ateneo de Manila University
Katipunan Avenue, Loyola Heights, Quezon City, Philippines 1108

ABSTRACT

Operations Research (OR) is a required course in any applied math program in the Philippines. It involves complex and computation-heavy algorithms to guide and improve decision-making in organizations and relevant contexts. Despite the advent of software that have automated the computations or the implementation of algorithms, the teaching and learning of OR may still be rife with procedures being performed manually by hand. In this paper, we report on our initial progress on a research project that aims to revise the OR syllabi in one Philippine university, by integrating more technological tools in the teaching and learning of OR for undergraduate and graduate students. We present the study's conceptual underpinnings and methodology, and discuss some initial results on the syllabi revisions.

KEYWORDS

Technology-Enhanced Learning, Operations Research, Design Research

1. INTRODUCTION

Operations Research (OR) (also often referred to as management science) is focused on developing and applying analytical methods to guide and to improve decision-making in organizations and other contexts. Throughout history, OR has found applications in several fields. For instance, applications in banking (Doumpos et al., 2023), healthcare (Guo, 2023), maritime logistics (Weerasinghe, Perera, & Bai, 2023), and business and industries (Gunasekaran et al., 2023) have been recently reported.

Given this wide applicability of OR, it is not surprising that higher education programs, especially those in science and engineering, have integrated OR courses in their respective curricula. In fact, this is a required course in any applied math program in the Philippines. For example, the applied math programs offered by our university have OR courses in their undergraduate and graduate curricula. In addition, OR has been taught at our university as early as the 1970s. As one can imagine, the technology landscape in the 1970s is widely different from what we have today, and this has been reflected on how OR courses in our university have traditionally involved implementing relatively complex and computationally heavy algorithms iteratively by hand. However, with the advancement of technology in the 1990s, the use of spreadsheet software, as Ragdale (2001) reported, has become common practice in teaching OR courses in several universities. Following this trend, spreadsheets were also used for OR courses in our university, but only to some extent. Up to this day, these courses still retain a substantial amount of manual implementations of optimization algorithms. In fact, previous students of these courses have mentioned in their course evaluations that they felt that some of the course assessments were evaluating their arithmetic skills rather than their understanding of the algorithms. In addition, some students also mentioned that the manual calculations emphasized in the course would be better done using computers. This then begs the question: can't we just use computers?

2. THE RESEARCH PROJECT

In discussing the philosophy of teaching mathematics, Ernest (2018) posed two issues pertinent to the integration and presence of digital tools vis-à-vis written algorithms. His first point questions the timing in which digital tools are introduced — should it be before, during, or after the teaching of manual algorithms? Meanwhile, his second issue revolves on the presence of technological tools — how much emphasis should these have over written procedures? While the debate on these questions has yet to be settled, it is widely recognized that educational technology has the power to positively impact the learning of mathematics. Through the strategic implementation of digital tools, students are accorded more opportunities to engage with the mathematical content (Calder, 2015). Since their focus is shifted away from complex calculations, this allows them not only to explore relationships among concepts and procedures, but also to develop problem-solving and critical thinking skills (Apostolopoulou et al., 2014).

With respect to OR, technology is indeed one of its important components, especially because real-world OR problems are often so large that using computers is the only feasible way to solve them. In fact, the widely used OR textbooks by Hillier and Lieberman (2010) and by Taha (2017) integrate the use of technology throughout their books. For example, Hillier and Lieberman (2010) incorporated several software options such as MS Excel, LINDO (Linear, Interactive, and Discrete Optimizer), and Queuing Simulator, while Taha (2017) developed his own software TORA, aside from other existing technological tools.

In light of the aforementioned, we have embarked on a project that aims to revise the OR course syllabi of our university's applied math programs by integrating more software-based implementations of different optimization algorithms. Nonetheless, technology integration in our case does not mean the complete removal of the paper-and-pen aspect of learning OR. Students will be exposed to several forms of implementing optimization algorithms: automated (e.g., using built-in functions), computer-aided (e.g., using spreadsheets), and manual (e.g., using pens, papers, and calculators). This pedagogical choice is anchored on the principle that procedural variation (Gu, Huang, & Marton, 2004) supports students' conceptual understanding (Rittle-Johnson, Schneider, & Star, 2015). Allowing them to experience various approaches in solving OR problems may potentially foster better understanding of the content. More so, it has its practical benefits in terms of opportunities to learn more advanced content or investigate more challenging problems, thereby ideally honing their higher-order thinking skills as well.

In addition, the project will also gather and analyze feedback from both OR teachers (i.e., implementers of the revised syllabus) and students of their experiences and perspectives on automated, computer-aided, and manual implementations of optimization algorithms. Such inputs can guide, but not necessarily dictate, how much technology should be integrated and how much manual implementations should be retained in these OR courses. Moreover, these inputs may inform further syllabus revision efforts. In this paper, we report on our work-in-progress qualitative study, particularly on its methodology and some initial outputs, such as on the revisions of the OR courses' syllabi for applied math students.

3. METHODOLOGY

The present study employs the design-research-redesign framework as characterized by the cyclical approach of a design research project (van den Akker et al., 2006; Nührenbörger et al., 2019). This framework is suitable for the project since the target output is a refinement of the revised syllabus as informed by inputs from teachers and students. To this, we likewise integrate some elements that Huang et al. (2019) have identified in their scope of educational technology: needs assessment, requirements analysis, design/redesign, development, deployment, management, and evaluation. This is illustrated in Figure 1.

In the design phase, the OR teachers (who are also co-authors of this paper) identified the need to increase the presence of technology in OR courses, through reflection on teaching OR and a review of textbooks and relevant literature (i.e., needs assessment). They then aimed to design a revised syllabus that would integrate more software-based implementations of different optimization algorithms, and balance those with manual implementation (i.e., requirements analysis). Afterwards, the teachers drafted a revised syllabi for OR courses that will be implemented during the Second Semester of School Year 2023-2024 (i.e., design and development).

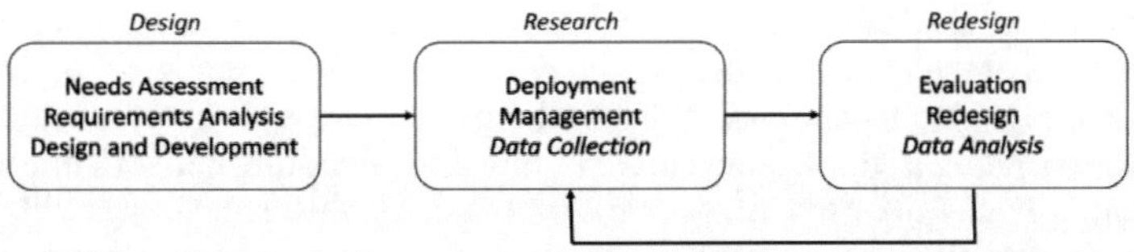

Figure 1. Research phases

The research phase commences once the revised syllabus has been implemented (i.e., deployment). In addition, teachers might encounter unforeseen circumstances during the implementation that might require them to be flexible and adaptive in modifying the syllabus (i.e., management). Furthermore, data collection shall also be carried out towards the second half of the semester. The target participants are both the OR teachers and applied math students. The teachers shall be interviewed of their introspections and experiences in implementing the revised syllabus. Likewise, a survey form shall be administered to consenting students; those who volunteer will be interviewed individually or in focus group discussions. For both respondents, the lines of inquiry will revolve on their experiences of more software-based implementations for certain topics, their perceived impact of such on their learning and achievement, and their suggestions and recommendations for future iterations of the course.

Lastly, the redesign phase involves analyzing the qualitative data (i.e., evaluation) that will inform the teachers on the possible modifications that they may implement in the future. In this regard, qualitative data shall be analyzed through content analysis, by first identifying meaning units (i.e., significant statements), then assigning codes to each, thereby generating categories and themes (Erlingsson & Brysiewicz, 2017). This phase will likewise consider the questions posed by Ernest (2018) on the pedagogical timing and presence of software-based implementations with respect to their manual counterpart.

4. REVISED OPERATIONS RESEARCH SYLLABI

In the undergraduate OR course taken for a full semester, students are primarily introduced to linear programming and its extensions. To solve these linear programming problems, the simplex method and its modifications are used. Alongside the manual implementations of the said algorithm, the theoretical underpinnings and automated implementations (i.e., using MS Excel Solver) are also discussed in the course. However, given the mechanical nature of the simplex method, more time is allocated for the manual rather than the automated implementation. Moreover, students are left on their own to explore computer-aided implementations. In this study, we will shift the focus of the undergraduate syllabi from manual and automated implementations, to computer-aided and automated implementations. That is, instead of using calculators for matrix operations, students will be using spreadsheets (such as MS Excel and Google Sheets). While manual calculations will still be illustrated when proving the theoretical justifications of the algorithms, implementing these algorithms will involve more computer-aided and automated approaches. This computer-aided approach to doing matrix operations will only need basic spreadsheet functionalities (see Figure 2 for examples), and not any special function or add-in package. On the other hand, more time shall be devoted to discussions in using MS Excel Solver. This will include having more examples on how to use and interpret results. Finally, students will be allowed to use computers during onsite assessments.

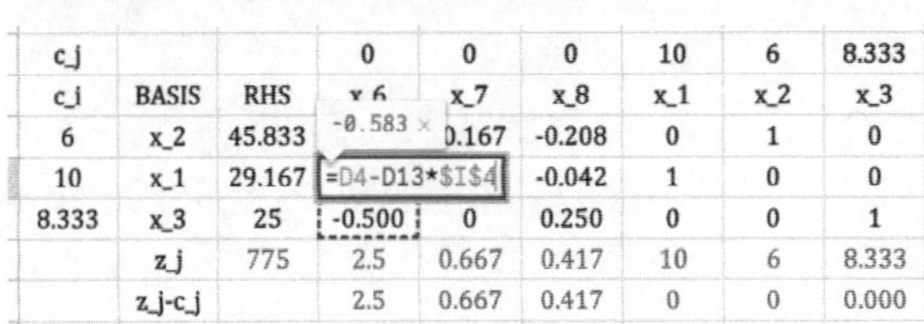

c_j			0	0	0	10	6	8.333
c_i	BASIS	RHS	x_6	x_7	x_8	x_1	x_2	x_3
6	x_2	45.833	-0.583	0.167	-0.208	0	1	0
10	x_1	29.167	=D4-D13*I4		-0.042	1	0	0
8.333	x_3	25	-0.500	0	0.250	0	0	1
	z_j	775	2.5	0.667	0.417	10	6	8.333
	z_j-c_j		2.5	0.667	0.417	0	0	0.000

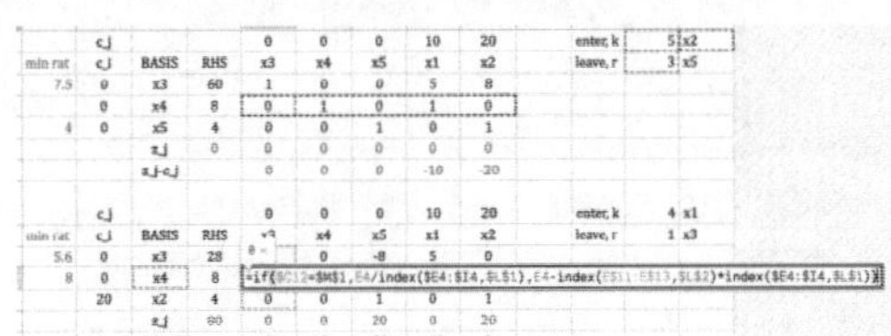

Figure 2. Examples of computer-aided approach to matrix operations using spreadsheet formulas. Students will be given the freedom to decide which spreadsheet formulas they will use when implementing the optimization algorithms

On the other hand, the graduate OR course, taken for a full semester as well, is primarily divided into two parts, with the first half of the course focused on network optimization models. For the purposes of this study, the focus will be on integrating technology in the teaching of these network optimization models. Traditionally, this course involves spending a significant amount of time implementing network optimization algorithms (e.g. Dijkstra's algorithm, Ford-Fulkerson algorithm) by hand. In this study, we will implement three initial revisions to the graduate course syllabi: reducing the time devoted to the manual implementation of all network optimization algorithms covered, using the free software Gephi (gephi.org), and integrating some programming (i.e., using Python) for the topic on the maximal flow problem. While less time will be devoted to manual implementations, they will be retained as they are important in understanding how network algorithms work and when they can or cannot be applied.

Gephi is an open-source and free software that can be operated on different operating systems. It has a wide range of visualization, exploration, and analysis features for networks. Gephi has a point-and-click interface that can facilitate the setting up of networks (Figure 3(a)). Alternatively, networks can be set up by importing network information (e.g., nodes, edges, weights) from a source file (e.g., spreadsheet); this makes Gephi ideal for analyzing large networks that may arise from real problems. For the purposes of the course, Gephi has a readily available function for finding a shortest path (Figure 3(b)) between two nodes in a network. Moreover, a freely available plugin can be installed to generate a minimum spanning tree (Figure 3(c)) of a network. Gephi also has readily available sample networks (e.g., Figure 3(d)) that can be used for examples and illustrations in lectures.

For the topic on maximal flow problems, computer programming will be incorporated. The Ford-Fulkerson algorithm, which can be used to solve maximal flow problems, will first be discussed in class and examples will be done manually. Students will then be asked to write a computer program to implement the algorithm. While this approach builds towards automating the implementation of an optimization algorithm, it will require students' understanding of its manual implementation as this will be necessary in writing the computer program correctly.

Given these initial revisions in the graduate OR course, examples and problems that may be covered in class can also be enriched. Given the access to the technologies discussed above, more attention can be devoted to formulating different real-world problems into network optimization algorithms. Additionally, solving problems that involve larger networks may now become accessible to the class.

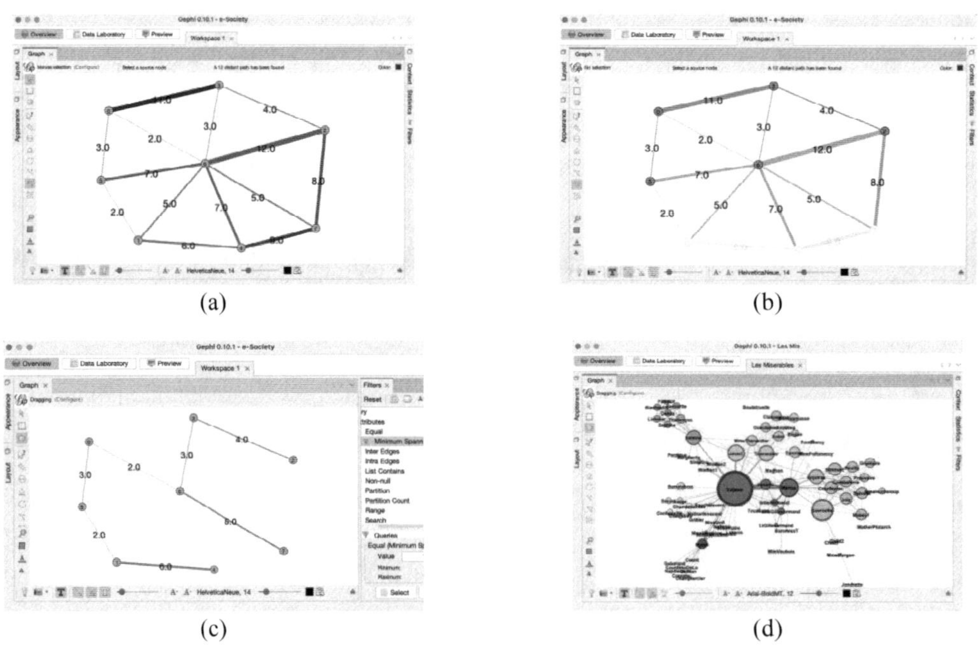

(a) (b)

(c) (d)

Figure 3. Screenshots from Gephi

5. CONCLUSION

In this paper, we presented an overview of a research project that aims to technologically enhance the teaching and learning of OR in a Philippine university. This is to be achieved by revising the OR syllabi for undergraduate and graduate courses, in which more software-based implementations of optimization algorithms will be utilized. To this, we reported on the outputs of the project's design phase, i.e., the intended syllabi revisions, and highlighted the topics and their corresponding software, in which students will be exposed to various forms of optimization algorithm implementations. In particular, the OR syllabi will focus more on computer-aided and automated implementations, with the manual implementation mostly to be used to build on the discussions of the algorithms involved. Moving forward, the revised syllabi will be implemented during the Second Semester of School Year 2023-2024, wherein the last two phases of the project will commence. In these last two phases, qualitative data from both teachers and students will be gathered and then analyzed towards guiding future syllabi modifications.

REFERENCES

Apostolopoulou, D. et al. (2014). Theories of learning in math and science educational software. In C. Karagiannidis et al. (Eds.), *Research on e-Learning and ICT in Education: Technological, Pedagogical and Instructional Perspectives* (pp. 25–36). Springer Science+Business Media, New York. http://doi.org/10.1007/978-1-4614-6501-0_3

Calder, N. (2009). Affordances of spreadsheets In mathematical investigation: Potentialities For learning. *Spreadsheets in Education (eJSiE)*, Vol. 3, No. 3, Article 4. http://epublications.bond.edu.au/ejsie/vol3/iss3/4

Calder, N. (2015). Apps: Appropriate, applicable, and appealing? In T. Lowrie, R. Jorgensen (Zevenbergen) (Eds.), *Digital Games and Mathematics Learning, Mathematics Education in the Digital Era 4* (pp. 233-250). Springer Science+Business Media, Dordrecht. http://doi.org/10.1007/978-94-017-9517-2_12

Doumpos, M. et al. (2023). Operational research and artificial intelligence methods in banking, *European Journal of Operational Research*, Vol. 306, No. 1, pp. 1-16. https://doi.org/10.1016/j.ejor.2022.04.027.

Erlingsson, C. and Brysiewicz, P. (2017). A hands-on guide to doing content analysis. *African Journal of Emergency Medicine,* Vol. 7, No. 3, pp. 93–99. https://doi.org/10.1016/j.afjem.2017.08.001

Ernest, P. (2018). The philosophy of mathematics education: An overview. In P. Ernest (ed.), *The Philosophy of Mathematics Education Today, ICME-13 Monographs*(pp. 13–35). Springer, Cham. https://doi.org/10.1007/978-3-319-77760-3_2

Gu, L. et al. (2004). Teaching with variation: A Chinese way of promotive effective mathematics learning. In L. Fan, N.-Y. W., J. Cai, & S. Li (Eds.), *How Chinese learn mathematics: Perspectives from insiders* (pp. 309–347). World Scientific, Singapore.

Gunasekaran, A. et al. (2023). Applications of Operational Research in Business and Industries. *Proceedings of 54th Annual Conference of ORSI*. Springer Nature.

Guo, J. (2023). Application of Operations Research to Healthcare. New Research in Nursing - Education and Practice [Working Title]. *IntechOpen*. http://dx.doi.org/10.5772/intechopen.109919

Hiller, F. and Lieberman, G. (2010). *Introduction to operations research* (9th ed). McGraw-Hill.

Huang, R. et al. (2019). *Educational technology: A primer for the 21st century*. Springer Nature, Singapore. https://doi.org/10.1007/978-981-13-6643-7

Nührenbörger, M. et al. (2019). Design science and design research: The significance of a subject-specific research approach. In H. N. Jahnke & L. Hefendehl-Hebeker (Eds.), *Traditions in German-speaking mathematics education research* (pp. 61–90). Springer, Cham.

Ragsdale, C. (2001). Teaching Management Science with Spreadsheets: From Decision Models to Decision Support. *INFORMS Transactions on Education*, Vol. 1, No. 2, pp. 68-74. https://doi.org/10.1287/ited.1.2.68

Rittle-Johnson, B. et al. (2015). Not a one-way street: Bidirectional relations between procedural and conceptual knowledge of mathematics. *Educational Psychology Review,* Vol. 27, No. 4, pp. 587–597. https://doi.org/10.1007/s10648-015-9302-x

Taha, H. (2017). *Operations Research: An Introduction* (Tenth Edition, Global Edition). Pearson Education Limited.

Van den Akker, J. et al. (2006). Introducing educational design research. In J. van den Akker, K. Gravemeijer, S. McKenney, & N. Nieveen (Eds.), *Educational Design Research* (pp. 3–7). Routledge, London.

Weerasinghe, B. A. et al. (2023). Optimizing container terminal operations: a systematic review of operations research applications. *Marit Econ Logist*. https://doi.org/10.1057/s41278-023-00254-0

DID THE COVID-19 PANDEMIC BOOST THE SPREAD OF DIGITAL DEVICES IN HOUSEHOLDS? THE ITALIAN SITUATION FROM AN EDUCATIONAL PERSPECTIVE

Marco Lazzari[↓] and Federica Baroni
Università di Bergamo, Dipartimento di Scienze Umane e Sociali
Bergamo, Italy

ABSTRACT

Digital devices and platforms have been of great help in overcoming the COVID-19 pandemic period. In the educational field, they made it possible to cope with social distancing through the delivery of remote teaching. This was even more felt in Italy, which was among the first countries to be affected by the pandemic and among those hardest hit. In this article, we ask ourselves whether the digital endowments of families with young children at this time have increased compared to the pre-pandemic period and whether the families themselves would be able to withstand the impact of a new period of distancing. Comparing data from our pre- and post-pandemic questionnaires, and from interviews we conducted over the past two years, against data from the Italian National Institute of Statistics, we conclude that the digital endowment of families of primary school children is not significantly more robust than it was for families who faced the pandemic period. This evidence must be kept in mind by policymakers and educators, so that, if a new confinement period occurred, steps might be taken with the utmost urgency to bridge any dangerous digital divides.

KEYWORDS

COVID-19 Pandemic, Household's Digital Equipment, Distance Education, Digital Divide, Educational Poverty, Families with Adolescents and Children, Virtual Learning Environments, E-Learning Political and Social Aspects

1. INTRODUCTION

The COVID-19 pandemic not only accelerated the adoption of digital technologies for pandemic management and response (OECD 2021, Whitelaw et al. 2020), but also the spread of digital devices in households in several scenarios:

1. Since lockdown and social distancing measures forced many people to work and study from home, there was an urgent need to adapt digital equipment to new necessities by adopting laptops, tablets, microphones, and webcams; many families, who did not have these essential devices to cope with domestic confinement, had to somehow obtain them.
2. Video conferencing tools saw a quick increase in usage for business meetings, distance learning, and social events; as a result, the demand for webcams, large screens, and microphones increased as well.
3. Due to the need to shop in online stores, the demand for smartphones and computers to access e-commerce platforms increased.

Given the hectic times in which it became necessary to adjust the ICT equipment of institutions, businesses and households, several countries invested significant funds in purchasing digital equipment to promote distance learning. The Organisation for Economic Co-operation and Development (OECD 2021) estimated that 'about two-thirds of OECD and partner countries increased their education budget in response to the pandemic'. The consequent diffusion of devices and connections took forms that went beyond the classic patterns of technology adoption (Davies 1979; Rogers and Shoemaker 1971; Venkatesh et al. 2003), in some ways generating a spike in the representation curve of adoption trends (European Commission 2021), with effects that went beyond the classic geographic distinction between cities and small towns.

[↓] The authors contributed equally to this work

The pandemic also highlighted some dangerous effects of the digital divide (Beaunoyer et al. 2020; Ramsetty and Adams 2020), as the biggest driver of people's propensity and ability to stay at home and, therefore, to self-protect from contagion was the availability of adequate devices and high-speed Internet connections (Chiou and Tucker 2020).

Even in the most developed countries, a non-negligible number of families, did not have equal access to the digital equipment and telematics facilities, that have become indispensable for accessing smart working, e-commerce, telehealth-based care, and distance learning. Studies in a number of countries have found a significant relationship between the socioeconomic status of families and forms of digital divide in the exploitation of distance learning resources, whereby wealthier families had more educational opportunities for their children (Azubuike et al. 2021; Francis and Weller 2022; Martínez-Domínguez and Fierros-González 2022). In order to bridge this gap, which threatened to worsen already precarious situations of educational poverty, institutions and governments in many countries stepped in to provide devices and connections to underserved communities.

The pandemic also significantly boosted the spread of digital devices among children and adolescents, producing an impact on education, socialisation and entertainment for young people. This implied an increase in screen time for children and adolescents, which raised concerns about potential threats to their physical and mental health (Camerini et al. 2022; Pandya and Lodha 2021; Tso et al. 2022; Wong et al. 2021). For their part, parents became more aware of the need for monitoring tools and parental controls to manage their children's digital behaviours.

Based on these data and reflections, one might imagine that the diffusion of technologies among households, at least as far as our country is concerned, has reached a level that enables us to face future occurrences such as the COVID-19 pandemic with confidence in our level of preparedness.

The considerations we present in this paper, however, are not so comforting. Evidence of various kinds, from in-field and desk-based investigations, suggests that the digital endowments of Italian households are not so different from what they were before the contagion broke out in February 2020, despite the pressure that was exerted during the pandemic period to digitally equip families and despite school interventions to help families by providing free loaner devices.

The aim of the paper is thus to suggest an alternative reading to those that consider high levels of domestic technology diffusion as having been acquired, and to propose more in-depth lines of inquiry for the future, that will contribute to supporting informed decision making.

2. HOUSEHOLD ENDOWMENTS STRADDLING THE PANDEMIC

The ideas set forth in this paper arose serendipitously while our working group was engaged in the fifth edition of a survey that started fifteen years ago (Lazzari and Jacono Quarantino 2010) to investigate the ways, places, and times of communication by adolescents and children in physical spaces and on the Internet. In the course of the survey, which was based on a mixed-methods methodology of information collection through focus groups and questionnaire administration, we happened to compare some data with others collected before the COVID-19 pandemic and were surprised by what we found.

We were particularly struck by the data on households' digital equipment. When asked 'Is there (at least) a personal computer (PC) or laptop in your home?', the percentage of children in the fifth grade of primary school (aged 10–11) who provided a positive response was lower than in the pre-pandemic surveys. Such evidence is counterintuitive and contrary to mainstream communication that reads a general increase in the spread of digital tools as a consequence of the COVID-19 pandemic. It is also surprising because it concerns young families, that is a segment of the population that one might expect to be more inclined than others to use digital technology.

We then wanted to delve deeper into the topic by selecting and comparing data from four of our questionnaires, two administered before the pandemic (2018 and 2019) and two after (2022 and 2023). We focused our attention on three questions related to families' digital endowments (see Table 1), circumscribing the data to those of fifth-grade primary school respondents (although the questionnaire was administered to a total of 2,798 pupils, the number of respondents considered for 2018 is lower because, on that occasion it was also intended for fourth graders, who were excluded from this analysis).

The three questions were:

1. Do you have your own phone?
2. Do you have your own tablet?
3. Is there (at least) a personal computer (PC) or laptop in your home?

Table 1. Possession of digital devices among households (respondents aged 10-11 years)

Respondents	Year	Do you have your own phone? (%)	Do you have your own tablet? (%)	Family PC equipment (%)
1803	**2018**	48.9	59.1	92.0
3639	**2019**	49.2	59.8	91.9
3881	**2022**	49.4	56.9	91.9
3388	**2023**	49.7	53.1	90.2

As shown in Table 1, the figure for the domestic equipment just before the pandemic and immediately after is unchanged, and stands at 91.9%. In the latest survey the percentage even decreased. The percentage of tablets owned by respondents also gradually decreases, but in this case, we know that the specificity of the question could hide situations of sharing among siblings. Only the value related to smartphone ownership is very slightly increasing, but it seems to be asymptotically approaching a saturation value of around 50% (with an average value of the date of entry into possession of the first phone of around eight and a half years, linked to the First Communion event).

Since the data seemed to go against the grain of common belief, we looked for comparisons with other investigations, thus conducting some desk research. In particular, we triangulated our evidences with a large amount of data collected by the Italian National Institute of Statistics (Istituto Nazionale di Statistica (ISTAT) 2023): even these data actually confirm the countertrend that we have identified. We have selected two indicators from the data that seem particularly interesting for our purposes and are in agreement with our finding.

As summarised in Table 2, the percentage of people in Italy (aged three years or older) who use a computer daily reached its peak during the pandemic, and now has fallen back just as sharply; and the number of people who do not use computers, which was compressed during the pandemic, has returned almost to pre-pandemic values.

Table 2. Frequency of personal computer use in Italy among people aged 3 years and older

Year	Use PC daily (%)	Do not use PC (%)
2019	31.0	43.8
2020	32.7	43.2
2021	37.0	40.2
2022	32.9	42.2

(Source: Italian National Institute of Statistics, https://www.istat.it/it/cultura-comunicazione-viaggi?dati)

Finally, we focused our attention on data from an interview campaign that we administered to 378 parents of primary school children; 256 interviews took place between March and May 2022, half in-person and half on online platforms, while 122 were conducted in spring 2023, 77 in person and 45 online (average age 42 years; 81% female). The theme of the investigation was the use of technological devices by children, with a focus on time spent with the family and strategies adopted in educational management.

The data reported by the interviewees were treated with quantitative methods and descriptive intent, while the answers to the open-ended questions were analysed with the support of a qualitative research software (Weft QDA).

Even from the interviews, it seems possible to infer that the lockdown period did not affect early endowment either quantitatively or qualitatively. We can plausibly state that for the sample we intercepted, the phenomenon of early endowment was already in place before the pandemic and that, due to the pandemic containment, there has not been a real push to digital for those who were not yet properly equipped.

3. DISCUSSION

The data set out in the previous chapter, which come from field surveys of large samples of primary school pupils and a considerable sample of parents, as well as from the archives of the Italian National Institute of Statistics, converge to show that, despite the scenarios outlined in Chapter 1, the digital endowments of families of children currently attending the fifth grade of primary school, do not appear to have significantly increased as a result of measures to deal with the COVID-19 pandemic.

We would like to note that those children, who are in the fifth grade in the current school year, were already at school during the pandemic, although in the 2019-2020 school year—the one plagued by the lockdown—they were only in the first grade; it is therefore possible that not everyone had obtained the necessary tools, or even that some families had received them on free loan from the school and returned them at the end of the distance learning period.

This means that a non-negligible segment of families (as in Table 1, Column V) could have inadequate digital equipment to cope with a new lockdown period so as to undermine any new recourse to distance learning. Should this finding worry the educational world? What might happen if another pandemic wave calls for social distancing and online teaching again in the future?

Although the data just reviewed give us a panorama of households (in our Region) not dissimilar to that which preceded COVID-19, the answer to the question must recognise that the school world is surely far better equipped today in terms of devices and networks, software, and, most importantly, skills acquired by teachers and managers than during the 2020 lockdown.

This means that the response to a new pandemic event could be prompter and more effective and that the data we have examined should be used to devise early intervention protocols in favour of that segment of families who, probably for reasons linked to their socio-economic backgrounds, would go into lockdown lacking adequate tools to deal with it.

We are aware that the conclusions drawn are based on data collected in a rather limited area of our country. It should be noted, however, that they are consistent with the trends of the Italian National Institute of Statistics; in addition, if the hypothesis is correct that socio-economic conditions have an influence on the data we collected, then it is to be expected that in the rest of Italy the percentages of households with inadequate endowments are higher, given that our district lies in one of the more developed and richest areas in Western Europe.

Therefore, we believe that policymakers, educators and school principals who want to be ready to cope with a possible new domestic confinement period and the subsequent switch to emergency remote teaching and distance learning must pay close attention to the problem and not be misled by figures that, taken alone, might seem particularly high.

To work towards providing more solid evidence, two lines of future development of our research can be envisaged:

- First, despite the difficulties that can be imagined, we intend to investigate some socio-economic characteristics of the households considered (such as education, employment status, income and migratory background), and possibly other characteristics, for example related to the personality types of the parents, that might differentiate less digitally-inclined families from the rest;
- Second, we are planning to broaden the geographic base of the sample, to incorporate areas, and therefore families that are more disadvantaged from a socio-economic point of view (if this causal link emerges from the previous step).

ACKNOWLEDGEMENTS

We would like to thank all the students in the 'Primary Education' degree programme at the University of Bergamo for their help in administering our surveys. We also want to thank all the schools that graciously and patiently hosted our research assistants.

REFERENCES

Azubuike, O.B. et al. (2021). Who Gets to Learn in a Pandemic? Exploring the Digital Divide in Remote Learning during the COVID-19 Pandemic in Nigeria. In *International Journal of Educational Research Open*, Vol. 2, Art. 100022, doi: 10.1016/j.ijedro.2020.100022.

Beaunoyer, E. et al. (2020). COVID-19 and Digital Inequalities: Reciprocal Impacts and Mitigation Strategies. In *Computers in Human Behavior*, Vol. 111, Art. 106424, doi: 10.1016/j.chb.2020.106424.

Camerini, A.-L. et al. (2022). The Impact of Screen Time and Green Time on Mental Health in Children and Adolescents during the COVID-19 Pandemic. In *Computers in Human Behavior Reports*, Vol. 7, Art. 100204, doi: 10.1016/j.chbr.2022.100204.

Chiou, L. and Tucker, C. (2020). *Social Distancing, Internet Access and Inequality*. National Bureau of Economic Research, Cambridge, USA, doi: 10.3386/w26982.

Davies, S. (1979). *The Diffusion of Process Innovations*. Cambridge University Press, Cambridge, UK.

European Commission (2021). *2030 Digital Compass: the European Way for the Digital Decade*. European Commission, Brussels, Belgium.

Francis, D. V., and Weller, C. E. (2022). Economic Inequality, the Digital Divide, and Remote Learning during COVID-19. In *The Review of Black Political Economy*, Vol. 49, No. 1, pp. 41-60, doi: 10.1177/00346446211017797.

Istituto Nazionale di Statistica (ISTAT). (2023). Dati e microdati. In *Istat.It Cutura, comunicazione e viaggi*. https://www.istat.it/it/cultura-comunicazione-viaggi?dati. Accessed 6 Feb. 2024.

Lazzari, M. and Jacono Quarantino, M., eds. (2010). *Adolescenti tra piazze reali e piazze virtuali*. Sestante, Bergamo, Italy.

Martínez-Domínguez, M. and Fierros-González, I. (2022). Determinants of Internet Use by School-age Children: The Challenges for Mexico during the COVID-19 Pandemic. In *Telecommunications Policy*, Vol. 46, No. 1, Art. 102241, https://doi.org/10.1016/j.telpol.2021.102241.

Organisation for Economic Co-operation and Development (OECD). (2021). *The State of Global Education: 18 Months into the Pandemic*. OECD Publishing, Paris, France, doi: 10.1787/1a23bb23-en.

Pandya, A., and Lodha, P. (2021). Social Connectedness, Excessive Screen Time during COVID-19 and Mental Health: a Review of Current Evidence. In *Frontiers in Human Dynamics*, Vol. 3, Art. 684137, doi: 10.3389/fhumd.2021.684137.

Ramsetty, A. and Adams, C. (2020). Impact of the Digital Divide in the Age of COVID-19. In *Journal of the American Medical Informatics Association*, Vol. 27, No. 7, pp. 1147-1148, doi: 10.1093/jamia/ocaa078.

Rogers, E. M. and Shoemaker, F. F. (1971). *Communication of Innovations. A Cross-cultural Approach*. The Free Press, New York, USA.

Tso, W.W.Y. et al. (2022). Vulnerability and Resilience in Children during the COVID-19 Pandemic. In *European Child & Adolescent Psychiatry*, No. 31, pp. 161-176, doi: 10.1007/s00787-020-01680-8

Venkatesh, V. et al. (2003). User Acceptance of Information Technology: toward a Unified View. In *MIS Quarterly*, Vol. 27, No. 3, pp. 425-478, doi: 10.2307/30036540.

Whitelaw, S. et al. (2020). Applications of Digital Technology in COVID-19 Pandemic Planning and Response. In *The Lancet Digital Health*, Vol. 2, No. 8, pp. e435-e440, doi: 10.1016/S2589-7500(20)30142-4.

Wong, C.W. et al. (2021). Digital Screen Time during the COVID-19 Pandemic: Risk for a Further Myopia Boom? In *American Journal of Ophthalmology*, No. 223, pp. 333-337, doi: 10.1016/j.ajo.2020.07.034.

UTILIZING TECHNOLOGY IN A PROFESSIONAL DEVELOPMENT PROGRAM ON PROBLEM-SOLVING FOR FILIPINO MATHEMATICS TEACHERS

Chara Deanna F. Punzal, Lester C. Hao, Eden Delight P. Miro and Romina Ann S. Yap
Ateneo de Manila University, Quezon city, Philippines

ABSTRACT

This paper presents a report on a work-in-progress on utilizing technology in ProbSET, a problem-solving professional development program for Filipino mathematics teachers. It is part of a study that aims to utilize technology to transcend geographical gaps and to create more equity of access in problem-solving professional development for teachers and training for students. The paper first discusses details about the program and the principles guiding its use of technology. It then shares initial findings from the first iteration during School Year 2022-2023. Results show that participants were satisfied with the implementation of digital communication platforms in the program, while suggesting more onsite activities in the future. Likewise, the use of software in designing and solving geometry problems was very well-received by the teachers. The paper concludes with a brief remark on the future directions of the program with respect to technology utilization.

KEYWORDS

Problem-Solving, Professional Development, Educational Technology

1. INTRODUCTION

The revised Philippine K-10 mathematics curriculum espouses developing mathematically proficient and critical problem-solvers as the goal of mathematics teaching and learning in basic education (Department of Education, 2023). Local problem-solving programs have been conducted in support of achieving these goals, in which it was emphasized that successful high-level problem-solving requires excellent master teachers, among other factors such as cultural beliefs (Nebres & Lee-Chua, 2005). However, these programs are mostly organized and conducted in the National Capital Region (NCR); hence, teachers and students in other regions and provinces are not accorded much opportunity for such training and exposure.

Responding to the call to capacitate teachers and students outside the NCR in problem-solving, Ateneo de Manila University's Department of Mathematics (henceforth referred to as Ateneo) launched the Problem-Solving Enrichment and Training program (ProbSET) during the COVID-19 pandemic last April 2022. It is a professional development (PD) program on problem-solving harnessing technology to provide Filipino mathematics teachers access to excellent continuous learning opportunities and exposure to a network of problem-solving teachers across the country by forging partnerships with State Colleges and Universities (SUCs) and Department of Education (DepEd) divisions. The program aims to inculcate problem-solving ideals by fostering teachers as problem-solvers, thereby imparting pertinent ideas such as Pólya's (1981) problem-solving model (i.e., understanding the problem, devising a plan, carrying out the plan, checking and reflecting) and Schoenfeld's (1985) elements of successful problem-solving (i.e., resources, metacognition, beliefs, heuristics). In addition, the program also aspires to imbibe the critical problem-solving skills identified by Zeitz (2021), such as developing mental toughness (or grit), getting one's hands dirty, and viewing problems from various perspectives.

1.1 The Structure of ProbSET

During the pilot implementation of ProbSET in School Year 2022-2023, there were two main stages: ProbSET A, the Problem-Solving Enrichment component for teachers, and ProbSET B, the Problem-Solving Training component for senior high school students. Throughout the initial implementation, online synchronous sessions were held via Zoom; meanwhile, Facebook Messenger was utilized to facilitate communication among the organizers and participants. These digital platforms allowed non-NCR participants to be trained by Ateneo's pool of veteran problem-solving coaches who are mostly based in NCR.

In ProbSET A, high school and college instructors were exposed to mathematical problem-solving across different content strands, namely recreational problems, algebra, discrete mathematics, and geometry, in several online synchronous sessions. A session was then devoted to problem-solving tools and manipulatives, in which there was emphasis on using technology as a tool for problem-solving. To this, dynamic geometry software such as Desmos and Geogebra were utilized. To help the teacher-participants imbibe the appropriate mindset and acquire effective pedagogical skills in doing and teaching problem-solving, the main sessions of ProbSET A were led by content coaches from Ateneo.

On the other hand, ProbSET B centered on the teachers implementing their own online problem-solving classes in their respective communities, therefore providing opportunities for their local students to gain experience and exposure to the content and ideals of mathematical problem-solving. This stage also featured sessions in which the speakers were the coaches from Ateneo. ProbSET B culminated with the ProbSET Olympiad, the only activity in the project's pilot implementation that was conducted in a hybrid manner. While each locality's teachers and students were gathered onsite, each site was connected to a central Zoom meeting facilitated by Ateneo's team. In this activity, students participated in a small-scale problem-solving competition. This not only aimed to foster camaraderie among the students (and even their teachers), but also to celebrate the spirit of problem-solving as a community.

1.2 The Present Paper

The present paper is a work-in-progress report about utilizing technology in ProbSET across two school years, of which the focus is two-fold: the use of digital communication platforms to deliver the training sessions and facilitate the program, and the implementation of educational technology to do mathematical problem-solving. This forms part of a research endeavor on acquiring insights in harnessing technology to transcend geographical gaps and to create more equity of access in problem-solving PD programs for teachers and training for students.

2. CONCEPTUAL UNDERPINNINGS

The use of technology in ProbSET is grounded on the principle that technology, when strategically utilized and implemented, indeed provides teachers more meaningful opportunities to participate and collaborate in an online PD program. This is further supported by the technological pedagogical content knowledge (TPCK) framework, an important conceptual underpinning of the present study.

2.1 Technology and its Affordances on Problem-Solving

The advancement of technology across hardware and software (and even *peopleware*) offered more possibilities and opportunities for its integration into the mathematics classroom, particularly with regard to the teaching and learning of problem-solving (Kariadinata et al., 2017; Amornrit, 2019). This was especially true in the advent of the shift towards educational modality brought about by the coronavirus contagion. It was found that teachers value and believe in the potential that information and communication technology (ICT) has in improving their pedagogy, as long as sufficient training and development is provided (Kaur, 2019). To this, the affordances provided by improvements in ICT allowed for teacher PD programs to be conducted online without consequence to training quality (Meletiou-Mavrotheris, 2012).

2.2 Technological Pedagogical Content Knowledge

The TPCK framework is built upon Shulman's (1987) framework for teacher's pedagogical content knowledge. Mishra and Koehler (2006, p. 1025) emphasize that the TPCK's focus is on "the connections, interactions, affordances, and constraints between and among content, pedagogy, and technology". They further argued that TPCK is tantamount to teachers being equipped with the appropriate technological know-how on representing and teaching content matter using technological tools. Hence, teachers should not only possess knowledge on subject matter and teaching strategies so as to effectively deliver the specific content across to learners. In maximizing the utilization of technology in the teaching-learning experience, teachers are thus required to have a good understanding of how technological tools (both hardware and software) can possibly aid in addressing the issues students face.

3. METHODOLOGY

The present study utilizes an exploratory research design, specifically in the form of an informal exploratory study (Swedberg, 2020). In such a study, the goal is to garner insights and to generate new ideas; hence, the sample size can be small. In addition, the results of exploratory research may be utilized as the foundation for future research projects (George, 2022).

Several sources of data were used for the present study. An online survey questionnaire was distributed to consenting teachers and students. They were asked to rate their level of satisfaction on the implementation of digital platforms and to provide their thoughts on the program's setup. In addition, interviews and focus group discussions were also held with the coaches, teachers, and students. Quantitative data from the survey instrument were analyzed using frequency counts. As for the qualitative data, content analysis was used; it is a method of qualitative analysis in which themes are generated through the coding and categorization of significant statements (Erlingsson & Brysiewicz, 2017). Significant statements were identified from the survey and interviews, which were then coded and categorized before generating pertinent themes.

4. INITIAL FINDINGS

In this section, we share our findings on the use of digital communication platforms and educational software from the initial implementation of the program. The respondents consisted of 7 coaches and mentors from Ateneo, together with 15 teachers and 18 students from three non-NCR institutions.

4.1 Digital Platforms and Modality

As previously mentioned, Zoom was used for all synchronous training sessions across the different stages, whereas Facebook Messenger was the primary communication platform among the organizers and participants. As shown in Table 1, 14 of 18 students, together with all 15 teachers, expressed satisfaction with the implementation of the aforementioned platforms. Quoting a teacher on the perceived strength of the program: "Communication is consistent and you really know that the team is doing their best in this project." In addition, coaches from Ateneo expressed that the use of Zoom allowed them to reach out to teachers and students in other provinces and regions, therefore making it much easier to nurture talent outside NCR.

Table 1. Participants' level of satisfaction on the implementation of digital platforms

Respondent	Very Dissatisfied	Dissatisfied	Satisfied	Very Satisfied	Total
Teachers	0	0	1	14	15
Students	1	3	9	5	18

Two themes from the qualitative data, gratitude and challenges, highlight how most of the participants were satisfied with the implementation of digital platforms, but had contrasting thoughts on the online modality of ProbSET. In terms of gratitude, participants acknowledged and appreciated the opportunities brought about by ProbSET's setup, as it allowed them not only to be trained by expert coaches, but also to collaborate and interact with their fellow Filipino teachers and students who are based in other provinces or regions. To this, a student remarked: "It's really interactive, I'm learning from the coaches and my co-participants." Moreover, teachers also noted how they learned strategies to teach problem-solving and to do such in a virtual environment during ProbSET A. The aforementioned corroborate ProbSET's ideal of promoting equitable access to capacity-building programs, especially in enhancing problem-solving skills.

On the other hand, the theme on challenges echoes how some teachers and students recommend more onsite sessions for ProbSET B, should the COVID-19 pandemic restrictions fully ease. They remarked that the virtual environment, along with infrastructural issues, such as intermittent internet connectivity or power supply, hampered their experience of teaching and learning problem-solving. To illustrate, a student wrote in the survey: "There were many that had internet connection problems that caused them to either can't join the meetings or leave mid-session." Moreover, from a pedagogical standpoint, coaches and teachers alike lamented how it was quite a challenge during training sessions to elicit feedback from participants and to identify those who need more support.

4.2 Utilizing Software for Mathematical Problem-Solving

One of the PD sessions in ProbSET A during the initial implementation centered on training teachers on using technology to foster problem-solving skills and attitudes. Geometry was chosen as the content strand to develop teachers' TPCK and to deliver the problem-solving experience through the use of GeoGebra and Desmos (i.e., the technology component). It could also be argued that to an extent, the actual mathematical content delivered in the session was problem-solving, in which geometry was utilized to demonstrate it. Lastly, pedagogy focused on the coach actively modeling the problem-solving ideals, and also included demonstrating to teachers the possible scripts they may use when eliciting student ideas or providing encouraging remarks, as inspired by the lesson plans by Toh et al. (2011).

To illustrate the aforementioned, we share a task posed by the coach in which the participants had to set up the problem using Geogebra. They were asked to create a dynamic representation of the problem "Let circles Γ_1, Γ_2 be tangent to one another at *P*. *A* line through *P* intersects Γ_1, Γ_2 at B_1, B_2 respectively. Prove that triangle $A_1PB_1 \sim \Delta A_2PB_2$." The participants were observed to initially make two arbitrary circles that intersect at a point, as shown in Figures 1(a) and 1(b). It was immediately apparent that at certain instances, the two circles may overlap or would be intersecting at two points and would not be tangent. A participant then suggested that after Γ_1 and point P are drawn, the center of Γ_2 should be determined first on a line that passes through the center of Γ_1 and the supposed point of tangency P. Then, circle Γ_2 should be drawn from the new point to the point of tangency P, as shown in Figure 1(c). This is an accurate illustration since even if points are moved on the software interface, the two circles remain tangent. This was a short exercise on problem solving since the activity posed smaller hurdles with nonroutine and possibly varied solutions.

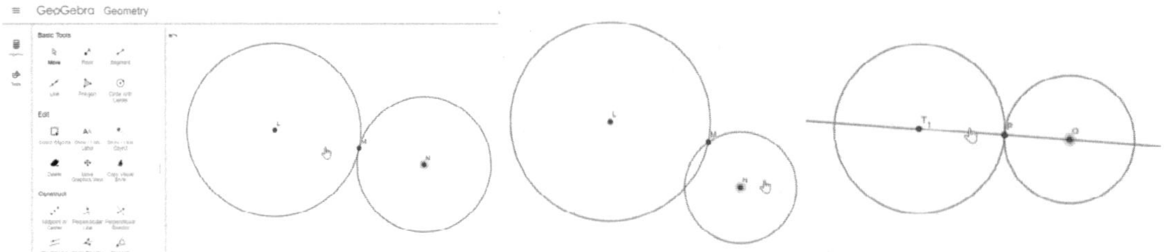

(a) (b) (c)

Figure 1. The participants' attempts in representing the given problem on Geogebra

Qualitative data reveal that the session was very well-received by the teachers, receiving positive remarks in terms of the session being insightful and interactive. One teacher wrote: "This session was an eye-opener. I never thought that math app[s] such as GeoGebra or Desmos could be that helpful." This is supported by the survey results as can be seen in Table 2; teachers were asked to rate their level of agreement towards several statements pertinent to the session. Despite the positive feedback, a few hoped that the session could have been longer, so as to have ample time to strategize and design their solutions to more complex geometry problems using the software.

Table 2. Teachers' level of agreement on statements about the session on using technology for problem-solving (n = 15)

Statement	Strongly Disagree	Disagree	Agree	Strongly Agree
The coach was effective in delivering content.	0	0	0	15
The coach included a variety of heuristics and strategies problem-solving.	0	0	1	14
The coach demonstrated appropriate teaching strategies.	0	0	0	15
The content discussed was appropriate to developing my problem-solving skills.	0	0	0	15
The content discussed varied in terms of strategies/heuristics.	0	0	1	14

5. MOVING FORWARD

For the iteration of ProbSET in School Year 2023-2024, the general structure is retained, along with each stage's purpose. However, preparations for ProbSET B shall be held fully onsite at Ateneo in January 2024. The onsite sessions will feature several workshops that will further strengthen the presence of technology in problem-solving. One workshop will focus on developing computational thinking, while another will concentrate on problem posing. A separate workshop will be organized in which both coaches and participants will share their best practices with the digital mathematical tools they use. Lastly, in ProbSET B, teachers will be provided the flexibility to conduct their own local problem-solving classes in in either onsite or online modalities, or a combination of both.

REFERENCES

Amornrit, P. (2019). Using OER through open educational practices to enhance creative problem solving skills. *In Proceedings of ICEMT 2019*. ACM, Nagoya, Japan, pp. 197-200. https://doi.org/10.1145/3345120.3345145

Department of Education [DepEd]. (2023). *Matatag Curriculum: Mathematics Grades 1, 4 and 7.* DepEd, Manila, Philippines.

Erlingsson, C. and Brysiewicz, P. (2017). A hands-on guide to doing content analysis. *African Journal of Emergency Medicine,* Vol. 7, No. 3, pp. 93-99. http://doi.org/10.1016/j.afjem.2017.08.001

George, T. (2022). *Exploratory research | Definition, guide, & examples*. Retrieved from https://www.scribbr.com/methodology/exploratory-research/

Kariadinata, R. et al. (2017). The implementation of GeoGebra software-assisted DDFC instructional model for improving students' Van-Hiele geometry thinking skill. *In Proceedings of ICEMT 2017*. ACM, Singapore, 58-62. https://doi.org/10.1145/3124116.3124129

Kaur, M. (2019). ICT in teacher education: Examining perceptions, needs and attitudes of prospective teachers. *In Proceedings of TEEM'19*. ACM, León, Spain, 4 pages. http://doi.org/10.1145/3362789.3362917

Meletiou-Mavrotheris, M. (2012). Online communities of practice as vehicles for teacher professional development. In A. Juan et al. (Eds.), *Teaching mathematics online: Emergent technologies and methodologies*. IGI Global, USA, pp. 142-166. http://doi.org/10.4018/978-1-60960-875-0.ch007

Mishra P. and Koehler, M. (2006). Technological pedagogical content knowledge: A framework for teacher knowledge. *Teachers College Record* Vol. 108, No. 6, pp. 1017-1054.

Nebres, B. F. and Lee-Chua, Q. N. (2005). Successful high-level problem solving in the Philippines. *In Proceedings of the Third East Asia Regional Conference on Mathematics Education* (EARCOME 3), Shanghai, China.

Pólya, G. (1981). *Mathematical discovery: An understanding, learning, and teaching problem solving* (Combined Edition). John Wiley & Sons, USA.

Schoenfeld, A. H. (1985). *Mathematical problem solving*. Elsevier, London.

Shulman, L. (1987). Knowledge and teaching: Foundation of the new reform. *Harvard Educational Review*, Vol. 57, pp. 1-21.

Swedberg, R. (2020). Exploratory research. In C. Elman et al. (Eds.), *The production of knowledge: Enhancing progress in social science (Strategies for social inquiry)*. Cambridge University Press, pp. 17-41. http://doi.org/10.1017/9781108762519.002

Zeitz, P. (2021). *Art and Craft of Problem Solving*. John Wiley & Sons, USA.

COMMOGNITIVE CONFLICTS IN A VIRTUAL LEARNING ENVIRONMENT: EXPLORING THE AFFORDANCES OF MOBILE LEARNING FOR DISCOURSE ANALYSIS

Mark N. Cumayas and Maria Alva Q. Aberin
Ateneo de Manila University
Quezon City, Philippines

ABSTRACT

This paper explores the affordances of mobile learning in developing frameworks for discourse analysis. Specifically, this paper examines the commognitive analysis of classroom discourses in virtual learning environments (VLEs) and how it resolves the challenges of discourse analysis in face-to-face (F2F) settings. With the ongoing social turn of mathematics education research comes the widespread adoption of discourse analysis in educational research. The shift towards virtual learning technologies necessitated by the recent COVID-19 crisis has led to the development of various tools and processes that enable the teaching-learning process to occur in the virtual environment. While the initial drive to adapt these tools has since subsided, the advantages of utilizing them remain apparent. As the teaching-learning process moves into virtual environments, so should research methodologies. As part of a broader study that attempts to develop a framework for characterizing commognitive conflicts and the corresponding teacher actions, this paper presents insights from the initial phases in the framework development process where a virtual learning environment was used to examine the integrity of the discourse analytic framework. This paper will discuss how the framework development benefited from using a virtual learning environment—how it mitigated the challenges of discursive approaches and the unique insights it offers for refining the framework compared to applying the framework directly in face-to-face classroom settings. Results from this work suggest that essential components of the mobile learning experience, such as VLEs, are advantageous to the development of discursive research approaches, such as in the case of developing a framework for identifying commognitive conflicts.

KEYWORDS

Commognition, Commognitive Conflict, VLE, Discourse Analysis

1. INTRODUCTION

Recent decades have seen the focus of mathematics education research (MER) shifting towards the social aspect of the teaching-learning process. For one, there has been a proliferation of theories concerning mathematics education that has grown from socially oriented fields of studies such as anthropology, sociology, and psychology. This is what Lerman (2000) refers to as the 'social turn' in mathematics education research. This might be driven by the impetus of interests in the 'learning' half of the teaching-learning process early in the 21st century. This 'learnification of education' (Biesta, 2009), while not problematic per se, has led to an imbalance that has muddled up the purpose and direction of mathematics education. In response, researchers have begun employing methodological approaches that center on the interaction between the students and the teacher rather than on the performance of the 'learner' alone. One evidence of this is the growing trend in the use of discourse analysis as an approach to mathematics education research. However, the use of discursive approach in research is not without challenges.

Attempting to capture various components of social interaction during classroom instruction is filled with many challenges. For one, faithfully capturing classroom interaction requires the use of multiple devices such as video-cameras and audio-recorders which adds to the cost of doing research. To clearly capture both the teacher's and the students' contributions, there is a need to use multiple audio-recorders placed strategically inside the classrooms. There is also the need to capture non-verbal actions, hence, the rise of videorecording as a method of data collection. Another concern is the comfort that participants while being involved in a recorded interaction. Known to most as the Hawthorne effect, this concern poses a risk on the integrity of the data gathered. Then, even with a faithful copy of the social interactions in the classroom, there lies the daunting task of discourse analysis. As teachers know too well, the classroom is seldom a one-to-one correspondence with a student at a time. Rather, classroom interactions fall under the category of multichannel communication. Hence, there is the challenge of keeping track of who-said-what on top of the task of analyzing what is being said.

In this regard, this paper presents how employing a discourse analysis framework to characterize a virtual learning session led to benefits in comparison with directly using conducting analysis of classroom instruction in a face-to-face setting. Results from studies that attempted to capture instances of commognitive conflicts during mathematics instruction will be used to illustrate the affordances provided by the VLEs in the development of discourse analytic tools as compared to F2F settings.

1.1 MER in Virtual Learning

During the COVID-19 crisis, educational institutions were pushed to adopt new modes of instructional delivery. This has led to the development of various tools and practices that enabled mass adoption and the continuation of education. One such practice is the employment of mobile learning through virtual learning environments using teleconferencing programs like zoom and google meet. While the initial drive for utilizing these tools for instructional purposes have since subsided, the advantages of having them even as optional cannot be understated. On top of that, many education providers such as universities has had to invest a great deal both in the development of resource materials and the training of their educators. To leave all that behind would clearly be a waste. It is for these reasons that distance education, in its various forms, is becoming a staple in many educational institutions. Universities that once shrugged even at the idea of virtual learning now offers it as an option especially for graduate studies and professional development. The Department of Education in the Philippines has since institutionalized the use of alternative delivery modes in the even that face-to-face instruction becomes less viable due to inclement weather conditions amongst other reasons. Rising above the pandemic has led the educational landscape forward with no going back.

As the educational landscape embraces this new normal, it would only be sound for educational research to do the same. With much of mathematics instruction happening virtually, so must mathematics education research look upon the affordances of virtual learning for informing our process of knowledge production. The call herein is not merely to conduct research on mobile learning in virtual learning environments. In fact, most of the critical decisions for education in the pandemic were made possible only through the works of researchers who have previously conducted educational research on innovative platforms. Rather, what is being suggested here is to look upon how mobile learning and particularly VLEs can inform our research practices—including the development and refining of theoretical frameworks and research methods. Novel tools for education are in of themselves novel tools for educational research.

The next section describes an endeavor driven by this insight. It involves the development of an operative characterization of the construct of commognitive conflict as it occurs during mathematics instruction. The conceptualization of the construct is then appraised through a characterization of interaction during mathematics instruction in mobile learning in comparison to that of an f2f setting.

1.2 Sfard's Theory of Commognition

Sfard's commognitive theory of mathematical thinking is one of the paradigms in mathematics education that utilizes a discursive approach to research. As a 'home-grown' theory—that is, developed from within mathematics education research—commognition attempts to fuse the dualistic view of behavior and thought by focusing on the human act of communicating. As such, the term 'commognition' is a portmanteau of the words communication and cognition (Sfard, 2008) suggesting that these communicating and thinking may be explored as visages of the same phenomenon. Thus, in the tradition following this theory, analysis is centered on the discourses between actors within a context which may involve a lone actor interacting with themselves.

Studies in mathematics education within this tradition aims to characterize changes in the mathematical discourse. This demands a high level of fidelity in capturing the interactions during classroom interactions. A researcher who wishes to follow this tradition is enjoined to adhere to a few principles in the analysis of data

(Sfard, 2018). The principle of wholeness means that the entire discourse must be taken in whole as the unit of analysis instead of its constituent structures. There is also the principle of operationality which demands a definition of codes based on perceptually accessible qualities and the principle of alternating perspective where a researcher must be conscious of how their own discourse contributes to the analysis of the discourses of the participants. All these research principles present a unique set of challenges to the commognitive researcher.

1.3 Commognitive Conflicts

Sfard (2008) defines commognitive conflict as a 'situation that arises when communication occurs across incommensurable discourses' (p.296). Since communication can be both *interpersonal* (between two or more individuals) or *intrapersonal* (within an individual), so could commognitive conflicts. To illustrate, a student whose only experience with multiplication is within the discourse of whole numbers subscribes to the narrative that multiplying makes numbers bigger. However, when the teacher introduces the concept of fractions within the discourse of integers, this narrative may fail to hold. Hence, the student may experience commognitive conflict when dealing with fractions. A student may then correct compute ½ x ¾ = 3/8 but still believes that 3/8 is bigger than either ½ or ¾ since 'multiplying makes bigger'. This points to an intrapersonal commognitive conflict. The significance of commognitive conflicts in pedagogy lies in the notion that learning occurs through discursive change resulting from the resolution of commognitive conflicts through various teacher discursive moves.

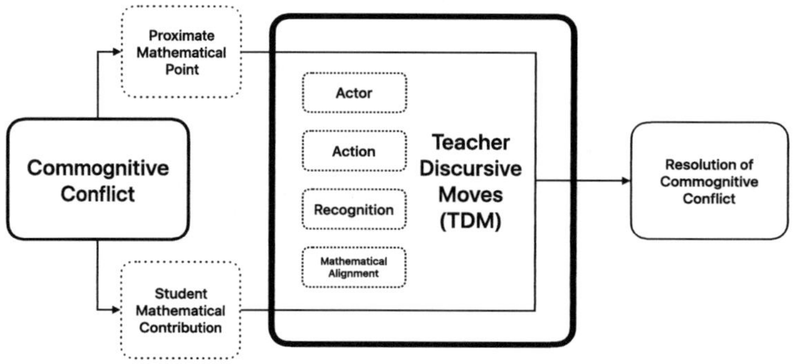

Figure 1. Resolution of Commognitive Conflicts through Teacher Discursive Moves

To aid in identifying commognitive conflicts, this study borrows the notions of *student mathematics* and *mathematical point* from Van Zoest and colleagues' (2022) Teacher Response Coding (TRC) Scheme. The difficulty of identifying commognitive conflicts during classroom instruction stems from the act of extracting two ideas from a student's mathematical contribution. What appears clear in theory is more elusive during commognitive analysis of a classroom instruction. The multimodal nature of communicative actions makes identifying commognitive conflicts a challenge during instruction. Factor in the multichannel communication that goes inside a face-to-face classroom setting and the challenge grows exponentially. Hence, this study turns to different platforms for assessing the viability of this conceptualization of commognitive conflicts.

2. COMMOGNITIVE CONFLICTS IN CLASSROOM DISCOURSES

This section examines the affordances of utilizing mobile learning for refining a framework for identifying commognitive conflicts during classroom discourse. It does through a comparison between commognitive analyses of classroom discourses from an F2F setting and from a mobile learning setting. The section begins with a brief overview of the methodology used for both the studies. Finally, the affordances of employing the conceptual framework against a session of virtual learning is discussed including the difficulties that the platform help mitigate and other unique insights from this endeavor.

2.1 Methodology

Results from the commognitive analyses of classroom discourses from two sessions will be discussed—one in an f2f setting and another in a mobile learning setting. Both these studies utilize commognitive analysis to identify commognitive conflicts in a classroom discourse. Another similarity is in the number of participants for each study which helps highlight the difference in commognitive analysis between the two studies.

The f2f classroom discourse is from a case study focusing on a remediation class in a public secondary school in the Philippines. The class consists of one teacher and six students in Grade 7. There were three sessions of classroom observations with around 40 minutes to 60 minutes of class time. Observations for each session were audio recorded and transcribed. The mobile learning classroom discourse study follows a qualitative interpretive approach to identify commognitive conflicts in a virtual learning class session. The topic is part of a mathematics class in a Problem Solving and Investigations in Mathematics course. There are 6 participants in total including 1 mathematics instructor and 5 students. The class was conducted using zoom which provided the recording of the sessions. Each recording was transcribed and commognitive analysis was conducted aimed at identifying commognitive conflicts.

2.2 Identifying Commognitive Conflicts in an F2F Classroom Discourse

As a pilot test for the framework on identifying commognitive conflicts on classroom discourse, a case study was conducted on a remediation mathematics class in a face-to-face setting. A remediation class was selected for the pilot since there are fewer students (six, in this instance) in the group compared to actual classroom teaching (usually 40-50 students, in a typical Filipino class). The small number allows for the researcher to capture more clearly the discourse between the teacher and the students and consequently, in theory at least, would have helped focus on evaluating the capacity of framework to capture commognitive conflicts within the discourse. However, even with the small number of participants, challenges to commognitive analysis remains evident in f2f classroom settings. One clear challenge is the multichannel flow of discourse in a face-to-face classroom, that is, the conversational turns tangent to different individuals throughout the discussion. This leads to a difficulty in tracking the commognitive conflicts in individuals as well as how the teacher responds to each one of them. While this paper recognizes that there are practical benefits to acknowledging this challenge in actual classroom instruction, the purpose of the pilot study which is to evaluate how effectively the framework capture instances of commognitive conflicts gets buried under the work of tracing the flow of responses. On top of that, there is the issue of positioning the devices for capturing the discourse of both the teacher and the students. There are instances where relevant conversational turns are overshadowed by noise from students closer to the devices. Clearly this issue can be resolved by additional devices, however, resources may not be as easily accessible in a pilot testing than with a full study. Furthermore, additional devices are needed to capture the visual elements such as responses written in the board along with other non-verbal cues which affects the flow of meaning in the discourse. Then there is the issue of participants' comfort to being surveilled. More commonly known as the *Hawthorne effect*, students—and even teachers—act differently when they become conscious of being recorded. This potentially muddies the integrity of the pilot testing which hinders the effective evaluation of the framework's effectiveness.

Acknowledging these barriers to the assessment of the framework for identifying commognitive conflicts, the researcher decided to turn to other platforms to pilot the use of the framework. The next section discusses the potential of mobile learning as an avenue to refine frameworks for discourse analysis.

2.3 Affordances of Mobile Learning for Commognitive Analysis

The use of a virtual learning platform to assess the viability of the conceptualization of commognitive conflicts showed promising potential. There are three direct advantages gathered from this endeavor. For one, the video-conferencing platform of choice, Zoom, already has a recording function built in. The process of capturing the class interactions is already embedded in the virtual learning environment. With this, researchers planning to employ discursive approaches to their work can do so without needing to invest in auxiliary devices for video or audio recording. Another benefit is related to the integrated recording of class interaction. Since the participants are already aware of that their participation is being recorded, this reduces the effect caused by the discomfort of being observed. While it can be argued that knowledge of being recorded in virtual learning may discourage participation, those who participate do so willingly with less discomfort if not none at all. This means that the quality of data from the participation of those who do participate could be better than that of those who are being recorded in face-to-face settings.

There are also benefit for the analysis beyond the fidelity of the data gathered. In particular, the limitation of videoconferencing tools such as zoom along with tacit etiquettes of having only one person speak at a time makes it easier to analysis the interactions during classroom instruction. This makes it easier for the analysis to track the switch in conversational turns between participants during the interaction. One practice during virtual learning is the presentation of the content during instruction. This way, the content being discussed is recorded alongside the discussion and the interaction between the students and the instructor. This allows the analysis to keep the context in mind when analyzing the communicative actions.

3. CONCLUSION

This paper shows the potential of utilizing mobile learning platforms as a tool to inform the development of operational definitions and frameworks for discourse analysis. Leveraging the recording functions embedded in virtual learning environments for data gathering can increase cost efficiency in educational research and improve the fidelity of the data gathered. This also makes the experience less intrusive for the participants. At the current pace of advancements in educational technology, novel platforms such as mobile learning are not going away. It is high time to capitalize on how these technologies can help inform our practices in mathematics education research.

REFERENCES

Biesta, G. (2009). Good education in an age of measurement: On the need to reconnect with the question of purpose in education. Educational Assessment, Evaluation and Accountability (Formerly: Journal of Personnel Evaluation in Education), 21(1), 33–46. https://doi.org/10.1007/s11092-008-9064-9

Leatham, K. R., Peterson, B. E., Stockero, S. L., & Zoest, L. R. V. (2015). Conceptualizing Mathematically Significant Pedagogical Opportunities to Build on Student Thinking. Journal for Research in Mathematics Education, 46(1), 88–124. https://doi.org/10.5951/jresematheduc.46.1.0088

Lerman, S. (2000). The social turn in mathematics education research. Multiple Perspectives on Mathematics Teaching and Learning, 1, 19–44.

Sfard, A. (2008). Thinking as Communicating: Human Development, the Growth of Discourses, and Mathematizing. Cambridge University Press.

Sfard, A. (2018). Commognition. In S. Lerman (Ed.), Encyclopedia of Mathematics Education (pp. 1–7). Springer International Publishing. https://doi.org/10.1007/978-3-319-77487-9_100031-1

Van Zoest, L. R., Peterson, B. E., Rougée, A. O. T., Stockero, S. L., Leatham, K. R., & Freeburn, B. (2022). Conceptualizing important facets of teacher responses to student mathematical thinking. International Journal of Mathematical Education in Science and Technology, 53(10), 2583–2608. https://doi.org/10.1080/0020739X.2021.1895341

IMPACT OF A GROWTH MINDSET INSTRUCTION ON MOBILE LEARNING IN GRADUATE TEACHER EDUCATION

Yuliang Liu
Phd, Southern Illinois University Edwardsville, USA

ABSTRACT

Online education should foster a growth mindset to promote active mobile learning in graduate education. This proposal describes how the author has used a growth mindset to deliver his online graduate educational technology course in a midwestern public university in the United States in an eight-week course in fall 2023. The author with over 20 years experiences of online instruction will share how he has used several deliberate and structured practices to properly foster a growth mindset to engage and challenge learners to maximize mobile instruction and learning in graduate students in education. The presentation has potential implications for online education internationally.

KEYWORDS

Growth Mindset, Engage, Challenge, Online, Mobile Learning

1. INTRODUCTION

Online education has grown rapidly in recent decades. However, there is a misconception about online courses. That is, many learners think it is easier to take online courses. In fact it is not true, and online courses are harder and more time-consuming for both students and the instructor. As online adult learners, they will have to spend a fair amount of time studying weekly in order to successfully complete the requirements of online courses. Therefore, it's not surprising that there is a high dropout in online education, compared with the traditional in-person instruction.

Lots of research has indicated that online discussion has been widely used to encourage learners' interactive communication. Such an emphasis will not only help learners exchange information, but also enable and promote learners' reflection of their own understanding and connections between theory and practice or experience, as well as promote peer learning from each other (Gasparič & Pečar, 2016). However, according to Stott (2016), many online courses in higher education involving "poor levels of student engagement pose challenges to institutions, instructors and learners" (p. 51). Recent research has indicated that there are various ways to address the poor levels of student engagement in online courses in higher education.

This study emphasizes the examination of fostering a growth mindset technique to promote online graduate learners' learning. Based on Dweck (2015), fixed and growth mindsets are quite different mindsets, and they can be changed from fixed to growth. The growth mindset was intended to help close achievement gaps in learners, not hide them. When online educators face challenges in the course, they should ask students lots of related questions, then accept those related thoughts and feelings, work and keep working with and through them instead of avoiding them.

This study reports a practical action research project that aimed to examine how the author has fostered a growth mindset in his recent teaching to promote online learning in graduate students in education. The author has over 20 years' experience of online instruction. He has employed several deliberate and structured practices to properly foster a growth mindset to engage and challenge learners to maximize online instruction and learning in graduate students in education. Those are primarily related to the asynchronous online discussion on the discussion board and weekly blogs submissions in Blackboard for learners to complete course assignments. In addition, students were required to write term papers related to the course.

1.1 Research Questions

The purpose of this study was to investigate the impact of fostering a growth mindset to promote graduate students' mobile learning. The study analyzed related qualitative data to examine whether the author's weekly use of growth mindset instructional method had helped engage and challenge online graduate learners in mobile learning. Two specific research questions guiding the study were:

1. RQ1: How did online learners perceive the impact of the instructional strategy of growth mindset on their learning?
2. RQ2: How did the strategy of growth mindset impact online students' learning outcomes?

2. METHOD

2.1 Participants

Participants were from a graduate educational technology teacher education course at a midwestern public university in the United States in the first 8 weeks of fall semester 2023. The course entitled "Foundational Issues for Educational Technology Specialists" is one of the ten required courses in the master's degree. The students involved ten full-time in-service teachers. Seven were females and three were males. All were Caucasians. Their ages varied in the 20s to 40s. The author of the study was the instructor who taught the course and who had not taught the course previously since it was a newly added course to the curriculum.

2.2 Research Design and Instructional Intervention

The research design in the study was the individual's practical action research (Gay et al. 2012) since the author planned to improve the capacity and subsequent practices. The learning management system used in the course was the Blackboard. There was no required textbook. All course readings primarily included related journal articles, book chapters, and videos per week. Course assignments included weekly discussion posts and peer reviews, weekly blog posts, two separate reflection papers, and a final paper of educational technology philosophy.

Major instructional practices included, but were not limited to: the instructor required all students to read and electronically sign the Faculty Expectations Message (FEM) on the first class day in the Blackboard. Then, the online instructional approach started with learners' initial written reflection posts based on the assigned readings and personal experience, then followed by the instructor's challenging questions based on the Socratic method and learners' written responses to those questions. The questioning method was primarily based on Golding's (2011) community of inquiry model. This method included discipline-specific questioning, creating a community where learners replied to the instructor's and learners' questions through modelling and facilitation, as well as promoting the instructor's thinking-encouraging approach. In addition, for the weekly discussions and blogs, the author provided additional detailed thoughts and resources in the feedback for students to keep on thinking beyond the black box, rather than just provided students the correct or direct answers.

2.3 Data Collection

The author conducted an anonymous online mid-point course evaluation survey including three open-ended questions to collect qualitative data in the third week. The three questions were (1) "What have you learned so far?," (2) "What have you liked so far?," and (3) "Any suggestions for instructional improvement in the rest of the semester?" Six students responded to the survey. He then presented a summary of the midpoint survey for sharing in the Blackboard. Although some students mentioned that the course assignments were challenging and overwhelming, no major suggestions were offered. In addition, the author found some interesting and positive results from grading the course assignments including weekly posts, weekly blogs, and philosophy paper. Finally, results of the university's student evaluation indicated that students liked the focused application to their current teaching careers, with the means of mostly 4 and 5 in all of the 10 multiple choice items.

3. RESULTS

The results from data mentioned previously were consistent. That is, overall, learners were surprisingly very positive about the online innovative reflection and questioning instructional methods used. The innovative instructional intervention used in the study was effective.

First, the qualitative data from the midpoint survey involved the thematic analysis, which is the most common form of analysis in qualitative research (Gay et al. 2012). Its results showed that all feedback was positive and no major suggestion was offered. So the author did not change any instructional strategies in the second half of the semester. Major related excerpts included as follows: "…I fully believe that Dr. L is interested in helping me learn…."; "…I have no concerns or advice for Dr. L. He is respectful and responsive to emails and questions. I have enjoyed taking courses with him as my professor…."

Second, based on students' course assignments, all students indicated that they learned a lot from the course although they felt the course was difficult. Sample excerpts included as follows: "…I feel like I'm learning a lot…."; "...I like how he has us read the information and finds many ways for us to retain the information. This includes the discussions boards and the weekly blogs. Therefore, I am very happy with this class…."; "…It is nice to have a professor who actually responds to messages in a timely manner and puts forth the communication needed for a class…."

Further, a careful analysis of the learners' qualitative data indicated two major themes below.

1. Learners worked hard to write and post the journal article and reading reflection essays and blogs online based on the topic and question prompts by the deadline. It is clear that learners enjoyed such assignments and were motivated to find additional articles and sources related to their own interests and to make connections between the articles/sources and their own experience or observations accordingly. A majority of learners' posts were of high quality and received a grade of "A" based on the assessment rubrics.

2. Learners enjoyed being challenged to work hard to address and reply to the content-specific challenging questions from the instructor and the peers accordingly every week. Generally, they exhibited higher order thinking in their peer reviewing and critiquing every week using reflection, questioning, organization, applications, connections, and synthesis. In addition, they engaged in critical reflections of their own work and work of their peers by giving and receiving positive and negative feedback that leads to furthering their thinking in the field. A majority of learners' responses to the instructor's and peers' questions every week were of high quality and detailed, as well as received a grade of "A" based on the assessment rubrics.

4. DISCUSSION

As indicated in the above "Results" section, both research questions were clearly answered. That is, first, most online learners favorably perceived the impact of a growth mindset instructional strategy on their learning. Most students not only liked positive challenging feedback, but they also got used to like constructive feedback about the assignments from the instructor and the peers. The constructive feedback including challenging questions was good at enabling dialog and reciprocity among the instructor and the students, connecting to learners' personal experiences and expressing their own opinions, as well as providing learners opportunities to comment on their own experiences led to more monolog exchanges.

Second, the strategy of a growth mindset positively and actively impacted online students' learning outcomes. All students made meaningful connections to their work while taking the course. Sampe learning outcome excerpts from students included as follows. "….IT-590 was a class that I talked to my co-workers about daily. I shared pieces of information from articles, gave data that supported specific components of technology and even allowed me to discuss that research data is often tied back to what the researcher wanted…."

4.1 Limitations and Implications for Future Research

Similar to other studies, this study has its limitations too. The study only focused on one instructor in a small online graduate course among a group of homogenous participants in education. It primarily focused on the online learners' perception of the impacts of online reflection assignments and the instructor's growth mindset strategy. Therefore, further research is needed to better understand the long-term impact of such an instructional technique across the disciplines in the world.

5. CONCLUSION

Having recently used the growth mindset instructional method and witnessed its positive effects described previously, the author likes this approach more and more due to several reasons. First, it engages learners actively and deeply in discipline. The constructive and challenging feedback forced learners to go beyond traditional thinking and to think deeply and critically for alternative possibilities. Second, it is a rewarding experience as an instructor and a researcher to see how learners have grown professionally by being intellectually challenged in the class all the time. The results of student assignments indicated that the use of growth mindset instructional method was very effective in engaging and challenging online graduate learners. International implications for online college teaching across the discipline will result from the study. However, care should be taken when generalizing the results to other situations since this study was limited to one small graduate online course in education.

REFERENCES

Dweck, C. (2015). Carol Dweck revisits the "growth mindset". *Education Week, 35*(5), 20-24.

Gasparič, R. P., & Pečar, M., (2016). Analysis of an asynchronous online discussion as a supportive model for peer collaboration and reflection in teacher education.

Gay, L. R., Mills, G. E., & Airasian, P. (2012). *Educational research* (10th ed.). Upper Saddle River: Pearson, USA (ISBN-13: 9780132613170).

Golding, C., (2011). Educating for critical thinking: thought-encouraging questions in a community of inquiry. *Higher Education Research and Development, 30*(3), 357–370.

Journal of Information Technology Education, 15, 377–401 Retrieved from http://www.informingscience.org/Publications/3538.

Stott, P. (2016). The perils of a lack of student engagement: Reflections of a "lonely, brave, and rather exposed" online instructor. *British Journal of Educational*

Technology, 47(1), 51–64 Wiley. Retrieved April 13, 2018 from https://www.learntechlib.org/p/171299/.

EXPLORING EDUCATOR EXPERIENCES WITH MOBILE LEARNING SOFTWARE: UNDERSTANDING THE INTERPLAY OF THEMES

Zandile Mboneni and Johannes Cronje
Cape Peninsula University of Technology, Cape Town, South Africa

ABSTRACT

Mobile technologies illustrate a positive effect when used in mathematics learning. However, user experience evaluations are mostly quantitative. The study adopted a qualitative case study approach using semi-structured interviews to examine the experiences of educators at a special needs school in the Western Cape, South Africa.
Thematic analysis of the interview data was performed using an inductive approach. The data revealed five themes, and the connections between these themes shed light on the educators' experiences with Siyavula.

KEYWORDS

Mobile Learning, Siyavula, Special Education, Educator Experiences, Qualitative Research, Theme Relationships

1. INTRODUCTION

Siyavula, a South African educational organization, prioritizes increasing access to education by utilizing open educational resources (OERs) and digital materials. Siyavula optimizes its resources for mobile accessibility by seamlessly integrating with mobile technologies, ensuring learners and educators can easily access their responsive website and digital materials. This is consistent with the widespread use of mobile devices for educational purposes. Siyavula has received recognition for its potential to support mathematics learning. Siyavula's approach to mobile learning is multifaceted, encompassing adaptability, interactivity, accessibility, and real-time assessment. By incorporating these features, the software emerges as a powerful tool for advancing mathematics education, catering to the diverse needs of South African learners and educators.

Using mobile learning software is becoming more popular, with an increased interest in its effectiveness in specific subjects and special needs education contexts (Crompton et al., 2017; Crompton & Burke, 2017; Svela et al., 2019). Research shows that there is an interest in the experiences that users with special needs have when interacting with mobile technology (Barbareschi et al., 2019; Jahan et al., 2020).

User experience evaluation studies illustrate that mobile technologies effectively support mathematics learning for learners with special needs (Benavides-Varela et al., 2020; Chelkowski et al., 2019; Pitchford et al., 2018). However, user experience studies on the use of mobile technologies within education focus on usability and are mainly quantitative (Maia & Furtado, 2016; Nur et al., 2021).

While quantitative research is proper for testing hypotheses, making predictions, and determining cause-and-effect relationships (Apuke, 2017; Eyesi, 2016), qualitative research is better suited for studying subjective experiences and perspectives which can be challenging to understand when using quantitative measurements (Strydom & Bezuidenhout, 2021).

A variety of research designs are used in qualitative research. Phenomenological, narrative, grounded theory, ethnographic, and case study designs are the most used qualitative designs for understanding people's subjective experiences (Asenahabi, 2019; Creswell & Poth, 2018). The nature of the data and research design guides the analysis process in qualitative research (Miles et al., 2020; Yin, 2018).

This paper focuses on the theme that emerged during data analysis to investigate educators' experiences with Siyavula when teaching mathematics to learners with special educational needs. The observed gaps in the effectiveness of mobile learning technology in special needs settings and the call for additional qualitative studies in user experience evaluation motivated this choice.

2. THEMATIC ANALYSIS AND THEMES

Thematic analysis is a popular method for analysing qualitative data (Gibbs, 2018; Miles et al., 2020). Braun and Clarke (2022:224) point out that it works well for research attempting to understand people's subjective experiences. Braun and Clarke have consistently emphasized the importance of understanding themes as complex and meaningful patterns, rather than just simple summaries of the data, throughout their research since 2006 (Braun et al., 2016; Braun & Clarke, 2022; Terry et al., 2017). Themes provide insights into the participants' experiences, perspectives, and beliefs, allowing for a more in-depth understanding of the research problem (Maguire & Delahunt, 2017; Miles et al., 2020).

Both Braun and Clarke (2022) and Miles et al. (2020) acknowledge that effective thematic analysis necessitates a thorough understanding of the data, research context, and theoretical framework. They stress the importance of paying close attention to the nuances of the data, the relationships between themes, and the implications of the interpretations.

Adu (2019a:158) also emphasized the significance of investigating the relationships between themes to adequately address the research questions. (Adu, 2019a) points out that these relationships are formed by comparing one theme to the other in terms of meaning, what the theme represents, and the empirical indicators and codes to which it is linked. Furthermore, once a link is established between two themes, the relationship between the two themes is then determined (Adu, 2019a).

Adu (2019a) employs various types of relationships discussed by Dey (1993:77-200) to determine the connection between themes, which can be:

Table 1. Definitions of the relationships among themes (adapted from Adu, 2019a:159-160)

Causal	"Two concepts have a causal relationship if the existence of or change in a concept leads or contributes to the emergence or adjustment of another."
Chronological	"Two concepts have a chronological relationship if one concept precedes or follows the other."
Concurrent	"Two concepts have a concurrent relationship if they exist, happen, change, or impact at the same time."
Embedded	"Two concepts have an embedded relationship if the entire characteristics of one concept are completely shared with a portion of another concept's features in terms of explaining a phenomenon, influencing another concept, or representing a process, behaviour or an event."
Explanatory	"Two concepts have an explanatory relationship if one concept plays the role of clarifying, elaborating or exemplifying another."
Overlapping	"Two concepts have an overlapping relationship if they have aspects of their characteristics in common in terms of explaining a phenomenon, influencing another concept or representing a concept, process, behaviour or an event."

These connections add to the richness of qualitative analysis. Some themes may complement or reinforce one another, resulting in a more complex understanding of a phenomenon or they may contrast or diverge, revealing contradictions or variations within the data (Braun & Clarke, 2022; Miles et al., 2020). Recognizing these relationships helps to provide a more complete interpretation of the underlying meanings, shedding light on the complexities of the subject under investigation (Gibbs, 2018; Saldana, 2021).

3. METHODOLOGY

To investigate the experiences of educators at a special needs school in the Western Cape, South Africa, who use Siyavula to teach mathematics, a qualitative case study design was chosen. The study included four senior-phase mathematics educators. Two of the educators have extensive experience, having taught mathematics for over 25 years and using Siyavula for the past six years. The third educator has been using Siyavula for two years and has six years of teaching experience. The fourth educator is new to the field, having taught mathematics for two years and using Siyavula for two months.

Semi-structured interviews were used to collect data, which was then analysed using thematic analysis. Thematic analysis is useful for capturing rich and contextually meaningful insights (Guest et al., 2020).

Data from interview transcripts were coded using interpretation-focused coding to better understand the educators' experiences using the Siyavula software to teach mathematics. The main characteristic of interpretation-focused coding is meaning creation, which entails locating significant information in the data and developing a code that represents our understanding of the data (Adu, 2019b). The interpretation-focused coding strategy successfully structured and simplified the data from the interviews, transforming it into meaningful and manageable codes, categories, and themes.

4. THEMES IDENTIFIED

Themes identified from the data, included technical challenges, ease of use, progress tracking, teaching and usage background, and learner perceptions. Technical challenges were one of the core themes that was identified from the data analysis. The theme encompasses the difficulties that educators encounter when using the software. It focuses on identifying and understanding specific technical difficulties faced when using Siyavula. These challenges encompass software glitches, repetitive content, numerous tabs, complex entry methods, content overload, and limitations in customisation.

The "Ease of Use" theme focuses on how educators use Siyavula and interact with its features and functionalities. It includes educators' experiences with the software's user interface, accessibility, and overall usability. This theme highlights the immediate feedback that learners get about their answers. It also shows that educators appreciate being able to track learner progress, the alignment of questions with the curriculum, and the flexibility of learning allowed by the software. Furthermore, educators found the leaderboard feature (P02) as one of the positive aspects as it motivates learners.

P02: *Ya, I particularly like it because I can use it. You know, there are some programs that I'm useless at manoeuvring through, but this is very easy and intuitive. So, I like it from that standpoint. I like it from the standpoint of having a view of what the kids are doing, checking that leaderboard, and just checking the number of assignments that they're doing, it tells me something about their motivation, so I like it from that standpoint.*

The progress-tracking theme centres on how educators use Siyavula for assessing and monitoring learner progress. Educators highlighted the progress tracking feature as one of the features they found most engaging (P01). Being able to track assignments, view learner performance data, and monitor engagement, provides critical insights into the learning process.

P01: *One of the benefits that I see is the instantaneous feedback that the kids get if their answer is right, or the answer is wrong, and it allows them a second stab at the answer to correct their thinking. So, it doesn't just mark it wrong. It says, "Are you sure? Remember, you've got to do this and this before you can get to your answer, and then they get a second chance at the answer. So, I think in other software that I've used, it's either right or wrong. Siyavula is nice in the sense that it gives you that second chance at answering the question again because you may have made a careless mistake in your calculations the first time around. Then from a teacher's point of view, the feedback that we get, we can instantaneously see specific areas that are trouble areas.*

The Teaching and Usage Background theme includes educators' years of teaching experience and familiarity with Siyavula. It investigates how educators' prior exposure to the software and their teaching background influence their interactions and experiences with Siyavula, shedding light on the role of expertise in the context of using the software.

P01: *So, I've been teaching math for the last 25 years, and have been using Siyavula over the last five to six years.*

P03: *Mm, I've been in class for four years. I'm teaching math for two years and I have been using Siyavula only for like the past two months.*

The Learner Perception theme is concerned with understanding the interaction between educators and students in terms of how the students perceive Siyavula (P01). It gathers insights from learners on their experiences, challenges, and overall feelings toward the software. This theme provides a crucial perspective from the end-users of the software.

5. RELATIONSHIPS BETWEEN THEMES

The findings illustrated several relationships between the themes (figure. 1). One of the key findings is the concurrent relationship between "Technical Challenges" and "Ease of Use." Educators frequently encounter both positive and negative aspects of using Siyavula simultaneously. Technical challenges, such as software glitches and cluttered interface, have a direct impact on educators' perceptions of ease of use. When technical challenges are resolved, educators find the software more user-friendly, while unresolved issues lead to frustration and hampered experiences.

In addition, an explanatory relationship exists between the theme of "Technical Challenges" and the theme of "Teaching and Usage Background." Educators' extensive teaching experience and familiarity with Siyavula have a significant impact on how they engage with technical challenges and navigate the platform. More seasoned educators exhibit greater adaptability in handling technical challenges and swiftly acquaint themselves with the software's functionalities.

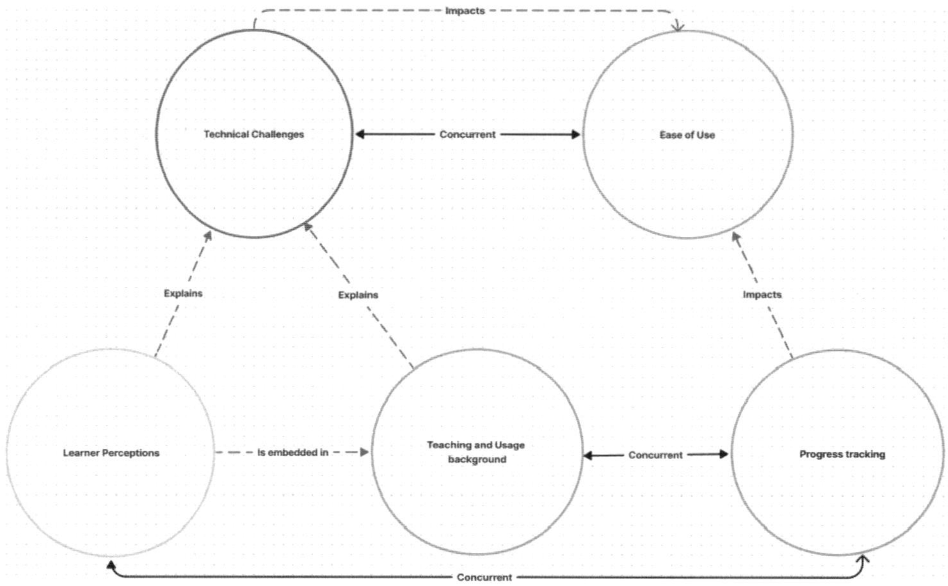

Figure 1. Relationships exist between the themes.

Another concurrent relationship emerges between "Ease of Use" and "Teaching and Usage Background." The teaching experience and adoption of Siyavula by educators influence their perceptions of the software's ease of use, with experienced educators finding the software more user-friendly. The themes "Educators' teaching and usage background" and "progress-tracking" are also concurrent. This is because educators value the ability to track learner progress, which aligns with their interest in understanding learner motivation and engagement. Another concurrent relationship is also apparent between the themes of "Learner Perceptions" and "Progress Tracking. When learners use Siyavula consistently and enjoy the motivating feature of "Are you sure", educators can track their performance and improvements.

A causal relationship is evident between "Ease of Use" and "Progress Tracking." The user-friendliness of Siyavula improves educators' abilities to navigate and use the progress-tracking feature, which contributes to their positive perceptions of the software's effectiveness. An explanatory relationship is observed between "Learner Perceptions" and "Technical Challenges," as learners' feedback helps understand specific technical difficulties encountered by educators.

Lastly, an embedded relationship emerged between "Learner Perception" and "Teaching and Usage Background." Effective use of the software by educators influences perceptions, shaping their feedback and facilitating a more tailored approach to teaching.

6. CONCLUSION

In conclusion, the connection between these themes highlights the importance of continuous improvement and user support in mobile learning platforms, particularly in special education. A more positive and impactful learning experience can be created for both educators and learners by improving personalisation, reducing content repetition and overload, and providing robust technical support.

Recognizing relationships between themes, as emphasised by Braun and Clarke (2022), Miles et al. (2020), and Adu (2019a), contributes to a more comprehensive interpretation of underlying meanings. The acknowledgement that themes can complement, reinforce, contrast, or diverge aligns with the proposed enhancements for a more impactful learning experience in the context of special education (Gibbs, 2018; Saldana, 2021). This study contributes significantly by emphasising the significance of these relationships and their implications in the context of mobile technology integration in special education.

As the study was based on a single case, the findings' generalizability may be limited. Furthermore, because the study is qualitative, the results are context-specific and may not be directly transferable to other settings. Despite the study's sample size being small, it allowed for a detailed exploration of educators' experiences with Siyavula within a specific context. This level of comprehension could be useful for future studies that aim to replicate or extend these findings in larger and more diverse settings.

REFERENCES

Adu, P. (2019a). connecting themes and developing tables and diagrams. In *A step-by-step guide to qualitative data coding*. New York: Routledge, 158-182.

Adu, P. (2019b). Understanding the art of coding qualitative data. In *A step-by-step guide to qualitative data coding*. New York: Routledge, 23-58

Apuke, O. D. (2017). Quantitative research methods: a synopsis approach. *Arabian Journal of Business and Management Review*, *6*(11), 40–47. https://doi.org/10.12816/0040336

Asenahabi, B. M. (2019). Basics of research design: a guide to selecting appropriate research design. *International Journal of Contemporary Applied Researches*, *6*(5), 76–89.

Barbareschi, G., Aranda Jan, C., Nique, M., Ramos Barajas, F., & Holloway, C. (2019). Mobile phones as assistive technologies: gaps and opportunities. In M. MacLachlan & R. Berman-Bieler (Eds.), *Proceedings of the GReAT Summit*: 294–308: WHO.

Benavides-Varela, S., Zandonella Callegher, C., Fagiolini, B., Leo, I., Altoè, G., & Lucangeli, D. (2020). Effectiveness of digital-based interventions for children with mathematical learning difficulties: a meta-analysis. *Computers and Education*, *157*(November), 103953.

Braun, V., & Clarke, V. (2022). Thematic analysis: a practical guide. London: SAGE publications Ltd.

Braun, V., Clarke, V., & Weate, P. (2016). Using thematic analysis in sport and exercise research. In B. Smith & A. C. Sparkes (Eds.), *Routledge handbook of qualitative research in sport and exercise*. London: Routledge, 191-205

Chelkowski, L., Yan, Z., & Asaro-saddler, K. (2019). The use of mobile devices with students with disabilities: a literature review. *Preventing School Failure: Alternative Education for Children and Youth*, *63*(3), 277–295.

Creswell, J. W., & Poth, C. N. (2018). Qualitative inquiry and research design: choosing among five approaches. 4th ed. Thousand Oaks, California: Sage Publications Inc.

Crompton, H., & Burke, D. (2017). Research trends in the use of mobile learning in mathematics. In Information Resources Management Association (Ed.), *Blended Learning: Concepts, Methodologies, Tools, and Applications*. Hershey, Pennsylvania: IGI Global, 2090-2104

Crompton, H., Burke, D., & Gregory, K. H. (2017). The use of mobile learning in PK-12 education: A systematic review. *Computers and Education*, *110*, 51–63. https://doi.org/10.1016/j.compedu.2018.04.007

Dey, I. (1993). Qualitative data analysis: a user-friendly guide for social scientists. New York: Routledge.

Eyesi, D. (2016). The usefulness of qualitative and quantitative approaches and methods in researching problem-solving ability in science education curriculum. *Journal of Education and Practice*, *7*(15).

Gibbs, G. (2018). Analyzing qualitative data. 2nd ed. New York: SAGE publications Ltd.

Guest, G., Namey, E., & Chen, M. (2020). A simple method to assess and report thematic saturation in qualitative research. *PLOS One*, *15*(5).

Jahan, N., Barbareschi, G., Jan, C. A., Mutuku, C. M., Rahman, N., Austin, V., & Holloway, C. (2020). Inclusion and independence: the impact of mobile technology on the Lives of Persons with Disabilities in Kenya and Bangladesh. *IEEE Global Humanitarian Technology Conference (GHTC)*: 573–580. Seattle, WA: IEEE

Maguire, M., & Delahunt, B. (2017). Doing a thematic analysis: a practical, step-by-step guide for learning and teaching scholars. *All Ireland Journal of Teaching and Learning in Higher Education*, *8*(3), 3351–33514.

Maia, C. L. B., & Furtado, E. S. (2016). A systematic review about user experience evaluation. In Marcus, A. (ed) Design, User Experience, and Usability: Design Thinking and Methods, 5th International Conference, DUXU 2016, 17-22 July 2016: 445-455. Toronto, Canada: Springer Cham.

Miles, M. B., Huberman, M. A., & Saldana, J. (2020). Qualitative data analysis: a methods sourcebook. 4th ed. Los Angeles: SAGE publications Ltd.

Nur, I. A., Santoso, H. B., & Putra, P. H. O. (2021). The method and metric of user experience evaluation: a systematic literature review. *10th International Conference on Software and Computer Applications*, 23 March 2021: 307–317, Kuala Lumpur: ACM.

Pitchford, N. J., Kamchedzera, E., Hubber, P. J., & Chigeda, A. L. (2018). Interactive apps promote learning of basic mathematics in children with special educational needs and disabilities. *Frontiers in Psychology*, *9* (MAR), 262.

Saldana, J. (2021). The coding manual for qualitative researchers. 4th ed. London: SAGE publications Ltd.

Strydom, A., & Bezuidenhout, R.-M. (2021). Qualitative data collection. In F. du Plooy-Cilliers, C. M. Davis, & R. Bezuidenhout (Eds.), *Research matters* (2nd ed.). Juta & Company Ltd.

Svela, A., Nouri, J., Viberg, O., & Zhang, L. (2019). A systematic review of tablet technology in mathematics education. *International Journal of Interactive Mobile Technologies*, *13*(8), 139–158. https://doi.org/10.3991/ijim.v13i08.10795

Terry, G., Hayfield, N., Clarke, V., & Braun, V. (2017). Thematic Analysis. In Willig, C.& Stainton-Rogers, W. (Eds.). *The SAGE Handbook of Qualitative Research in Psychology*. 2nd ed. Thousand Oaks, California: SAGE Publications, 17-37.

Yin, R. K. (2018). Case study research and applications: design and methods. 6th ed. Thousand Oaks, California: Sage Publications.

DIGITAL RESOURCES IN MOBILE LEARNING AND SOME ASPECTS OF TEACHING AND EDUCATION ENVIRONMENT

Albena Nakova[1], Emilia Chengelova[1] and Valentina Milenkova[1,2]
[1]*Institute of Philosophy and Sociology, 13a Moskovska str., Sofia, Bulgaria*
[2]*South-West University, 66 Iv.Mihailov str., Blagoevgrad, Bulgaria*

ABSTRACT

This article focuses on the work of teachers in the conditions of mobile learning, since theachers perform various activities related to preparation of classes, training and students' assessment in digital learning environment. The analysis emphasizes the fact that the responsibilities of modern teachers are becoming more complicated, following the challenges of information technologies and the expectations of the new generation of learners. The paper examines various digital resources used by teachers, tracks their effectiveness, and presents the results of conducted researches.The main idea of the article is to present the restructuring of the learning environment related to the introduction of various digital tools, requiring more interactivity and improving students' achievements, as well as increasing the digital skills and competences of the teachers themselves. It is concluded that the use of digital resources stimulates students' interest and increases their activity.

KEYWORDS

Mobile Learning, Digital Resources, Teaching, Learning Environment

1. INTRODUCTION

Digital transformations have a significant impact on the quality of life of modern people and lead to the formation of the so-called digital generations who have continuous access to diverse information sources. Prolonged contact with the Internet and various computer games have developed in students speed and versatility of reactions, non-traditional visual thinking, dynamic perceptions and maintaining a continuous connection in their network of friends and peers. In this situation, the school education system is faced with a great challenge - to provide adequate education to modern students, whose way of thinking, behavior, preferences, expectations and learning style are radically different from those of teachers, parents and previous generations (Kukulska-Hulme at al., 2021).

Information and communication technologies (ICT) provide a variety of methods and digital tools that open up new opportunities for mobile learning in formal and nonformal learning. They make it possible to support the mobile learning process by organizing it in a way that takes into account the individual needs of the learners. Information technologies stimulate the development of digital competences necessary for the dynamic world in which we live. They provide an opportunity, through the use of specialized software and hardware, to carry out activities that are difficult to implement with classical training tools.

This article analyzes some of the available digital tools and their application in the Bulgarian school. It highlights the fact that different digital tools exist, but not all of them are used equally actively by teachers. The type of learning content is important, as well as the stage in which it is applied - teaching, testing, discussion, teamwork, quiz, practical activity. The article shows that expectations for teachers are rising, which is restructuring the entire work environment. In the conditions of mobile learning, the status of the teacher himself is reformatted, who fulfills not only the role of a teacher, but also of an innovator, accepting the challenges of technology and the expectations of the new generation of learners. This requires that, in addition to the skills and qualifications in the professional-pedagogical field, the teacher must also have digital competencies corresponding to the performance of the educational activity itself. The main idea of the article is to present the widely used digital learning resources in the Bulgarian school environment, requiring activity in mobile learning, aiming for more interactivity and improving student results, as well as the preparation of teachers themselves.

Digitization and the use of computer and information technologies covers the entire system of education: from kindergartens, through higher education and postgraduate qualifications. Effective work and training in an information environment is related to building digital skills and abilities, which are a prerequisite for accessing and using various information resources, for their combination, structuring and creation of new content with a view to solving specific tasks and identifying needs. Today, various interactive methods can be applied to increase the motivation to learn and the commitment of students to the learning process, increasing academic success. In this context, teachers strive to develop interdisciplinary lessons through which to develop students' critical, non-standard, creative thinking, looking for effective ways of communicating with generations. The aspiration is for the teachers themselves to build competences corresponding to innovative digital technologies and working with cloud services, preparation and distribution of didactic materials in cloud space.

2. BASIC CONSIDERATIONS

2.1 Policy Documents

In recent years, there has been a lot of political activity related to understanding the significant role of digitization in the field of education. The process of digitization of education in Bulgarian conditions was strengthened by the creation of a national cloud-based ICT infrastructure for mobile learning: the new national e-learning platform was launched in April 2022 and began to function from the academic year 2022/2023. The platform allows teachers to create digital learning materials - lessons, exercises and tests using various electronic resources. The start was made through the activities of the project "Education for Tomorrow" (https://oud.mon.bg/) under the Operational Programm "Science and Education for Smart Growth 2014-2020", co-financed by the European Structural Funds. The national program "Digital Bulgaria 2025"provides the basis for modernization and implementation of smart solutions, including ICT in schools.

Another important policy is the Recovery and Sustainability Plan of Bulgaria, approved in May 2022, which defines the development of STEM infrastructure as a priority area. Reforms and investments, according to the document, support the development of digital technologies and the expansion of STEM subjects in schools, by building STEM laboratories and creating high-tech classrooms. On a national scale, the creation of one national and three regional STEM centers is envisaged, which aim to train teachers, develop teaching materials and create electronic portals and libraries. Significant political practice is represented by innovative schools aimed at improving learning outcomes through modern teaching methods, development of learning content, curricula and programs. In the academic year 2020/2021, 504 schools from 28 districts in the country received the status of "innovative school", and for the academic year 2022/2023, their number was increased to 542 (https://web.mon.bg/bg/1682). In addition, over the past three years, all public and municipal schools have built secure wireless networks, including a new generation of firewalls and access points. This guarantees full coverage and rapid exchange of information in accordance with the latest standards, allowing the use of all types of devices from anywhere in the school with a high level of security. Kindergartens and schools have been provided with over 20,000 personal computers, laptops and tablets, and about 4,000 classrooms are equipped with the latest high-tech visualization equipment, including interactive whiteboards and displays with built-in computer modules and Internet access. In this way, access to quality educational resources and services is ensured.

From March 2023 launched the National Program "Digital Qualification", financed by the Ministry of Education and Science (https://www.strategy.bg/StrategicDocuments/View.aspx?lang=bg-BG&Id=1583). The program meets the need for high-quality training of pupils, students, secondary school teachers and university professors, in accordance with the digital transformation of education. The main focus of the program is the creation of staff with a high level of digital competence, with an attitude to improve and transfer their experience and knowledge. The focus of the program is also teaching methods, which should include innovative approaches and modern learning platforms. Within the framework of the program, it is planned to increase the digital skills and competences of teachers in various subjects in secondary education, as well as the possibility of retraining them as informatics and information technology teachers. The program is also aimed at business personnel who want to practice teaching. This program aims to make digital training and skills a key focus of learning, including business practitioners to bring their expertise to the learning environment.

The listed policy documents and practical actions taken are indicative of the awareness of digitization and mobile learning at the national level and the search for different solutions for introducing more digital devices and tools as part of the educational environment into the educational practice.

2.2 Digital Educational Tools

Digital tools are programs, websites, or online resources that can facilitate various learning-related tasks. Many of them are accessible through web browsers without the need to download them, and in general, they can be accessed anytime and from anywhere, making learning easier. To help the teacher, there are many technological solutions to achieve an effective learning process, starting with the most familiar and common form - the presentation, and going through flash cards, mind maps, electronic test creation tools, virtual laboratories, dynamic software, artificial intelligence and come to learning platforms that integrate webcams and provide advanced opportunities for learning and connection, for sharing resources and collaboration.

Efforts to implement ICT in education at all levels, however, presuppose teachers' technical literacy and skills in handling digital tools. This requires teachers to increasingly move from the role of users of e-resources to creators of e-resources. In the 21st century, the skills to search, find and use already created content are no longer enough, but a more active attitude towards digital competences is needed (Kukulska-Hulme at al., 2021). In this context, the implementation of digital tools goes through several stages.

- Choice of methodology.
- Development of content (teachers must develop their own programs, adapting them to the relevant context for the specific needs of their students).
- Choice of devices (the best device is the one that can be used for different educational tasks).

It is also important that teachers have the attitude to modernize and update educational tools, adequately responding to the challenges of the situation. Online education tools are diverse and they are related to the advancement of hardware and software. Their main functions consist in: 1) maintaining communication between the participants in the training. 2) Creation of an electronic register to store grades, tasks completed, meetings held. 3) Content sharing and teamwork.

Knowledge of the main characteristics of educational platforms and digital environments, as well as the possibilities for their integration in the learning process and in extracurricular activities, must take into account the age characteristics of the students. The use of educational digital tools is becoming more and more important in modern education, because interactive learning resources can be created through them. Students can use these resources using different electronic devices: computer, tablet, phone, accessing their learning materials.

Digital platforms are related to organizing and managing learning, delivering materials, maintaining databases for storing student results. These platforms are used at the school level, with each participant having personal access to the platform with a username and password. To get the most out of the platforms, students and teachers need to be active participants in the learning process. Teachers have the ability to create lessons, manage their content, add quizzes, homework and videos, and encourage discussions. Students, in turn, have access to all available resources and can ask questions and complete a variety of tasks.

Most Bulgarian schools use platforms offered at the national level. In Bulgaria, Office 365 and G Suit are currently used with their virtual classrooms Teams and Google Classroom, respectively. They integrate applications for real-time communication, ongoing and periodic assessment.

2.2.1 Tools for Creating Online Tests

An important element of mobile learning is the tools for checking and evaluating students' knowledge and skills, for which teachers invest a lot of time in a traditional learning environment. The development and implementation of electronic tests greatly facilitates teachers, helping them to check achievements more quickly and qualitatively. Electronic tests give instant access to results, making grading easier. In addition, the student can immediately see which are the right and wrong answers. Methods of testing and assessment reflect ways of teaching and learning and enrich the experience of learners within the relevant discipline. Testing and assessment in an online environment is characterized by a number of advantages, such as flexibility in terms of time and place, accurate and rapid feedback. In learning in a mobile environment, methods for assessing learner knowledge are based on different technologies. Taking a test measures a specific piece of knowledge or the level at which a student has mastered a given skill.

There are a number of electronic platforms for creating online tests - SmarTest, ClassMarker, Google Forms, Microsoft Forms, the last two being the most common. Both Google Forms and Microsoft Forms offer the same basic features: question and answer templates, different question types, sharing tests with students and with teachers.

Data from the educational software platform Shkolo.bg (https://www.shkolo.bg/) show that teachers create various online tests. Students on the platform, who are 84% of all in the country, have completed 1.2 million tests, 400,000 more than in 2021. Teachers and principals share that digitization saves them 200 hours a year, in which teachers can do other activities.

2.2.2 Effectiveness of Digital Educational Tools

The wide application of electronic tools to create digital resources raises the question of evaluating their effectiveness. In the most general case, effectiveness is seen as the main characteristic of functional learning. It shows the degree of fulfillment of the set goals and the achieved results when using and applying digital resources with the smallest possible expenditure of time, labor and financial resources on the part of the trainees and the training organization. In general, the effectiveness of the electronic tools used and the digital resources applied is determined by a large number of factors:

- Autonomy in work (teachers' ability to creatively organize the teaching and learning process themselves);
- Digital skills of the teacher him/herself;
- Creative teacher attitudes towards creating digital content.

In Bulgarian secondary schools, the most widely used learning platform is Microsoft Teams. Some teachers share that they have difficulties (https://diuu.bg/emag/14268/) and make efforts to create a virtual classroom and communicate with students, as well as in sharing learning materials, preparing electronic lessons, tests, assignments, generate homework, get feedback.

The behavior and attitudes of the individual teacher and his contribution to adapting the learning process to the new technological environment is key to increasing the effectiveness of learning with digital means. In the focus groups held with teachers on the project КП-06-ПН80/12 "Quality of life and well-being in the context of professional communities and their activity", funded by the National Science Fund – Bulgaria, the teachers also shared that in their work they use both digital educational resources developed by them and resources developed by their colleagues.

Here are some views:

„The most important criterion for using any online tool is - whether it corresponds to the topic under consideration, and to what extent it will make students more active and they will understand and learn the educational content" (female, 43 years old).

„I prefer to independently develop the materials on each topic I teach, but regarding the tests I often use tests that have already been developed by colleagues" (female, 39).

„I prefer to work with online materials that I can download from the platforms and that are ready and working in the training. This way I feel safer, because I don't always manage to cope with digital tools" (female, 60).

From the presented results, it can be seen that some of the teachers prefer to develop their online materials independently, while others prefer to use ready-made digital tools. A factor in the preference shown is the extent to which teachers are digitally skilled and confident; in general, younger teachers are more likely to be digitally independent and active. At the same time, older teachers are putting in more effort, encountering more difficulties, but all now have the necessary digital literacy, which was dictated by the Covid pandemic when almost three years of training took place online. In this regard, efforts are generally being made at the national level to promote the experiences of successful teachers of today who are applying innovative approaches to their work and striving to provide a multifaceted education for students. Innovative methods imply digital, virtual and visual literacy of teachers, making their methods flexible in the learning process.

3. CONCLUSION

This article shows that it is important to consider several things: 1) the political commitment and will to ML. 2) the digital competences of teachers. 3) the equipping the environment with digital devices and tools.

Digital learning implies the active use of home or mobile devices by students in order to participate in class and perform various tasks. The preparation of the lessons themselves requires the reorganization of the whole lesson, the rearrangement of the different activities and, in general, their successful implementation depends to the greatest extent on the teacher. Pedagogical practices based on digital learning themselves require testing in the learning context itself, and the decision to use them, and to what extent, is the result of the teacher's judgment about how a tool or platform will be useful in their classes. Moreover, the use of digital tools always directly or indirectly develops students' digital skills. It's only natural that students of all ages use technology in every aspect of their lives. Using digital resources in education stimulates students' interest, increases their activity and leads to more effective learning and understanding.

ACKNOWLEDGEMENTS

The article has been developed in the framework of the research project “Quality of life and well-being in the context of professional communities and their activity” КП-06-ПН80/12, funded by National Science Fund.

REFERENCES

"Digital Qualification" https://www.strategy.bg/StrategicDocuments/View.aspx?lang=bg-BG&Id=1583

"Education for Tomorrow" https://oud.mon.bg/ of Operational Program

Educational software platform Shkolo.bg https://www.shkolo.bg/

Electronic resources to help the modern teacher https://diuu.bg/emag/14268/

Kukulska-Hulme, A., Bossu, C., and Coughlan, T. (2021). *Innovating Pedagogy* 2021. Retrieved from the Open University: http://www.open.ac.uk/blogs/innovating

List of innovative schools in the Republic of Bulgaria for the academic year 2022/2023: https://web.mon.bg/bg/1682

VIRTUNITA: ENRICHING UNIVERSITY EXPLORATION THROUGH MOBILE LEARNING WITH A GAMIFIED VIRTUAL TOUR

Barbara Bruschi[1], Theofild-Andrei Lazar[2], Manuela Repetto[1], Fabiola Camandona[1], Melania Talarico[1], Damaris Baciu[2] and Simone Zamarian[1]

[1]*University of Turin, Italy*

[2]*West University of Timisoara, Romania*

ABSTRACT

This study presents an innovative approach to promoting the international attractiveness of the University of Turin (UniTo) through synergy with the University of the West Timişoara in the "UNITorientA" project. In particular, the focus is developing a gamified virtual tour to offer students an interactive immersion in university spaces. Mobile technology plays a central role, enabling students to explore university environments and access multimedia content via personal devices. In this context, mobile learning emerges as a critical element in enhancing the learning experience by expanding access to information and promoting student mobility. The present study, conducted in collaboration between UniTo's Department of Philosophy and Educational Sciences and the University of the West of Timişoara, aims to explore how the convergence of mobile technology and virtual tours can significantly contribute to the knowledge and experience acquisition process of university students, highlighting the transformative potential of technology.

KEYWORDS

Mobile Learning, Virtual Tour, Gamification, University Students

1. INTRODUCTION

Nowadays, many operations are supported by technologies revolutionizing how we explore the world around us. The pandemic has forced a profound change in educational institutions, which have had to adapt to continue with distance learning-educational activities (Toquero, 2021). Emergency Remote Education (Mobo, 2020; Morgan, 2020) highlights the shift from "in-presence" and "distance" teaching, resulting in the deployment of those who argue for a loss of student learning and those who emphasize the possibility of reflecting, rethinking the role and spaces of digital, but also the potential, through conscious and competent use of digital educational technologies (Oliverio, 2020). Moreover, the latter has revolutionized how we explore the world around us, a change reflected in the digitization of products and services and the virtualization of everyday consumption experiences, such as the museum and institutional sector (Calveri & Sacco, 2021). Indeed, the use of technology has had a significant impact on the learning process and the development of teaching techniques (Coskun-Setirek & Tanrikulu, 2021; Lee & Hsu, 2021). This form of learning, mobile learning, combines universal communication technology and advanced user interfaces (Sharma & Kitchen Al-Hamad et al., 2021) by facilitating access to content. Users are only required to have a mobile device equipped with an Internet connection to access distance learning spaces (AlMajali & Masa'deh, 2021). Research shows that mobile learning positively affects learning in terms of strategy seeking, peer collaboration, and motivation toward learning (Bernacki et al., 2020). Today, more than ever before, the use of mobile learning is complemented by the use of virtual or augmented reality tours that enhance the learner experience. Virtual tours are becoming an excellent teaching approach to increase knowledge about realities perceived as distant to the learner. Virtual tours have become very important in heritage enhancement, educational, and orientation contexts, especially during the pandemic. The use of tools such as 360-degree imagery (Susanti, 2016), for example, show that it is possible to enhance the sensory and cognitive experience of people, who can very easily connect to media content using their device and explore virtual environments of all kinds (Argyriou et al., 2020).

Starting also from studies in education (Oliveira et al., 2023) and in virtual tours for tourism (Wei, Zhang, Wuang, 2023) on gamification, i.e., the use of game mechanisms to non-game contexts, it plays a key role in keeping user motivation high.

A virtual and gamified journey carried out within universities is illustrated here. These tools provide an extraordinary opportunity to explore university campuses and all their facets from anywhere globally, facilitating access to both domestic and international students eager to explore options and evaluate campuses akin to their academic careers (Nugraha, 2017).

2. RESEARCH DESIGN

The present study began in March 2023 and is still ongoing and is part of a larger research project aimed at enhancing the international dimension and promoting UniTo's educational offerings through the development and strengthening of research and teaching networks. The synergistic work was carried out in collaboration with an academic partner based in Romania, specifically at the University of the West in Timişoara. The main objective involved implementing a gamified virtual tour to improve academic orientation actions for domestic and international students not yet enrolled in the university and/or belonging to the United Alliance (Universitas Montium). A gamified virtual tour was constructed that would present the places of student habitation, attracting and guiding the visitor's gaze in order to be able to interpret and rework the content, extending it beyond the tour (Panciroli, & al. 2022, p.251).

2.1 VirtUniTa: A Virtual Tour of The University

This initiative is part of an academic landscape increasingly influenced by student mobility and evolving technology. Various mobile learning projects have shown promising results, such as environment simulation (Klopher & Squire, 2008) and design literacy (Matthews, 2010). Mobile media, virtual and augmented reality, can combine the advantages of educational video games with place-based learning (Squire & Jan 2007). Mobile devices may be particularly well suited for creating educational experiences in informal settings (Gagnon, 2010; Squire, 2009). However, it is important to delve into how students interact with these learning experiences and how they are designed (Squire, 2009). Information technology is increasingly being used to enrich the communication of information; in fact, whatever the context, alongside the traditional poster, there are codes to be activated to access additional multimedia content (audio, video, hypertext, three-dimensional), enriching the individual's opportunity for deeper learning (Orlandi, & al. 2014). Among the innovations of recent years are virtual tours, which rest their foundation on a technology developed by Apple dating back to the mid-1990s (Quicktime Vr) and now enhanced by the peculiarities of the available devices (Di Marino, 2018). The increased available hardware and the greater simplicity of software have seen wide-spectrum deployment through three-dimensional reconstructions and explorable environments. (Zaccarini, 2013).

In the following paragraphs, we will discuss the creation of the VirtUniTa, which takes the form of a pilot project carried out by the Department of Philosophy and Educational Sciences in Turin in collaboration with the Department of Social Sciences at the University of Timişoara that aims to create a gamified virtual tour that offers innovative immersion in university spaces, highlights how mobile technology revolutionizes students' access to information and learning experience. Student mobility, enhanced by advanced technological devices, thus becomes a critical element of acquiring knowledge and experiences, in line with Sharples et al.'s (2007) considerations on the potential of technology in transforming learning.

The project starts with the following research question: What is the potential of virtual tours applied to the orientation of pre-college and college students in the field of education science?

2.2 Aims

The objectives of the research were:

- To develop an interactive gamified virtual tour to expand access to information to enable students to explore university environments' multimedia content through their devices virtually.
- Use technology to promote student mobility by expanding the learning experience and enabling students to discover university options flexibly.

2.3 Methods and Tools

The creation of the virtual tour for mobile learning involved using two fundamental tools for its construction: the 360° Ricoh Theta camera and the Thinglink program. The stages of realization of the project can be described in the following list:

- Identification of information about places and services: services and places essential to university life, including academic buildings, libraries, study rooms, administrative offices and research laboratories, residence halls, university cafeterias, sports centers, parks, green areas, and city curiosities are brought to the fore.
- Storytelling design: Prior to the design, it was decided to create a story, starting with the creation of a guiding character, both on the United and Timişoara sides, to focus on emotional involvement on the part of the participant. The story also conveys the content by following a more elastic and light-hearted mode, helping the user to maintain high motivation toward the task.
- Design of the game flow and play activities: Several levels and a sequential flow were implemented to encourage the player to solve the puzzles in one room to gain access to the next.
- Multimedia materials were created: 360-degree images of the university spaces and neighboring places of interest to university life, and videos with helpful information for students were created.
- The photographs and videos were implemented within the ThingLink platform. The tour pages include the navigation menu, icons for the menu and places of interest, and a gallery button.
- Verification and evaluation: An initial evaluation will be conducted with a small group of students from the University of United and Timişoara who will evaluate the product regarding the tour's technical and content dimensions. They will be given evaluation grids so that they can follow precise criteria. A second evaluation phase will involve the student players administering satisfaction questionnaires.

Figure 1. The virtual tour begins. The user can view the University of Turin or the University of Timişoara

Figure 2. Insertion of icons aimed at guiding accessible services and spaces

2.4 Expected Results

This research hopes to achieve the following results:

- Increase the visibility and attractiveness of the universities involved among domestic and international students.
- Engage and orient through a gamified virtual tour, providing the tools to locate classrooms, libraries, study rooms, and student-oriented services.
- Increase accessibility by enabling remote exploration of university spaces facilitating access to information.

3. CONCLUSION

Among the many experiments and projects conducted by museums (and others) during lockdowns around the world, it is evident that virtual tours represent a "format" of particular interest (Coates, 2020; Khalel, 2020). The combination of real and virtual, physical and simulated, presence and distance, will accompany our consumption habits for a long time, which is why virtual tours play a driving role in diversifying cultural institutions' proposals (Vilardo & Mazali, 2022). Using new tools and the openness to digital languages lead to a positive disruption, increasing offerings and integrating traditional values and practices with new forms of valorization (Giannini, Bowen 2019). Cost is a limiting factor in the continuation of this path taken, both in terms of the technologies themselves and the need to employ specialized personnel to put (and maintain) them in operation. Despite these difficulties, the importance of harnessing digital to rethink the offerings that institutions cherish and enhance creatively should be highlighted. Literature (Dragoni, 2017) highlights how the gamified virtual tour experience can maximize engagement, experience, and learning effectiveness. Starting in December, the tour will be piloted by department students, disseminated on the University network, and with the support of faculty. In this way, data can be collected from questionnaires providing a wide range of how the tour can be further enhanced and what tangible benefits it brings to students and academic institutions.

REFERENCES

Al-Hamad, M.Q., Mbaidin, H.O., Alhamad, A.Q.M., Alshurideh, M.T., Kurdi, B.H. & Al-Hamad, N.Q. (2021). Investigating students' behavioral intention to use mobile learning in higher education in UAE during the Coronavirus-19 pandemic. International Journal of Data and Network Science, 5(3). https://doi.org/10.5267/j.ijdns.2021.6.001

AlMajali, D., & Masa'deh, R. (2021). Antecedents of students' perceptions of online learning through the COVID-19 pandemic in Jordan. International Journal of Data and Network Science, 5(4), 587-592. https://doi.org/10.5267/j.ijdns.2021.8.009

Argyriou, L., Economou, D., & Bouki, V. (2020). Design methodology for 360 immersive video applications: the case study of a cultural heritage virtual tour. Personal and Ubiquitous Computing, pp. 24, 843-859

Bernacki, M. L., Greene, J. A., & Crompton, H. (2020). Mobile technology, learning, and achievement: Advances in understanding and measuring the role of mobile technology in education. *Contemporary Educational Psychology*, *p. 60*, 101827.

Calveri, C., Sacco, P.L. (2021). La trasformazione digitale della cultura. Milano: Editrice Bibliografica.

Coates, C. (2020). Virtual reality is a big trend in museums, but what are the best examples of museums using VR? Museum Next, July 17. Preso da: https://www.museumnext.com/article/how-museums-are-using-virtual-reality/

Coskun-Setirek, A., & Tanrikulu, Z. (2021). M-universities: Critical sustainability factors. SAGE Open, 11(1), 2158244021999388. https://doi.org/10.1177/2158244021999388

Di Marino, B. (2018). Segni sogni suoni: quarant'anni di videoclip da David Bowie a Lady Gaga. Mimesis.

Dragoni, M., Tonelli, S., Moretti, G. (2017). A Knowledge Management Architecture for Digital Cultural Heritage. Journal on Computing and Cultural Heritage, 10 (3), 1–18. doi:10.1145/3012289

Khalel, S. (2020). Devastated ancient sites return to life in VR exhibit. Middle East Eye, February 10. Preso da: https://www.middleeasteye.net/discover/ancient-sites-mosul-palmyra-aleppo-war-virtual-reality-exhibitionKwastek

Klopher, E. (2008). Augmented Learning - Research and Design of Mobile Educational Games.

Klopher, E., & Squire, K. (2008). Environmental Detectives: The development of an augmented reality platform for environmental simulations. Education Tech Research 56, 203–228.

Lee, C.-J., & Hsu, Y. (2021). Sustainable Education Using Augmented Reality in Vocational Certification Courses. https://doi.org/10.3390/su13116434

Morgan, H. (2020). Best Practices for Implementing Remote Learning during a Pandemic. The Clearing House: A Journal of Educational Strategies, Issues and Ideas, 93(3), 134–140. https://www.tandfonline.com/doi/full/10.1080/00098655.2020.1751480.

Oliveira, W., Hamari, J., Shi, L., Toda, A. M., Rodrigues, L., Palomino, P. T., & Isotani, S. (2023). Tailored gamification in education: A literature review and future agenda. *Education and Information Technologies*, *28*(1), 373-406.

Orlandi, M., Zambruno, S., & Vazzana, A. (2014). Tecnologia, Beni Culturali e Turismo: I Tour Virtuali (Virtual Tours) come strumento per una corretta comunicazione dei Beni Culturali. Storia e Futuro, 34.

Panciroli C., Corazza L., Russo V., Sghinolfi, M. C., (2022). Ambienti digitali di co-creazione partecipata per nuove forme di narrazione del patrimonio culturale. FrancoAngeli.

Sharma, S.K., & Kitchens, F.L. (2004). Web services architecture for m-learning. The Electronic Journal of E-Learning, 2(1), 203-216

Squire, K. & Jan, M. (2007). Mad City Mystery: Developing scientific argumentation skills with a place-based augmented reality game on handheld computers. Journal of Science Education and Technology, 16(1) 5–29.

Vilardo, G., & Mazali, T. (2022). La virtualizzazione dei Musei alla prova del Covid-19: Un caso studio. Mediascapes journal, 19(1), 177-203.

Wei, Z., Zhang, J., Huang, X., & Qiu, H. (2023). Can gamification improve the virtual reality tourism experience? Analyzing the mediating role of tourism fatigue. *Tourism Management*, p. *96*, 104715.

Zaccarini M., Iannucci A., Orlandi M., Vandini M., Zambruno S. 2013, From a multi-disciplinary approach to the virtually augmented preservation of Cultural heritage, Atti del convegno "Digital Heritage 2013", Marsiglia, 28 ottobre – 1 novembre 2013.

COCO: A SYSTEM FOR SUPPORTING COLOCATED COLLABORATIVE LEARNING WITH TABLETS

Mia Čarapina[1] and Klaudio Pap[2]
[1]*Zagreb University of Applied Sciences, Vrbik 8, 10000 Zagreb, Croatia*
[2]*University of Zagreb, Faculty of Graphic Arts, Getaldićeva ul. 2, 10000 Zagreb, Croatia*

ABSTRACT

This paper introduces CoCo, a system designed to support and encourage collaborative learning among colocated students sharing a single mobile device. It provides teachers with the possibility to create digital lessons, configure parameters for collaborative activities such as the number of students and tablets, and monitor students' progress. On the other side, students use the tablet mobile application with an implemented split screen feature which can support up to four colocated users. This approach could be advantageous for organizations with limited technology resources and a restricted budget.

KEYWORDS

Collaborative Learning, Mobile Learning, Multiuser Interaction, Tablet Computers, Split Screen

1. INTRODUCTION

The distribution of devices during the mobile learning activity generally falls into one of two categories: 1) one-per-one (1:1) or one device per student, and 2) one-per-many (1:m) or one device per many students. The literature overview in the mobile learning domain shows the prevalence of educational activities favoring 1:1 distribution (Čarapina & Botički, 2015) and the evident popularity of the numerous 1:1 learning initiatives or bring your own device (BYOD) solutions (Song, 2014; Tamim et al., 2015; Tubplee, 2019). Nevertheless, a significant digital gap persists in terms of global access to information and communication technologies (ICT) in education. For example, this is evident in the findings of a study performed by the European Commission on ICT in education (European Commission, 2019). The causes behind this phenomenon are diverse, with budgetary considerations frequently being the primary cause of restricted technology integration in public schools (Gray & Lewis, 2021; Heinrich et al., 2020; Tamim et al., 2015; Tubplee, 2019). In such circumstances, instructional activities utilizing technology are often organized in a one-per-many distribution, where several students use a single device. However, working on a single device in 1:m distribution is typically facilitated with software support specifically designed for individual use. Moreover, as a result of the cost infeasibility of providing each student with an individual device, equipment like mobile devices is often not purchased at all.

Building upon the existing research that 1:m distribution can be as effective as favored 1:1 distribution (Čarapina & Pap, 2023a; Heinrich et al., 2020; Lin et al., 2012; Wang et al., 2021), this paper presents a system for supporting collaborative learning activities of colocated students who can share a single tablet device. This is achieved by partitioning a tablet's screen into many distinct sections that are visually distinguishable from each other. This study extends prior research exploring the effectiveness of 1:m device distribution among early elementary school students solving a set of mathematical assignments on tablets with implemented split screen feature (Čarapina & Pap, 2023a) as well as the proposed prototype of a tablet split screen application for collaborative learning (Čarapina & Pap, 2023b).

2. THE SYSTEM FOR COLOCATED COLLABORATION ON TABLETS

The system developed for supporting collaboration between colocated students was named CoCo, which is a symbolic name derived from the combination of the words "colocated" and "collaboration". The name reflects the system's purpose, which is to facilitate and support collaborative activities involving a group of students who are physically located in the same place, next to each other, so they can work around a single mobile device. Up to four students can simultaneously share one device, yet many different groups can participate in the same activity.

The system has three main components (Figure *1*):

- client web application with three different modules for creating the content of educational lessons, defining the settings of the educational activity, and analyzing the data collected during the learning activity,
- client mobile application for displaying the content of the educational lesson, and
- database server.

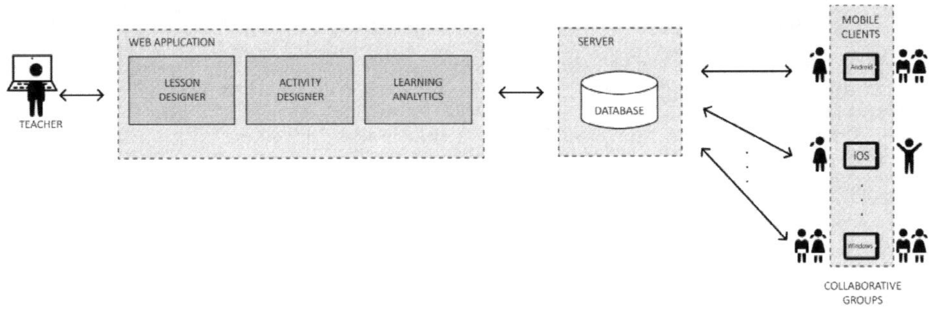

Figure 1. CoCo system architecture

Each component of the system is designed as an independent subsystem that functions relatively independently from other components of the system. The server acts as an intermediary between the web and mobile application and is accountable for retrieving and storing essential information necessary for the overall operation of the system. The educational content is created through the web application and stored on the server. There is no direct communication between the web application and the mobile application. The mobile application only communicates with the server during specific events such as when it is launched and when working settings are downloaded, and after the completion of collaborative activities when information collected on tablets, which is necessary for learning analytics, gets uploaded to the server. Thus, the system's architecture allows for the client mobile application to be developed using different technologies, such as native development for Android and iOS or one of the multiplatform development technologies, and easily integrated into the system. In other words, the client mobile application can run on different types of devices with different operating systems. Furthermore, the system design facilitates the connection of several client mobile applications, allowing for their concurrent usage during the carrying out of educational activity. The first functioning prototype of the client mobile application was developed employing native development for Android OS tablets. The web application was developed using the Angular framework and Google Firebase[1] Firestore was used as a database.

2.1 Web Application for Teachers

The web application is organized into three different modules: the lesson designer, the activity designer, and the analytics module. The web application enables teachers to create educational lessons, define the settings for the educational activity they wish to carry, and afterward they can analyze the data collected from tablets during the learning activity.

Interacting with the lesson designer teachers can create educational content that will be displayed in the mobile application. The technology allows for the production of instructional materials for any subject as long as students sharing a mobile device are presented with mutually exclusive questions as described in more detail in a paper by Čarapina & Pap (2023b). For example, if two students work in pairs one should get a question "*Select all animals that can fly.*" and the other student should get a question "*Select all animals that can't fly.*".

[1] https://firebase.google.com/

To complete the assignment, each student must choose answers from the same set of available answers and engage in discussion if any discrepancies arise. The answers can be presented as text or as images. The collaborative process is in more detail described in section 2.2.

Through the activity designer module (Figure 2(a)), teachers can configure the settings for the activity planned to be carried out in the classroom, such as the number of students per device and the duration of the activity. One notable characteristic of the system is its ability to adapt the execution of activities depending on the number of devices and pupils present in the classroom when the instructor intends to use digital lessons. In other words, a teacher can set up the activity to be carried out in any combination of 1:2, 1:3, or 1:4 distributions with a desired number of students and available mobile devices.

Furthermore, in the analytics module (Figure 2(b)) teachers can analyze the data gathered from the mobile application. The purpose of this module is to display the performance of individuals within a specific group and showcase the outcomes of all groups that participated in the classroom activity.

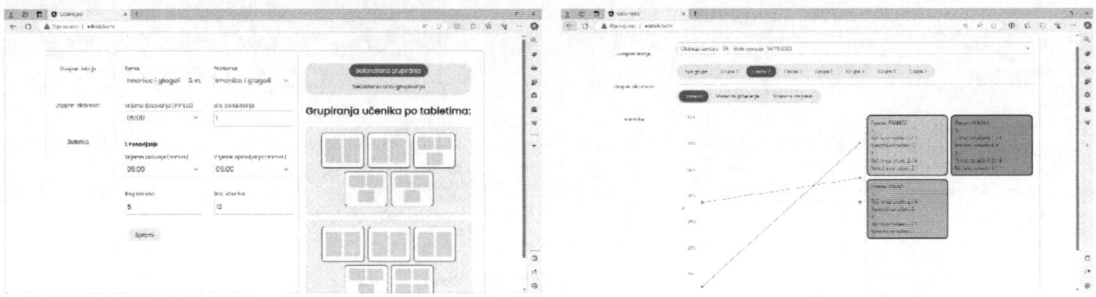

(a) (b)

Figure 2. Web application with (a) activity designer module and (b) analytics module

2.2 Mobile Application for Students

The primary role of the client mobile application is to deliver educational content to students. The content is displayed by employing the split screen feature and supports up to four colocated users. In other words, educational content can be displayed to a pair of students sharing a mobile device (Figure 3(a)), a group of three students (Figure 3(b)), and a group of four students (Figure 3(c)). The split screen functionality was implemented under the notion that it could help the organization and implementation of collaborative learning activities in early grades of elementary education. This was based on the premise that sharing a device would encourage them to exchange knowledge as indicated in the research on the effectiveness of the 1:m split screen approach applied for supporting independent activities on a shared tablet by Čarapina & Pap (2023a).

(a) (b) (c)

Figure 3. Representation of screen partitioning on a mobile device with the split screen feature into (a) two independent segments, (b) three independent segments, and (c) four independent segments

The designed activity for supporting colocated collaboration is broken down into three distinct phases: an initial phase that promotes individual effort, followed by a variable number of rounds of discussion and a correction phase. With the designed process (Figure 4), it was attempted to encourage the active participation of all students in the group while at the same time nurturing a sense of personal accountability in each individual through an individual task that is integrated into the overall activity. That is, the student is encouraged to think independently about the assigned task and work on a separate segment of the device's screen during the first phase. To encourage student engagement and knowledge sharing, the discussion phase follows the initial phase of answers submission. During this phase, students are presented with visually distinguished correct answers and potentially erroneous answers that can then be debated among the group of students sharing a device. If there are discrepancies in the answers within a set of tasks, the answers will be highlighted as possibly incorrect on every instance they appear on the device screen, for both students (Figure 5). To promote a focused discussion on questionable responses corrections are not allowed during the discussion phase. During the correction phase, students are given a chance to correct their responses, but without any visible highlighting of potentially erroneous answers.

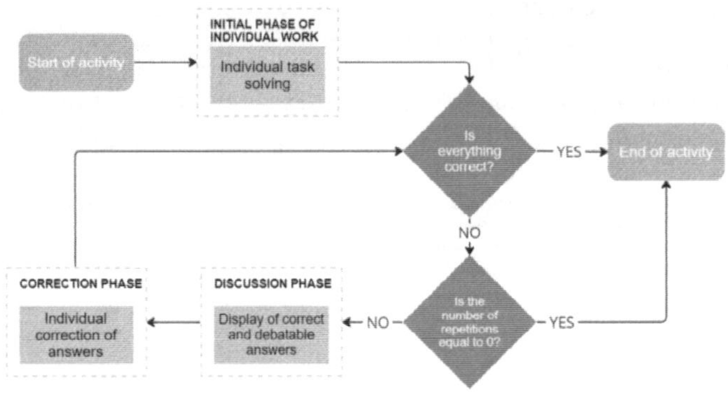

Figure 4. Collaborative process diagram

Upon launching the mobile application, all necessary data for the activity's execution is downloaded from the server. The content of the educational lesson is obtained together with a set of questions and answers, the configuration in which the application should be started on the device, that is, the number of segments that must be instantiated, and other data such as the duration of each phase of the activity. The collaborative learning activity is then carried out in the split screen mode (Figure 3). The process also allows for the early ending of each phase, but all students must agree that each phase stops before the time limit expires. On top of that, the application has a feature that allows students to rotate their segment, enabling them to move and position themselves relative to the device. In October and September 2023, the system was tested on a variety of topics (e.g. mathematics, Croatian language, etc.) among students of the first four grades (6 to 10 years old) of elementary education in Croatia (Figure 6) and the preliminary results indicate this approach could be beneficial for supporting and encouraging collaborative activities.

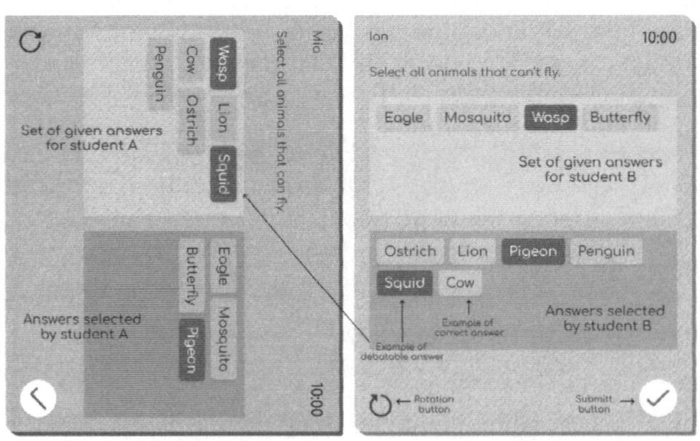

Figure 5. An example of the discussion phase with the display of highlighted debatable answers for a pair of students

(a) (b)

Figure 6. An example of (a) educational content displayed on Android tablet for pairs and (b) pair of first grade students sharing tablet

3. CONCLUSION

The CoCo system was developed to support and encourage collaboration between colocated students sharing a single mobile device. Throughout web modules teachers can create content, organize activities and track students' progress when working on tablets with implemented split screen functionality. The utilization of a split screen approach for device sharing offers a novel alternative for organizing educational activities. Initial trials undertaken with first-grade children suggest that this method has the potential to facilitate and encourage collaborative learning, thus creating new opportunities for organizations operating on tight budgets or with limited equipment.

REFERENCES

Čarapina, M., & Botički, I. (2015). Technology trends in mobile computer supported collaborative learning in elementary education from 2009 to 2014. *Proceedings of the 11th International Conference on Mobile Learning 2015*, 139–143.

Čarapina, M., & Pap, K. (2023a). Exploring colocated synchronous use of tablets based on split screen feature. *IEEE Access*, 11, 123418–123432. https://doi.org/10.1109/ACCESS.2023.3329478

Čarapina, M., & Pap, K. (2023b). The prototype of a tablet split-screen application for collaborative learning. *17th International Technology, Education and Development Conference*, 1437–1444. https://doi.org/10.21125/inted.2023.0415

European Commission. (2019). *2nd Survey of Schools: ICT in Education*. https://data.europa.eu/euodp/data/storage/f/2019-03-19T084831/FinalreportObjective1-BenchmarkprogressinICTinschools.pdf

Gray, C., & Lewis, L. (2021). *Use of educational technology for instruction in public schools: 2019–20*. https://nces.ed.gov/pubs2021/2021017.pdf

Heinrich, C. J., Darling-Aduana, J., & Martin, C. (2020). The potential and prerequisites of effective tablet integration in rural Kenya. *British Journal of Educational Technology*, *51*(2), 498–514. https://doi.org/https://doi.org/10.1111/bjet.12870

Lin, C.-P., Wong, L.-H., & Shao, Y.-J. (2012). Comparison of 1:1 and 1:m CSCL environment for collaborative concept mapping. *Journal of Computer Assisted Learning, 28*(2), 99–113. https://doi.org/https://doi.org/10.1111/j.1365-2729.2011.00421.x

Song, Y. (2014). "Bring Your Own Device (BYOD)" for seamless science inquiry in a primary school. *Computers & Education, 74*, 50–60. https://doi.org/https://doi.org/10.1016/j.compedu.2014.01.005

Tamim, R. M., Borokhovski, E., Pickup, D., & Bernard, R. M. (2015). *Large-Scale, Government-Supported Educational Tablet Initiatives*. https://oasis.col.org/server/api/core/bitstreams/3348c70b-eee3-47d9-ac29-83d595520b3a/content

Tubplee, E. (2019). One Tablet per Child Policy in Thailand. *Academic Journal Bangkokthonburi University*.

Wang, C., Wang, J., Shi, Z., & Wu, F. (2021). Comparison of the effects of 1:1 and 1:m CSCL environments with virtual manipulatives for scientific inquiry-based learning: a counterbalanced quasi-experimental study. *Interactive Learning Environments*, 1–18. https://doi.org/10.1080/10494820.2021.1948431

Reflection Papers

TWO 'USE CASES' OF CHATGPT IN MEDICAL EDUCATION IDENTIFIED IN THE LITERATURE: INTERACTIVE DIALOGUE AND CONTENT GENERATION

Heather L. Green[1] and Yulong Gu[2]
School of Health Sciences, Stockton University, 101 Vera King Farris Drive, Galloway, NJ 08205, USA
[1]Ed.D., [2]Ph.D.

ABSTRACT

Major shifts are occurring in higher education since the inception of Artificial Intelligence (AI) tools such as ChatGPT. With AI's growing integration into academia, understanding its usage and impact is imperative. We reviewed literature on ChatGPT use in medical education and identified two 'use cases' as: (1) an interactive dialogue tool to enrich student learning, and (2) a content generation tool to assist educators in course content creation. Literature also reported concerns around information accuracy, academic integrity, and potential bias. We call for more research to inform the development of pedagogical activities using ChatGPT, and to examine its impact and the effectiveness of risk mitigation strategies.

KEYWORDS

ChatGPT, Artificial Intelligence, Higher Education, Medical Education, Use Case

1. INTRODUCTION

ChatGPT is a language model developed by OpenAI that interacts with users in a conversational way (Schulman et al. 2022). The chatbot ChatGPT falls into the category of generative Artificial Intelligence (AI). ChatGPT-3.5 was first released for free public use in November 2022 and the most recent version (ChatGPT-4) was released in March 2023 with a paid subscription. ChatGPT was trained on vast text data which enables it to generate coherent text and perform complex natural language processing tasks (Lin 2023). The integration of AI and chatbots into academia was predicted to increase (Kooli 2023). ChatGPT further inspired substantial public interest and debate including in higher education. To the best of our knowledge, there is no established evidence on its effectiveness in improving learning outcomes. Thus, there is an urgent need to identify the potential opportunities and challenges presented by ChatGPT in higher education and to identify possible strategies to effectively integrate AI tools in teaching. This paper reports on our scoping literature review findings and synthesizes research evidence on the use of ChatGPT specifically in medical education to identify key areas of its potential use. Key research questions of this study are: What research studies have investigated the use, opportunities, and challenges of ChatGPT in medical education (including medical education programs, nursing programs, health science programs, etc.)? And what have they found?

2. METHODOLOGY

We searched in peer-reviewed articles published in academic journals and grey literature using search terms such as *ChatGPT, medical education, health education, health science, higher education,* and *effectiveness.* We focused on ChatGPT use in medical education in higher education and also included studies that discussed general AI use in education. By synthesizing the literature-identified opportunities and risks associated with using ChatGPT in medical education, we describe two 'use case scenarios' that represent two key areas of its use with the most expected benefits; and offer two recommendations for future research that may critically examine ChatGPT impact on medical education and inform risk mitigation strategies.

3. TWO USE CASES FOR MEDICAL EDUCATION

Two key ChatGPT 'use cases' for medical education suggested in literature are to support 1) interactive dialogues with students and 2) content generation for teachers (Benoit 2023, Choi et al. 2023, Khan et al. 2023, Lee 2023, Liu et al. 2023, Seetharaman 2023, Sun and Hoelscher 2023, Totlis et al. 2023, Tsang 2023).

3.1 An Interactive Dialogue Tool for Students

ChatGPT may enhance student's learning and engagement as a "Q&A" tool or a "virtual tutor". Medical students are expected to learn a large amount of complex information, they may benefit from quick access to information on subjects of human anatomy, pharmacology, disease, treatment, and medical procedure in nontechnical language via interactive 'dialogues' with ChatGPT (Choi et al. 2023, Khan et al. 2023, Nisar and Aslam 2023, Totlis et al. 2023). Students may type in ChatGPT their detailed, specific questions and receive insightful answers immediately (Totlis et al. 2023). Such insight may support medical students in preparing for licensure exams (Kung et al. 2023, Tsang 2023). Students may also use ChatGPT to generate "knowledge-check questions" to solidify their understanding of the licensure exam questions (Tsang 2023). ChatGPT may also simulate standardized patient (SP) and generate real-world case scenarios to interact with students in clinical (reasoning) skill training (Khan et al. 2023, Liu et al. 2023, Seetharaman 2023).

ChatGPT is capable of summarizing texts, hence may provide concise summaries of clinical guidelines in easy-to-understand language to support learning (Tsang 2023). Literature reported ChatGPT use by students (university and high school) to support writing/editing as it can rapidly paraphrase text, rewrite sentences, correct grammatical and spelling errors, generate ideas, and provide a framework for students' written work (Alkaissi and McFarlane 2023, Athanassopoulos et al. 2023, Salvagno et al. 2023, Sun and Hoelscher 2023).

ChatGPT may be accessed by students at their own time, in their own way, which may engage and optimize the learning experience (Choi et al. 2023). ChatGPT may also adapt to students' personal learning styles and abilities (Zhai 2022, Alves de Castro 2023, Khan et al. 2023). Since ChatGPT does not follow a fixed script, it generates responses based on user input ("prompt"), allowing for tailored instruction for each user. Given appropriate prompts, ChatGPT may outline rationales for decision making in complex clinical scenarios to help students grasp difficult concepts such as pathophysiology, pharmacology, diagnostic reasoning, and critical thinking (Sun and Hoelscher 2023).

3.2 A Content Generation Tool for Teachers

Literature also suggests potential use of ChatGPT to generate and evaluate course content and teaching materials, including realistic clinical vignettes/customized clinical cases and exam questions (Benoit 2023, Khan et al. 2023, Kung et al. 2023, Moore et al. 2023, Totlis et al. 2023). For instance, ChatGPT has been used to generate a multiple-choice quiz for medical students on musculoskeletal anatomy including questions of varying levels of difficulty (Totlis et al. 2023). ChatGPT may also generate open-ended questions for critical thinking and diagnostic reasoning, and provide rationales for the given responses (Sun and Hoelscher 2023). Research on ChatGPT integration in medical education is needed to confirm its effectiveness and to investigate its limitations and challenges (Choi et al. 2023, Lee 2023, Liu et al. 2023, Seetharaman 2023, Sun and Hoelscher 2023, Totlis et al. 2023, Tsang 2023).

4. RISKS, CONCERNS, AND FUTURE RESEARCH

Notwithstanding the wide-spread interest, recognized opportunities, and expected benefits from implementing ChatGPT in the above use cases, literature also acknowledges potential risks and unintended consequences including a main concern related to inaccurate information generated by ChatGPT. Several studies have measured the accuracy of ChatGPT-generated information, which is reported as good or acceptable in most studies (Alkaissi and McFarlane 2023, Benoit 2023, Kung et al. 2023, Nisar and Aslam 2023, Sng et al. 2023, Totlis et al. 2023, van Dis et al. 2023, Yeo et al. 2023). But all have acknowledged varied rates of inaccurate information, which is a concern given the medical education objectives on **gaining**

factual knowledge (Sng et al. 2023, van Dis et al. 2023). On the other hand, since ChatGPT's performance on the United States Medical Licensing Examination (USMLE) reached (near) passing grade (Gilson et al. 2023, Kung et al. 2023) and ChatGPT-4 is said to "exhibit human-level performance on various professional and academic benchmarks" (OpenAI 2023), the technology's potential to revolutionize medical education cannot be ignored. Several studies have highlighted an urgent need to establish guidelines for ChatGPT's optimal use and application in medical education (Rudolph et al. 2023, Totlis et al. 2023, Tsang 2023). We propose two recommendations on research to investigate ChatGPT for medical education.

4.1 Integrate ChatGPT as a Pedagogical Tool and Evaluate its Impact

ChatGPT has the potential to become a useful pedagogical tool for medical education with the two above-mentioned use cases supporting students and teachers respectively. We suggest future research should inform the development of evidence-based best practice of using ChatGPT in teaching. Experimental studies could focus on positive uses of ChatGPT identified in the literature (İpek et al. 2023). Some research topics might include 1) how to quickly construct effective prompts in building course materials – e.g., by drawing on clinical guidelines, using established licensure test questions, or other standardized practices? 2) how to guide students' dialogues with ChatGPT to enable effective learning – e.g., by preparing simulated standardized patients, or teaching students how to ask effective prompts to address their learning needs? 3) are ChatGPT-assisted medical education activities efficient and effective (in terms of learning outcomes, critical skills such as interprofessional collaborative practice competencies, licensure exam passing rate, etc.)?

4.2 Develop ChatGPT Risk Mitigation Strategies and Evaluate their Impact

ChatGPT may be susceptible to producing inaccurate information, plagiarism, risk of bias, and digital divide (Alkaissi and McFarlane 2023, Haq et al. 2023, Lee 2023, Lin 2023, Sallam 2023, Sng et al. 2023, Sun and Hoelscher 2023, van Dis et al. 2023). ChatGPT is also limited in its ability to conduct real-time searches, to cite sources, and provide proper references (Alkaissi and McFarlane 2023, Sallam 2023, Sun and Hoelscher 2023). Similar conversational AI tools based on large language models such as Google's Bard might outperform ChatGPT in terms of retrieving real-time information and citing sources (Google 2023). But these technologies' black-box nature continues to pose challenges for 1) constructing effective prompts, and 2) interpreting and evaluating the information they generate – e.g., to identify inaccurate content with the risk of "hallucination", out-of-date/limited knowledge, and lack of citation. These issues may pose limits regarding the technology's usefulness and ease of use for medical educators and students, hence need to be addressed. Recommendations have been made for faculty to establish ChatGPT use guidelines (Sun and Hoelscher 2023, Totlis et al. 2023) and for medical schools to develop university-wide policies (Tsang 2023). Research is needed to inform the development of and examine impact of risk mitigation strategies that target the above known issues, and potential medical, legal, ethical issues, as well as possible changing education paradigm.

5. CONCLUSION

ChatGPT offers promising new approaches for enhancing medical education. Current evidence highlights two main use case scenarios: 1) an interactive dialogue for students learning and 2) course content generation for educators. While ChatGPT has the potential to support both the student and the teacher, our review indicates it is not without limitations. Concerns have been reported around the accuracy, academic integrity, and bias with the need to address these issues. Research efforts should prioritize the development and testing of effective ways to use ChatGPT in pedagogical activities and risk mitigation strategies.

REFERENCES

Alkaissi, H., & McFarlane, S. I. (2023). Artificial Hallucinations in ChatGPT: Implications in Scientific Writing. *Cureus,* 15(2): e35179.

Alves de Castro, C. (2023). A Discussion about the Impact of ChatGPT in Education: Benefits and Concerns. *Journal of Business Theory and Practice,* 11(2): 28-34.

Athanassopoulos, S., et al. (2023). The use of ChatGPT as a learning tool to improve foreign language writing in a multilingual and multicultural classroom. *Advances in Mobile Learning Educational Research,* 3(2): 818-824.

Benoit, J. R. A. (2023). ChatGPT for Clinical Vignette Generation, Revision, and Evaluation. Retrieved Sep 18, 2023. https://www.medrxiv.org/content/medrxiv/early/2023/02/08/2023.02.04.23285478.full.pdf.

Choi, E. P. H., et al. (2023). Chatting or cheating? The impacts of ChatGPT and other artificial intelligence language models on nurse education. *Nurse Educ Today,* 125: 105796.

Gilson, A., et al. (2023). How Does ChatGPT Perform on the United States Medical Licensing Examination? The Implications of Large Language Models for Medical Education and Knowledge Assessment. *JMIR Med Educ,* 9: e45312.

Google. (2023). Bard FAQ. Retrieved Sep 20, 2023. https://bard.google.com/faq.

Haq, Z., et al. (2023). Comparing human and artificial intelligence in writing for health journals: an exploratory study. https://www.medrxiv.org/content/medrxiv/early/2023/02/26/2023.02.22.23286322.full.pdf.

İpek, Z., et al. (2023). Educational Applications of the ChatGPT AI System: A Systematic Review Research. *Educational Process International Journal,* 12(3): 26-55.

Khan, R. A., et al. (2023). ChatGPT - Reshaping medical education and clinical management. *Pak J Med Sci,* 39(2): 605-607.

Kooli, C. (2023). Chatbots in Education and Research: A Critical Examination of Ethical Implications and Solutions. *Sustainability,* 15: 5614.

Kung, T. H., et al. (2023). Performance of ChatGPT on USMLE: Potential for AI-assisted medical education using large language models. *PLOS Digit Health,* 2(2): e0000198.

Lee, H. (2023). The rise of ChatGPT: Exploring its potential in medical education. *Anat Sci Educ.*

Lin, Z. (2023). Why and how to embrace AI such as ChatGPT in your academic life. *R Soc Open Sci,* 10(8): 230658.

Liu, X., et al. (2023). ChatGPT: when the artificial intelligence meets standardized patients in clinical training. *J Transl Med,* 21(1): 447.

Moore, S., et al. (2023). Assessing the Quality of Multiple-Choice Questions Using GPT-4 and Rule-Based Methods. *European Conference on Technology Enhanced Learning*, Springer.

Nisar, S. & Aslam, M. S. (2023). Is ChatGPT a Good Tool for T&CM Students in Studying Pharmacology? Retrieved Sep 14, 2023. https://papers.ssrn.com/sol3/papers.cfm?abstract_id=4324310.

OpenAI. (2023). GPT-4 Technical Report. Retrieved Sep 14, 2023. https://cdn.openai.com/papers/gpt-4.pdf.

Rudolph, J., et al. (2023). ChatGPT: Bullshit spewer or the end of traditional assessments in higher education? *Journal of Applied Learning and Teaching,* 6(1).

Sallam, M. (2023). ChatGPT Utility in Healthcare Education, Research, and Practice: Systematic Review on the Promising Perspectives and Valid Concerns. *Healthcare (Basel),* 11(6).

Salvagno, M., et al. (2023). Can artificial intelligence help for scientific writing? *Critical Care,* 27(1): 75.

Schulman, J., et al. (2022). "Introducing ChatGPT." *Product Announcements.* https://openai.com/blog/chatgpt 2023.

Seetharaman, R. (2023). Revolutionizing Medical Education: Can ChatGPT Boost Subjective Learning and Expression? *Journal of Medical Systems,* 47.

Sng, G. G. R., et al. (2023). Potential and Pitfalls of ChatGPT and Natural-Language Artificial Intelligence Models for Diabetes Education. *Diabetes Care,* 46(5): e103-e105.

Sun, G. H. & Hoelscher, S. H. (2023). The ChatGPT Storm and What Faculty Can Do. *Nurse Educ,* 48(3): 119-124.

Totlis, T., et al. (2023). The potential role of ChatGPT and artificial intelligence in anatomy education: a conversation with ChatGPT. *Surg Radiol Anat.*

Tsang, R. (2023). Practical Applications of ChatGPT in Undergraduate Medical Education. *J Med Educ Curric Dev,* 10: 23821205231178449.

van Dis, E. A. M., et al. (2023). ChatGPT: five priorities for research. *Nature,* 614(7947): 224-226.

Yeo, Y. H., et al. (2023). Assessing the performance of ChatGPT in answering questions regarding cirrhosis and hepatocellular carcinoma. *Clin Mol Hepatol,* 29(3): 721-732.

Zhai, X. (2022). ChatGPT User Experience: Implications for Education. Retrieved Sep 15, 2023 https://papers.ssrn.com/sol3/papers.cfm?abstract_id=4312418.

INTERSECTION OF ECONOMIC INTELLIGENCE, BLOCKCHAIN AND PUBLIC ADMINISTRATION

Frédérik Sinan Bernard
Centre d'Etudes Diplomatiques et Stratégiques, 100-110 Espl. du Général de Gaulle, 92400 Courbevoie, France

ABSTRACT

The paper explores intersections of Economic Intelligence (EI), Blockchain Technologies (BCT), and Public Administration (PA). Despite the attention devoted to blockchain, including in public administration, economic intelligence considerations remains notably absent. Leveraging the ontological similarities of EI and PA, the paper proposes to adopt an EI approach when analyzing blockchain projects in the public sector (BCTiPS) and trying to understand whether these projects display an EI function.

KEYWORDS

Blockchain, Economic Intelligence, Governance, Public Management, Transdisciplinary Study, BCTiPS

1. INTRODUCTION

The emergence of blockchain technologies sparked interest across private (entrepreurship), public (Central Bank Digital Currencies) and multiple academic domains, showcasing versatile applications in B2B, B2C, voting systems, supply chain, governance structures, and more. Despite literature exploration, economic intelligence (EI) remains noticeably absent in the general blockchain discourse, even more so between blockchain (BCT) and public administration (PA). This paper endeavors to bridge this gap by providing the rationale for an EI approach to blockchain and its applications in the public sector (BCTiPS).

Recognizing parallels between EI and PA, the study proposes an initial theoretical framework. This framework will then be used to observe real-world implementation cases of BCTiPS, employing a qualitative approach to assess applicability, coherence and performance. The validation of this framework through empirical cases would establish a solid groundwork for further investigation.

Leveraging definitional traits and methods of PA and EI, the study proposes an analytic frame to be used for observations of BCTiPS' EI elements. This frame considers levels of analysis (micro, macro and meso) and key items (governance models). Variables such as stakeholders' technological knowledge, political orientation, and power dynamics, are presently excluded from this construct. However, these aspects could potentially play a crucial role in further refining the understanding of the relationship between blockchain projects in public administration and economic intelligence.

2. ECONOMIC INTELLIGENCE IN PUBLIC ADMINISTRATION

2.1 BCT and BCTiPS

Initially exemplified through the Bitcoin experiment (Nakamoto, 2009) which presented a relatively well working prototype for a decentralized currency system, BCT usage is rooted into the historical process of divorcing currencies from material backings going up until 1971 (Valori 2018). At its core, BCT offers an alternative digital and trustful registration system for actions between multiple actors without human intervention. Fundamentally, the protocol distributes and secures data exchanges among nodes, ensuring authenticity, traceability, and auditability while optimizing time and cost efficiency (Choo et al. 2020).

However, rather than replacing trust entirely, BCT serves as a confidence machine distributing trust among identifiable actors via consensus algorithms governing the blockchain (De Filippi et al. 2020). Algorithms help define the governance regime of the blockchain; and further so does the public, private, or hybrid nature of BCT (Morabito 2017). Elaborate governance policy research such as "governance by/of blockchain" (Tan & Crompvoets 2022) contribute to indicate the complexity of establishing governance on this platform.

Public administration are historically challenging to define and encapsulate the perspectives shaped by legal, political, economic, and sociologically leading ideologies. Initially, Wilson's (1887) emphasis on law application evolved to encompass relational elements highlighted by Hodgson (1969). Governance in public administration delineates decision-making mechanism regimes governing a public unit, shifting through approaches: Weberian, New Public Management, or New Public Governance. These approaches coexist in practice and reflect the shifts' impacts on policy, cycles and interaction depths within single governed unit (Campbell-Verduyn 2018, Finck 2018, Van Rijmenam 2019). PA's use of BCT (governance "by" blockchain) might contribute to these shifts. BCTiPS projects currently heavily focuses on governance complexities (Brinkmann & Heine 2019,2021&2022, Tan et al., 2022). However analytical, political and legal (Casey and Vigna, 2018) the visions, literature suggests a need for a nuanced understanding emphasizing BCTiPS's practice and potential to reclaim activities previously outsourced to the private sector (Bustamante et al. 2022, Cagigas et al. 2021). BCTiPS' adoption is also associated with transformations and effective decision-making effects in public organizations, highlighting enhanced privacy, robust data security, and cost-efficiency (Sousa 2023, Huang et al. 2021, Toapanta et al. 2018). The literature is still young and associating economic intelligence "good practices" scrutiny might be of relatively important use.

2.2 Economic Intelligence (EI), State EI and BCTiPS

Economic intelligence, is characterized by a difficult definition due to cultural practices, private and public connotations, legal framework of operations, etc... While private EI aims at market advantage and economic efficiency through informed decision-making (Porteous 1995, Potter 1998), state EI serves similar interests at the national level by gathering and utilizing economic data to ensure national prosperity, security, and competitive edges (Martre 1994, Malecki 2017). State EI's coordinated research activities align with national strategies, integrating internal and external functions to support decision-making and national objectives (Allain-Dupré & Duhard 1996, Carayon 2004). The intricate nature of EI, influenced by security, legal, and economic factors, relates closely to governance styles and national agendas (Revel 2010). This synergy between state economic intelligence and public administration also emerges from their common focus towards the state: EI and PA share such a focus on innovation, knowledge management, or efficient service deliveries (Cengiz 2023, Zuboff 2015) further showing their conceptual compatibility.

EI and PA can be considered through ontological categories (Table 1)– an exercise that could help inform the existence of dynamics between governance styles, national agendas and agile policy-making.

Table 1. Economic Intelligence (EI) Public Adminstration (PA) Ontological Similarities observed by author

Ontological characteristic	Public administration	Economic intelligence
Generation	The public administrations are all based on a legal framework determined by the state and the legal framework's appraisal and future direction is highly dependent on the political bias of the decision-makers.	Economic intelligence is a strictly legally grounded field of activity, where interpretation of knowledge acquired is highly susceptible to the practitioner or agents' political biases.
Function	Empirically, PA fundamentally serves the state units, is mainly informed by agents and beneficiaries feedbacks.	Empirically, EI fundamentally is a state tool - it is mainly actionable through information, analyses of the competitive environment
Internal	Governance and structure are politically dependent and decision-making takes place at macro-level	Governance of national EI is politically-structured and decision-making takes place at meso/micro
External	PA's governance share is a relatively new concept. This process takes place at meso or micro levels	EI limitatively shares governance with external actors. This process takes place at macro-level
Levels of analyses	Macro/Meso/Micro - International and regional / National or State / Local or community level	Macro/Meso/Micro - International political economics / State-unit competitive environment / Individual and unit related knowledge creation

Aiming to convey the strategic implications of economic intelligence concerns when it comes to BCTiPS, a building block is thus proposed (Table 2) that seeks to provide an analytical tool. It is based upon Moinet & Deschamps (2017) 6-dimensional view of EI.

Table 2. EI analysis frames in BCTiPS

Dimension	Public administration	Is BCTiPS compatible	EI Tools available
Integrating EI Elements	Aligning project goals with organizational/sectoral strategic intelligence (EI) objectives.	Secure and transparent data sharing for collaborative EI analysis.	System mapping, competitive environment, SWOT, information mapping and audit, ethical charter
Environment Surveillance	Continuous monitoring of relevant external factors impacting the project.	Real-time environmental data tracking and analysis on a trusted platform.	Surveillance parameters, R&D, knowledge modes, search engines, e-reputation
Leveraging Information	Extracting insights from gathered data to inform decision-making.	Secure auditable data analysis with clear provenance for informed decision-making.	PESTEL, network analyses, biases, IP research, mind mapping, red hat analysis
Managing Information & Knowledge	Effectively capturing, storing, sharing, and utilizing project knowledge.	Immutable and transparent knowledge storage and sharing, enhancing collaboration and trust.	Press review, benchmarking, document management, knowledge co-creation, war-room
Protect Immaterial Material	Safeguarding sensitive project information and intellectual property (IP).	Enhanced data security and tamper-proof record-keeping for sensitive information and IP.	Security analysis, social engineering, IPI protection, job and skill forecast
Influence Environment	Shaping the external environment to be more favorable to the project.	Decentralized and transparent stakeholder engagement using blockchain platforms.	Internal communication, PR, crisis coms, lobbying

2.3 Concluding Remarks

The exploration of EI in BCTiPS offers for a compelling set of tools to decipher the complexities of governance, decision-making, and information dynamics in organizations. Despite the elementary nature of its EI-PA scale and subsequent preliminary analytical framework, such approach could present promising policy research interest. Expanding the construct through bibliometric systematic reviews would strengthen its conceptual foundation – as in-depth analyses would help ensure the tools validity for BCTiPS practice.

The objective of providing an EI analysis tool for BCTiPS is to inform policy-making and BCTiPS practices: better understand knowledge leveraging in highly informational environments; establish good practices for governance, and implications of adopting hybrid digital governance; help bridge growingly complex policy-making to transparency and privacy concerns, particular to the public service units.

REFERENCES

Allain-Dupre, P., & Duhard, N. (1996). Les armes secrètes de la décision. Gualino Editeur. ISBN: 9782842000721

Brinkmann, M., & Heine, M. (2019). Can blockchain leverage for New Public Governance? A conceptual analysis on process level. In Proceedings of the 12th International Conference on Theory and Practice of Electronic Governance (ICEGOV'19) (pp. 338–341). ACM, New York, NY. DOI:10.1145/3326365.3326409

Bustamante, P., Cai, M.,Gomez, M., Harris, C., Krishnamurthy,P., Law, W. Madison, M.J., Murtazashvili, I., Murtazashvili, J.B., Mylovanov, T., Shapoval, N., Vee, A., Weiss, M., Government by Code? Blockchain Applications to Public Sector Governance (June 21, 2022). Frontiers in Blockchain, Vol. 5, Art. 869665, p. 1, June 2022, U. of Pittsburgh Legal Studies Research Paper No. 2022-2022, Available at SSRN: https://ssrn.com/abstract=4156869

Cagigas, D., Clifton, J., Fuentes, D., & Fernández-Gutiérrez, M. (2021). Blockchain for Public Services: A Systematic Literature Review. IEEE Access, 9, 13904-13921. https://doi.org/10.1109/ACCESS.2021.3052019

Campbell-Verduyn, M. (Ed.). (2018). Bitcoin and Beyond: Cryptocurrencies, Blockchains, and Global Governance. RIPE Series in Global Political Economy. London, UK: Routledge.

Carayon B. (2003). Intelligence économique, compétitivité et cohésion socials, Rapport au Premier Ministre, Paris, La Documention Française

Casey, M. J., & Vigna, P. (2018). The Truth Machine: The Blockchain and the Future of Everything. HarperCollins.

Cengiz, F. (2023). Blockchain governance and governance via blockchain: decentralized utopia or centralized dystopia? Policy Design and Practice, 6(4), 446-464. https://doi.org/10.1080/25741292.2023.2247203

Choo, K.-K. Raymond., Dehghantanha, Ali., & Parizi, R. M. (2020). Blockchain cybersecurity, trust and privacy. Springer. https://doi.org/10.1007/978-3-030-38181-3

De Filippi, P., Mannan, M., & Reijers, W. (2020). Blockchain as a confidence machine: The problem of trust & challenges of governance. Technology in Society, 62, 101284. https://doi.org/10.1016/j.techsoc.2020.101284

Finck, M. (2018). Blockchain Regulation and Governance in Europe. Cambridge, UK: Cambridge University Press. https://doi.org/10.1017/9781108609708

Forrester, J.W. (1968) Principles of Systems. Productivity Press, Cambridge, MA.

Hodgson, J. S. (1969). Public Administration. New York: McGraw-Hill.

Huang, H., Wang, L., Wu, Y., & Choo, K.-K. R. (2021). Blockchains for Network Security: Principles, Technologies and Applications. Stevenage: Institution of Engineering and Technology.

Malecki, G. (2017). The economic intelligence system as a crucial factor in the success of the responsible development plan. Pulaski Policy Papers.

Martre, H. (1994), « Intelligence économique et stratégie d'entreprise », Rapport du commissariat général au plan

Moinet, N. & Deschamps C. (2017). *La boîte à outils de l'intelligence économique*. Dunod.

Morabito, V. (2017). Business innovation through blockchain: The B3 perspective. Management/business for professionals. Cham: Springer International Publishing.

Nakamoto, S. (2008) Bitcoin: A Peer-to-Peer Electronic Cash System. https://bitcoin.org/bitcoin.pdf

Porteous S. D., (1995) Economic/commercial interests and the world's intelligence services: A Canadian perspective, International Journal of Intelligence and CounterIntelligence, 8:3, 275-306, DOI: 10.1080/08850609508435285

Potter, E. H. (Ed.). (1998). Economic Intelligence and National Security. McGill-Queen's University Press. https://doi.org/10.2307/j.ctt7zt2xt

Revel C., (2010). Economic Intelligence: An Operational Concept for a Globalised World (ARI). Elcano Royal Institute. https://www.realinstitutoelcano.org/en/analyses/economic-intelligence-an-operational-concept-for-a-globalised-world-ari/

Sousa, M. J. (2023). Blockchain as a driver for transformations in the public sector. Policy Design and Practice, 6(4), 415-432. https://doi.org/10.1080/25741292.2023.2267864

Tan, E. (2023). The missing piece: the link between blockchain and public policy design. Policy Design and Practice, 6(4), 488-504. https://doi.org/10.1080/25741292.2023.2233160

Tan, E., & Crompvoets, J. (Eds.). (2022). The New Digital Era Governance: How New Digital Technologies Are Shaping Public Governance [Edited Collection]. ISBN: 978-90-8686-378-5. eISBN: 978-90-8686-930-5. https://doi.org/10.3920/978-90-8686-930-5

Tan, E., Mahula, S., & Crompvoets, J. (2022). Blockchain governance in the public sector: A conceptual framework for public management. Government Information Quarterly, 39(1), 101625. https://doi.org/10.1016/j.giq.2021.101625

Toapanta, M., Mero, J., Huilcapi, D., Tandazo, M., Orizaga, A., & Mafla, E. (2018). A Blockchain Approach to Mitigate Information Security in a Public Organization for Ecuador. IOP Conference Series: Materials Science and Engineering, 423, 012164. https://doi.org/10.1088/1757-899X/423/1/012164

Valori G., E., (2018), The Geopolitical and Financial Significance of Bitcoin. In Israel Defense. Retrieved September 29, 2018, from http://www.israeldefense.co.il/en/node/33017.

Van Rijmenam, M. (2019). A Distributed Future: Where Blockchain Technology Meets Organisation Design and Decision-Making. Medium. https://medium.com/swlh/a-distributed-future-where-blockchain-technology-meets-organisation-design-and-decision-making-ce7430e1a196

Wilson, T.W. (1887) The Study of Administration. Political Science Quarterly, 2, 210. http://dx.doi.org/10.2307/2139277

Zuboff, S. (2015). Big other: Surveillance Capitalism and the Prospects of an Information Civilization. Journal of Information Technology, 30(1), 75-89. https://doi.org/10.1057/jit.2015.5

SHAPING ONLINE LEARNING FOR THE NEXT MAJOR HEALTH EVENT: INSIGHTS FROM COVID-19 PANDEMIC LEARNING RESPONSE

Heini Utunen, Ranil Appuhamy, Anne-Sophie Allegre, Corentin Piroux and Mafalda Dançante
World Health Organization, Avenue Appia 20, CH-1211 Geneva 27, Switzerland

ABSTRACT

OpenWHO, launched by the World Health Organization (WHO) in 2017, is a global online learning platform designed to disseminate essential scientific, technical, and operational knowledge relevant to health emergencies. The COVID-19 pandemic witnessed substantial growth in the platform, marked by an increased number of courses, enrolments, and expanded demographics. In anticipation of future health crises, it is imperative to reflect on achievements and lessons learned. This reflection serves as a foundation for refining and fortifying the approach to online learning, ensuring equitable and timely access to critical health knowledge for everyone. We reviewed internal course production processes, learning platform metadata, published papers, and feedback to determine key lessons learnt and areas to improve for a future health emergency. The paper explores crucial considerations for a robust learning response in the context of large-scale global health emergencies - anticipating learning needs, enabling content adaptation, improving production efficiency, utilizing multiple formats, promoting multilingual learning, exploring public access formats, evaluating registration policies, designing for a global audience, creating engaging content, and enhancing the visibility of learning content during a health emergency.

KEYWORDS

Public Health, Elearning, Pandemic, Health Emergencies, Health Education, Preparedness

1. INTRODUCTION

OpenWHO is the World Health Organization's (WHO) online learning platform that was launched in 2017 to share essential WHO scientific, technical, and operational knowledge with frontline responders and the public with a focus on learning topics relevant to health emergencies. It provides free, self-paced, multilingual courses accessible in low-bandwidth and offline formats.

OpenWHO experienced significant growth throughout the COVID-19 pandemic, reflected in the increased number of courses, enrolments, and extended platform reach (Utunen, Appuhamy, et al., 2023). The platform has 230 courses with the number of enrolments rising from 160,000 in January 2020 to 8 million by November 2023. There was also a shift in learner demographics with more women and the elderly accessing the platform post pandemic (Utunen, George, et al., 2020; Utunen et al., 2021). OpenWHO courses have been translated into over 71 languages.

While OpenWHO has achieved significant and equitable global reach (George et al., 2022), there remain challenges and gaps in disseminating health knowledge where it is most crucial. These include difficulties in reaching individuals with restricted access to technology, limited internet connectivity, and those encountering barriers in digital literacy (Utunen, Appuhamy, et al., 2023).

As we prepare for the next health emergency, it is essential to analyze the factors that led to the growth and reach of the OpenWHO, reflect on the lessons learnt and determine ways to enhance our learning response. This paper aims to delve into key learnings that must be considered to achieve this objective.

2. METHODS

We reviewed internal course production processes and metadata from the learning platform to derive key metrics such as number of courses, enrollments, geographic distribution and learner demographics. We also reviewed published papers on OpenWHO and analyzed feedback from technical teams, learners, and production staff. We used this information to determine lessons learnt and areas to consolidate for a future health emergency.

3. KEY CONSIDERATIONS FOR AN EFFECTIVE LEARNING RESPONSE

Connecting the WHO normative work with ongoing health operations through learning responses, OpenWHO offers a unique comparative advantage to anticipate needs and address them readily, while continuously evaluating and re-adjusting offerings to respond to major health threats. During the COVID-19 pandemic, OpenWHO published in total 36 articles. Investing in operational research and publications helps to validate and share findings that can feedback again into WHO normative and operational work.

Figure 1 presents the key findings from the pandemic learning response 2020-2023, which are further expounded upon in the subsequent text.

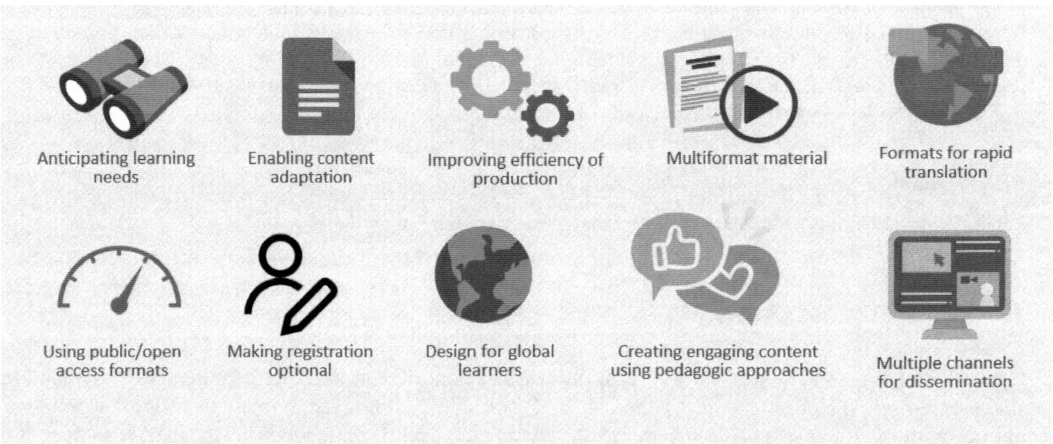

Figure 1. Summary of key findings from the WHO pandemic online learning response 2020-2023

The following key considerations are important when providing a learning response for a large-scale global health emergency.

1. Anticipating learning needs and proactively preparing to address them facilitates a more timely and efficient learning response during a health emergency. This ensures that frontline responders, the public, and other stakeholders have access to up-to-date knowledge aligned with current evidence and technical guidance, particularly in the crucial early stages of the health emergency. This preparedness involves monitoring normative work, such as infectious diseases and health responses to natural hazards and complex humanitarian settings, utilizing pre-prepared material in templates, and developing capacity of content creators.

2. Enabling content adaptation proved to be an efficient strategy in ensuring that learning material could be adapted to local contexts and specific requirements. OpenWHO's learning resources such as videos, presentations and transcripts are downloadable and can be transformed or modified for offline use, an attribute referred to as the learning multiplier effect. Throughout the COVID-19 pandemic, OpenWHO content was extensively utilized across many countries through various modalities such as face-to-face training, local dissemination, distribution on social networks, integration into local curricula, microlearning and distribution to remote/rural setting via USB devices (Utunen *et al.*, 2022). This can ensure that the reach of learning extends beyond the confines of the online format.

3. Improving efficiency of production is important to ensure fast production of course content for a health emergency. This efficiency is crucial to ensure that health professionals and other stakeholders deployed and/or involved in the response can all access the latest guidance from WHO. For example, in 2017 a course on diphtheria was launched on the platform on the same day as the emergency medical teams were about to board the plane to Bangladesh (Rohloff *et al.*, 2018) and in 2020, an introductory COVID-19 course was published four days before the declaration of COVID-19 as a public health emergency of international concern (Utunen et al., 2020). This can be achieved by having pre-prepared course templates, timely collaborations between learning and operations teams, a standardized production pathway (Gamhewage *et al.*, 2020) and the flexibility to quickly update material as evidence or guidance evolves.

4. Producing learning products in multiple formats enhances accessibility and accommodates diverse learning preferences. OpenWHO learning content is available as presentations, videos and documents which are downloadable. This versatility caters to a broad audience with varying learning backgrounds and styles, allowing individuals to engage with the content in a manner that aligns with their preferences and needs. In addition to this, offering content in various formats supports learners with different technological constraints or sovereign restrictions, ensuring broader accessibility and outreach.

5. Enabling multilingual learning not only reduces language related barriers but can enhance the reach and accessibility of learning material. Providing learning material in the native language of a community has been shown to increase learners' comprehension of information (Perera *et al.*, 2012; Arora *et al.*, 2014; Translators Without Borders, 2015). Language usage data from the platform has demonstrated that, regardless of where learners resided, they preferred to learn in their native languages (Utunen et al., 2020). OpenWHO has undertaken the translation of courses into over 71 languages, with a specific focus on languages spoken by vulnerable or underserved populations, aiming to maximize accessibility and enabling learners to access educational content in their preferred languages. Rapid translation of OpenWHO material is done through a network of translators and working with regional and country offices to adapt course materials in national and local languages. An automated transcription and translation tool called "Transpipe" is also used to increase the speed and efficiency of translation (Utunen et al., 2023). Computer-generated transcription offers an efficient and cost-effective alternative to translation services for most languages. With the significant progress of Artificial Intelligence in the past years, this model may prove to be the most effective solution in a future learning response to an acute public health emergency.

6. Using public/open access formats to host courses in addition to the OpenWHO platform is likely to enhance the dissemination of learning content, particularly in the context of a large-scale health emergency. Leveraging diverse platforms and dissemination methods for public/open access formats enhances the reach and impact of learning content during global health emergencies, ensuring timely and broad-based access to critical information across different communities and regions. However, it is important to strike a balance between this broader dissemination and the ability to provide uniform updates across all platforms.

7. Making registration optional could prove beneficial for certain learners, enhancing accessibility by eliminating potential barriers. Some individuals may be hesitant to provide personal details to access. However, the disadvantage of this is that learners would be unable to track their learning progress or receive a certificate of completion.

8. Designing for a global audience is important for a global learning platform, to ensure universal access and equity. When developing learning materials, it is crucial to consider variations in literacy, learning styles, language, technological access, and cultural backgrounds. Tailoring content to accommodate these factors leads to a more equitable educational experience, fostering a broader reach and impact (George *et al.*, 2022).

9. Creating engaging content using adult education approaches is crucial for a learning platform because it enhances the effectiveness of the learning experience. Applying evidence-based instructional design strategies to OpenWHO courses is important to facilitate better retention, nudge behavior change, increase motivation and promote comprehension of the learning material (Utunen et al., 2023). For example, an analysis of pre-and post-test scores from COVID-19 vaccine courses showed an impact on knowledge gained. On average, learners scored 76% on the pre-course quiz and showed improvement to 85% on the post-course quiz (Goldin *et al.*, 2021).

10. Improving visibility of learning content during a health emergency is important so that it can be found and used by health responders, the public, and other stakeholders. Additionally, this accessibility plays a pivotal role in mitigating the 'infodemic,' defined here as an excess of information of varying quality, including false and/or misleading information in digital and physical environments during an acute public health event. The COVID-19 pandemic underscored the extensive use of technology and social media on a massive scale, exacerbating the infodemic and impeding effective pandemic control measures, and leading to loss of lives (Islam *et al.*, 2020; WHO *et al.*, 2020). Hence, enhancing the searchability of learning content becomes imperative. Strategies to achieve this goal include the implementation of effective and pertinent search engine optimization (SEO) strategies, utilization of existing tools and platforms to raise awareness and guide learners to relevant courses, and collaboration with partner institutions to promote courses and extend their reach.

Health emergency learning production can be at its most efficient when using multiple formats that work for different use cases, both for learners and learning multipliers. Ability to translate quickly is of key essence, to be able to reach diverse learners groups with constantly evolving needs. Expecting more complex health-related crises, which will present a combination of vulnerabilities with climate change consequences and multi-hazards, it will be important to also prepare for multi-pathogen learning responses readily deployable on a large scale (Figure 2). While preparing for the next major health event, it will be critical to continue innovating in health emergency learning, and to continue focusing on the learners for more personalized just-in-time and on-the-go learning that helps save lives and alleviate suffering.

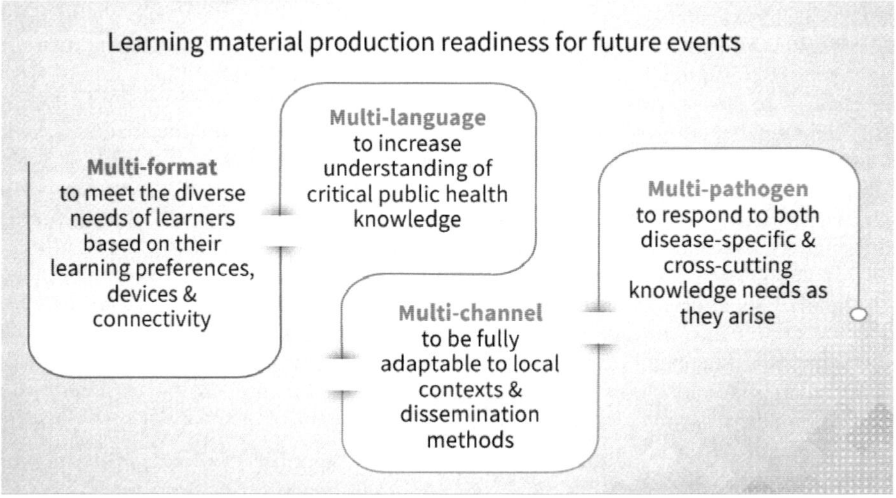

Figure 2. Summary of core considerations for online learning material readiness for future major epidemic events

4. CONCLUSION

The COVID-19 pandemic revealed to be a turning point for public health and online learning, unveiling both strengths and limitations of our own current systems. This has prompted us to reflect on key takeaways that could serve as a blueprint for a learning response for future health emergencies.

The ability to anticipate learners' needs and proactively and timely set up necessary systems and approaches, ensures a more efficient and effective learning response to a health emergency. Timely and efficient content production, combined with the adaptability of learning materials to local contexts and language requirements allows for addressing diverse learning needs and preferences. Designing materials in multiple formats, in line with the latest evidence in adult learning enhances accessibility and learning uptake. Finally, the use of additional open-access systems for course hosting, with the option of non-mandatory registration is likely to augment learning dissemination and reduce potential barriers.

REFERENCES

Arora, A. *et al.* (2014) 'What do these words mean? A qualitative approach to explore oral health literacy in Vietnamese immigrant mothers in Australia', *Health Education Journal*, 73(3), pp. 303–312. Available at: https://doi.org/10.1177/0017896912471051.

Gamhewage, G. *et al.* (2020) 'Fast-tracking WHO's COVID-19 technical guidance to training for the frontline', *WHO Weekly epidemiological record*, 23/24(95), pp. 257–264. Available at: https://apps.who.int/iris/bitstream/handle/10665/332276/WER9523-24-eng-fre.pdf.

George, R. *et al.* (2022) 'Ensuring equity in access to online courses: Perspectives from the WHO health emergency learning response', *World Medical & Health Policy*, 14(2), pp. 413–427. Available at: https://doi.org/10.1002/WMH3.492.

Goldin, S. *et al.* (2021) 'Learning from a massive open online COVID-19 Vaccination training experience: Survey study', *JMIR Public Health and Surveillance*, 7(12), p. e33455. Available at: https://doi.org/10.2196/33455.

Islam, M.S. *et al.* (2020) 'COVID-19–Related Infodemic and Its Impact on Public Health: A Global Social Media Analysis', *The American Journal of Tropical Medicine and Hygiene*, 103(4), pp. 1621–1629. Available at: https://doi.org/10.4269/AJTMH.20-0812.

Perera, K.Y.S. *et al.* (2012) 'Medium of language in discharge summaries: would the use of native language improve patients' knowledge of their illness and medications?', *Journal of health communication*, 17(2), pp. 141–148. Available at: https://doi.org/10.1080/10810730.2011.585926.

Rohloff, T. *et al.* (2018) *OpenWHO: Integrating Online Knowledge Transfer into Health Emergency Response, Conference: The 13th European Conference on Technology Enhanced Learning At: Leeds, UK Volume: EC-TEL 2018.* Available at: https://ceur-ws.org/Vol-2193/.

Translators Without Borders (2015) *Does Translated Health-Related Information Lead to Higher Comprehension? A Study of Rural and Urban Kenyans*. Available at: https://translatorswithoutborders.org/wp-content/uploads/2017/04/TWB_WoR_ImpactStudy_FINAL.pdf.

Utunen, H., Ndiaye, N., *et al.* (2020) 'Global reach of an online covid-19 course in multiple languages on openwho in the first quarter of 2020: Analysis of platform use data', *Journal of Medical Internet Research*, 22(4), p. e19076. Available at: https://doi.org/10.2196/19076.

Utunen, H., George, R., *et al.* (2020) 'Responding to Global Learning Needs during a Pandemic: An Analysis of the Trends in Platform Use and Incidence of COVID-19', *Education Sciences*, 10(11), p. 345. Available at: https://doi.org/10.3390/EDUCSCI10110345.

Utunen, H. *et al.* (2021) 'Changes in Users Trends Before and During the COVID-19 Pandemic on WHO's Online Learning Platform', *Studies in health technology and informatics*, 287, pp. 163–164. Available at: https://doi.org/10.3233/SHTI210838.

Utunen, H. *et al.* (2022) 'Learning multiplier effect of OpenWHO.org: use of online learning materials beyond the platform', *WHO Weekly epidemiological record*, Nos 1/2(97), pp. 1–7. Available at: https://www.who.int/publications/i/item/WER9701-02-1-7.

Utunen, H., Appuhamy, R., *et al.* (2023) 'Observations from three years of online pandemic learning response on OpenWHO', *International Journal of Information and Learning Technology*, 40(5), pp. 527–540. Available at: https://doi.org/10.1108/IJILT-12-2022-0220.

Utunen, H., Crowder, R., *et al.* (2023) 'Promoting Learning Retention and Nudging Behavior Change through Learning Design Practices for WHO Online Platform', *Journal of Educators Online* , 20(3), p. 2. Available at: https://doi.org/10.9743/JEO.2023.20.3.2.

Utunen, H., Staubitz, T., *et al.* (2023) 'Scale Up Multilingualism in Health Emergency Learning: Developing an Automated Transcription and Translation Tool', *Studies in health technology and informatics*, 302, pp. 408–412. Available at: https://doi.org/10.3233/SHTI230162.

WHO *et al.* (2020) 'Joint Statement. Managing the COVID-19 infodemic: Promoting healthy behaviours and mitigating the harm from misinformation and disinformation', *WHO News*, 23 September. Available at: https://www.who.int/news/item/23-09-2020-managing-the-covid-19-infodemic-promoting-healthy-behaviours-and-mitigating-the-harm-from-misinformation-and-disinformation.

DESIGN PATTERNS FOR MOBILE LEARNING IN DIGITAL MULTICULTURAL ACADEMIC COURSES

Liat Eyal[1, 2*] and Talia Traister[3*]
[1]*Levinsky-Wingate Academic Center, Shoshana Persits St 15, Tel Aviv-Yafo, Israel*
[2]*MOFET R&D Institute, Shoshana Persits St 15, Tel Aviv-Yafo, Israel*
[3]*Ono Academic College, Pinsker 18a Herzeliya, Israel*
[*]*Ph.D*

ABSTRACT

Multicultural classes in academia present challenges, intensified further in the context of online learning. Addressing these disparities requires innovative solutions to the challenges stemming from the diverse cultural backgrounds, religious affiliations, age disparities, varying learning skills, and differences in technology access.
This study employs Design-Based Research (DBR) methodology to tackle these challenges. Through iterative processes involving expert collaboration, several Design Patterns (DPs) were identified and refined. All design patterns revolve around digital and visual literacy. The study's findings indicate that implementing various Design Patterns in a multicultural class using mobile learning and a shared visual language can be highly effective.
These Design Patterns foster a common vocabulary, and cultivate essential learning skills to bridge existing gaps, they facilitate recognition of the learning space and interactions between the students. This paper presents four design patterns that serve as the didactic foundation for designing visual academic learning using smartphones: 'The Power of Selfies' – Leveraging selfies for active learning; 'Album Anchored Theory' – Utilizing personal picture repositories to grasp abstract theoretical models ; 'Between Image and Word' – Utilizing metaphors to enhance vocabulary; 'Research in a "Physital" Environment' – Collaborative learning without textual overload in an intriguing virtual setting.
These patterns offer the basis to structure multicultural online lessons effectively.

KEYWORDS

Multicultural Classes, Visual Literacy, Mobile Learning, Design-Based Research (DBR), Design Patterns (DPs)

1. INTRODUCTION

Academia is a multicultural environment. Each culture identified by a unique set of symbolic tools that are internalized, consequently leading to diverse cognitive behaviors. These cultural attributes further compound the inherent complexities within digital platform learning processes. The challenges stem from language barriers, variations in learning aptitudes, deficiencies in self-organizational skills, digital illiteracy, disparities in learning perceptions, and ability to articulate personal and critical viewpoints (Eyal & Gil, 2020).

Additionally, there are technical challenges such as internet accessibility and the availability of sufficient computers, particularly when all family members are mandated to engage in remote learning, as witnessed during the Covid-19 pandemic.

To bridge both cultural and technical gaps, Visual Literacy using mobile phones was chosen. Mobile Learning created a platform for active and collaborative learning. In parallel, an active WhatsApp group complemented the learning process, providing quick access to support and material, fostered a sense of belonging, enhanced motivation, and nurtured a feeling of capability.

2. GOALS

This study aims to conceptualize the cumulative knowledge acquired through multicultural groups during their academic courses. The courses employed Visual Language within a dialogue-driven, active, and collaborative

Mobile Learning environment. The repetitive nature of the design-based research (DBR) enabled successful creation and distribution of the best practices using the design patterns.

3. METHODOLOGY

Design-based research (DBR) was chosen for this study. It represents a research approach tailored for analyzing teaching practices within the learning environments. It endeavors to enhance teaching through a cyclical process of design, implement, evaluate, improve, test, iterated until optimal levels are achieved. DBR facilitates the development of effective practices and their distribution through the utilization of Design Patterns.

Such Design-based Research was undertaken within expansive multicultural academic online courses. The cultural differences spanned many areas such as religion, language, learning capabilities, technological access, efficacy, motivation for learning, and other factors.

Various instructors taught each unit across multiple courses, with class sizes ranging from 50 to 100 students. Feedback was collected from students, instructors, and expert groups. This feedback, coupled with insights gathered from the WhatsApp groups that accompanied each class, contributed to refining and enhancing the course material before its next iteration.

By employing this iterative process of design, implement, evaluate, improve, and test, four distinct Design Patterns (DPs) were extracted and applied to structure the accumulated knowledge. These patterns articulate actionable methods and expertise intended for reuse across diverse contexts as well as aid trainees. It includes didactive organization of units, each one can include any content in different ways (Eyal & Gil, 2020).

4. KEY FINDINGS

Each design pattern template centers around a distinct challenge, offering its contextual background, the specific challenge it poses, and the research's focal question. It further presents a solution, delineates the activity steps at the student level, acknowledges solution limitations, and provides recommendations for instructors' assimilation. This paper exclusively focuses on the questions (Q) and solutions (S) sections within the framework of the four design patterns, the remaining elements will be elaborated during presentation.

The power of selfie

Q: How can passive learners, particularly those hesitant to speak in a large group, be encouraged to become active participants?

S: A collective exhibition showcasing student-created selfies serves as a foundation for group analysis. Each selfie symbolizes a concept or idea, complemented by a verbal explanation.

Utilizing a picture album for model representation

Q: How can an abstract theoretical model be transformed into an accessible learning tool?

S: Students leverage their existing mobile photo libraries to select images that symbolize elements of the theoretical model. Working in pairs, they engage in a comparative process, matching photos to represent different facets of the model. Subsequently, students present their interpretations within a shared environment for group analysis.

Between image and word

Q: How to bridge the linguistic gap between students and build a shared vocabulary?

S: Utilizing visual metaphors such as photographs, images, sketches, and more to introduce concepts, ideas, or processes. Decoding these visual representations initiates dialogue, establishes a shared vocabulary, and clarifies messages collaboratively.

Collaborative learning through research in a "physital" environment

Q: How to cope with deficient learning skills without over textualization?

S: Transition the research activities into a "physital" environment that simulates physical reality in a virtual way. The environment incorporates additional learning scaffolding that open on demand.

5. DISCUSSION AND CONCLUSIONS

To navigate complex multicultural classrooms, we embraced a Visual Language utilizing mobile phones as a teaching tool in workshop-style academic courses.

The symbols of the visual language and their combinations are linked with society, culture, time, and space that influence how the material is absorbed and understood (Peshat, 2021). The transition to distance learning does not automatically make learning multicultural (Jørgensen et al. 2020). The multicultural approach aspires to promote learning while honoring diversion. It enforces exposure to other cultures while committing all its participants to contribute to the learning process (Paul-Binyamin & Reingold, 2020). Teaching and learning using visual tools, especially ones created and interpreted by students, enables them to find common grounds. This promotes trust and respect between group members. The ability to express themselves visually in familiar surroundings encourages dialog and a deeper understanding of the experiences of the rest of the group (Yenawine, 2013). Sharing personal stories that are hidden behind the visual gives a positive experience, enhances self-esteem, and gives a feeling of capability – all of which motivate learning and academic success (Paul-Binyamin, Reingold, 2020).

The study shows that making use of Mobile Learning with visual approach, ignites excitement, curiosity, and motivation among students. Leveraging the camera and authentic photographs fosters a connection to the students' world, promoting increased engagement.

Our approach aims to uncover meaning and interpret text by deconstructing, verbalizing, and promoting awareness of reading and thinking processes. Employing Visual Thinking Strategy (VTS) encourages observation, theorization, and evidence-based reasoning, supporting robust thinking and learning (Yenawine, 2013). Utilizing artifacts: student-created representations, sketches, and artwork - break language barriers, fostering dialogue that enriches vocabulary and promotes active, collaborative learning. Transitioning learning into a visual virtual environment facilitates additional explanations, serving as scaffolding to support students with learning gaps, enabling them to catch up, achieve success, and bolster their sense of accomplishment.

The WhatsApp group played a pivotal role in fostering a sense of belonging and accomplishment, enabling immediate resolution of challenges, discussions, and real-time adjustments of teaching, ensuring up-to-date information tailored to current needs. Furthermore, the use of visual language fosters an environment of relative equality among students, requiring all, regardless of background, to acquire new tools and skills.

REFERENCES

Ben Peshat, M. (2021). The Field of Visaul Literacy: Local Insights into Theory, Practice and Interpretation, Mofet institute.

Eyal, L., & Gil, E. (2020). Design patterns for teaching in academic settings in future learning spaces. *British Journal of Educational Technology, 51(4),* 1061-1077.

Jørgensen, M., Mason, A., Pedersen, R., & Harrison, R. (2020). The transformative learning potential in the hybrid space between technology and intercultural encounters. *Journal of Studies in International Education, 26(3)*, 318–333. ISSN 1028-3153.

Paul-Binyamin, I., Reingold, R., Editors (2020). Shared Spaces in the Education System and Academia, Beit Berl College and Mofet Institute (Hebrew).

Yenawine, P. (2013). *Visual thinking strategies: Using art to deepen learning across school disciplines*. Harvard Education Press.

Posters

EXPECTATIONS FOR THE USE OF TELEPSYCHOLOGY IN THE PROMOTION OF HEALTHY HABITS IN MEXICAN ADULTS FOR THE DEVELOPMENT OF A MOBILE APP

Lorena Alejandra Flores Plata, Anabel de la Rosa Gómez, Javier Darío Ríos Castillo, Zuleyca Pérez Martínez, Blanca Anel Perea Aguirre and Liliana Moreyra Jiménez
Faculty of Higher Studies Iztacala, SUAYED, National Autonomous University of Mexico, Mexico

ABSTRACT

A qualitative study was carried out as part of the developing a mobile application for the prevention of mental health issues in the Mexican population, taking advantage of the increasing use and positive evidence of Telepsychology. A focus group was carried out with 10 participants aged 18 to 50, focusing on mental health services and attitudes toward receiving such services through Telepsychology and an e-health application. The UTAUT model, with a panel of experts, was used for deductive content analysis. The results highlight the importance of previous experiences, privacy, infrastructure, and trust in the therapist as crucial factors in designing services that meet the needs and preferences of users.

KEYWORDS

Mobile App, Telepsychology, Prevention, E-Health

1. INTRODUCTION

Mental disorders impact over 970 million individuals globally, with only one in five receiving treatment, WHO (2022) emphasizes the need for preventive actions at the primary level due to factors like stigma, time constraints, economic aspects, and challenges in accessing preventive services. Telepsychology, a technological advancement in psychological care, employs various communication tools to provide services, aiming to inform, generate preventive actions, evaluate, and perform interventions (APA, 2013). Mobile applications utilizing techniques such as mindfulness, sleep regulation programs, and AI chatbot, contribute to demonstrating the effectiveness of application use (Aislaity et al., 2022).

This study, guided by the UTAUT model, qualitatively explores the perspectives of the Mexican population regarding mental health and telepsychology services. The research employs deductive content analysis and open coding to analyze arguments and attitudes.

2. BODY OF PAPER

Telepsychology offers advantages over face-to-face therapy, including cost reduction, time savings, and expanded access to remote locations, especially for individuals with physical or emotional challenges (Lin et al., 2022). However, limitations exist, such as the reliance on a stable internet connection, technical issues, difficulties in crisis intervention, and the absence of physical contact, which is essential for some individuals (Perrin et al., 2020).

Therefore the increasing accessibility of the internet and smartphones has led to a surge in mental health applications. Smartphones, being readily available tools, contribute to treatment adherence through reminders (Gaviria-Mendoza et al., 2021). Mobile applications address various mental health concerns, including stress regulation, depression, modification of beliefs, OCD-related symptoms, and the promotion of well-being, self-compassion, and gratitude (Márquez et al., 2023; Karyotaki et al., 2021; Roncero et al., 2019; Serlachius et al., 2020).

It is also important to note that the UTAUT model is employed in studies related to technology adoption and use. UTAUT aims to explain technology acceptance and use, incorporating variables such as performance expectancy, effort expectation, social influence, and facilitating conditions (Staeck et al., 2022). This theory provides a framework for understanding the interaction and intervention in the use of technology in various contexts.

2.1 Method

The study employed a cross-sectional qualitative methodology using a grounded theory design, deductive content analysis, and open coding based on the UTAUT model. The research session involved a video call with a moderator, two observers, and an auditor. A convenience sample of 10 Mexican participants aged 18 to 52 (M=27, SD=11.9), including students and workers, was selected. This sample size was deemed appropriate for a comprehensive analysis of the shared information (Martinez, 2006). Inclusion criteria were established, requiring participants to be of legal age, not under psychological treatment or psychiatric medication during the sessions, committed to attending with the camera on, and consenting to participation. The entire session was subsequently transcribed for content analysis by a panel of experts.

2.2 Results

In the initial section of the study, which focused on users' performance expectations, the relevance of receiving preventive mental health tools and coping skills was underscored. Users expressed a tension between the convenience and intrusiveness of smartphone apps, particularly those related to mental health. While some users found automated tracking useful, others perceived it as disruptive to their daily routines. Additionally, challenges related to maintaining privacy during remote sessions and issues with internet connectivity emerged as influential factors. Furthermore, there was not unanimous agreement on the belief that establishing emotional connections with therapists at a distance was difficult.

Concerning the social influence variable, there was a positive appreciation for psychological care, with recognition of the importance of forming support communities in this context. However, traditional personal services remained the preferred choice. Participants addressed negative beliefs about mental health problems, with some feeling that these thoughts were misconceptions and did not align with their own thinking. There was emphasized need for applications to be more humane, provide up-to-date or novel information, and be adaptable for mental health care. The reiterated idea was the necessity for career guidance, in contrast to relying solely on a personal support network. The use of multimedia resources, especially videos and images, was highlighted as effective tools for intervention. Participants expected therapists to be knowledgeable and capable of using these resources to complement their work. In the discussion, participants reflected on the constant tension between in-person and online care. Considering a hybrid model, people could consult with a therapist in situations that require support but also rely on resources, particularly multimedia and reliable information.

3. CONCLUSION

This study provides valuable insight into the expectations and needs of a small sample of potential users of mental health services through technological and digital tools. It highlights the positive interest in mental health services, the use of technology to receive psychological support and the desirability of characteristics in the use of telepsychology. Some limitations are identified such as that the findings are based on this specific and limited sample of participants, which may not fully represent the diversity of general experiences, so it will be advisable for future research to diversify the samples. Although it is recognized that these findings can be an important guide for the development of telepsychology interventions, further research on the accessibility, effectiveness, and quality of technology-based services will be needed.

ACKNOWLEDGEMENT

Research carried out thanks to the project PAPIIT-UNAM TA300223.

REFERENCES

American Psychological Association. (2013). Telepsychology Guidelines for Psychologists. *Guidelines for the practice of telepsychology* Vol. 68, No. 9, 791-800. https://www.apa.org/pubs/journals/features/amp-a0035001.pdf

Aislaity, A., Suruliraj, B., Oyebode, O., Fowles, J., & Orji, R. (2022). Mobile Applications for Health and Wellness: A Systematic Review. *Proceedings of the ACM on Human-Computer Interaction*, Vol. 6, No. 171, 1-29.

Gaviria-Mendoza, A., Emura-Vélez, M. H., García-Ospina, D. A., Machado-Duque, M. E., & Machado-Alba, J. E. (2021). Cibersalud y salud móvil: adherencia al tratamiento en enfermedades crónicas. *Rev. Fac. Med.*, Vol. 69, No. 3, e78766. https://doi.org/10.15446/revfacmed.v69n3.78766

Karyotaki, E., Efthimiou, O., Miguel, C., Mass, F., Furukawa, T., Cuijpers, P., et al. (2021). Internet-based cognitive behavioral therapy for depression: a systematic review and individual patient data network meta-analysis. *JAMA Psychiatry*, Vol. 78, 361–371.

Lin, T., Heckman, T. G., & Anderson, T. (2022). The efficacy of synchronous teletherapy versus in-person therapy: A meta-analysis of randomized clinical trials. *Clin. Psychol. Sci. Pract.*, Vol. 29, 167–178. https://doi.org/10.1037/cps0000056

Márquez, L., Sánchez, L., & Jiménez, J. (2023). Aplicación móvil para realizar pruebas y recomendaciones relacionadas con el estrés en estudiantes universitarios. *Revista Electrónica Instituto Politécnico Nacional*, Vol. 15, No. 28, 1-5.

Martínez, M., 2006. *Validez y confiabilidad en la metodología cualitativa*. Trillas.

Organización Mundial de la Salud, [OMS]. (2022). La OMS subraya la urgencia de transformar la salud mental y los cuidados conexos. Organización Panamericana de la Salud. https://www.paho.org/es/noticias/17-6-2022-oms-subraya-urgencia-transformar-salud-mental-cuidados-conexos#:~:text=Las%20desigualdades%20sociales%20y%20econ%C3%B3micas,a%C3%B1o%20de%20la%20pandemia%20solamente.

Perrin, P. B., Rybarczyk, B. D., Pierce, B. S., Jones, H. A., Shaffer, C., & Islam L. (2020). Rapid telepsychology deployment during the COVID-19 pandemic: A special issue commentary and lessons from primary care psychology training. *J Clin Psychol.*, Vol. 76, No. 6, 1173-1185. doi: 10.1002/jclp.22969

Roncero, M., Belloch, A., y Doron, G. (2019). Can brief, daily training using a mobile app help change maladaptive beliefs? Crossover randomized controlled trial. Journal of Medical Internet Researc., Vol. 7, No. 2, 1-14. https://doi.org/10.2196/11443

Serlachius, A., Schache, K., Boggiss, A., Lim, D., Wallace-Boyd, K., Brenton-Peters, J., Buttenshaw, E., Chadd, S., Cavadino, A., Cao, N., Morunga, E., & Thabrew, H. (2020). Coping Skills Mobile App to Support the Emotional Well-Being of Young People During the COVID-19 Pandemic: Protocol for a Mixed Methods Study. *JMIR Res Protoc*, Vol. 9, No. 10, e23716. https://doi.org/10.2196/23716

Staeck, R., Drüge, M., Albisser, S., & Watzke, B. (2022). Acceptance of E-mental health interventions and its determinants among psychotherapists-in-training during the first phase of COVID-19. Internet Interventions, Vol. 29. https://doi.org/10.1016/j.invent.2022.100555.

PSYCHOLOGICAL AND ORGANIZATIONAL ASPECTS OF REMOTE INTERACTION BETWEEN DOCTOR AND PATIENT DURING TELECONSULTATIONS FOR REMOTE ROTATIONAL SETTLEMENTS USING FEEDBACK

Alexander Penkov, Roman Chertovskikh, Valery Stolyar, Maya Amcheslavskaya, Catherine Shimkevich and Tatyana Lyapunova
Department of Medical Informatics and Telemedicine,
Patrice Lumumba Peoples' Friendship University of Russia, Russia

ABSTRACT

This article is devoted to a comprehensive study of the organization and conduct of teleconsultations in the context of developing and young remote industrial areas, which will enable the organization and conduct of quality remote sessions between doctor and patient. This study investigated the influence of feedback from patients on the quality of telemedicine counseling sessions. The empirical part involved 57 physicians consulting residents of rotational settlements in the Far North of the Russian Federation. The doctors were randomized into experimental and control groups. In the experimental group, feedback from the patient on 5 parameters was provided after each consultation. The results showed that the introduction of feedback significantly improved patients' subjective evaluations of the quality of consultations in the experimental group compared to the control group ($p \leq 0.05$). Feedback from patients stimulates doctors to pay more attention to psychological aspects of interaction and increases the feeling of care from the medical organization. The obtained data can be used to improve the organization of telemedicine services in remote regions.

KEYWORDS

Telemedicine, Contact with the Patient, Teleconsultation, Remote Consulting Doctor-Patient, Client-Oriented Medical Organization, Remote Provision of Medical Care, Feedback

1. INTRODUCTION

There is a need to organize teleconsultation from the medical station with the nearest hospitals or medical centers in order to get a second opinion in case of health problems of the shift workers. This is especially important for resolving complex cases, including discussing the need for evacuation or discussing stabilization of the patient if immediate evacuation is difficult. However, equally important and interesting is the possibility to consult directly with doctors of the "big land" without the need to involve a member of the medical station staff.

Availability of medical services in remote rotational settlements is one of the most important tasks, the solution of which determines the health of rotational workers, their well-being, their quality of life and competitive advantage in employment. It is possible to ensure timely and prompt consultations with doctors of various specializations, who are absent among regular medical personnel in the rotational settlements, with the help of modern digital solutions and teleconsultations. Preparation of remote doctor-patient interaction has certain norms, rules and aspects - psychological, organizational and technical.

2. SPECIFIC FEATURES OF ESTABLISHING PSYCHOLOGICAL CONTACT IN THE CONDITIONS OF TELEMEDICAL CONSULTATION WITH THE USE OF FEEDBACK FROM PATIENTS

With the development of technology, telemedicine is an important aspect of health care delivery. For example, M. Hyder and J. Razzaq (2020) show that telemedicine has great potential to improve the quality of patient care, reduce re-hospitalizations, and increase cost savings for both patients and providers. That being said, the COVID-19 pandemic has led to a significant increase in the use of telemedicine for healthcare delivery. In addition, L. Ussher-Pines, for example, that in addition to direct teleconsultation for illness, "telemedicine services can act as a 'safety valve' for patients who have difficulty accessing care during a public health emergency" (Uscher-Pines et al., 2020)

According to researchers D.V. Melik-Guseynov et al (2019) telemedicine allows providers to deliver health care services to patients in remote locations by conducting "virtual visits" via videoconference. This is another factor in increasing the popularity of telemedicine on the one hand, and improving the quality of medical care in remote regions on the other.

Norwegian researchers report that the main services received through telemedicine in Arctic areas include teleconsultation (24%), teleradiology (22%), teledermatology and tele-education (8%), telemonitoring and telecardiology (telesonography) (3%) and other services (27%) (Woldaregay et al. 2017). At the same time, in the conditions of the Arctic in the Russian Federation, as A.A. Dudarev (2013) notes, the problems of lack of qualified assistance are only increasing. This makes the problem of organizing telemedical consultations in these regions particularly urgent.

At the same time, the problem remains the acquisition of telemedical counseling skills by specialists, as well as the allocation of key components of quality telemedical consultation. In foreign literature there are examples of development of special training courses for telemedical consultation. Thus, M. Mulcare et al.(2020) showed that special training with the use of simulation method seriously improved teleconsultation skills of medical students. Also a training program for nurses was tested by K. Rutledge. In Russian Federation A.V. Vladzimirsky and A.I. Andreev (2018) note in their review article that the system of teaching telemedicine skills should be built at several levels, starting with theoretical aspects in university courses and ending with practical skills at the level of master's and postgraduate education. At the same time, the authors of the review emphasize the highly specialized approach of telemedicine consultation skills for doctors of different profiles.

The first condition for a successful teleconsultation is a quality contact with the patient, which the doctor establishes at a distance, starts from the first seconds of teleconsultation - from what the patient sees and hears. From what he sees and hears and will depend on all further happening between him and the doctor - empathic contact, established trust and mutual understanding or dissatisfaction and disappointment in teleconsultations forever. In order for the patient to see an attentive, empathic, listening doctor - this doctor he needs to be shown - so very disembodied, the position of the doctor in the frame. In communicative interaction the interlocutor trusts more the one who is open, therefore in the frame should be not a "talking head", but an open, well-lit silhouette of the doctor, whose gaze is directed at the patient in the first place.

On the left in Figure 1, the position in the frame is incorrect; on the right, it is correct.

Figure 1. Position in the frame

Such a landing and position in the frame informs about the professional, businesslike approach of the doctor - he has specially prepared, equipped the workplace for teleconsultation, he is open, attentive to the patient and ready to start working.

The second component is psychological. To begin contact with a patient immediately and without preparation is a sure way to a cold conversation in which the two interlocutors are alienated from each other and separated by thousands of kilometers. It is very important to start the consultation with a "small talk" (small talk). It can be a compliment, not necessarily to the appearance, but, for example, to the fact that the meeting started on time, minute by minute.

The success of teleconsultation lies in the preliminary preparation of the patient. It is very good when the patient on the eve of receiving a small file - instructions for preparation for teleconsultation. It specifies the requirements for visual demonstration of the investigated place (burn, wound, rash, etc.), for lighting. It is desirable to indicate that the teleconsultation is better to "come" with a desktop computer or laptop, and smartphone or tablet, on the contrary, are not suitable for it - the patient's hands should be completely free.

The fourth component is technical means, the quality of the Internet network, bandwidth and hardware and software. It is possible to go to a remote interaction session only using a channel with a speed of at least 20 mbps.

The fifth component is the choice of platform for online contacts. Conducting a quality teleconsultation by using free platforms is not the best solution. Here we are talking about the security of personal data, the quality of the platform, and the service capabilities. It is best to use those platforms that are specifically designed and developed for remote consultations with a doctor.

Using a proprietary digital platform that also has the brand of the medical company adds credibility and disposes the patient more than using well-known free platforms.

The purpose of our empirical study was to investigate the use of feedback forms as a factor that improves the quality of teleconsultations for remote regions

Research methodology

Assessments. The quality of the teleconsultation conducted by patients was assessed based on a feedback form including the following questions: Communication skills and behavior of the doctor, Ease of establishing an emotional connection, Clarity of instructions and explanations, Quality of the technical component (video, audio, communication), Overall satisfaction with the teleconsultation experience.

Study Participants. The empirical part of the study involved 57 physicians providing teleconsultation services to residents of remote rotational settlements in the far north of the Russian Federation. Of these, 23 were women and 34 were men, aged 31 to 53 years.

Study procedure. The subjects were randomized into two groups. In the experimental group (Group 1), within 6 weeks, each doctor was provided with feedback from the patient after the teleconsultation with scores for each of the 5 parameters and an aggregated assessment of the quality of the consultation. Each of the doctors in the expert group conducted at least 27 teleconsultations.

Results. After the test period was over, the mean scores of the quality of the conducted counseling in the control and experimental groups were calculated. The results are summarized in Table 1.

Table 1. Comparison of telemedicine counseling quality indicators before and after the introduction of patient feedback in the control and experimental groups (according to patient assessment)

Statisitcs		**1-st group (experimental) (n=25)**		**2-nd group (control) (n=32)**	
		before	after	before	after
Mean		29,72	38,24	27,68	26,96
95% Confidence Interval for	Lower Bound	23,97	22,99	34,63	25,28
Mean	Upper Bound	35,46	32,38	41,84	28,65
Median		34,00	40,00	25,50	27,00
Variance		193,62	76,27	169,44	21,83
Std. Deviation		13,91	8,73	13,017	4,67
Fisher's F test empirical			***6.724***		***0.86***
p -level			***0.13***		***0.770***

Thus, we have shown that the introduction of feedback for a doctor conducting consultations remotely significantly ($p \leq 0.05$) improves patients' subjective assessments of the quality of counseling. The introduction of feedback seems to stimulate doctors, on the one hand, to pay attention to the psychological aspects of contact with the patient during the counseling session. On the other hand, providing a form of feedback may increase the feeling of importance and care on the part of the medical organization for patients.

3. CONCLUSION

With teleconsultations, it is possible to get a second opinion, which is especially important in remote areas. It is also important to be able to discuss evacuation of the patient and, if it is difficult, to discuss stabilization of the patient's condition.

Qualitatively prepared, organized and conducted in accordance with these rules, teleconsultation is a tool, an incentive and an opportunity to improve the health of workers and residents of remote communities, their timely treatment or referral to a face-to-face consultation. visit to the right specialist.

It is necessary to use the free time that a shift worker has to improve his or her health. This can be done with the help of a qualitatively organized and conducted teleconsultation, taking into account the above mentioned technological and psychological aspects.

The introduction of feedback forms in our study significantly improved patients' subjective evaluations of the quality of the conducted telecounseling. These results can serve as a basis for improving the organization of remote medical care for workers in rotational settlements who do not have direct access to quality medical care.

REFERENCES

Dudarev AA & Jon Øyvind Odland (2013). Occupational health and health care in Russia and Russian Arctic: 1980–2010, International Journal of Circumpolar Health, 72:1, DOI: 10.3402/ijch.v72i0.20456

Hyder MA, Razzak J. (2020). Telemedicine in the United States: An Introduction for Students and Residents. J Med Internet Res. 2020 Nov 24;22(11):e20839. doi: 10.2196/20839. PMID: 33215999; PMCID: PMC7690251.

Mulcare M, Naik N, Greenwald P, Schullstrom K, Gogia K, Clark S, Kang Y, Sharma R. (2020). Advanced Communication and Examination Skills in Telemedicine: A Structured Simulation-Based Course for Medical Students. MedEdPORTAL. 2020 Dec 17;16:11047. doi: 10.15766/mep_2374-8265.11047. PMID: 33365390; PMCID: PMC7751329.

Rutledge CM, Haney T, Bordelon M, Renaud M, Fowler C. (2014). Telehealth: preparing advanced practice nurses to address healthcare needs in rural and underserved populations. Int J Nurs Educ Scholarsh. 2014 Jan 14;11:/j/ijnes.2014.11.issue-1/ijnes-2013-0061/ijnes-2013-0061.xml. doi: 10.1515/ijnes-2013-0061. PMID: 24423469.

Uscher-Pines L, Thompson J, Taylor P, Dean K, Yuan T, Tong I, Mehrotra A. (2020). Where Virtual Care Was Already a Reality: Experiences of a Nationwide Telehealth Service Provider During the COVID-19 Pandemic. J Med Internet Res. 2020 Dec 15;22(12):e22727. doi: 10.2196/22727. PMID: 33112761; PMCID: PMC7744145.

Vladzimirskij A.V., & Andreev A.I. (2018). Obrazovatel'nye aspekty telemediciny. // ZHurnal telemediciny i elektronnogo zdravoohraneniya. 2018. 1-2 (6-7), S. 43-54. (in russian)

Woldaregay AZ, Walderhaug S, Hartvigsen G. (2017). Telemedicine Services for the Arctic: A Systematic Review. JMIR Med Inform. 2017 Jun 28;5(2):e16. doi: 10.2196/medinform.6323. PMID: 28659257; PMCID: PMC5508113.

INTEGRATION OF LANGUAGE LEARNING MOBILE APPLICATION IN UNIVERSITY LANGUAGE PROGRAM

Katarzyna Gajda
University of Warsaw,Krakowskie Przedmieście 26/28,00-927 Warsaw, Poland

ABSTRACT

The integration of mobile technology in language education represents notable progress, providing a versatile tool for learners of different ages to acquire a language. The poster will focus on research evaluating the efficacy of the Duolingo mobile app in augmenting Russian language proficiency for A1 and B1 level students at the University of Warsaw. The study aims to investigate the linguistic perspective and examine how the application enhances language proficiency in reading, writing, speaking, and listening. The research was conducted during the winter term of the academic year 2022/2023 and involved 80 participants. To assess the efficacy of Duolingo's digital solution compared to traditional teaching methods, a mixed-methods approach was employed. This entailed integrating engagement metrics, linguistic proficiency assessments, and user feedback to evaluate the app's efficacy across various age groups. The research indicates that Duolingo is a promising tool for improving learners' motivation and adaptability in educational contexts. The app's functions, such as real-time progress monitoring, prompt feedback, and community engagement, played a key role in creating a stimulating educational setting for students of different ages. The poster will include partial results of the study, which suggest that students at various stages frequently interacted with the Duolingo app. Most respondents confirmed that they used the app daily, with each learning session averaging around 30-40 minutes. Most students would recommend the app to others, noting its effectiveness and enjoyable user experience. Additionally, a correlation was found between the duration of app usage and language proficiency levels, with students who invested more time in the app generally achieving higher outcomes, although exercises aimed at developing speaking and writing skills were perceived as less effective. The data indicates that incorporating mobile applications could significantly transform traditional language education frameworks, potentially resulting in more tailored and efficient learning opportunities.

KEYWORDS

Mobile Assisted Language Learning, Language Acquisition, Mobile Applications, Duolingo Efficacy

1. INTRODUCTION

Over the past decade, the use of mobile technologies in education has significantly increased. This trend is particularly noticeable in foreign language teaching, where mobile apps have become increasingly popular. These apps offer a range of features, including mobility, personalization, interactivity, multimedia, flexibility, and access to online resources (Kukulska-Hulme & Traxler, 2013). Foreign language learning applications provide support for both independent language study and traditional teaching methods, enabling students to engage in practice outside the classroom. Additionally, Burston (2014) noted that these applications assist in the self-regulation of the learning process and offer immediate feedback, which is essential for effective language learning. The use of mobile applications for teaching foreign languages, also known as Mobile Assisted Language Learning (MALL), can be implemented by utilizing established concepts, strategies, and pedagogical models.

2. STUDY OBJECTIVE

The pilot study aimed to evaluate participants' opinions regarding the use of mobile applications and test the effectiveness of the Duolingo app. To achieve this objective, the study endeavored to answer the following questions: to what extent do students and course attendees use mobile applications, and to what extent do mobile applications assist with reading, writing, listening, and speaking? Hypothesizing that mobile tools can enhance foreign language proficiency across different linguistic levels, a preliminary analysis was conducted. The study involved analyzing popular language apps used by university students and attendees, followed by administering surveys, language proficiency tests, and a comprehensive pilot study. The pilot study provides an initial framework for a comprehensive experimental investigation that requires additional work, currently underway. However, this article concentrates on the results and conclusions obtained during the implementation phase of the pilot study.

2.1 Popularity of Language Learning

Russian is the fifth most popular language at the University of Warsaw, having ranked fourth in the 2021/2022 academic year. The School of Eastern Languages and the School of Foreign Languages offer Russian language classes, while the Open University of the University of Warsaw provides commercial courses. Lectures and courses catering to all levels of proficiency are available.

Table 1. Number of enrollments in language classes

Year	Russian	English	German	Spanish	French	Italian	Other
2022/2023	524	5222	663	625	608	261	1575
2021/2022	632	5632	742	671	625	280	1462
2020/2021	623	5785	760	712	699	272	1413
2019/2020	674	6003	702	634	677	322	1311

2.2 Research Group

In total, 78 individuals participated in the study, with 60 completing the full survey and partially engaging in proficiency test verification. Furthermore, 18 students at the A1 level took part in the entire pilot educational experiment, which consisted of both surveys and proficiency tests.

2.3 Method and Research Tool

The study utilized quasi-experimental methods and administered two surveys that were revised based on participant feedback. In the pilot study, a pretest and posttest were administered using two Russian language certification exams, TRKI (Test of Russian as a Foreign Language) at levels A1 and B1.

2.4 Analysis of Survey Data

The survey gathered responses from 46 female and 32 male participants, with 45% of these being under the age of 20, 38% aged between 21 to 30, 10% aged between 31 to 40, 5% aged between 41 to 50, and 1% being over the age of 50. The location of the participants revealed that a significant 72% lived in cities with a population of over 1 million people, followed by 11% from cities ranging from 100,000 to 1 million people, and 17% from towns with up to 100,000 people. Out of the 78 individuals examined, only 18 fully participated in the experimental final study.

2.5 Proficiency Test Results Compilation

All 18 participants in the certification test successfully passed it. Ten individuals scored above 95%, six scored above 85%, and two scored 75%. There was a noticeable correlation between the amount of time students spent on the Duolingo application and their success rate. The most commonly used types of exercises show that when designing them, the creators of the Duolingo platform aim primarily to develop two language subsystems in users - grammar and vocabulary (Aleksandrowska, Stanulewicz, 2020). This is evident in the test results, as in the blocks related to grammar and vocabulary, students using the Duolingo application achieved results that were 10% better in vocabulary and 8% better in grammar than students in the control group.

3. CONCLUSION

The majority of participants enthusiastically used the Duolingo application, accessing it regularly and engaging with it daily for an average of 30-40 minutes. While their primary goal was to expand their vocabulary, they found reading comprehension to be the most effective skill within the application. However, they rated speaking and writing as less effective teaching methods within the application. Most study participants had a positive view of Duolingo and would recommend it to others due to its effectiveness and enjoyable user experience. However, some participants questioned its comprehensiveness as a full-fledged language education resource. All participants passed the A1 level certification exam, with those who spent more time on the app achieving higher scores. To ensure maximum user engagement, regular discussions and instructor support were provided to offer necessary assistance with technical issues and platform modifications. The pilot study's results, presented on the poster, are only a portion of the research. Further details of this pilot study will be described in the article for issue 62/1 (2024) of the journal Neofilolog, which is currently under review. Future research on mobile language apps should examine their effectiveness, particularly with regard to the links between the design of the application's exercises, the effectiveness of developing specific language skills, and the implications for mobile learning.

REFERENCES

Aleksandrowska, O., Stanulewicz, D., (2020). Internetowa platforma do nauki języków Duolingo – opinie użytkowników. *Neofilolog*, No. 55/1, pp. 125–144.

Burston, J., (2014). The Reality of MALL: Still on the Fringes. *CALICO Journal*, No. 31 (1), pp. 103-125.

Kukulska-Hulme, A., Traxler, J. (ed.), (2005). *Mobile Learning: A Handbook for Educators and Trainers.* Taylor and Francis, London.

Morgana, V., Kukulska-Hulme, A. (ed.), (2021). *Mobile Assisted Language Learning Across Educational Contexts.* Routledge, London, New York.

Oxford, R. L., (2011). *Teaching and researching language learning strategies.* Pearson Education Limited, London.

Stockwell, G., (2022). *Mobile Assisted Language Learning Concepts, Contexts and Challenges.* Cambridge University Press, Cambridge.

LEVERAGING COGNITIVE STRATEGIES IN CONTENT DESIGN TO SUPPORT CREATIVE THINKING IN MOBILE LEARNING

Robert Zheng
Department of Educational Psychology, University of Utah, USA

ABSTRACT

The current examined the roles of cognitive strategies using Chi's framework in mobile learning. Three conditions (active, constructive, and interactive) were created for a college statistics I course where students were randomly assigned to each condition. The results indicate constructive and interactive support students' problem solving and number of solutions generated whereas active learning is less helpful in terms of students' problem solving and divergent thinking. It is suggested that mobile learning should take cognitive strategies into consideration when designing its content. Instructional designers should heed to the fact that constructive and interactive activities enable learners to become more productive in problem solving and solution generation.

KEYWORDS

Cognitive Strategies, Constructive Learning, Content Design, Mobility, Mobile Learning

1. INTRODUCTION

Creative thinking is perhaps one of the most important outcomes in education. It accounts for learners' cognitive abilities in making connections between concepts and information across domains and disciplines. Research has shown a significant correlation between learners' academic achievement and creative thinking, suggesting that creative thinking can enhance learners' academic performance in terms of deep understanding, multi-level problem solving, and far knowledge transfer within and outside academic domains and disciplines (Birgili, 2015; Goldschmidt, 2016; Lince, 2016; Zheng, 2020, 2022).

With the advancement of digital technology, new ways of teaching creative thinking skills have been introduced (Widiana & Jampel, 2016; Vale, et al., 2017). For example, the mobile learning is considered to be a viable platform to promote learners' creative thinking skills (DeSchryver, 2017). However, not much literature exists in exploring the use of cognitive strategies to support creative thinking such as divergent thinking in mobile learning. In this study, we investigated Chi's (2009) active-interactive-constructive framework in the quest of meaningful implementation for divergent thinking in mobile learning.

1.1 Active-Constructive-Interactive Framework

According to Chi (2009), there are three-levels of activities with each interacting with the content differently. The three-levels of activities are: active, constructive, and interactive. Active learning activities include learning activities like searching a term in the Internet, underlying a sentence in the textbook, or copying and pasting a text. By actively doing something, the learner becomes engaged with the content. However, being active in learning does not necessarily guarantee that the learner is processing the content deeply. Chi contended that for deep learning to occur, learners must be engaged in constructive and interactive activities in which they hypothesize, analyze, synthesize, and make inferences based on the data. Chi noted that being constructive is different from being active. The former involves producing new "content-relevant ideas that go beyond the information given" (2009, p.78) whereas the latter just shows the learner is doing something to being active.

2. THE STUDY

The current study applied Chi's framework to promoting learners' creative thinking in mobile learning. It was hypothesized that cognitive strategies (i.e., active, constructive, interactive) can influence learners' ability to think creatively. It was also hypothesized that learners' divergent think ability could affect the way they interact with the cognitive strategies deployed.

2.1 Design of Study

The study tested the role of cognitive strategies in mobile-based learning. The content (College statistic I) was hosted on an online platform that is accessible from laptop computer or mobile phone. Three conditions were created: Condition 1 requires students to focus on key concepts by highlighting or making the notes of the concepts or procedures they believe were important (Active). Condition 2 asks students to identify the concepts or procedures and apply them to a given problem. Students need to reason about which concepts or procedures were more effective in statistical problem solving. For example, under which circumstances, the T-test or ANOVA should be used and why since they both can be used to compare two groups (Constructive). Condition 3 asks students to manipulate certain variables in the procedure to explain or justify why a particular statistic method (T-test or ANOVA) should be applied to a problem (Interactive).

The study employed a 2 x 3 design in which levels of cognitive strategy (active, constructive, and interactive) interact with learners' divergent thinking (high vs. low) as measured by achievements and number of solutions generated.

2.2 Participants

Two-hundred forty participants were recruited from a Research I university in the United States. An institutional review board approval was obtained for the study. Participants were given consent to sign followed by a convergent thinking test with demographic information items. Guilford's (1967) Alternative Uses Task (AUT) was adopted to measure divergent thinking. After the divergent thinking test, the participants were randomly assigned to three groups: active, constructive, and interactive learning conditions. Participants then engaged in a 40-minute learning activity on College Level 1 statistics. At the end of learning activity, the participants took an achievement test which consists of 15 items with a possible max score of 30 and three application problems with a possible max score of 15. The max total possible score a participant can obtain is 45 points.

3. RESULTS

The 2x3 multivariate analyses have revealed significant differences across three cognitive strategies, $\lambda= .125$, $p <..001$, $\eta^2=.646$. There is a significant interaction between cognitive strategies and divergent thinking $\lambda= .851$, $p <..001$, $\eta^2=.077$. The follow-up multiple comparison analyses indicate there were significant differences between active condition and constructive/interactive conditions with regard to learner performance in conceptual questions. No significant difference was found between constructive and interactive by the same measure. In terms of problem solving, differences were found between active condition and constructive/interactive conditions. Again, no significant difference was found between constructive and interaction conditions. In terms of numbers of solutions generated, there was significant difference between active condition and constructive/interactive conditions. In addition, the difference between constructive and interactive conditions measured by learners' ability to generate number of problem solutions was significant.

By examining the differences between high and low divergent thinking learners in terms of their performance in conceptual questions, problem solving, and number of solutions generated, it was found that no significant differences were found between high and low divergent thinking learners in active conditions across three measures: conceptual questions, problem solving, and number of solutions. However, significant differences were found for constructive condition between high and low divergent thinking learners for problem solving and number of solutions but no significant difference was found for conceptual questions.

Finally, with regard to interactive condition, significant difference was found for number of solutions generated but no differences were found for conceptual questions and problem solving.

4. CONCLUSION

The results of current study suggest that embedding cognitive strategies in mobile learning can improve learners' performance in learning. In particular, constructive cognitive strategy supports high divergent thinking learners in their ability to solve problem and generate more solutions. It appears that interactive cognitive strategy helps solution generation for high divergent thinking learners but shows flat when measured by conceptual understanding and problem solving.

REFERENCES

Birgili, B. (2015). Creative and critical thinking skills in problem-based learning environments. *Journal of Gifted Education and Creativity, 2*(2), 71–80.

Chi, M. (2009). Active-constructive-interactive: A conceptual framework for differentiating learning activities. *Topics in Cognitive Science, 1*(1), 73-105.

DeSchryver, M. (2017). Using the web as a higher order thinking partner: Case study of an advanced learner creatively synthesizing knowledge on the web. *Journal of Educational Computing Research, 55*(2), 240–271.

Goldschmidt, G. (2016). Linkographic evidence for concurrent divergent and convergent thinking in creative design. *Creativity Research Journal, 28*(2), 115–122.

Guilford, J.P. (1967). Creativity: Yesterday, today and tomorrow. *The Journal of Creative Behavior. 1*, 3–14.

Lince, R. (2016). Creative thinking ability to increase student mathematical of junior high school by applying models numbered heads together. *Journal of Education and Practice, 7*(6), 206–212.

Zheng, R. (2020). Learning with immersive technology: A cognitive perspective. In R. Zheng (Ed.), *Cognitive and affective perspectives on immersive technology in education* (pp. 1-21). Hershey, PA: IGI Publishing.

Zheng, R. (2022). Foster transversal skills in game-based learning: A deep learning approach. In I. Rivera-Trigueros, A. López-Alcarria, D. Ruiz-Padillo, M. Olvera-Lobo, and J. Gutiérrez-Pérez (Eds.), *Using disruptive methodologies and game-based learning to foster transversal skills* (pp. 106-130). Hershey, PA: IGI Global Publishing.

Doctoral Consortium

AN EDUCATIONAL OUTCOME MEASURING INSTRUMENT FOR THREADED DISCUSSION LEARNING USING DEPTH SCORING

Ian McGowan
University of Technology, Jamaica

ABSTRACT

Online threaded discussion forums continue to be widely used at the higher educational level as a learning tool. An investigation of the computer-supported collaborative learning literature however as presented in this paper, is showing that assessing the effectiveness of this mode of learning is largely not studied. Therefore, using a combination of threaded message depth scoring and self-dialog act coding powered by a newly designed app for the mobile browser, a threaded discussion learning intervention outcome measuring tool using a statistical model was proposed in this study for development.

KEYWORDS

Depth Scoring, Threaded Discussions, Dialogue Acts, Equipose

1. INTRODUCTION

Widely used at the higher educational level, online threaded discussions hold a promise for collaborative knowledge construction. When participants in the discussions build on the comments of others, using dialog acts or pronounced utterances, a higher flow of communication and inference is being shown compared to the "turn-taking" face-to-face learning environment (Garrison, 2006). One of the key potential challenges facing threaded discussion learning (TDL) however, which is at the heart of this study, is the inadequate number of valid and reliable learning outcome measurement instruments available to TDL researchers and practitioners (O'Riordan, 2016). Absence of such learning outcome measuring instruments limits the comparisons of pedagogical approaches (Lim et al, 2012; Darko & Wang, 2021) and learning outcome assessments provide a direct measure of participants' educational outcomes following a learning activity (Liu et al, 2012; Keshavarz, 2011).

In this study, I will be taking the relationship between threaded discussions posted by participants and learning one step further: to examine how the discussions in depth and in small groups of participants, correlate with the educational outcomes. This study therefore, will seek to answer the following research questions:

1. Which of the dialogue acts present in the threaded discussion messages, individually or in combination, best explain the results presented by the developed educational outcome measuring instrument?

2. What were the depth scores of the dialogue acts present in the threaded discussion messages, individually or in combination that best explain the results presented by the developed educational outcome measuring instrument?

3. For which of the group sizes can the knowledge gain or loss results presented by the developed educational outcome measuring instrument, be best explained?

2. RESEARCH DESIGN

In this section, I discuss eight topics, namely, pretest-posttest design, research site, participants' sampling, treatment designs, participant groupings, the pretest, the intervention and the depth scoring method proposed.

2.1 Pretest-Posttest Design

This study uses the *randomized pretest-posttest* design, a research design vehicle for assessing the impact of and measuring of change resulting from experimental interventions. With this randomized design, all conditions are the same for al! the participants. In this study, I will be assessing participants at both ends of a threaded discussion learning intervention, with the aim of predicting learning outcomes and explaining knowledge gains/loss resulting from the intervention as the study's outcome. This aim thus supports my choice of using this research design approach.

2.2 Research Site

This study will take place in the School of Computing & Information Technology (SCIT), the second largest school at the University of Technology, Jamaica with an overall university population of over twelve and a half thousand. With a student population of approximately 1,480, the computer science program in SCIT exposes them all to the C/C++/Java/C# family which is central to a solid computer science education. The study of programming languages raises key issues that permeate computer science to include for example, the limits of computability, modularity and abstraction. For the school, it is imperative that every computer science student learns early on (by year 2) to be flexible in expressing his or her algorithmic thinking.

2.3 Methods

Following the ethical and equipoise considerations of Royall (1991) relating to randomized controlled trials in educational research, the randomized pretest-posttest design, and to gather the data needed for the study, this section will be presented as shown in Table 1.

Equipoise, important in this study to help ensure participants are not disadvantaged from the random assignments to particular treatment groups, will be discussed further in section 2.3.2.

Table 1. Method activities

Activities (in the following order)	Data to be gathered (variables)	RQ1	RQ2	RQ3
Pre-randomization				
Participant Sampling				
Treatment Designs				
Participant Groupings				
Pretest	*Pre*	√	√	√
Intervention (Orientation, Treatment Groups A, B and C)	Depth score per self-coded dialogue act	√	√	
Posttest	*Post*	√	√	√

2.3.1 Participants' Sampling

In this study, I will seek to recruit about one hundred and fifty-four first year computer science students from SCIT. This sample size is consistent with the recommendation of Bulus (2021) to achieve an MRES (minimum relevant *treatment* effect size) of 0.25 in education research and a r^2 (proportion of variance in the posttest that is explained by the pretest and threaded discussion depth scores) of 0.70 or better for conducting experiments under a randomized pretest-posttest design. I'm choosing from this population of approximately 540 first year computer science students as they are required to be engaged, not only individually, but in group coding work collaboratively, to discuss problems to be solved, share, test and criticize each other's codes in their programming modules. This population of computer science students faces the most serious threat of falling into academic probation due to inexperience in coding coming into the program. Hence sampling this population is not only timely, but is also important.

2.3.2 Treatment Designs

Parallel design is a standard design for randomized control trials (Berkman et al, 2014) & (Kabisch et al, 2012). In this design, following the randomization, participants will be assigned to receive treatment A, B or C (explained in Table 2) throughout the entire intervention period.

Table 2. Treatment designs

Treatment Elements	A	B	C
Group size	4 (Lou et al, 2001 & Tu et al, 2002)	5 (Miflin,2004)	6 (Miflin,2004)
Attend an orientation	Yes	Yes	Yes
App to use	Sync-asynchonous	Sync-asynchonous	Sync-asynchonous
Threaded discussion	Yes	Yes	Yes
Problem statement to solve	A	A	A
Access to tutor scaffolding & tutor interaction	Yes	Yes	Yes
Code example set	A	A	A

Table 3. Taxonomy of dialogue acts (Saab et al, 2007)

Code/Independent variable	Dialogue act	Code/Independent variable (cont 'd)	Dialogue act (cont' d)
Info	Informative	ResC	Responsive – Confirmation/acceptance
Argu	Argumentative	ResN	Responsive – Negative
EvaN	Evaluative – Negative	Dire	Directive
EvaP	Evaluative – Positive	OffT	Off task – social talk
EliU	Elicitative (Asking) – For understanding		
EliA	Elicitative – For agreement		
EliO	Elicitative – Open question		
EliC	Elicitative – Critical question		
ResI	Responsive – Informative		

In satisfying the requirements of equipoise, as prescribed by Royall (1991), (*a*) as the sole researcher on this study, I have no preferences for treatment A, B nor C, (*b*) the benefits of treatments A, B and C are truly evenly balanced with respect to each participant also in keeping with the ethical considerations of Zelen (1979), and (*c*) the participants are not likely to have a preference for one treatment or another.

2.3.3 Participant Groupings

In this study, participants will be selected at random into the three treatment groups (A, B and C) from the full pool of participants. These three batches will be asked to solve a problem collaboratively online (described in Section 3.3.5.) in small groups of a sizes 4, 5 and 6 respectively. These target group sizes are in keeping with Kooloos et al (2011) who write that when a small learning group is used, it cannot function well beyond eight members.

2.3.4 Pretest

I will administer a pretest programming knowledge assessment to all of the participants before they receive treatment protocols. To be gathered as data needed for research questions one, two and three, we call this pretest covariate *Pre*.

2.3.5 Intervention

For the intervention, I will administer the treatment protocols for groups A, B and C. Each small group, in threaded discussion mode and in creating a code solution to the problem statement given, is expected to perform the following steps internally: (1) discuss problem statement, (2) demonstrate understanding of the problem statement, (3) submit a code solution (4) test codes for correctness and efficiency, (5) submit challenges and feedbacks resulting from the tests, and (6) repeat from step 2 until a final version of the code solution is arrived at. Steps one to five are in keeping with the school's standard of delivery practice and program curriculum.

For each contribution or post, the owner participant will (1) self-code, and (2) relate the post to a previous post from another group member building the threads at multiple depths. Each self-coded post will then be scored automatically by the app against its owner (of the post) according to its depth in its corresponding thread.

I will now explain how the planned *self-coding* and contribution/post *depth-scoring* respectively are to work.

In exploring Jeong (2003)'s suggestion as a means of more accurately linking a taxonomy of dialogue acts to utterances, this study will allow participants to code their own posts using the taxonomy of Saab (2007) in table 4. This feature of the newly built app will work by, for each post entered, present participant with a drop list of the taxonomy along with corresponding utterance examples as used in Saab (2007) to be used as a guide for the participant in the writing of the post. On submission of the post, app will automatically tag the selected dialogue act code to it.

For this study, I will be scoring the depths of the utterances in relation to their respective levels in the threaded discussions. Defined by Hsu et al (2015, p. 7), "how extensively the participants elaborated on an argument", depth is a feature of the quality of collaborative argumentation (Asterhan, 2011) represented in the threaded discussions. Thus for this study, I will score each utterance (or post) by its level in the discussion. The deeper the discussion, the higher the score.

3. DATA ANALYSIS

For this study, a multiple linear regression (MLR) will be used for analyzing the data. This statistical method, used with a pretest-posttest design, is a powerful approach (Kraemer et al, 2002). This approach (1) aids researchers to determine cause-and-effect relationships (Zientek et al, 2016), and (2) according to Gliner et al (2003) and Linn & Slinde (1977), can be used by researchers to analyze group differences in posttest or gain/loss scores. These benefits of the MLR approach thus allow this study to (1) conduct an analysis on the resulting regression effects of the threaded discussions, and (2) assess the variance in the posttest that are uniquely associated with the threaded discussion learning intervention. Not only is the MLR approach most appropriate for this study, these benefits of a MLR approach therefore will allow for the answering of this study's research questions, better explain some of the learning outcomes from small group threaded discussions, and present a statistical regression model as my contribution to the threaded discussion learning outcome literature. The choice of the MLR approach for this study was in keeping with the recommendation of Zientek et al (2016) where studying the variances in the posttest is needed to answer the research questions.

MLR is used commonly in pretest-posttest analysis studies in the evaluation of intervention programs, examples Alessandri et al (2017), Dimitrov & Rumrill (2003) and Hennig et al (2010). This equation modeling approach however, as my literature review highlights, is not common in cause-and-effect nor learning outcome CSCL studies. Hence I think CSCL scholars would be ready to make use of the resulting output equations from this kind of data analysis.

For the MLR approach presented here, the posttest scores become the dependent or outcome variable. The independent or predictor variables are the pretest scores and each of the dialogue acts (shown in Table 4). The approach will allow me to test for the significance of each of the predictor variables and assess the impact of the treatment on the posttest scores (Gliner et al, 2003). On this basis, I will follow the hierarchical multiple regression process of Leech et al (2003) in answering research questions one and two. In this process considering the treatment group data, variables are entered or replaced in steps then the change in the output represent by a r^2, is examined at each step.

Research Question 1: *Which of the dialogue acts present in the threaded discussion messages, individually or in combination, best explain the results presented by the developed educational outcome measuring instrument?*

$$\text{Model 1: } Pre + \text{DialogueAct}_m + \mathcal{E} = Post$$
$$\text{Model 2: } Pre + \text{DialogueAct}_m + \text{DialogueAct}_q + \mathcal{E} = Post$$

For this study, the final output in answering RQ1 is the corresponding equation or regression model with the highest r^2 recorded.

Research Question 2: *What were the depth scores of the dialogue acts present in the threaded discussion messages, individually or in combination that best explain the results presented by the developed educational outcome measuring instrument?*

To understand how much each predictor present in the model selected from answering RQ1 is contributing to the r^2, the standardized coefficients (ß weights) will then be computed to answer this research question. This selected model with the reflected coefficients would represent *the final educational outcome measuring instrument*.

Research Question 3: *For which of the group sizes can the knowledge gain or loss results presented by the developed educational outcome measuring instrument, be best explained?*

The regression analysis procedure for assessing the correlation between the pretest and net gain in scores for this study will follow Dalecki & Willits (1991) in answering this research question. In this approach, the pretest (*Pre*) covariant is to be incorporated into the predictive equation as a control variable so that the net relationships of the gain score to the independent variables in the model are adjusted for the confounded effects of the pretest. I am expecting some level of pretest sensitizing among some of the participants in this study who did programming at the senior high school level. For this study, I am interested in a general comparison of the treatment groups by size with respect to the net gain scores.

$$\text{(Treatment group A) Model 3: } Pre_A + \mathcal{E} = (Post_A - Pre_A)$$
$$\text{(Treatment group B) Model 4: } Pre_B + \mathcal{E} = (Post_B - Pre_B)$$
$$\text{(Treatment group C) Model 5: } Pre_C + \mathcal{E} = (Post_C - Pre_C)$$

The outputs would be the resulting r^2s for each group which would indicate the respective statistical relationships between the pretest and the overall learning outcome. The group with the strongest r^2 would represent the group with the best explained gain or loss measure.

REFERENCES

Alessandri, G., Zuffianò, A., Perinelli, E. (2017). Evaluating intervention programs with a pretest-posttest design: A structural equation modeling approach. Frontiers in psychology, 8, 223.

Asterhan, C. (2011). Assessing e-moderation behavior from synchronous discussion protocols with a multi-dimensional methodology. Computers in Human Behavior, 27(1), 449–458

Berkman, N. D., Santaguida, P. L., Viswanathan, M. (2014). The Empirical Evidence of Bias in Trials Measuring Treatment Differences. Rockville, MD: Agency for Healthcare Research and Quality (US)

Bulus, M. (2021). Sample size determination and optimal design of randomized/non-equivalent pretest-posttest control-group designs. Adiyaman Univesity Journal of Educational Sciences, 11(1), 48-69.

Darko, E., Wang, X. (2021). Research on the Influence of Collaborative Learning among Bachelor of Education (Management) Students in University of Cape Coast, Ghana. Open Journal of Business and Management, 9, 2816-2833.

Dimitrov, D. M., Rumrill P.D. Jr. (2003). Pretest-posttest designs and measurement of change. Work;20(2):159-65. PMID: 12671209.

Garrison, D. (2006). Online collaboration principles. Journal of Asynchronous Learning Networks, 10(1)

Gliner, J. A., Morgan, G. A., Harmon, R. J. (2003). Pretest-posttest comparison group designs: Analysis and interpretation. Journal of the American Academy of Child & Adolescent Psychiatry, 42(4), 500–503.

Hennig, C., Müllensiefen, D., & Bargmann, J. (2010). Within-Subject Comparison of Changes in a Pretest-Posttest Design. Applied Psychological Measurement, 34(5), 291–309

Hsu, P., Van Dyke, M., Chen, Y. (2015) Examining the Effect of Teacher Guidance on Collaborative Argumentation in Middle Level Classrooms, RMLE Online, 38:9, 1-11

Jeong, A. C. (2003). The Sequential Analysis of Group Interaction and Critical Thinking in Online Threaded Discussions. The American Journal of Distance Education, 17(1), 25–43

Kabisch, M., Ruckes, C., Seibert-Grafe, M. (2012). On the proper use of the crossover design in clinical trials: part 18 of a series on evaluation of scientific publications. Dtsch Arztebl Int.;109: 276–281

Keshavarz, M. (2011). Measuring Course Learning Outcomes. Journal of Learning Design. Designing for Effective Learning

Kooloos, J. G. M., Klaassen, T., Vereijken, M., Van Kuppeveld, S., Bolhuis, S., Vorstenbosch, M. (2011). Collaborative group work: Effects of group size and assignment structure on learning gain, student satisfaction and perceived participation. Medical Teacher.

Kraemer, W. J., Adams, K., Cafarelli, E., Dudley, G. A., Dooly, C., Feigenbaum, M. S., Hoffman, J. R. (2002). American College of Sports Medicine position stand. Progression models in resistance training for healthy adults. Medicine and science in sports and exercise, 34(2), 364-380

Linn, R.L., Slinde, J.A. (1977). The determination of the significance of change between pre-and posttesting periods. Review of Educational Research, Vol. 47, pp. 121-150

Liu, O., Bridgeman, B., Adler, R. (2012). Measuring Learning Outcomes in Higher Education: Motivation Matters. Educational Researcher.

Lou, Y., Abrami, P. C., D'Apollonia, S. (2001). Small Group and Individual Learning with Technology: A Meta-Analysis. Rev. Educ. Res. 71, 449–521

Miflin, B. (2004). Small groups and problem-based learning: Are we signing from the same hymn sheet? Med Teach 26(5):444–450

Royall, R. M. (1991). Ethics and Statistics in Randomized Clinical Trials. Statistical Science, Statist. Sci. 6(1), 52-62

Saab, N., Van Joolingen, W. R., Van Hout-Wolters, B. H. A. M (2007). Supporting Communication in a Collaborative Discovery Learning Environment: The Effect of Instruction. Instructional Science, 35:73–98

Tu, C. H., McIsaac, M. (2002). The Relationship of Social Presence and Interaction in Online Classes. Am. J. Distance Educ. 16, 131–150.

Zelen, M. (1979). A new design for randomized clinical trials. New England Journal of Medicine. 300 1232-1246

Zientek, L.R., Thompson, B. (2009). Matrix summaries improve research reports: secondary analyses using published literature. Educational Researcher, Vol. 38, pp. 343-352

Zientek, L., Nimon, K., Hammack-Brown, B. (2016). Analyzing data from a pretest-posttest control group design: The importance of statistical assumptions, European Journal of Training and Development, Vol. 40 No. 8/9, pp. 638-659

AUTHOR INDEX

International Association for Development of the Information Society (IADIS)
Rua Sao Sebastiao Da Pedreira
No. 100, 30, 1050-209
Lisbon, Portugal

ISBN 979-8-3313-0141-5

9 798331 301415

CURRAN ASSOCIATES INC.
proceedings.com